# DRUGS IN AMERICAN SOCIETY

Seventh Edition

# DRUGS IN AMERICAN SOCIETY

**Erich Goode**

*University of Maryland*

**McGraw-Hill**
**Higher Education**

Boston   Burr Ridge, IL   Dubuque, IA   New York   San Francisco   St. Louis
Bangkok   Bogotá   Caracas   Kuala Lumpur   Lisbon   London   Madrid   Mexico City
Milan   Montreal   New Delhi   Santiago   Seoul   Singapore   Sydney   Taipei   Toronto

**McGraw-Hill**
**Higher Education**

Published by McGraw-Hill, an imprint of The McGraw-Hill Companies, Inc., 1221 Avenue of the Americas, New York, NY 10020. Copyright © 2008. All rights reserved. No part of this publication may be reproduced or distributed in any form or by any means, or stored in a database or retrieval system, without the prior written consent of The McGraw-Hill Companies, Inc., including, but not limited to, in any network or other electronic storage or transmission, or broadcast for distance learning.

This book is printed on acid-free paper.

2 3 4 5 6 7 8 9 0 DOC/DOC 0 9 8 7

ISBN:  978-0-07-340149-2
MHID:  0-07-340149-8

Editor-in-chief: *Emily Barrosse*
Publisher: *Frank Mortimer*
Sponsoring editor: *Katie Stevens*
Marketing manager: *Lori DeShazo*
Developmental editor: *Teresa Treacy*
Production editor: *David Blatty*
Designer: *Andrei Pasternak*
Photo researcher: *Nora Agbayani*
Production Supervisor: *Dennis Fitzgerald*
Typeface: *10/12 Times Roman*
Composition: *Aptara*
Printing: *R. R. Donnelley & Sons*

Cover photo: *Matthew J. Johnston*

Credits: The credits section for this book begins on page C-1 and is considered an extension of the copyright page.

**Library of Congress Cataloging-in-Publication Data**

Goode, Erich.
    Drugs in American society / Erich Goode.—7th ed.
     p. cm.
    Includes bibliographical references and index.
    ISBN-13: 978-0-07-340149-2
    ISBN-10: 0-07-340149-8
    1. Drug abuse—United States.  2. Drugs—United States.  3. Drug utilization—United States.  4. Drug abuse and crime—United States.  I. Title.

HV5825. G63 2008
362.290973—dc22                              2007015667

The Internet addresses listed in the text were accurate at the time of publication. The inclusion of a Web site does not indicate an endorsement by the authors or McGraw-Hill, and McGraw-Hill does not guarantee the accuracy of the information presented at these sites.

**www.mhhe.com**

# ABOUT THE AUTHOR

ERICH GOODE received his Ph.D. in sociology from Columbia University and has taught at New York University, the University of North Carolina, Chapel Hill, The Hebrew University of Jerusalem, and the University of Maryland, and is Sociology Professor Emeritus at the State University of New York, Stony Brook. Prof. Goode is the author of ten books, including *The Marijuana Smokers* (Basic Books, 1970), *Deviant Behavior* (8th edition, Prentice Hall, 2008), *Moral Panics* (with Nachman Ben-Yehuda, Blackwell, 1994), *Between Politics and Reason: The Drug Legalization Debate* (St. Martin's Press, 1997), and *Deviance in Everyday Life* (Waveland, Press 2002). His articles have appeared in scholarly and professional journals as well as newspapers, magazines, and literary journals. His areas of specialization are drug use and deviance.

# BRIEF CONTENTS

# CONTENTS

**PART III**

DRUGS AND THEIR USE   *203*

**CHAPTER 8**

Legal Drugs: Alcohol, Tobacco, and
Psychotherapeutic Drugs   *205*

**CHAPTER 9**

Marijuana, LSD, and Club Drugs   *237*

**CHAPTER 10**

Stimulants: Amphetamines,
Methamphetamine, Cocaine, and Crack   *276*

**CHAPTER 11**

Heroin and the Narcotics   *307*

**PART** IV
DRUGS, CRIME, AND DRUG
CONTROL   *329*

**CHAPTER** 12
Drugs and Crime: What's the
Connection?   *331*

**CHAPTER** 13
The Illicit Drug Industry   *354*

**CHAPTER** 14
Drug Control: Law Enforcement, Drug
Courts, and Drug Treatment   *385*

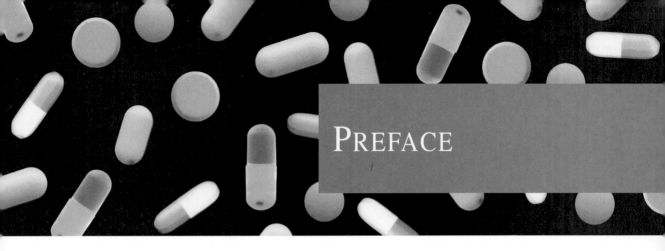

# PREFACE

Since President George W. Bush's "war on terrorism," launched after the attacks on the World Trade Center and the Pentagon on September 11, 2001, the "war on drugs" rhetoric has subsided. Indeed, the war on drugs, it seems, has been harnessed to the war on terrorism. The latest edition of the White House's keynote drug-fighting document, *National Drug Control Strategy* (2006), mentions "terror," "terrorism," and "terrorist" ten times in 40 pages, indicating the rhetorical importance of fighting the drug war in the administration's war against terrorism.

Referring specifically to Afghanistan, the *National Drug Control Strategy* states: "We are committed to a counternarcotics strategy that aims to enhance stability in this fledgling democracy by attacking a source of financial and political support for terrorist organizations that threaten the United States and our allies" (p. 38). Terrorist organizations are funded by many sources, of course—oil and diamonds among them—but what makes the drug war especially advantageous for its supporters is that it a war against the use of *illegal* substances. The convergence of the two "wars" underscores the importance of this mission and simultaneously severs the distribution of illicit drugs from that of harmful *legal* products and activities (not only oil and diamonds but also alcohol and tobacco), making the drug war solely and exclusively about illegal substances. Fighting

alcoholism and reducing tobacco consumption are not part of the drug war. The vision of a "drug-free" society, so often invoked by speechifying politicians, does not include a society without the pleasures of a beer during a ballgame, a glass of wine during mealtime, or an after-dinner smoke.

Fighting the drug war has always been partly a war of words, and so the Bush administration's recent rhetoric serves to remind us that drug use is a socially constructed phenomenon—a materially real action with materially real consequences, to be sure, but created and re-created by the social, cultural, and legal world. This book is a testament to that fundamental truth; in it, I stress both the essential facts of the matter and the ways in which we see, talk about, and react to the facts of the matter. Hence, social constructions are more than words; they are embodied in deeds as well. And whether it is wise policy or not, we still arrest and imprison drug offenders—another facet of the current reality of drug use.

In this book, I argue that drug use is an activity in which humans engage; it is socially patterned and it has important social consequences; drug users are looked upon, dealt with, judged, evaluated, and reacted to; and they, and their activity, are socially constructed in ways that demand investigation. Consequently, from the point of view of social theory—that is, devising general explanations of human behavior—the subject is very much in need of sociological consideration.

A study of drug use is also crucial from a practical standpoint. It is, in fact, a life-or-death proposition. Drug abuse kills. In the United States alone, cigarette smoking claims roughly 440,000 victims a year. The consumption of alcohol claims some 85,000 victims annually. And illicit drug use, or the recreational use of prescription drugs, kills between 20,000 and 30,000 people each year. To be blunt about it, a systematic study of the causes and consequences of substance abuse can save lives. In addition, drug use, whether directly or indirectly, causes a swarm of sublethal social problems, including disease, a lower quality of life, enslavement to a chemical, lower academic and job performance, and less safe streets. A mistaken policy, based on distorted or fallacious views of drugs, their effects, use, misuse, and users, as well as the consequences and accompaniments of use, can be deadly. Are these problems remediable? Some critics of the current policy argue that drugs don't kill—it is a mistaken drug policy that kills. Would a different drug policy reduce these social harms? Would it make things worse? Either way, we cannot base policy on ignorance, and the only cure for ignorance is an open and frank discussion of the subject, based on the best available evidence and reasoned conclusions drawn from that evidence. I believe that this book is exactly such a discussion; I leave it to the reader to draw his or her own conclusions about that.

Every edition of this book has represented an effort to teach students about the reality of drugs and drug use, as I interpret the available evidence. And in this effort, it is the evidence above all that guides my approach. Examining the evidence entails looking at facts and figures—statistics, if you will. Some students find an examination of statistics dull and sometimes incomprehensible. But to me, a consideration of a data-relevant issue—especially one so replete with evidence as drug use—without considering statistics is like groping around in the dark.

But behind the facts and figures, the surveys and statistics, there is also the human drama. People ingest drugs, for good or ill, and as a result, they are dealt with by the rest of the members of the society, again, for good or ill. Real people's lives are affected in myriad ways by drug consumption and drug law enforcement, and the rest of us have to live with the consequences—or try to change the world so that these consequences are minimized or eliminated. The story of drug use, then, is the confluence of the hard, material facts of the consumption of psychoactive substances and the reactions to that consumption by the many actors in this drama, users and nonusers alike. How we are all caught up in this confluence is the story I tell in this book.

The division of this book into parts makes a great deal of sense to me. Part I provides background to our understanding of drug use—the sociological, pharmacological, and historical background, and the ways in which drug use is explained by experts and presented in the media. This background is necessary for understanding the chapters that follow. Part II gives us a bird's-eye view of prevalence of use and changes in prevalence figures over time, and discusses how we can have confidence in these figures to begin with. Part III homes in on the details of the use of the specific drugs that are widely used in this society—the drugs, naturally, that are of most interest to anyone concerned with the subject. And Part IV takes a step back from the drugs, their use and use patterns, and their abuse, to ask how they are entangled in the world of crime—in terms of influencing criminal behavior and illuminating what we can do to reduce the incidence of crime. For many observers, good policy is the payoff in any study of a social problem, and hence, Chapters 14 and 15 address this issue.

For this edition, I have updated information, especially the data published in the National Survey on Drug Use and Health (NSDUH), the Drug Abuse Warning Network (DAWN), and the Arrestee Drug Abuse Monitoring (ADAM) Program. I have condensed or deleted some sections, expanded others, and rewritten still others. And I have considered and made use of the comments and criticisms of the reviewers of the seventh edition of this book; I gratefully acknowledge their suggestions for revision. I would also like to thank the people who agreed to allow me to publish their personal accounts, which illustrate and enliven the principles discussed in many chapters.

*Erich Goode—*

# DRUGS IN AMERICAN SOCIETY

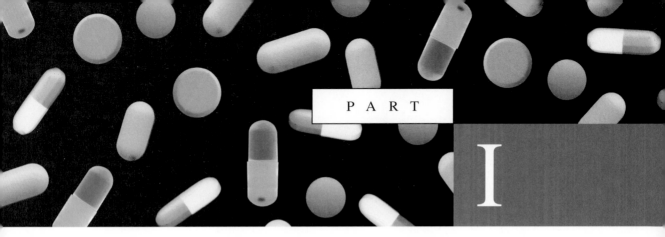

# INTRODUCTION

# DRUGS 1

## *A Sociological Perspective*

It's called the "power hour," or "21 for 21." At the stroke of midnight, with the arrival of the first moment of the first day of a 21-year-old's birthday, the legal drinking commences—21 shots in one hour. "We've all done it," says a friend of the initiate into the club of adult drinkers. Mike Hatch, a Minnesota attorney general, whose daughter was arrested a year ago in the midst of her rite, declared the practice "a parent's nightmare." The Fargo, ND, police seized a videotape of a birthday boy downing his quota of drinks in the Bison Turf bar. After his thirteenth shot, the young man vomits into a metal pail—provided by the bar—and then continues drinking toward his goal. "It's a tradition," explains one of his pals. In 2004, 21-year-old Jason Reinhardt died of an alcohol overdose after a "21 for 21" celebration in a Fargo bar, putting a serious dent in the tradition (Zernike, 2005).

"Marijuana will be the wonder drug of the beginning of this millennium," explains Lester Grinspoon, "just as penicillin was the wonder drug of the forties." Grinspoon, 76, is a physician, retired Harvard professor of psychiatry, and the author of six volumes on drugs, two of them devoted to cannabis. To the advocates of marijuana legalization, he is a guru. To the anti-legalization forces, he is the devil himself. With collaborator James Bakalar, he literally wrote the book on medical cannabis: *Marihuana: The Forbidden Medicine* (1997). Over the years, he's recommended the drug to hundreds of his patients who have sought relief from ailments as varied as multiple sclerosis, migraines, menstrual cramps, and nausea from chemotherapy. Through his book and his website, he has encouraged many thousands more to use the drug therapeutically. "I use it," he declares. "I have osteoarthritis. Both of my knees are going to have to be replaced. Bone is rubbing on bone, and it's painful. Walking in the woods is painful to me. But if I take a few puffs of marijuana, that resolves the problem."

Robert DuPont, founder and former director of the National Institute on Drug Abuse, and author of *The Selfish Brain: Learning from Addiction* (1997) disagrees: "People need to see medical marijuana for what it is: A hoax and a fraud." According to federal law, it's completely illegal. Ed Childress, special agent for the Drug Enforcement Administration, declares, "As it stands right now, there *is* no medical marijuana" (statements by Grinspoon and Childress, personal communications with the author).

It's "like something out of *The Godfather*," explains John Hamilton, American ambassador to Guatemala. Hamilton describes a recent bloody incident in which drug kingpin hit men walked into a hospital and killed a rival drug trafficker who was lying in a bed, along with the victim's attending nurses. Dozens of torched planes, once loaded with cocaine, lie in a nearby airplane graveyard, littering the tropical rain forest, discarded "like old soft drink cans" after their flight from Colombia. Within minutes of landing, smugglers offload their cargo, set their plane on fire, and disappear into the jungle. Officials estimate that 10 percent of the cocaine shipped through Guatemala is sold and used there, much of it distributed by street gangs. Crack cocaine, now a minor problem in the United States, has become a major economic enterprise for Guatemalan gangs. Since so many members smoke it, violence has escalated there. Organized crime uses gang members as hit men. Poverty and unemployment in Guatemala are rampant, nearly a third of the population is illiterate, and youths under 18, more than half the nation, have no hope of getting a job. Says a government official, they see only two options: "Migrate to the United States or get involved in the drug trade" (Jordan, 2004).

"It's almost like drinking a lot of coffee," explains Chris Langley, an English major at the University of Maryland, "but to a higher degree. . . . Adderall is a . . . stronger way of getting me to concentrate. It almost makes it like you don't mind studying." Adderall, the brand name for amphetamine sulfate, is a stimulant commonly prescribed to treat attention deficit/hyperactivity disorder (ADHD). It increases the capacity to concentrate, whether the user has ADHD or not. As a result, its use is widespread, especially on college campuses, as a study aid. Chris took a 10-milligram tablet and read 100 pages of the textbook in three hours; he got a 92 on the exam. "I know a lot of people who take Adderall," he says. A study conducted at the University of Wisconsin found that one out of five students there said that they had taken at least one attention deficit disorder drug without a prescription. Becky, who did not give her last name, another Maryland student, took a 30-milligram Adderall pill to study for her philosophy exam. "I just felt like I had constant energy," she said. The side effects included dehydration and "the jitters." She didn't mind, though, because she got an A on the exam. Dr. Robert Herman, a staff psychiatrist at the University of Maryland, warns that taking amphetamines in high doses "can cause paranoia and hallucinations, increase the heart rate, and even bring on a heart attack" (Nicholl, 2004, p. A41). There is no indication that the drug's potentially harmful side effects act as much of a deterrent for millions of college students taking shortcuts to do well in their courses.

Jan and Terry share a nightly bottle of Chardonnay during dinner. Both enjoy the slightly fuzzy feeling that comes over them after consuming two glasses of wine. They purchase the wine at a local liquor store located in a shopping mall a dozen blocks from their house. They are not breaking the law when they purchase, possess, or drink their alcoholic beverage. Neither engages in criminal behavior of any kind, nor has either ever been arrested.

Pat and Dale share a nightly marijuana joint before bedtime. Both enjoy the slightly fuzzy feeling that comes over them after smoking the joint. They purchase an ounce of marijuana each month from Stephanie, a close friend, who grows cannabis in her basement.

Five years ago, with fear and trepidation, Max took a bus to an inner-city neighborhood, spotted a dealer, purchased a rock of crack cocaine, took it home, and smoked it. The experience, he said, was fabulous, orgasmic, even better than sex. Nevertheless, he has never taken the drug again, nor does he intend to. In every other respect, Max is a law-abiding citizen.

James is an alcoholic. When drunk, he becomes belligerent. He has been in dozens of fistfights and has twice been arrested for assault, once for hitting his girlfriend. He has also totaled two cars and been arrested once for burglary.

Sally snorts "ice," or recrystalized methamphetamine. She admits to being addicted to the drug. Unemployed, she sells her body and shoplifts from department stores to pay for her habit.

Sam is a physician who considers himself a "controlled" user of prescription-strength narcotics. He never injects the drugs, uses them only for relaxation and recreation, confines his use to weekends, rarely uses them more than once in a given day, and never uses up the supply of narcotics he keeps on hand.

Veronica, 17, a high school senior, takes Ecstasy (or MDMA) several times a month at "raves," parties, and concerts with her friends. She enjoys the feeling of empathy or emotional closeness with others when she takes the drug. Her parents do not know about her use, and she pays for the drug by working at a part-time job. Her schoolwork seems not to be affected by her indulgence, and she plans on attending college in the fall. She regards her use of "E" as "no big deal."

We might think that drug use is confined to the present or recent past, that Veronica, Sam, Sally, James, Max, Pat, and Dale are distinctly modern creatures, sharing a practice never experienced by our ancestors. This is not the case at all. Human drug use is

## True-False Quiz

At the beginning of a recent class I taught in a course on drugs and crime, I administered a quiz. I asked the 165 students in this class to tell me if each of 32 statements was true or false. Each statement, in my judgment, was fairly straightforward, concrete, and, given the empirical evidence, clearly either true or false. Overall, my students gave right answers 45 percent of the time; that is, on average, 14.5 out of 32 of their answers were correct. In other words, flipping a coin would have yielded more accurate responses. This quiz illustrates that a high proportion of the public, including college students—a fairly well-educated segment of the public—believe in drug myths. It should be clear that we cannot rely on intuition and common sense to guide us to valid observations and conclusions. For that, we need to take a close look at the evidence and to have the courage to accept what is true. While I do not believe that the truth will necessarily "set you free," I do believe two things: It is a great deal better to know than not to know, and acting on what is true is more likely to lead to reasonable policies than is acting on what is false.

ancient, predating the fashioning of metal. Archaeologists have found the leaves of the coca plant, which contains cocaine, in graves dating back prior to the cultivation of corn. Researchers have unearthed caches of peyote "buttons," cut from the peyote cactus and collected into piles that were carbon-dated to 4,000 years ago. Paleontologists believe that humans cultivated the cannabis or marijuana plant and the opium poppy contemporaneously with the rise of agriculture over 10,000 years ago. The discovery and consumption of alcohol is equally as old. Even more remarkable, in an essay titled "The Signs of All Times," two anthropologists argue that many cave drawings feature optical patterns that correspond to the visions induced by psychoactive mushrooms and plants (Lewis-Williams and Dowson, 1988; Nicholl, 2000). If true, this would place early human drug use at tens of thousands of years ago. Some observers even speculate that animals used drugs even before humans did (Siegel, 1989), which throws the initial use of mind-active drugs back into the distant, indecipherable mists of time.

## WHAT IS A DRUG?

Many people imagine that words define clear-cut objects, that using a word is like picking up a rock and holding it in their hand. They think that everyone does—or should—agree on what a word means, that there is one and only one valid definition of each and every word. This belief is false. The fact is, for many words, observers strongly disagree as to their meaning. (See the accompanying box.) Try getting a group of intelligent, inquisitive, educated people to agree on the meaning of the concepts "truth," "justice," "love," "deviance," or "evil," and you'll see what I mean.

Over the years, I've asked the students in my drug courses to define what a "drug" is. A useful dictionary should contain an adequate definition, with all phenomena covered by it included, and all phenomena not covered by it excluded. For instance, to define a drug as a substance that is "addicting" is inadequate because of the problem of *overexclusion*—that is, it is too *narrow*. Such a definition excludes some substances that are referred to as drugs that are *not* addicting—for instance, LSD and psilocybin. To define a drug as "a chemical" is inadequate because of the problem of *overinclusion*—that is, it is far too broad. Many chemicals, such as water and sulfuric acid, are covered by this definition but are not considered drugs. Even a fairly standard definition such as "a drug is a substance that influences biological processes" is too inclusive. Why? Because many substances that no one would call drugs influence biological processes, including perfume, a warm shower, caviar, and a bullet fired from a gun.

The question "What is a drug?" cannot be answered strictly objectively (that is, based on a substance's pharmacological properties alone) or strictly subjectively (that is, the way a substance is seen, thought of, reacted to, and defined in a society). Each is necessary to define "drugness"—that is, what a drug "is."

In an unpublished paper, sociologist David Matza draws an analogy between how we categorize the concept "drugs" and the common use of the term "weed" (see Howard S. Becker's discussion at http://home.earthlink.net/~hsbecker/drugs.html). What we call "weeds" do not constitute a biological category "but rather a moral category." A weed is "a plant out of place," a place that a gardener or a homeowner doesn't want that plant to be. For instance, blackberry bushes might be "fine in their place," but on a lawn or in a patch of petunias, "they are in another plant's place." Drugs—substances that, in some contexts, might have a certain "place" in the world (as medicine, for example)—can be seen as "pharmacological weeds." They are ingested substances that, in certain contexts, are regarded by some observers as "out of place," used in a setting and for a purpose considered illegitimate.

"Drugs" as a concept can be defined both *materially*—that is, with respect to their essential or physically real properties—and *socially*—that is, as a construct that is both in our minds, in the way we picture or represent the world, and in the institutions we have built to deal with certain substances. In other words, drugs have a cultural, conceptual, and legal reality. In short, drugs can be defined by what they *are* and *do*—in a real-world bio-chemical and pharmacological sense—as well as what they are *thought* to do, including how the law defines them and how they are depicted in the media. The first definition delineates the "objective," or **essentialistic,** reality of drugs; the second definition delineates the "subjective," or **constructionist,** reality of drugs. Every phenomenon that has ever existed can be looked at through the lens of these two definitions or perspectives.

Definitions may be more—or less—useful according to a specific setting or context. For drugs, three such contexts come to mind: medical utility, psychoactivity, and illegality. The "medical utility" definition regards a drug as a substance that is used by physicians to treat the body or mind; the "psychoactivity" definition regards a drug as a substance that influences the workings of the brain or mind, that has an impact on cognitive and emotional processes; and the "illegality" definition regards as a drug any substance whose possession and sale are against the law. If we use one definition, certain logical implications unfold that may—or may not—be fruitful. On the other hand, if we use another definition, different implications make their appearance that, again, could be useful or counterproductive, depending on what we wish to achieve. In other words, even though both are tools, we don't use a hammer to saw wood or a saw to hammer a nail. Definitions, like tools, are useful only according to their context, that is, what we want to use them for.

## Medical Utility

A drug can be defined as *a substance that is used to treat or heal the body or mind*. According to this definition, drugs are used to return the user to a state of normalcy or "ordinariness." Drugs are used to remove that which is pathological, abnormal, or unnatural (the disease or medical condition). What about a medical definition? Can we define a drug by the criterion of medical utility? For instance, since heroin is not approved for medical use in the United States, does our medical definition exclude heroin? Does it mean that heroin is *not* a drug? Well, if we were to follow that definition alone, yes, it does dictate that, in the United States, we may not regard heroin as a drug. And is penicillin a drug? Well, if we were to adopt a strictly medical criterion as defining what a drug is, *of course* penicillin is a drug; it is used to treat bacterial infection. Hence, within a medical context, penicillin *is* a drug. But is penicillin used illegally on the street? No, because it does not produce a "high" or intoxication. In the context of illicit use, penicillin is *not* a drug.

Obviously, the medical definition contains both an objective (or "essentialistic") and a subjective (or "constructionist") element. In order for a drug to be used medically, we assume that it *does* something to the body—that is, it acts as a healing agent. This is its **objective reality.** But in addition, a drug has to be *recognized* as therapeutically useful by physicians, and physicians in a given society may not adopt it as medicine even if it works as a therapeutic agent. Controversy may exist with respect to whether some drugs are medically useful. For instance, as of this writing, marijuana is recognized and legitimated as medicine in 11 states but not the other 39, and it is not so recognized by the federal government. Heroin can be used as a painkiller in the United Kingdom but not in the United States. This means that heroin is medically a drug in the UK, but not in the States. This is the **subjective reality**—"socially constructed" side of the medical definition of how drugs are defined.

Hence, the same substance can be defined as a drug and not as a drug—depending on the context. Within the context of medicine, a medical definition of what a drug is, is useful. Outside that context, it may be less useful. However, it's also true, as we'll see, that a medical definition may *determine* a substance's legal status; that is, if it is *not* recognized as medicine by the government, this makes its possession and sale a crime. Since most of the drug use we'll be looking at in this book is recreational—that is, users engage in it for the purpose of getting high, for the effects themselves—the medical definition of drugs is not always useful to us in our quest to understand the causes, consequences, and implications of drug use.

## Illegality

Another possible definition of a drug is based on a substance's *legal* status, that is, whether possession and sale of a given substance is legal or illegal. According to this definition, it is the law and law enforcement that define what a drug is. If the possession and sale of a substance are against the law and likely to generate criminal punishment, then that substance is a drug. The legal status of drugs is a socially constructed definition: When a drug law is enacted, a category of illegal substances is created. Societies vary with respect to their drug laws. The same substance may be legal (and therefore not a drug according to the definition of illegality) in one jurisdiction and illegal (and therefore a drug) in another. Same substance, different status with respect to "drug-ness." In addition, drug laws change over time; substances move from being legal to illegal, and vice versa. Of course, presumably, the possession and sale of certain drugs result from their physical or material properties. That is, they are *considered* harmful because, presumably, they *are* harmful and are, as a consequence, prohibited by law. In other words, though the legal definition of what drugs are is a social construct, it is a construct that is hypothetically based on their physical (or "essentialistic") properties.

But here, as in the medical world, controversy is the rule. For instance, some marijuana users proclaim, "Marijuana's not a drug—it's a gentle, natural herb! How can you outlaw nature?" The fact is, according to federal law and the law of all but 12 states, the possession and sale of any quantity of marijuana are against the law and can result in arrest and incarceration. Moreover, in all states, the possession of large quantities (usually more than one ounce) is a crime. Hence, by the criterion of illegality, marijuana is most decidedly a drug. That is, any substance for which possession and sale can be punished by the law is a drug—regardless of how its users may feel about the matter.

In contrast, according to the definition based on a substance's legal status, alcohol is *not* a drug, since its sale is authorized and controlled by the state, and nearly anyone above the age of 21 may possess it. Hence, if someone who uses a definition based on a substance's legal status refers to the drug problem, it is clear that alcohol is *not* part of the drug problem, since its possession and sale are not illegal. The definition that is based on illegality uses a kind of double standard when it comes to psychoactivity: Certain substances that influence the mind are included, while others are excluded. To the federal government, the "drug problem" involves *only* the use and abuse of illicit substances—not alcohol.

A definition of a drug that is based on criminality is woefully inadequate if we wish to examine the full range of the use of psychoactive substances—that is, why drugs are used and what consequences this use has. Why? Because the "illegality" definition, based on a drug's legal status, excludes alcohol, a psychoactive substance with an extremely strong connection to both the use of illicit drugs and the behaviors that illicit drugs cause or are correlated with. Alcohol consumption can never be neatly separated from the use of illegal drugs, because the same people who use the latter consume the former. It is not enough to say, well, yes, but they also drink milk, because consumers of alcohol are *much more* likely to use and abuse illegal drugs than are persons who do not use alcohol. Alcohol tends to be used in addition to—not instead of—illegal drugs. In addition, people who commit crimes are much more likely to drink than are people who do not engage in criminal behavior, but these two groups don't consume milk at different rates.

In addition, illegality is absolutely crucial when considering the process of criminalizing the possession and sale of certain substances and enforcing the laws outlawing them. The criminalization of certain substances is a central topic when thinking about the issue of drug use. The fact that a given substance is illegal—regardless of its effects—determines the sorts of lives users and sellers lead. A consumer of alcohol may be using a psychoactive substance, but that fact alone does not make him or her a potential target of law enforcement. The same cannot be said for the consumers of illicit substances.

## Psychoactivity

"Pharmacology" is the study of the effects of drugs on biological organisms. "Psychopharmacology" is the study of the effects of drugs specifically on the brain, that is, on the mind. And "psychoactive," as we saw, refers to influencing the working of the mind. Hence, one way of defining a drug is *any substance that has an effect on the mind.* The scientists who study the effects of drugs are called pharmacologists. To the pharmacologist, **psychoactivity** is an extremely important property of chemical substances. A psychoactive substance is one that effects the workings of the central nervous system (that is, the brain and the spinal column) and thus influences thinking, mood, feeling, sensation, perception, and emotion—and, as a consequence, behavior as well. In short, the psychopharmacological definition—what a drug does to the brain, and therefore the mind—is a definition based *entirely* on the materially real or essential properties of substances. According to this definition, some substances (such as LSD) are drugs because they influence mood, emotion, and cognitive processes, while other substances (such as penicillin) are not drugs because they are not psychoactive. By this definition, a drug serves exactly the opposite purpose as that focused on in the medical definition. Medically, drugs are used to return the body or mind to a state of normalcy, ordinariness, or stasis. In contrast, from the perspective of psychoactivity, drugs are used to take the mind *out of* a state of normalcy, or ordinariness, into a state that the ancient Greeks referred to as *extasis*—ecstasy. Of course, this condition may be very mild (such as puffing on a cigarette or sipping a cup of coffee) or very powerful (such as swallowing a tab of LSD or smoking crack cocaine). But in principle, the functions of medical and recreational drugs, as implied by their respective definitions, are very different, almost the opposite of one another.

Different types of drugs have different sorts of effects, and we'll be looking at some of these effects in later chapters. But whenever a substance influences how the brain works, pharmacologists refer to it as psychoactive. In addition, to any social scientist, including the criminologist, psychoactive drugs are interesting because they influence human behavior, including drug-taking behavior. As a consequence, societies all over the world have decided that the possession and sale of certain substances should be illegal. This will be a central theme throughout this book.

To sum up: According to the "psychoactivity" definition, a substance is a drug if it alters the workings of the brain, and hence the mind—and consequently, human behavior. Any substance, regardless of its legal or medical status, that significantly and pharmacologically alters the workings of the brain *is* a drug. Any substance that does not is *not* a drug.

All substances that are taken recreationally on the street are psychoactive. This is the reason *why* they are taken—to get high, that is, *because* of their effect on the mind. Users seek the very effects that define or constitute the psychoactivity of certain chemical substances. For many users, the effects of particular drugs are felt as pleasurable, and it is this pleasurable state that users wish to achieve when they take the drug. Drug researchers refer to drugs that are taken primarily for their effects, that is, for the purpose of getting "high," as **recreational drugs.** Of course, pleasure comes in many guises and is achieved with many consequences. With all drugs, pleasure is a "package deal," and some of the contents of the package may be undesirable to all concerned, user and nonuser alike.

As to specifics, to return to our earlier question: Is alcohol a drug? According to the definition of psychoactivity, *of course* alcohol is a drug! Alcohol is psychoactive. It has effects on the brain; it influences mood, emotion, feeling, and cognitive processes. In addition, it powerfully influences human behavior. For instance, coordination diminishes under the influence. Human speech is impaired at low-to-moderate doses of alcohol. After drinking a sufficient quantity of alcohol, inhibitions are lowered and behavior that is unlikely to be attempted under most circumstances is all too often seized upon with great enthusiasm. To reiterate: from a psychoactive or psychopharmacological point of view, yes, most emphatically, alcohol is a drug! And so are cocaine and amphetamine; heroin, oxycodone (one brand name: OxyContin), and the other narcotics; marijuana; LSD ("acid"); and the so-called club drugs—Ecstasy ("XTC" or MDMA), ketamine ("special K" or "super K"), GHB ("G"), Rohypnol ("roofies"), and methamphetamine. But please notice: Pharmacologically speaking, alcohol is a drug *in exactly the same way* as these illicit substances are. Alcohol, like these illegal drugs, influences the mind, and hence behavior. In this respect, it is no different from all the controlled substances that law enforcement is concerned about.

Psychoactivity is a matter of both degree and kind. By "degree," I mean that some drugs are extremely mild in their effects. For instance, coffee is a mild stimulant. Technically, objectively, and psychopharmacologically, coffee is a drug. But it is such a weak substance that, for our purposes, it does not quite qualify as a drug; it does not produce effects that have relevance for most significant and important forms of human behavior. By "kind," I mean that drugs are classified according to their effects or action; some are referred to as stimulants, some as depressants, and so on. The kind of effects a drug has influences the way it influences and intertwines with human behavior. We'll look at drug effects and drug actions in detail in the next chapter.

## Defining Drugs: A Summary

For our purposes, two definitions, based on two different criteria, define what drugs are; these criteria are psychoactivity and illegality. The first is based entirely on an essentialistic or (presumably) materially real property, while the second is partly a socially constructed property and partly a consequence of the effects of certain substances. To the sociologist and criminologist interested in naturalistic behavior, a third definition of what a drug is, the *medical* definition, is far less useful. The fact that penicillin is used as a medicine is not interesting or relevant to the work of the criminologist or the sociologist studying recreational drug use. Of course, some substances are defined as drugs according to one of our two definitions (psychoactivity and illegality) but not the other; many substances are drugs according to both of these criteria. Morphine is a drug according to *all three* of our definitions: It is psychoactive; it is illegal if used for recreational purposes; and it is used by physicians to treat pain. Of course, many substances are not drugs according to any of our criteria.

## DRUG USE AND DRUG ABUSE

By themselves, sitting on a shelf, drugs are inert substances; they have effects only when they come into contact with other chemicals or with biological tissue. What makes drugs interesting to the researcher, the sociologist, the criminologist, the legislator and politician, the law enforcement officer, the journalist, and the general public is the fact that they are used and that their use has crucial consequences for both the user and for society at large. The fact that use is the be-all and end-all of the drug equation raises the issue of the distinction between *use* and *abuse*. "Use" is the more generic or general category. Drug use is simply ingesting a given substance or set of substances in any quantity with any frequency over any period of time; it covers the entire spectrum of consumption. "Abuse" is a specific subset or type of use. But how exactly should abuse be defined?

A great deal of nonsense has been written about this distinction. Some observers argue that abuse is the use of a psychoactive substance outside a medical context. Hence, following this definition, smoking one marijuana joint a month—or a year—for the purpose of getting high would qualify as drug abuse. Moreover, this definition adopts a legalistic or criminal criterion for what a drug is, thereby excluding alcohol. By this definition, since alcohol is not a drug, drinking a quart of whiskey a day is not drug abuse. (It is the abuse of alcohol, true, but it is not *drug* abuse.) It is not clear what such a definition seeks to achieve, aside from confirming that the drug laws are fair and just, demarcating "bad" substances (drugs) from "good" substances (nondrugs, such as alcohol and tobacco). For the purposes of this book, such a definition simply confuses the issues we wish to make clear.

"Drug abuse" connotes or conveys the impression that a given level of consumption of a substance is harmful. It implies that a certain type of use causes or is the manifestation of a medical or psychiatric pathology or illness of some kind, a sickness in need of treatment. It implies that certain varieties of use have deleterious effects on the user's life and/or the lives of persons around the user and/or the society as a whole.

One problem with this definition is that there is no exact, one-to-one correspondence between any level of use of any drug and any resulting harm. It is possible to be addicted to heroin for the better part of a lifetime and suffer no medical harm whatsoever. Contrarily, it is possible to get high on marijuana once, climb into a car, and smash it into a tree, killing oneself and three passengers. Is that an example of drug abuse? What about someone who smokes marijuana heavily for a lifetime and suffers no ill medical or social effects whatsoever? The fact is, *abuse* is a very inexact and loaded term. It cannot be pinned down with scientific exactitude—yet it *suggests* scientific exactitude. In this book, I'll use **drug abuse** as a purposely inexact term to refer to the level of use of a given drug at which harm is at least moderately likely.

Snorting two lines of powder cocaine once a month is unlikely to cause harm of any kind to the user; smoking two grams of crack cocaine every day is almost certainly harmful. Drinking a glass of wine at dinner causes harm to practically no one; drinking a quart of vodka a day will harm almost anyone. Exactly where we should draw the line between ordinary use and use that is so highly likely to be harmful that it qualifies as abuse cannot be determined with any precision. What we do know, however, is that higher levels of use cause more harm and are therefore more likely to qualify as abuse than are lower levels of use. As a general rule, the term *abuse* should be avoided except at levels of use that are by their very nature likely to be harmful, and hence abusive. Of course, any activity at any level carries a certain measure of risk of physical and mental harm, and this includes driving a car, flying on an airplane, taking a shower—and consuming psychoactive substances. In *Living Dangerously,* John Ross argues that ordinary, natural toxins in foods, the soil, and our home put our lives at greater risk than do synthetic chemicals (1999, pp. 123–148). "Where do we draw the line?" he asks rhetorically. "It's never quite clear" is his implied answer.

## TYPES OF DRUG USE

### Dimensions of Drug Use

At least two dimensions distinguish the many varieties of drug use: legal status and the goal or purpose of use. With respect to legal status, the possession and sale or distribution (or "transfer") of some drugs are criminal acts: They are against the law; they are crimes. If you are apprehended possessing, buying, or selling certain controlled substances, you may be arrested; if convicted, you may be sent to jail or prison. For example, heroin and LSD may not be possessed or purchased by anyone for any purpose. On the other hand, it is legal to sell, purchase, and possess certain drugs. Any nonincarcerated person above a certain age can legally buy alcoholic beverages in the United States. A number of psychoactive substances can be found in a wide range of legally purchasable products, including nicotine (in cigarettes and other tobacco products), caffeine (in coffee, tea, cola, and chocolate), and various substances in over-the-counter remedies (aspirin, Tylenol, No Doz, Sominex, Allerest, Dexatrim, and so on). In addition, many drugs are legal if taken for a medical purpose with a physician's prescription, but those same drugs are illegal if taken without a prescription, especially if used for recreational purposes.

With respect to the second dimension of drug use—goal or purpose—it would be a mistake to assume that all drugs are used for the same purpose by everyone. The same drug will be used for a variety of reasons by different users, and even the same person will use the same drug for different reasons at different times and in different situations. All drugs have multiple effects. Some users will seek one effect from a given drug, while others will take it for another. For example, in low-to-moderate doses, amphetamines produce mental alertness. Thus, many thousands of individuals who need to stay awake for many hours at a stretch use amphetamines to offset drowsiness and fatigue. These individuals include long-haul truck drivers, students cramming for exams, medical professionals on multihour rounds, and business executives attempting to remain alert after long work hours or sleepless nights. Here, we have instances of illegal **instrumental use:** Users are taking the drug not because they enjoy the effects they experience when they take it, but in order to achieve more effectively a goal of which most members of the society approve: working at a job, pursuing an education, or advancing a career. In this case, although the *goal* is approved, the *means* by which it is attained are considered unacceptable and illegitimate to most Americans. On the other hand, if you were to take that same drug, amphetamine, simply for the purpose of getting high, you would be engaged in illegal **recreational use.**

Calling an activity recreational does not imply that it is harmless. Many recreational activities are extremely dangerous: any extreme sport, motorcycles racing, hang-gliding, mountain and rock climbing, cave exploring, skydiving, scuba diving, even skiing. However, the term does imply that the activity is considered enjoyable by some. Recreational drug use involves taking a chemical substance to receive the pleasurable effects the drug generates in users—in short, *to get high.* Here, the effects are pursued not as *a means to an end* (as they are with instrumental use), but as *an end in themselves* (that is, to enjoy the effects).

There are vast and crucial differences among the effects of different drugs, both in quality or kind and in intensity or degree. Some drugs take you up, some down, and some take you in an altogether different direction. The effects of some drugs are relatively mild in the doses typically taken, and for most activities, the user can cope with the everyday world more or less normally—for instance, smoking one joint of marijuana of medium potency. The effects of other drugs are far more intense, even in fairly low doses, and the user must withdraw from the demands of the everyday world while under the influence or suffer the consequences. We cannot equate drinking two glasses of wine at dinner with an intense eight-hour LSD "trip" or the one- or two-minute "rush" that seizes the crack cocaine smoker. But all these activities—smoking marijuana, drinking wine, taking LSD, and smoking crack—represent taking a chemical substance *for the effects themselves,* that is, for the pleasure or euphoria the user experiences.

Combining these two dimensions—legal status and goal—yields four quite different types of drug use: (1) legal instrumental use, (2) illegal instrumental use, (3) legal recreational use, and (4) illegal recreational use. The combination of these two dimensions can be schematically represented as follows:

|  | Legal Status | |
| --- | --- | --- |
| **Goal** | **Legal** | **Illegal** |
| *Instrumental* | Taking Ambien with a prescription | Using amphetamines to study all night |
| *Recreational* | Drinking alcohol | Taking LSD to get high |

Each of these types of drug use will attract different users whose patterns and frequencies of use contrast significantly. Consequently, it is necessary to devote a separate discussion to each one.

## Legal Instrumental Use

There are two principal forms of legal instrumental drug use—over-the-counter and pharmaceutical. (Drinking coffee to wake up or stay alert might make up a third variety—with somewhat milder effects than the first two.)

Over-the-counter (OTC) drugs may be purchased directly by the public, off the shelf, without a physician's prescription. Examples of OTC drugs include aspirin, Tylenol, No Doz, Sominex, Allerest, and Dexatrim. The retail sales of OTC drugs totaled nearly $20 billion each year in the 2000s. OTC drugs are not strongly psychoactive and are rarely used for the purpose of getting high. There is one partial exception to this rule: Ephedrine and pseudoephedrine are used, illegally, to manufacture a decidedly psychoactive drug—methamphetamine. We'll look at this seductive, dangerous drug in the chapter on stimulants.

For the most part, OTC drugs are fairly safe if used instrumentally, and they do not normally represent a threat to human life. But no chemically active substance can be completely safe, and deaths have been known to occur from these products. As we'll see shortly, through a program called the Drug Awareness Warning Network (DAWN), the federal government collects information on hospital emergencies and deaths by drug overdose. Each year, acetaminophen (its most popular brand name is Tylenol) is judged to have contributed to tens of thousands of nonlethal medical emergencies nationwide; in addition, acetaminophen directly or indirectly causes several hundred deaths. Hence, acetaminophen is far from harmless. But *millions* of doses of this and other OTC drugs are taken every day. In relation to their total use, the toxicity of all OTC drugs is *extremely* low, and they need not be considered in detail in this book.

Prescription drugs are manufactured, bought, sold, and used legally, for medical purposes. They are prescribed by physicians to patients for the alleviation or cure of physical or psychiatric ailments, and the prescriptions are filled and sold at licensed pharmacies. In the United States, over 300,000 physicians are legally permitted to write prescriptions, and 150,000 pharmacists working at 60,000 locations are legally permitted to fill them. According to the trade journal *Pharmacy Times,* more than half of the prescriptions written in the United States are for the nation's most popular 200 drugs.

Pharmaceutical trade journals track the sales of prescription drugs on a year-by-year basis. Roughly 80 percent of the drugs sold by prescription are not psychoactive (that is, do not influence the workings of the mind), and a very small proportion of the hundreds of currently available prescription drugs are used illegally, on the street, for recreational purposes (that is, to get high). At the same time, prescription drugs—those that are taken legally, via prescription, for medical and psychiatric problems—are a major source of psychoactive drug use. In addition, the effects of some psychoactive drugs (mainly antipsychotics) are not experienced as pleasurable, and hence are never, or almost never, used for recreational purposes. Still, in absolute terms, illegally diverted or manufactured prescription drugs represent a major source of illicit recreational drug use in America.

In 2004, the pharmaceutical drug industry sold about $235 billion worth of drugs in the United States at the retail level. According to Scott-Levin, a corporation that tracks prescription drug sales (its website is PharmClips), 3.5 billion prescriptions were written in the United States in that year. As the American population ages, and as a higher proportion of the population lives into their eighties and even nineties, the sales of prescription medications will continue to rise. Most prescription drugs, as I said, are not psychoactive. Most medications work exclusively on the body and are used for the treatment of chronic physical conditions, such as high cholesterol (Lipitor, Zocor, Prevachol), ulcers (Prevacid), gastrointestinal disorders (Nexium), anemia (Procrit, Epogen), arthritis (Celebrex, Remicade), and asthma (Singulair, Aranesp). Only one of the nation's top 25 prescription drugs in dollar sales (OxyContin, a painkiller) is used illegally, recreationally, on the street. The drugs in which we are mainly interested in this book, however, are psychoactive; they do influence the workings of the mind and are widely taken for the purpose of getting high. Hence, ulcer, arthritis, and osteoporosis remedies are only marginal to our interests.

However, one reason prescription drug use could be interesting to us, is that, *if* a drug is psychoactive and its effects are experienced as pleasurable, it rarely remains permanently confined to the context of approved medical usage. Heroin, cocaine, morphine, barbiturates, amphetamines—all these widely used psychoactive drugs were originally extracted or synthesized, and then marketed, for medical purposes, and all eventually "escaped" into the world of recreational street usage. Many psychoactive drugs were initially sold over the counter; eventually, they came to be used on the street for the purpose of getting high. As a consequence, legal access to them was restricted via prescription, in order to cut down on their recreational use. In addition, for hundreds or even thousands of years, many of the psychoactive plants of the world—marijuana, coca, and psychedelic mushrooms and cacti—have been used for both healing and euphoria, often within a religious context. Hence, it is misleading to think that medical and recreational use occupy totally distinct worlds. Many of the drugs used in both worlds are identical, and the major motive for use in each of these two worlds—taking drugs to feel better— is the same. In other words, though in principle the licit medical and the illicit recreational worlds of drug use are distinct, in practice they overlap.

Even today in a number of instances, the legal instrumental use of drugs is controversial. For instance, at the federal level, possession and sale of marijuana for therapeutic purposes is completely illegal. However, in 11 states, physicians can legally (by state law) *advise* patients that smoking marijuana may ease their symptoms; they cannot *prescribe* the drug. Yet, even in these states, in which physicians and patients cannot be prosecuted by state law, they can be arrested and imprisoned by enforcers of federal law. Hence, the therapeutic status of marijuana currently remains controversial and unsettled.

Another example of a controversial therapeutic use of a psychoactive drug, as we saw, is the fact that heroin—even more effective as an analgesic than morphine—is approved in the United Kingdom to alleviate pain in terminally ill cancer patients. But in the United States, the federal government, fearing that approving therapeutic heroin will represent a "foot in the door" encouraging more illicit use, maintains its all-but-complete ban. Once again, we have legal therapeutic use in one setting but not another. Hence, these categories and the instances of drug use that fall in each should not be seen as immutable, as carved in stone. Definitions of what's legal or illegal, or what's instrumental or recreational, shift somewhat from one year to the next. For example, methaqualone was once a legal prescription drug but is now completely banned. Even in the same state or country, some physicians regard certain substances (marijuana, for instance, or heroin) as effective medicines, while other physicians do not—or at least the dominant, established medical organizations do not. Hence, not only may a drug's medical status vary from one jurisdiction to another and over time, it may also vary from one observer to another.

## Legal Recreational Use

Legal recreational drug use refers to the use of alcohol, tobacco, and caffeine products. In each case, a psychoactive substance is consumed in part to achieve a specific mental or psychic state. Of course, not every instance of the use of these three drugs is purely for pleasure or euphoria. Nevertheless, these drugs are consumed to attain a desired psychic state. Coffee drinkers do not achieve a high with their morning cup, but they do use caffeine as a pick-me-up to achieve a mentally alert state, a slight "buzz" to begin the day. Coffee drinking can be described as both recreational and instrumental. Many— probably most—cigarette smokers are driven by a compulsive craving at least as much as by the pleasure achieved by inhaling a psychoactive drug; still, the two dimensions are not mutually exclusive. If smokers do not achieve a true high, they at least achieve a psychic state that is more pleasure to them than abstinence.

Most individuals who engage in a given behavior have mixed motives for doing so, and subeuphoric pleasure cannot be discounted as a major reason most people use alcohol, tobacco, and, to a lesser degree, caffeine products. What is important about legal recreational drug use is not that it is identical to illegal recreational drug use (it is not—there are interesting differences between them), but that there are some interesting parallels and continuities that must be explored. Moreover, pleasure must not be viewed as an either-or proposition, but as a continuum.

Currently, the Substance Abuse and Mental Health Services Administration (SAMHSA) sponsors a survey, referred to as the National Survey on Drug Use and Health, of a nationally representative sample of American households. The survey asks respondents questions about the drug use, legal and illegal, of everyone age 12 or older living in the households it contacts. I'll describe this survey in more detail in Chapter 6. Suffice it to say at this point that, in the most recent survey (conducted in 2005), half of the sample (51.8%), or about 121 million people, said that they drank alcohol once or more during the past month, and were therefore defined by SAMHSA as "current" users. Nearly half of current drinkers or nearly a quarter of the total sample (55 million, or 22.7%) said that they consumed five or more alcoholic drinks on one or more occasions in the past 30 days. And a quarter of the total population age 12 or older (60 million, or 25%) said that they used cigarettes at least once in the past month—in fact, most of these are daily smokers—and, by definition, can be considered "current" or at least monthly users of cigarettes.

The extent of legal recreational drug use, then, is immense. (One qualification: The purchase of alcohol by anyone under the age of 21, and of tobacco products by anyone under 18, is illegal.) Excepting caffeine, the most popular legal recreational drug is alcohol, which, as we saw, is used regularly or currently by a majority of the American population. Even the second most commonly consumed legal recreational drug (again, excepting caffeine products), tobacco, is used by more individuals *than are all illegal recreational drugs combined*. Of all drugs, tobacco, in the form of cigarettes, is used most frequently. In the United States, smokers use their drug of choice on average 18.5 times a day—that is, they smoke just under a pack a day—whereas the vast majority of drinkers of alcohol do not use alcohol that much during an entire week. Alcohol is used by the population, on average—alcoholics, moderate drinkers, and abstainers included— roughly once a day. Consequently, alcohol and tobacco are so important as drugs of legal recreational use that I'll devote a separate chapter, Chapter 8, to them.

## Illegal Instrumental Use

Illegal instrumental use includes taking drugs without a prescription for some instrumental purpose of which society approves, such as driving a truck, studying for an exam, working at an all-night job, falling asleep, achieving athletic excellence, or calming feelings of anxiety so as to cope with the events of the day. People who purchase drugs illegally, without a physician's prescription, typically do not think of themselves as "real" drug users. They do not (primarily at least) seek the intoxication or high associated with ingesting the drug, but rather aim to achieve a goal of which conventional members of society approve. These users regard their behavior as merely technically illegal, and therefore not really criminal in nature, and completely nondeviant. They do not make a sharp distinction between the use of legal, over-the-counter drugs and the use of pharmaceuticals without a prescription. Both types of drug use have the same purpose: to achieve a mental, psychic, or physical state to facilitate the accomplishment of a socially approved goal. These drug users are only half right: Most Americans would approve of their goal but disapprove of the means they have chosen to attain it. And because they approve of the goal, most Americans would not condemn illegal instrumental use as strongly as they would drug use for the primary or exclusive purpose of achieving euphoria or intoxication. Again, instrumental use highlights the continuities among different kinds of drug use even while pointing out their differences as well.

As we'll see when we explore the use of some of these prescription drugs, illegal but instrumental has a variety of manifestations. It can occur through chemical diversion of legally manufactured pharmaceuticals; the mercenary, unethical, unprofessional, and thoroughly illegal writing—for a fee—of prescriptions by "script mill" doctors for anyone who asks for them; the illicit, clandestine production, either in the United States or abroad, of chemicals that are otherwise used in the manufacture of legal prescription drugs; and the illicit or semi-illicit importation (smuggling) into the United States of quantities of drugs that are manufactured elsewhere. Of course, the same drugs, derived from the same source, can be used for instrumental ends or for recreation and intoxication.

## Illegal Recreational Use

As we will see in Chapter 6 in more detail, the federal government invests millions of dollars a year in research to determine the extent of illicit drug use in the United States. It sponsors two major annual surveys that ask members of nationally representative samples, consisting of tens of thousands of respondents, questions about their consumption of illegal (and legal) psychoactive substances (see Figure 1-1). According to the most recent survey in 2005, 4 out of 10 Americans (46.1%), or 112 million, had at least tried one or more illegal drugs; 1 out of 7 (14.4%), or 35 million, had done so during the previous year; and 1 out of 13 (8.1%), or 19.7 million, had done so in the 30 days prior to the survey (SAMHSA, 2006). The illegal recreational drug use of school-age children and young adults is even more extensive. In 2005, half of high school seniors (50%)

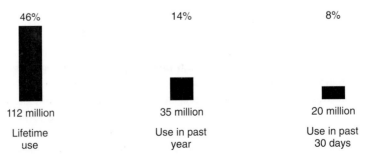

**Figure 1-1** Percentage of Americans saying they used at least one illicit drug during the period of time indicated, 2005.

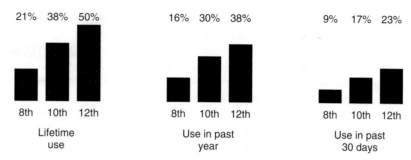

**Figure 1-1** concluded  **Percentage of American schoolchildren in each class using at least one illicit drug during the period indicated, 2005.**
*Source:* Johnston et al., 2006.

had taken an illicit drug once or more in their lifetimes; two-fifths (38%) had done so during the previous year; and a quarter (23%) had done so during the previous month. For tenth-graders, these figures were 38, 30, and 17 percent, respectively, and for *eighth-*graders, they were 21, 16, and 9 percent, respectively (Johnston et al., 2006, pp. 44–55). In other words, a great many people are using drugs not only casually but regularly. This book will uncover the whys and wherefores of these statistics.

## THREE ERAS OF DRUG USE: TECHNOLOGY AND SOCIOECONOMIC CHANGE

Drug use has undergone several revolutionary changes since its prehistoric origins. The first era of drug taking began in the corridors of prehistory when our ancestors ingested plants that contain psychoactive ingredients, such as marijuana, coca leaves, psychedelic mushrooms, peyote, and opium, as well as the alcohol that issues from fermented fruit. This can be referred to as the **natural era** of drug consumption. In ancient and tribal societies, the use of mind-altering drugs tended to take place either in a religious and ceremonial context or in a medicinal setting. Opium smoking, a major exception to this rule, probably began as a medical remedy but for centuries has also been for the purpose of recreation, that is, for getting high. In all likelihood, the dominant motive for the consumption of alcohol has always been recreational. However, a major portion of that recreational use was linked to collective and ceremonial goals. For instance, the Dionysian cult of ancient Greece seems to have been oriented toward drinking oneself into an ecstatic frenzy, dancing to music, engaging in orgiastic sex, and ripping apart and eating the bodies of sacrificial animals. The current use of wine in religious ceremonies is an extremely diluted and temperate version of this early Dionysian cult.

The natural era included at least one innovation that yielded psychoactive substances considerably more potent than their natural plant form: the distillation of alcoholic beverages. Wine is only 10–13 percent alcohol, but distillation—boiling fermented liquids, then recovering their more alcohol-potent vapors—produces drinks such as gin, vodka, brandy, and whiskey that have a much higher alcohol content (roughly 40–50%). Scholars place this innovation at roughly 800 C.E., in the Arabian peninsula; it required several centuries, however, for the practice of distillation to reach the shores of Europe, where it was more fully exploited. Higher-potency drinks have the capacity to get the consumer intoxicated more quickly, with a lower volume of beverage.

The second or **transformative era** began at the dawn of the nineteenth century with discoveries and innovations that produced substances more potent than natural plant products. The key to the transformative era was that a *new* substance was created from the natural plant product by means of a chemical extraction. The 1800s generated a dozen or so innovations and discoveries that vastly increased the potency of the drugs found in nature. For instance, in 1803, morphine, a much more potent narcotic, was extracted from opium, a natural plant product. In 1831, codeine was synthesized from opium. In 1859, cocaine was isolated from coca leaves, a natural product containing roughly 1 percent cocaine. And in 1874, diacetylmorphine (heroin) was synthesized from morphine. In addition, these more potent substances were delivered into the body by means of new routes of administration or ways of taking drugs. For instance, in 1853, the hypodermic syringe was devised, and three years later, it was brought to the United States. It was used to administer calibrated—and very potent—intravenous (IV) doses of morphine.

In short, nineteenth-century America witnessed a virtual explosion of inventions, discoveries, and applications that virtually guaranteed that the country would be awash in drugs—and, moreover, drugs vastly more potent than their natural progenitors. An IV administration of morphine, heroin, or cocaine, for example, can reach and activate the pleasure centers of the brain considerably more quickly and vastly more effectively and efficiently, and consequently can generate a physical and psychological dependency more readily, than can the natural forms of the drugs, less efficiently administered. (As we'll see in the next chapter, smoking is a slightly more efficient and effective route of drug administration than IV injection.)

The third or **synthetic era** dawned early in the twentieth century, when scientists began to create drugs entirely from chemicals not found in nature. Scientists synthesized the first barbiturate drug, Barbital, in 1903 and over time continued to isolate different barbiturate compounds with slightly different pharmacological effects—for instance, Luminal (1912), Amytal (1923), and Nembutal (1930). In all, some 2,500 barbiturate compounds have been created in the lab. In the late 1920s, scientists synthesized amphetamines, a potent stimulant. These early chemicals were developed by scientists seeking some medical or therapeutic benefit from the synthetic compounds they discovered. (Nearly all drugs—natural, transformative, and synthetic—had their origin in medicine.) This effort spawned what has been called "the pharmacological revolution" (Ksir, Hart, and Ray, 2006, pp. 7–8), that is, the development of entirely synthetic chemicals used in the treatment of mental illness. In the 1950s, psychiatrists administered the first of the many antipsychotics, Thorazine, to mental patients; today, nearly all schizophrenics and clinically depressed patients take or are administered one or more chemicals to treat their mental disorders.

For our purposes, what is most interesting about the synthetic era, and the pharmacological revolution it spawned, is that not only are these drugs psychoactive, many also produce effects that recreational users enjoy and seek. In other words, a number of the psychotherapeutic drugs "escaped" into the street, to be used for the purpose of getting high. (Some of them—the antipsychotics and the antidepressants, for instance—are not used recreationally because they do not have effects that users regard as pleasurable.) LSD, first synthesized in 1938 and whose effects were discovered in 1943, was initially studied as a possible cure for schizophrenia. PCP, or phencyclidine, synthesized in the 1950s, was first used as an anesthetic and tranquilizer for animals. In the early days of the recreational use of psychotherapeutic drugs—mainly barbiturates, tranquilizers, and amphetamines—young people stole a few pills from their parents; faked symptoms of psychic distress, thereby convincing their physicians to write prescriptions; or located and paid unethical doctors to give them prescriptions for bogus ailments. Later, illicit labs sprang up to manufacture the chemicals that went into these drugs, and distributors sold them to a clientele interested more or less exclusively in taking the drugs to get high. Even today, the recreational use of the synthetic psychotherapeutic drugs rivals that of drugs whose recreational use stretches back much further in time. For instance, in the latest government survey (conducted in 2005), twice as many people illegally used a prescription drug for nonmedical purposes, that is, to get high, during the previous month (2.6%) than used cocaine to get high (1.0%). The synthetic era, spawned by the search for psychotherapeutics, is extremely important for our understanding of the use of psychoactive drugs for recreational purposes.

Superimposed on the technological changes that delivered more potent drugs into the hands of users are sociocultural and economic changes that radically transformed the world of drug use. Of such changes, perhaps two stand out as most influential: (1) the availability to the young of a disposable income, and (2) globalization.

Using drugs in a market economy for recreational purposes presupposes a source of discretionary, disposable income, or access to the largesse of someone who has such an income. In economies in which the young have no such income, the segment of the population typically most likely to use drugs recreationally is denied access to them, and hence is unlikely to use or is capable of using only under nonroutine circumstances, such as generating an income illegally. Therefore, in tribal, agrarian, and early industrial societies, it was adults, not adolescents, who were most likely to use drugs recreationally. However, beginning in the second half of the twentieth century, income in the hands of the young increased enormously, and as a result, their capacity to spend that income on any and all recreational activities, including drugs, has increased as well. Consequently, over the past century or so, the center of gravity in drug use has shifted from young adulthood to late adolescence.

**Globalization**—the expansion of the international economic network, drawing many previously local and national markets into a single worldwide economy—has influenced drug use by transforming the drug trade. The degree to which drugs are distributed on an international basis varies from substance to substance. Still, a certain proportion of the distribution of all drugs depends on interconnections that reach across national borders. Beginning in 1972 with the dismantling of the so-called French Connection, which previously had supplied 80 percent of the heroin sold in the United States, the number of source countries, the different routes through which drugs have traveled, and the number of national and ethnic groups involved in the trafficking of all drugs, have exploded. Since the 1970s, the drug trade has been transformed from a cottage industry with a small number of country-to-country linkages into a global enterprise with multiple international linkages, whose profits are greater than that of three-quarters of the national economies of the world. The movement of persons, goods, and information across national boundaries constitutes a literal superhighway for traffickers to transport drugs from source to user. In addition to an economy that is increasingly globalized, and hence increasingly favorable to the worldwide distribution of drugs, the past half-century has seen a globalization of information, travel, and the media, all of which have facilitated drug use and distribution.

## AN OVERVIEW OF DRUG USE IN THE TWENTY-FIRST CENTURY

The drug situation in the first few years of the twenty-first century can be summed up in the following generalizations, which will form much of the core of this book.

- With respect to death and disease, tobacco and alcohol remain the country's number-one and -two drug problems, killing more than half a million people annually. In comparison, the illicit drugs, or the illicit use of prescription drugs, cause roughly 20,000 deaths a year.
- Drugs vary enormously with respect to their capacity to cause acute (that is, immediate or short-term) medical complications, including death by overdose. On a dose-for-dose basis, heroin is the most harmful in this respect, but cocaine and alcohol appear extremely frequently in the nation's overdose statistics. Unfortunately, the overdose statistics for alcohol, for adults, are tabulated only when it is used in combination with another drug; if use by itself were tallied, alcohol's totals would be six or seven times greater than for cocaine and heroin (Goldstein, 2001, p. 11).
- Drugs also vary enormously in terms of generating or being associated with acute, problematic behavioral changes, such as discoordination, violence, and poor impulse control. Alcohol, barbiturates, cocaine, and the amphetamines are heavily implicated here, while tobacco ranks low in this respect.
- Seriously involved, abusive users of cocaine number roughly 3 million, and of heroin, close to a million—perhaps a fifth the number of alcoholics and problem drinkers. Nearly all the country's 30 million smokers use tobacco abusively.
- Chronic, abusive cocaine and heroin use is most likely to be concentrated in the inner cities, mainly among racial and ethnic minorities.
- The high-level, abusive use of cocaine and heroin is declining, albeit slowly. The addict population is getting older (and sicker), and there are relatively few fresh young recruits to their ranks.
- Marijuana use, especially among the young, is higher than it was a decade ago, but since 1996, the percentage of use has either remained stable or decreased.
- Marijuana is by far the most commonly used illicit substance. There are roughly as many episodes of marijuana use as of all the other illegal drugs combined. In addition, the chronic, abusive use of marijuana is more common than for cocaine and heroin, but it is associated with far less crime and vastly fewer psychological and medical pathologies.
- The use of several "club" drugs introduced in the past two decades—most notably, Ecstasy, ketamine, Rohypnol, and GHB—has become widespread, but so far, it has not rivaled that of the older, more entrenched illicit substances. Since 2000, the percentage of eighth-, tenth-, and twelfth-graders using Ecstasy and the other club drugs has declined significantly.
- Although over the past decade and a half, methamphetamine has become one of the more widely used drugs in the country, its use remains fairly regionalized, with high

levels of use in some, mainly western and midwestern, cities, and little or no use in most eastern and southern cities. Even so, in the past half dozen years, "meth" has been seeping into areas that previously had no experience with the drug.

- Drugs vary with respect to how "loyal" their users are to them. As a general rule, users tend to continue using the legal drugs—alcohol and tobacco—strikingly more than is true of the illegal drugs. Among the latter, marijuana, the most "legal" of the illegal drugs, manifests the highest continuance rate. LSD and PCP tend to be drugs of episodic, sporadic use.

- Alcohol is the only drug that a majority of at-least one-time lifetime users have taken during the past month. The nicotine in cigarettes is the only drug that over 8 out of 10 of at-least one-time past-year users have taken during the past month. For *all* illicit drugs, the vast majority of users either discontinue use after experimenting with them or take them on a noncompulsive, recreational basis.

- The federal government spends nearly $20 billion annually fighting the drug war, roughly two-thirds of that on law enforcement; states spend roughly the same amount and in roughly the same proportion.

- In the United States, the sale of illicit drugs is a $65-billion-a-year business at the retail level, a steep decline over the past 20 years; over half of that expenditure is for cocaine. Some 260 tons of cocaine and 13 tons of heroin were imported into the United States in 2000.

- The country's rate of incarceration generally and for drug offenses specifically is the highest in the world. At the dawn of the new millennium, there were roughly 1.5 million prisoners in the United States, exclusive of jails. A majority of federal and a quarter of state inmates are drug offenders. African Americans are disproportionally on the receiving end of these sentences. At the federal level (about 10% of all inmates) sentences for drug offenses are only slightly more than a year shy of those for violent offenses.

- In spite of the country's stepped-up vigilance against drug offenses, heroin and cocaine are now purer and cheaper than they were two decades ago.

- It is clear from the vast research literature that drug courts and drug treatment programs are more effective than incarceration for nonviolent drug offenders. Indeed, for every dollar spent on the former, taxpayers receive three or four dollars back in savings to the community.

## SUMMARY

Drug use exists both as a material or essentialistic reality and as a constructed or conceptual reality.

Drugs are chemicals, and they cause materially real effects in the bodies and minds of real people who ingest drugs. But drugs are also phenomena that are talked and thought about, reported on and reacted to, and enshrined into law. Any investigation of drug use must walk along these two paths, if you will, simultaneously.

This means that when someone drinks a certain quantity of alcohol, intoxication and discoordination are an inevitable, measurable product of the interaction between the substance, alcohol, and a human body. But it also means that alcohol, a drug, is depicted in the media in a certain way, is thought about by the population at large in a certain way, and is handled by the law in a certain way.

Drugs are substances with effects, and these effects (or supposed effects) have objective, essentialistic, or intrinsic properties. In this book, the effects of substances on the workings of the mind are paramount. They manifest themselves in material or real-world effects—a reality that transcends perception, myth, law, and image. But drugs are also substances that are seen, defined, judged, conceptualized, and socially and legally constructed in certain ways. Indeed, the ways that substances are defined may even influence the effects substances have. This is one of the beauties of our subject, and it is a theme that runs throughout this book. The twin tracks along which we run, so seemingly separate, are inextricably intertwined.

"Drug abuse" is a term that has been employed both objectively and pejoratively by observers whose intention is to vilify the consumption of illicit (but not legal) psychoactive substances. As an objective term, it refers to drug consumption that is harmful and/or risky to users and to persons who come in contact with users. This can be measured by specific, concrete, material indicators. As a pejorative term, it argues that only illegal substances can be drugs, and hence only the use—*any* use—of illegal substances can be drug abuse. This means that slugging down a quart of vodka a day is *not* drug abuse while smoking one marijuana cigarette a week *is*. This makes no sociological sense, although it may be useful for propaganda purposes. The term "use," in contrast, seems to be a more neutral term, referring to any consumption of a psychoactive substance.

Drug use can be divided into distinctly different although overlapping types based on two dimensions, the recreational-instrumental and the legal-illegal dimensions. Some types of drug use are pursued for the purpose of getting high ("recreational"), and others to achieve a state that facilitates the achievement of a goal of which society approves ("instrumental"). Most people identify drug use only with the illegal-recreational pattern, but illegal use can also be instrumental (taking amphetamines at night to cram for an exam), and legal use can be both recreational (drinking a glass of wine at meals) and instrumental (taking Ambien to ease anxiety and get to sleep). Each type has its characteristic patterns and extent of use, its own caste of users, and its own networks of distribution.

The history of psychoactive drug use, which stretches back into prehistory, can be roughly divided into three eras. The first is the "natural" era, during which the drugs that humans consumed derived from natural substances, such as plants (cannabis, opium, psychedelic mushrooms) and fruits and starchy vegetables (which produce alcohol). This era encompassed the eighth-century innovation of distillation, which produced more potent alcoholic beverages—specifically, distilled spirits—by boiling off and then recovering the more alcohol-rich vapors of naturally occurring alcoholic substances.

The nineteenth century was the "transformative" era, during which scores of innovations transformed botanical products that occurred in nature into new, semisynthetic psychoactive substances. These substances were not only new, they were vastly more potent than the botanical forms from which they were derived; that is, they contained a higher concentration of the psychoactive drug. Opium, a natural substance, was transformed into morphine (1803) and heroin (1874), and cocaine was synthesized from coca leaves (1859). In addition, inventions, including the hypodermic syringe, delivered these semisynthetic substances into the human body more efficiently and effectively.

With the dawn of the twentieth century, innovations in chemistry permitted the synthesis of completely artificial substances that did not previously exist in a state of nature. The barbiturates were the first of such substances; amphetamines followed soon after. Modern chemistry has produced countless compounds, including "designer drugs," that alter the workings of the brain, dozens of which are used recreationally: Ecstasy (MDMA), PCP, methamphetamines, GHB, ketamine, and Royphnol, to list just a few.

In addition to technological innovations that revolutionized the world of drug use, several social and economic changes produced equally momentous changes. Two are worthy of note: the earning and accumulation of a disposable income by adolescents, that segment of the population most likely to use drugs recreationally; and globalization, or the development of a worldwide network in communications, transportation, trade, and the flow of income—and hence, the distribution of drugs.

## KEY TERMS

| | | |
|---|---|---|
| constructionism   7 | natural era   19 | recreational drug use   13 |
| drug abuse   12 | objective approach to reality   8 | subjective approach to reality   8 |
| essentialism   7 | psychoactivity   10 | synthetic era   20 |
| globalization   21 | recreational drugs   10 | transformative era   20 |
| instrumental drug use   13 | | |

## ACCOUNT:  The Illegal Instrumental Use of Adderall, an Amphetamine

*The following interview was conducted by Laura Franz, a University of Maryland undergraduate. The interviewee is a student at a major state university. He routinely uses Adderall, an amphetamine and controlled substance, not for the purpose of getting high but mainly to stay up at night and study for exams. "A" indicates the interviewee's name; "L" refers to Laura, the name of the interviewer. At the beginning of the interview, "A" is breaking up a 20-milligram tablet of the drug into a powder.*

**L:** How does your body feel [when you take Adderall]?

**A:** Well, my body feels more alert and active and more awake like when you take any stimulant, like when you take too much

caffeine. It's like a double-edged sword, it feels good to have the high, but . . . , when you start coming down, that feels bad. For that reason I just try to completely ignore the high so all it is is me being focused and being able to work. . . .

**L:** Did you have any trouble earlier in school?

**A:** When I was younger it was a lot easier to study and prepare for an exam. I would study the night before a test. I wouldn't have any problems paying attention or staying focused. But as soon as I came to college . . . , in the middle of my first semester, I discovered Adderall, 'cause, well, like, my first math test, I studied for 42 hours straight without Adderall, just on

Red Bulls [a high-energy soft drink] and caffeine trying to stay awake. I studied a day and a half beforehand and went to sleep and got a good night's sleep, woke up, took the test the next day. I got a 38 on it. And this semester, I'm retaking the course and I've taken Adderall before each test and the lowest grade I've gotten is an 87, and I haven't studied nearly as long.

**L:** So the Adderall really seems to improve your grades?

**A:** It cut my study time by more than half and has improved my grades, like, threefold.

**L:** Has it improved your grades because you stay awake [on it]?

**A:** No, it's not about staying awake. It's about being focused, being able to concentrate on the work.

**L:** Do you have a learning disability? Because the symptoms of ADD [attention deficit disorder] are being distracted, an inability to focus, etc. Have you been diagnosed with a learning disability?

**A:** I haven't been diagnosed but I am 99.9 percent sure that I have ADHD [attention deficit/hyperactivity disorder].

**L:** And why do you believe this?

**A:** Well, for one, [because of] the effectiveness Adderall has on me. And [two,] I have a lot of problems paying attention to anything. . . .

**L:** What were your grades?

**A:** My weighted GPA at the end of high school was 3.98. My GPA at the end of my first year of college was 1.4. In high school I was all-honors. I took advanced-placement courses, [and] my senior year, I took courses at the community college. . . .

**L:** Do your parents know about this?

**A:** My parents have no clue that I do Adderall. I doubt they even know what Adderall is. I told my mom that I think I have ADHD and that I would like to go to the school psychiatrist and see if I can get a prescription for Ritalin [a stimulant used to treat ADHD] or something . . . , but they weren't really supportive. They don't

like the idea that I have a mental problem; they don't like the idea that I need medication of any sort. They think their son is perfect.

**L:** Have you explained to them your difficulty?

**A:** Oh yeah, I explained to them that I have so many problems concentrating and, I mean, it's reflected in my grades, but, I don't know, it's not really their choice, so . . . , whatever.

**L:** Are you scared of them finding out?

**A:** I'm scared of them finding out that I snort things [drugs] because that is . . . frowned upon. My parents know I smoke weed, but that's not too bad because a lot of people smoke weed and are open about it. But snorting coke and stuff [other drugs used for recreational purposes] is a whole level above.

**L:** Do you think this [taking Adderall] is as bad as doing coke?

**A:** Oh, no, that's the thing. I don't think it's nearly as bad as coke. I don't see anything wrong with doing Adderall. It just helps you get shit done.

**L:** What other drugs have you done? Or still do?

**A:** Currently, I smoke weed and drink alcohol, basically every day. Every once in a while, I do coke. I'm trying to stop though, because it's really, really bad. I've done E, I've snorted it. I've done [psilocybin] mushrooms, I've used Percocet and Vicodine recreationally, Ambien recreationally, I've tried acid [LSD], I've tried PCP. . . . Let me think. . . . I know there's more. I've smoked opium, I've smoked hash. Oh, and Adderall, obviously. . . .

**L:** When do you take Adderall?

**A:** I take it whenever I have work to get done that is usually due the next day. . . . If there is something large like a test for a course I haven't been to for three weeks, then it's necessary.

**L:** Do you take Adderall for your job?

**A:** No.

**L:** Do you take Adderall to stay awake, because it's a stimulant?

**A:** It's not about staying awake at all. It's about performance improvement. . . . Adderall makes it so that if I am typing I can keep typing. I hate to sound like a hippie, but it expands your mind. It makes you so you are more able to do things like write a paper on a topic you don't know much about, or getting a lot of research done. A couple of weeks ago, I took 60 milligrams of Adderall, read a 300-page book, and wrote a six-page paper on it. And I got an A on it—for a course I've been to only twice. I didn't even have any background knowledge [in the material I wrote the paper about] either. If I hadn't been on Adderall, I wouldn't have had the focus to get through.

**L:** So do you feel that you wouldn't have gotten that work done if it wasn't for Adderall?

**A:** Well, I would have turned something in but I wouldn't have read that whole book and 90 percent of the term paper would have been BS. . . . Without Adderall, I would be able to get everything done, but the level of work would not be as good and it would take me at least five times as long to get everything accomplished. . . .

**L:** Where do you get the pills from?

**A:** I have a couple people who have prescriptions I can get it from.

**L:** Do they have ADD?

**A:** Well, yeah, they have been diagnosed with ADD. That doesn't necessarily mean that they have it [the disorder]. Either way, they have a bottle full of it and they figure "spread the wealth" because it is such a good thing. They sell it for a couple bucks apiece, enough to cover the price of the prescription. . . .

**L:** Are you worried about getting in trouble?

**A:** No. I mean, there's not much of a way to get into trouble, unless a cop walks into my room and sees me snort it. One thing I have

to say is, people act like it is really secretive, but it's not that secretive. It's just that you take it when you are studying and when you are studying, you need to be alone because the distractions will screw up your studying. . . . So when you are taking Adderall, you are usually getting into the mind-set to study, so you are usually alone. . . .

**L:** What about hiding it from your friends?

**A:** I don't hide it from any of my friends. Most of them use it. I'd say 80 percent of college students use Adderall or have used it at one time.

**L:** You are in a fraternity. . . . Do your [fraternity] brothers know you use Adderall?

**A:** I would guess that all except for four or five of my brothers use Adderall. Just to study—not recreationally. Further, I would say that it is roughly the same statistic for every fraternity and every sorority on campus. . . . I have friends in a bunch of other fraternities and it's the same thing. . . . It's the same all across the board.

**L:** Do you ever use the drug with them?

**A:** I've used it to study with other people before, but it wasn't for fun.

**L:** So pretty much it is a private drug to do?

**A:** Yeah, but like I said before, it's only private because the purpose it fulfills is kinda a private thing. You don't go out to a party and study. Adderall is for studying. Therefore, you study in private.

**L:** So you are saying you do not use it recreationally?

**A:** No, I don't use it recreationally.

**L:** You use it strictly for the purpose of studying?

**A:** Exactly.

**L:** So you are no different from the kid who has his prescription and takes his medicine before he goes to class?

**A:** Exactly. I use it strictly to get work done. If I don't have work to do, then I don't see any reason to waste the Adderall and waste my time. . . .

**L:** Do you think anything contributes to the desire to take Adderall?

**A:** Actually, I think there is one common denominator.

**L:** What is that?

**A:** Kids have the desire to do well, so much so that they know how to do well by getting Adderall and recognizing that it helps. They can recognize what they need to do in order to do well.

## QUESTIONS

Do you see a basic difference between the illegal instrumental use of an amphetamine and the illegal recreational use? Do you see a difference between the legal instrumental use of a psychoactive prescription drug (obtaining a prescription from a physician for a medical or psychiatric condition) and using the same controlled drug instrumentally, but without benefit of a prescription? Do you think this student is correct—that 80 percent of college students today use a controlled substance to study and write papers? Is it as widespread as he says? Would it make a difference to you if that were true? Is this student's instrumental use of psychoactive drugs as separate and distinct from his recreational use as he claims? What should be done about the illicit, nonprescription use of controlled substances for instrumental purposes? Do you believe "the ends justify the means"?

# DRUGS

2

## *A Pharmacological Perspective*

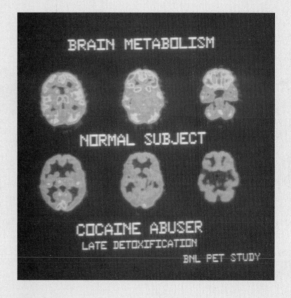

In the previous chapter, we learned that reality may be looked at from both an essentialistic (or "objectivistic") and a constructionist (or "subjectivistic") perspective. Everything in the world, anything we could point to, indeed, any concepts we can imagine—all can be approached from the same two perspectives—and that includes drugs.

Understood essentialistically, drugs are substances that are attributed with material or physical properties and/or effects.[1] The essentialistic definition of drugs points to a real-world quality that (presumably) resides *within* or is *intrinsic to* substances that are referred to by the term "drugs." If a substance possesses that internal or intrinsic quality, it is a drug; if such quality is lacking, it is not a drug. The quality is within, not external to, outside of, or imposed upon, that substance. To the essentialist, that quality can (supposedly) be determined as a result of investigation, evidence, and introspection—that is, scientific investigation. So, the essentialist would say that the concept of drug is defined by a substance's real-world, material or physical characteristics, such as its chemical structure or its effects—that is, what it *does* to living organisms.

In contrast, understood from a constructionist perspective, drugs are defined subjectively—that is, in terms of what they are *thought* to be, of how the public, law enforcement, the media, and politicians *regard* them. To the constructionist, the defining quality of drugs stems not from what's inside or intrinsic to substances, but from what's *external* to them, what's imposed on them by the society. To the constructionist, "drug-ness" is imposed on substances by how they are seen, judged, legislated, reacted to, represented, or thought about.

Both the essentialist and the constructionist perspectives are important in the world of drugs, but the relevance of each perspective emerges specifically within certain contexts. In this chapter, I adopt the perspective of the natural scientist and look at drugs as physical substances with material or real-world effects—in short, as having an objectivistic or essentialistic reality. The fact is, independent of how psychoactive substances are thought about and looked at by the society in which they are used, they are chemical agents with specific actions that have to be understood. It is the mission of this chapter to understand the pharmacological action of psychoactive drugs. This means that in this chapter, it is the essentialistic perspective that will be central.

As we've seen, the drugs in which sociologists and criminologists are interested are chemical substances that have mind-altering or psychoactive properties. To us, as students of drug use, what makes drugs interesting and distinctive is their capacity to influence mood, emotions, and intellectual processes. This is the case because it is the psychoactivity of certain chemical substances that gives them their popular appeal, that impels substantial members of society to experiment with and use them. It is precisely this appeal that initiates the chain of events that leads to their scrutiny by social scientists.

People who take a drug typically experience psychic effects, enjoy the experience, and tell others about what they experienced. Neophytes—persons who have never ingested a given drug—hear descriptions of a drug's effects from friends and acquaintances who have used the drug. Most of these descriptions are positive. "It's great—you gotta try it" is such a common theme in such descriptions that it is something of a cliché. Most of these positive descriptions are inspired by a drug's pharmacological action: how its chemical structure

---

[1]Essentialism is *not* what's true, while constructionism is what is falsely *thought* to be true. Essentialist definitions are those that are based on *notions* of ultimate truth—that is, what something, presumably, "really, truly" is, as manifested in the way they are in the material world. Such definitions are not always or necessarily correct according to scientific evidence. For instance, someone may define a drug as a substance that causes violent behavior. This is an essentialistic definition, but no scientist would find it valid or terribly useful. In the same vein, constructionist definitions may or may not be false; for instance, drugs may (or may not be) as harmful as the members of society think they are. The two definitions are, however, based on entirely different dimensions.

interacts with the central nervous system. It is the effects that users enjoy that (along with other factors such as availability and individual motivation) prompts their use which, in turn, influences or causes behavior *associated* with their use. *Drug* effects are absolutely central to drug use. Hence, drug effects are likewise central to why societies attempt to control access to psychoactive substances.

But psychoactivity is not the only effect of psychoactive drugs. In the material world, we rarely get something for nothing, and psychoactivity is always accompanied by a host of other effects as well. At a certain dose, taken over a sufficiently extended time, psychoactive drugs produce significant side effects. Some chemical substances are capable of producing a powerful **dependence** in users. Others have extreme **toxicity**—that is, when using them, a drug "overdose" may take place. Still others produce medical damage; they kill body tissue by damaging the lungs, the liver, the brain, and/or the hormonal system. Damaging side effects of psychoactive substances are interesting to the researcher because they suggest one reason (among others) why societies attempt to control access to and the use of drugs.

Psychoactive drugs are interesting for a variety of reasons; one is their potential impact on human behavior, and a second is society's attempt to control them. The psychoactive appeal of drugs leads to their potential for widespread use, which, in turn, leads to the possibility of widespread harm or untoward behavior, which further result in some members of the society deciding that legal controls over their distribution and use are necessary. In other words, societies raise the question, Is this drug harmful to users? When the answer seems to be in the affirmative, the next question becomes, How can we limit and control the use of this drug? Hence, the objectivistic or essentialistic and the constructionist or subjectivistic dimensions are intertwined—although always imperfectly.

The second reason why we have to understand the **psychopharmacology** of drugs—that is, the impact of a given drug on the mind—is that the action of some drugs **conduces** users to engage in certain actions ("conduce" means to "lead or contribute" to something). For instance, to the sociologist and the criminologist, one extremely interesting effect of certain drugs is that they make violent or criminal actions more likely. If a drug lowers inhibitions, certain behaviors that would normally be unthinkable to the user become acceptable under the influence. Alcohol, a drug that is intimately intertwined with violent and criminal behavior, plays precisely such a disinhibiting role. In addition, if a drug is strongly physically addicting or dependency producing *and it is illegal—and hence, relatively expensive*—it may not be possible to pay for a steady supply without resorting to a life of crime. To the sociologist, whether and to what extent drugs influence the enactment of untoward, unacceptable, and/or criminal behavior is worth investigating.

By itself, the pharmacology of drugs does not cause the drug laws to materialize out of thin air. Nor is pharmacology the only factor in drug-related behavior. What people do under the influence, again, is partly a consequence of a society's cultural and legal structure—the social and legal norms spelling out and sanctioning appropriate and inappropriate behavior. Still, what a drug does to the neurochemistry of the human brain—and hence, the body—is relevant to the social scientist's interests, namely, human behavior and, ultimately, along with other factors, legal controls. Hence, we need to take a look at drugs as psychopharmacological substances.

## DRUG ACTION

In order to understand what drugs do to the brain and the body, it is necessary to distinguish between a drug *action* and a drug *effect*.[2]

A **drug action** is specific and takes place at the molecular level. Drugs are chemicals that interact with the body's neurochemical system; the outcome of this interaction is what is referred to as the drug's "action." As we'll see, drugs act in certain ways on receptor sites located at nerve endings. These actions are measurable and take place, with some variation, in laboratory animals as well as humans. Indeed, they take place in tissue that has been removed from an organism's body.

**Drug effects** are **nonspecific** and more highly variable, and result from more than a given dose of a particular drug. For instance, by its very nature, alcohol *always* binds to a receptor site, located in the cerebellum, that controls coordination (a drug action), and as a result, the consumption of a stipulated quantity of alcohol *usually* produces **ataxia,** or motor discoordination, in users (a drug effect). In other words, a drug action is a molecular product of chemistry, while a drug effect is a nonspecific product of chemistry interacting with the organism, plus the personal and social environment. An action that takes place in the body—again, a biophysical reaction, as predictable as mixing two chemicals in the lab—often, although not always, results in human responses or behavior that we refer to as a drug effect.

Drugs have one or more actions because their chemistry interacts in specific ways with the biochemistry of the central nervous system. The nerve cells, called **neurons,** send electrical impulses or signals from one part of the body to another. When neurons send signals, they release chemicals that are conducted from one site or locus to another. These chemicals are called **neurotransmitters;** they act as chemical messengers. Neurotransmitters, when accompanying drugs that are conveyed to the brain, influence such absolutely crucial functions as emotions, moods, sexuality, appetite, anger, waking and sleeping, and depression. The body has many neurotransmitters. In effect, neurotransmitters may be regarded as **endogenous drugs**—chemical substances, produced internally by the body, that influence the workings of the brain and powerfully influence behavior.

At the end of each neuron are **receptors;** between the receptor of one neuron and the receptor of the one next to it is a microscopic space called a **synapse.** Neurotransmitters are released into this space and travel toward the receptor of the next neuron. The receptors of specific neurons are able to detect and react to only certain neurotransmitters; the neurotransmitters "fit into" a specific receptor in a distinctive and unique fashion, much as a key fits into a lock. Some keys (that is, specific drugs) will not "fit"—and hence, not act upon—certain locks (that is, receptor sites of specific areas of the nervous system); they will pass by the site without exerting an effect. When neurons recognize or fit into specific neurotransmitters, they translate their signals into a certain neurological action. They bind or attach to a receptor, causing a current or signal to flow from one neuron to another, across the synapse between them. Once binding is achieved, the signal goes to a certain location in the brain and from there, to an organ, in effect, telling it what to do—for instance, to speed up or slow down. All organic functions in the body—including those that regulate emotion, coordination, and cognition—are controlled by this system of electrical impulses that are activated by these chemical reactions in the central nervous system.

---

[2]For detailed discussions on behavioral psychopharmacology, consult Goldstein, 2001; Ksir, Hart, and Ray, 2006; McKim, 2007.

Here's where psychoactive drugs come in. When introduced into the body, drugs *mimic* or *block* the neurotransmitters used to communicate with one another (Goldstein, 2001, p. 20). In other words, drugs, including those that are taken for the purpose of getting high, "hijack," or take over, certain functions of neurotransmitters. When neurotransmitters engage in the usual communication processes, communicating with nerve cells such vital functions as hunger, pleasure, fatigue, anger, and sexual arousal, psychoactive drugs overpower these functions either by taking them over, sending their own chemicals to the appropriate sites, or blocking them by fitting their chemicals into receptor sites and short-circuiting certain chemical reactions. In this way, then, under the influence of one or more psychoactive drugs, our usual capacity to feel pleasure is stimulated many times over; when we would normally feel hungry or tired, that sensation is blocked; in situations when our neurological pathways would usually communicate no (or at least modulated) irritation, a flood of anger overtakes us.

The sites in the brain that control certain organs are rich in receptors into which specific drugs "fit," as I said, much like a key in a lock. These same sites may lack receptors for other drugs. When a drug passes through the brain, a given drug (the "key") will be attracted to and will bind to a specific site in the brain (the "lock"), which controls a certain function or organ. Hence, the drug will act on that organ. Another drug, which lacks the chemical configuration to fit into the lock and therefore will not bind to that site, will simply pass that site by and not act on the organ that that site controls.

For example, heroin enters the body, breaks down into morphine, and flows toward and then acts on receptors in the brain that control breathing and heartbeat rate. Because morphine has an affinity for and fits into those sites, the drug hijacks the usual neurotransmitters that control these functions and itself affects these functions. As a consequence, a sufficiently large dose of heroin can shut down breathing and heartbeat and cause death by overdose.

In contrast, the chemical keys of **THC** (tetrahydrocannabinol, the major psychoactive chemical in marijuana) do not fit into and hence do not bind with—and as a consequence do not act on—the receptor sites in the brain that control breathing and heartbeat rate. Because of its chemical structure, marijuana does not powerfully act on breathing and heartbeat rate the way that heroin does, so it is almost impossible to die of a marijuana overdose. On the other hand, two areas of the brain—the hippocampus and the cerebral cortex—which control thinking and short-term memory, are rich in receptors to which THC provides the chemical key. When THC approaches these sites, it is attracted to them, binds to them, and acts on them. Therefore, sufficient doses of marijuana can diminish the user's short-term memory and disorganize his or her thinking processes. In addition, there is a dense binding of THC to the **cerebellum** and basal ganglia, which control movement and coordination.

The relationship between a specific drug and a specific receptor site is not absolute. Just as a poorly made key may open a lock with a certain amount of jiggling, a drug that fits poorly into a receptor site may produce an action, but more weakly than a better-fitting drug does. Drugs with the best fit in a given receptor will be more potent and will produce a greater effect than those with a less-than-perfect fit. For instance, methamphetamine, a stimulant, is more potent than amphetamines, to which it is closely related. As a result, it elicits a greater response in the relevant organs. In short, the affinity of a receptor for chemicals with a specific configuration or structure is a matter of degree. Some receptors have a high affinity or "specificity" for a certain drug molecule, while for others it has a lower affinity, and for still others, there is no fit at all.

## A Few Basic Pharmacological Concepts

In this section, we look at four basic and crucial pharmacological concepts you should understand to have a good idea of how drugs work: the acute-chronic distinction, the ED/LD ratio, drug tolerance, and drug fate.

### The Acute-Chronic Distinction

**Acute effects** refer to the short-term effects of a drug, those that take place within the period of its administration and during the immediate aftermath of a single episode of use. Motor discoordination is an acute effect of downing four drinks, each containing an ounce of alcohol. Getting high after smoking crack or marijuana, or snorting four lines of cocaine, likewise is an acute effect of administering these substances. So is dying of an overdose after an intravenous injection of a massive dose of heroin. These are effects that occur *during* or *immediately after* taking one or more drugs.

**Chronic effects** are long-term effects, those that occur after the chronic use of one or more drugs. Developing cirrhosis of the liver after 30 years of heavy drinking, lung cancer after decades of two-pack-a-day cigarette smoking, or brain damage after a period of methamphetamine dependence are all chronic effects from which users can suffer after the long-term period of the use and abuse of each respective drug. Some chronic effects are a direct consequence of the long-term action of the drug itself. The fact is, heavy, frequent use of alcohol damages the liver as well as most other organs of the body; the heavy, frequent use of nicotine damages the lungs as well as most other organs of the body. These are **direct effects** of drugs.

Then there are the **indirect effects** of taking the drug. These effects are not caused by the action of the drug itself but by the circumstances of use—for instance, using contaminated needles or leading an unhealthful lifestyle. By itself, heroin does not cause AIDS, but using shared needles that are contaminated by HIV, a common practice among addicts, does cause AIDS. Distinguishing between direct effects and indirect consequences of drug taking is crucial because that has extremely important policy implications, as we'll see in Chapters 14 and 15.

### The ED/LD Ratio

**ED** stands for effective dose. Also known as "active dose," this refers to the dose of a given drug that is required to produce a given effect. More specifically, since all organisms vary in their receptivity to the effects of drugs, ED is represented with respect to the *percentage of a given population* (including humans and such animals as mice, rats, and beagles) among which the dose in question produces the specific effect. ED50 would mean that the drug in question produces a given effect for 50 percent of the stipulated population; ED100 refers to the same thing for 100 percent of the population.

For instance, if we stipulate ED50 for morphine in humans for a reduction in pain among a population of postoperative patients, we are spelling out the dose of morphine that is required to achieve a pain-killing effect for half the patients tested. We can do this for any drug, any specific effect, any percentage, in any population. Obviously, for different effects or functions, ED will differ. For instance, alcohol will slow down reaction time in humans at lower doses (that is, at a lower ED50) than the dose at which it produces motor discoordination, or ataxia. And obviously, larger organisms require larger doses to produce a given effect—humans versus mice, for instance. Doses are often expressed per kilogram of body weight.

LD refers to the lethal dose, the quantity of a given drug that is required to kill a stipulated population. LD refers to a drug's toxicity. More specifically, the **ED/LD ratio** measures its toxicity—how much of a danger to life and limb its use represents to organisms that ingest it. The ED/LD ratio—that is, the *size* of the difference or the gap between ED and LD—can be referred to as its **safety margin** or **therapeutic margin.**

The larger the ratio between a dose that has a given effect and a dose that is lethal, the safer the drug; the smaller the ratio, the more dangerous it is. For a drug to be considered safe, its ED/LD ratio should be *much* higher than 1:1. The closer a drug's ED/LD is to 1:1, the more dangerous it is. If a hypothetical drug were to have an ED/LD ratio of exactly 1:1, this would mean that in order to achieve a given effect (say, intoxication or getting high), everyone or everything that ingested it would end up dead—an extremely dangerous drug indeed! But if this ratio is on the order of 1:1,000,000, it is an extremely *safe* drug. Most drugs are somewhere in between 1:1 (the most dangerous drug known) and 1:1,000,000 (an extremely safe and nearly totally nontoxic drug).

Realistically, a drug that has a safety or therapeutic margin of 1:10 or so is an extremely *unsafe* drug. If the quantity that can kill a user is only 10 times higher than the quantity that causes the desired effect, a very substantial number of users who take it will end up dead. On the other hand, a drug with an ED/LD ratio or safety margin on the order of 1:1,000 is extremely safe; that is, it will be very difficult for a user to die of an overdose of this drug.

Drugs vary enormously with respect to their safety or therapeutic margin. Heroin is a remarkably unsafe drug; the dose that causes death in a substantial proportion of users is only 10 to 15 times higher than the dose at which a substantial proportion of humans achieve a given effect—and obviously here, getting high is the effect in which we are interested. Since illicit heroin is highly variable in purity and potency, this means that it is not terribly difficult to die of a heroin overdose. As we'll see, considering the relatively small number of heroin users, heroin makes a remarkably substantial contribution to the nation's overdose statistics.

As I have already discussed, one reason for this is the affinity of the receptor sites in the brain that control breathing and heartbeat rate for the chemical structure of morphine, which is the substance heroin breaks down into after entering the body. In contrast, as we have also seen, marijuana has a remarkably high safety margin. It is extremely difficult to die of an overdose of marijuana because its ED/LD ratio is so enormous. Of course, drugs have effects other than their capacity to kill in an acute episode of use. Hardly anyone dies of a nicotine overdose (although if the quantity of nicotine in one cigar were injected intravenously, it would be lethal), but the *chronic* effects of tobacco are devastating.

## Drug Tolerance

**Tolerance** refers to the fact that repeated administration of a given dose produces diminishing effects. Over time, the body requires a larger and larger dose to achieve the same effect.

**Pharmacological tolerance** refers to the fact that the neurons become increasingly insensitive to a given drug, and so that drug becomes decreasingly effective. For instance, as a general rule, drug users must increase the dose of their drug of choice in order to get high. The flip side of this is the fact that as habituation rises along with tolerance, the lethal quantity of a given drug rises as well. In other words, it requires much more of a given drug to kill a habituated or long-term user than it does a neophyte or inexperienced user.

**Cross-tolerance** refers to the fact that the same principle of diminishing effects that takes place for a given drug also applies to another drug within the same type. An example: Tolerance to LSD will also produce tolerance to psilocybin, a related substance. Another example: Tolerance to heroin will also produce tolerance to morphine, another narcotic.

**Behavioral tolerance** reflects how an experienced user learns to compensate for the effects of a given drug, as a given dose of the drug produces a decreasing impact on his or her behavior. For instance, experienced drinkers claim that they can drive as well under the influence as normally. This is false, of course, but what *is* true is that they can drive better under the influence than an inexperienced drinker can. Over time, as a result of trial and error, they have inadvertently trained themselves to "handle" or compensate for the effects of alcohol in such a way that these effects are not nearly as discoordinating as they are to the novice drinker.

## Drug Fate

Drugs are metabolized or broken down in the body in different ways; this is **drug fate.** As we've seen, once it enters the body, heroin breaks down into morphine. If you were to examine the body of a deceased person who took heroin, you would not be able to determine whether he or she took heroin or morphine, since the former converts into the latter. The same is true of crack cocaine and powder cocaine; in the body, both convert to the same chemical. The body acts on a number of drugs and converts them into **metabolites**—the chemical by-products of drugs. Even if the original drug is no longer present, the presence of metabolites tell a toxicologist which drugs were taken.

Drugs are also excreted or eliminated from the body in specific ways: through the breath, the pores, in urine, or in feces. Different drugs are excreted from the body at different rates. Pharmacologists refer to the **half-life** of drugs, which is the length of time it takes to eliminate half of a given dose of a given drug from the body. Some drugs are eliminated very quickly, whereas others require a much longer time. Of all widely used drugs, marijuana is excreted most slowly; it has the longest half-life. THC has a special affinity for fatty tissue; it is stored in fat cells for long periods. THC itself has a half-life of 20 hours, and its metabolites, about 50 hours; complete elimination may take as long as three weeks. All other things being equal, drug tests are more likely to detect the use of slowly metabolized drugs than drugs that are eliminated more swiftly. Whereas a week after use, a marijuana smoker will test positive, a cocaine user will test negative, simply because metabolites of THC linger in the body much longer than do traces of cocaine.

## FACTORS THAT INFLUENCE DRUG ACTION

In order to exert a mind-altering or psychoactive effect, drugs must enter and act on the **central nervous system (CNS),** that is, the brain and the spinal column. As I have noted, not all drugs are psychoactive, and even psychoactive drugs exert many actions in addition to psychoactivity. In order to exert an action on the brain, a drug must enter the bloodstream and cross the blood-brain barrier. The body's entire volume of blood circulates roughly once a minute. Hence, when a drug enters the body, it circulates throughout the body rapidly and evenly.

At least four major factors influence the action of drugs: route of administration, dose, potency and purity, and drug mixing. Each one demands attention.

## Route of Administration

Drugs may be ingested in a variety of ways. Pharmacologists refer to a method of taking a drug as a **route of administration.** Some routes of administration introduce drugs into the body in an extremely rapid and efficient manner. Injecting directly into a vein a liquid solution into which a drug has been mixed is called **intravenous (IV) administration.** Obviously, only a drug that dissolves in water can be injected in this way. IV administration is one of the most effective means of administering drugs. Injecting a drug under the skin (**subcutaneously**) or directly into a muscle (**intramuscularly**) rather than into a vein are much slower and more inefficient routes of administration. Oral administration, such as drinking a liquid (like alcohol) or swallowing a pill, is an even slower and more inefficient method of ingestion. This is the case because taken orally, a drug must pass through the stomach and be absorbed from there or even further down, through the small intestine, all of which takes a long time. Drugs can also be administered via a dermal patch or through a rectal or vaginal suppository, or placed directly on mucous membranes such as the eye or the gums, or under the tongue or elsewhere on the inside of the mouth.

Smoking is the most rapid and efficient route of administering a psychoactive drug. A substance will produce the quickest, strongest reaction when smoked. This is the case because the air sacs of the lungs are densely surrounded by capillaries; as a result, drugs move rapidly from the lungs into the bloodstream, and from there they "swamp" the brain.

The difference between IV administration and smoking is that when a drug that is injected into a vein enters the heart, the blood that carries it to the heart is diluted with blood that does not contain the drug. In contrast, blood that travels from the lungs through the capillaries to the brain is completely undiluted and enters the brain at full strength (Goldstein, 2001, p. 119). Hence, if heroin or crack cocaine is injected intravenously, the high, felt as a "rush" or "flash," will take hold in 12–14 seconds. If these drugs are smoked, the rush will take place in 6–8 seconds.

The route of administration is a crucial factor because a focus on it and it alone may confuse observers into thinking that drugs taken in different ways are actually different drugs. For instance, federal law mandates much harsher penalties for crack cocaine than for powder cocaine possession: A five-year prison sentence is mandated for the possession of 5 grams of crack and 500 grams of powder cocaine. The justification for the discrepancy is that crack is a more dangerous and addicting drug than powder cocaine. In fact, crack and powder cocaine are very nearly the same drug, taken via different routes of administration. Crack is more dangerous and addicting—it has different "effects" from powder cocaine—specifically because it is taken in a more efficient, effective, and reinforcing fashion. Because powder cocaine combusts at a higher temperature than crack, it is more difficult to smoke, but smoking it would produce a similar effect as crack cocaine. Of course, as a result of the way they are used, practically speaking, crack cocaine *is* more reinforcing, and hence, more dependency producing, than powder cocaine. Consequently, the legal distinction is not totally absurd.

To summarize: Crack both *is* and *is not* a different drug from powder cocaine. It is different in that, when taken via the usual route of administration, it is extremely pleasurable, and therefore very likely to result in abuse and dependence. But it is not different in the sense that the active ingredient in crack and powder cocaine is chemically identical, and both substances break down into the same chemical in the body. The world of drugs is not a simple either-or, black-or-white phenomenon.

The important point about route of administration is that it influences the effects a drug has. The same drug will have different effects according to the manner in which it is taken. In addition, because of their physical form, some drugs cannot be taken by certain methods.

For example, marijuana is not soluble in water and hence, cannot be injected into the bloodstream. In some societies, marijuana is brewed in tea; here, its effects are much milder, more muted, and less intense than if it is smoked. In the United States, it is mainly smoked. The fact that a low proportion of marijuana users become dependent on it indicates that it has an extremely low *potential* for dependence, because the method by which most users take it is normally highly reinforcing. Since alcohol is only used orally, its effects tend to be considerably less powerful and instantaneous than if it were taken in more reinforcing ways. As a result, most people who drink do not become dependent on alcohol. The leaves of the coca plant contain roughly 1 percent cocaine; if they were chewed, the effects would be very different from the experience of snorting a line of powder cocaine, which, in turn, is very different from smoking crack. Some gasses (nitrous oxide or amyl nitrite, for instance) are too volatile, too unstable, and too chemically active to be taken in any manner other than by inhalation. Both cocaine and heroin are smoked, administered intravenously and sniffed or "snorted" intranasally, that is, into the nostril. Each means of taking these drugs will produce a different set of effects—although recognizably "cocaine" or "heroin" effects.

## Dose

A discussion of drug effects is meaningless without considering the factor of dose. There are minuscule dosage levels at which a normally potent drug would exert no psychologically discernible effect whatsoever, and there are massive doses of a relatively weak or safe drug that would be overwhelming, even fatal. Aspirin, a safe drug taken by millions of people every day with no harmful effects whatsoever, can cause death if taken in a sufficiently large dose. As we know, it is almost impossible to die of a marijuana overdose, yet if several kilograms of the drug were forcibly shoved down one's throat, the dose could be fatal. Heroin, a drug that can shut down the body's heartbeat and breathing mechanisms, can be extremely safe if taken in a dose as minuscule as several micrograms, which will exert no recognizable effect at all. In sum, the issue of dose is inevitably intertwined with drug effects.

The customary dose at which a drug is taken by users is crucial. Drug effects are most meaningful at the dosage levels users customarily take. And dose is influenced not in the laboratory but on the street. For each drug, traditions that dictate the appropriate dose for users to take have evolved and vary from one society to another. In addition, the availability of drugs influences what doses are taken. During a period of great abundance, when an illicit drug is not only readily available but inexpensive as well, users will take it at higher doses; during a "drought," when the drug is expensive and difficult to obtain, each dose users take will be lower. It is possible that when a drug is studied in the laboratory, the doses administered are not realistic in that the drug may not be used at that dosage level in real life.

Drugs generally exhibit what pharmacologists refer to as a **dose-response curve** (see Figure 2-1). To be more precise, each drug exhibits a characteristic dose-response curve *for each effect*. As a general rule, the higher the dose, the greater or more extreme the effect. For most drugs, there are doses at which a given effect does not occur at all. Plotted on

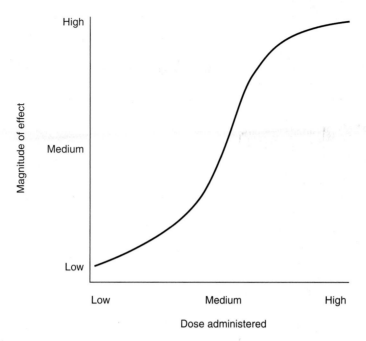

**Figure 2-1** **Model dose-response curve.**

a graph, the lower end (that is, at low doses) of the dose-response curve will be almost flat, rising very slowly. As the dose increases and the drug's effects begin to kick in, there will be a kind of "takeoff" point, where the dose-response curve rises rapidly. Then, for most drugs and for most effects, at even higher doses, the dose-response curve will flatten out again, after which a higher dosage does not produce more extreme effects. With alcohol, for instance, the range of doses between one drop and roughly half an ounce will produce no discernible effect in adults. This is the nearly flat lower part of the dose-response curve. Then, for most adults, after a half ounce, the effects of the drug start to kick in, and the imbiber begins to feel intoxicated. Most effects begin to flatten out again at a certain point, although with alcohol, death by overdose occurs at extremely high doses. In short: To know a drug's effect, it is absolutely necessary to consider the dosage taken.

## Potency and Purity

**Potency** is defined as the quantity of a drug it takes to produce a given action or effect; the lower the quantity, the greater the potency of the drug. Drugs vary in potency between and among themselves.

For example, LSD is vastly more potent than psilocybin, a related psychedelic. This does not mean that LSD produces more extreme effects, but it does mean that it takes less LSD to produce the same effect. In addition, the same drug will be variable in potency from one batch to another.

For instance, "ditch weed" marijuana, which grows by the side of the road, will usually have an extremely low level of potency, that is, will contain considerably less than

1 percent THC, the drug's active ingredient. Other batches of marijuana that are bred and grown to achieve maximum effect will contain 10 percent or more THC. Alcoholic beverages, likewise, are variable in potency; beer is 4–5 percent alcohol, wine is 12–13 percent alcohol, and distilled spirits such as gin, vodka, whiskey, and tequila are 40–50 percent alcohol. (Technically, the alcohol itself is not variable in potency, it is alcoholic *beverages* that vary with respect to the percentage of alcohol they contain.) Hence, drinking the same quantity of each beverage will produce different effects because of the factor of potency.

**Purity** refers to the fact that batches containing the same drug will vary as to the percentage of the drug they contain. Two users, for example, may each ingest the contents of packets containing 100 milligrams of something that is sold as "heroin." But one packet may be only 10 percent pure; that is, it may contain 10 milligrams of actual heroin and 90 milligrams of adulterants, such as quinine, lactose, or milk sugar, which are not psychoactive. The second packet may also contain 100 milligrams of "heroin"—but 30 milligrams of actual heroin and 70 milligrams of adulterants. Hence, in effect, the second user is getting three times as much heroin as the first, even though they both purchased packets of the same size. This is because some illicit drugs are "hit," "cut," or "stepped on" with cheap, nonactive fillers so that dealers can increase their profits. Heroin is much more potent today (the average potency is roughly 25%) than it was 25 years ago, when the average potency of street heroin was 3–5 percent. Purity is a crucial consideration when thinking about drug effects.

## Drug Mixing

**Drug mixing** is extremely common. Many users who take one drug take one or more other drugs simultaneously, that is, *in combination* with it. Roughly three-quarters of all persons who die of a drug overdose have more than one drug in their system. A popular street drug called a "speedball" contains a combination of cocaine and heroin, or methamphetamine and heroin. Alcohol is frequently imbided at the same time as marijuana is smoked; people who take "downers" such as barbiturates, methaqualone, or tranquilizers often drink at the same time.

Drug mixing is extremely important to consider because drugs can *interact* in important ways when they are taken together. Some drugs may have **antagonistic effects** with one another, meaning the effect of one drug nullifies or cancels out the effect of another. For instance, Antabuse not only blocks the effects of alcohol but makes the drinker violently ill when alcohol is ingested. For antagonistic drugs, one plus one equals zero.

Other drug combinations produce **additive effects.** For instance, one aspirin and one Tylenol will produce the same effect as two aspirin or two Tylenol taken separately. Additive effects can be represented by the formula one plus one equals two.

Some drugs have **synergistic effects** when taken in combination. "Synergy" refers to the **multiplier effect:** The effect of one drug plus the effect of another equals more than twice as much of either, taken alone. We can represent synergy by the formula one plus one equals four.

Many drug combinations produce synergistic effects. For example, alcohol and barbiturates are synergistic with one another. If you were to ingest half a quart of vodka plus ten 10-milligram capsules of the barbiturate Seconal, you would be much more likely to die of a lethal overdose than if you drank a full quart of vodka *or* took twenty 10-milligram capsules of Seconal. This is because alcohol and barbiturates interact with one another to produce a more powerful, synergistic, or "multiplier" effect in combination than they produce by themselves.

Synergy is especially important because drugs are more likely to be mixed today than was true a generation ago and, as we have seen, synergy produces not only more powerful but more dangerous effects, such as death by overdose.

## DRUG DEPENDENCE

### The Classic Addiction Model

Until the 1970s, the model of drug dependence that dominated the field of drug studies was the "classic" **drug addiction** model. In the classic model, an "addicting" drug is defined by the appearance of withdrawal symptoms. If an organism takes a sufficient quantity of a given drug over a sufficiently long period, and then administration is discontinued, withdrawal symptoms appear. These symptoms—depending on the prior dose and the duration of the use—include chills, fever, gooseflesh, diarrhea, muscular twitching, muscle spasms, nausea, vomiting, cramps, and bodily aches and pains, especially in the joints. These effects are pharmacological, not psychological; they can be reliably reproduced in laboratory animals and in patients who do not even know they have been administered an addicting drug.

The classic addiction model also recognized the existence of the phenomenon of **cross-dependence.** When the addict becomes physically dependent on a given drug and is withdrawn from it, painful withdrawal symptoms appear. These symptoms can be alleviated by the administration of a dose of the drug. But more than that, administration of any drug in that same *category* of drugs will alleviate withdrawal. For example, withdrawal from heroin can be alleviated by the administration of morphine, since both are narcotics. Thus, heroin and morphine are cross-dependent with one another. Withdrawal from alcohol can be alleviated by taking a barbiturate, since both alcohol and barbiturates are sedatives. Again, alcohol and barbiturates exhibit cross-dependence. Of course, cross-dependence applies only to drugs that produce a classic addiction.

Not all psychoactive drugs are "addicting" according to the classic model. In the classic sense of the word, the narcotics, including heroin and morphine, are addicting, as are alcohol, the barbiturates, and other depressants. However, no withdrawal symptoms even remotely like those spelled out by the classic model appear with the discontinuation of cocaine, marijuana, or LSD. What we see instead is more psychological discomfort than physical manifestations of genuine withdrawal symptoms. Since some observers have theorized that the avoidance of withdrawal symptoms explains the continued use of narcotic drugs (Lindesmith, 1968), the puzzle that once confronted researchers was why such a high proportion of users took *nonaddicting* drugs on a chronic, abusive basis. In other words, **behavioral dependence**—engaging in continued, compulsive, chronic use to the point at which that use becomes a threat to everything one once valued, including life and limb—is not the same thing as **physical dependence,** or the pharmacological capacity of a drug to cause withdrawal symptoms. Drugs that are not physically dependency producing (or addictive) *often* produce a behavioral dependence, and drugs that are physically addicting, *in the typical case,* do not produce a behavioral dependence. To be plain about it, cocaine (a nonaddicting drug) is more likely to produce behavioral dependence than is alcohol (an addicting drug); on the other side of the coin, *most* drinkers are *not* alcoholics. Physical addiction is only a part of the dependence puzzle.

A series of animal experiments with cocaine indicated that this supposedly nonaddicting drug—at least, with respect to the classic model—was taken as chronically and as abusively as heroin is taken by addicts. How could an addictive drug like heroin and a supposedly non-addictive drug such as cocaine produce similar patterns of use and abuse? If addiction, the product of a pharmacologically induced craving, culminating in the avoidance of withdrawal symptoms at all cost, is the principal explanation for compulsive use, how is this possible?

Laboratory experiments have verified cocaine's capacity to generate compulsive patterns of abuse. Animals such as rats, mice, and monkeys that were rigged up to self-administer a drug by pressing a bar worked very hard to receive cocaine, pressing the bar thousands of times to receive a single dose. When the animals were withdrawn from the drug they had self-administered, they continued to press the bar without receiving the drug for a much longer period of time for cocaine than for heroin, which is an addicting drug. And when the animals were given the choice between cocaine and food, they consistently self-administered cocaine in preference to food—even to the point of death by starvation (Brady and Lucas, 1984; Clouet, Asghar, and Brown, 1988; Johanson, 1984).

Remarkably, most animals who take cocaine end up taking it uncontrollably, even to the point of killing themselves; animals who take heroin take it more reasonably and controllably, typically keeping themselves alive and healthy in the process. Animals that self-administer cocaine *ad libitum*—that is, at will, as much or as little as they choose—exhibit an erratic pattern of use, with periods of bingeing alternating with periods of abstinence; do not maintain their pretest weight; cease grooming behavior; and maintain poor physical health. In contrast, when animals self-administer heroin *ad libitum,* they develop a stable pattern of use, maintain their pretest weight, continue grooming behavior, and, for the most part, remain in good health. In one experiment, after 30 days, 90 percent of the mice that self-administered cocaine *ad libitum* were dead (Bozarth and Wise, 1985).

In short, without fail, animal experiments indicate that animals take cocaine, a supposedly nonaddicting drug, *even more compulsively* than heroin—a classically addicting drug. Cocaine gives these animals something that other drugs do not.

Humans are not laboratory animals, and laboratory conditions are not the same as real life. But laboratory experiments give us the broad outline of how drug effects can be understood; they establish the inherent pharmacological properties of drugs. Just how people take them may be a different matter. But laboratory experiments do give us an important clue to what a drug's potential is.

## The Dependence/Reinforcement Model

What these and other experiments show is that the classic conception of addiction does *not* explain the continued use of drugs. An altogether different mechanism is at work here, and most contemporary researchers believe that positive **reinforcement,** or the pleasure that organisms derive from taking a drug, is the driving force in generating continued, compulsive, abusive drug use. In other words, a drug does not have to be addicting in the classic sense of the term—that is, produce physical withdrawal symptoms—to produce a dependency in users, whether animal or human. So irrelevant has physical dependence become to the way most specialists view continued, compulsive drug abuse that they now prefer the term "dependence" to "addiction." Typically, little or no distinction is made between the physical dependence that a drug like heroin produces and the psychic dependence that cocaine and amphetamines produce.

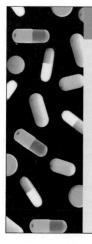

## True-False Quiz

One of the statements in my true-false quiz was this: "By defini-tion, *all* drugs are addictive; in fact, that is how they are defined—they all create a chemical dependency in users over time." As you now know from the discussion, this statement is false. Drugs vary enormously in their capacity to generate dependency in users. In the sense that they are not powerfully reinforcing and do not pro-duce chronic, repeated administration in a high proportion of users, some drugs (LSD is an excellent example) are not at all "addictive." My students were evenly split on the issue: 49 percent said that this statement is true, and 49 percent said that it is false. But the conjunction of "drugs" with "addiction" is so strong that it is difficult for many people to separate.

Heroin generates both a physical dependence or "addiction" (that is, withdrawal symptoms ap-pear when chronic use is discontinued) and a psychic dependence (that is, it is highly reinforc-ing upon administration). Today, when the term "addiction" is used, it refers not to the classic addiction syndrome, complete with a full-blown physical withdrawal, but to dependence. For instance, physician and neuropharmacologist Avram Goldstein titles his book on drugs *Addiction* (2001); in it, he discusses the dependency-producing properties of substances rang-ing from caffeine to heroin. In short, the original meaning of "addiction" has been buried.

Using an extremely reinforcing drug alters the chemistry of the brain such that the neurons "remember" having been reinforced, that is, having once been administered a jolt or rush of an intensely pleasurable stimulus. Events in the current milieu of former users may remind them of the sensations they experienced at one time, and such stimuli will produce actual physical sensations in their bodies. For instance, watching a smoker light up will result in the firing of neurons in a former smoker's central nervous system, which generate a craving for cigarettes. Former cocaine users watching a film in which actors snort a white power up their noses will experience sensations in the brain that cause their sinuses to tighten up and their nostrils to di-late, and they will involuntarily begin sniffing—a biochemical reminder of their experiences in days gone by. Many former users of cigarettes, cocaine, and heroin report that these sensations never go away. The less reinforcing drugs are less likely to produce such reactions.

Not all or even most human users of even the most pleasurable or reinforcing of drugs will become dependent on them. *Most* users of cocaine do not become cocaine "addicts." Other factors are at work. Compulsive drug taking is caused as much by the characteristics of the user as the characteristics of the drug being used. But a drug's capacity to deliver a reinforcing jolt of pleasure is perhaps the most important factor in generating a dependence on it. The more reinforcing a drug is, the stronger the desire to repeat the experience, and the greater the sacrifices the user will make to continue doing so. Because of this shift from the "classic" model, based on withdrawal symptoms, to the more contemporary "dependence" model, based on reinforcement, most researchers today have abandoned the term "addiction." It is true that reinforcement helps explain continued, compulsive use—behavioral dependence—much better than addiction does, but addiction *does* produce clear-cut withdrawal symptoms, and it cannot be dismissed as an archaic relic of a bygone age.

Substances vary in their potential for causing dependence, with cocaine ranking at the top, methamphetamine and amphetamines next, heroin in a slightly lower category, and the other drugs trailing substantially behind these three. It is highly likely that the potential for dependence is closely related to and is caused by how reinforcing each drug is, that is, how intense the pleasure each delivers to the user. The more reinforcing the drug, the higher is its potential for dependence. In other words, substances vary with respect to their **immediate sensual appeal** (Grinspoon and Bakalar, 1976, pp. 191–194; Lasagna, von Felsinger, and Beecher, 1955). This is closely related, but not identical, to the capacity to generate pleasure. More precisely it means the capacity to generate intense pleasure *without the intervention of learning or other cognitive processes*. Some drugs deliver a jolt of intense, orgasmlike pleasure, much like a flash or rush of electricity to the brain.

In contrast, the pleasure that other drugs deliver is more subtle, as much mental as physical, more cultivated, less immediate and intense. For the most part, users have to learn to enjoy marijuana. The same is true of alcohol, LSD, and nicotine. These are drugs that animals don't like to take initially and have to be taught to self-administer. Many pleasurable activities, much like alcohol, have to be cultivated, including reading classic books, appreciating fine art, and eating caviar. The pleasure these activities generate is great, even intense, but people must *learn* to appreciate them. Contrarily, cocaine requires no such learning process. When human subjects are experimentally administered cocaine and amphetamines without knowing what they are taking, they usually enjoy them the first time and want to take them again. This is what "immediate sensual appeal" means. Drugs with this quality are highly reinforcing and have a high dependence potential.

Of course, humans vary with respect to their degree of susceptibility or vulnerability to becoming dependent on a chemical substance. The variation from one person to another is vastly greater than from one representative of the same animal species to another. Indeed, especially among humans, there is enormous variation from one person to another with respect to their initial experience with a given drug. Says physician David Smith:

> Some people will take the drug—any drug—and not get addicted [or dependent]. Others will take it once and be inexorably drawn to it. The drug is the same; the people are different. . . . Interestingly, the person who is addicted to cocaine responds very differently the very first time he [or she] uses it [from the person who uses it but does not become dependent]. Later, he'll [or she'll] use terms that are qualitatively different from those that others use to describe the experience of taking cocaine the first time: "This is the greatest thing that's ever happened to me," or words to that effect. (quoted in Gonzales, 1984, p. 114)

Once again, the pharmacological properties of a given drug are not the only factor that explains its continued, compulsive use, but they are a major reason for chemical dependence and must be kept in mind when discussing the abuse of psychoactive drugs.

## A CLASSIFICATION OF PSYCHOACTIVE DRUGS AND THEIR EFFECTS

All classifications of drugs are somewhat misleading, because all drugs have multiple effects. How we divide up the world of drugs depends on our interests. One of our interests here is the relationship between psychoactive substances and crime. Many of the drugs that are interesting to the psychiatrist, for example, or the physician have little or no relevance to the criminologist. The sociologist interested in the behavioral impact of psychoactive substances and the criminologist interested in the criminogenics (crime-causing properties) and legal control of these substances, however, do study drugs and crime. For researchers and students of psychoactive drugs, the most relevant categories of drugs are included in Table 2-1.

---

### TABLE 2-1   A Classification of Psychoactive Drugs, with Representative Examples

**Sedative-Hypnotics/General Depressants**

alcohol (ethyl alcohol, or ethanol)

barbiturates (Nembutal, Tuinal, Amytal, Seconal, phenobarbital, pentobarbital)

benzodiazepines (Librium, Valium, Xanax, Halcion, Rohypnol, Ativan)

miscellaneous sedatives: meprobamate (Miltown, Equanil), methaqualone (Quāālude, Mandrax, Sopor), GHB (gamma-hydroxybutyrate)

**Antidepressants or Mood Elevators**

Prozac, Elavil, Zoloft, Sinequan, Tofranil, Paxil

**Antipsychotic Agents**

phenothiazines (Thorazine, Stelazine, Mellaril, Haldol)

**Hallucinogens/Psychedelics**

LSD ("acid"), mescaline ("mesc"), psilocybin ("'shrooms")

**Narcotics**

opiates (opium and its derivatives): opium, morphine, heroin, codeine

opioids (synthetic narcotics): methadone, oxycodone (OxyContin), Darvon, Percodan, fentanyl, Dilaudid, Demerol

**Stimulants**

cocaine ("coke"), crack cocaine

amphetamines (Adderall, Benzedrine, Dexedrine, "speed")

methamphetamines (Methedrine, Desoxyn, "meth," "crank," "crystal," "ice")

Ritalin (methylphenidate)

caffeine

**Disassociative Anesthetics**

PCP (Sernyl, Sernylan, "angel dust")

ketamine ("K," "special K," "super K")

Nicotine

**Drugs Not Easily Classifiable in a General Category**

marijuana

MDMA (Ecstasy, "XTC," "E," "X")

---

*Note:* A number of these substances are classified as Schedule I drugs and therefore are not legally available. Hence, their trade names, referred to here, are those that were used when they were sold as prescription drugs; they are not currently manufactured under these trade names.

## Stimulants

The drugs that excite or stimulate the central nervous system (CNS) are called **stimulants.** Stimulants produce arousal, alertness, an elevation in mood, even excitation. They also inhibit fatigue and lethargy, and provoke physical activity. For our purposes, cocaine and amphetamines (along with methamphetamine) are the most important stimulants.

Pharmacologist Avram Goldstein refers to the use of cocaine and amphetamines as "the wild addictions" (1994, p. 155). The immediate subjective effects of these two stimulants are euphoria and a sense of self-confidence and well-being. As we saw on page 44, administering cocaine and amphetamines is extremely reinforcing; they possess what pharmacologists call "immediate sensual appeal." Taking them generates the impulse to take them regularly, regardless of the obstacles, pain, or cost. In popular or lay terms, they are pleasurable.

It should come as no surprise that these two drugs are widely used for recreational purposes, that is, to get high. Most users can overcome the impulse to become dependent on cocaine and amphetamines; they have better things to do with their lives than devote all their time to self-indulgence. But the seductive pleasure principle is always present, always exerting an effect, and a minority of experimenters—perhaps one in ten—will escalate to more serious use and eventually to abuse.

Stimulants speed up signals passing through the CNS. They activate organs and functions of the body, heighten arousal, increase overall behavioral activity, and suppress fatigue. In low doses, stimulants can heighten the body's sensitivity to stimuli, increase concentration and focus, and improve mental and physical performance. At higher doses, however, many of these functions seem to go haywire. Behavior becomes unfocused, supersensitivity translates into paranoia, and mental and intellectual performance becomes uncontrollable, ineffective, counterproductive, and compulsively repetitive.

Because the stimulants are highly pleasurable, they often lead to compulsive use and abuse, which, in turn, not infrequently cause medical complications, including death. Hence, it should come as no surprise that societies everywhere have instituted legal controls on the distribution and use of stimulants. These legal controls cause stimulants to become expensive, and hence profitable to sell, which means enormous criminal empires are based on the sale of cocaine and amphetamines. In addition, since both drugs activate bodily processes, we are led to ask what their role is in influencing or causing untoward, "deviant," and criminal behavior. The criminogenics of cocaine and amphetamines is an important feature of their use.

## Sedative/Hypnotics

General **depressants** or **sedative/hypnotics** have effects that are more or less precisely the opposite of those of the stimulants. They inhibit and slow down signals passing through the CNS, affecting a wide range of bodily functions. At low to moderate doses, they induce relaxation and reduce anxiety. At higher doses, they produce (or potentiate) drowsiness and eventually sleep. Alcohol (known to pharmacologists as ethyl alcohol or ethanol) is a general depressant or sedative, as are methaqualone (once sold commercially as Quāālude); the barbiturates, such as Seconal and GHB (gamma-hydroxybutyrate), a semipopular "club drug"; and the tranquilizers or anti-anxiety agents (mostly benzodiazepines), including Valium, Halcion, and Royphnol. At a sufficiently high dosage, all general depressants produce a high or intoxication, all produce a physical addiction or dependency, and all can cause death by overdose. PCP, once sold under the trade name of Sernyl as an animal anesthetic and tranquilizer, has complex and contradictory effects because it produces "disassociation" (a feeling of being detached from reality) and, sometimes, hallucinations. It is often classified as a hallucinogen. ketamine ("special K") is closely related to PCP but with somewhat less of a disassociative effect.

All of the general depressants, alcohol included, slow down, retard, or *obtund* many functions of the body, especially the CNS. In other words, organs become more sluggish, slower to respond to stimuli. If the dose is too high, the body's organs will shut down altogether, and death will result. The depressants also disorganize and impede the brain's ability to process and use information. Hence, they may impair the perceptual, cognitive, and motor skills needed for coordination and decision making.

At a sufficiently high dose, all sedatives produce mental clouding and motor discoordination. This is especially relevant for alcohol, the most widely used sedative. In the United States alone, roughly 15,000 people die each year of alcohol-related road fatalities. At low doses, sedative users feel a mild euphoria; a diminution of anxiety, fear, and tension; and a corresponding increase in self-confidence and, usually, what is called a "release of inhibitions." Fear of engaging in risky activities also generally diminishes, an effect that can be observed in laboratory animals as well as humans. Ingestion of higher doses of a number of sedatives, including alcohol and barbiturates, often results in paranoia, distrust, heightened anxiety, belligerence, and even hostility.

Of all drugs, nationally, internationally, and cross-culturally, alcohol is by far the one that is most likely to be implicated in violent crimes. The empirical evidence linking alcohol to violent behavior is overwhelming. More individuals who commit violent offenses are under the influence of alcohol than is true for any other single drug. For this reason, any examination of drugs and crime cannot possibly omit the role of alcohol in potentiating, influencing, and facilitating criminal, especially violent, behavior.

In short, the role of sedatives, especially alcohol, is crucial to any investigation of human behavior, including—and perhaps especially—drugs and crime. It is entirely possible that the effects of alcohol, GHB, barbiturates, PCP, and ketamine *conduce to* criminal behavior. Barbiturates are prescription drugs, illegal for nonmedical use, and the others are not legally available in the United States. Hence, the issue of the criminalization of drugs, or drugs as crime, is crucial for the sedatives as well.

## Narcotics

Narcotics are more specific in their action: They act to depress or inhibit a particular function—the perception of pain. Referred to as painkillers or **analgesics,** the major representative of this category is the narcotics. The narcotics are the most efficient and effective of all painkillers and are essential in the practice of medicine. However, at a sufficiently high dosage, narcotics also produce mental clouding, a euphoric high, or intoxication. In addition, narcotics have, as we have seen, a fairly narrow safety margin: They are physically addicting and can produce death by overdose. The "opiates" are the natural derivatives of opium: morphine, heroin, and codeine. The "opioids" are the entirely synthetic narcotics with effects very similar to the opiates: methadone, Demerol (meperidine), Dilaudid, OxyContin, and fentanyl.

It is the painkilling property of narcotics that makes them of interest to the physician. But it is their narrow safety margin, their euphoria inducing, and their addicting properties that make them of interest to any social scientist. The narrow safety margin of narcotics tells us that they are dangerous drugs. Compared with other drugs, they are highly likely, on a dose-for-dose basis, to lead to death by overdose. Their euphoria-inducing and addicting properties tell us that many users are likely to be motivated to take them on a compulsive basis. Societies are likely to control or criminalize such behavior ("drugs as crime"), and such behavior is likely, in turn, to produce or conduce to criminal acts ("drugs and crime"). Narcotics are among the drugs in which sociologists and criminologists are most likely to be interested.

## Hallucinogens/Psychedelics

**Hallucinogens** have effects on the CNS that are not easily classified in terms of stimulation or depression. They occupy their own territory and include LSD, mescaline (a naturally occurring chemical found in the peyote cactus), psilocybin (the naturally occurring chemical found in the mushroom of the same name), and the synthetic, extremely short-acting DMT (dimethyltriptamine). The hallucinogens stimulate a wide range of psychic effects, including **eidetic imagery** (vivid closed-eye visual imagery), **synesthesia** (the mixing or translation of one sense into another—for instance, "seeing" sound), subjective exaggeration, the "eureka" experience (the ordinary becoming the extraordinary), emotional lability (extreme mood shifts, from ecstatic to depressive), a sense of timelessness, sensory overload (a bombardment of the senses), and striking alterations of visual stimuli.

Most of the harms attributed to the **psychedelics** in the 1960s—hallucinations, psychotic episodes, psychosis, suicidal behavior, violence, and genetic damage most prominent among them—turn out to have little or no factual foundation whatsoever. Perhaps the most remarkable fact about the hallucinogens is that they are hardly ever abused. By that I mean that they are used episodically, sporadically, and infrequently; very few users take them frequently, chronically, or compulsively. Of all well-known drugs or drug types, the hallucinogens are the least frequently used. For instance, of the entire universe of at-least-one-time users, for all drugs, LSD is among the *least* likely to have been taken within the past 30 days. This is almost certainly because LSD and the other psychedelics are not reinforcing in the usual sense of the word. (If permitted to take them at will, laboratory animals do not repeat their use of LSD.) The enjoyment of taking them is a cultivated taste. In addition, apart from their illicit sale, the hallucinogens are extremely unlikely to be implicated in criminal behavior. On the other hand, LSD's impact on human emotion, cognition, and behavior is so profound and disruptive to everyday life that it is very rarely used on a compulsive basis. And the legal controls on the distribution of LSD are interesting sociological and criminological topics in themselves.

## Marijuana

What is referred to as "marijuana" is the dried buds and flowers (now, increasingly less commonly, the leaves) of the **cannabis** plant; its Latin name is *Cannabis sativa*. Hashish is the dried resin of the cannabis plant and is usually, although not always, more potent than marijuana. The main psychoactive ingredient in marijuana is THC (Δ-9-tetrahydrocannabinol).

Marijuana varies enormously in THC content, from less than 1 percent to more than 10 percent. Many specially tended, home-grown **hydroponic** plants (those grown in water rather than soil) contain buds that are well over 10 percent THC. Hashish, which is much less readily available in the United States than marijuana preparations, usually contains 10–15 percent THC.

At different times, observers have classified marijuana as a stimulant, a depressant, a psychedelic and a hallucinogen—even a narcotic. Actually, it is none of these. Although marijuana does produce sedation in users, this is not regarded by most pharmacologists as its central effect. A few users have reported psychedelic-like effects, but this is rare. Today, marijuana is regarded as occupying its own unique category. Marijuana is not cross-tolerant with any of the psychedelics, which means that it belongs in a category by itself.

In spite of the fact that marijuana is smoked—an extremely efficient and effective route of administration—the effects of marijuana are not powerfully reinforcing, nor does the drug have a high potential for producing a strong dependence. Recent research on laboratory animals supposedly indicates that marijuana may be a "harder" drug than was previously thought, given that withdrawal-like symptoms appeared when the drug was discontinued (Swann, 1995; Tanda, Pontieri, and Di Chiara, 1997; Tsou, Patrick, and Walker, 1995; Wickelgren, 1997). But the fact that the vast majority of human users take the drug in moderation, do not become dependent, and do not experience withdrawal symptoms when they stop indicates that these studies may not be sufficiently lifelike for researchers to draw conclusions from them about the abuse or dependence potential of marijuana.

Marijuana, like alcohol, is used extremely frequently among people who violate the law. Studies show that arrested offenders are as likely to test positive for marijuana as any other drug, with the partial exception (depending on the city and the sex of the arrestee) of cocaine. Unlike alcohol, however, it is not clear what marijuana's role is in the commission of crimes. Marijuana is much less likely to be associated with violence than alcohol. And, since it does not produce the same kind of compulsive drug taking as heroin and crack cocaine, it is not as likely to be as closely implicated in money-making crimes. But to the interested sociologist, the enormous distribution of marijuana, an illegal substance used currently–that is, within the past month—by nearly 15 million Americans, is fascinating. And the marijuana industry—America's number one agricultural crop—make the drug a worthy subject of inquiry for the inquisitive criminologist. In addition, the **criminalization**—and the attempted ***de*criminalization**—of marijuana is as interesting to the sociologist and criminologist as for any other drug or drug type.

## Ecstasy

MDMA—"XTC," "E," or Ecstasy—is usually classified as a hallucinogen. However, it possesses none of the major properties of LSD and the other psychedelics, such as spectacular alterations of visual stimuli. As with marijuana, it seems reasonable to classify Ecstasy as belonging in its own category. Some observers argue that the fact that MDMA induces extremely strong feelings of closeness with others suggests that it is an **empathogen**—an agent that induces empathy. The drug induces a sense of trust, openness, peacefulness, and serenity, along with the sense that one is experiencing the world afresh, for the first time. Like LSD, Ecstasy is not often used on a compulsive basis. Moreover, the effects of the drug are not normally associated with criminal behavior. However, critics of the drug argue that, in animal experiments, continued use of Ecstasy produced a permanent depletion of **serotonin,** an extremely important neurotransmitter that regulates emotion, mood, cognition, sexuality, and sleep. If this effect took place in humans, it would make Ecstasy an extremely dangerous drug. Between the early 1990s and 2000, the use of Ecstasy grew faster than for any other major drug; use since 2000, however, has leveled off or declined slightly. Possession and sale of Ecstasy became illegal at the federal level in 1985.

# APPENDIX: Drug Names

Some drugs are manufactured, sold, and used legally for medical and psychiatric therapy; they are prescribed by physicians and are called prescription drugs or pharmaceuticals. If used recreationally as well as legally, prescription drugs have four different names: (1) a category name that identifies their general type, (2) a generic or chemical name, (3) a brand or specific name, and (4) a street or slang name (or names). For instance, methaqualone (generic name), a nonbarbiturate sedative (category name), once sold under various brand or specific names (Quāālude, Sopor, Parest), is known on the street as "'ludes" or "soaps." (Methaqualone is no longer legally prescribed in the United States.) Ecstasy (a street name) is chemically known, in shorthand, as MDMA, and is often referred to as "X" or "E"; it does not belong to a convenient pharmacological category, although it is chemically related to the amphetamines.

As a general rule, if a generic or chemical name is spelled out, it begins with a lowercase letter (although if its initials are used, it is usually capitalized). If it is referred to by its brand or specific name, it is capitalized. In this book, all brand or specific names will be capitalized; brand names are trademarked, like Ford, Xerox, and Coca-Cola. My practice follows that of most other drug authors. I quote Paul Gahlinger (2001), from his book's copyright page: "The book includes many drug names that are registered trademarks. For ease in reading, the trademark symbols are not used; instead, all terms known, or suspected to be, trademarks . . . are appropriately capitalized. Generic drug names are given in lowercase. For instance, the brand name Valium is capitalized, but its generic name diazepam is not capitalized."

Illegal drugs taken for recreational purposes (that is, for the purpose of getting high) may also have several names. Marijuana is known to botanical science as *cannabis* because it is taken from a plant with the name of *Cannabis sativa.* Technically, marijuana (like tobacco) is not a drug but a vegetable substance that contains a drug, tetrahydrocannabinol, or THC for short. In addition, marijuana has acquired a number of street nicknames, including "weed," "pot," "grass," "dope," and "smoke."

## SUMMARY

Drugs are physical substances with measurable effects as well as symbols, socially and legally constructed entities that society thinks about and reacts to in certain ways. Pharmacologists study the molecular action of drugs on organisms, and psychopharmacologists study how a drug's chemistry interacts with the body's neurology, and hence its brain and spinal column—in other words, its mental processes. Many of these actions translate into the real-world "effects" we observe when people take drugs. Much of the most innovative and influential research on drug use is being conducted at the molecular and neurochemical level. Drugs can be thought of, in conjunction with substances called neurotransmitters, as a "key" that unlocks a site in the brain (a "lock") that causes a chemical reaction to take place. Neurotransmitters—which are, in effect, endogenous drugs—regulate countless functions, from the molecular level through the brain to the relevant organs of the body. The functions include hunger, emotion, pleasure (sexual pleasure included), fatigue, and anger. Drugs mimic or block the usual chemical reactions caused by neurotransmitters and either prevent certain functions from taking place or exaggerate those that usually take place. Many of these chemical reactions produce behavior in which we, as sociologists and criminologists, are interested, with addiction or behavioral dependence perhaps foremost among them.

To understand drug use, it is necessary to pay attention to two dimensions—first, four basic pharmacological concepts, and second, four factors that influence drug effects. Our basic pharmacological concepts are the acute-chronic distinction, the ED/LD ratio, drug tolerance, and drug fate. Our four factors that influence drug effects are dose, potency and purity, route of administration, and drug mixing.

Some drug effects ("acute") occur within the span of a single episode of use, that is, under the influence of the drug—the marijuana smoker's high, the heroin addict's overdose, the LSD user's dilated pupils. Other drug effects ("chronic") take place over an extended period of time—the cigarette smoker's lung cancer, the alcoholic's damaged liver, the methamphetamine addict's damaged brain. The acute-chronic distinction is crucial to any student and researcher of drug use.

Before the 1970s, the dominant perspective on drug dependence was the "addiction" model. Certain drugs (such as the narcotics, alcohol, and barbiturates), if consumed in moderate-to-heavy quantities over a period of time, supposedly produced what was known as an abstinence or withdrawal syndrome. And if their use was abruptly discontinued, the user would undergo a painful reaction, including nausea, vomiting, muscular twitching, gooseflesh, chills, aches and pains, and the like. It was assumed that the avoidance of withdrawal was the primary motive of addicts for continued, compulsive use. But the results of laboratory experiments with animals demonstrated that cocaine, a drug that does not produce these classic withdrawal symptoms, produces a far more powerful pattern of continued, compulsive use than heroin, a drug that does. Psychologists began to realize that psychological reinforcement is a more adequate explanation for abusive, compulsive drug use than is addiction. Certain drugs, such as cocaine and methamphetamines, produce a strong, orgasmlike "rush" that generates in some users a behavioral pattern we identify as dependence. Not all (or even most) users develop such a pattern, however, and understanding why some do and some don't is a central mission of drug researchers.

Drugs may be looked at with respect to the dosage at which certain effects take place. The "effective dose" (ED) is the dosage at which a certain relevant effect occurs (among a specific percentage, usually 50 percent, of a designated population) that is of interest to a given observer. To the marijuana smoker, the relevant ED is the amount that causes a high or intoxication. To the physician, the relevant ED is the amount of morphine,

Percodan, or Darvon that is necessary to alleviate pain in patients with a certain level or degree of pain.

In contrast, the "lethal dose" (LD) is the dosage that produces death in a certain percentage of a designated population. Most drug-related acute deaths take place as a result of the shutting down or inhibition of the signals from the brain commanding breathing and/or heartbeat. Some drugs have an affinity for specific sites in the brain that control these functions. Fifty percent of humans will die if they have four-tenths of 1 percent (0.4%) of the volume of alcohol in their bloodstream; 100 percent will die if their blood contains more than 0.8 percent alcohol, by volume. Hence, for alcohol, the LD50 is 0.4 percent blood-alcohol concentration, and the LD100 is 0.8 percent.

Drugs differ with respect to the ratio or gap between ED and LD. For some drugs (barbiturates and heroin are excellent candidates here), it takes only ten times as much to kill an organism (LD) as it does to produce a given effect, such as intoxication or sedation (ED). For these drugs, the ED/LD ratio is 1:10, narrow enough to cause a very substantial number of deaths by overdose. For other drugs, such as marijuana, the ED/LD is enormous, almost incalculable. Hence, hardly anyone dies of an "overdose" of marijuana. (But marijuana, through its principle psychoactive ingredient, THC, does influence other functions of the body, such as coordination and cognition.) Hence, our twin concepts, ED and LD, as well as their relationship *for specific drugs,* is central to any social scientist's understanding of how and why drugs are used, and with what consequences.

Drug tolerance is a crucial pharmacological concept because, over time, with most drugs, to achieve the same effect, a user needs to take an increasing dose. Addicts take a quantity of heroin that would kill a nonuser; their bodies have become habituated to the drug. Behavioral tolerance refers to the fact users are able to comport themselves under the influence in such a way that minimizes the negative effects of the drug. Some drinkers say they can drive as well under the influence as normally. This is not true, but they *are* able to drive better than an inexperienced drinker who is under the influence.

What happens to drugs once they enter the body? How are they broken down? How are they eliminated? How swiftly are they eliminated? Drugs vary with respect to how and how quickly they move through the body. Alcohol and cocaine are relatively quickly metabolized (and hence eliminated) drugs; methadone and marijuana are metabolized (and eliminated) much more slowly. Other things being equal, drug tests are likely to detect substances that are metabolized slowly simply because they remain in the body longer.

Aside from the chemical composition of the drugs themselves, of the many thousands of factors that influence drug effects, four stand out as crucial for us, as students of the intersection between drugs and human behavior, to pay attention to.

Route of administration is central to any understanding of drug use and drug effects. How drugs are taken influences what they do. "How" refers to techniques of use—for our purposes, mainly smoking, injecting, sniffing ("snorting"), and swallowing. The same drug may be taken in different ways and have very different effects. (Not different "actions," but different effects.) In the Andean region of South America, coca leaves (containing 1% cocaine) are chewed; such a route of administration produces effects vastly milder than smoking crack, also a cocaine product. Both routes entail "taking" cocaine, but they produce such different effects that it is difficult to think of both as entailing the use of the same drug. Both smoking and intravenous (IV) administration of drugs are extremely swift, efficient, and effective routes through which to take psychoactive substances. Snorting and oral administration are vastly less efficient and produce slower and less intense "highs."

Dose is central to understanding drug use. While pharmacologists study drug effects in laboratory settings, social scientists look at the impact of drug use in naturalistic settings. What's more important here is the dose characteristically taken, not the potential effect of a drug in an artificial context. In all societies, norms and rules regulate the use of drugs and the amount that is regarded as acceptable to use. Most consumers of alcohol do not become intoxicated when they drink because they usually consume moderate quantities, but if their dose were to increase drastically, they would become not only intoxicated but seriously debilitated as well. To know the effects of drugs in real-life situations, it is necessary to know the doses taken—and the doses customarily taken.

Potency and purity are central to drug taking and its impact. In the early 1980s, heroin was available, illegally, on the street at a purity of roughly 3–5 percent heroin. This means that most of what addicts were taking was inert, nonactive fillers. Today, heroin is available on the street at a purity of 25 percent. This means that users are taking nearly ten times more heroin per packet than they did two decades ago. Different batches of marijuana will contain varying percentages of THC, the drug's psychoactive ingredient, ranging from less than 1 percent THC for wild marijuana growing in roadside ditches to more than 10 percent THC for hydroponic or sinsemilla cannabis. Batches of greater potency will produce more extreme effects, or the same effects at lower doses.

Lastly, drug mixing influences drug effects. Increasingly, different drugs are used together, with many users enjoying the effects of two or more drugs simultaneously. For instance, a "speedball," a popular concoction on the street, is a mixture of heroin and cocaine or methamphetamines. Most drug episodes that result in trips to the hospital and, even more seriously, death by overdose, are a consequence of taking two or more drugs at the same time. Hence, their pharmacological interaction is crucial. The effects of some drugs, when taken together, are additive. With other drugs, taken together, the effect is synergistic—that is, they multiply one another; their effect, together, is greater than twice as much as each single drug, taken alone. Alcohol and barbiturates are the classic example here.

Drugs are classified in different ways. For our purposes, psychoactive drugs fall into the following categories: general depressants, or sedatives, which have a generalized inhibiting effect on organs and functions of the body; narcotics, which dull the mind's perception of pain; stimulants, or substances that speed up signals passing through the central nervous system; and hallucinogens or psychedelics, which generate profound alterations in the perception of sensory stimuli. Sedatives include alcohol, GHB, barbiturates, methaqualone, and the benzodiazepines, or the tranquilizers, including Rohypnol. The "disassociatives,"—PCP and ketamine ("special K")—have sedative-like properties. Narcotics include opium and its derivatives—morphine, heroin, and codeine—as well as the many potent synthetic analgesics, such as methadone, oxycodone, Darvon, Dilaudid, Percodan, and fentanyl. The stimulants are made up mainly of cocaine and crack cocaine, amphetamines, and methamphetamines, a chemical relative of amphetamine. Marijuana and Ecstasy do not easily fall into any broader class of drugs, and hence occupy separate and independent categories.

## KEY TERMS

acute effects   34

additive effects   40

analgesics   47

antagonistic effects   40

ataxia   32

behavioral dependence   41

behavioral tolerance   36

cannabis   48

central nervous system   36

cerebellum   33

chronic effects   34

conducement   31

criminalization   49

cross-dependence   41

cross-tolerance   36

decriminalization   49

dependence (drug)   31

depressants   46

direct drug effects   34

dose-response curve   38

drug action   32

drug addiction   41

drug effects   32

drug fate   36

drug mixing   40

ED (effective dose)   34

ED/LD ratio   35

eidetic imagery   48

empathogen   49

endogenous drug   32

half-life   36

hallucinogens   48

hydroponic   49

immediate sensual
  appeal   44

indirect drug effects   34

intramuscular injection/
  administration   37

IV administration   37

LD (lethal dose)   35

metabolite   36

multiplier effects   40

narcotics   47

neuron   32

neurotransmitter   32

nonspecific effect   32

pharmacological
  tolerance   35

physical dependence   41

potency   39

psychedelics   48

psychopharmacology   31

purity   40

receptors   32

reinforcement   42

route of administration   37

safety margin   35

sedative/hypnotics   46

serotonin   50

stimulant   46

subcutaneous
  administration   37

synapse   32

synergistic effects   40

synesthesia   48

THC (tetrahydrocannabinol)
  33

therapeutic margin   35

tolerance (drug)   35

toxicity   31

## ACCOUNT:   Multiple Drug Use

*Fred, a college student in his late 20s, contributed this account.*

While I was working on my car, a man sporting dreadlocks came up to me and began talking. We became good friends. I asked him if he had a weed connection. He said he needed to talk to his friends. A few days later he came over to my apartment with a couple of his friends. They hung out for a while and offered me some weed. We passed the bowl around and had a nice time talking. His friends told me that they didn't usually have weed but that they could get crack for me any time. The next night I bought $100 worth of crack. I sat in my apartment and smoked it all by myself. It was an amazing experience. I felt whole again. The crack lasted for several hours. I had incense burning, music playing, and I was really happy to be all by myself with my crack. The only weird thing about that night was that I kept peeking out the window every few seconds. For some reason I felt that someone was watching me. It was like I was paranoid or something. . . . All I really wanted to do was smoke crack and work on my car. My credit card bills were mounting, but I continued to make the minimum payments with what little money I had left. Eventually I ended up buying merchandise with my credit cards just so I could sell it to buy crack. I started becoming more and more paranoid, so I bought a .45 caliber Beretta handgun with a night scope and a laser built into the barrel. I even bought a box of hollow-point bullets. I practiced loading and unloading the gun. I had become extremely paranoid, so I bought a pit bull to protect me and to keep me company. His name was "Chunks." He was a great dog, but he ate practically everything I owned.

I remember one night smoking $300 worth of crack all by myself. I started around 6:00 P.M. and by 9:00 the next morning I was still smoking crack. I was afraid I was going to die, so I flushed the little bit that was left down the toilet. I just sat there on my bathroom floor listening to music waiting to see if I was going to die. Three hours later, while Maria [my girlfriend] was on her lunch break, she called and asked to be picked up from school. My lips were completely burnt from the hot crack pipe, and I couldn't talk because my throat was burnt from inhaling the hot gas from the crack all night long. I told her what had happened. She took care of me and kept bringing me cold beer until I fell asleep.

At this point I was no longer a nice person. I felt invincible. Anyone who got in my way was immediately run over. I was constantly fighting with Maria, my parents, and with Maria's family. Her father hated me and I hated him. One time Maria got in a fight with her mom and asked me to come pick her up. When I arrived, the police pulled in behind me and surrounded my car. Maria's mom had told them that I had a gun and that I was going to hurt someone. Fortunately I had removed the gun from the car just prior to going over to her house. The police threw me up against the car and searched me. They asked to search the car and I gave them permission, because at the time I had nothing to hide. Maria's mom kept telling the police that I had a gun, so I responded, "The constitution gives me the right to bear arms, bitch." Eventually the police let me go, but I was really angry and I wanted revenge. . . . I hated her father so much that I wouldn't talk to him.

My rent was three months behind, I owed $60,000 to American Express, and I was flat broke. . . . I sold my television to the crack dealer and managed to scrounge together a few thousand dollars. . . . I threw Chunks onto the passenger seat, and we headed south [to Miami, to visit my brother]. . . . [Several days later, my brother and I] were walking down the strip, we ran into a friend of mine from home. He invited us back to his friend's house to hang out. We smoked some weed, and then everyone including my brother took XTC [Ecstasy, MDMA]. I really wanted to do it, but for some reason XTC really scared me, so I didn't do it that night. Everyone decided to go out to the beach, but I wasn't really in the mood, so I stayed at the apartment building. I met a family who lived down the hall, and decided to hang out with them. They had seven little kids and lived in roach-infested, two-bedroom apartment. They fed me dinner, and we drank a few beers together. I was talking to the father, and he asked me if I had ever done cocaine. I said yes, and he said he could get us some. He asked if I wanted crack or powder. I told him crack. I gave him $50, and he returned with a bag. We went into the bathroom, and he pulled out a thin copper pipe. I had never smoked crack out of a pipe like this, but it really intensified the delivery. We continued smoking for several hours, and then I crashed on their couch. . . .

My brother dragged me outside for some fresh air, but my mind had snapped, like a bone breaking in half. My brother thought it had something to do with the . . . crack I had smoked the night before, but nothing he did seemed to help. He even brought me a shot of liquor thinking it might help bring me down, but it didn't help. He then decided maybe I just needed something to eat, so he carried me to the car and drove me to the Ale House. We walked inside, and I started to feel better, but I was still really confused. The hostess seated us at a bench, and then we ordered some wings and soft drinks. We had just started to eat our wings when I looked over my brother's shoulder, and an evil-looking man was staring at me as if he were going to devour me. It was the Devil. I grabbed my brother's hand and told him the Devil was sitting behind him and we had to get out of the restaurant. He told me to calm down, but I couldn't. My brother looked over at the hostess and told her we had to leave and asked if she could wrap up our wings. Before he could finish what he was saying, the hostess looked at me with an evil smile and said, "You're leaving so soon?" I glanced back over my brother's shoulder, and the Devil was still sitting there with an evil grin on his face, staring me down.

I ran out of the restaurant, pushing everyone out of my way. I jumped in the car and waited for my brother, but he wasn't returning. My mind was racing, and I thought the Devil had taken my brother. I ran back into the restaurant, and as I opened the door, he came out. I was so relieved to see him. We jumped in the car, and my brother frantically called everyone, telling them that something was seriously wrong with me. . . . [Later that night,] I fell asleep, but I was having terrible nightmares. When I woke up, I was ranting and raving about Nostradamus and that I had to save the world. I continued to rant uncontrollably for several days, and eventually my brother couldn't take it anymore. We were driving to his house, and he started screaming at me. . . . I . . . asked him to get out of the car. He got out, and I drove back to his house. Ten minutes later he showed up and he was steaming mad. He started kicking the car and telling me to get out and that he was going to kick my ass. I was really scared, but I got out of the car and asked him to calm down. He punched me in my stomach and tried to hit me over the head with a metal lantern. We rolled around on the ground for several minutes before I was able to get the upper

hand. I had him on the ground, and I was kicking him in his stomach. He pretended to be hurt, so I stopped kicking him. I jumped in my car and tried to leave, but as I was starting the car, he jumped up and started kicking the car again. I frantically locked the doors, and took off. . . .

I continued to have terrible nightmares about the world coming to an end. . . . I didn't want to be left alone, but I had no choice. . . . I went outside to get some fresh air, but I couldn't escape my thoughts. As I paced around the pool, I kept looking up at the sky frantically. The house was in the flight path of the airport, and I felt that the airplanes were going to crash into the house. I also kept having visions of nuclear bombs going off and the world coming to an end. I couldn't handle being outside, so I went inside and turned on the television. As I was changing the channels, I realized that the people in the programs were talking directly to me. I thought it was God, but I couldn't figure out how He could talk to me through the television set. It was as if he knew personal things about my life, and was able to say just the right things to frighten the hell out of me. I ran outside and jumped in my car.

The rest of that day I raced around Orlando trying to find my sanity. I started following white cars and running from black cars. At this point, I had truly lost my mind. . . . I kept trying to drive south, but every time I saw a black car I turned off the road. I continued to drive in circles for hours. I remember finally seeing signs to Miami, but I couldn't get on the highway, because the wind was howling, and the birds were swirling around against the dark gray sky. I thought it was God telling me that there was going to be a tornado and I shouldn't get on the plane. [A friend] called my brother, and they decided I needed to go to the hospital. I agreed, so my brother came over . . . and he drove me to the emergency room.

This was not just any emergency room. These patients looked as if they were headed for hell. Every face was filled with pure evil. And everyone had serious wounds. While sitting there, I felt this was . . . a place for God to judge me. I wanted to show God I was a good person, and I didn't belong in hell, so I went around helping the patients. I put a blanket on a guy sitting in a wheelchair and held a baby because it wouldn't stop crying. I was willing to do anything to show God I didn't belong in hell. Just then a doctor came out, and told me they didn't have room for me at this hospital. When he looked up from his clipboard, I freaked out. It was the Devil, the exact same man who was sitting behind my brother in the Ale House, but this time, he didn't have such a sinister look. He looked sophisticated and godlike, whatever that might mean. He said I would need to go to another hospital because they had more room there. The three of us got in the car and drove to the other hospital. On the way there, I was elated because I felt God was not going to kill me. We arrived at the hospital and walked into the waiting room. That's when I freaked out again.

*Friday the Thirteenth* was playing on the television. I told my brother that there was no way I was going into that hospital. He convinced me to relax and reminded me I needed help. I went up to the desk to sign in. . . . A few minutes later they called my name. The three of us walked back to a room, and I sat on the hospital bed. They handed me a "Living Will" and asked me to sign it. I told them I needed to read it over. A few minutes later, the nurse asked my brother and Maria to leave the room. They left, and I sat there with this paper trying to figure out if I was going to sign it. I thought that it was God asking me if I wanted to live or die. I couldn't sign the form and I started to freak out because I thought these people were going to execute me.

After several minutes of contemplating, I burst out of the room, ran through the lobby, and out the front door of the hospital. I ran for about a mile, when I finally reached a payphone. I dialed 911, and told the police these crazy people in the hospital were trying to kill me. He instructed me to wait at the phone until the police arrived. Within a few seconds, there was a helicopter swirling over my head, with a spot light pointed at me. Simultaneously, the police surrounded me, and told me to lie down on the ground, and a bunch of men in white coats showed up. I told the police those were the men who were trying to kill me. The police told me . . . I needed to go with the men in the white coats. I told the police officer I was going to hit him in his face so he could take me to jail, because I was afraid the people in the hospital were going to kill me. He handcuffed me and drove me back to the hospital. They placed me in a wheelchair, and rolled me up a long ramp into the psychiatric ward of the hospital.

## QUESTIONS

How typical is this case? Which basic principles discussed in this chapter does this person illustrate? After reading this chapter, what would you have predicted about the effects on him of the drugs he took? Are the consequences of taking drugs described here simply a product of those drugs' pharmacological properties? Or is something else at work? Do other users experience the same effects using the same drugs? Why do you think this person had such untoward drug experiences? What can you learn from this account?

CHAPTER

# 3

# THEORIES OF DRUG USE

In this chapter, we look at the causes of drug use. To understand the cause of a phenomenon such as drug use, we need a theory. A theory is simply an explanation for a general category of phenomena, that is, any set of events or conditions. The word "general" is important, because scientists don't usually apply the term "theory" to a single event or condition, such as the assassination of John F. Kennedy or Martin Luther King. Accounting for why assassinations take place *in general*

would be a theory. Astrophysicists have theories or explanations about the birth, movement, and death of stars; biologists have theories about genetic changes in organisms over time; sociologists and political scientists have theories about voting behavior.

One major type of theory or explanation of drug use would be the attempt to explain why people use drugs. There are two absolutely necessary preconditions for use—the **predisposition,** or motive and susceptibility, to do so, and the **availability** of one or more psychoactive substances. Each of these two preconditions is *necessary but not sufficient* to explain drug use. If a drug is not available in a particular locale, drug use is not possible—whether or not a predisposition to use is present. Likewise, without the predisposition to use, use cannot take place; *by itself,* availability does not explain use. Each is an essential—or necessary—condition for use; neither is sufficient for it to take place. In this chapter, we focus mainly on the predisposition or motive, that is, on the factors that make drug use seem desirable and enticing—an activity in which someone wants to engage.

For millennia, humans have asked, Why do they do it? about a variety of anomalous, unconventional, or deviant behaviors. The ancient Greek philosophers began thinking about the forces and factors that lead some of us astray. But, for the most part, until just a few hundred years ago, the dominant theory for wrongdoing was **demonology,** meaning the devil (or evil spirits) made them do it. Demonology has not disappeared from the popular or public mind, however. Toward the end of a course on criminology taught at a small Bible Belt college, Frank Schmalleger asked his students to speculate on which theory of crime they thought made the most sense: biological, psychological, or sociological. The overwhelming majority of the class chose none of these three, and instead agreed that "the devil made them do it" was the most valid (1996, p. 88).

In contrast, nearly all intellectuals and experts on human behavior favor a *materialistic* explanation, one rooted in the social, psychological, or biological worlds. Social scientists look to such forces as childhood socialization, urban decay, poverty, and bonds to conventional society to account for why people do the things they do. However, once we agree that it is forces in the material world that best explain drug use and abuse, and not evil demons and spirits, we are still left with a bewildering array of theories.

Dozens of explanations have been proposed for drug use and abuse. In the early 1980s, the National Institute of Mental Health (NIDA) published a volume that spelled out more than 40 theories of drug abuse (Lettieri, Sayers, and Pearson, 1980). The number of theories proposed by experts today is even greater than this number. As I just said, the dictionary defines "theory" as an explanation for a general class of phenomena. To most people, then, a theory of drug use would be an explanation as to why people use and abuse drugs. However, not all the theories that have been proposed address this particular issue. Most theories do not attempt to explain the entire spectrum of use; some are more narrowly focused. Most concentrate either on illicit use (often referred to as "abuse") or on alcoholism. Some focus entirely on addiction, usually to narcotics. Some focus on the individual, others on society, and still others on the individual's relationship to the society. While a number of theories deal with initiation into drug use, several focus on continued or habitual use. Nearly all these theories are *partial* in scope: They select one factor or a limited number of factors that are believed to cause drug use or abuse. Most theorists admit that the factor they focus on, *in combination with others,* influences drug taking. Hardly any researcher in the field believes that one factor, and one alone, explains the phenomenon under investigation. Moreover, a factor is not a theory; most theories put several factors together to form a coherent explanation, an argument with several different pieces that articulate with one another. All of this means that most theories of drug use are not contradictory or in competition with one another. Most cover different aspects of the same phenomenon and may be regarded as complementary rather than contradictory.

As is true of theories of crime, there are three broad *types* of explanations for drug use: (1) biological theories, (2) psychological theories, and (3) sociological theories. Each focuses on a different range of factors as crucial in determining why people use and abuse psychoactive substances. Of course, even within each broad type, there is a range of specific theories. All biological theories, and nearly all psychological theories, are individualistic in that they focus on differences between and among people. They can be referred to as "kinds-of-people" theories: Person X is different in some way from person Y (or has had different kinds of experiences from person Y), and therefore, person X is more likely to use drugs than person Y. In contrast, most sociological theories tend to focus not on individual differences but group or category differences (persons belonging to group X are different from persons belonging to group Y), or structural differences (the larger structures or circumstances in which persons are located differ, such as cities, neighborhoods, time periods, social conditions, or countries). At the same time, some sociologists do promulgate more individualistic explanations; in this chapter, we'll encounter a few. Since most of these theories explain only a piece of the puzzle, most of them are complementary rather than contradictory. Still, some explanations do contradict others: If one is true, one or more others cannot be true. It's important to understand the implications of each one so that we have a clear idea of what manner of evidence confirms or falsifies it.

## BIOLOGICAL THEORIES

**Biological theories** are those that postulate specific physical mechanisms in individuals that impel or influence them either to experiment with drugs or to abuse them once they are exposed to them. Some are constitutional, that is, are based on mechanisms that are present at birth and vary from one person to another. Others are partly environmental; that is, inborn factors *in conjunction with* environmental factors generate drug-using behavior. Two of these explanations are genetic theories and the theory of metabolic imbalance.

### Genetic Factors

According to one line of thinking—**genetic theories**—the genetic makeup of individuals predisposes them toward drug abuse and alcoholism. A gene or combination of genes influences the specific biological mechanisms relevant to substance abuse—such as being able to achieve a certain level of intoxication when using drugs, becoming ill at low doses as opposed to much higher doses, lowering or not lowering anxiety levels when under the influence, or having the capacity to metabolize chemical substances in the body. Any and all these factors could vary from one individual to another, or from one racial or national group to another, and could influence continued use. This "genetic loading," in combination with environmental and personality factors, could make for a significantly higher level of drug abuse or alcoholism in certain individuals or groups in the population (Schuckit, 1980). Indeed, the tendency to prefer alcohol to other beverages can be bred in animals, suggesting the relevance and strength of the genetic factor in drug use and abuse.

Most of the research attempting to demonstrate a genetic factor in drug abuse has focused on alcoholism. Studies have shown that adopted children have rates of alcoholism closer to those of their natural parents than to those of their adoptive parents (Schuckit, 1984, p. 62). One study found that 30–40 percent of natural children of alcoholics become alcoholics themselves, as opposed to a rate of 10 percent for the general population (Kolata, 1987). Some experts conclude that the rate of heritability of alcoholism—the chance of inheriting the disorder—is "similar to that expected for diabetes or peptic ulcer disease" (Schuckit, 1984, p. 62). Now that the entire human DNA sequence has been "decoded," it is entirely possible that during the coming decade scientists will discover a genetic link with alcoholism.

No researcher exploring the inherited link with alcoholism asserts that genetic factors represent the only or even the principal factor in compulsive drinking. Rather, they posit a genetic *predisposition* toward alcoholism. Inheritance is one factor out of several. Alone, it does not "make" someone a compulsive, destructive drinker. In combination with other variables, genetic factors may facilitate or make the process more likely, however.

What are some precise mechanisms that may push someone in the direction of alcoholism? What's the lynchpin between biology and abusive drinking? One study found that the sons and daughters of alcoholics tend to be less affected by alcohol than are the sons and daughters of nonalcoholics: Their coordination is less debilitated, their bodies produce a lower hormonal response, and they feel less drunk when they imbibe a given quantity of alcohol. According to researchers Marc Schuckit, Jack Mendelson, and Barbara Lex, 40 percent of the children of alcoholics exhibit a significantly lower sensitivity to alcohol in these three respects, while this was true of only 10 percent of members of control groups (Kolata, 1987). In addition, researcher Henry Begleiter found that boys who do not drink but whose fathers are alcoholics have brain waves significantly different from boys who are sons of nonalcoholics (Kolata, 1987). Although some researchers doubt that such physical or biological differences produce real-world differences in drinking patterns, others point out that inherited mechanisms, in combination with other factors, could lead to an increased likelihood of compulsive, destructive, chronic drinking.

## Metabolic Imbalance

A second theory postulates **metabolic imbalance** as a possible causal factor in at least one type of drug abuse—narcotic addiction. Developed by physicians Vincent Dole and Marie Nyswander (1965, 1980; Dole, 1980), this theory argues that heroin addicts suffer from a metabolic disease or disorder, much as diabetics do. Once certain individuals begin taking narcotics, a biochemical process "kicks in," and physiologically, they begin to crave opiate drugs in much the same way that the bodies of diabetics crave insulin. Repeated doses of a narcotic complete their metabolic cycle; narcotics act as a stabilizer, normalizing an existing deficiency. The narcotic abuser can never be withdrawn from drug use because his or her body will continue to crave opiates, just as diabetics cannot be withdrawn from insulin; in both cases, the substance provides what the body lacks and cannot provide.

No precise biological mechanism corresponding to metabolic imbalance has ever been located. The best that can be said about this theory is that the treatment program based on it, methadone maintenance, has helped a certain proportion of addicts—a far lower proportion than its proponents claim, but a higher proportion than its critics claim. We'll explore the various available drug treatment modalities in more detail in Chapter 14. Here, it is enough to know that hormonal imbalance has been proposed as a factor influencing drug abuse in certain individuals, even though its existence has never been established empirically. The only evidence supporting it is that some addicts behave *as if* they suffer from a metabolic imbalance. Comparing their early thoughts with their later writings on the subject, it becomes clear that the proponents of the metabolic imbalance theory have retreated somewhat from their original insistence on the importance of this factor (Dole and Nyswander, 1980). It is possible that the theory is relevant only on the clinical, and not the theoretical, etiological, or causal, level. Indeed, it may remain as a relevant theory only in order to justify the maintenance of addicts on methadone for life.

## PSYCHOLOGICAL THEORIES

Theories relying on **psychological factors** fall into two basic varieties: those emphasizing the mechanism of reinforcement, and those stressing that the personalities of the drug user, abuser, and especially addict are different from those of the abstainer, and are causally related to use and abuse. The mechanism of reinforcement is fairly straightforward: People tend to maximize reward and minimize punishment; they continue to do certain things because they have a past history of being rewarded for doing them. Drug users are individuals who have been rewarded for use, and hence they continue to use. While **reinforcement theories** underplay personality factors, personality theories, as you might expect, emphasize their important role in causing drug use and abuse. The precise personality configuration that is said to determine drug use and abuse varies with the theorist; a range of personality factors is invoked here. The key factor that binds these **psychodynamic theories** together, however, is that they postulate that certain individuals have a type of personality that impels them to drug use and abuse.

### Reinforcement

A major psychological theory underplays the idea of personality differences between users and nonusers, and emphasizes the role of reinforcement. Even animals use certain drugs compulsively under the right experimental conditions, casting doubt on the need to invoke psychodynamic variables in the development of addiction (McAuliffe and Gordon, 1980, p. 139; Wikler, 1980, p. 174). In addition, experiments have shown that, independent of personality factors, human subjects who are administered opiates without knowing what they have taken wish to repeat taking the drug; their desire grows with continued administration (McAuliffe, 1975). For some aspects of the drug-taking process, a consideration of personality variables is not necessary. (At the same time, there is individual variation in reactions to and experiences of drug effects.) However, it is an axiom in science that *you can't explain a variable with a constant*. After all, if two people are taking the same highly reinforcing drug (a constant), and one becomes addicted to it while the other does not (a variable), it is insufficient to argue that reinforcement explains continued use because it does not account for the difference in behavior. Consequently, we need to bring into the picture variables or factors in addition to simple reinforcement.

There are two distinctly different types of reinforcement—positive and negative—and consequently two different theories that cite reinforcement as a mechanism in continued drug use. (Actually, some approaches make use of both these mechanisms—different types of reinforcement for different types of drugs or drug abusers.) **Positive reinforcement** occurs when the individual receives a pleasurable sensation and, because of this, is motivated to repeat what caused it. In brief, "The pleasure mechanism may . . . give rise to a strong fixation on repetitive behavior" (Bejerot, 1980, p. 253). With respect to drug use, this means that getting high is pleasurable, and what is pleasurable tends to be repeated.

According to this view, the continued use of all drugs that stimulate euphoria is caused by their "extremely potent reinforcing effects" (McAuliffe and Gordon, 1980, p. 137). Inferring from the way that users behave, it is difficult to draw a sharp distinction between a strong psychological and a physical dependency. Indeed, physical dependence is not even a necessary mechanism for the proponents of the theory of positive reinforcement. What is referred to as addiction is simply an end point along a continuum indicating that "a sufficient history of reinforcement has probably been acquired to impel a high rate of use" in the user (McAuliffe and Gordon, 1980, p. 138). This also means that ongoing, even compulsive, use and abuse do not require the mechanism of a literal physical addiction to continue taking place. Many users are reinforced—that is, they experience euphoria—from their very first drug experience onward, and the more they use, the more intense the sensation and the greater the motivation to continue use.

**Negative reinforcement** occurs when an individual does something to seek relief or to avoid pain, thereby being rewarded—and hence motivated—to do whatever it was that achieved relief or alleviated the pain. In the world of drug use and addiction, when someone who is physically dependent on a particular drug undergoes painful withdrawal symptoms upon discontinuing the use of that drug, and takes a dose to alleviate withdrawal distress, he or she will experience relief with the termination of the pain. Such an experience will motivate the addict to do what has to be done to obliterate the painful sensations associated with withdrawal.

While positive reinforcement can occur with *any* euphoric drug—indeed, with any pleasurable sensation (Bejerot, 1972, 1980)—the theory emphasizing the mechanism of negative reinforcement as a major factor in drug abuse is largely confined to drugs that produce a physical dependence, especially the opiates. Relatively little attempt has been made to apply this theory to explain either the continued use of nonaddicting drugs or the use of opiates that does not involve a literal physical dependence. (However, some nonaddicting drugs, such as cocaine and marijuana, may provide relief from depression; this factor has also been mentioned as a reason for continued use.)

The argument invoking negative reinforcement goes as follows. Initially, pleasure dominates as a motivating force in use. Hence, the first few weeks of narcotic drug use have been called the "honeymoon" phase of addiction. However, the user gradually becomes physically dependent without realizing it. Because of the body's growing tolerance to narcotics, the user, in order to continue receiving pleasure, is forced to increase the doses—eventually to a point at which addiction takes place. If use is discontinued, whether because of arrest, disruption in supply, or lack of money to purchase the drug, painful withdrawal symptoms wrack the addict's body. Because the user recognizes that doses of a narcotic drug can alleviate these symptoms, an intense craving is generated for the drug over time.

According to Alfred Lindesmith (1947, 1968), the earliest proponent of this theory:

> The critical experience in the fixation process is not the positive euphoria produced by the drug but rather the relief of the pain that invariably appears when a physically dependent person stops using the drug. This experience becomes critical, however, only when an additional indispensable element in the situation is taken into account, namely a cognitive one. The individual not only must experience withdrawal distress but must understand or conceptualize this experience in a particular way. He [or she] must realize that his [or her] distress is produced by the interruption of prior regular use of the drug. (Lindesmith, 1968, p. 8)

In short, the "perception of withdrawal symptoms as being due to the absence of opiates will generate a *burning* desire for the drug" (Sutter, 1966, p. 195). According to this theory, addicts continue taking their drug of choice *just to feel normal*.

Recent evidence suggests that, as originally stated, the theory does not account for most narcotic use among addicts. The majority of addicts and other compulsive drug abusers *do* experience euphoria, and this is a major factor in their continued drug use. In one study of addicts, all of whom used heroin at least once a day, 98 percent of the sample (63 out of the 64 interviewed) said that they got high or experienced euphoria at least once a month, and 42 percent did so *every day* (McAuliffe and Gordon, 1974, p. 804). In this sample, euphoria was consciously desired and sought: 93 percent said that they wanted to be high at least once a day, and 60 percent wanted to be high all the time (McAuliffe and Gordon, 1974, p. 807). Heavy, compulsive heroin users continue to seek and achieve euphoria, and its attainment is a major motivating force behind their continued use.

A resolution to the apparent conflict between the positive and the negative reinforcement models of drug addiction has been offered. (While the negative reinforcement school argues that only the avoidance of pain and the desire to feel normal motivate the addict, the positive reinforcement advocates argue that both factors, as well as others, may be operative.) It is likely that there are actually two types of narcotic addicts—the *maintainers* and the *euphoria-seekers*. The maintainer takes just enough narcotics to avert withdrawal distress. Some addicts lack the financial resources, and are unwilling to engage in a life centered around the commission of crime, to obtain enough heroin to attain euphoria. They are simply staving off the agony of withdrawal, "nursing" their habit along (McAuliffe and Gordon, 1974, p. 826). To achieve the high they really want would require taking such substantial quantities of the drug that their lives would be transformed utterly and completely. They would have to work very hard and run a substantial risk of harm and arrest. Not all users want to commit crimes to get high; not all think the chance of arrest is worth threatening such valued aspects of their lives as their jobs, families, and freedom to come and go where and when they want. They prefer to maintain a habit to risking what they have in order to achieve euphoria. They retain most of their ties with conventional society and "let loose only periodically" (McAuliffe and Gordon, 1974, p. 822).

In contrast, the pleasure-seeking addict takes narcotics in sufficient quantities and at sufficiently frequent intervals to achieve euphoria. This habit is extremely expensive, and hence, typically requires illegal activity to support it. In addition, the lifestyle of the euphoria-seeking addict is sufficiently disruptive that a legal job is not usually feasible; he or she must resort to criminal activity instead. It is also difficult for the nonaddict to fit in with and be capable of tolerating the addict's lifestyle, so marriage and a family are a chancy proposition unless the addict's spouse is also addicted. Further, since heavy opiate use depresses the sexual urge, intimate relationships are difficult. In short, the euphoria-seeking addict sacrifices conventional activities and commitments for the hedonistic pursuit of pleasure, and to engage in this pursuit, a commitment to a deviant and criminal lifestyle is also necessary. Such sacrifices would make no sense "if they were directed solely toward reducing withdrawal symptoms, which could be accomplished with much less effort, as every addict knows" (McAuliffe and Gordon, 1974, p. 828).

## Inadequate Personality

Several psychological theories of drug use rely on the notion of a psychological pathology, defect, or inadequacy: There is something wrong in the emotional or psychic life of certain individuals that makes drugs attractive to them. They use drugs as an escape from reality, as a means of avoiding life's problems and retreating into euphoric bliss and drugged-out indifference. Euphoria, says one inadequate-personality theorist, is adaptive for the immature individual who lacks responsibility, a sense of independence, and the ability to defer hedonistic gratification for the sake of achieving long-range goals (Ausubel, 1980, pp. 4–5). Although drug use is adaptive for the defective personality in that it masks some of life's problems, it is adaptive only in an exclusively negative way: The problems never get solved, only covered up, and meanwhile, drug use itself generates a host of other, more serious problems. Normal people, who do not share this inadequacy, do not find drugs appealing and are not led to use them. Of course, not all drug users share personality inadequacies and defects to the same degree; some will be impelled to experiment or use simply because of social pressure or availability. However, the more inadequate the personality, the greater the likelihood of becoming highly involved with drug use, and the more that use becomes abuse and eventually addiction. In short, for the weak, drug abuse is a kind of crutch; for the strong, experimentation leads to abstention, not abuse. To the inadequate-personality theorist, drug abuse is an adaptation or a defense mechanism, a means of obliterating feelings of inferiority (Wurmser, 1980, pp. 71–72).

One major variety of the inadequate-personality approach is the self-esteem or **self-derogation perspective.** This theory holds that drug use and abuse, like deviant and criminal behavior generally (Kaplan, 1975), are responses to low self-esteem and self-rejecting attitudes. (But it does not apply in societies in which the particular type of drug use being explained is practically universal and normatively accepted by the majority.) Low self-esteem could come about as a result of "peer rejection, parental neglect, high expectations for achievement, school failure, physical stigmata, social stigmata (e.g., disvalued group memberships), impaired sex-role identity, ego deficiencies, low coping abilities, and (generally) coping mechanisms that are socially disvalued and/or are otherwise self-defeating" (Kaplan, 1975, p. 129). For some, normatively approved activities and group memberships are sources of painful experiences; deviant or disapproved activities and memberships, however, are effective sources of self-enhancement. Drug use provides exactly such a deviant activity and group membership, and one that permits a deadening of the painful feelings stirred up by self-rejection. It is difficult to reconcile such self-derogation theories, which explain drug use as being brought on in part as a consequence of social rejection, with the fact that illicit drug users tend to have more, not fewer, intimate friends than do nonusers (Kandel and Davies, 1991), as the theory would predict. In addition, in recent years, the entire edifice of self-esteem theory—that low self-esteem "is to blame for a host of social ills, from poor academic performance and marital discord to violence, crime, and drug abuse" (Erica Goode, 2002, p. D1)—has come crashing to the ground. Most researchers no longer believe that a poor sense of oneself accounts for any of the behaviors that were once attributed to it, and that includes drug abuse.

## Problem Behavior Proneness

In a third type of psychological theory of drug use, researchers see the phenomenon as a form of deviant or problem behavior. In sociology and in social psychology, the branch of psychology most influenced by sociology, the term "deviant" has no negative, pejorative, or pathological connotations. Instead, it refers to behavior that is not in accord with the norms of, and that tends to be condemned by, the majority. Likewise, "problem" behavior is not necessarily bad or pathological; the term simply denotes behavior that has a certain likelihood of getting the individual who enacts it in trouble. Social psychologists have found that drug users typically have attitudes, values, personalities, and norms that depart significantly from those of the nonuser majority. And these, in turn, make it likely that users will engage in behavior that, likewise, departs from the conventional path. Of course, these are statistical, not absolute, differences; many users and nonusers may be similar to one another in a number of ways, and substantially different from one another in other important respects. Still, the statistical differences are there, and they are often quite striking. What are they?

Before examining the literature on the subject, it must be stressed that **problem behavior proneness** is a dimension, the key elements of which are unconventionality and the willingness to take risks. Not all problem behavior–prone individuals stand at the extreme end of the spectrum, that is, are so unconventional and so willing to take risks that they are unlikely to survive in polite society. In fact, *moderately* unconventional and *moderately* risk-taking persons are often among society's most creative, innovative, and successful individuals: artists, inventors, writers, scientists, academics. Without unconventionality, risk taking, and a certain tolerance for both, society is likely to be repressive, and social change is likely to be sluggish or nonexistent (Sunstein, 2003). Many problem-prone youngsters are bright, do well in school, and are headed for successful careers. The concept has no meaning outside a specific social and cultural context, and a society that provides a place for eccentrics may also profit from their often considerable contributions—just as it often also punishes their unconventional behavior. But the fact is, other things being equal, the problem-prone youngster is more likely to use a wide range of drugs than the one who follows the rules, plays it safe, and takes few risks.

With respect to users' personality and attitudes, a great deal of research (Jessor, 1979; Jessor and Jessor, 1977, 1980; Robins, 1980; Smith and Fogg, 1977, 1978) demonstrates that users, in comparison with nonusers, tend to be more rebellious, independent, open to new experiences, willing to take a wide range of risks, tolerant of differences, accepting of deviant behavior and transgressions of moral and cultural norms, receptive to uncertainty, pleasure seeking, hedonistic, peer oriented, nonconformist, and unconventional. (Again, some of these qualities are also related to imagination, creativity, and certain kinds of talent, ability, and accomplishment.) Users also tend to be less religious, less attached to parents and family, less achievement oriented, and less cautious. This personality manifests itself in a wide range of behavior, much of it not only unconventional but problematic for the individual and for mainstream society: earlier sexual behavior, and with a wider range of partners; underachievement in school and on the job; and at least mildly delinquent behavior.

Researchers who emphasize the unconventional personality as a key factor in drug use can demonstrate the validity of their approach with longitudinal studies. That is, they can predict *in advance,* before they have used drugs, with a high degree of accuracy, which youngsters will experiment with and use psychoactive substances and which ones will not. With respect to personality, the adolescent *less* likely to experiment with and use drugs "is one who values and expects to attain academic achievement, who is not much concerned with independence, who treats society as unproblematic rather than as an object for criticism, who maintains religious involvement and a more uncompromising attitude toward normative transgression, and who sees little attraction in problem behavior relative to its negative consequences." The adolescent *more* likely to experiment with and use drugs "shows an opposite pattern: a concern with personal autonomy, a lack of interest in the goals of conventional institutions, like church and school, a jaundiced view of the larger society, and a more tolerant view of transgression" (Jessor and Jessor, 1980, p. 109). In other words, a "single summarizing dimension underlying the differences between users and nonusers might be termed conventionality-unconventionality" (Jessor and Jessor, 1980, p. 109).

Like most theories, in the view that drug users are more unconventional and risk taking than nonusers, the relationship is a matter of degree. That is, the more unconventional the youth, the greater the likelihood that he or she will use drugs. In addition, the more unconventional, the more serious the drug involvement. *Mildly* unconventional youngsters are likely to drink, experiment with marijuana, but do little else. *Moderately* unconventional youngsters will drink alcohol more heavily, use marijuana regularly, and experiment with other drugs. *Highly* unconventional youth have a much greater chance of becoming seriously involved not only with alcohol and marijuana but also with more dangerous drugs as well. It is possible that this explanation accounts for the typical or modal drug user—mainly, the "recreational" drug user—but an account of why some recreational users become compulsive, abusive, and addicted consumers of psychoactive substances requires a separate theory or the introduction of additional factors. What causes someone to *use* drugs may be different from what causes her or him to *abuse* them.

## SOCIOLOGICAL THEORIES

Biological and psychological theories tend to emphasize individualistic factors, although the researchers who propose them usually indicate that broader factors are at work. For instance, two psychologists associated with the problem behavior–proneness line of thinking (Jessor and Jessor, 1980, p. 105) incorporate the environment or, to be more specific, the "perceived environmental system"—especially parents and friends—into their model. However, their focus is on the characteristics of the individual.

In contrast, sociologists tend to make broader, structural factors the focus of their theories. For most sociologists, the crucial factor to be examined is not the characteristics of the individual, but the situations, social relations, or social structures in which the individual

| TABLE 3-1 | Sociological Theories of Drug Use | |
|---|---|---|
| **Theory** | **Explanatory Factor** | **Proponents** |
| Anomie/strain theory | Disjunction between means and ends | Robert Merton; Richard Cloward and Lloyd Ohlin |
| Social control theory | Absence of bonds to conventional society | Travis Hirschi; others |
| Self-control theory | Inadequate parenting, leading to lack of self-control | Michael Gottfredson and Travis Hirschi |
| Social learning and subcultural theory | Deviant socialization | Edwin Sutherland; Ronald Akers; Howard Becker |
| Selective interaction/ socialization | Attraction to unconventionality, and influence by peer groups | Bruce Johnson; Denise Kandel |
| Social disorganization | Community or neighborhood disorganization | Many |
| Conflict theory | Differences in power, resources, and opportunities | Elliott Currie; Harry Levine; many others |

is, or has been, located. More specifically, it is the individual *located within* specific structures. (I summarize the sociological theories in this section in Table 3-1.)

The field of sociology proposes seven partially overlapping **sociological theories** to help explain drug use: (1) anomie, (2) social control, (3) self-control, (4) social learning and subcultural, (5) selective interaction/socialization, (6) social disorganization, and (7) conflict. (I'll mention an eighth theory, routine activities theory, only in passing.) The overlap among these theories is sufficiently great that some of the theorists who endorse one of them also support one or all of the others.

## Anomie Theory

In the 1930s, sociologist Robert K. Merton generated what came to be referred to as the **anomie theory** of deviant behavior. In his view, deviant behavior—illicit drug use included—takes place when avenues to material success are blocked off. Anomie theory, as Merton developed it (1938, 1957, pp. 131–160; 1968, pp. 185–248), argues that in a competitive, materialistic, achievement-oriented society, success is *encouraged* as attainable for all members but actually is attainable to only a small proportion of the society. Individuals who do not succeed must devise "deviant" or disapproved adaptations to deal with their failure. Those who have given up on achieving society's materialistic goals, whether by approved or disapproved means, become **retreatists.** "In this category fall some of the adaptive activities of psychotics, autists, pariahs, outcasts, vagrants, vagabonds, tramps, chronic drunkards, and drug addicts" (Merton, 1957, p. 153). An extension of this theory holds that the person most likely to become a drug addict has already attempted to use both legal (or legitimate) and illegal (or illegitimate) means to achieve success, and has failed at both. The addict is a "double failure" who has "retreated" into the undemanding world of addiction (Cloward and Ohlin, 1960, pp. 179–184).

Anomie theory has been applied by others to drug use and abuse (Cloward and Ohlin, 1960, pp. 178–184; Palmer and Linsky, 1972, pp. 297–301), but, some believe, never entirely successfully. Indeed, devastating critiques have been leveled at anomie theory and its application to drug use and abuse. (Lindesmith and Gagnon, 1964, is one of the most thorough.) The perspective experienced an eclipse in the late 1960s and remained at a low ebb throughout the 1970s and early to mid-1980s. At that time, many researchers believed that the perspective had been discredited and "disconfirmed" (Kornhauser, 1978, p. 180) as completely irrelevant to an understanding of the etiology, or causality, of drug use. Some argued that the theory had become something of an embarrassment to the field and, as it applied to drug use and addiction, was utterly fanciful, generated in the almost total absence of knowledge of the world of drug use (Lindesmith and Gagnon, 1964; Preble and Casey, 1969).

The model addict that predominates in anomie theory is that of the Chinese opium addict, puffing on his pipe in a dreamy, somnolent state. However, the world of the addict is anything but undemanding. It is a brutal, abrasive world requiring extreme skills and maximum effort to survive (Preble and Casey, 1969). Moreover, it is not the poorest members of poor communities—the most clear-cut "failures"—who turn to heroin, but those who are a rung above them financially and occupationally. In the view of many, anomie theory explained *no* significant feature of drug use, abuse, or addiction.

However, beginning in the late 1980s, anomie theory experienced a renaissance; scholars began to look at the perspective in a fresh way, revised some concepts and assumptions, and pursued fresh lines of research (Adler and Laufer, 1995; Messner and Rosenfeld, 1997). Is the anomie approach relevant to drug abuse after all?

It is possible that the earlier judgments about the theory were premature and overly harsh in at least one sphere of behavior—that of drug selling. Since legitimate achievement is blocked off for a significant proportion of the members of society, one avenue of illegitimate achievement is rendered more attractive as a consequence. What is drug dealing but an *innovative* attempt to maintain the goal of achieving material success by engaging in an illegitimate, illegal, and deviant enterprise? Drug dealing is an innovative adaptation to blocked or frustrated material success for many members of society who have learned to expect that success but who live in a setting in which high levels of achievement are all but impossible. Hence, anomie theory has a great deal to say about one major aspect of the drug scene (dealing), but not, as it turns out, drug use, abuse, or addiction.

## Social Control and Self-Control Theory

Two major theories whose adherents attempt to explain deviant and criminal behavior—and, by extension, drug use and abuse as well—are social control or bonding theory and self-control theory or the "general theory of crime." Both are individualistic theories, and not group or structural, which is the approach adopted by most sociologists. These two theories make extensive use of the concept of control and focus on why some people *conform* to society's norms and laws. Both assume that deviance and, by extension, drug use do not need to be explained. If left to their own devices, everyone would deviate, break the law, use drugs, and get high; they would simply be doing what comes naturally. What really needs to be explained is why some people do *not* deviate from the norms, violate the law, use drugs, or get high. However, they differ considerably in the emphasis they place on the dynamics of deviance, crime, and drug use, and the relevant explanatory time frame.

According to **social control theory,** what causes drug use, like most or all deviant behavior, is the absence of social controls encouraging conformity. Most of us do not engage in deviant or criminal acts because of strong bonds with or ties to conventional, mainstream persons, beliefs, activities, and social institutions. If these bonds are weak or broken, we will be released from society's rules and free to deviate—and this includes drug use. It is not that drug users' ties to an unconventional subculture attract them to drugs; it is their *lack* of ties to the conforming, mainstream sectors of society that frees them from the bonds keeping them from using drugs. It is the absence of these bonds that explains illicit, recreational drug use.

Of course, delinquency, deviance, and criminal behavior—including recreational, non-medical drug use—are matters of degree. Just as most of us engage in at least one technically illegal act in our lives, a very high proportion of the American population eventually uses at least one drug outside a medical context. Social control theory does not assert that persons with strong ties to conventional society will *never* engage in any deviant action, regardless of how mild, including using a drug recreationally. It would, however, assert that both deviance and control are matters of degree: The more attached we are to conventional society, the lower the likelihood of engaging in behavior that violates its values and norms. A strong attachment does not absolutely insulate us from mildly deviant behavior, but it does make it less likely.

Social control theory emphasizes the actor's stake in conformity. The more we have "invested"—with respect to time, emotion, energy, money, and so on—in conventional activities and involvements, the more conventional our behavior is likely to be. A "stake" could be anything we value, such as a loving relationship, good relations with our parents, a family, children, an education, a satisfying job, and/or a career. Someone who has "invested" in these positively valued, reward-laden enterprises is less likely to engage in behavior that threatens or undermines them than is someone who has no such investments. One or more stakes in conformity tend to act to keep us in line, away from the potential clutches of drug abuse.

The more *attached* we are to conventional others—parents, teachers, clergy, employers— the less likely we are to break society's rules and use drugs. The more *committed* we are to conventional institutions—family, school, religion, work—the less likely we are to break society's rules and use drugs. The more *involved* we are in conventional activities— familial, educational, religious, occupational—the less likely we are to break society's rules and use drugs. And the more deeply we *believe* in the norms of conventional institutions—again, family, school, religion, occupation—the less likely we are to break society's rules and use drugs. Drug use is "contained" by bonds with or adherence to conventional people, institutions, activities, and beliefs. If they are strong, recreational drug use is unlikely. Control theory has a kind of commonsensical flavor to it, and it also has a loyal following in the fields of criminology, the sociology of deviance, and the sociology of drug use (Hirschi, 1969).

**Self-control theory** represents another explanation of drug use and other unconventional, deviant, and/or criminal behavior. Self-control theory sounds a great deal like the "social" control theory we just looked at; however, the two are really very different. Many of the assumptions made by the latter are rejected by the former. Travis Hirschi, a sociologist, has been a major proponent of social control theory; starting in the late 1980s, in collaboration with Michael Gottfredson, he developed an altogether different, and to some degree contradictory, perspective; in 1990, these two sociologists presented self-control theory in book form—*A General Theory of Crime*.

Self-control theory does share with social control theory the assumption that drug use and crime are "doing what comes naturally"—that is, in the absence of controls, most people would engage in them. What is necessary to explain, then, is *how* controls come to be absent. However, here, the two theories diverge. To begin with, the proponents of self-control theory conceive of crime as including not only crime itself but also a variety of other illegal, illegitimate, deviant, and self-interested actions. The authors define crime as "force or fraud in pursuit of self interest." This encompasses an extremely diverse kettle of fish, but the authors explicitly state that drug use and abuse qualify (Gottfredson and Hirschi, 1990).

Drugs and crime are similar activities, Gottfredson and Hirschi argue, because "both provide immediate, easy, and certain short-term pleasure" (p. 41). Crime and drug use are basically *the same sort of behavior*. They represent grabbing what someone wants without regard for the social or legal consequences. Getting high is fun—why not do it? Stealing gets you what you want—go ahead, do it! Both behaviors manifest low levels of self-control (pp. 233–234). Compared with law-abiding citizens and nonusers, criminals and drug users (whose personnel overlap heavily) are impulsive, hedonistic, self-centered, insensitive, risk taking, short-sighted, nonverbal, impulsive, inconsiderate, and intolerant of frustration. In a nutshell, the "general theory" of crime's explanation of drug use is that some people find drugs attractive because they lack self-control. They take the easy, self-indulgent route; they are impulsive and pleasure oriented. They do not think about the consequences—the possible harm—to themselves or others in using drugs or anything else. They take shortcuts; they do whatever yields immediate gratification. They are grabbers, exploiters, liars, thieves, cheaters; they are reckless, careless, and violent; and they have no concern for long-range consequences of their actions. Drug use is simply a manifestation of their general orientation toward life; Do whatever gets them what they want, whatever feels good, regardless of whether their actions harm others or even, in the long run, themselves. The usual controls that keep the rest of us in check are simply not operative in their lives.

What causes low self-control? Here again, social control and self-control theories diverge. According to self-control theory, a lack of self-control is caused by inadequate parental socialization. Parental socialization is a factor that operated in the past but exerts a lifetime influence, whereas social control is a factor that operates only in the present. Parents who are lacking in strong affection for their children are unable or unwilling to monitor their children's behavior, and in failing to recognize that their children are engaging in wrongdoing, they are more likely to raise offspring who both engage in criminal behavior and indulge in drugs. Hence, as we have seen, self-control is caused by a factor that takes place very *early* in one's life, whereas social control can operate more or less *throughout* one's lifetime.

The most important reason why self-control theory and social control theory are incompatible or contradictory is that, in order for the forces of *social* control to operate, it is necessary for someone to have attained a certain level of achievement to begin with—and that requires *self*-control. In other words, if individuals lack self-control, they cannot get to the point where social control is relevant. Social control theory says that persons with a stake or investment in conformity—such as a house, a marriage, children, or a college education—are more likely to conform to society's norms. How can persons who lack self-control achieve such a stake? The fact is, they can't; their lack of self-control makes it difficult if not impossible for them to purchase a house, hold down a job, sustain a meaningful marriage, have a rewarding relationship with their children, or do well enough in school to enter, stay in college, and graduate. According to this theory, self-control is prior to and more pervasive than social control. Hence, in the book that articulates self-control theory, *A General Theory of Crime,* co-author Travis Hirschi barely acknowledges the existence of a theory he once embraced.

Once again, as with all other factors or variables, self-control is a continuum, a matter of degree. The theory would predict that self-control and drug use are inversely or negatively correlated with one another: the lower the level of self-control, the greater the likelihood of drug abuse; the higher the self-control, the lower that likelihood is. It does not argue that all drug users lack self-control, only that they are *less likely* to be governed by self-control. Further, it would predict that the experimenter is more likely to possess self-control than the occasional user, and the occasional user more than the regular user; that the weekend marijuana smoker is more likely to possess self-control than the crack or heroin addict; and so on. As with all sociological theories or explanations, self-control theory makes comparative or relative rather than absolute statements: the greater the self-control, the lower the likelihood of drug abuse.

Gottfredson and Hirschi argue that their theory demolishes all other explanations of drug use, including anomie and learning theory, with the exception of two: social disorganization and routine activities theory. Self-control theory is **social disorganization theory** writ small. The key to drug use, as with crime and deviance in general, in social disorganization theory is that members of the neighborhood are unwilling or unable to monitor or control wrongdoing, and so it flourishes. The same applies to inadequate parenting. To the extent that parents are unable or unwilling to monitor or control their child's behavior, that child will manifest low self-control and hence will get high, steal, and engage in violent behavior. Neighborhood social disorganization and individual low self-control are different levels of essentially the same factor.

**Routine activities theory** argues that deviance and crime will take place to the extent that three factors are present: a **motivated offender,** something worth offending against (a **suitable target,** such as a quantity of cash), and someone who can defend or protect that which is offended against (a **capable guardian,** such as the presence of a police officer). But routine activities theory ignores the motivated offender. To that extent, it is very different from self-control theory, which focuses *entirely* on the offender, and simply assumes that low self-control leads to drug use, delinquency, deviance, and criminal behavior. But self-control theory is (at least partly) consistent with routine activities theory in that, for both, opportunity is a major piece of the puzzle. Routine activities theory argues that persons offend to the extent that a suitable target is available and a capable guardian is absent—in a word, to the extent that the opportunity to offend exists. People will use drugs to the extent that the drugs are available and agents of social control are not in the picture. Again, the theory does not raise the question of which people will follow up on the available opportunity, only that there are enough motivated offenders in the population to keep the enterprise of offending healthy and strong. In any case, routine activities theory has not been used much by researchers in the area of drug use; it applies most strongly to money-making crimes.

## Social Learning and Subcultural Theory

The theory that criminal or deviant behavior is a product of learning was first elaborated by sociologist Edwin Sutherland in the third edition of his *Principles of Criminology* (1939). He called this formulation the theory of *differential association* because the key mechanism in becoming criminal or deviant is the fact that one associate differentially with social circles whose members define crime and deviance in favorable terms. The central tenets of this theory are that crime and deviance are learned in intimate, face-to-face interaction with significant others, or people to whom one is close. A person engages in deviant and criminal behavior to the extent that the definitions to which he or she is exposed are favorable to violations of the law—that is, because of an excess of definitions favorable to legal and normative violations over definitions unfavorable to such violations. The key to this process, according to Sutherland, is the *ratio* between definitions favorable and unfavorable to legal and normative violations. When favorable definitions exceed unfavorable ones, the individual will turn to deviance and crime.

The social learning approach has been extended by several sociologists who have blended Sutherland's theory of differential association with the principles of behaviorism in psychology. **Social learning theory** holds that behavior is molded by rewards and punishment, or reinforcement. Past and present rewards and punishments for certain actions determine the actions that individuals continue to pursue. Reward and punishment structures are built into specific groups. By interacting with members of certain groups or social circles, people learn definitions of behaviors as good or bad. It is in the group setting, differentially for different groups, where reward and punishment take place, and where individuals are exposed to behavioral models and normative definitions of certain behaviors as good or bad.

Social learning theory has a clear-cut application to drug use: It proposes that the use and abuse of psychoactive substances can be explained by differential exposure to groups in which use is rewarded. "These groups provide the social environments in which exposure to definitions, imitations of models, and social reinforcements for use of or abstinence from any particular substance take place. The definitions are learned through imitation and social reinforcement of them by members of the group with whom one is associated" (Akers et al., 1979, p. 638). Drug use, including abuse, is determined "by the extent to which a given pattern [of behavior] is sustained by the combination of the reinforcing effects of the substance with social reinforcement, exposure to models, definitions through association with using peers, and by the degree to which it is not deterred through bad effects of the substance and/or the negative sanctions from peers, parents, and the law" (Akers, 1992; Akers et al., 1979, p. 638). Social learning theory, then, proposes that the extent to which substances will be used or avoided depends on the "extent to which the behavior has been differentially reinforced over alternative behavior and is defined as more desirable" (Radosevich et al., 1980, p. 160). In short, we tend to repeat what we like doing. Of course, the theory does not explain why a given activity, such as drug use, is liked by one individual and not another.

**Subcultural theory** and the theory of differential association are related but distinctly different. The central thesis of subcultural theory is that involvement in a particular social group with attitudes favorable to drug use is the key factor in fostering the individual's own drug use, whereas involvement in a group with negative attitudes toward drug use tends to discourage such use. Drug use is expected and encouraged in certain social circles, and actively discouraged and even punished in others. Although subcultural theory has certain parallels with the theory of differential association, there are crucial differences as well. For one thing, Sutherland's theory of differential association, and the learning theory that grew out of it, does *not* require that the process of socialization take place within stable, identifiable social groupings. Indeed, Sutherland postulated that, in principle, deviant or criminal socialization could be effected through association with a single individual such as a friend or with a small group of individuals such as a delinquent gang. In contrast, subcultural theory identifies the socialization process as taking place through the assimilation of individuals into specific groups or social circles, with a resultant transformation in identity, values, norms, and behavior.

The first systematic application of subcultural theory to drug use was done by Howard S. Becker (1953, 1955, 1963), who focused on the process of becoming a marijuana user. Becker, like the other interactionists, was not concerned with issues of etiology or with cause-and-effect explanations; the traditional question of why someone uses marijuana and someone else does not did not capture Becker's attention. His focus was not so much on the characteristics that distinguish the user from the nonuser—what it was about the user that impelled him or her to the drug—but rather on how someone came to use and experience marijuana in such a way that it continued to be used to achieve pleasure. For this to take place, three things must happen, according to Becker's model.

First, one must learn how to use marijuana so that the drug is capable of yielding pleasure, that is, one must learn the proper technique of smoking marijuana. Second, since the effects of the drug are subtle and ambiguous, one must learn to perceive them: One must learn that something is happening to one's body and mind, and that it is the marijuana that is causing this effect. And third, one must learn to enjoy the effects. By themselves, the sensations that the drug generates are not inherently pleasurable. Without knowing what is happening to one's body, the feelings attendant upon ingesting marijuana may be experienced as unpleasant, unsettling, disorienting, uncomfortable, confusing, even frightening. The drug's effects must be conceptualized, defined, and interpreted as pleasurable. How do these three processes come about? They depend, Becker said, "on the individual's participation with other users. Where this participation is intensive, the individual is quickly talked out of his feeling against marijuana use" (1963, p. 56).

Learning to enjoy marijuana "is a necessary but not a sufficient condition for a person to develop a stable pattern of drug use" (Becker, 1963, p. 59). Marijuana use is, after all, a deviant and criminal activity (and it was even more so in the 1950s and early 1960s, when Becker wrote about the subject). The individual must also learn how to deal with the social control that exists to punish users and eliminate use. Deviant behavior can flourish when "people are emancipated from the controls of society and become responsive to those of a smaller group" (p. 60), that is, a subculture or, in Becker's words, a "subcultural group." To continue smoking marijuana, users must have a reliable supply of the drug, keep their use secret from relevant disapproving others, and nullify the moral objections raised by mainstream society. These three processes, again, require normative and logistic support from the marijuana-using subculture.

An interesting feature of Becker's model is that it turns the traditional view of drug use on its head. Far from motives causing use, Becker proposed the opposite—that *use causes motives*. One does not learn that drug use is acceptable and then use drugs as a result; rather, one first uses drugs, and, during the course of drug use, learns the necessary justifications and explanations that provide the motivations for further use. In a group setting, one is furnished with "reasons that appear sound for continuing the line of activity" he or she has begun (1963, p. 39). As Becker summarized:

> To put a complex argument in a few words, instead of deviant motives leading to the deviant behavior, it is the other way around; the deviant behavior in time produces the deviant motivation. Vague impulses and desires . . . are transformed into definite patterns of actions through the social interpretation of a physical experience which is in itself ambiguous. Marihuana use is a function of the individual's conception of marihuana and of the uses to which it can be put, and this conception develops as the individual's experience with the drug increases. (1963, p. 42)

In short, the individual's involvement with the marijuana-using subculture is the key factor in use. People do not begin using the drug on their own; individualistic theories cannot account for use. The characteristics of individuals count for nothing in the absence of social circles whose members explain use to the novice, supply the drug, and provide role models. It is only through contact with other users, Becker reminds us, that use, especially regular use, can take place.

Becker's model does not include any discussion of specific individual or group characteristics that are compatible with use. His theory is very close to a "pure" subcultural model, discussing the processes and mechanisms of the socialization of the novice—and only with reference to the use of the drug—without mentioning the fact that only certain types of individuals and members of only certain types of groups are likely to be attracted to marijuana use. Becker was totally uninterested in the fact that people who have certain attitudes, beliefs, and personality characteristics, or who engage in certain forms of behavior, are much more likely to be attracted to subcultural groups that use drugs. Becker's model seems to presuppose an almost random recruitment into drug subcultures (although, once an individual is recruited, selective interaction and socialization are the major mechanisms at work).

It should be noted that, for Becker, the *content* of the user subculture—apart from its use of the drug and its definition of the drug and its use—is secondary. Becker did not touch on any potentiating factors in use at all. He does not explain which individuals are more likely to be attracted to the use of the drug or which are likely to be attracted to other individuals or groups who are users. He did not deal with the issue of the compatibility between a given individual and the content of a specific subculture—what it is that draws a novice to a circle of individuals who use marijuana. Following the interactionist approach, Becker underplayed the question of cause or etiology. Why someone finds him- or herself in the company of others who smoke marijuana and actually ends up using the drug—rather than turning down the chance—is something of an unexplained or "black box" factor in Becker's analysis. He assumed that the user's subculture is favorable toward use and defines it as such. But he made no assumption about any other values or behavior that might or might not be consistent or compatible with use itself.

## Selective Interaction/Socialization

The term "selective interaction" refers to the fact that potential drug users do not randomly "fall into" social circles of users; they are attracted to certain individuals and circles— subcultural groups—because their own values and activities are compatible with those of current users. There is a dynamic element in use: Even before someone uses a drug for the first time, he or she is "prepared for" or "initiated into" its use—or, in a sense, *socialized in advance*—because his or her values are already somewhat consistent with those of the drug subculture. As a result, the individual chooses friends who share these values and who are also likely to be attracted to use and to current users. I call this process "selective recruitment." In addition, once someone makes friends who use drugs, she or he becomes socialized by a using subcultural group, both into those values compatible with use and by values consistent with use. This is why I call this the **selective interaction/socialization** model. Bruce Johnson (1980) calls it the subcultural model, and Denise Kandel (1980a, pp. 256–257) calls it the socialization model. It is both a subcultural and a socialization perspective, but it does not follow the lines of Becker's classic argument, and it is a somewhat different process of socialization from the traditional model.

Studying drug use in a college setting, Johnson (1973) made use of both the subcultural and the socialization models. He demonstrated that drug use occurs because adolescents are socialized into progressively more unconventional groups (p. 5). Briefly, Johnson argued that the more adolescents are isolated and alienated from the parental subculture, and the more involved they are with the teenage peer subculture, the greater the likelihood that they will experiment with and use a variety of drugs. The peer subculture provides a transition between the parental and the drug subcultures. For the most part, the parental generation is conventional and antidrug, and also opposes a number of other unconventional and deviant activities. Adolescents who are strongly attached to, influenced by, and committed to the parental subculture tend to adhere more closely to its values and follow its norms of conduct. As a consequence, they are more likely to abstain from drugs than the teenager who is isolated from his or her parents and involved with peers, who favor more unconventional norms, and therefore is more likely to accept certain forms of recreational drug use, especially marijuana smoking.

Not only does the peer subculture exist somewhat independently of the conventional parental generation, it also emphasizes activities in contexts in which parental control is relatively absent. There is something of a competition for prestige and status ranking within peer groups. Higher status is granted in part as a consequence of engaging in activities and holding values that depart significantly from parental demands and expectations. These include alcohol consumption, marijuana use, the use of certain hard drugs, some delinquent activity (including what Johnson calls automobile deviance—speeding, driving without a license, and so on), shoplifting, hanging out, and cruising.

Johnson's study found that if one has marijuana-using friends, one tends to use marijuana; if one does not have marijuana-using friends, one tends not to use marijuana. The more marijuana-using friends one has, the greater the likelihood of using marijuana regularly, buying and selling marijuana, and subsequently using hard drugs. In addition, having marijuana-using friends and using the drug regularly tend to be strongly related to sexual permissiveness (having sex early and with a number of partners, and approving of sex in a wide range of circumstances), political leftism, plans to drop out of college, and engagement in delinquent acts (Johnson, 1973, p. 195). Note that marijuana use is instrumentally involved in this process; using marijuana vastly increases the chance of engaging in numerous other drug-related activities. But Johnson's study suggests that it is not the physiological action of the drug itself that does this, but the subcultural involvement that marijuana use entails. Marijuana use is an index or measure of subcultural involvement, and the more involved one is with the drug subculture, the more socialized by it, influenced by its values, and engaged in its activities one is.

The selective interaction/socialization model of drug use has been explored most systematically and in the greatest empirical detail by sociologist Denise Kandel. Kandel can be said to be the principal proponent of the perspective. Kandel's approach is eclectic and makes use of concepts taken from learning theory, the social control model, and the subcultural approach. She placed less emphasis on "selective recruitment"—the fact that young people who eventually use drugs are different from those who never use, even before use takes place—and relatively more on the processes of selective interaction and socialization.

Adolescents vary with respect to a range of individual and social background characteristics. Likewise, adolescent social gatherings or groups have different and varying characteristics. Some are more compatible with a given adolescent's own traits; others are less so. As a general rule, people of all ages, adolescents included, tend to gravitate to groups whose characteristics are compatible with or similar to their own, and to avoid those that are incompatible or dissimilar. However, in early adolescence, young people tend to be "drifters"—that is, their early drug use, mainly of beer and wine, or nonuse is dependent mainly on accidental, situational factors. If they are in a circle of adolescents who drink, their chances of drinking are greater than if they are in a circle of nondrinkers. Early on, general peer climate powerfully influences patterns of substance use, and young adolescents are not strongly motivated to select a peer group that reflects their own interests and inclinations.

Adolescents are socialized by a number of different "agents." Socialization theorists locate four main agents of socialization: parents, peers, school, and media. Two are tightly related to drug use—parents and peers. Adolescents tend to internalize definitions and values and to engage in behavior enacted and approved by significant others. The impact of the various agents of socialization depends on the values and behavior in question. For broader, long-term values and behavior, such as religion, politics, and lifetime goals, parents tend to be most influential; for more immediate lifestyle behavior and values, peers are most influential (Kandel, 1980a, p. 257).

The parental influence on the drug use of teenagers is small but significant: Parents who use legal drugs (alcohol, tobacco, and prescription drugs) are more likely to raise children who both drink hard liquor and use illegal drugs than are parents who abstain from drugs completely. In the earliest stages, parental example will influence substance use in the form of beer and wine and, a bit later on, hard liquor. However, peer influence on drug use is even more formidable. Teenagers, especially older ones, tend to associate with one another partly on the basis of similarities in lifestyle, values, and behavior—and drug use or nonuse is one of those similarities. Friends typically share drug-using patterns: Users tend to be friends with users, and nonusers friends with nonusers. Of all characteristics that friends have in common—aside from obvious social and demographic ones, like age, gender, race, and social class—their drug use or nonuse is the one they are most likely to share (Kandel, 1973, 1974).

Selective peer group interaction and socialization represent probably the single most powerful factor related to drug use among adolescents. Imitation and social influence play a significant role in initiating and maintaining drug use among teenagers. Over time, participation in specific groups or social circles reinforces certain values and patterns of activity. Association with friends whose company the individual enjoys reinforces the values shared and behavior engaged in with those friends. And the closer the bond, the greater the likelihood of maintaining the values and behaviors that are shared. Note, however, that adolescents do not choose friends at random. Rather, they are, in a sense, socialized "in advance" for participation in certain groups. They choose and are chosen by certain groups because of that socialization process, and likewise, participation in those groups socializes them toward or away from the use of illicit drugs. We have something of a reciprocal or dialectical relationship here.

Kandel's model of adolescent drug use is dynamic in that she did not end her analysis with substance use per se—that is, at the point when someone has experimented with a psychoactive substance or with continued use over time. Kandel is interested in drug use *sequences*. For her, to focus on a single drug would be fallacious; adolescents use several drugs, and they use them in specific patterns and in specific "culturally determined" and "well-defined" developmental stages. The "use of a drug lower in a sequence is a necessary but not a sufficient condition for progression to a higher stage indicating involvement with more serious drugs" (Kandel, 1980b, pp. 120, 121). These stages can be reduced to four: (1) beer and/or wine, (2) cigarettes and/or hard liquor, (3) marijuana, and (4) other illegal drugs (1980b, p. 121). Adolescents rarely skip stages; drinking alcohol is *necessary* to smoking marijuana, just as marijuana use is necessary to moving on to more dangerous drugs such as cocaine and heroin.

Kandel supported the idea that unconventionality is related to drug use generally. However, she argued that the relevance and importance of specific variables are dependent on the young person's stage in life and the drug in question; in other words, there is a *time-ordering* of specific factors. In the early stages of substance use, early in adolescence, as I said above, the most important drugs used are beer and wine, and the most crucial causal factor is general peer climate. The less serious the drug use (beer and wine versus heroin and cocaine), and the more widespread it is, the more important the role played by accidental situations' features and by broad peer-subcultural attitudes and drug-related behavior. Here, most adolescents are "drifters" with regard to drug use; users' attitudes and beliefs about drugs are not significantly different from nonusers. At this point, most adolescents are "seducible" with respect to psychoactive substances, particularly beer and wine.

At later stages, different factors come into play. For marijuana, in middle adolescence, attitudes toward the drug are very important, peer influence remains strong, and parental influence is fairly weak. In later adolescence, three factors that were less crucial earlier loom especially large. The first is psychological pressures: More troubled adolescents will tend to progress from marijuana to "harder" drugs; less troubled ones will be less likely to do so. The second is the relationship with parents: The more alienated an adolescent is from his or her parents, the greater the likelihood that he or she will progress from marijuana to more dangerous drugs. Intimate relations with parents tend to "shield" the adolescent from the more serious forms of drug use. And finally, while peer climate in general declines in importance over time, having at least one specific friend who uses one or another dangerous drug assumes central importance. Here, the adolescent breaks away from peer circles that do not favor the use of more dangerous drugs and gravitates toward specific individuals who use them. "The individual who progresses to the use of other illicit drugs may, as a result of his drug-related behavior, factors of availability, or family difficulties, move away from long-term friendships and seek less intimate relationships with those who share his attitudes, behaviors, and problems" (Kandel, Kessler, and Margulies, 1978, p. 36). This adolescent is no longer a "drifter" but a "seeker."

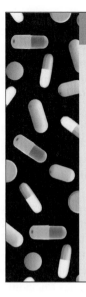

## True-False Quiz

In my quiz, I asked the students to tell me whether the following statement is true or false: "There are no social or demographic differences between user and nonusers. Anyone can become a drug user or abuser, and everyone's odds are the same. Drug use strikes the population randomly and seemingly without explanation." Clearly, this is a false statement. In fact, if it were true, the entire basis of this chapter would be undermined; that is, no conceivable theory or "explanation" could possibly account for drug use and/or abuse. Theorists of drug use assume that there *are* differences between user and nonusers and that, by examining these differences, an explanation can be devised for why some people with certain backgrounds or life experiences, or in certain settings, are attracted to the consumption of psychoactive chemicals. Only 40 percent of my students thought that this statement is true; 56 percent were correct in saying that it is false.

## A Conflict Theory of Drug Abuse

In a National Institute on Drug Abuse (NIDA) publication (Lettieri, Sayers, and Pearson, 1980), one theory of drug abuse was conspicuously absent: **conflict theory.** This perspective is distinctly "macro" in its approach: It examines the big picture—larger, structural factors, forces that influence not merely individuals but members of entire societies, cities, neighborhoods, and communities. Conflict theory applies more or less exclusively to the heavy, chronic, compulsive abuse of heroin and crack, and only marginally to the use of alcohol, tobacco, and marijuana. Hence, conflict theory explains a portion of the drug abuse picture; it is not a complete explanation of drug abuse—no explanation can be that—but one that addresses the issues that much of the public finds most troubling.

Proponents of conflict theory hold that the heavy, chronic abuse of crack and addiction to heroin are strongly related to social class, income, power, and locale. A significantly higher proportion of lower- and working-class inner-city residents abuse hard drugs than is true of more affluent members of society. More importantly, this is the case because of the impact of a number of key structural conditions, conditions that have their origin in economics and politics. Specifically, several key economic and political developments over the past three decades or so bear directly on differentials in drug abuse.

Some version of this theory is endorsed by a substantial proportion of left-of-center African-American politicians and commentators, such as the Reverend Jesse Jackson and the Reverend Al Sharpton. Sociologist Elliott Currie spells out this perspective in *Reckoning: Drugs, the Cities, and the American Future* (1993), as does Harry Gene Levine in his paper "Just Say Poverty: What Causes Crack and Heroin Abuse" (1991). In my view, it is the most adequate and comprehensive explanation for a number of recent developments in the world of drug abuse. Connections that have always existed between income and neighborhood residence on the one hand, and drug abuse and addiction on the other, have been exacerbated by these developments. So what are these crucial recent developments?

First, since the early 1970s, economic opportunities for the relatively unskilled and the relatively uneducated sectors of the society have been shrinking. In 1970, it was still possible for many, perhaps most, heads of households with considerably lower-than-average training, skills, and education to support a family by working at a job that paid them enough to raise their income above the poverty level; this was especially the case if more than one member of the household was employed. Today, this is much less likely to be true. Far fewer family breadwinners who lack training, skills, and education can earn enough to support a family and avoid slipping into poverty. Decent-paying manual-level jobs are disappearing. Increasingly, the jobs that are available to the unskilled and semiskilled, the uneducated and semieducated, are dead-end, minimum-wage, poverty-level jobs. In other words, the bottom third or so of the workforce is becoming increasingly impoverished. One consequence of this development: the growing attractiveness of drug selling.

As a result—and this is the second of our recent developments—the poor are getting poorer; ironically, at the same time, the rich are getting richer. Between 1945 and 1973, the incomes of the highest- and lowest-income strata grew at roughly the same annual rate. However, since 1973, the income of the top fifth of the income stratum has grown at a yearly rate of 1.3 percent, while that of the lowest stratum has decreased at the rate of 0.78 percent per year (Cassidy, 1995). Additional factors such as taxes and entitlements (including welfare payments) do not alter this picture at all. We are living in a society that is becoming increasingly polarized with respect to income. A few relevant facts should put these developments into perspective. (All figures are adjusted for inflation, of course.)

- Over the past 30 years, the share of the richest 1 percent of the population in the nation's total income doubled. Meanwhile, the income of the bottom fifth of families "actually fell slightly" (Krugman, 2002, p. 67).
- Today, the nation's top 1 percent in income earn as much as the poorest 40 percent combined. The nation's 13,000 richest families earn nearly as much as the country's 20 million poorest households put together.
- In 1992, the richest 400 families in the United States earned 0.5 percent of total income. In 2000, they earned double that share—1.1 percent. During this period, their incomes increased at 15 times the rate of the bottom 90 percent of the population (Johnston, 2003).
- Thirty years ago, the richest 0.01 percent of taxpayers earned 70 times the average family income; today, they earn 300 times that (Krugman, 2002).
- Over the past 30 years, the average salary of the top 100 chief executive officers zoomed from $1.3 million (39 times the pay of the median worker) to $37.5 million (more than a *thousand* times an average worker's pay).
- During the past 30 years, among the nation's top 10 percent of income earners, *most* of the gains went to the richest 1 percent of all families; and in that 1 percent, 60 percent of the gains went to the top 0.01 percent of families (Krugman, 2002).

This development is not primarily a racial phenomenon. In fact, the income gap between African-American and white households hasn't changed much since the end of World War II. What has changed is that, among both Blacks *and* whites, the poor are getting poorer and the rich are getting richer. Among married couples, both of whom have jobs and work year-round, the Black-white income gap has practically disappeared. However, among Blacks, there is a growing underclass whose members are sinking deeper and deeper into poverty. Ironically, at the same time that the Black middle class is growing, the size of the poverty-stricken inner-city underclass is growing. Again, one consequence of the polarization of the class structure is the increased attractiveness and viability of selling drugs as a means of earning a living. Not only are the poor becoming poorer, but the visibility of the display of affluence among the rich acts as a stimulus for some segments of the poor to attempt to acquire that level of affluence, or a semblance of it, through illicit or illegitimate means—again, a factor that increases the likelihood that some members of the poor will see drug dealing as an attractive and viable livelihood.

A third development is especially relevant to the issue of the distribution of illegal drugs: community disorganization and political decline. In large part as a consequence of the economic decline of the working class and the polarization of the economy, as well as the "flight" of more affluent members of the community, the neighborhoods in which poor, especially minority, residents live are becoming increasingly disorganized and politically impotent (Wilson, 1987, 1997). Consequently, they are less capable of mounting an effective assault against crime and drug dealing. The ties between such neighborhoods and the municipal power structure have become weaker, more tenuous, even conflictual. The leaders of such communities increasingly become adversaries rather than allies with city hall, or they have learned that they cannot expect resources once extended to them. As with the other two developments, this makes drug dealing in such communities more attractive.

In such neighborhoods, criminals and drug dealers make incursions in ways that would not be possible in more affluent, more organized communities, which have stronger ties to the loci of power. In cohesive, unified, and especially prosperous neighborhoods, buildings are not abandoned to become the sites of "shooting galleries"; street corners do not become virtual open-air markets for drug dealing; the police do not as routinely ignore citizens' complaints about drug dealing, accept bribes from dealers to look the other way, steal or sell drugs, or abuse citizens without fear of reprisal; and innocent bystanders do not become victims of drive-by gangland turf wars. In communities where organized crime becomes entrenched, it does so either because residents approve of or protect the criminals or because residents are too demoralized, fearful, or impotent to do anything about it. Where residents can and do mobilize the relevant political forces to act against criminal activities, open, organized, and widespread drug dealing is unlikely; in contrast, where communities have become demoralized, disorganized, and politically impotent, drug dealing is far more likely to thrive. And the fact is, many poor, inner-city, minority communities have suffered a serious decline in economic fortune and political influence over the past generation or so. The result: Drug dealers have been able to take root and flourish (Hamid, 1990).

These three developments—the decay of much of the economic structure on which the lower sector of the working class rested, the growing economic polarization of the American class structure, and the physical and political decay of poorer, especially minority, inner-city communities—have contributed to a fourth development: a feeling of hopelessness, alienation, depression, and anomie among many inner-city residents. These conditions have made drug abuse especially attractive and appealing. For some, getting high—and getting high frequently—has become an oasis of excitement, pleasure, and fantasy in otherwise dreary lives. Let us be clear about this: *Most* of the people living in deteriorated communities *resist* such an appeal; most do *not* abuse drugs. Our structural or macro-oriented conflict theories do not explain why some members of a blighted community turn to drugs but others—*most* residents—do not. But *enough* succumb to drug abuse to make the lives of the majority unpredictable, insecure, and dangerous. A violent subculture of drug abuse flourishes in response to what some have come to see as the hopelessness and despair of the reality of everyday life for the underclass.

A crucial assumption of the conflict approach to drug abuse is that there are two overlapping but conceptually distinct forms or types of drug use. The first, which accounts for the vast majority of illegal users, is "casual" or "recreational" drug use. It is engaged in by a broad spectrum of the class structure, but it is perhaps most characteristic of the middle class. This type can be characterized as "controlled" drug use, drug use for the purpose of pleasure, drug use that takes place experimentally or, if repeated, once or twice weekly, once or twice a month; it is drug use in the service of other pleasurable activities. This type of drug use is caused by a variety of factors: unconventionality, a desire for adventure, curiosity, hedonism, willingness to take risks, sociability, and, as we saw, involvement with a subcultural group. Relatively few of these drug users become an objective or concrete problem for society, except for the fact that they are often targeted or singled out *as* a problem.

The second type of drug use is abuse—compulsive, chronic, or heavy drug use, drug use that often reaches the point of dependency and addiction; it is usually accompanied by social and personal harm. A relatively low percentage of recreational drug *users* progress to becoming drug *abusers*. For all illegal drugs, there is a pyramid-shaped distribution of users, with many experimenters at the bottom, fewer occasional users in the middle, and a small number of heavy, chronic abusers at the pinnacle. This second type of drug use is motivated, as we've seen, by despair, hopelessness, alienation, poverty, and community disorganization and disintegration. By abusing drugs, users are harming themselves and others, including the community as a whole. Use results in medical complications, drug overdoses, crime, violence, imprisonment, and even a trip to the morgue. Experts argue that moving from the first type of drug use (recreational) to the second (abuse) is far more likely to take place among the impoverished than among the affluent, by residents of disorganized rather than intact communities (Currie, 1993; Johnson, Elmoghazy, and Dunlap, 1990; Levine, 1991). And, while drug abuse is facilitated by the political developments discussed above, when abuse becomes widespread in a community, it contributes to *even greater* community disorganization. Inner-city residents become trapped in a feedback loop: Powerlessness and community disorganization contribute to drug abuse and drug dealing in a community, which, in turn, entrench these communities in even greater powerlessness and disorganization.

Let me be crystal clear about this point: Drug abuse is not unknown among members of the middle class and residents of politically well-connected communities. Significant proportions of *all* categories of the population fall victim to drug abuse. For all of us, both "micro" and "macro" forces operate. The micro forces discussed in relation to the theories above may be sufficient to impel some members of affluent communities into drug abuse. In contrast, most members of communities subject to the macro forces addressed by conflict theory resist the blandishment of drug abuse. The key point is this: While *some* members of *all* economic classes abuse cocaine and heroin, those members of the bottom economic stratum are more likely to do so. To deny this would be to deny that living at the bottom of the economic hierarchy in this society creates problems for those who do so (or that there is any connection between economic misery and drug abuse). But my second point is even more important: Even if there were no class differences in drug abuse, the fact is, *drug abuse has especially harmful consequences in poor, minority communities.* The class and community differences in drug abuse rates are important but secondary. The main point is that drug abuse more seriously disrupts the lives of persons who lack the resources and wherewithal to fight back effectively than is true of the lives of those who possess these resources. Poor neighborhoods are especially vulnerable to intrusions by drug dealers and increases in drug abuse.

Poor and minority people and neighborhoods are already struggling with a multitude of problems; drug abuse is another major exacerbating difficulty. Members of more affluent neighborhoods are more likely to have connections, ties with city hall and the state house, "clout" or political influence, money to tide them over, a bank account, mobility, autonomy, and so on—a variety of both personal and institutional resources to deal with problems they face. Hence, the drug abuse of some of their members is not as devastating as it is among the poor and the powerless. And the communities in which they live, likewise, get favored treatment from the powers that be; they are less likely to fall victim to the many marauders and exploiters that prey on the powerless and the vulnerable.

In contrast, poor, minority communities are shortchanged by local, state, and federal governments, and bypassed by developers and entrepreneurs. Banks are reluctant to lend money to open businesses in such communities; stores that do open are undercapitalized and frequently fail; landlords abandon buildings that then become the sites of shooting galleries. It is the vulnerability and relative powerlessness of such neighborhoods that makes them a target for both petty and organized criminals, for drug dealers small and large, for corrupt officials and police officers. And vulnerability and powerlessness enable drug abuse to flourish in such communities and to wreak havoc with residents' lives. In short, when we ask, "Why drug abuse?" our answer must be tied up in issues of economics and politics (Goode, 1997, pp. 32–39).

## SUMMARY

A number of factors are at work in encouraging drug use; no single factor or variable can possibly completely answer the question of why some people use drugs and others do not. The main theories of drug use and abuse can be boiled down to three: biological, psychological, and sociological explanations.

Biological theories are based on constitutional or inborn differences between persons who become drug users and those who do not. One such theory is genetic. Some progress has been made in locating a genetic predisposition to alcoholism, but it is only one factor among many. Another theory locates the cause of one type of drug abuse, narcotic addiction, in metabolic imbalance. Methadone maintenance providers argue that once persons with a metabolic imbalance begin using heroin, a physiological process "kicks in" to make their bodies "crave" narcotics and render them prone to becoming heroin addicts. No concrete evidence supports this theory, but methadone maintenance seems to be one therapeutic program that lowers narcotic addiction and criminal behavior.

Psychological theories focus on one of three factors—positive and/or negative reinforcement and two personality theories, inadequate personality and problem behavior-proneness. Do drug users and abusers have "inadequate personalities"? Users' personalities are no doubt different from those of nonusers. However, this would have to be established *before* use takes place, since socialization by user groups is likely to transform the individual's personality, or at least her or his values. One value common in deviant or unconventional groups, these theorists argue, is self-deprecation—in a phrase, low self-esteem. In contrast, other theorists argue that users who continue to take narcotics, once addicted, do so to avoid the painful withdrawal symptoms of discontinuing the administration of heroin. Still others claim that continued use results from the jolt of pleasure users get from administering a reinforcing drug. Of course, all or nearly all persons who administer one or more reinforcing drugs receive that jolt of pleasure, but not all continue using these drugs. Clearly, other factors are at work.

The "problem behavior proneness" perspective offers a somewhat different take on drug use. Individuals with certain kinds of personalities and values are more likely to get into trouble than are those with other personalities and values. This can be predicted in advance by the degree of the individual's unconventionality: Someone who strays from society's mainstream values and behavior in one dimension is likely to stray in other dimensions as well (Robins and Wish, 1977). Users are more rebellious, critical of and alienated from conventionality, independent, open to new experience, pleasure seeking, peer oriented, and risk taking, and less mindful of real-life consequences, than are nonusers. The evidence linking "traits, values, and behaviors indicative of unconventionality and rejection of social institutions" and the use of psychoactive drugs "is overwhelming" (Kandel, 1980a, p. 266). One problem that arises, however, is this: Are these personality characteristics, or are they subcultural in nature? Sociologists would tend to see them as originating in the subcultural group, as values that characterize certain social circles. In contrast, psychologists would emphasize their individualistic psychodynamic origin. This dispute is unlikely to be resolved overnight. Still, the differences between users and nonusers are statistically significant, powerful, and causally connected to use, and they increase in relevance with higher levels of involvement. Hence, such differences cannot be ignored.

All the sociological perspectives shed light on the phenomenon of substance use and abuse—anomie theory, social control and self-control theories, subcultural or learning theories, selective interaction/socialization theory, and conflict theory.

Anomie theory argues that drug use is explained in terms of people being socialized to want, need, and expect material success and failing to attain that success. As a result, they "retreat" into a state of drugged-out bliss and oblivion. One adaptation to failing to obtain success in the legal or legitimate realm is attaining success in illegal or illicit enterprises— drug dealing, for instance.

Social control theorists argue that deviant, delinquent, and criminal activities are explained by weak or absent bonds to conventionality or a "stake" in conformity. Self-control theorists argue that drug use, nothing more or less than a manifestation of a selfish quest for short-run, hedonistic self-indulgence, is a by-product of poor or inadequate parenting, which leads to low self-control.

Drug use is learned and reinforced within a group setting. Future drug users interact with current users and learn appropriate definitions of the drug experience, which has a strong impact on their future experiences and behavior. Individuals learn how to smoke, snort, and inject; how to recognize and enjoy drug effects; how to ensure a drug supply; and how to keep their use secret from conventional society. All of this is part of the "lore" of the user subculture.

However, the interaction and the subcultural perspectives do not address themselves to the question of why some people use and others don't. Here, the selective interaction/ socialization approach must be mobilized. Personality factors, especially problem behavior proneness, must be combined with group and subcultural factors. Social background, parental, personality, behavioral, and value characteristics predict which young people will gravitate toward one another—toward peer circles whose values and behavior are compatible with use. Once someone is selectively "recruited" into such a circle or group, his or her likelihood of use increases rapidly. Young people are socialized into values favorable to drug use by the social circles they interact in and are involved with. The more consistent these values, and the more concentrated and intense the interaction, the greater the likelihood of use. In addition, involvement in a using circle also provides role models for use, so imitation comes into play here. Youngsters do not magically and independently devise a solution to a psychological problem they may have, and then rush out in search of a chemical substance to alleviate that problem, as the inadequate-personality theory seems to predict. Future users turn to drugs because they have friends who use and endorse use, and because they are relatively isolated from peers who don't use and who actively discourage use.

However, as the theorists of this perspective emphasize, the relative importance of certain dimensions, factors, and variables shifts with the stages in a youngster's life, with his or her drug history, and with the drug in question (Kandel, 1980b; Kandel, Kessler, and Margulies, 1978). The dynamics or causal sequence of using (or not using) different drugs is somewhat different for each stage. In early adolescence, beer and wine are the drugs of choice, and here, peer factors—simply falling into or drifting toward a certain circle of users—play the most prominent role. Moreover, parents set a pattern for alcohol use: Parents who drink are more likely to raise children who also drink. Warnings not to drink have little impact in the face of parental examples. Once in a specific social group, the process of socialization takes over, and such socialization prepares the youngster for more serious drug use—initially, cigarettes and hard liquor and, a bit later on, marijuana. In middle adolescence, general beliefs and values, especially about drugs, play a more prominent role, as does peer influence. At this stage, strong differences in values and lifestyles predict marijuana use, and these differences increase with greater levels of use and involvement (Kandel, 1984, p. 208).

Marijuana users generally display a lower level of involvement in conventional roles, values, and activities than do nonusers. In later adolescence, a progression from marijuana to more dangerous drugs may occur. In this process, parental influences—especially in the form of the degree of intimacy of the adolescent with his or her parents—loom especially large, as does the example of a friend who provides a role model for illicit drug use even as generalized peer influence begins to retreat into the background. Psychological problems assume prominence at this time and predict the use of drugs more serious and dangerous than marijuana. This model shows that explaining drug use is not a simple matter. A number of factors play a key role, each fits into a coherent system or pattern of causality, and each plays a somewhat different role according to the time in someone's life and the drugs in questions. Anyone peddling a simplistic theory of drug use cannot be taken seriously.

The conflict perspective shifts our attention squarely into the "macro" or big picture level of causality; it is the larger structural forces that influence or determine drug use, abuse, and sale. Differences in control of economic and political resources help us understand why members of some communities and neighborhoods are more likely to use drugs and become victims of abuse. Recent developments—especially the collapse of the lower rungs of the working class, the polarization of the economy, and an escalation of social, political, and economic disorganization in the poorest neighborhoods—have speeded up processes that have always existed. Over time, as the poor become poorer, the communities in which they live become increasingly politically impotent. Drug dealers are more able to gain a foothold in them, and their residents find drug dealing an attractive career option.

Politicians learn that the demands of the leaders of such communities can be ignored without consequence. The physical decay of the community, the economic decline of its residents, its shrinking political clout—all contribute to the growing drug abuse of some of its residents and to the institutionalization of drug dealing on its streets. (Conflict theory is partially dependent on social disorganization theory.) Naturally, this approach does not explain why some residents of such neighborhoods turn to drug abuse and/or dealing while most do not. As with most other theories, conflict theory has to be supplemented with others.

In spite of what some theorists argue (for instance, Gottfredson and Hirschi, 1990), the validity of one theoretical perspective does not imply the falsity of another. Each explanation addresses a portion of a large, complex phenomenon. No single theory of drug use or abuse could possibly explain everything that we might want to know about the drug scene. Macro processes may or may not be relevant to micro phenomena, and vice versa; explaining alcoholism says next to nothing about heroin addiction; accounting for drug experimentation says nothing about dependence; subcultural processes may operate alongside psychodynamics; and so on. In attempting to answer the question "Why drug use?" we need to be broad and eclectic in our approach rather than narrow, parochial, and dogmatic.

## KEY TERMS

anomie theory   68

availability (drug)   59

biological theories of
   drug use   60

capable guardian   72

conflict theory   79

demonology   59

genetic theories of
   drug use   60

metabolic imbalance   61

motivated offender   72

negative reinforcement   63

positive reinforcement   63

predisposition   59

problem behavior
   proneness   66

psychodynamic theories
   of drug use   62

psychological theories
   of drug use   62

reinforcement theories of
   drug use   62

retreatism   68

routine activities theory   72

selective interaction/
   socialization theory
   of drug use   76

self-control theory   70

self-derogation theories
   of drug use   65

social control theories   70

social disorganization
   theory   72

social learning theories   73

sociological theories of
   drug use   68

subcultural theory   73

suitable target   72

## ACCOUNT:   Multiple Drug Use

*The subject of the following account, Sam, is a college student.*

Most people think that hard-core drug users come from poor neighborhoods or broken homes, so I guess I'm not your typical drug user. I grew up in a small town in Ohio. The worst thing I ever saw was this long-haired kid smoking a cigarette on the steps of my school one day. I was confused because

I thought cigarettes were only for adults. He looked like a loser, and from what I remember, he was a trouble maker.

I didn't even know anything about drugs or alcohol until I moved to the suburbs of DC at the age of 13. At first I didn't have any friends. Kids made fun of me because I wore imitation Adidas shoes from Kmart. This was considered taboo in my school, but in Ohio, Kmart was a cool place to shop. One day at school, this guy Steve started talking to me. We became friends, and before I knew it, I was wearing Calvin Klein, and I was part of the "in crowd." I started hanging out at other kids' houses, and eventually they hung out at mine. I told Steve that my parents were going out of town, and he said that I should have a party. I said okay, and then we started planning. We handed out directions and fliers for about a month prior to the party! (I can honestly tell you that I had no idea what I was doing, but I didn't want to let my cool friends down, and I didn't want to go back to being a loser in Kmart tennis shoes.) We all took the bus to my house after school and set up for the party. We each grabbed a bottle of alcohol from my parents' bar and started drinking! I picked up a pretty green bottle with a yellow label, took a sip and choked on it! I really didn't like the taste of the Scotch, but I carried the bottle around all night, taking little sips of it! Before I knew it, a few hundred people were in my house, and everything was being destroyed. Eventually the police arrived and kicked everyone out, but the damage was already done! My parents' house was trashed, and I had opened the door to an ugly world that I would have to live in for the next 15 years.

We continued to drink occasionally in junior high, and I tried a few cigarettes, but the real addiction started in high school. I had just started ninth grade at [a very affluent] high school. From time to time I would make eyes with this really pretty girl in the hallways. One day I saw her at a football game, and I told her she was cute. By the end of the game, we were kissing under the bleachers! Jody asked me if I wanted a cigarette, and I said sure! I remembered trying it, in junior high, and I figured if she was smoking it must be wonderful. As it turned out, she became my girlfriend,

and I became a smoker. I feel that this evil habit was my biggest downfall. Nicotine took my normal mind and turned it into a nicotine-dependant, drug-craving machine. I loved smoking! I couldn't wait for class to end so that I could light up with my friends. What I didn't know was that I would spend the next 15 years trying to quit. For 15 years my lungs burned, I coughed all the time, and I couldn't exercise. But I loved my cigarettes! One day we skipped school, and went down by the railroad tracks. I knew that Jody smoked pot, but I had never tried it. She pulled out a joint and started smoking it. I took a couple of hits, but I didn't feel much of anything. A few days later we smoked another joint in her apartment. This time I got high. I couldn't really tell what had happened to me, but I felt confused and overwhelmed. Over the next few months, we continued to smoke cigarettes and pot. Jody and I started skipping school to get high, and our grades started slipping. We didn't really care about school anymore.

My brother asked Jody and I if we wanted to go to the railroad tracks with him and his friends. We said sure. My brother's friend, John, offered us each a hit of acid. We were excited because we had talked about doing acid, but we could never find any. We each took a hit and waited for the fun to begin. Before I knew it I had lost my friends, and I was talking to a bear that had been painted on the wall. My brother came up to me and told me to come with him because everyone was lying on the tracks waiting for the train to come, and he wanted me to try it. I lay down on the track and forgot about everything. Apparently the train was coming down my track, and I wasn't moving. My brother and his friend had to pull me off the track. I really don't remember this, but my brother tells me about it all the time.

My parents became so fed up with my behavior and performance in school that they sent me away to military school. While in military school, I was able to get my act together and finish out my freshman year. . . . Summer came around, and we were allowed to go home. I convinced my parents to take me to the beach because I felt that I deserved a break. While at the beach, I met some guys on the boardwalk. I told them my story, and they said that I could live with them for the rest of the summer. I begged my parents until they gave in. So my parents went home without me. I had no money, very few clothes, and no job. My new friends and I spent the summer going out and having parties at our house every other night. I was never quite sure as to who really lived in the house because so many people crashed there every night. We drank alcohol every night, smoked cigarettes all the time, and smoked weed whenever we could get our hands on it. I remember one time when one of the guys smoked some pot laced with PCP. He became really angry and kept punching the wall. Eventually, he had punched a hole big enough to walk from the kitchen into the bedroom without using the door. We thought it was really funny. Luckily, some of the guys worked at restaurants, so we could get free food sometimes. I also remember filling up cups with the free chili sauce from 7-Eleven, and sometimes that's all we had to eat. After a while the landlord kicked us out, and we all went back home. I was 14 and had decided that I didn't want to go back to military school, so I floated around from public school to public school, and then I quit going to school all together. I started working as a part-time cashier at a gas station and moved into a group house with some strangers. I met this Nigerian guy at my work, and he loved to smoke pot. He came over quite often, and we smoked pot on a regular basis. Our lease eventually ran out on our house, and I was forced to move back home with my parents.

My father decided that if I was going to graduate, he needed to get me into a school. He quit his job as a stockbroker and got a job teaching at a private school. . . . I was able to return to school. I studied hard, got straight A's my senior year, and was able to graduate. I was accepted by many schools, but my parents chose [a particular university] because it was affordable and close to home, and they had a great engineering program. I had no idea what I was getting into.

I moved into [a dorm] my freshman year. It was just one big party. Everyone was smoking pot, drinking alcohol, and no one really cared about school. I met this guy, Jan, who lived on my floor, and we became best friends. He was pledging a fra-

ternity, and the following semester he convinced me to rush his fraternity. I was given a bid and decided to pledge. These guys seemed really different from me, but I trusted Jan and pledged the fraternity anyway. I was voted pledge class president, so I was responsible for all of my pledge brothers. I needed money to pay for the fraternity so I got a job bartending at [a local bar]. I would get drunk at work every night, come home at four in the morning, and have to be at the fraternity house at 7 A.M. to clean up after the parties. Pledging was really difficult. There was hazing, rampant drug use, alcohol and alcoholics everywhere. One time I was kidnapped by an older fraternity brother and taken to the [mountains]. We hiked for several miles and then set up our tents. Later, we built a fire, and he handed us each a bag of mushrooms. We made mushroom tea, and ate the rest of the mushrooms. I waited about a half an hour and then started hallucinating. I remember being really sad and then really happy and then really sad again. I would cry for a while, and then I would laugh uncontrollably. I remember seeing ballerinas in the trees, and the rocks were breathing. It was an exhausting trip, and I continued to hallucinate for a few days afterwards. I also remember one really bad experience when I was lined up with my pledge brothers and pissed on by one of the fraternity brothers. It was degrading, but in the end, there was supposed to be some great reward. I never found it, even after living in the fraternity house for two semesters. To this day, I still wonder what purpose my fraternity served.

## QUESTIONS

Which theory of drug use does this account illustrate? Would Sam have used drugs without social contact with friends who supplied them and endorsed their use? Does Sam's background strike you as one characterized by poor parenting? Is his life characterized by low self-control? How does anomie or "strain" fit into his pattern of drug use? What about his bonds to conventional others? His stake in conformity? Can theories explain individual cases—or are they generalizations that apply only to patterns?

# 4

# CONTROLLING DRUGS

*The Historical Context*

For most of human history, the use, sale, and distribution of psychoactive substances were regulated mostly by informal custom and personal predilection. True, the use of certain substances (like mandrake and henbane) was associated with witchcraft and magic, and practitioners of such uses of these drugs were rooted out by the authorities and punished. In addition, when a new psychoactive drug first entered a society—for instance, in the very early 1500s, when tobacco hit the shores of Europe—steps were taken to control its use. And with the coming of Islam during the seventh century, devout Muslims punished purveyors and consumers of alcoholic beverages. However, for the most part, until a bit more than a century ago, the legal authorities in societies around the world tended to adopt a "live and let live" attitude toward most psychoactive substances. For our purposes, drug legislation dawns somewhere between the end of the nineteenth century and the beginning of the twentieth.

The history of drug use in America is marked by wild swings between legal and social tolerance on the one hand and repression on the other (Musto, 1991); this stretch of time can be summed up as follows:

- During the 1600s and 1700s, Americans drank substantial, even enormous, quantities of alcohol but consumed relatively few, and fairly modest levels of, natural psychoactive substances, mostly as medicines.
- In the 1800s, alcohol consumption declined and the social and legal control of alcohol tightened, but there was an explosion in the use of a range of other drugs, as well as a shift away from natural to semisynthetic—and more powerful—substances. During the first half of the nineteenth century, an accepting, laissez-faire attitude toward consumption was the rule, with high levels of use, substantial public tolerance, virtually no antidrug laws, and an extensive system of distribution.
- The second half of the nineteenth century witnessed the beginnings of alcohol control (at the state level) and, beginning in 1875, drug control, with lower levels of tolerance, the passage of restrictive legislation—and declining levels of use. The first substance that was legally controlled was alcohol, and the second was opium.
- During the early twentieth century, drug legislation on a substantial scale was enacted, including national alcohol prohibition and the passage of the Harrison Act controlling narcotics and cocaine. Several crucial Supreme Court decisions were handed down ruling that the medical maintenance of addicts by physicians was illegal, which led to a huge rise in drug arrests and incarcerations, and a further decline in use. The media began to depict drug use and users in sensationalistic, exaggerated, and propagandistic terms, and there was a rejection of the idea that drug addiction is a medical matter along with a corresponding acceptance of the idea that illicit drug users are criminals and degenerates who should be arrested. Staunch antidrug attitudes and policies remained in place more or less until the 1960s.
- Between the late 1960s and the mid-to-late 1970s, public opinion and public policy were more supportive of the treatment and rehabilitation of substance abusers, and less staunchly in favor of law enforcement as the sole solution to the drug problem. A majority of high school students favored marijuana legalization and did not believe that casual use of the drug was harmful. During this era, methadone maintenance was implemented, and small-quantity marijuana possession was decriminalized in a dozen states. Drug use rose during the mid-1960s and reached a twentieth-century peak in the late 1970s; twentieth-century alcohol consumption peaked at just about the same time.
- After 1980, once again, America's drug attitudes, laws, and law enforcement stiffened. The use of illicit drugs, tobacco, and alcohol declined; the percentage of young people favoring penalizing marijuana use, and believing that the drug is

harmful, rose; two states recriminalized marijuana. The federal government switched its priorities from treatment to law enforcement. Marijuana and cocaine once again became a target of law enforcement. Many experts abandoned the belief that marijuana and cocaine were not harmful drugs, and several Schedule II drugs were reclassified as Schedule I drugs. The advertising of alcohol and cigarettes was restricted, and numerous laws controlling smoking were enacted. Drug arrests and incarcerations rose sharply, reaching an all-time high. We are currently living in that era which may be characterized as a period of a "war on drugs."

An exploration of these massive fluctuations is essential to our understanding of the place of drug use in American society.

## DRUG USE IN NINETEENTH-CENTURY AMERICA

Nineteenth-century America "could quite properly be described as a dope fiend's paradise" (Brecher et al., 1972, p. 3). Psychoactive substances were freely available from a variety of sources, and levels of public consumption of these substances were immense—in all likelihood, on a per-population basis, equaling or surpassing today's volume of use. What stimulated such high levels of use a century or so ago? How did tolerance for drug taking emerge? And what brought about a change in attitudes and public policy? How did we get from a society in which no one was imprisoned on drug charges to one in which hundreds of thousands are? What does history have to teach us about changes in the drug laws?

### Medical Drug Use

In order to understand the scope and nature of nineteenth-century drug use, it is important to keep in mind the extremely primitive state of the medical profession a century or more ago. Opium's painkilling property was discovered by the ancient Sumerians roughly 6,000 years ago, but during the intervening years, physicians did not usually have the drug at their disposal. In past centuries, surgery practiced without opium was savage, brutal, and horrifyingly painful. Limbs were sawed or hacked off, bodies were cut open, teeth were yanked out—and the patient, if still conscious, often screaming and held down by force, suffered indescribable agony. Prior to the twentieth century, an extremely high proportion of surgical patients died on the operating table or soon after.

Under such primitive medical conditions, opium seemed quite literally a godsend. So important was opium in the healing arts that many prominent physicians declared it to be the most useful medicine at doctors' disposal. Oliver Wendell Holmes, Sr. (1809–1894), physician and father of the famous Supreme Court justice, stated that all the medicine available to nineteenth-century physicians "could be sunk to the bottom of the sea [and] it would be all the better for mankind"—with the single exception of opium, a medicine, he said, "which the Creator himself seems to prescribe" (1891, pp. 202–203).

Prior to the twentieth century, treatment for most diseases was ineffective and, in a substantial percentage of cases, dangerous. It is entirely possible that prior to 1900, medical intervention was more likely to be harmful than beneficial, more likely to kill than to save. Supposed cures for diseases, such as drilling holes in the skull, purging (evacuation of the bowels with an enema), bloodletting (the application of leeches), and administering mercury, a poison, were routinely practiced. It was not until the 1850s that a Hungarian physician, Ignaz Semmelweis (1818–1865), discovered that infections could be communicated from one patient, through the medical staff, to another patient, or from cadavers, to the hands of physicians, to patients. So ignorant were physicians at the time that doctors would dissect a diseased cadaver, then walk to the next room and deliver babies without washing their hands—those same hands that had just cut up a rotting corpse. Semmelweis insisted that his attendants wash their hands, thereby sharply reducing the mortality rate of the women in his care who were giving birth. He designed a controlled experiment, testing his proposition, demonstrating conclusively that by washing their hands, medical staff could save the lives of women delivering children. Ridiculed for his discovery and driven out of the medical profession, Semmelweis went insane and eventually committed suicide. It was only in the 1890s that his insight—one of the most important discoveries in the history of medicine—was universally recognized as valid.

It should come as no surprise, therefore, that in centuries past, opium was widely—and today, we would say indiscriminately—administered as a medical treatment. Prior to the twentieth century, administration of opiates was one of the very few medical treatments that was effective in obliterating pain; in addition, it was one of the very few medical treatments that *seemed* to cure a variety of illnesses. Of course, opium did not cure disease so much as mask its painful symptoms. Often, by the time the drug was withdrawn, the body had spontaneously cured itself; with more serious, chronic illnesses, of course, the drug did far more harm than good. And sometimes, the patient was left with an additional medical problem: addiction.

Over-the-counter medications containing opium, morphine, marijuana, and cocaine were freely available in nineteenth-century America, without prescription, and at low cost from physicians, traveling salesmen, drugstores and pharmacies, and general and grocery stores, and through the mail. Bearing names such as Mrs. Winslow's Soothing Syrup, Godfrey's Cordial, Scott's Emulsion, and McMunn's Elixir of Opium, these quack cure-alls or panaceas were taken for a bewildering array of conditions and illnesses, including flat feet, baldness, toothaches, the common cold, cancer, diarrhea, "female troubles," rheumatism, and dysentery. So unregulated was the industry that dispensed these supposed medications that, prior to 1906, their manufacturers *did not even have to list the ingredients of these products*. Hence, patients taking an off-the-shelf patent medicine were never informed that they were taking a psychoactive, dependency-producing substance.

In addition, opium, morphine, marijuana, and cocaine could be obtained by prescription from most physicians for a myriad of ailments. As an indication of how accepted and widely available prescription drugs were, the 1897 edition of the Sears Roebuck catalogue advertised hypodermic kits, which included a syringe, needles, vials, and a carrying case.

In the last decade of the nineteenth century, a number of states passed laws that required patients taking drugs containing morphine or cocaine to first obtain a prescription from a physician. But these laws were ineffective because they were not enforced. Moreover, patients could obtain these drugs without prescription in adjoining states or seek out "dope doctors" who had purchased their supply of drugs by mail in states where such legal controls were lacking, thereby dispensing them freely to their patients (Musto, 1999, pp. 8–9).

## Cocaine-Based "Soft" Drinks

In addition to prescription drugs and numerous drug-based patent medicines, a variety of popular beverages (ironically referred to as "soft" drinks) sold at the time contained one or more psychoactive substances, mainly cocaine. In 1863, a French chemist named Angelo Mariani marketed "Vin Mariani," a drink composed of wine and an extract of coca. Billed as a "tonic," a stimulant, and "a powerful nervous excitant," this beverage was so popular that it received testimonials from numerous celebrity users, including an American president, two popes, several well-known writers, a famous inventor, and at least one king. Mariani became a multimillionaire from its sale (Ashley, 1975, pp. 41–44; Grinspoon and Bakalar, 1976, p. 20).

The success of Mariani's coca concoction spawned countless imitators. John Pemberton of Atlanta, a pharmacist and purveyor of a line of patent medicines, introduced his coca-based Peruvian Wine Cola—an "Ideal Nerve and Tonic Stimulant." Critics agreed that the product was inferior to Vin Mariani (in 1886, Atlanta banned its manufacture), so the following year, Pemberton introduced Coca-Cola, a syrup containing caffeine and a mild extract of coca leaves.

In 1891, when Asa Candler, another pharmacist, bought the rights to Coca-Cola and took control of Pemberton's company, the beverage skyrocketed to national success. Like Mariani's product, the drink also generated a swarm of imitators, in fact, a total of 69 (Grinspoon and Bakalar, 1976, p. 28)—including Cafe-Cola, Afri-Cola, Kos-Kola, Kola-Ade, Celery-Cola, Koca-Nola, Rococola, Vani-Kola, and Koke (Spillane, 2000, p. 77). Coca-Bola, the most potent of the lot, contained an astounding 710 milligrams per ounce of liquid beverage (Spillane, 2000, p. 84)! Early in the twentieth century, companies that manufactured these drinks were pressured to "decocainize" their products (Ashley, 1975, p. 46; Brecher et al., 1972, pp. 270–271; Spillane, 2000, pp. 132, 134, 140). The public and media furor over cocaine products in soft drinks was enormous—and ultimately influential. One W.A. Starnes, who ran a drug treatment clinic in Atlanta, declared that Coca-Cola "is doing more injury to the human race than all other drugs put together" (quoted in Spillane, 2000, p. 131). As a result of removing the cocaine from their beverages, the producers of nearly all of these drinks eventually went out of business. By 1906, Coca-Cola had removed the cocaine but kept the noncocaine ingredients of the coca leaf, paving the way to become the most popular commercial beverage in history.

## Medical, Scientific, and Technological Innovations

In addition to the primitive state of nineteenth-century medicine and a "live and let live" attitude toward the content of beverages and pseudomedicines sold to the public, a number of remarkable scientific, medical, and technological innovations took place during the 1800s that made psychoactive substances not only more available but available in purer form and via a much more efficient and effective route of administration. Prior to the nineteenth century, drugs were ingested in their milder, natural form. For instance, natural opium is considerably less potent than morphine, from which it is extracted. And coca leaves contain only about 1 percent cocaine, while cocaine hydrochloride is roughly 90 percent pure cocaine. In addition, prior to the nineteenth century, the drugs that were ingested, and the forms in which they were ingested, placed a pharmacological limit on their potential for producing dependency in humans. It is true that opium was addicting in its natural form. But heroin builds a dependency more quickly and more surely than does opium, and during the first half of the nineteenth century, cocaine did not exist in its pure form. By 1900, however, nearly all the innovations that currently make highly potent drugs available in a highly reinforcing form had taken place. Most notably:

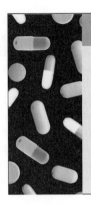

## True-False Quiz

In my quiz, I offered students the following statement: "During the 1800s, drugs such as cocaine, opium, and marijuana were legal and could be purchased openly from physicians, at pharmacies, grocery stores, general stores, and out of catalogs." As we see in this section, this is indeed true; almost without exception, all the drugs whose possession and sale are a crime today could, in the past, be purchased openly and legally from a wide range of retail outlets. And most of my students were aware of this fact: 80 percent said that the statement is true; only 20 percent said that it is false.

- In 1803, morphine, a much more potent narcotic, was extracted from opium.
- Codeine, another derivative of opium, was synthesized in 1831.
- The hypodermic syringe, devised in Europe for the specific purpose of injecting morphine, was brought to the United States in 1856; by the early 1880s, "virtually every American physician possessed the instrument" (Courtwright, 1982, p. 46). The syringe enabled physicians to administer a calibrated—and very potent—intravenous dose of morphine to their patients. (So unaware of the effect of drugs were physicians at the time that, initially, some believed that, unlike oral doses, injected drugs did not have addicting properties.) Hypodermic injection of morphine was used extensively during the Civil War (1861–1865).
- In 1859, cocaine was isolated from coca leaves, and in the 1880s, a German physician discovered that soldiers fortified with the drug were a great deal less likely to become tired. In 1884, a letter was published in a medical journal proclaiming that cocaine possessed anesthetic properties; the drug almost instantly becoming, in many medical circles, "a miracle of modern science" (Spillane, 2000, pp. 7–24).
- In 1874, diacetylmorphine (heroin) was synthesized from morphine; it was marketed commercially by the Bayer Company in 1898.

In short, nineteenth-century America witnessed a virtual explosion of inventions, discoveries, and applications that practically guaranteed that the country would be awash in drugs. More specifically, these innovations assured that *more potent* forms of potentially harmful drugs would be available and used via a more potent route of administration.

### Numbers of Addicts and Abusers

Given the free and easy availability of so many addicting and dependency-producing substances, it should come as no surprise that the United States housed an extremely large user and addict population in the nineteenth century. No national records were collected at the time; moreover, even the concept of drug dependence was poorly understood until well into the twentieth century. Estimates of the number of narcotic addicts ranged from a low of 100,000 (the estimate provided by the Bureau of Narcotics) to a high of a million or more. The two most reliable estimates place the total at 250,000 (Musto, 1999, p. 5) and 313,000 (Courtwright, 1982, p. 9). A century ago, three more or less distinct populations or social circles of narcotic users existed in the United States: (1) medical and pseudomedical addicts, mostly white, middle-class, middle-aged women; (2) opium smokers, mostly Chinese immigrants; and (3) criminal, underworld, and less-than-respectable morphine addicts. The largest of these three populations was made up of medical addicts. Two researchers estimate the number of cocaine habitués at the turn of the century at 80,000 (MacCoun and Reuter, 2001, p. 194).

All such estimates are based partly on records of the importation of the drug in question and partly on physician and hospital records. However, since the distribution and use of marijuana has always been much more informal and rarely tabulated in medical records, the size of the marijuana-using segment of the population a century ago can probably never be known. We do have, however, fairly good estimates of the impact of state bans on the distribution of alcohol: Drinking sharply declined between the early to mid-1800s (roughly 7.10 gallons of absolute alcohol per person per year in 1830) and the late 1800s and early 1900s (roughly 2 gallons per person per year).

Beginning late in the nineteenth century, a substantial number of lawmakers and re-formers decided that local, state, and federal legislation was necessary to stem the tide of substance abuse that was presumably flooding the country. Their motives were complicated and irreducible to a single formula. Different reformers had different motives; even the same reformers were driven by mixed motives. And the motives that dominated the debate over the control of a particular drug were different from those that moved the sponsors of bills to control other drugs. No single explanation can account for the criminalization of psychoactive substances beginning in the last quarter of the nineteenth century. The drug laws that were enacted during this period emerged out of a cultural and political ferment that was composed of a mixture of conventional moralism, racism, the protection of economic and political interests, and the "social workerly" impulse to prevent the weak and vulnerable from harming themselves, their loved ones, and vulnerable, innocent members of the society.

## THE MOVEMENT TO PROHIBIT ALCOHOL: 1784–1920

We'll look at the impact of national alcohol **prohibition** in more detail in the next chapter, but here we need to look at the forces and factors related to the government's attempt to control drinking, which was part of a more general effort to curtail untoward behavior of all kinds. As we'll see in more detail in Chapter 7, eighteenth- and early-nineteenth-century Americans drank truly *immense* quantities of alcohol. In the year 1790, the year of the first U.S. Census, Americans consumed a per-capita average of 5.8 gallons of pure alcohol (see the box on the next page). By 1830, this had increased to an astonishing 7.1 gallons—or two and a half drinks containing an ounce of pure alcohol *per day, per person*. Since this includes the entire population (age 15 and older), including teetotalers, a substantial segment of the population clearly drank considerably more than the average.

Many observers recognized that uncontrolled drinking carried a heavy price and set out to control the consumption of alcohol in the United States. Dr. Benjamin Rush, prominent Philadelphia physician and signer of the Declaration of Independence, wrote a pamphlet, *An Inquiry into the Effects of Ardent Spirits on the Human Mind and Body* (1784), which challenged the view that drinking was an unmixed blessing. Rush's targets were heavy rather than moderate drinking, and "ardent spirits" (distilled alcoholic beverages) rather than wine and beer.

**True-False Quiz**

When I asked my students about the statement "Americans drank considerably more alcohol during the 1700s than they do today," only a third (36%) believed it to be true, while two-thirds (64%) said that it is false. In fact, the statement is true. In the 1700s, Americans drank more than they do today, and by a considerable margin. It is difficult to believe that the country drank *three times* as much as it does today, on a per-person basis, but historical records, including transactions of the sale of alcoholic beverages, clearly indicate that this was the case.

While rejecting absolute prohibition, Rush nonetheless urged his fellow citizens to "unite and beseech" their leaders to demand fewer taverns and heavier taxes on liquor (Lender and Martin, 1987, p. 38). Regarding the pulpit as a promising source of reform, he sent thousands of copies of his pamphlet to the general assembly of the Presbyterian Church for distribution. As a result of Rush's arguments, the church fathers became aware that excessive drink stimulated un-Christian vices and took up the cause of temperance. Soon, other Protestant denominations followed; within three years, hundreds of antiliquor organizations became active across the country. By the 1810s, temperance reform "constituted a burgeoning national movement" (p. 68).

During the 1820s and 1830s, clergymen debated the question of whether temperance was sufficient to control the sin of excessive alcohol consumption. Many began to argue that total abstinence rather than moderation was necessary. In 1826, Lyman Beecher, prominent Presbyterian minister, published his *Six Sermons on Intemperance,* which argued that total abstinence "was the only sure means of personal salvation and societal stability." Any drinking, Beecher claimed, was one step along the path of "irreclaimable" slavery to liquor. A Methodist report agreed. There is "no safe line of distinction between the *moderate* and the *immoderate* use of alcohol," the report argued; moderate use was "almost . . . certain" to lead to immoderate use. The report's conclusion questioned "whether a man can indulge . . . at all and be considered temperate" (Lender and Martin, 1987, p. 69).

To judge by their results, these sermons and publications began to have an impact on American drinking patterns. Employers stopped supplying their workers with liquor breaks; increasingly, farmers harvested their crops without bringing the communal jug to the field; railroad employers began firing workers who drank on the job; rowdy, troublesome taverns were closed down when local governments refused to renew their licenses; and liquor rations were no longer distributed to army soldiers. By the 1840s, prohibition sentiment was so strong that statewide alcohol bans became feasible. In 1846, Maine became the first state to outlaw the manufacture and sale of distilled spirits. By the mid-1850s, roughly one-third of the population lived in a state in which the sale of alcohol was prohibited. But the conflict over the abolition of slavery overshadowed the issue of prohibition, and a number of states repealed their "dry" laws. Still, the Civil War (1861–1865) did not resolve the issue of prohibition; but merely delayed it.

For the prohibitionist, the urban saloon remained a symbol of the degeneracy brought on by drink. Its patrons were frequently immigrants, usually from Catholic regions of Europe, who did not share the Anglo-Saxon Protestant temperance virtues of abstinence from sensuous pleasures. Prostitution, gambling, and violence were frequently accompaniments of local barroom activity. Moreover, corrupt political bosses made the neighborhood tavern a meeting place and recruiting locale, which both encouraged their constituency to drink and involved them in undemocratic practices, such as stuffing ballot boxes and intimidating and assaulting political opponents (Lender and Martin, 1987, p. 104). The local saloon became the most important target of prohibitionist reformers, representing, as it did, the perfect example of what they were fighting against. The Anti-Saloon League was organized in 1893, and by 1910, it was a major political force to be reckoned with; its single purpose: national alcohol prohibition.

From today's vantage point, it is simple—but misleading—to regard the nineteenth-century prohibitionist as a hide-bound conservative trying to stamp out a harmless vice and eliminate one of the working man's few worldly pleasures, a "meddling busybody, interested in forcing his [or her] own morals on others" (Becker, 1963, p. 148). But the fact is, prohibitionist factions represented a most decidedly mixed bag. Motives that today we would recognize as both backward and progressive together formed the prohibitionist impulse.

For one thing, most "drys"—who were supporters of prohibition—harbored and expressed strong ethnic chauvinism. Opposition to the manufacture and sale of alcohol often went hand in hand with opposition to immigration because most immigrants came from "wet" cultures and strongly opposed prohibition. And anti-immigrant sentiment easily translated into hostility to Catholics and the Irish, the Italians, and, during World War I, the Germans. Many prohibitionists harbored "nativist" (strongly pro-American) and xenophobic (antiforeign) sentiments that seem racist today—and they did not hesitate to express them.

At the same time, the Women's Temperance Christian Union (WTCU), founded in 1874 and perhaps the single most powerful late-nineteenth-century antiliquor lobby, supported women's rights, women's suffrage (the right to vote), world peace, and laws against statutory and forcible rape. The WTCU may very well have represented the entry of American women into the organized political process. The very fact that wives were called upon to control the drinking of their husbands reconfigured power relations between men and women, and may very well have been a first step in asserting women's rights and establishing women's liberation. In the short run, women were instrumental in establishing national alcohol prohibition; in the long run, it was women's interactions with men that eventually "domesticated" drinking to its current, more moderate form (Murdock, 1998).

During the first decade of the twentieth century, big business became involved in a big way in the prohibitionist cause. An antidrinking stance was consistent with a disciplined and cooperative workforce. Between 1911 and 1920, 41 states passed workmen's compensation laws, which meant that employers had to compensate workers for industrial accidents. In 1914, the National Safety Council cited alcohol consumption as a cause of industrial accidents; "safety through sobriety" became the employer's watchword, adding to the chorus of prohibitionist voices (Cashman, 1981, p. 6; Rumbarger, 1989).

In January 1919, Nebraska became the thirty-sixth state to ratify the Eighteenth Amendment to the Constitution, which called for the prohibition of the manufacture, sale, transportation, importation, and exportation of "intoxicating liquors" for "beverage purposes" within, into, and from the United States and its territories. A year later, the amendment went into effect. Over a veto by President Woodrow Wilson, Congress passed the National Prohibition Act. Referred to as the **Volstead Act,** it legally banned the distribution of all beverages containing more than 0.5 percent alcohol. The act also empowered the federal government to enforce the law.

The passage of the Volstead Act represented the triumph of Protestants over Catholics, native-born Americans over immigrants, rural and small-town dwellers over urban residents, the South over the North, Anglo-Saxons over ethnics from southern and eastern Europe, farmers and the middle class over the working class, and Republicans over (nonsouthern) Democrats. In effect, **Prohibition** marked the dying gasp of a traditional way of life that was to be forever cast to the winds by the Great Depression (1929–1939) and beyond.

As we'll see in more detail in the next chapter, although Prohibition was widely ignored and circumvented, alcohol consumption did decline between 1920 and 1933. Nonetheless, enforcement created more problems than it solved; the decline in drinking was bought at a very high price. For one thing, comparing the pre-Prohibition era to the 1920–1933 period, the national murder rate increased from 6.8 to 9.7 per 100,000 in the population. For another, the opportunity to sell alcohol was enormously profitable to organized crime—in effect, Prohibition subsidized the criminal organizations that eventually developed into the organized drug gangs that were so successful until the breakup of the French Connection in the 1970s. All in all, Prohibition proved to be a *disastrous* experiment in legislative reform.

## EARLY ANTI-OPIUM LEGISLATION

With the exception of alcohol, the earliest drug legislation enacted in the United States was directed specifically at the use and distribution of opium. In one form or another, opium had been an essential ingredient in a wide variety of medications and nostrums. Dover's Powder, introduced commercially in England in 1709, contained an ounce of opium per bottle; it remained in use for roughly 200 years (Inciardi, 2002, p. 16). In the last years of his life, Benjamin Franklin used laudanum—opium soaked in alcohol—to soothe the pain of kidney stones. Samuel Taylor Coleridge (1772–1834), author of the hallucinatory poem "Kublai Khan," was addicted to laudanum, from his student days to the end of his life. Edgar Allan Poe (1809–1849), author of many intense, dreamlike tales, wrote that he "had become a bounden slave in the trammels of opium" (Hodgson, 1999, p. 102); Poe, an alcoholic, died after an evening of overindulgence of alcohol. While nearly all pre-twentieth-century practicing physicians recognized the benefits of opium in medicine, most agreed that it had a negative side as well: Its use brought on a dangerous dependency. The turn-of-the-century debate over whether self-regulation among physicians was sufficient to control medical addiction or whether legal controls were necessary split the profession into two opposing factions.

However, the earliest drug laws were not aimed at medical addiction at all but were designed to stamp out the recreational use of opium—specifically, opium smoking. Chinese immigrants began arriving in the United States in 1848, originally to work on the railroad, in mines, and in the gold fields. By the 1850s, substantial numbers of Chinese had arrived, and Chinatowns sprang up in San Francisco and other towns and cities in California and the Southwest. When jobs were plentiful, the Chinese were welcome, but an economic depression in 1875 made them less than welcome. One contemporary figure, Benjamin Brooks, who testified in 1877 on behalf of continued Chinese immigration, estimated that roughly 1 Chinese man out of 20 smoked opium, and 1 out of 100 was addicted to it (Courtwright, 1982, p. 69). Less sympathetic observers hugely exaggerated these figures (p. 70), and perhaps the perception was more important than the reality. The fact is, many whites felt threatened by the "alien" presence of the Chinese and their "Oriental" ways, and opium smoking by a small minority among them became a particular focus of contention among elements of the white majority who sought to exclude the Chinese from the U.S. shores.

Prior to 1870, opium smoking had been confined to the Chinese immigrant community. With "little incentive to abandon old ways and adapt to the new culture," the Chinese tended to band together with other Chinese and avoid whites on a social basis. Racism on the part of many, perhaps most, whites contributed to the mutual estrangement. "There was, however, one element of the white community willing to mix with the Chinese: the underworld. Operating beyond the bounds of respectability, gamblers, prostitutes, and assorted other criminals would have had fewer scruples about associating with Orientals and experimenting with their vices" (Courtwright, 1982, p. 71). In opium dens, men vastly outnumbered women, whites were relatively rare, and "respectable" white women rarer still.

Nonetheless, some conservative members of the white community feared that opium smoking "had spread or was about to spread to the upper classes" (Courtwright, 1982, p. 64), particularly young white women who had been seduced into "degenerate practices" by the "cunning Oriental." Fear of interracial sex made such concerns all the more pressing. San Francisco physician Winslow Anderson wrote of the "sickening sight of young girls . . . lying half-undressed on the floor or couches, smoking with their lovers. Men and women, Chinese and white people" he wrote indignantly, "mix in Chinatown smoking houses" (quoted in Courtwright, 1982, p. 78).

"Public outrage at this sort of behavior was soon translated into restrictive legislation" (Courtwright, 1982, p. 78). San Francisco passed the first anti-opium legislation in 1875; many other similar municipal laws soon followed. In 1881, California enacted a state statute penalizing anyone who operated or patronized an opium den (p. 79). And in 1882, the federal Chinese Exclusion Act banned the immigration of Chinese laborers for ten years. Both demographic and legal factors contributed to limit opium smoking in the United States. As a result of restrictions on Chinese immigration, between 1890 and 1920, the Chinese population in the United States fell by nearly half, from 103,000 to 53,000. In 1909, the Smoking Opium Exclusion Act was passed, making access to the drug more difficult. And as a result of the law and its enforcement, a substantial number of whites drifted away from the practice—some of them only to take up "new and more potent varieties" of addicting drugs (p. 86).

# THE PURE FOOD AND DRUG ACT OF 1906

As we saw, during the nineteenth century, not only were ineffective patent medicines containing psychoactive drugs freely available, off the shelf, to anyone with the wherewithal to purchase them, but they did not even have to list their ingredients. In 1905, President Theodore Roosevelt called for a law "to regulate interstate commerce in misbranded and adulterated foods, drinks, and drugs."

In 1905, *Collier's* magazine and the *Ladies' Home Journal* ran articles attacking the bogus claims and misleading labels of patent medicines that contained cocaine, morphine, opium, and alcohol. In 1906, Upton Sinclair published a shocking, muckraking novel titled

*The Jungle*, which exposed the horrifically unsanitary and unhealthful conditions of the meat-packing industry. The public was outraged, and Congress was moved to pass the **Pure Food and Drug Act,** which prohibited interstate commerce in adulterated or misbranded food and drugs. The act created the Food and Drug Administration (FDA), which was empowered to oversee its provisions. From the beginning, however, compliance has been more voluntary than enforced, with persuasion rather than punishment being the rule.

The Pure Food and Drug Act did not outlaw the sale of patent medicines that contained opiates and cocaine. Instead, such contents had to be listed on the product's label. But such labeling, along with media exposure, brought about a keener public awareness of the lack of curative powers of these so-called medications. Within a few short years, the patent medicine industry suffered a steep decline in sales. In 1912, an amendment to the act outlawed "false and fraudulent" claims for the therapeutic powers of patent medicines. However, the government permitted enormous latitude to manufacturers, assuming their "good faith" in making clearly false claims. It was not until the 1960s that the federal government applied moderately strict standards regarding the safety and effectiveness of medications sold to the public. Nonetheless, the Pure Food and Drug Act was a pioneering piece of legislation, one that provided a model for countless laws that followed.

## THE SHANGHAI COMMISSION AND THE HAGUE CONFERENCE

The Chinese government banned opium in 1729, but the British illegally smuggled the drug into the country from India. In 1839, increasingly distressed by the growing number of addicts, the emperor empowered Chinese authorities to seize and destroy a large shipment of opium in the city of Canton. In retaliation, a British expeditionary force attacked and defeated Chinese military forces; in the settlement that followed, the emperor was forced to pay $18 million in compensation—equivalent to about $18 billion today—cede Hong Kong to the British, and open a half dozen ports to British trade. In 1856, a minor incident served as an excuse for the British, now allied with the French, to sail into Peking and sack and burn the emperor's palace. Once again, the emperor was forced to pay compensation, and the opium trade was legalized. These two **Opium Wars** were deeply humiliating to the Chinese, both as a reminder of their subjugation to foreign powers and as the source of an unwanted social problem—opiate addiction. In effect, not only was the British government meddling in the internal affairs of a sovereign state, it was doing this to satisfy its own greed for profit. As the Chinese government saw it, Britain was forcing opium down the throats of the Chinese populace, thereby exacerbating the country's addiction problem.

By the early 1900s, the U.S. government was keenly aware of the enormous potential in trade with China. In addition, American missionaries in China made it plain that opium smoking was an evil that had to be eradicated if China was to be a productive trading partner. The United States had inherited the Philippines as a result of the Spanish-American War of 1898. To fight opium addiction there, authorities banned the drug in 1905 (for the Chinese living in the Philippines) and 1908 (for all residents of the Philippines). Their experience in that colony proved to be a major spur to apply similar prohibitions elsewhere. Humiliated by the mistreatment of Chinese immigrants in the United States, Chinese merchants launched a boycott of American goods in 1905.

A year later, an American bishop, Charles Henry Brent, who was instrumental in the opium bans in the Philippines, persuaded President Theodore Roosevelt that an international treaty was necessary to placate Chinese interests. The International Opium Commission, usually referred to as the **Shanghai Commission,** convened representatives from 13 countries, presided over by Dr. Hamilton Wright, "the father of American narcotic laws" (Musto, 1999, p. 31). The American delegation presented evidence demonstrating the evils of narcotics, but the lack of national American drug bans "embarrassed the commission officials" (p. 33).

Following the Shanghai Commission, Wright drafted a bill that sought to control drug traffic "through federal powers of taxation. His bill would require every drug dealer to register, pay a small tax, and record all transactions" (Musto, 1999, p. 41). Introduced as the Foster bill, this "direct antecedent of the Harrison Act" was "designed to uncover all traffic in opiates, cocaine, chloral hydrate, and cannabis regardless of the minute quantities that might be involved" (p. 41). Although the bill did not ban the sale of drugs, its penalties for noncompliance with record-keeping were severe, presumably making "retail sales more troublesome than profitable" and thereby eliminating the drug trade altogether (p. 42). But in 1911, the bill was defeated in Congress as a consequence of extremely strong opposition from the pharmaceutical lobby, which found its provisions meddlesome, unnecessary, and very possibly damaging to sales (p. 48).

The International Conference on Opium, usually referred to the **Hague Conference,** opened late in 1911. Representatives from 12 nations attended. Once again, the United States proved to be the most insistent that each country enact its own narcotics legislation, and again, representatives from the other countries proved to be reluctant or skeptical. And, once again, the American delegation was placed in the embarrassing position of urging narcotics legislation on other countries while not having any of its own. Several other countries had already enacted drug legislation; was it not hypocritical that the United States did not? "What assurances could be given that, having signed and ratified the Convention, the United States would enact implementing legislation?" Wright was asked (Musto, 1999, p. 51).

The meetings at the Hague proved to be "one more instance in which enactment of exemplary domestic laws became necessary in order to avoid international embarrassment" (Musto, 1999, p. 51). The Hague Conference ended with less-than-unanimous agreement on the need for international drug laws. But it did open the door to domestic narcotics legislation, which took the form of the **Harrison Act,** the source of all subsequent American drug laws. The Harrison Act was the single most important piece of drug legislation ever enacted in the United States.

## The Harrison Act of 1914

In 1912, after the meetings in China and the Netherlands, and the defeat of the Foster bill, Dr. Wright resolved to draft a bill that would eliminate all nonmedical use of narcotics. Representative Francis Burton Harrison, a New York Democrat, agreed to shepherd Wright's bill through Congress. However, the bill was not appreciably different from the defeated Foster bill of 1910 (Musto, 1999, p. 54). Moreover, a powerful coalition of forces opposed the bill—most notably, Southerners, because they believed that any strong federal legislation challenged states' rights, and the pharmaceutical lobby, because druggists believed the regulations to be inconsistent, complex, and unnecessary.

But at the time, the American Medical Association (AMA) approved of drug control. (By 1918, the AMA would change its tune.) And after the election of 1912—with Woodrow Wilson in the White House, the Democrats in control of both houses of Congress, and William Jennings Bryant, who approved of the bill, as secretary of state—the alignment of political forces now favored the Harrison Act. With some tightening, simplification, and compromises, the pharmacists' lobby was won over, and on December 14, 1914, Congress passed the Harrison Narcotic Act. President Wilson signed it into law three days later. "Finally the American government had redeemed its international pledges; a federal law brought some control to the traffic in opiates and cocaine" (Musto, 1999, p. 61).

Contemporary observers argue that the passage of the bill was facilitated by an association in the general public's mind between the recreational use of opiates and cocaine and stigmatized minorities. Medical use, already on the decline, was less than influential in the legislators' decision, and besides, everyone agreed that medicine had relied on a far-too-liberal—and dangerous—administration of opiates. Opium smoking had been indulged in by Chinese immigrants and underworld whites; morphine was used by criminals and prostitutes; and cocaine, whether rightly or wrongly, was associated in the minds of many Southerners with African-Americans. "Cocaine was especially feared in the South by 1900 because of its euphoric and stimulating properties" (Musto, 1999, p. 6). Many southern whites believed that, under the influence of cocaine, Blacks would rape white women and attack white society (Ashley, 1975, pp. 66–71). Nonetheless, unlike the public furor and debate—and media attention—that attended the issue of alcohol prohibition during the 1900–1920 era (and the marijuana problem in the 1930s), the Harrison Act slipped through Congress virtually unnoticed. It was approved in a matter of minutes, and even *The New York Times* failed to note its passage (p. 66).

There was only one problem with the Harrison Act: The law was ambiguous. There was no agreement as to how to interpret it. Under its provisions, it was not even clear what was legal and what was illegal. On the surface, the Harrison Act was clear. Any and all dispensers of narcotics and cocaine had to be licensed physicians and were required to register with the government and pay a nominal tax. It was illegal to sell or otherwise dispense opium or opium derivatives and cocaine without first obtaining an order from the commissioner of revenue, and only medical professionals could register. The registered medical professionals were required to keep a record of the drugs they sold and fill out prescriptions for the drugs they dispensed. At the time, hardly anyone questioned the legitimacy of keeping heroin, morphine, opium, and cocaine out of the hands of the recreational user. Everyone agreed that physicians alone should be allowed to dispense prescriptions for narcotics. The sticking point was the medical maintenance of the addict on narcotics by physicians.

The Harrison Act stated that only the dispensation of narcotics "prescribed in good faith" was legal. According to the government's strict interpretation, this *excluded* the maintenance of addicts on narcotics. To many physicians, however, the prescription of narcotics for the purpose of maintenance constituted a legitimate "good-faith" medical use of drugs, and hence was legal. Given the lack of clarity on the matter, it was up to the Supreme Court to interpret what the law meant. Less than a year after the passage of the Harrison Act, Jin Fuey Moy, a Pittsburgh physician, was arrested for prescribing 1.8 grams (about one-sixteenth of an ounce) to an addict. A year later, the case was brought before the Supreme Court, which, in a 7-to-2 vote, *rejected* the government's case, ruling that the provisions of the Harrison Act were not required by international treaty and that the phrase "prescribed in good faith" was impossibly vague. Many observers believe that the *Jin Fuey Moy* decision could completely emasculate the Harrison Act, making narcotics control all but impossible (Musto, 1999, p. 130).

In 1915, a San Antonio physician named Charles Doremus was arrested for dispensing 500 tablets of morphine to a known addict. In 1919, in a five-to-four decision, the Court upheld the constitutionality of the Harrison Act and convicted Doremus. In the same year, by the same margin, the Court also decided against a pharmacist and a physician, and in favor of the law, arguing that maintaining an addict "for the sake of continuing his accustomed use" is such a "plain perversion of meaning that no discussion is required" (Musto, 1999, p. 132).

The fact is, by 1919, America had become a very different place from what it was in 1914. The United States had fought in World War I, and narcotics addiction was "perceived as a threat to the national war effort" (Musto, 1999, p. 133). Prohibition had been ratified, which verified, for a time at least, that the federal government had the power to prohibit the distribution of psychoactive substances. And the country began to experience a growing fear of communism—the Russian Revolution took place in 1917, and fear of the same thing happening elsewhere radiated to representatives of governments throughout the Western world—which increasingly served to chill public dissent over and opposition to federal programs. "Indulgence in narcotics tended to weaken the nation and was associated with other un-American influences which would dissolve the bonds of society" (p. 134).

Interestingly, beginning in 1918, nearly 50 narcotic maintenance clinics were set up around the country by local, state, and federal agencies. These clinics proved to be the swan song of narcotic maintenance. The clinic in New York City registered 7,500 addicts before it was closed down in 1920. All of the remaining clinics treated no more than 3,000 addict-patients. Though these clinics were never a major source of drugs, "they were nevertheless obstacles to the agents' efforts to indict the major purveyors [of narcotics]: physicians, druggists, and peddlers" (Musto, 1999, p. 152). One after another, they were investigated by the Treasury Department's Narcotic Division and closed down. The last one, located in Shreveport, Louisiana, was closed in 1923.

By the early-to-mid-1920s, it had become crystal clear that drug maintenance was doomed. Between 1914 and 1938, nearly 30,000 physicians were arrested for dispensing narcotics, and nearly 3,000 actually served jail or prison sentences. Eventually, the medical profession withdrew from the business of dispensing narcotics to addicts, and addicts, in turn, were forced to abstain or seek out an illicit drug supply. By the 1920s, narcotic addiction had become, by its very nature, a criminal offense. The Harrison Act had created a new class of addict-criminals.

## THE IMPACT OF THE HARRISON ACT: DID IT MAKE MATTERS WORSE?

The history of American drug laws, especially subsequent to the Harrison Act, is absolutely central to any mission attempting to understand the issue of the legal control of drug use. Many observers argue that the change in the addict's legal status wrought by the Harrison Act produced our current, extremely serious, drug problem, and that the solution to the drug problem is to return to pre–Harrison Act drug laissez-faire. Consider this: The majority of pre–Harrison Act addicts were medical addicts, mostly white, respectable, middle-class, middle-age females, who harmed no one but themselves. But the majority of the post–Harrison Act addicts were predatory street criminals, increasingly inner-city minority males, who lived by stealing from the law-abiding citizen.

Doesn't it make sense, some critics of drug prohibition argue, that the drug laws and their enforcement *caused* this unfortunate transformation? Isn't the disastrous impact of the Harrison Act and its legal descendants a clear lesson to us all? We should return to nineteenth-century laissez-faire legal policy, these critics argue, when drugs were freely available to all and caused relatively few problems for society. A close scrutiny of the harmful impact of the Harrison Act, they say, teaches us a very clear lesson: Legalize the currently illicit drugs. This conclusion has been reached by a substantial number of authorities, most of them politically liberal, who have examined the history of the American drug laws, including Edwin M. Schur (1962), Alfred R. Lindesmith (1965), Edwin M. Brecher (1972), and Rufus King (1972).

Not all observers are convinced that our drug laws had such disastrous effects. And not all agree that the laws were responsible for the transformation of the addict population from medical to criminal addicts. David Courtwright (1982), a historian, argues that this transformation did *not* take place between 1914 (the year the Harrison Act was passed) and 1924, when all the maintenance clinics had been closed and the courts had decided that maintenance was illegal, but at least a decade *earlier*. Courtwright's argument is that the decline in the number of narcotic addicts in the United States came about *not* as a result of the passage and enforcement of the Harrison Act, but through voluntary changes in medical practice.

Prior to 1900, writes Courtwright, "most addiction resulted from the activity of physicians; it was, to use a shorthand term, iatrogenic," that is, caused by medical intervention itself. "Doctors liberally dispensed opium and morphine to their patients," but "as a wider range of effective therapies, improved sanitation, and improved medical education became available," Courtwright argues, the number of medical addicts diminished. "The net result was that opiate addiction, while declining relative to the population, began to assume a new form: it ceased to be concentrated in upper-class and middle-class white females and began to appear more frequently in lower-class urban males, often . . . members of the underworld" (pp. 2–3).

Courtwright assembled his evidence from surveys of physicians', pharmacists', and maintenance programs' records, military medical examinations, and the statistics on the importation of opiate drugs. His conclusion is that "the rate of opiate addiction in America increased throughout the nineteenth century from not more than 0.72 addicts per thousand persons prior to 1842 to a peak of 4.59 per thousand in the 1890s; thereafter the rate began a sustained decline. In round figures there were never more than 313,000 opiate addicts in America prior to 1914" (p. 9) (see Figure 4-1). If, as Courtwright argues, the addict population began to change *prior* to 1914—indeed, prior to 1900—the Harrison Act and its enforcement could not have been responsible for the change. Instead, he says, we have to look elsewhere for its causes. The reason for the sharp decline in medical addicts—and, as a result, the number of addicts overall—can be traced, first, to more sophisticated medical care and self-monitoring of the dispensation of opiates by physicians to their patients, and second, to an aging, and hence dying, addict population.

But the other side of the coin (the shrinking of the absolute size of the medical addict population) was the growing *relative* size of the criminal addict population. Courtwright believes that the number of recreational addicts remained more or less stable—with year-

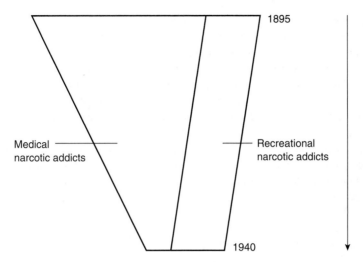

1895

Medical
narcotic addicts

Recreational
narcotic addicts

1940

**Figure 4-1** **Number of narcotic addicts, 1895–1940.**
*Source:* Adapted from Courtwright, 1982.

to-year fluctuations—between the early twentieth century and World War II, when drug supply lines were cut off. But recreational addicts formed an increasingly greater *proportion* of all addicts because medical addicts declined in number after 1895 (see Figure 4-1). In addition, and just as important, the drug of choice among recreational addicts shifted from opium and morphine to heroin.

Heroin was synthesized from morphine in 1874, but it was not sold commercially, and then as a cough suppressant, until 1898. The number of medical or iatrogenic addicts generated by the reckless administration of heroin was small; most physicians recognized its addicting property extremely quickly. But news of its euphoric property leaked out early on, and within the first decade of the twentieth century, a substantial number of young, mainly white, criminally inclined males began using it recreationally. Roughly 90 percent of them lived within striking distance of New York City.

Initially, heroin was cheap. For some users, it substituted for opium, which had become scarce and expensive as a result of an effective federal ban on its importation. For others, it served as a substitute for cocaine, since the supply of this drug had dried up as a consequence a series of pre–Harrison Act anticocaine state laws. And because heroin was extremely potent, it could be sniffed or snorted to excellent effect.

While morphine maintenance was being debated in the courts, illicit heroin was gradually spreading from New York City. For both addict and dealer, its appeal lay in its potency. Heroin could be diluted several times over and still remain potent. But the more diluted and less pure it became, the greater the tendency of addicts to switch from snorting to intravenous injection. In 1924, recognizing the threat to the country's youth, Congress passed a law specifically banning the domestic use of heroin, a bill, it almost need not be said, that failed to curtail the drug's use (Courtwright, 1982, p. 107). As an indication of the growing importance of heroin relative to morphine as a street drug during the 1920s and 1930s, consider the fact that in 1927, 4 pounds of morphine were seized by the federal government for every pound of heroin; by 1932, 3.4 pounds of heroin were seized for every pound of morphine; and by 1938, the figure was up to 7.7 pounds (pp. 108, 110).

By 1940, says Courtwright, "the heroin mainliner had emerged as the dominant underworld addict type" (p. 112). Think back to the respectable, middle-age, middle-class females who made up most medical addicts at the end of the nineteenth century. The transformation of the addict population turns out to be the switching of one population for another rather than a literal "transformation" of the same population. And the magnitude of this change "can be described by the etymology of a single word, *junkie*. During the 1920s, a number of New York City addicts supported themselves by picking through industrial dumps for scraps of copper, lead, zinc, and iron, which they collected in a wagon and then sold to a dealer. Junkie, in its original sense, literally meant *junkman*" (p. 113). The mind reels at the image of nineteenth-century addicts—respectable, middle-aged ladies—pawing through piles of junk to support a drug habit. Within a single generation, then, the locus of addiction "shifted from the office and parlor to the desolate piles of urban debris" (p. 113).

## THE MARIHUANA TAX ACT OF 1937

Marijuana's use stretches back thousands of years. In the United States, research suggests, the practice began on the Mexican border among working- and lower-class Mexican immigrants, particularly migrant farmworkers. From there, in the 1920s and 1930s, it spread to New Orleans among some members of the African-American working-class community, and from there to Black and white jazz circles, and then to bohemians, intellectuals, gamblers, prostitutes, and criminals. During the period when this diffusion was taking place, popular images of marijuana use were so unrealistic as to be amusing today. Sixty or 70 years ago, users were said to be "addicts," and were thought to become violent, dangerous, and insane under its influence. In the 1940s and 1950s, the furor died down, only to erupt again in the 1960s, when the use of marijuana became extremely widespread. However, by this latter era, the image of the marijuana user had shifted from that of a violent, deranged psychopath to a hippie, a drop-out, a shiftless ne'er-do-well (Himmelstein, 1983, pp. 121–136).

Judging from comments by journalists and lawmakers in the 1920s and 1930s, members of the white majority were almost entirely critical of the "vicious weed." An army botanist who observed Mexican railroad workers' and prison inmates' use of marijuana said that "under its baleful influence reckless men become bloodthirsty, trebly daring and dangerous to an uncontrollable degree." Said an American consul stationed in Nogales, a border town, the use of the drug "causes the smoker to become exceedingly pugnacious and to run amuck without discrimination" (Bonnie and Whitebread, 1974, p. 37). Lawmakers responded with legislation. By the early 1930s, practically every state west of the Mississippi River had passed anti-marijuana legislation, practically without publicity, debate, or opposition (pp. 39, 52).

This era, roughly 1914–1931, can be referred to as the "local" phase of marijuana prohibition (p. 51). During this period, a distinctly grassroots opposition to the drug developed that was rooted in anti-Mexican racism and an association of marijuana with ethnic minorities and otherwise "immoral" populations, such as, as we saw, criminals, prostitutes, longshoremen, gamblers, and jazz musicians. During this era, marijuana was regarded as an alien presence, an addictive narcotic no different from opium, and a stimulant to violence, lawlessness, and crime. Moreover, there was fear that the marijuana habit would spread from society's fringes and underworld to respectable whites, especially women and children (p. 52).

As early as 1915, lawmakers and law enforcement officers in the Southwest urged that marijuana be included in the Harrison Act. Interestingly, however, federal authorities rejected these appeals, believing that Washington "had its hands full with the enforcement of the Harrison and the Volstead Acts" (p. 55). In 1930, the **Federal Bureau of Narcotics (FBN)** was created, with Harry J. Anslinger, a former Prohibition agent, as its first commissioner. One of the first items on the Bureau's agenda was to pass a Uniform State Narcotic Act, ensuring that the same drug laws were enacted across the United States. However, at first, marijuana was not on the FBN's radar screen.

But Anslinger's mind was changed in 1934, thereby shifting efforts at marijuana prohibition into its "national" phase. During the mid-to-late 1930s, the Bureau undertook a major, comprehensive media campaign, as well as lobbying in legislatures, to convince the public of the evil effects of the "killer weed." Anslinger wielded anecdotes and stories about the drug's supposed criminogenic and violence-inducing effects to convince voters and legislators that marijuana had to be criminalized. For instance, he widely publicized a letter the Bureau received, published in the *Alamosa Daily Courier*, which described an attack by a Mexican-American presumably under the influence of marijuana, on a young girl. It read: "I wish I could show you what a small marihuana cigaret can do to one of our degenerate Spanish-speaking residents. That's why our problem is so great; the greatest percentage of our population is composed of Spanish-speaking persons, most of who are low mentally, because of social and racial conditions" (p. 101). Anslinger piled one fanciful tale on another, all with the same moral: Marijuana causes users to become violent. In his classic "Marihuana—Assassin of Youth," published in 1937, he describes a young man "walking along a downtown street after inhaling a marihuana cigarette." Suddenly, "for no reason, he decided that someone had threatened to kill him." Spotting an elderly man, a shoe-shiner, in the vicinity, he decided that he had found his assassin. Rushing home, he got a gun and shot the man, killing him. "I thought someone was after me," the young man babbled. "That's the only reason I did it. I had never seen the old fellow before. Something just told me to kill him." Today, observers agree that Anslinger's documentary evidence for the drug's violence-inducing properties was anecdotal at best and bogus at worst—but at the time, it was taken very seriously.

In short, the Federal Bureau of Narcotics "wanted to arouse public opinion against marihuana, and Commissioner Anslinger enlisted an army of public opinion makers and legislative pressure groups to accomplish this task" (Bonnie and Whitebread, 1974, p. 112). Anslinger's goal was the adoption of the Uniform State Narcotic Act, as well as marijuana legislation, in all states. In spite of the Bureau's aggressive and sensationalistic campaign, the public was more apathetic than outraged (p. 117).

In 1935, two federal legislators representing New Mexico introduced bills to prohibit shipment of marijuana across state lines and into and out of the United States. In 1930, Anslinger had been opposed to bills attempting to criminalize interstate and international marijuana commerce, arguing that there was very little of it to prohibit. But interest in the bills encouraged Anslinger, and the FBN decided to jump on the bandwagon. The **Marihuana Tax Act** became law in August 1937. It had three provisions: (1) "a requirement that all manufacturers, dealers, and practitioners register and pay a special occupational tax"; (2) "a requirement that all transactions be accomplished through use of written order forms"; and (3) "the imposition of a tax on all transfers in the amount of $1 per ounce for transfer to registered persons and a prohibitive $100 per ounce for transfer to unregistered persons" (p. 124). In other words, under the guise of a revenue measure, the federal government effectively banned all possession and sale of marijuana products. The Marihuana Tax Act was to remain federal law until 1970, when the Comprehensive Drug Abuse Prevention and Control Act was passed.

## THE CONTROLLED SUBSTANCES ACT
## AND THE NIXON/FORD ADMINISTRATION

In 1970, Congress approved the Comprehensive Drug Abuse Prevention and Control Act. Referred to as the **Controlled Substances Act,** this bill superseded and replaced all prior federal drug legislation. Though states could still enact their own legislation, in the case of conflicts between state and federal law, federal law always has precedence over state law.

The Controlled Substances Act was originally designed to address drug research, rehabilitation, and education. For instance, it authorized substantially increased funding for Public Health Services hospitals. It also authorized a two-year study by the **National Commission on Marihuana and Drug Abuse,** which published its findings in a multivolume report in 1972 and 1973. The Commission was authorized to make recommendations about drug policy, but its recommendations, which included the decriminalization of marijuana, were largely ignored by President Richard Nixon. In addition, the National Institute on Drug Abuse (NIDA) was authorized to become the federal government's primary agency for drug research, education, and prevention.

However, when the Controlled Substances Act was passed, it became clear that its priority lay mainly in enforcement, not education, research, or rehabilitation. Most observers attribute this emphasis to the law-and-order climate that dominated both Congress and the Nixon administration in the early 1970s. One of the first orders of business of the Controlled Substances Act was to abolish the Federal Bureau of Narcotics, then an agency of the Treasury Department, and to move its replacement, the Bureau of Narcotics and Dangerous Drugs (BNDD) to the Justice Department, a vastly more enforcement-oriented agency. The act increased the strength of the BNDD by 300 agents.

Perhaps the Controlled Substances Act's primary impact was the establishment of categories of "controlled substances" or a program of schedules. It established five "schedules" based on a drug's "potential for abuse" and its medical use (as determined by the federal government).

Schedule I drugs have a "high potential for abuse" and, according to the **Department of Health and Human Services (DHHS),** have "no medical use." (Even though some physicians, and some states, may disagree.) These drugs are illegal under any and all conditions (except for extremely restricted experimental or research circumstances), and penalties for possession and distribution are imposed. Heroin, LSD, marijuana, Ecstasy (as of 1987), and GHB (as of 2000) are representative Schedule I controlled substances. For the manufacture or distribution of narcotics, such as heroin, the maximum penalty is a 15-year sentence; for nonnarcotics manufacture and sale, the penalty is a 5-year sentence. Simple possession entails a 1-year sentence. Subsequent offenses, obviously, increase the penalty.

Schedule II substances are regarded as having a high potential for abuse but, according to the DHHS, do have some medical utility. Possession and distribution for illegal (that is, nonmedical) possession, manufacture, and distribution are the same as for Schedule I drugs. Cocaine, methamphetamines, opium, morphine, methadone, and codeine are Schedule II drugs.

The DHHS regards Schedule III–V drugs as having medical utility and a lower potential for abuse. And the penalties attached to their illicit possession, manufacture, and distribution are likewise correspondingly lower. Examples of Schedule III drugs include slow-acting barbiturates, nonamphetamine stimulants, and narcotics such as Percodan and Darvon. Examples of Schedule IV drugs include Valium and other tranquilizers, and extremely slow-acting barbiturates, such as Phenobarbital. Schedule V drugs are regarded as having an extremely low potential for abuse; examples include Robitussin, Kopectate, Lomotil, and Cheracol.

One of the more fascinating stories in the history of the American drug laws and their enforcement concerns President Nixon's uneasy relationship with drug prohibition. A law-and-order politician with impeccable conservative credentials, Richard Nixon's position on drugs was expected to feature a strong emphasis on enforcement and repression. But the fact is, Nixon was the only recent president whose record reflected a stronger domestic commitment to rehabilitation and treatment than to enforcement. As we might expect, the reasons are complex and revealing.

In the 1960s, two medical researchers, Vincent Dole, a specialist in metabolic diseases, and Marie Nyswander, a psychiatrist, began experimenting with stabilizing addicts on methadone, a long-acting narcotic. In 1965, a psychopharmacologist named Jerome Jaffe attended a lecture by Dr. Dole, was impressed with the results of Dole's research, and began administering methadone to his patients. In 1968, at the University of Chicago, Dr. Jaffe began the Illinois Drug Abuse Program (IDAP), a large-scale adoption of the methadone program. In June 1970, a White House policy advisor named Jeffrey Donfeld called Dr. Jaffe and asked to review IDAP. "Donfeld's visit . . . was to have profound consequences . . . for the nation's drug policy" (Massing, 1998, p. 96).

Elected president in 1968, Richard Nixon "felt a reflexive disgust for illegal drugs and the people who used them" (p. 97). In a campaign speech in California, Nixon referred to narcotics as the "modern curse of the youth. . . . Just like the plagues and epidemics of former years," he said, drugs "are decimating a generation of Americans." If elected, Nixon pledged, he would triple the number of customs agents and work with source countries to eliminate drugs where they grow (p. 97). Just as Nixon took office, the District of Columbia experienced a sharp upturn in the crime rate. A presidential secretary's purse was snatched right outside the White House grounds (p. 99). Nixon was more determined than ever to quell crime in the district, and he entrusted the job to Egil ("Bud") Krogh, considered the White House's "Mr. Fix-It."

At the time, a local methadone program was being run by Robert DuPont. Working with the DC Department of Corrections, Dr. Dupont conducted a study that revealed that 45 percent of the inmates of the district jails were heroin users, demonstrating an extremely strong link between drug use and crime. Suspecting that treatment might be the answer to the crime problem, Krogh sent Jeff Donfeld around the country to survey treatment programs, including Dr. Jaffe's IDAP. Donfeld's report to the White House dismissed all programs then in place, with the exception of one: IDAP. DuPont's own experience and Donfeld's report convinced Krogh of methadone's feasibility. Both Jaffe and a government task force were asked to prepare position reports on drug treatment. The government's report, prepared by

**National Institute of Mental Health (NIMH)** aides, underplayed the seriousness of the drug problem and was extremely skeptical of methadone maintenance. In contrast, Jaffe's report framed heroin addiction as a serious problem that demanded innovative solutions. Jaffe argued that addicts are resistant to treatment, and because methadone shows promise, the government should commit millions to the program to set up IDAP-type programs nationwide (Massing, 1998, pp. 104–105).

In April 1971, two congressmen, as members of a House Foreign Affairs Committee, visited Vietnam "to investigate reports of growing heroin addiction among U.S. troops there" (p. 107). Representative Robert Steele, the Republican, reported his findings to the White House. Not only were 10–15 percent of servicemen in Vietnam addicted to heroin, Steele said, but with the United States mustering out a thousand servicemen a day, many were returning to the United States with their drug habits. If the spread of drugs among troops abroad continued, he stated, "the only solution" would be "to withdraw American servicemen from Southeast Asia" (p. 109). As it turns out, Steele's initial estimates were inflated; between 4 and 5 percent of American soldiers stationed in Vietnam tested positive for narcotics. But the perception of huge numbers of GI addicts was an important impetus to immediate action—and a justification for treatment. After all, these men were not street junkies; they were "our boys," risking their lives abroad for their country. And while a hard-liner on drug enforcement, President Nixon recognized that seizures, arrests, and incarcerations were not reducing the size of the addict population. Something else had to be done—and soon.

In June 1971, Nixon escorted Dr. Jaffe to a bipartisan meeting in the Cabinet Room of the White House and announced that he was creating the Special Action Office for Drug Abuse Prevention (SAODAP) with Jaffe as its director; $155 million in new funds were being requested, with $105 million of that earmarked for treatment. Jaffe was caught completely by surprise. "And so, for the first time in U.S. history, a president had declared war on drugs. And Richard Nixon, the apostle of law and order, was going to make treatment his principal weapon" (p. 112). No other American president had decided to solve the drug problem by making a commitment to reducing the demand for drugs rather than the supply (p. 113).

In the meantime, Nixon remained committed to the policy of eradicating the drug supply. In the summer of 1972, the Turkish government agreed to ban all poppy production in exchange for $35 million in American aid. The farmers who had previously grown the opium poppy would be encouraged to substitute other crops. In addition, in 1972, federal agents, in cooperation with the French and the New York City police, dismantled the so-called French connection, a major drug ring that stretched from Turkey and Lebanon, through Italy and southern France, into the United States. For a time, seizures were up and heroin supplies and drug overdoses were down; experts saw a heroin shortage in the eastern United States. Remarkably, the crime rate in East Coast cities declined correspondingly. (Unfortunately, the decline in the heroin supply proved to be short-lived; within months, Mexico, Iran, Afghanistan, and countries in Southeast Asia began to bring heroin into the country.) It seemed as if Nixon's two-pronged attack on both demand and supply had born fruit in the form of a diminished drug problem—along with a lower crime rate.

In fiscal 1973, federal spending on drug treatment and prevention totaled $420 million—eight times the sum when Nixon took office; by the time he left office, this sum had reached $600 million. And a remarkable two-thirds of the federal budget was earmarked for the demand side, that is, treatment. Only a third went into the supply side, that is, enforcement. Given Nixon's law-and-order orientation, this distribution was astonishing. By late 1972, the number of addicts in federal drug treatment programs had reached 60,000, three times the October 1971 total (Massing, 1998, p. 123); by October 1973, methadone programs nationwide enrolled 80,000 addicts (Musto, 1999, p. 253).

But soon after President Nixon's 1972 reelection, the storm clouds began to gather. In January 1973, New York governor Nelson Rockefeller, considered a liberal Republican, unveiled a harsh, punitive, draconian set of drug laws that would eliminate plea bargains and parole and make the penalty for selling heroin stiffer than that for murder. Although severely criticized, Rockefeller's proposals became law, and they represented the turning of the tide that had been flowing toward treatment and away from punishment. A poll indicated that in New York State, two-thirds of respondents favored the Rockefeller bill. Within months, Nixon asked his aides to draft a similar punitive federal bill; its provisions, while not so harsh as those in Rockefeller's bill, represented a stiffening of federal drug penalties. Dr. Jaffe's objections carried little weight with the president. In March 1973, the Heroin Trafficking Act was sent to Congress; two months later, a federal "superagency," the Drug Enforcement Agency (DEA), was created.

The methadone experiment seemed to be paying off; in cities where it was instituted, both overdoses and the crime rate declined. But now, simple statistics were not enough. The public mood seemed to be swinging away from treatment and toward punishment; a new era in drug enforcement was about to unfold. Funding for Jaffe's Special Action Office was reduced, and seeing the handwriting on the wall, in May 1973, Jaffe resigned. Jaffe's successor, Robert DuPont, oversaw the dismantling of SAODAP, whose offices had been close to the White House, and the creation of NIDA, the National Institute on Drug Abuse, which was located in the suburbs far from Washington, both physically with respect to distance and symbolically in terms of its diminished power.

An event seemingly unrelated to drug treatment and enforcement accidentally and most forcefully inserted itself into the picture. On June 17, 1972, five employees of the Committee to Reelect the President were apprehended breaking into and attempting to wiretap the offices of the Democratic National Committee in the Watergate office complex in Washington. A number of close presidential advisors and aides were forced to resign, and some, including Egil Krogh, served federal prison sentences. In August 1974, in exchange for a pardon, Richard Nixon resigned the presidency. Since Nixon's vice president, Spiro Agnew, had resigned in disgrace a year earlier as the result of an unrelated scandal, Gerald Ford, the speaker of the House of Representatives, became president.

Ford had little interest in the drug problem and even less in drug treatment; interestingly, he was less concerned than Nixon was about both enforcing the drug laws and treating drug addicts. Federal support for treatment programs, including methadone maintenance, declined year by year during the Ford administration (1974–1977). For Ford, drug abuse had a low priority. Once again, almost by default, the federal focus—and funding—reverted to enforcement. Still, in 1975, a surprisingly enlightened document issued from the White House, the *White Paper on Drug Abuse*. It stated that total elimination of drug abuse "is unlikely," but the government "can contain the problem and limit its adverse effects." The white paper also stated: "All drugs are not equally dangerous, and all drug use is not equally destructive." However, the enforcement-treatment imbalance began to assert itself, and this position would be discarded within the decade. In 1976, the federal government committed itself to a program of helping Mexico eliminate illicit poppy plants by paying millions to spray its fields. That same year, federal spending for drug enforcement caught up with the budget for treatment and prevention (Massing, 1998, p. 135). A tidal wave of drug incarcerations was about to begin.

## THE BACKLASH GATHERS STRENGTH: THE CARTER YEARS

In 1976, Jimmy Carter, a Democrat, was elected president of the United States. This seemed to be a positive sign for drug treatment, since Carter, regarded as left of center, supported a variety of humanitarian programs. But Carter's seeming promise was short-circuited in fairly short order, on one front after another. His drug advisor, Peter Bourne, had worked with Jerome Jaffe and was strongly committed to treatment. In 1977, Carter asked Bourne for a position statement on drugs; in it, Bourne came out strongly for marijuana decriminalization— a position Carter adopted in a statement he sent to Congress.

At the time, the president seemed to be in the vanguard of public opinion. While a majority of the general population remained at least moderately opposed to marijuana decriminalization, Monitoring the Future polls indicated that young Americans approved of it. Only 25 percent of 1976's high school seniors indicated that they would support the outright criminalization of marijuana; 29 percent said that marijuana use or possession should be a violation, like a parking ticket; and 33 percent said it should be "entirely legal." In 1973, Oregon decriminalized the possession of small quantities of marijuana, in the mid-to-late 1970s, 11 states followed suit. Marijuana decriminalization seemed to be an idea whose time had come. And Robert DuPont, head of the National Institute on Drug Abuse, agreed.

In 1976, an event took place that represented something of a turning point in drug law enforcement. While it did not cause the changes that followed, it reflected future developments with dead-on accuracy. A suburban Atlanta couple, Ron and Marsha Schuchard, both English instructors at nearby institutions of higher learning, had a 13-year-old daughter whose life seemed recently to have taken a turn for the worse. Normally cheerful and active, she had turned moody and sour, interested only in hanging out with her friends. They decided to throw a birthday party cookout for her. During the barbecue, the Schuchards noticed unusual behavior in their daughter's friends. One girl, red-eyed and discoordinated, could barely dial the phone; a boy barged into the house without announcing himself. Cars full of teenagers showed up, shouting "Where's the party?" (Massing, 1998, p. 143). That night, peering out a second-floor window, the Schuchards noticed lights flickering in the bushes. At one o'clock in the morning, after all the kids had departed, the couple went outside with a flashlight and found empty malt liquor cans and wine bottles, and marijuana roaches and roach clips (p. 142)."We had a sense of something invading our families, of being taken over by a culture that was very dangerous, very menacing," said Mrs. Schuchard. She decided to act.

In 1977, after scouring the available literature and not finding much on marijuana's impact on teenagers, Marsha Schuchard fired off a letter to Dr. DuPont expressing her concern with the drug and the indifference of the medical fraternity toward the dangers it presented. DuPont was impressed. "The heart of the drug problem, he felt, was not heroin addiction, which affected a small, marginalized population, but pot smoking, which touched many families" (Massing, 1998, p. 145). Seemingly, overnight, DuPont was converted to the cause of the parents Schuchard spoke for—parents who felt that marijuana was harmful, especially to adolescents, and should not be decriminalized, but rather should become the central target of drug legislation and enforcement. Along with a neighbor, Schuchard formed **Families in Action,** dedicated to fighting teenage drug abuse. This organization spawned many others like it, and during the 1980s and 1990s, the proparent, antidrug movement became the most powerful nongovernment force influencing drug policy.

In 1978, Carter's drug advisor, Peter Bourne, wrote an illegal prescription for a White House staff member. The bearer of the prescription was caught, and the story made front-page headlines in *The Washington Post:* "Carter Aide Signed Fake Quāālude Prescription." Bourne was suspended, pending the results of an investigation. Meanwhile, rumors began to spread that Bourne, who believed (and still believes) cocaine to be harmless, was present at a party, sponsored by the National Organization for the Reform of the Marijuana Laws (NORML), a marijuana legalization lobby, at which cocaine was used. The head of NORML, Keith Stroup, was asked about the rumor, and Stroup, angry at Bourne for supporting the spraying of Mexican marijuana fields, said that he would not deny the story (Massing, 1998, p. 149). The story broke, and Bourne was asked to hand in his letter of resignation.

"The departure of Peter Bourne [from Carter's administration] would mark a watershed in U.S. drug policy. . . . Bourne had remained an adherent of the Jaffe code, with its belief in the primacy of hard-core drug use [as the central issue in the drug problem] and the government's responsibility to treat it. Though battered, the public-health model had remained largely intact on his watch" (p. 149). With Bourne's demise, "zero-tolerance" became the government's watchword, drug treatment was given low priority, and recreational marijuana use became the government's central drug problem.

The brief stretch of time, roughly from the mid-to-late 1960s to the late 1970s, was an era of comparative tolerance for drug use. Use shot up sharply between 1965 and 1979. Although the number of arrests also increased during this period, the likelihood of incarceration, especially for mere possession of small quantities, and particularly for a marijuana offense, was extremely low. Moreover, the drug enforcement community was poorly funded, and dollars for treatment outstripped those for law enforcement. At the time, cocaine, whose use was just beginning to take off, was barely on law enforcement's radar screen. And during this era, the methadone maintenance program was born, became institutionalized, and received generous federal funding. A dozen states decriminalized the possession of small quantities of marijuana. Teenagers thought that marijuana was fairly harmless—as did many experts—and most supported liberalizing the pot laws. Public interest in and concern over the drug problem was fairly low. All of this was to change in very short order. In fact, 1980—give or take a year or two—can be considered a watershed; after that, in the world of drug use in the United States, nothing was ever the same.

## THE CONTEMPORARY ERA: THE REAGAN YEARS AND AFTER

The contemporary era of drug law enforcement, and incarceration for drug offenses began in 1980; it dawned with the election of Ronald Reagan as president of the United States. As we saw, historical developments that produced the contemporary laws and their enforcement were already percolating as early as the Ford years (1974–1977), for instance, in the form of cutbacks in federal spending for drug treatment and the reversal of President Nixon's two- or three-to-one treatment-to-enforcement spending ratio. And certainly during the Carter years (1977–1981), events were unfolding that helped usher in a more repressive era—for instance, the birth of the parents' anti-marijuana movement and the germ of the idea of "zero tolerance" for illicit drug use. Zero tolerance was pushed, ironically, by Robert DuPont—the man who once advocated marijuana decriminalization. But it was during the Reagan years (1981–1989) that the "war on drugs," originally launched by Richard Nixon, was rejuvenated with special vigor. And it was during the Reagan years that the outlines and foundation of the current drug policy were shaped and laid down. But whereas Nixon's war on drugs stressed treatment, Reagan overwhelmingly emphasized enforcement. And it is enforcement that has remained the centerpiece of government policy toward illicit drugs. Hence, any story on the contemporary "drugs as crime" issue begins in earnest with the Reagan era.

In 1980, Ronald Reagan, a staunch conservative, defeated Jimmy Carter in the presidential election. In 1981, Carlton Turner, a chemist of psychoactive plants, was appointed White House drug advisor. Turner's views on drugs were extremely conservative. He rejected the distinction both between "hard" and "soft" drugs, and between "hard-core" and "recreational" users. For Turner, all drugs were equally dangerous, and any and all levels of drug involvement were likewise equally dangerous (Massing, 1998, p. 160).

Moreover, Turner rejected the very morality of treatment, believing that it sent a message that it was "all right" to abuse drugs, then get bailed out by being treated—courtesy of the federal government. He believed that the government should get out of the drug problem altogether—except, of course, for law enforcement. President Reagan seemed to agree; in the first fiscal year of Reagan's administration, taking inflation into account, federal spending on drug treatment shrank to one-fourth of what it had been in 1974. "Rather than deal with inner-city addicts, the government was now going to get on with its really important business: stopping teenage pot use" (p. 161). Carlton Turner needed an advocate.

Shortly after Turner took office, Nancy Reagan, the First Lady, attended the wedding of Prince Charles and Lady Diana. Traveling with "four hat boxes, twenty dresses, a hairdresser, a photographer, sixteen security agents, [and two] official chaperones," the trip "had been a public relations disaster" (p. 161). The press attacked her extravagance with a vengeance; she was dubbed "Queen Nancy." On the same day that she ordered over $200,000 worth of china for the White House table, the Agriculture Department announced that for the purpose of government-supported school lunches for the poor, catsup would be defined as a vegetable. Mrs. Reagan was in hot public relations water, and she needed to adopt a cause to boost her image with the public. At a meeting in the White House, Turner suggested the issue of drug abuse, pushing his, and the antipot parents' lobby, position. "Nancy was won over" (p. 162).

Early in 1982, the First Lady made a speech in Florida stressing the proparent, antidrug theme. She was an instant hit. Throughout 1983 and 1984, Mrs. Reagan continued to crisscross the country giving antidrug speeches. At a meeting in an elementary school in Oakland, Mrs. Reagan and the rest of the audience, consisting of both adults and schoolchildren, watched a NIDA-produced film in which a child was asked what he would do if he were offered drugs. "I'd say no," he replied on camera. "The phrase had been coined by the Advertising Council for a NIDA campaign the previous year, but no one had paid much attention. Now Mrs. Reagan picked up on it" (p. 174). Shortly thereafter, a club was formed to keep schoolchildren off drugs: the Just Say No Club. Early in 1985, several of the Oakland schoolchildren plus a television child star were invited to a White House antidrug event; there, the phrase "Just say no" was repeated. It caught on and gained national attention, and Mrs. Reagan's campaign suddenly shifted into warp speed. A fawning cover story published in *Time* magazine (January 14, 1985) expressed "new respect" for the First Lady. CBS, once critical of Mrs. Reagan's lavish expenditures and apparent insensitivity to human suffering, gushed with admiration over her recent adoption of a worthy, humanitarian cause. "Just Say No was on its way to becoming the most remembered phrase of the Reagan presidency" (p. 174).

Meanwhile, the federal drug treatment budget had shrunk to one-fifth of what it was in 1973, holding the value of the dollar constant. Only 20 cents of the government's drug dollar was being spent on the demand side, that is, on treatment; 80 cents went to the supply side, that is, to enforcement (p. 180). From Nixon to Ford to Reagan, drug enforcement had supplanted treatment as the federal government's number-one priority.

It is interesting that the crack epidemic exploded during the administration of Ronald Reagan, the country's most conservative, antidrug recent president. Five weeks after the meeting that launched Nancy Reagan's catchy slogan, on November 29, 1985, *The New York Times* ran a page-one headline that read: "A New Purified Form of Cocaine Causes Alarm as Abuse Increases." But public attention to crack abuse did not reach hysterical proportions until two events took place that virtually seized the country by the throat.

Len Bias, University of Maryland basketball star and the number-one pick in the draft, had just signed a long-term contract with the Boston Celtics. On the night of June 19, 1986, Bias, partying with friends, took some cocaine. The next morning, he was found in a dorm room, dead of a heart seizure, brought on, the police said, by an overdose. A week later, Don Rogers, a defensive back who played for the Cleveland Browns, also died of a cocaine overdose. The death of Bias was especially earth-shattering. "Prior to June 19, drugs had been a second-tier issue in Washington; after it, people wanted to talk about little else" (p. 182). A moral panic was launched.

In June, New York City mayor Ed Koch proposed the death penalty for any dealer convicted of possessing a kilogram (2.2 pounds) of heroin or cocaine. Two months later, New York governor Mario Cuomo called for a life sentence for anyone convicted of selling three vials of crack—at that time, roughly $50 worth of the drug. The drug problem preoccupied politicians and lawmakers at all levels of government, all "scrambling to put their imprint on the issue" (Fuerbringer, 1986). In a series of speeches delivered between June and September 1986, President Reagan called for a "nationwide crusade against drugs, a sustained, relentless effort to rid America of this scourge." He called for legislation totaling $2 billion in federal monies to fight the problem.

In September 1986, the House of Representatives approved, by a vote of 393 to 16, a package of drug law enforcement, stiffer federal sentences, and penalties for drug-producing nations that refused to cooperate in eradication programs. Called the Anti-Drug Abuse Act of 1986, this legislation introduced mandatory minimum sentences for cocaine possession. The most remarkable aspect of this bill was the 100-to-1 discrepancy between the volume of powder versus crack cocaine necessary to draw a 5- to 40-year sentence. The penalty was the same for simple possession of 5 grams of crack as for 500 grams (just over a pound) of powder cocaine. Two years later, Congress approved the Anti-Drug Abuse Act of 1988, which called for the death penalty for major traffickers as well as for anyone who, in the course of a drug felony, caused someone's death. The act also called for penalties for drug money laundering, and asset forfeiture in cases involving drug dealing. The language of the bill is just as interesting as its penalties: The phrases "hard and soft drugs" and "recreational use" should not be used, the bill stated, because "all illicit drugs are harmful" and "no drug use is recreational" (Musto, 1999, p. 278).

Public opinion went hand in hand with the passage of harsher, stiffer laws. During the debate over Reagan's 1986 drug bill, Claude Pepper, a Florida member of the House of Representatives, said cynically: "Right now, you could put an amendment through to hang, draw, and quarter," drug dealers. "That's what happens when you get an emotional issue like this," he added (Kerr, 1986). In April 1986, only 2 percent of Americans named drug abuse as the nation's number-one problem; by August, this had grown to 13 percent. The figure continued to grow until September 1989, when a whopping 64 percent of respondents in a *New York Times*/CBS News poll named drugs as the most important issue facing the nation. This is close to the most intense preoccupation of the American public on any issue in polling history. Although the prominent place of drugs as the country's most serious problem declined after 1989, the issue remained prominent, and the priority of enforcement over treatment likewise has never diminished.

Clearly, the public and legislative antidrug mood of the country was firmly in place when President Reagan left office in 1989. George H. W. Bush, Reagan's vice president, was elected to the presidency. While not nearly so conservative as Reagan, Bush maintained Reagan's emphasis on law enforcement in the drug war. Bill Clinton, a moderately liberal Democrat, was elected president in 1992 and reelected in 1996. Some observers expected him to temper drug law enforcement, increase federal funding for treatment, and perhaps even push for the decriminalization of marijuana. (Clinton admitted to having tried marijuana in his youth, but, he claimed, he "didn't inhale.") But under President Clinton's administration, federal spending to control drug abuse increased more than tenfold, from $1.5 billion in 1989 to $18.5 billion in 2000, and drug arrests grew by 400,000. In 2000, the number of persons arrested for drug violations in the United States stood at just under 1.6 million. Regardless of which administration was in office, after 1980, law enforcement remained the dominant approach to fighting drug abuse, while the treatment or public health approach was given low priority. The combination of legislative ferment and public concern that was generated in the second half of the 1980s translated into an intensification of drug law enforcement and incarceration that has continued unabated to this day.

## SUMMARY

Understanding the historical context of drug use is essential to get a clear picture of today's patterns of drug use. Especially crucial to that picture is an understanding of drug control during the past century or so, since the drug laws and their enforcement influence use.

Nineteenth-century America has been described as a "dope fiend's paradise," because for nearly its entire sweep, the distribution of psychoactive substances was unregulated and uncontrolled. Anyone could purchase and use nearly any drug, at a wide range of establishments and in a wide range of forms. Medicine at that time, primitive and ineffective, relied heavily on administering painkilling drugs. Over-the-counter patent medicines frequently contained opium, morphine, and/or cocaine, and dozens of so-called soft drinks contained significant quantities of cocaine. In addition, numerous drugs were available as purchasable products from a variety of sources, including grocery and general stories and pharmacies, and by order from catalogues. Historians estimate the number of addicts late in the nineteenth century at a figure, on a per-capita basis, as high as or possibly higher than it is today.

To collapse a century or more of the history of drug use into a couple of paragraphs, two discoveries radically transformed the nature of drug consumption around the globe; the first took place mainly in the nineteenth century, and the second mainly in the twentieth. The first discovery was the process of extracting chemical psychoactive agents from natural raw materials—for instance, cocaine from coca leaves (1859), and morphine (1803), codeine (1831), and heroin (1874) from the opium poppy. And the second was the discovery of entirely synthetic psychoactive chemicals—for instance, barbiturates (Veronal, the first barbiturate, was marketed in 1903), amphetamines (patented in 1932), and chlordiazepoxide (synthesized in 1947 and marketed as Librium in 1960).

What the development of semisynthetic and synthetic drugs has done for modern medicine is to permit administering standard, easily calibrated doses of drugs to patients. What it has done for recreational drug use is to produce and make available very nearly pure and, therefore, relative to their natural state, extremely potent, forms of drugs. As a result, certain psychoactive substances are capable both of generating stronger, more reinforcing effects and causing far more harmful effects as well.

It is important to emphasize that natural agents can be extremely potent, dangerous, and dependency producing. For example, alcohol is a chemical naturally found in fermented fruit; the distillation process, which produces drinks that are 50 or more percent pure alcohol, is simple and straightforward. The addictive property of opium has been known for hundreds, possibly thousands, of years. And the natural product leaf tobacco, if smoked, is just as dangerous today as it was centuries ago.

However, what the processes of chemical extraction and synthesis have done for the world of recreational drug use is to deliver extremely high-potency and far more dangerous and more reinforcing substances into the hands of consumers and potential consumers. Death by overdose from opium is practically unknown; death by overdose as a result of using heroin is more common than for any other drug, with the exception of the vastly more commonly used drug alcohol. Dependency on cocaine is widespread; in contrast, the use of the coca leaf, roughly 1 percent cocaine, barely qualifies as a chemical dependency. As a general rule, natural psychoactive agents are less potent, and hence less dangerous, than purer semisynthetic and synthetic substances. In addition, entirely laboratory-produced drugs require little space, and their production is not dependent on the vagaries of climate, harvest, or season; they can be produced virtually anywhere, anytime. And lastly, the production of synthetic drugs is not dependent on a social or cultural tradition of harvest; it is driven more or less by the marketplace. In a sense, then, technology has freed the illicit drug market from the usual time and place constraints that prevail in the buying and selling of natural products. With the necessary chemicals and the requisite know-how, all drug dealers need to run a successful business is customers—and they can be found virtually anywhere.

In colonial, eighteenth-, and early-nineteenth-century America, the alcohol consumption rate was more than three times higher than it is today. Early in the nineteenth century, the temperance movement began to target the free and easy consumption of alcohol. The social history of the regulation of alcohol is mixed with elements of altruism, nativism, ethnic chauvinism, racism and xenophobia, feminism, and simple, old-fashioned conservative moralism, as well as the intervention of big business. Though strong evidence suggests that alcohol consumption declined during Prohibition, that decline was bought at a very high cost—an increase in the murder rate, huge profits and an increase in power and influence for organized crime, disrespect for the law, and an increase in deaths as a result of consuming toxic substitutes. Most Americans were happy to see the end of Prohibition. But the temperance movement had spawned the effort to control a wide range of psychoactive substances, and once this ball began rolling, there seemed to be no way of stopping it.

Except for alcohol, the first drug to be regulated by law in the United States was opium. Today, historians agree that the earliest local anti-opium laws were motivated by anti-Chinese prejudice.

The Pure Food and Drug Act was the first piece of federal legislation to protect consumers from fraud; although it did not outlaw any drug per se, it moved against misbranded and adulterated foods, drinks, and drugs. It was instrumental in bringing about the downfall of the patent medicine industry and provided a model for later antidrug legislation.

Federal anti-narcotics legislation has its roots in two meetings—the Shanghai Commission and the Hague Conference. The United States engineered the meetings partly to curry trade favor with the Chinese, who wanted to fix their opium addiction problem, and partly because missionaries in China and the Philippines pressured the government to deal with the problem. Embarrassed by the fact that the United States was attempting to regulate the distribution of narcotics in other countries while it had no federal drug legislation of its own, activists influenced legislators to consider anti-narcotics legislation. Interest groups on both sides of the debate had reasons for supporting or opposing the law, but compromises resulted in the Harrison Act of 1914.

The Harrison Act was ambiguous, however; it did not so much outlaw narcotics (and cocaine) as require that sellers and purchasers of these drugs record and register their transactions and pay a tax. It was up to the Supreme Court, in a series of decisions from 1916 to the early 1920s, to *interpret* the Harrison Act as outlawing the distribution of narcotics to addicts, even by physicians for maintenance purposes. Clinics set up to dispense narcotics to addicts were all closed down by 1923. Narcotic addiction, once seen as an unfortunate illness, came to be treated as a crime. All opium, heroin, and morphine addicts were *by definition* criminals. Tens of thousands of physicians caught dispensing narcotics were arrested, and several thousand were imprisoned. Quickly, doctors abandoned their addict patients.

Two schools of thought exist concerning the Harrison Act. Some observers believe that the act made matters worse by criminalizing addiction and creating a criminal class of junkies. They propose that addiction be treated as a medical problem, that narcotics be legalized, controlled, and dispensed to junkies. But recent historical evidence calls this view into question. By the middle of the last decade of the nineteenth century, some two decades before the act, addiction had been declining as a result of improvements in medical care and more careful monitoring by physicians of the drug use of their patients. But in the two decades before the act, as the number of medical addicts was declining, the criminal addict subculture was already growing. Because of its euphoriant properties, the use of heroin in particular, marketed in 1898, was growing alarmingly, again, well before the act was passed or took effect. The act did not so much create a class of criminal addicts as it took note of the fact that criminals used narcotics, especially heroin, well before its passage. Rather than creating a class of addicts, what was happening all along was that, due to extralegal developments, the addict population was drastically changing its composition.

The federal Marihuana Tax Act was passed in 1937. It was the culmination of more than two decades of control and regulation that began in the Southwest at the local level. Most historians believe that anti-marijuana legislation had its origin in anti-Mexican prejudice. In the early 1930s, Harry Anslinger, commissioner of the federal Bureau of Narcotics, initially opposed a federal marijuana law, but public and political opinion on the matter had by 1935 changed his mind. Under the guise of a revenue measure, largely modeled after the Harrison Act, the federal government effectively banned the possession and sale of marijuana products. The Marihuana Tax Act remained in effect until passage of the Comprehensive Drug Abuse Prevention and Control Act, usually referred to as the Controlled Substances Act, in 1970.

The Controlled Substances Act superseded and replaced all federal drug legislation; it remains in effect to this day. State laws differ from federal law, but in principle, federal law takes precedence over state law. It was the Controlled Substances Act that authorized drug research, education, and treatment. But its principle arm lay in enforcement. The law created categories of "schedules" based on their supposed potential for abuse and medical utility. Schedule I drugs (marijuana, heroin, Ecstasy, methamphetamine, LSD, and GHB), according to the law, have "no medical utility," even if individual physicians decide otherwise. In effect, the law usurps expertise from the medical profession. Schedule II drugs (morphine, most amphetamines, cocaine) have medical utility but a high potential for abuse.

In spite of the fact that Richard Nixon (president 1969–1974) was very conservative, especially on matters of law and order, he was also influential in allocating federal expenditures to drug treatment rather than drug law enforcement. He was the political force behind the federal commitment to the methadone maintenance program. But when Nixon had to resign the presidency, in disgrace, as a result of the Watergate scandal in 1974, the federal emphasis on treatment was doomed.

Nixon's replacement, Gerald Ford, was indifferent to the drug issue, and Jimmy Carter, elected in 1976, found out that a liberal policy on drugs was politically dangerous. Liberal policies and attitudes that had developed in the 1970s along with higher rates of use, soon fizzled out. The "parents' movement," a staunchly anti-marijuana organization, was born in 1976 with the discovery, by an Atlanta couple, that young teenagers smoke pot. And in 1978, Carter's drug advisor, Peter Bourne, was discovered to have written a bogus prescription for Quāāludes (methaqualone) and, later, charged with having attended a party at which cocaine was present. The resignation of Bourne and, two years later, the election of Ronald Reagan (president 1981–1989) marked a watershed in the history of drug use and control in the United States. Since the 1970s, the country has moved from adopting a relatively tolerant, treatment-oriented orientation to one in which "zero tolerance" is the watchword. Enforcement has remained the centerpiece of government drug policy for a quarter century. By 1985, the federal budget for treatment had shrunk 80 percent, holding the value of the dollar constant. In that same year, only 20 percent of the federal drug dollar was being spent on treatment; 80 percent went for enforcement. The election of a liberal-centrist president, Bill Clinton in 1992, did not alter the picture. Drug arrests grew by 400,000, and the allocation of the federal dollar to law enforcement increased tenfold. We live in an era in which, to use Peter Reuter's term, the drug "hawks" are "ascendant."

## KEY TERMS

Controlled Substances
 Act   108

Department of Health and
 Human Services
 (DHHS)   108

Families in Action   113

Federal Bureau of
 Narcotics (FBN)   107

Hague Conference   101

Harrison Act   101

Marihuana Tax Act   107

National Commission on
 Marihuana and Drug
 Abuse   108

National Institute of Mental
 Health (NIMH)   110

Opium Wars   100

prohibition   95

Prohibition   98

Pure Food and Drug
 Act   100

Shanghai Commission
 101

Volstead Act   98

# DRUGS IN THE NEWS

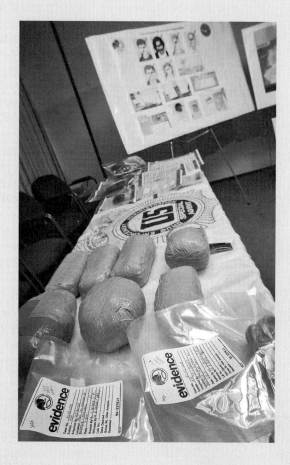

In Chapter 1, we saw that drugs and drug use can be looked at from both the objectivistic (or essentialist) and the subjectivistic (or constructionist) perspectives. Recall that the essentialist perspective focuses on drugs and drug use as materially real phenomena while the constructionist perspective looks at depictions or representations of or beliefs about drugs and drug use as well as what is done about them. In this chapter, we' examine one aspect of the social construction of drug use—how drugs are depicted in the media. The media create the reality of drugs by presenting stories about them. During a particular period, the media seize on drug use as a major social problem, stirring up public fears and concern. By focusing on the issue, the media generate talk, politicians and community organizers launch plans to control use, legislators pass laws, law enforcement arrests users in greater numbers—all, in part, because the media depict drug use in a certain way. At other times, the media present a portrait of drug use in more nuanced, more complex, and less negative, less denunciatory terms. As a result, the public, legislators, and law enforcement become less concerned about the issue. Clearly, the issue here is the *how* and *why* of drug reporting. This issue underscores the importance of the concept, so crucial throughout this book, of the social construction of reality—how the reality of drug use is constructed and, more specifically, how the media depict drug use, and with what consequences.

How do the news media depict the reality of drugs? Is it portrayed in an accurate, unbiased, and—to use an overworked word—"objective" fashion? Or is the coverage biased, unfair, and—to adopt a term used by two media critics to refer to the cocaine story— "cracked" (Reeves and Campbell, 1994)? Just as important, if bias is evident in the media's coverage of the drug story, does it influence legislation and law enforcement?

One brief digression before we plunge into the media's representation of drugs. "The media" encompass an enormous number of separate yet overlapping enterprises: newspapers and magazines; television news, drama, comedy, and documentaries; films; videotapes, CDs, and DVDs; books, both fiction and nonfiction; comic books and graphic novels; advertising of every conceivable description; government informational materials; leaflets, flyers, and solicitations; interest group propaganda; and of course, the Internet. To discuss how each and every one of these enterprises depicts drug use would require an entire book-length treatment. Here, I will focus specifically on what is regarded as news, as opposed to fictional representations. In addition, I'll concentrate mainly on the print media (magazines and newspapers), since they are more accessible to the researcher than are the broadcast media (mainly television). The depiction of drugs in the electronic media (the Internet) requires a separate treatment.

## ARE THE NEWS MEDIA BIASED?

What is "bias"? Is any assertion or argument with which someone disagrees "biased"? In the 1960s and 1970s, many Marxist criminologists accused sociologists investigating deviance and crime of bias for not supporting a socialist revolution to destroy the capitalist system (Quinney, 1979, pp. 12–14, 422). With the collapse of Marxist-inspired regimes in Eastern Europe and the downfall of Marxism as a dominant—or even a viable—intellectual, theoretical, and political framework among academics and activists around the world, the earlier charge of bias no longer seems plausible. Many fundamentalist Christians accuse scientists and the mainstream media of bias because they support the idea of the evolution of the species. Scientists argue that the evidence supports their position, asserting that it is creationists, not they, who are biased. So—who's biased? Moreover, critics who charge the American or the Western media with bias do not compare these media with those in other societies—for instance, Saudi Arabia, Nigeria, Nepal, China, Nazi Germany, or the former Soviet Union—but with journalism's own stated ideal of objectivity (Parenti, 1993).

So, once again, what is "bias"? Is it merely in the eye of the beholder? It's not as easy to determine bias as critics who charge the media with it claim. Taken as a neutral, descriptive term rather than a refusal to accept the observer's version of truth, "bias" can have at least two meanings. The first is *factual* bias—making factually and empirically false claims or assertions in order to justify a particular moral, ideological, or political position. The second is *selection* bias—focusing on facts that support a particular slant or position and ignoring those that undermine it. In principle, these two forms of bias are quite different, although in practice, they are intertwined. Let's start with the first form of bias—making factually false statements.

Journalists will say that it is their job to tell the truth about the significant and important events of the day; they will say that it is their responsibility to ensure that established interests don't shove lies down the throat of the public. They claim that they serve as a "watchdog" for the truth, that they are on the lookout for the facts, that they want to get it right.

Nearly all reporters are distressed if they are lied to by their informants, and editors become doubly so when their reporters swallow factually false tales spun by their informants and sources. Journalists say that when a story is unmasked as factually false, there are usually harmful consequences for its writer, editor, and publisher. In this chapter, we'll encounter precisely these consequences for all concerned. All reporters know the consequences of being found out to have written stories that are fabricated or factually erroneous. Any journalist whom editors and publishers find to be "error-prone" will be fired (Mencher, 1997, p. 34). Hence, journalists will emphatically deny that the news media practice factual bias.

Of course, it is also true that not all news media are equally concerned about issues of factual accuracy. The higher the prestige of a particular media institution, the more professional embarrassment factually false stories cause. Publications with very low prestige, such as the *Weekly World News*—which carries stories about Bigfoot sightings, snake tattoos coming to life, and women being raped by extraterrestrials—do not concern themselves about whether their stories have been fabricated. No one fact-checks these stories because nearly everyone in the tabloid business knows they are bogus. On the other hand, highly prestigious publications such as *The New York Times* and *The Washington Post* do care a great deal about factual accuracy and spend a great deal of money, time, and effort engaging in fact-checking.

However, this does not mean that everything in even the most highly respected newspapers and magazines is true. Given the enormous volume of factual assertions made in them every day, and the immense number of sources the press must rely on, errors inevitably slip through the cracks. (It is usually the press itself that uncovers the relatively infrequent serious factual slipups that do occur.)

But notice that what editors and publishers consider factually wrong assertions are nearly always *specific, concrete* facts—facts about events that either happened or did not happen. Editors are a great deal less distressed about big or general assertions that are based on putting together and drawing conclusions from many specific, concrete facts. Editors and publishers permit much more latitude to writers for interpretations from the facts than for the specific facts themselves. For instance, whether drug treatment is effective or ineffective can be interpreted in a variety of ways. Most researchers believe that if we agree on what we mean by "effectiveness," yes, drug treatment is at least modestly effective. (The evidence to support that assertion is presented in Chapter 14.) But enough researchers can be located and quoted to make it seem that there is disagreement in this area, and many journalists have presented the case that drug treatment is a failure. Conservative publications will welcome articles criticizing drug treatment programs even though expert consensus is that such programs work. What editors and publishers will become distressed about is when a reporter gets the specific facts wrong—for example, if a given treatment program is located in California rather than New York, or if it treats heroin addiction rather than cocaine addiction, or if it treats 100 clients, not 1,000. They will become especially distressed if a reporter makes up facts, fabricates interviews, or steals quotes from other journalists (Barry et al., 2003). But what editors and publishers will not be distressed by is errors of reasoning from the facts—big-picture conclusions or generalizations that are no less factually relevant than specific facts—since, in most cases, such errors square with the biases of the publication they work for or own.

Hence, the kind of bias we're interested in here is less an issue of factual correctness than of the slant or focus of stories based on—more or less—factually correct facts. This is our "selection" bias. Of course the media are biased—that is, they tend to present a particular angle or point of view on the events of the day. No story can present "the truth, the whole truth, and nothing but the truth." In fact, there is no such thing as the whole truth. In narrating a story, it is impossible to present each and every relevant fact about a particular phenomenon or set of events. *Some* selectivity is necessary and inevitable. The question is, what *form* does this selectivity take?

This type of bias isn't necessarily a bad thing—indeed, it is impossible to avoid—but it is important to know how it operates in the news. After all, all narrators select and focus on particular features of a phenomenon and leave others out of the picture. Yes, many news stories are a factually inaccurate representation of reality. But the most important thing about how the press handles the drug beat is their "take" or slant—how it construes and narrates their stories, what is *newsworthy* about a given story. Other institutions and entities, such the general public, criminologists, other social scientists, law enforcement personnel, politicians, lawmakers, and educators, have their own slant and construe and narrate the same phenomena, but in somewhat different ways. What is the special slant of the media, and why do they hold it?

## FOUR THEORIES OF MEDIA BIAS

Four theories that attempt to explain the direction of media slant or bias come to mind.

The first is the **ruling elitist theory** (or "top-down" theory), which argues that the media consciously and purposely serve the interests of the ruling elite. In one version of this theory, mainstream society, including representatives of the media, has been socialized to accept the ruling elite's version of truth; this is referred to as **hegemony** or **institutional dominance.** In another version of the theory, there is something of a conspiracy among members of the elite to coerce representatives of society's mainstream institutions, including the media, to accept versions of the truth that agree with their own class interests. In both versions of ruling elite theory, the media distort the truth by presenting the news in a manner that favors the ruling class, and hence maintains the status quo. Says Michael Parenti, a major advocate of this position: "We do not have a free and independent press in the United States but one that is tied by purchase and persuasion to wealthy owners and advertisers and subjected to the influence of state power" (1993, p. 4). In this theory, *ideology* is the key factor, not profits.

A related but distinctly different theory of media bias is the **money machine theory.** This perspective argues that owners of newspapers and television stations are interested in the bottom line, not political indoctrination. The "elite dominance" theory would argue that earning a profit depends on maintaining ideological hegemony, but the fact is, many ideologically motivated systems do not turn a profit. Chinese audiences avoid films attempting communist indoctrination and flock to action movies made in Hollywood—in principle, the very lair of capitalism. In addition, many profitable enterprises may, each in its own way, challenge the status quo. Top dogs—successful corporate executives, the CIA, shadowy, powerful figures pulling society's strings to their own advantage—are typically presented as villains in popular Hollywood films. In principle, profits and ideology are separate and distinct from one another. Journalists Leonard Downie, Jr., and Robert Kaiser, summing up the money machine theory, suggest that the American news media are "being degraded by pressure from the top to squeeze unrealistically high profits out of newspapers and TV news operations." They argue that news coverage "is now being cut to the demand of bottom-line zealots." Delivering a profit—and a substantial one at that—has become the guiding principle of news organizations, leading to triviality, sensationalism, bias, and irrelevancy. Stories of pollution in local waters and body bags being carted out of school busses are being turned "into gold" (Baker, 2002, pp. 4, 6; Downie and Kaiser, 2002). Meanwhile, the important stories of the day are ignored.

The third theory of media bias is the **grassroots theory** (also known as the populist or "bottom-up" theory), which argues that the press responds to the interests of the public at large by reporting stories and in ways that are appealing to their readership as a whole. Hence, it is the general public's view that determines the slant of the news. If the media can be said to have a bias, it is the bias of their audiences. The grassroots theory doesn't necessarily hold that the general public has interests that oppose or support those of the ruling class. Some views of the public at large are populist and antielitist, while others are consonant with the interests of the elite. In the grassroots theory, the elite are more or less irrelevant to shaping media content. Interestingly, this theory is not radically different from the money machine theory, since what appeals to the masses is also likely to make a profit—hence the saying "If it bleeds, it leads." Journalists refer to this slant as the "Hey, Mabel!" principle. (To be nonsexist, it could just as easily be referred to as the "Hey, Fred!" principle.) A man is sitting at the kitchen table, sipping coffee and reading the morning newspaper. He comes across an item that he finds especially remarkable. He shouts out to his wife, who's preparing breakfast, "Hey, Mabel! Listen to this!" In this case, the remarkableness of the story was a "grassroots" phenomenon: It spontaneously struck the ordinary, grassroots reader as remarkable.

The fourth theory of media bias is the **professional subculture theory.** On this view, the media approach the events of the day according to the distinct norms, expectations, and ethics of practitioners of the profession of journalism. For instance, a norm among journalists is to verify a story with two or more sources. A second is to always keep in mind the cardinal rule of journalism: "Accuracy, accuracy, accuracy" (Mencher, 1997, p. 34). A third is "Tell the story in human terms. . . . Human interest is an essential ingredient of news" (p. 51). And a fourth is shape the story with a specific audience in mind (pp. 66–67). The first two of these principles guide the journalist away from bias and toward objectivity, whereas the second two (stressing the human interest angle and keeping the audience in mind) may—and often do—contradict the norm of factual accuracy and push the journalist toward biased reporting. Hence, the media's bias, if they can be said to have one, is slanted toward the norms of reporters, editors, and publishers. It is those subcultural norms that determine the content, and hence the slant or bias, of the news.

These four theories are not mutually exclusive or contradictory in every detail. And no advocate of a given theory would argue that this view explains every single story or every single media source. There will always be exceptions to any rule. What's important is not to pick and choose examples or illustrations to verify one or another of these theories, but to determine whether one or another of them explains the basic structure and dynamics of how news in general is reported. Of course, it is entirely possible that the way the media work is a mixture of different processes spelled out by all four of these theories. Still, the question is relevant: Which of these theories *best* explains the slant the media adopt in their stories on drugs?

## SENSATIONALISM IN THE MEDIA: THE DRUG STORY

Of the many different forms of bias of which the media are accused, the one that is most directly relevant to stories on drugs is **sensationalism.** Dictionaries define "sensationalism" as intending to amaze, thrill, or excite intense reactions through the use of exaggerated, superficial, or lurid elements. The charge of sensationalism goes directly to the heart of all four of our theories of media bias—the ruling elite, the money machine, the grassroots, and the professional subculture.

Sensationalism is relevant to the ruling elite theory of media bias because, its advocates argue, sensationalistic stories divert attention away from the fundamental, structural problems of society—such as racism, inequality, and poverty—whose solution would require that the elite relinquish power and resources. When the public is fed sensationalistic stories of celebrity stalkers, road rage, crack whores, and child molesters, they tend to forget about what needs to be done to make society a more humane and just place in which to live. In other words, the media serve the function of maintaining social control—that is, preventing the masses from demanding significant, meaningful social change.

Sensationalism is clearly relevant to the money machine theory because it argues that what counts in making a profit is attracting a large audience. To be more precise, in the world of print media, especially magazine publishing, success means carrying stories and attracting ads that appeal to specialty "niche" audiences, such as those interested in skiing, interior decorating, cooking, computers, gardening, or wrestling. More specifically, it argues that attracting advertising revenue is fundamental to making a profit, and advertising flows from the size, the affluence, and the interests of specific audiences. Hence, a large audience within a specific market is a good thing. An audience need not be large for advertisers to recognize that well-placed ads in a specific media venue are likely to attract customers, and hence sales. Jaguar and Porsche advertise in the pages of *The New Yorker,* as do the St. Regis Hotel, Giorgio Armani, and Rolex—all corporations whose exclusive, expensive products or services attract customers earning a six- or seven-figure income. But, the money machine theory would argue, while affluent specialty audiences are, taken as a whole, enormously profitable, the bigger the media outlet—and hence its audience—the larger the total profit. After all, television networks (with vastly larger audiences) earn a great deal more than does *The New Yorker.* Moreover, affluent, sophisticated audiences, while they are attracted to a wide range of stories, are no less fascinated by sensationalistic stories than are larger mass audiences. In magazine publishing, then, specialization is the rule; in network television broadcasting, mass marketing is the rule, although this is changing as the large networks lose viewers to cable and satellite hookups.

Sensationalism is relevant to the grassroots theory because it addresses the fact that the general public loves an exciting story, and the more sensationalistic it is, the more it grabs an audience by the throat. To much of the grassroots populace, fact-checking is secondary; to a populist, that a story *feels* true is more important than whether it has been *verified* as true. Anyone interested in what a populist-driven publication looks like should peruse the tabloids in the supermarket checkout counter. Here, human interest, sensationalism, and a low priority on factual accuracy are dominant features.

And sensationalism is relevant to the professional subculture theory of media bias because journalists believe they have an obligation to personalize, dramatize, and individualize the news, and to approach it from the perspective of one or more relevant audiences, so that readers (and viewers) identify with their stories. Reputable media sources always walk a fine line between news as drama and news as verified fact; often, news as drama slants stories in a sensationalistic, distorted, and biased fashion. Among the more reputable and prestigious media sources (such as *The New York Times*), the norm of factual accuracy will dampen sensationalism; among less prestigious media sources (such as the *Weekly World News*), the norm of personalization will permit sensationalism to run wild.

Do the media sensationalize stories on drug use? Do they exaggerate a moderately threatening situation into a far graver, more ominous threat? Do they emphasize lurid details? Through the use of a biased selection and presentation of the facts, do they lead audiences to false conclusions? Sensationalism comes in a variety of forms in the phenomenon of drug use, including exaggerating the number of people engaged in the behavior, the amount of harm the behavior causes, and the number of victims who are harmed; advocating the "enslavement" theory of the behavior ("once you start, you can't stop"); claiming that all social groups and classes are equally at risk for engaging in the behavior, that it is randomly distributed in the population rather than socially patterned; claiming that victimization is random rather than socially patterned, that everyone in the society has an equal chance of becoming a victim of the offending behavior; implying that drastic, harsh, draconian measures are necessary to deal with the offending behavior, that "lock 'em up and throw away the key" is the only solution.

## NEW DRUGS IN THE MEDIA: VIOLENCE, INSANITY, AND GENETIC DAMAGE

When a previously unknown drug begins to be used on a widespread basis, or a drug begins to be taken by a group in the population that had not previously used it, the media all too often indulge in sensationalistic reports of this brand-new "scary drug of the year" (Akers, 1990). The details are different, but the common element is the hysteria generated over the use of a novel substance, initially believed to be far more harmful than it eventually turns out to be. More specifically, new drugs are usually, although not always, attributed with a *criminogenic* effect—that is, it is believed that they cause violence and crime.

Even though the subject of the stories—that is, the specific drug that is the focus of media stories—changes, the structure of news reporting has remained the same. A few untoward episodes, whether alleged or real, are presented as if they were the *paradigmatic* (typical, characteristic) experience with this new drug. In the heat of a drug panic or scare, such episodes come to be regarded as *summary* events, representing or standing in for the experience most or many users have with the substance. The worst-case scenario is depicted as if it were common, even typical. This pattern has prevailed for over a century, beginning with alcohol, opium, and cocaine in the nineteenth and early twentieth centuries. And it was true for marijuana in the 1930s, LSD in the 1960s, PCP in the 1970s, crack cocaine in the 1980s, and methamphetamine beginning in the 1980s and extending into the twenty-first century.

### Marijuana in the 1930s

"An entire family was murdered by a youthful [marijuana] addict," claimed a typical—and very famous—article published in the 1930s, authored by the commissioner of the Federal Bureau of Narcotics (FBN). "When officers arrived at the home, they found the youth staggering about in a human slaughterhouse." The boy was "pitifully crazed." The cause? Marijuana! (Anslinger and Cooper, 1937, p.19). As it turns out, the young man was mentally ill *before* using marijuana, but this fact was conveniently overlooked in this sensationalistic story.

The 1930s was an interesting era in the history of drug use and legislation, as we saw in Chapter 4. Beginning in 1934, the FBN lobbied each state to adopt the Uniform Narcotic Drugs Act. (In the early 1930s, interestingly enough, the FBN had resisted proposals to criminalize marijuana [Himmelstein, 1983, p. 57].) In order to generate public and legislative support for this act, it had to "conjure up the specter of a marihuana 'menace'" (p. 59). Once committed to this cause, the FBN launched a moral crusade against the drug. "Policymakers and the media faithfully adopted the bureau's image of marihuana, repeating [its] examples of marihuana-related violence and ignoring the data that the bureau chose to ignore. . . . Marihuana was believed to be not just dangerous but a menace. Its . . . effects on consciousness were said to lead . . . to a maniacal frenzy in which the user was likely to commit all kinds of unspeakable crimes" (p. 59).

In an analysis of the articles on marijuana published in popular magazines between 1935 and 1940, Himmelstein found that 95 percent depicted the drug as "dangerous," and 85 percent specifically mentioned violence as an effect of its use; 73 percent regarded moderate use as impossible (1983, pp. 60–67). "Addicts [meaning marijuana 'addicts'] may often develop a delirious rage during which they are temporarily and violently insane," stated Harry Anslinger, the FBN's chief during the 1930s; "this insanity may take the form of a desire for self-destruction or a persecution complex to be satisfied only by the commission of some heinous crime" (Anslinger and Cooper, 1937, p. 150). Violence was the central guiding principle of the media's depiction of marijuana's effects. "In short," says Himmelstein, "nearly every effect imputed to marihuana was also linked to violence and was interpreted in its light. Insanity, destruction of the will, suggestibility, distortions of perception, and alterations of consciousness all carried the connotations of violence and crime. The image of the violent criminal tied these disparate effects together and gave them coherence" (1983, p. 65).

Marijuana does not cause or induce users to violence, of course, as an examination of the scientific literature will tell you. By the 1960s, anti-marijuana propagandists and the media quietly dropped the violence theme, and instead emphasized almost exactly the opposite effect—passivity. In short, between the 1930s and the 1960s, marijuana was transformed "from killer weed to dropout drug" (Himmelstein, 1983, pp. 121ff). Nonetheless, Harry Anslinger used his atrocity-oriented articles on marijuana in popular magazines as a bully pulpit from which to argue for the passage of the Uniform Narcotic Drugs Act. In the mid-1930s, only 10 states had passed the act. But by 1937, all of the then-48 states had enacted an anti-marijuana law, and the federal government had approved the Marihuana Tax Act. Harry Anslinger's media-driven campaign to convince the public of the "menace" of marijuana was successful, and his effort to criminalize the possession and sale of marijuana was a complete triumph.

## LSD in the 1960s

"Under the influence of LSD," read a June 17, 1966, article in *Time* magazine, "nonswimmers think they can swim, and others think they can fly. One young man tried to stop a car . . . and was killed. A magazine salesman became convinced that he was the Messiah. A college dropout committed suicide by slashing his arm and bleeding to death in a field of lilies." Prior to 1967, the media theme for LSD's effects was psychosis. The danger posed by users of LSD was not so much crime and violence against others but insanity and self-destruction. The pre-1967 media stories conveyed a distinct impression that anyone who ingested LSD stood an unwholesomely strong likelihood of losing one's mind—temporarily and possibly even for good.

The effects of LSD were described in the media as "nightmarish"; "terror and indescribable fear" were considered common, even routine. *Life* magazine ran a cover story on March 25, 1966, titled "The Exploding Threat of the Mind Drug That Got Out of Control." Psychic terror, uncontrollable impulses, unconcern for one's own safety, psychotic episodes, delusions, illusions, hallucinations, and impulses leading to self-destruction—these themes fueled the early articles on the use of LSD.

As sensationalistic as these magazine articles were, those published in newspapers were even more lurid, sensationalistic, and one-sided. While magazine stories usually qualified their scare stories by saying that not everyone "freaked out" when they took the drug, newspaper articles rarely offered such qualification. Newspaper headlines trumpeted stories such as "Mystery of Nude Coed's Fatal Plunge," "Thrill Drug Can Warp Minds and Kill," "Strip-Teasing Hippie Goes Wild on LSD," and "LSD: For the Kick That Can Kill"

(Braden, 1970). Public hysteria at the time was summed up in the statement by the New Jersey Narcotic Drug Study Commission in 1966. LSD, the Commission declared, "is the greatest threat facing the country today" (Brecher et al., 1972, p. 369).

Today, as measured by Drug Abuse Warning Network (DAWN) data on untoward, or sudden and undesirable, emergency department (ED) episodes, LSD's role in causing panic or psychotic reactions is minuscule. In 2002, DAWN recorded only 891 LSD-related episodes requiring medical intervention. This is only a bit more than 0.01 percent of all ED episodes. And, based on the total number of users and the average number of times the drug is taken, this is 1 untoward LSD episode out of 10,000 incidents of use. (Keep in mind, however, that DAWN is not complete in its enumeration of all untoward drug episodes.) In other words, today, ingesting LSD hardly ever leads to the kinds of extreme episodes widely reported in the media in the 1960s.

Why the discrepancy? One possible explanation is that the media seized upon and reported the very small number of untoward LSD-related episodes that did take place and ignored the immense volume of peaceful experiences that users had with the drug. Another possible explanation is that, over time, users learned to handle the novel, strange, and unsettling LSD experiences they had, and hence no longer "freaked out" under the drug's influence (Becker, 1967). In any case, it's clear that the media were guilty of sensationalistic coverage of the effects of LSD in the 1960s. Certainly, the fact that LSD does not typically cause untoward effects has not received the same amount of attention that was given to the story that it did. Once again, media bias rears its ugly head. Clearly, in the context of the 1960s, LSD "freak-outs" were news; the story that LSD does *not* cause psychotic outbreaks was *not* news.

In March 1967, the prestigious scientific journal *Science* published an article about the research of a geneticist and two associates, who found that when human blood cells were placed in a culture containing LSD the cells underwent some chromosome breakage. In addition, one schizophrenic mental patient who was treated with LSD 15 times in a therapeutic setting was found to have a higher-than-normal rate of chromosome breakage (Cohen, Marinello, and Back, 1967).

Within 24 hours, news of the study had swept the country like wildfire. The findings from this research report were somehow translated into the inescapable fact that LSD would damage one's offspring. News stories intimated that if youths began taking the drug, uncountable generations of infants would be born deformed. Numerous articles in popular magazines appeared, explaining that the drug would cause genetic mutations and birth defects. "If you take LSD, even once," intoned an August 1967 article in *Look* magazine, "your children may be born malformed or retarded." Just below the title of this article was this statement: "New research finds it's causing genetic damage that poses a threat of havoc now and abnormalities for generations yet unborn" (Davison, 1967, pp. 19–22).

An indication of how seriously these early findings were taken is the fact that even in the decidedly pro-marijuana underground newspapers, such as *The East Village Other* (*EVO*), a number of articles appeared during the summer of 1967 affirming that genetic damage would take place in anyone who ingested LSD. One such article published in *EVO* was titled "Acid Burned a Hole in My Genes." Antidrug propaganda campaigns rarely failed to mention LSD's supposedly "monster-producing" properties. The National Foundation–March of Dimes distributed a leaflet containing photographs of deformed, legless, or armless children pitifully attempting to perform simple tasks such as writing or picking up toys with their flipperlike limbs or artificial hands or feet. The text contained the warning that "there is evidence that LSD and other similar drugs may cause chromosome damage." Though the leaflet included the qualification that "there is no proof that chromosome breaks cause birth defects in humans," the impact of the photographs was so devastating that the caveat was completely lost on readers.

As it turns out, the media seized on the *Science* article, broadcasting its findings as if they were clear-cut evidence of LSD's harmful effects on human chromosomes. Just four years later, a team of four scientists conducted an exhaustive survey of the findings reported in nearly 100 scientific papers on the subject of LSD and genetic damage (Dishotsky et al., 1971). These researchers concluded: "We believe that pure LSD ingested in moderate dosages does not produce chromosome damage detectable by available methods." Clearly, the media stories reporting that the drug caused damage to human chromosomes were a premature rush to judgment. Interestingly, the story that LSD does not damage chromosomes was not given the fanfare accorded the earlier stories that it does.

In short, the panic generated by the early use of LSD led many reporters and journalists to find plausible the conclusions of a shoddy piece of research that supposedly indicated that the drug is harmful. Had the same findings been published on the effects of alcohol, hardly anyone would have written stories about it. Given that, in the context of the 1960s, the subject of the article was LSD, the findings that the drug had horrendous effects made the story newsworthy and believable. It is out of the raw material of (1) the introduction of a new drug into the society, (2) claims of unusual, damaging effects, and (3) a resultant panic or scare that sensationalism in the media is born.

Media attention to LSD triggered—or at least preceded—criminal legislation. The federal Drug Abuse Control Amendments, which penalized the manufacture and sale of hallucinogens, including LSD (along with barbiturates and amphetamines), was passed in 1965 and became effective in 1966. In May 1966, Sandoz, the only pharmaceutical company to manufacture LSD, withdrew the drug from the market. In 1966, California and New York passed laws criminalizing LSD. In 1968, the Drug Control Amendments were revised, rendering the sale of LSD a felony and its possession a misdemeanor. And in 1970, the Controlled Substances Act declared LSD a Schedule I drug, indicating that it had a high potential for abuse and no medical utility. Possession of LSD for personal use calls for a one-year penalty; possession with intent to sell calls for a maximum of five years' imprisonment. Since 1970, nearly all the states have adopted their own version of the federal act, and for a number of them, penalties are even more severe than under the federal law. For example, in New York State, possession of LSD with intent to sell brings a prison term of up to seven years (Grinspoon and Bakalar, 1979, p. 310). Whether intentionally or unwittingly, the media hysteria led to criminal legislation penalizing the possession and sale of LSD.

## PCP in the 1970s

PCP, or phencyclidine (whose trade names are Sernyl and Sernylan), is an animal tranquilizer and anesthetic, whose use is not medically approved for humans. PCP began to be used illegally on the street in substantial numbers in the second half of the 1970s. During that period, the media devoted enormous attention to the drug and its effects. Two researchers examined 323 newspaper and 23 magazine articles, as well as a number of television news broadcasts and dramas on the use of PCP (Morgan and Kagan, 1980). Most of the coverage of PCP took place in the single year 1978; after that, the number of stories dropped off sharply.

Media accounts of PCP were extremely narrowly focused. In a quarter of the newspaper articles, "violent or shocking themes" predominated, and in one, an especially gruesome story appeared. In 1971, a Baltimore student named Charles Innis blinded himself in jail. This real-life event served as the inspiration for 17 newspaper articles in which a person under the influence of PCP gouged out his or her eyes. The story also appeared in 7 out of the 23 magazine articles on the horrors of PCP and in a large number of television broadcasts. The identity of the person who supposedly committed this horrific act of self-mutilation changed from story to story. In one, the victim was a woman, arrested for assault, who gouged out her eyes in jail; in another, a young man, arrested for indecent exposure, gouged out his eyes in prison; in still other versions, he was (correctly) a Baltimore college student, the son of a Massachusetts congressman, a man from a midwestern city, and a man from San Jose (Morgan and Kagan, 1980, p. 197). These different identifications suggest that the tale, though based on an initially true event, is as much an urban legend as a real-life event. It became a story that was a little "too good to be true" (Brunvand, 1999), moving "from anecdote to apocrypha" (Morgan and Kagan, 1980, p. 201). Years after the supposed event, the story is "exhumed, polished and transformed into part of the PCP mythology" (p. 202).

In the other "horror stories," a "nude, unarmed man refuses to halt on police command" and is killed "after [a] varying number of bullets are fired" (13 stories); a "person drowns in [a] shower stall with four inches of water" (12 stories); a "young man shoots and kills [his] own father, mother and grandfather" (9 stories); a "person sits engulfed in flames, unable to perceive danger" (9 stories); a "person amputates a bodily part: [a] nose, breast or penis" (9 stories); a "man crosses [an] eight lane freeway, enters a house, randomly stabs [a] pregnant woman and toddler" (8 stories); a person "pulls out [his or her] own teeth with pliers" (7 stories). And so on. The theme in each of these stories was that, under the influence of PCP, the user became deranged, psychotic, and completely unconcerned for his or her safety, and engaged in horrific self-destructive and/or violent behavior (Morgan and Kagan, 1980).

Fictionalized television dramas made especially strong use of this "mindless violence and self-destructive acts" theme. In one, a young woman, attempting to evade her pursuers, tries to fly off the roof of a building. In another, the "strength and invincibility" of a PCP-high youth is stressed. In yet another, the police have to fire "multiple bullets" into the user's body to halt his advance. In still another, a young man, high on the drug, breaks the handcuffs and leg shackles used to restrain him.

The way the PCP story is reported in the media bears strong parallels with how other drugs are covered. According to Morgan and Kagan:

> Every new drug experience in America is handled in a stereotypical fashion by the media. Emphasis is placed on individual tales of dangerous, criminal or self-destructive behavior by the drug-crazed. The myth is newly erected and slightly embellished with each new drug, and the stories come to resemble the myths, ballads and folk-tales previously generated and transformed by oral transmission. Indeed, the best model seems to be the Frankenstein monster who advances impervious to pain, bullets and . . . fire in order to murder, dismember or bugger men, women, children and the household pets. The myths are compelling because they touch

an emotional core that has meaning in the individual and the culture, and they exploit our fascination with horror. . . . The monster must die bizarrely: drowning in inches of water, attempting to fly from a building or trying to halt a speeding two-ton vehicle with its bare hands or body. If it lives it should commit the most . . . meaningful of self-mutilations–removal of the eyes or castration. These tales are the archetypical expressions of human inner terrors and exist in the preserved ballads and epic tales of most languages. (p. 201)

Were some of the anecdotes narrated in the news about persons who, high on the newly introduced drug, committed terrible acts of violence and self-destruction, actually true? Almost certainly! But "myth feeds on fact nearly as well as it feeds on fancy" (p. 201). The fact is, PCP *is* extremely dangerous, very possibly the most dangerous currently used drug in the United States. But in the 1970s, the horrifying effects attendant upon use of this drug were sometimes fabricated—and nearly always exaggerated. In 2002, DAWN reported 7,648 PCP-related ED episodes, indicating that it isn't quite as harmful as the media said or, as with LSD, that the subculture of users has learned to deal with its bizarre effects (p. 203). One study estimated that in the late 1970s, out of the roughly 20 million instances of use experienced each year by some 300,000 regular users, only about 5,000–6,000 resulted in such unpleasant or life-threatening effects that they required a trip to an emergency room—approximately 0.03 percent of all such episodes (Newmeyer, 1980, pp. 214–215).

It is easy to see that the media sensationalized PCP use and exaggerated the most extreme effects of the drug to the point at which what is actually unusual and atypical is described as common and routine. While the user does take a certain psychological and physical risk by ingesting PCP, and while that risk is probably higher than it is for any other illicit drug currently in use, at the doses that are usually taken, the risk is quite small. Once again, we have this formula: New drug equals media sensationalism. And just as new drug equals media sensationalism, media sensationalism leads to criminalization.

## Crack in the 1980s

Beginning in late 1985, a substantial number of Americans began using an old drug in a new form. On November 17 of that year, in what was the first mention of this drug in the mass media, *The New York Times* journalist Donna Boundy described a substance referred to as "crack" as "rock-like pieces of prepared 'freebase' (concentrated) cocaine." Crack is neither freebase nor concentrated, but the brief piece was the first in an avalanche of over 1,000 stories that appeared in the media in less than a year. In the following year, two major television stories, CBS's "48 Hours on Crack Street" and NBC's "Cocaine Country," were broadcast. Within six months, over 400 television broadcasts on the same topic were aired. Crack became what is probably the biggest drug story of all time (Inciardi, 2002, pp. 145–146).

Just as previous media constructions of drugs focused on a core theme, the earliest stories on crack concentrated on a theme: the drug's supposed addictive property. A March 17, 1986, *Newsweek* article quoted one drug expert as saying, "Crack is the most addictive drug known to man." Smoking the drug, he said, produces "instantaneous addiction. Try it once and you're hooked! Once you start, you can't stop!" Using crack, claimed a June 16, 1986, *Newsweek* story, immediately hurls the user into "an inferno of craving and despair."

A theme in media stories about crack that emerged slightly later than the addiction theme emphasized that the use of crack was becoming widespread and threatened to turn into a virtual "tidal wave" of substance abuse. Crack now "infested" every community and group in the country, these stories announced, and had become a "plague" comparable to the Black Death in fourteenth-century Europe. The use of metaphors and mental images often leads audiences to think about something in a particular way. The common use of the term "plague" to refer to the emergence of a new drug in general, and to crack use in the second half of the 1980s in particular, is especially revealing (Reinarman and Levine, 1997, pp. 33–36). When, in 1986, both *Newsweek* and *U.S. News & World Report* compared the devastation of illicit drug use to that of medieval plagues; in effect, readers were being asked to regard substance abuse as a catastrophe of unimaginable proportions.

In the sixth century, the bubonic plague killed about 100 million people in Europe and the Middle East. In the fourteenth century, the bubonic plague returned as the "Black Death," killing roughly a third of the population of Europe—about 75 million people. Each of these episodes came and went in a matter of a couple of years. Since the use of *all* illicit drugs in the United States is associated with a total of no more than 25,000 deaths a year, the comparison seems remarkably biased, twisted—indeed, one is tempted to say, sensationalistic. Even cigarette use (which kills 440,000 smokers in the United States each year) and alcohol consumption (which kills 85,000 annually) are positively benign in comparison with the medieval plagues.

A third theme found in the media made the claim that not only was crack use becoming "pervasive" and "universal," it had become as common among the educated, middle-class sectors of the society as among unemployed, poverty-stricken school dropouts. In its March 17, 1986, issue, *Newsweek* proclaimed that crack "is rapidly spreading into the suburbs." Three days later, *The New York Times* stated that crack was spreading from the inner cities to "the wealthiest suburbs of Westchester county." Said a representative of the New Jersey Health Department, "It's all over the place." On June 8, the *Times* ran a story that proclaimed "Crack Addiction Spreads Among the Middle Class." Three weeks later, the *Times* announced the "growing use of crack" in several suburban counties; in them, the newspaper stated, the "per capita use of cocaine is the heaviest in the state." On August 11, referring to crack use, *Newsweek* declared that "nearly everyone now concedes that the plague is all but universal" (Reinarman and Levine, 1997, pp. 3–4).

And the fourth theme that emerged in the media to capture the reality of crack use was the "crack baby" phenomenon. Between 1989 and 1991, following the publication of several medical reports, a flood of news stories indicated that if pregnant women smoked crack (or used powder cocaine—the distinction was never made clear), their children would be born with a range of neurological and anatomical defects. These children would be permanently impaired, these stories indicated, and would cost the society many billions of dollars in hospital bills, remedial educational programs, and, ultimately, other immense expenses associated with criminal offenses and incarceration. It became an established fact that crack babies represented a major social and medical problem.

William Bennett, then federal drug "czar," claimed that in the late 1980s, 375,000 crack babies were born each year—1 out of 10 of all births! This figure was echoed by respected *Washington Post* columnist Jack Anderson and *New York Times* editor A. M. Rosenthal (Gieringer, 1990). The cost of medical care of crack babies, stated one of the most widely quoted articles to appear in a mass magazine on the subject, is 13 times as expensive as that of normal newborns—$7,000 versus just under $500 (Toufexis, 1991). The fear was that these youngsters would become "an unmanageable multitude of disturbed and disruptive youth. Fear that they will be a lost generation" (p. 56). A Pulitzer Prize–winning journalist described the crack baby crisis in dramatic, heart-wrenching prose: "The bright room is filled with baby misery: babies born months too soon; babies weighing little more than a hardcover book; babies that look like wizened old men in the last stages of a terminal illness, wrinkled skin clinging to chicken bones; babies who do not cry because their mouths and noses are full of tubes. . . . The reason is crack" (Quindlen, 1990, p. E19). According to common media wisdom in the late 1980s, crack cocaine use among pregnant women caused serious—in all likelihood, irreparable—medical problems in babies. This condition was extremely widespread, we learned from the news, and would be extremely costly to the society.

What of these four media crack themes—universal addiction; widespread use; use as great in the middle class as among poor, inner-city residents; and devastating, irreparable harm to children born to crack-using expectant mothers, or the so-called crack baby syndrome? Were these assertions actually true?

First, crack never became a popular drug, even at its height of use. And after the early 1990s, its use declined rather sharply. According to the Monitoring the Future survey, even at its peak no more than 5 percent of American high school seniors had even tried the drug, and only 0.1–0.2 percent had used it in the prior 30 days. (Of course, let's remember, this survey does not include dropouts and absentees.) According to the National Survey on Drug Use and Health, in 2005, only 0.5 percent of respondents ages 12–17 had even tried crack, and only 0.1 percent had used it in the prior 30 days. In 1992, just after crack's use peaked, only 0.6 percent of 12- to 17-year-olds, 3.2 percent of 18- to 25-year-olds, 3.3 percent of 26- to 34-year-olds, and 0.4 percent of persons ages 35 and older said that they had *ever* used the drug—even once. Statistics on use in the past year for these four groups were 0.3, 1.1, 0.9, and 0.1 percent, respectively. In other words, this "tidal wave" of use never developed. Crack never became a drug of widespread use, and most users experimented with the drug, then stopped using it.

The fact is, precisely the opposite of widespread use was the case. Crack use was, and remains, anything but universal. In addition, not only did—and does—a very small proportion of the population use the drug, but its use tends to be very strongly patterned according to social class and education. The higher up on the occupational and educational ladder, the lower the likelihood that one will use crack cocaine; the lower one is on this continuum, the higher that likelihood is. Crack use is relatively rare—although it does exist—among middle-class, suburban youngsters. Its use tends to be concentrated mainly in poverty-stricken, inner-city communities. There are plenty of exceptions to this rule, but as a pattern, this generalization is sound.

Going back to the 1992 National Household Drug Abuse Survey, among 18- to 25-year-olds, the percentage who had at least tried crack was 7 percent of high school dropouts, 3 percent high school graduates, 1.6 percent of those with some college, and only 0.6 percent of college graduates. In other words, as education increased, the likelihood of crack use decreased. The same pattern prevails for the older age categories, for more frequent use, and for later and earlier surveys as well. In other words, the media's claim that crack abuse was as common in the middle-class suburbs as in the inner cities was bogus.

What about the "crack baby syndrome"? To be fair to the media, the views expressed reflected the opinions of the researchers who published the early articles in the medical literature. However, even in the late 1980s, a few experts were challenging the veracity of the crack baby stories. But it was not until the early 1990s that enough medical evidence was assembled to indicate that the crack baby syndrome is, in all likelihood, mythical in nature. By 2001, in an article published in the most prominent medical journal in the country, the *Journal of the American Medical Association (JAMA),* a panel of experts, summarizing the entire research literature on the subject, concluded that there is "no consistent negative association between prenatal cocaine exposure and physical growth, developmental test scores, or receptive or expressive language" (Frank et al., 2001, p. 1613). The problem with the earlier studies, these researchers argued, was that they had no controls—that is, they did not sort out the many other factors that could have caused impairment, such as cigarette smoking, alcoholism, inadequate or nonexistent medical care, the use of other drugs, and poor diet. Mainstream medical opinion now holds that these other factors caused the medical problems observed in the late 1980s and early 1990s. In all likelihood, they were not caused by their mother's ingestion of cocaine. In short, it is entirely possible that the crack baby issue was a hysteria-driven rather than a fact-driven syndrome.

Interestingly, while the media were quick to pick up on and publicize the early research that seemed to show that powder and crack cocaine caused medical problems in newborns, infants, and school-age children, very little media attention was devoted to correcting this—in all likelihood—mistaken view. One rare exception was *Boston Globe* columnist Ellen Goodman (1992). Wrote Goodman: "It turns out that 'crack babies' may be a creature of the imagination as much as medicine, a syndrome seen in the media more often than in medicine." Dr. Ira Chasnoff, whose work originally pointed in the direction of indicating problems for these children, was quoted by Goodman as saying, "Their average developmental functioning level is normal. They are no different from other children growing up." According to Dr. Clair Coles, another researcher cited by Goodman, the crack baby story became a "media hit" in part because crack is not used by "people like us," that is, well-educated, middle-class people who constitute the principal audience for the majority of the print media (Goodman, 1992). "Why all the hullabaloo about crack babies?" asked Dr. Wendy Chavkin in a commentary on the Frank et al. (2001) summary of the available medical literature. Crack babies, she argued, "have become a convenient symbol for an aggressive war on drug users because of the implication that anyone who is selfish enough to irreparably damage an innocent child for the sake of a quick high deserves retribution. This image, promoted by the mass media, makes it easier to advocate a simplistic punitive response than to address the complex causes of drug use" (Chavkin, 2001, p. 1627).

How did the media's coverage of the crack story influence drug laws? Drug bills and drug legislation followed in the wake of the 1980s media panic over drug use generally and crack abuse specifically: In a series of speeches between June and September 1986, President Ronald Reagan called for a "nationwide crusade against drugs, a sustained, relentless effort to rid America of this scourge." His proposed legislation added $2 billion in federal funds to fight the problem, including $56 million for drug testing of federal employees. In September 1986, the House of Representatives approved, by an overwhelming vote of 393 to 16, a package of drug law enforcement measures, stiffer federal sentences, and penalties against drug-producing countries that did not cooperate with U.S.-sponsored drug eradication programs. Approved by the Senate in October 1986, the drug bill, ultimately costing $1.7 billion, was signed into law by President Reagan. In it, a death penalty provision (unlikely ever to be carried out) was included for drug kingpins. Except for some antidrug provisions enacted in 1984, the 1986 legislation represented the first effort by Congress in

15 years to enact a major antidrug law. Much the same was happening at the state level all over the country (Goode and Ben-Yehuda, 1994, pp. 208–209). In addition, it was the crack baby stories that inspired the many court interpretations, beginning in 1989, that pregnant women could be convicted of delivering a drug to a minor, that is, the fetus they were carrying. In addition, in 1986, the federal Anti-Drug Abuse Act was passed, which dictated that the same ten-year penalty be imposed for the possession of 50 grams of crack cocaine as for the possession of 5,000 grams of powder cocaine. "Crack cocaine is the only drug for which there exists a mandatory minimum penalty for a first offense of simple possession" (Kennedy, 1997, p. 364). Almost certainly, the media hysteria surrounding drugs—and more specifically, crack cocaine—was instrumental in the punitive legislation that followed.

## Methamphetamine in the Late 1980s and After

Beginning in the late 1980s, the media began reporting on a terrifying epidemic of a new form of an old drug—metaphetamine. The drug was sweeping the country "like wildfire." Within a few short years, the United States would be "awash" in "ice"—recrystalized methamphetamine sulfate. Methamphetamine was, according to the media in the late 1980s, the drug of choice for a "new generation." Methamphetamine would replace heroin, cocaine, and even marijuana as the nation's premier problematic drug. Law enforcement was put on notice; "crystal meth," "crank," "crystal," or "glass" (other terms for illicit methamphetamine sulfate) was the drug to watch for. Or so the media announced in the late 1990s (Lerner, 1989; Young, 1989). But the media drumbeat to the meth epidemic did not fizzle out, as it did for PCP and LSD; it continued well into the 2000s. Between October 2004 and March 2006, *The Oregonian* ran a series of over 250 stories on the horrors of methamphetamine. Steve Suo, the key reporter in these stories, became the chief advisor for the Public Broadcasting System's sensationalistic 2006 broadcast "The Meth Epidemic." In its cover story of August 8, 2005, *Newsweek* proclaimed methamphetamine "America's Most Dangerous Drug."

To make the public acutely aware of the dangers of meth, some members of the press quoted officials who compared methamphetamine with crack cocaine. "Meth makes crack look like child's play," declared one law enforcement officer to veteran *New York Times* reporter Fox Butterfield, "in terms of what it does to the body and how hard it is to get off" (Butterfield, 2004). "It makes the crack epidemic of the '80s look like kids eating candy" (Williams, 2006), said another law enforcement official to a South Carolina reporter. In neither case did the official present any corroboration or empirical evidence of his claim; in a climate of fear, a mere assertion, it seems, is sufficient. The public's—largely distorted—knowledge of crack became a measuring rod against which to compare the new drug menace. And like crack cocaine, methamphetamine was said to be instantly addicting. Asserted a Milwaukee law enforcement official: "If you use it once, you'll become an addict" (Zielinski, 2005).

In addition to methamphetamine's supposed cracklike addictive properties, news stories stressed the drug's inexorable spread from coast to coast and up the socioeconomic ladder. On December 31, 2004, *The Oregonian* ran a story titled "East Coast Horror Stories Reflect New Map of Meth," implying that communities east of the Mississippi had been invaded by methamphetamine and were now as swamped as those in the West and Midwest.

The *Newsweek* story proclaimed that the drug not only had "marched across the country" but also had moved "up the socioeconomic ladder" (Jefferson, 2005). The implication of the story was that the meth epidemic was so widespread that it was not confined to poverty-stricken rural whites but could also strike a "good" family "with two children, a six-figure income, a dog and a Volvo in the garage" (King, 2006, p. 17).

As we'll see in more detail in Chapter 10, on the stimulants, as of the first decade of the 2000s, methamphetamine remains a regionalized drug—it has not "invaded" the East Coast to any appreciable degree; its use and abuse levels remain below that of at least a half-dozen more commonly used illicit drugs; use rates have not risen in the past half-dozen years or so; and among high school students, its use has actually declined somewhat (King, 2006, pp. 2–3). Make no mistake about it: Methamphetamine is a harmful, dangerous drug. It is one of the most dependency-producing drugs known to humanity, and its abuse causes a wide range of medical pathologies. But most of the claims of the hysteria-driven news stories—including its "instantly addicting" property, its widespread use nationwide, its invasion of all communities, and a recent massive increase in its use and abuse, not to mention huge increases in overdose deaths—have turned out to be false. As a result of these media exaggerations, a media "boomerang" took place, with dozens of stories refuting these original claims (Shafer, 2005, 2006; Valdez, 2006).

## STORYTELLING VERSUS FACTUAL ACCURACY: THE JANET COOKE SAGA

At the same time that journalists seek to tell an interesting, dramatic, and personal story, they are enjoined by their professional ethics to "get it right," that is, to tell stories that cannot be unmasked as conventionally and factually false. Perhaps the classic drug-related case of the clash between telling "one hell of a good story" and adhering to the professional ethic of journalism is the saga of reporter Janet Cooke.

On September 28, 1980, *The Washington Post* ran a feature story titled "Jimmy's World," which detailed the horrifying life of an 8-year-old heroin addict (Cooke, 1980). Jimmy, claimed Cooke, had been an addict since age 5. His mother, repeatedly raped by her mother's boyfriend, had become pregnant with Jimmy. Using heroin to obliterate her anguish, she had turned to prostitution to pay for her habit. Unconcerned with Jimmy's use of narcotics, she allowed Ron, her live-in boyfriend, to routinely inject the boy with heroin, "plunging a needle into his bony arm, sending the fourth grader into a hypnotic nod." Cooke claimed that heroin had "become part of life" among inner-city residents; its use, she wrote, was "filtering down to untold numbers of children like Jimmy who are bored with school and battered by life."

The publication of Cooke's article created a sensation. Marion Barry, then mayor of Washington DC, became so incensed by the story that he assigned hundreds of police officers and social workers to find Jimmy. They combed the city for three weeks, enlisting teachers, searching through the housing projects, even threatening Cooke with a subpoena to locate and "save" the boy from the morass of addiction. But *The Washington Post* refused to cooperate with Barry, citing the First Amendment rights of reporters to protect their sources.

Six months later, in April 1981, Janet Cooke was awarded the prestigious Pulitzer Prize in Feature Writing for "Jimmy's World." However, the attention the prize focused on the story's author turned into the harsh glare of a spotlight that ultimately exposed the story as a fraud. The editors of *The Toledo Blade,* Cooke's previous employer, asked the *Post* for the rights to reprint the story. When the *Post* editors sent the Toledo paper the résumé she had submitted to them, the *Blade* editors, knowing her actual educational and occupational background, realized that Cooke had given the Washington paper certain biographical particulars they knew to be false. For instance, Cooke claimed to have graduated from Vassar College, to have studied at the Sorbonne, to have a master's degree, to be fluent in four languages, and to have won a number of regional journalism awards. Editors at the *Blade* called the Associated Press, and before long, the editors of the *Post* were appraised of these discrepancies.

After grilling her, the *Post*'s editors, realizing that Cooke's résumé had been fabricated, began questioning the veracity of her "Jimmy's World" story. After repeatedly denying it, finally Cooke broke down, admitting that the story had been "a fabrication. . . . There was no Jimmy and no family. . . . I want to give the prize back." *Post* editor Benjamin Bradlee asked for a written admission of guilt and a resignation, and Cooke complied (Green, 1981). The ensuing scandal terminated the career of a talented journalist, seriously damaged the credibility of the second-most influential newspaper in the country, and tarnished the luster of the Pulitzer Prize.

Prior to publication, when the editors of the *Post* read Cooke's story, why did alarm bells or "red flags" not go off? Why did they not ask whether something might be wrong with this picture? Why were they taken in by the story? What misled them into thinking it was an authentic account of the life of a real 8-year-old heroin addict? And what does their mistake tell us about media bias when it comes to the drug beat? In the words of media critics Craig Reinarman and Ceres Duskin (1999), what are "the lessons learned" from the "Jimmy's Story" debacle?

Interestingly, the Janet Cooke scandal precisely exemplifies our two guiding but contrary norms of the journalistic community: Tell a story that readers can identify with, and get it right. Telling a dramatic, personal story does not always or necessarily mean telling a true story. All too often, a good story—that is, an exciting, entertaining, attention-grabbing, even sensationalistic story—is not a true story. Frequently, truth gets in the way of a good story. *True* stories are complicated, difficult, multisided, nuanced, often contradictory. In contrast, *good* stories—that is, stories that conform to the "Hey, Mabel!" principle—are usually simple, black-or-white, and unidimensional, quite often containing a clear-cut message. But they are also very often implausible. What made "Jimmy's Story" implausible?

First, though it may be possible to locate an 8-year-old addict (or may have been in 1980), "it is a virtual certainty that if such child addicts exist at all they are exceedingly rare." Did anyone bother to check the available data on the age distribution of addicts at the time? Even if a tiny handful of such youthful addicts did exist, what purpose did the paper serve by presenting such a shocking fact as if it were typical or far commoner than was actually the case? Remember, Cooke claimed that heroin was "filtering down to untold numbers of children like Jimmy." Why did the *Post* engage in the "routinization of caricature"—that is, "recrafting worst cases into typical cases," thereby "profoundly distorting the nature of drug problems in the interest of dramatic stories" (Reinarman and Duskin, 1999, p. 81)?

Second, how common is it for addicts to recommend heroin to their own children— and a child, at that, one who supposedly began using at age 5—or, for that matter, to anyone at all? "The media apparently knew so little about heroin that they *assumed* it induced depravity and transformed users into the sort of vile subhumans who think nothing of doing such things" (p. 83).

Third, why would any addict "give away the very expensive stuff for which they reputedly lie, cheat, and steal" (p. 83)? If anyone had thought to ask a cross-section of addicts if such a tale were plausible, nearly all would have thought it "absurd." If asked to read the Cooke story, "most addicts could have told the *Post* immediately that it was concocted" (p. 83). Just for veracity's sake, why didn't the newspaper's editors run the story by the souls who live the very lives the story supposedly described?

And fourth, once the story appeared and a citywide search turned up no clue of the existence of Jimmy, why didn't that fact alert the *Post* editors that, in all likelihood, he didn't exist? Hundreds of police officers and social workers, as well as a half dozen *Post* reporters, failed to confirm Jimmy's existence. "The intense police search continued for 17 days. The city had been finely combed. Nothing." After having been informed that "untold numbers of children like Jimmy existed," no one found an addict as young as 8—or even 12 (Green, 1981; Reinarman and Duskin, 1999, p. 83). Even so, the *Post* continued to stand by its story, and Cooke went on to win a Pulitzer. Why?

Cooke's motive was clear. By lying about her credentials, she moved from a relatively obscure, local daily to a job with one of the most prestigious and powerful newspapers in the country. Now she had to prove that she belonged on the staff of the *Post* by writing a story that shocked, astounded, and impressed her editors.

But why did the *Post* fail to catch the fabrication? Cooke's editors were sloppy about verifying her story because they leaned too far in the direction of the norm "Tell a good story" and not far enough in the direction of the norm "Get it right." In other words, they took a gamble. As the award of the Pulitzer Prize shows, initially, the gamble was rich with promise. As the scandal that erupted when the fabrication was uncovered demonstrates, the gamble also proved to be a landmine that exploded in the faces of the *Post*'s editors. The fact is, by itself, a story about 28-year-old addict is routine and not terribly exciting. But a story about an 8-year-old grade school boy being injected with heroin is sensational news. It is exciting, attention-grabbing, highly personal—a human-interest story of the highest order.

The ignorance of the *Post*'s editors about the basics of the lives of heroin addicts, circa 1980, is at once inexcusable and understandable. In spite of the fact that the *Post* is located in a city with a predominantly African-American population, most of the paper's readership is white. And in 1980, its editors and even reporters were largely out of touch and out of contact with the working-class Black residents of Washington. As a result, they trusted the veracity of a Black reporter, Janet Cooke, to convey for them the reality of the scene she described. When she handed them an implausible story, they were incapable of checking it against what they knew about the lives of working-class African-American addicts, because that was a world about which they knew next to nothing. The combination of their ignorance and their lust to grab their readers by the throat proved to be disastrous. It is unlikely that *The Washington Post* will make that mistake again.

## MEDIA ACCOUNTS OF CRACK-RELATED HOMICIDE: 1985–1990

One of the four major theories of media bias, as noted previously, is the ruling elite approach; it is exemplified by the work of criminologist Henry Brownstein (1991), whose book on how the media covered the biggest drug story of the late 1980s is subtitled *Crack Cocaine and the Social Construction of a Crime Problem* (1996). As we know, the late 1980s witnessed a huge increase in crack-related violence in the United States. More specifically, during those years, in many cities across the country, some 50 percent of homicides were drug-related, and roughly 80 percent of drug-related homicides were specifically traceable to the crack cocaine trade (Goldstein et al., 1989). Prior to 1985, hardly anyone used crack, and there were no crack-related homicides. As with all phenomena, this real and present condition—the sudden and startling increase in crack-related killings—was socially constructed by the press. In other words, the press reported the story of the connection between criminal homicide and drug selling in its own distinctive fashion. However, saying that the story was socially constructed does not necessarily mean that it was reported inaccurately. Did the media *distort* the reality of this phenomenon, or did they report it accurately?

Brownstein argued that the media seriously distorted and sensationalized the nature of crack-related violence. What was the image the press projected of a typical or modal drug killing in the late 1980s? Beginning early in 1989, the message conveyed in the news of crack-related criminal homicides was that they were random, that anyone could become a victim of a gangland shooting. More specifically, the message was that consumers of the media—readers of the newspapers and viewers of the television broadcasts in which such stories appeared—could have been gunned down in a crossfire between rival drug gangs. Middle-class people, people who live in communities that were not crack infested, people who consumed the media and paid attention to their stories, people who feared drug gangs and applauded the efforts of the police and the courts to root them out and incarcerate their members—these people constituted the audience at which such stories were aimed. And it was specifically they who were reported to have been the accidental victims of drug gang shootings.

A January 22, 1989, story that appeared in *The New York Times* was titled "Drug Wars Don't Pause to Spare the Innocent." Detailing the "killing of innocent bystanders" caught "in the crossfires of this nation's drug wars," the story argued that these killings had "suddenly become a phenomenon that greatly troubles experts on crime." The next day, the New York *Daily News* referred to such killings as "spillover," quoting a community leader as saying, "There are no safe neighborhoods any more." The following week, the *New York Post* ran a related story under the sensationalistic headline "Human Shield—Snatched Tot Wounded in Brooklyn Gun Battle." A 3-year-old boy, the story reported, had been "critically injured yesterday when a teenager snatched him from his mother's grasp and used him as a human shield in a gun battle."

The message was loud and clear: Many innocent bystanders had become victims of the drug wars. Drug-related killings were indeed "random"; spillover was a fact of life on the urban landscape. In record numbers, innocent white, middle-class people were being gunned down on the street because they happened to be in the wrong place at the wrong time. The media "constructed" the problem of crack-related violence as an issue that was central to the concerns of their audience: It was a serious problem because *they* could become victimized. The conclusion was obvious: Something had to be done to deal with this extremely serious problem.

In actual fact, drug-related violence was not random, of course. Indeed, during the late 1980s, a middle-class person innocently sipping a latte at Starbuck's was *extremely* unlikely to be gunned in a random shooting. During the first six months of 1990, for example, the New York City Police Department determined that just a shade over 1 percent of all its homicides involved innocent bystanders. Researchers determined that of the 414 criminal killings they studied that took place in New York City in 1988, again, just over 1 percent were of non-involved bystanders (Goldstein et al., 1989). A study of four American cities up to the late 1980s concluded that "bystander shootings are a rare event" (Sherman et al., 1989, p. 303).

So why the bias? Why did the media report random, senseless killings as common when they were actually extremely rare? Why did they run so many news stories about random, drug-related killings when, overwhelmingly, dealers were killing one another and their employees and customers—not middle-class bystanders? And why did the media target their message specifically to middle-class whites? What was the media's agenda? What did the press hope to accomplish with such biased reporting?

Brownstein adopted the power-elitist position that the media are working hand in glove—in a sense, *colluding*—with the powers that be in their reactionary program to convince the public that society's problem is not structural inequality but individual immorality. Drug scares are hoked up, Brownstein argued, to divert attention away from the problems of racism, inequality, poverty, and unemployment—and away from any actual solution to these problems and toward "solutions" that are both nonexistent and, supposedly, locatable in the "bad" motivations of a few violent, greedy, and evil drug dealers. In other words, the attention the media paid to random, crack-related violence represented *scapegoating in the service of right-wing politics.*

Presumably, this line of reasoning goes, it is in the interests of the rich and the powerful to maintain injustice and inequality because they profit from them. And focusing on sensational stories maintains injustice, the power elitists argue, by diverting attention from the fundamental problems of society, like inequality. All the while, the poor and the powerless receive society's crumbs, and the public receives biased news stories. Anything the elite can do to perpetuate that inequality serves their interests. And since challenges to inequality would undermine their interests, the rich and the powerful do whatever they can to stifle such challenges. Instilling fear in the middle class over the possibility that its members could, say, be accidentally cut down in a hail of bullets targeted for a drug dealer is precisely such a smokescreen. And media overlords, anxious to please—and also controlled by—the powers that be, collude with elite interests by publishing articles and broadcasting stories that instill fear in the public over nonexistent problems.

Is this a valid explanation for why so many stories appeared on crack-related violence in the late 1980s? As we saw, an entirely different perspective toward the functions of the media looks at the profession of journalism as the conveyor of a distinctive subculture. The job of the journalist, according to this view, is not to defend the interests of the ruling elite, but to practice a craft in a fashion compatible with the norms of the profession of journalism. Just as physicians possess and promulgate a sense of what constitutes good and bad doctoring, journalists learn and practice their own special notion of what their journalistic agenda is.

Interestingly, while most members of the ruling elite occupy the right or conservative wing of the political spectrum, most members of the profession of journalism occupy the left or liberal wing. Most professional journalists regard themselves as liberal, hold liberal ideological and political beliefs and values (pro-choice, pro–affirmative action, pro–gun control, anti–prayer in public schools, anti–death penalty, and so on), and vote for the Democratic candidate in presidential elections (Goldberg, 2002, pp. 122–126). And most conservatives—as well as the majority of the wealthiest and most powerful members of society—believe that the press holds a liberal bias.

The fact is, media biases do exist, but they neither automatically favor the interests of the ruling elite, as radicals and ruling elite theorists charge, nor are they slanted to favor liberal causes automatically, as conservatives charge. As we have seen, journalists claim it is their job to tell an important story fairly and accurately. However, in addition to getting it right, journalism has a second task, and that task has a kind of slant or bias: to grab the public's attention by telling an interesting, exciting, human-interest story that emotionally resonates with their audience's lives.

What moves readers is news; what's uplifting is news; what's distressing is news; what's in the audience's face is news. The press operates, as I explained, on the basis of the "Hey, Mabel!" principle. This principle is that whatever attracts the reader's attention and causes him or her to exclaim to another person, "You've gotta hear this!" is a successful story.

To address Brownstein's thesis, media representatives do not think of themselves as depicting reality in a totalistic, generalizing fashion. By that I mean that their stories do not necessarily reflect the actual incidence or rate of a phenomenon's occurrence in real life. Brownstein naively imagines that journalists should reason about and depict reality in exactly the same way that criminologists or social scientists do. For instance, he would argue, if 1 percent of all drug-related violence is "random" and "spills over" to innocent, middle-class victims, then newspaper stories ought to report that fact, or the distribution of their news stories should reflect that fact. But this is an extremely unrealistic expectation.

The murder of one drug dealer by another may be news, but it is not *major* news. In contrast, the killing by a drug dealer of a baby used as a human shield *is* major—indeed, sensational—news. The accidental killing by a drug dealer of a bystander—an executive, lawyer, or doctor who is sitting in an outdoor cafe having coffee—is major news. The fact is, "dog bites man"—which is the routine, expected story—is boring and not likely to grab the public's attention. But the "man bites dog" story—what isn't routine or expected, and what may be relatively rare—is exciting, is news, and will forever have a place in the headlines.

The fact that media stories about random, drug-related violence may (or may not) divert attention from the major problems of our day or support the interests of the ruling elite has nothing to do with why such stories receive attention from journalists. The fact is, such stories tell an exciting tale, provide a surefire human-interest angle, and hence, grab the public's attention. Therefore, according to the norms of journalism, they are newsworthy. In short, any claims about the ruling elite theorist's hidden political or ideological agenda, supposedly lurking behind media accounts of random, drug-related violence, are sheer speculation. In contrast, the explanation offered by professional subculture theory provides a view of how journalism actually practices its craft on a day-to-day, story-by-story basis. Biasing news stories toward the dramatic and the personal admittedly promotes sensationalism, but this is how journalism works.

## SUMMARY

We need not invoke conspiracies or hegemonic machinations to explain the phenomenon of how drugs are depicted in the media. The interests and the influence of the ruling elite do make it possible for certain themes to be woven into the news and certain stories to be planted in the media. The elite own the media, and they influence its content. But this does not explain why journalists find certain stories newsworthy or why certain stories capture the imagination of the public, and it does not explain the sweep and direction of drug stories.

The plain fact is, most of what criminologists and sociologists know about drug use is simply not newsworthy. Nor is the *way* most criminologists and sociologists approach and study drugs especially interesting to the public—that is, statistically and structurally, and on the basis of large numbers, general factors, and the configuration and interrelationship of society's major institutions. "Factors" and "variables" do not excite audiences—the lives of real people do. Media representatives and the media-consuming public find human-interest *anecdotes* engaging—not statistics. They find stories about *individuals* interesting—not analyses of the major social institutions. They find the offbeat, the unusual, the dramatic interesting—not the routine, the mundane, the ordinary. They find the plight of vulnerable souls, threats from monstrous villains, and the exotic lives of celebrities interesting—not an extension of the nuts-and-bolts, meat-and-potatoes lives all of us lead.

In the 1930s, the claim that puffing on a marijuana cigarette would cause men to assault and kill, and women to become sexually wanton, was wildly interesting and newsworthy. (The fact that these stories were, for the most part, planted by the Federal Bureau of Narcotics is an important, but not the only, issue.) The fact that marijuana possesses no such power was not especially worthy of media attention.

In the 1960s, the assertion that LSD would cause users to go crazy and bear children with birth defects was major, indeed, shocking news. The fact that the drug simply did not cause these effects was barely minor news.

In the late 1970s, the report that PCP would cause users to gouge out their eyes and attempt to fly off buildings to their deaths was sensational news. At the time, the fact that this was so rare as to be insignificant seemed trivial, irrelevant, a distraction.

In the late 1980s, as stories on the horrors of crack cocaine waned in volume and stridency, the media began to seize on methamphetamine as the new scary drug. Observers predicted a tidal wave of meth abuse. So far, this drug has not invaded states east of the Mississippi; moreover, experts have argued, the press has hugely exaggerated its addictive properties.

In 1980, the story that Jimmy, an 8-year-old heroin addict, lived in the nation's capital was astounding news. The fact that the boy did not exist in real life was news only because it had repercussions for Janet Cooke, *The Washington Post,* and the Pulitzer Prize committee.

In the 1980s, the fact that drug gangs gunned down innocent, middle-class bystanders was news. The fact that this happened extremely rarely was not especially interesting.

In short, what academics, researchers, criminologists, and sociologists consider "the truth" about drugs is not particularly newsworthy to the general public, and to most journalists as well. "The truth" is very rarely a "Hey, Mabel!" story.

Again, elite machinations need not even enter into the picture here. The news media are conveyors of myth, just as folktales and legends have been recounted in cultures around the world for thousands of years, long before capitalism existed, even long before any such entity as a ruling elite existed. Saying that the news tells "eternal stories" that serve a "mythological role" (Lule, 2001) does not mean that media stories are necessarily, or always, or even usually factually false. It means that certain eternal themes, themes that have always existed in the form of folktales, are emphasized in the media because they correspond to essential issues of societal and individual struggles, to notions of right and wrong, and to dilemmas and dichotomies that we humans face and deal with in our everyday lives. These themes include the victim, the scapegoat, the hero, the good mother, the trickster, the "other world," and disasters (Lule, 2001). One or more of these themes form the backbone of nearly all exciting news stories.

Yes, specific stories are *volatile,* in the sense that they erupt in the media, receive enormous attention, then recede from the limelight. The underlying themes that make stories exciting are ancient, but the specific stories that revolve around these themes are most exciting and newsworthy when they are new and fresh. And, though what's news is socially and culturally constructed, it is not *solely* and *exclusively* a social and cultural product. What's happening in the material world does provide raw material from which to draw news stories, and new developments happen to be more newsworthy than what is familiar to media audiences. And, though news stories are not necessarily "engineered" by the ruling elite to preserve the status quo, most often they *affirm* the existing order. (Occasionally, they may challenge hierarchies of power—for example, the Pentagon Papers, Watergate, or the "big tobacco" story.) In short, the ruling elite theory of the media is wrong because it is far too narrowly focused. In many authoritarian regimes, elites do control the media, but in modern capitalism, they do so only minimally. News is myth, news is legend, news is gossip, news is the magical tale—with its feet rooted in the ground and its eyes scanning the heavens. The plain fact is, forces far more ancient and far more powerful than capitalism determine what is news.

## KEY TERMS

grassroots theory of the
  media   125

hegemony   125

institutional
  dominance   125

money machine theory of
  the media   125

professional subculture
  theory of the
  media   126

ruling elitist theory of the
  media   124

sensationalism in the
  media   126

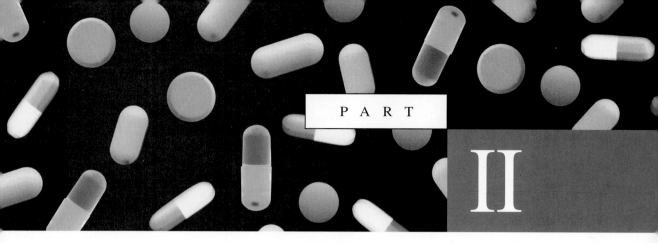

# DRUG USE

## *Methods and Data*

# HOW DO WE KNOW IT'S TRUE?

## *Methods of Research*

"**D**rug Abuse Skyrockets" screams one headline. "Drug Use Declines" announces another. "Drugs cause crime," one friend tells us. "No," says another, "crime causes drug use." How do we know when an assertion we read or hear is true? More specifically, how do researchers gather information about drug use? And how do they draw conclusions from the evidence they've gathered?

Researchers make use of a wide range of different kinds of information to determine what the drug picture looks like. Indeed, there is something of an "embarrassment of riches" here, since there are so many data sources. But not all of them are equally valid; in fact, there are flaws with each and every one. However, when we put two or more data sources together, we get a clearer sense of what that picture looks like. Researchers use the term **triangulation** to refer to using two or more sources of information to focus on a single phenomenon. If these data sources agree with one another, researchers call this **multiple confirmation.** And when two or more independent pieces of evidence say the same thing, our confidence that what the evidence says is true increases.

In Chapter 2, we looked at drugs from a pharmacological perspective—at issues pharmacologists and other medical and natural scientists are interested in. In this chapter, we think about drug use as a phenomenon that social scientists study. Sociologists and criminologists are interested, among other things, in *rates* of drug use, or how widespread it is. There are many different sources of information about how much drug use there is in the population. The systematic study of drug use entails making use of self-report surveys as well as drug tests, arrest data, and hospital and medical examiner reports. In addition, the sale of legal psychoactive drugs (alcohol, tobacco, and prescription drugs) is recorded and is therefore publicly available for study. Illegal drug use poses special problems for the social researcher, since it is, by its very nature, clandestine—hidden from public view. Hence, we must rely on a variety of *indirect* sources of information, including **surveys.** Before we examine these sources, however, we need to know a bit about some very basic principles of social research.

## SOCIAL RESEARCH ON DRUG USE: AN INTRODUCTION

To repeat the title of this chapter, How do we know it's true? How can we feel confident that the conclusions we read in a study on drug use are reasonably valid, reliable, and accurate? Here are a few things we need to know about three matters in social research: lying, sampling, and statistics.

### Lying

It is a half-truth that people will lie in surveys about their deviant, criminal, illegal, and controversial behavior. True, it is almost certain that a substantial proportion of respondents understate their drug use. When we compare what people say about their drug use in surveys with the results of drug tests, the latter figures tend to be significantly higher than the former. This discrepancy also tends to be much greater for some segments of the population than for others (Fendrich et al., 1999; Wish, Hoffman, and Nemes, 1997). But the fact is, in surveys on illicit and criminal behavior, *most* respondents tell the approximate truth, to the best of their ability—*if* they believe they will remain anonymous, their responses will remain confidential, and they will not get into trouble as a result of revealing incriminating information.

All of us make mistakes when we answer questions about the things we do, even if these things are legal. We forget, we imagine, we conflate, we distort, we telescope; there are many common flaws in recalling events that make answers to questions in surveys far from perfect. And not *all* respondents trust researchers to protect the information they give them. Hence, there is likely to be something of a dampening effect in answers people

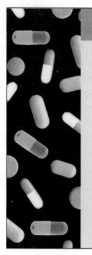

## True-False Quiz

One of the items in my true-false quiz was: "In surveys on illicit drug use, everyone lies; as a result, it is invalid for researchers to base their conclusions on the responses to surveys on illegal drug use." As we can see in this section, this statement is false. In fact, in drug surveys, most respondents tell the truth, to the best of their ability—if they believe that their answers are confidential, that they will not get into trouble as a result of revealing their participation in illegal behavior. Most of my students gave the correct answer to this question; only 36 percent said that the statement is true, while 63 percent said that it was false. What is true is that we cannot rely on anything like 100 percent validity in respondents' answers, and sometimes answers diverge considerably from being 100 percent true. But the cliché "everyone lies" is clearly false.

give to questions about illicit, illegal, deviant, and delinquent behavior. But the picture we get of drug use from surveys is *roughly* accurate. It is good enough to give us a *fairly* accurate idea what's going on; it provides us with enough information to make generalizations and predictions.

In an *absolute* sense, there is a great deal of inaccuracy in self-report surveys. That is, if 5 percent of a sample say they used cocaine last year, chances are, if we had more accurate measures (such as urine tests), we'd probably find a figure that's closer to 10 percent. In a study of young adults in a "high risk" community in Chicago (that is, in a neighborhood whose population had a high proportion of admissions to drug and alcohol treatment programs), researchers found that, in comparison with the results of drug tests based on hair samples, survey respondents significantly *underreported* their cocaine and heroin use (Fendrich et al., 1999). This study, however, was based on a small sample (322 respondents). It's not clear whether and to what extent the same technique could be used on a sample consisting of tens of thousands of respondents, one that was truly representative of the American population at large. In any case, it would be foolish to assume that in an absolute sense, self-report surveys on criminal or deviant behaviors are completely accurate.

But in a *relative* sense, our figures are likely to be reasonably accurate. By "relative" sense, I mean that respondents who said they used cocaine last year are statistically a great deal more likely to have done so than those who said they did not. In addition, surveys probably give a fairly accurate picture of drug use over time. If more respondents said they used illicit drugs in a survey conducted in 2006 than in one conducted in 2004, other things being more or less equal, I'd put my money on an increase. The same thing could be said about differences between and among populations in geographic categories (large cities versus small towns, for instance) or demographic categories (men versus women). For example, if surveys report that a higher percentage of males said they used marijuana in the past month than did females, in all likelihood, if we were to take blood or urine samples to verify this, the male edge would be confirmed. The reason this is so is that, when we compare categories, years, or geographic regions, we assume that whatever errors that prevail in one also take place in another; in other words, errors tend to cancel each other out. There is very little doubt that the results of self-report surveys are fairly valid sources of data in making comparisons. The fact is, given the controversial nature of what drug researchers are asking questions about, it's remarkable that respondents are as honest as they are.

This does not mean that more valid techniques for getting more honest answers in self-report surveys do not need to be developed. Researcher Eric Wish and his colleagues (1997) found that persons in a drug treatment program who were tested for the presence of drugs in their urine before being interviewed gave extremely accurate answers concerning their drug use. (He refers to this as the "test first" method.) Would this work for the population at large? If research is conducted using this method, we'll know the answer.

## Sampling

In surveys, sampling is typically a bigger problem than lying. **Sampling** refers to the way that respondents in a survey are chosen. No criminologist, sociologist, or medical researcher studies *every* person in a given population—that is, group, category, or universe. That would be wasteful and unnecessary—indeed, virtually impossible—not to mention silly. Instead, researchers rely on drawing samples of people that are similar in important ways to the whole group, category, or universe from which they are chosen. But the way a sample is drawn is extremely important. Researchers who conduct surveys do not pick people in a haphazard fashion. They select their samples so that everyone in the universe (the population at large) has an equal chance of appearing in the sample. That way, the sample will be a cross-section of, will look like, or will "represent" the universe. This means that the sample contains more or less the same proportion of men, women, Blacks, whites, younger and older people, liberals and conservatives, educated and less well educated, and so on, as the entire population. A sample that does not look like or reflect the population as a whole may be "biased" or **skewed** in one direction or another. Its respondents may be answering honestly, but not necessarily in the same way that a cross-section of the population would respond.

One problem with sampling the general population is that a lot of people can't be located or questioned; hence, samples that fail to include these hard-to-find segments of the population are not a true cross-section of the whole "universe," that is, the population as a whole. This matter is especially problematic for studies of drug use and criminal behavior because it is precisely the difficult-to-locate segments that have the highest rates of illicit drug use. How do we study runaways and the homeless when they don't live at a fixed address? Most surveys don't include the millions of people who are incarcerated in a jail, prison, or mental institution, or who are in the military. If we were to conduct a survey of drug use among high school students, what about dropouts and absentees? And, of course, no matter how much researchers try, some people refuse to take part in their survey.

## Statistics

Much information is conveyed in the form of statistics. Many students find reading discussions that make use of statistics unappetizing, even boring. Complaining about a course in which the instructor drew on statistical formulations, students often moan, "We had to memorize a bunch of statistics!" But the fact is, no instructor wants his or her students to "memorize a bunch of statistics" simply for their own sake. Statistics should be harnessed to a larger purpose: presenting important information in a condensed and powerful way.

For example, saying that more than 99 percent of all the people who have jumped off the Golden Gate Bridge in San Francisco were killed in the fall is a very dramatic way of saying that that particular act is extremely dangerous. Saying that smokers are more likely to die at age 65 than nonsmokers are to die at age 75 is an extremely vivid means of presenting the idea that smoking cigarettes shortens life. Saying that 20-year-olds are more than 30 times more likely to have taken an illicit substance during the previous month than are persons age 65 or older is an effective way of conveying the idea that age is related to recreational drug use. Statistics can be a powerful way of hammering home many basic facts of human existence. It is true that many statistics are so complex and difficult to understand that they do not tell most people much of anything. But presenting simple, direct, clear statistical facts about basic aspects of our lives can be a forceful, in-your-face way of imparting information that cannot be communicated by any other means.

The researcher is interested in two different types of statistics: descriptive and inferential statistics. **Descriptive statistics** describe what something is like in quantitative terms, that is, in the form of numbers. In descriptive statistics, the rough approximation "more" versus "less" is given exactitude. Descriptive statistics are the basic numerical facts of life, and they may be presented in the form of absolute numbers or rates and percentages.

For instance, in the 2005 National Survey on Drug Use and Health estimated that 19.7 million persons living in the United States (an absolute number), or 8.1 percent of the population age 12 or over (a rate or percentage), used one or more illicit drugs. In 2004, the National Crime Victimization Survey estimated that 24.1 million Americans were victims of violent or property crimes (an absolute number), for a violent crime rate of 22.0 per 1,000 households in the population and a property crime rate of 162.2 per 1,000 (Catalano, 2005, p. 2). Rates or percentages are standard measures that make possible a systematic comparison between different areas, social categories, or years. For instance, the 2005 rate of drug use represented a slight increase from the previous year. In contrast, both the violent and the property crime rates for 2004 represented a drop from the previous year.

In contrast to descriptive statistics, **inferential statistics** attempt to measure cause-and-effect relationships between and among two or more factors or variables. When things happen, we want to know what caused them to happen. The problem is, we don't necessarily see them happening before our eyes. From descriptive statistics, we simply see that two or more things are associated or related to one another. Rich people are more likely to vote Republican; poorer people are more likely to vote Democratic. But what *causes* these relationships? Why do they exist? Inferential statistics attempt to answer questions such as these.

For instance, we know from descriptive statistics that, generally speaking, drugs and crime are related. People who use illicit drugs are more likely to commit crimes of all kinds than are people who do not use drugs. Just as interesting, as their drug use increases, their likelihood of committing crimes increases as well. But does drug use cause criminal behavior? Or is it the reverse—does engaging in criminal behavior cause drug use? We also know that alcohol consumption is related to violent behavior: As the use of alcohol rises, so does violence. But is the consumption of alcohol causally related to violence? Or are other factors the reason why the two are related to one another? Many things are descriptively but not causally related to one another. We'll look at some of these issues in Chapter 12.

For example, the consumption of ice cream is statistically and "descriptively" related to rape: As ice cream consumption goes up, so does the incidence of rape. Using descriptive statistics alone, we'd find a strong correlation, relationship, or association between eating ice cream and committing rape. But does eating ice cream *cause* men to rape women? Is this a cause-and-effect relationship? Of course not, as inferential statistics will show us. The fact is, both ice cream consumption and rape rise during the summer; in the United States, consistently, the months with the highest rates of reported rape are July and August—precisely the months in which ice cream consumption reaches its peak. Here, the relevant factor is the season—summer—when it's warmest, and social interaction is more intimate and more frequent than during the rest of the year. When we control for or hold constant the season, it is clear that the consumption of ice cream has no independent or causal impact whatsoever on rape.

In a like fashion, inferential statistics attempt to weed out, control, or "hold constant" all the other factors that are related to the ones in which we're interested. They cast a clear, cold light on the precise cause-and-effect connection between and among them. Unlike descriptive statistics, which are usually very straightforward and easy to understand, inferential statistics are usually complex and extremely technical. But in order to answer the most important questions about how the social world is put together, researchers have to rely on them.

## RATES OF DRUG USE: AN INTRODUCTION

What's the best way of finding out about rates of drug use? The fact is, there is no single best way, but using a variety of research techniques will give a more accurate and complete picture of this interesting and important phenomenon than relying on only one. Pharmacologists study the effects of drugs in the lab or in hospital clinics. Criminologists and sociologists, unlike pharmacologists, are interested in drug use in *naturalistic* settings: on the street, in the home, among friends, on the job, in the school—anywhere people decide to alter their consciousness. Social scientists want to know who uses (and how many people use which drugs), why, with what frequency, and with what consequences.

As we have seen, when it comes to the "how many" question, with respect to the consumption of alcohol and tobacco, the researcher is in a fortunate position, because these are legal, taxable products. Hence, records are kept of how many bottles of beer, wine, and distilled spirits; cigars; containers of pipe tobacco; packs of chewing tobacco; and cartons of cigarettes are sold each year. The same applies to the prescription drugs: A record is kept of each and every prescription written for each and every legendary or pharmaceutical drug. We know, within very narrow limits, how frequently all of the prescription drugs are used in a legal, medical context.

Unfortunately, we don't have the same sort of hard and fast data for rates of illegal drug use. To get the full illicit drug consumption picture, researchers utilize drug tests, surveys, and hospital and coroner's records. The following four data sources make use of one or more of these research methods and convey crucial information about drug use and abuse in the United States: the Arrestee Drug Abuse Monitoring program, the Drug Abuse Warning Network, the Monitoring the Future survey, and the National Survey on Drug Use and Health, which, prior to 2002, was referred to as the National Household Survey on Drug Abuse. They are the four mainstays of the social science drug researcher's data sources when it comes to rates. Each data source tells a slightly different story, each is flawed, yet each has strengths. Let's look at them one by one.

# THE ARRESTEE DRUG ABUSE MONITORING (ADAM) PROGRAM

If you want to know about the relationship between drugs and crime, what better place to begin than with the drug use of people who have been arrested for criminal behavior? In 1987, at the initiative of drug researcher Eric Wish, the National Institute of Justice established the **Drug Use Forecasting (DUF)** program. In 1997, the name was changed to the **Arrestee Drug Abuse Monitoring (ADAM)** program. During each year, a sample of persons is drawn in the counties in which most of the nation's largest cities are located. The sample includes persons who have been arrested for violent crimes, property crimes, drug crimes, DWI, and domestic violence crimes. These arrestees are approached and asked if they would be willing to be interviewed and to supply urine samples. Responses are confidential, and neither testing positive for drugs nor giving information about illegal activities results in any legal consequences. Roughly 85 percent of the arrestees who are approached agree to an interview, and of these, nearly 95 percent agree to provide a urine specimen. Initially, 12 sites were in ADAM's program and only adult males were included in its samples. Today, four separate samples are drawn. In 2003, the adult male sample was 24,000 in 36 sites. What is so remarkable about ADAM is that it accesses populations that are inaccessible by means of more conventional research methods, such as surveys. Most of ADAM's respondents would not be drawn by the National Household Survey on Drug Abuse's or Monitoring the Future's samples, because many of them do not live in conventional households. For anyone interested in the relationship of drug use and crime, ADAM is probably the best place to start (Yacoubian, 2000; Wish, 1995).

Table 6-1 presents the median percentages for arrestees testing positive for the specific drugs indicated in all the metropolitan counties participating in ADAM's program for the years 1990 and 2003. (See also Figure 6-1.) This table tells several stories.

Obviously, the first story is that arrestees—presumably, all or almost all of whom are criminal offenders—are *extraordinarily* highly likely to use drugs. In 2003, in all sites, more than 50 percent of adult male arrestees tested positive for at least one drug, and the median percentage testing positive for one or more drugs was 67 percent. In stark contrast, only 6 percent of the American population says that they used at least one illicit drug once or more during the past *month*. With most tests employed, no drug (except for marijuana)

| TABLE 6-1 | Median Percentage of Adult Male Arrestees Testing Positive, 1990 and 2003 | | | |
|---|---|---|---|---|
| | **1990** | | **2003** | |
| | **Males** | **Females** | **Males** | **Females** |
| Any drug | 56% | 64% | 67.0% | 68.0% |
| Cocaine | 45 | 49 | 30.1 | 35.3 |
| Marijuana | 20 | 12 | 44.1 | 31.6 |
| Opiates/heroin | 6 | 11 | 5.8 | 6.6 |
| Methamphetamines | * | * | 4.7 | 8.8 |

*Not recorded or reported.

*Source:* Drug Use Forecasting (DUF) for 1990; Arrestee Drug Use Monitoring Program (ADAM) for 2003, released 2004.

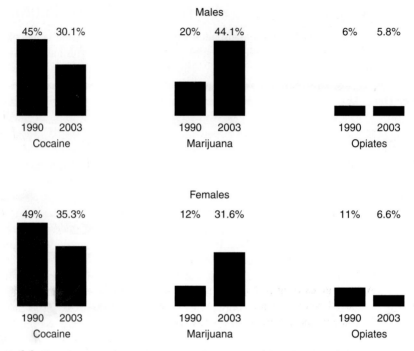

**Figure 6-1**  **Arrestees testing positive for various drugs, by median county, 1990 and 2003.**
*Source:* DUF, August 1991; ADAM, 2004.

can be detected a month or more since most recent use—most are detectable only within two to three days of most recent use. The chances are, if that 6 percent figure is accurate, less than 3 percent of the American population would test positive for an illegal drug—in other words, would have used a drug recently enough to have traces in their bodies. When we set this statistic against the fact that nearly *two-thirds* of arrestees test positive, the message is loud and clear: Compared with a cross-section of the population at large—most of whom are *not* criminals— criminal offenders are *extremely* likely to use psychoactive drugs, *hugely* more likely to do so than are nonoffenders. Table 6-2 documents the striking difference in drug use between arrestees and nonarrestees (and presumably between criminal offenders and nonoffenders).

The most interesting story about methamphetamine use is that it is extremely localized. While in three of the counties, no arrestees tested positive for meth, and in six of them, less than 1 percent did so, tests were positive for at least three out of ten arrestees in the counties in which Honolulu (40%), Phoenix (38%), Sacramento (38%), San Diego (36%), and San Jose (37%) were located. Another important story: Opiates (mainly heroin) are also fairly rarely used. Marijuana (a median of 44.1% for men and 31.6% for women) and cocaine (a median of 30.1% for men and 35.3% for women) are by far the two premier drugs that arrestees have taken recently. And between 1990 and 2003, while cocaine use *declined* significantly, marijuana use *increased*. To be more specific, for cocaine, arrestees testing positive in the median county declined 15 percent, while for marijuana, the figure more than doubled. Marijuana seems to have become the drug of choice of the nation's criminals, especially among the young (Golub and Johnson, 2001).

| TABLE 6–2 | Percentages of Persons Ages 18 and Older Reporting Past-Year Illicit Drug Use by Whether They Were Arrested for Any FBI Part I Offense in the Past Year, 2002, 2003, and 2004 |
|---|---|

| | Arrested for Any Part I Offense | Not Arrested for Any Part I Offense |
|---|---|---|
| Marijuana | 46.5% | 10.0% |
| Cocaine | 24.8 | 2.4 |
| Crack cocaine | 11.8 | 0.6 |
| Hallucinogens | 11.0 | 1.5 |
| Methamphetamine | 6.5 | 0.5 |
| Heroin | 4.3 | 0.1 |
| Nonmedical use of any prescription drug | 28.8 | 5.7 |

*Source:* "Illicit Drug Use among Persons Arrested for Serious Crimes," the NSDUH Report, December 15, 2006; based on NSDUH surveys conducted 2002, 2003, 2004.

In short, ADAM gives drug researchers a clear picture of use among arrestees on a drug-by-drug, county-by-county, and year-by-year basis. It is an absolutely essential tool for understanding one major link in the drugs-and-crime equation.

Researchers agree that ADAM's data are unique and valuable. But they do have limitations. First, ADAM's program draws arrestee samples only from the counties with the country's largest cities, which is important, because some drugs, such as methamphetamine and heroin, are beginning to be used at extremely high rates in rural areas (Egan, 2002; Ferdinand, 2003). Second, by definition, arrestees are offenders who get caught. Many offenders are able to escape detection; those who do may differ from arrestees in important ways, including their drug use patterns. In spite of these limitations, however, ADAM's sample of arrestees is as good as any comparable sample is likely to be, and data from its tabulations are extremely valuable to an understanding of the drugs-and-crime picture.

# THE DRUG ABUSE WARNING NETWORK (DAWN)

Through a program funded by the Substance Abuse and Mental Health Services Administration (SAMHSA), information is collected on two crucial drug abuse events: emergency department (ED) episodes and medical examiner (ME) reports. This program is referred to as the **Drug Abuse Warning Network (DAWN).** DAWN tabulates the number of acute medical complications that are caused by or associated with the use of certain drugs. Comparing DAWN's figures with the percentage of the population who use these drugs gives a rough idea of how dangerous their use is, at least within the time frame of a particular episode of use. As does ADAM, DAWN's ME reports collect data only in the metropolitan counties in and around which the nation's largest cities are located. Hence, its data do not represent the population of the country as a whole. In DAWN's 2004 ED data, for the first time, information was drawn from and is representative of hospitals in the entire 50 states and the District of Columbia. In its 2003 ME reports, detailed information was collected from 35 metropolitan areas and, separately, from six states (Maine, Maryland, New Hampshire, New Mexico, Utah, and Vermont).

An **emergency department (ED) episode** is any nonlethal, untoward, drug-related event that results in an emergency department visit to a facility with 24-hour services. Such episodes include a suicide attempt, a panic reaction, a psychotic episode, a hallucination, unconsciousness, poisoning, accidental ingestion, an extreme allergic reaction, and dependence for which the patient demands treatment. (A patient who comes or is brought to the emergency room for drug "detoxification" is the only nonacute episode that is tallied in ED figures.) In a given episode, recorded by a designated member of the ED staff, up to four different drugs may be mentioned as the cause of the untoward effect. (For patients under age 21, all alcohol "overdoses" are counted; for those 21 and older, alcohol is mentioned only if it was used in combination with one or more other drugs.) ED visits involved an average of 1.6 drugs. Obviously, in a given year, the same patient could visit one or more emergency departments on two or more occasions; hence, the yearly tabulation of episodes does not indicate the number of people who experienced untoward, drug-induced ED visits during that year. And since several drugs could be mentioned as having been used in a given episode, the number of times a drug is mentioned may be greater than the number of drug visits or episodes (in the case of ME reports, an "episode" is the drug-related death of the user) that took place. It should also be emphasized that drugs may be adulterated or bogus, and so tabulations of ED episodes may be misleading in that they may not tell us about the inherent dangers of a particular drug. Hence, all DAWN figures should be read with a measure of skepticism.

**Medical examiner (ME) reports** are tabulations of deaths caused directly or indirectly by one or more drugs, as reported by a city or county coroner or an ME. In the case of a nonroutine death, that is, a death that requires investigation, an autopsy is performed on the decedent. (Roughly 70 percent of all autopsies performed in the United States are included in the DAWN program.) If drugs are deemed to be a factor in the death, it is counted as an ME episode. In the most recent report, two-thirds of all ME episodes were deemed directly drug-induced (that is, were regarded as drug "overdoses"); in just under one-third of the cases, the drug or drugs played a contributory role. The rules medical examiners follow for including a case in their DAWN reports are not completely standardized. Hence, a case that is included in one jurisdiction may be excluded in another. As with ED figures, for adults, beginning in 2003, alcohol is counted only if it was taken in combination with one or more other drugs; for persons under age 21, all alcohol episodes are counted. For ME cases, up to six drugs may be counted; in the most recent report, in three-quarters of all ME episodes, more than one drug was tallied.

Keep in mind that DAWN tabulates only *acute* drug reactions, that is, those that take place specifically during the immediate aftermath of an episode of use. It does not tally the untoward *chronic* effects of drugs, that is, those that take place over the long run, after weeks, months, or years of use. (An exception to this rule, as we saw, is the users who appear at an emergency room seeking detoxification for drug dependence, which is a chronic rather than an acute effect.) If a heroin addict is hospitalized for hepatitis or a "crack whore" dies of AIDS, their deaths will not be tallied in DAWN's data. And keep in mind that many factors could cause a given untoward episode, including the dose and combination of drugs, any impurities in the drugs, and the route of administration. Also keep in mind that the methods of recording both ED and ME episodes is nonstandardized, varying somewhat from one metropolitan area to another. For instance, in 2003, in some counties, medical examiners mentioned marijuana in ME reports, while in a number of others, they did not.

This indicates that in the latter cases, the medical examiners did not believe that the drug played a contributory role in overdose deaths, even though decedents may have tested positive for the presence of the drug. In 2002, in Omaha, both nicotine and caffeine were mentioned as contributing to drug-related deaths! In Baltimore, quinine was listed as a drug that played a contributory role in drug-related deaths; in no other city was quinine mentioned. It is also true, however, that procedures for recording DAWN data are becoming more standardized over time.

With respect to population demographics, relative to their numbers in the population, drug overdose decedents are substantially more likely to be male (depending on the year, about 70% of decedents) than female (30%), about two-thirds (67%) are white, a quarter (25%) are African-American, and less than one in ten (7%) Hispanic. Perhaps the most startling demographic statistic for drug-related mortality is related to *age*. While teenagers and young adults are strikingly more likely to use drugs than older adults, they are vastly less likely to die of drug-related causes. In 2002, only 1 percent of drug overdoses were age 17 or younger, and only 8 percent were between the ages of 18 and 24. The reason for the discrepancy is that as age rises, the risk of dying of drug-related causes rises as well: A fifth of DAWN's decedents (20%) were between 25 and 34; a third (32%) were between 35 and 44; and a whopping 39 percent were 45 and older! Considering that persons in the oldest age category are, comparatively speaking, extremely unlikely to use illicit drugs, it becomes clear that taking psychoactive substances recreationally poses a much more serious health hazard to the middle-aged than to younger persons. By a certain age, illicit, recreational drug use becomes an enormous threat to the user's very existence.

In 2003, DAWN changed its procedures for tabulating ME reports. So much is this the case that its 2003 report (published in 2005) issues a warning: "None of the cases in new DAWN . . . are comparable to DAWN cases from prior years" (p. 9). Each of "new" DAWN's cases (that is, those after 2002) is assigned to one of seven "case types": suicide, homicide by drugs, accidental ingestion, adverse reaction, overmedication, all other accidental, and "could not be determined." Drug-induced homicide is extremely rare (only 5 out of 32 metropolitan areas reported any drug-related homicides). DAWN's category drug abuse/misuse excludes suicide. In addition, in 2003, DAWN combined the heroin/morphine category with other narcotics, such as methadone, oxycodone, and hydrocodone. For some reason, DAWN's 2003 report presented data only for the top-five drugs in each metropolitan area. Hence, any drug that consistently appeared in a number-six or lower spot as a cause of or a contributor to an overdose death would not appear at all in any of DAWN's tables. As a result, the drugs that do appear do so in much higher percentages than they would if all drugs were included, regardless of rank. And lastly, DAWN counted alcohol-only incidents if the decedent was under age 21, but counted alcohol-in-combination only when the decedent was 21 or older. In sum, the "new" DAWN data are only minimally useful in telling us about the dangers of drug use and abuse.

As with ADAM's data, Tables 6-2, 6-3, and 6-4 have several interesting stories to tell. The first is that alcohol is involved in a great many untoward drug reactions; it ranks first in ED mentions and third in drug-related deaths. Since alcohol is used so often by such a huge percentage of the population, on a dose-by-dose user-by-user basis, it is certainly a great deal *less* toxic than most of the other drugs in DAWN's tabulations. But consider this: DAWN tallies alcohol *only* if it is used in combination with another drug (but alcohol-only

### TABLE 6-2   Emergency Department (ED) Episodes, Selected Drugs, 2004

|  | Percentage of Visits | Number of Visits |
|---|---|---|
| Total alcohol visits* | 23 | 461,809 |
| Alcohol-in-combination | 18 | 363,641 |
| Cocaine | 19 | 383,350 |
| Marijuana | 11 | 215,665 |
| Sedatives/hypnotics (such as barbiturates) | 9 | 175,115 |
| Heroin/morphine | 8 | 162,137 |
| Benzodiazapines (Valium-type tranquilizers) | 7 | 144,385 |
| Stimulants (amphetamine and meth) | 5 | 102,843 |
| Antidepressants (Prozac- and Xanax-type drugs) | 3 | 62,743 |
| Hydrocodone combinations | 2 | 42,491 |
| Oxycodone combinations | 2 | 36,559 |
| Methadone | 2 | 31,874 |
| Antipsychotics | 2 | 30,846 |
| PCP | ** | 8,828 |
| MDMA (Ecstasy) | ** | 8,621 |
| GHB | ** | 2,340 |
| LSD | ** | 1,953 |
| Rohypnol | ** | 473 |
| Ketamine | ** | 227 |
| Illict drugs only | 30 |  |
| Pharmaceuticals only | 25 |  |
| Alcohol only (under 21) | 8 |  |
| Combinations | 37 |  |
| Total drug-related ED visits |  | 1,997,993 |
| Total ED visits |  | 106,000,000 |

*Includes all alcohol visits by a patient under age 21 (alcohol only as well as alcohol-in-combination) as well as alcohol-in-combination only for patients 21 and older. Hence, the two alcohol figures in this table overlap and cannot be added together.
**Less than 0.5 percent.
*Source:* DAWN, ED data, 2006.

### TABLE 6-3   Number of Mentions and Deaths, Medical Examiner (ME) Reports, 1996–2002

|  | 1996 | 1997 | 1998 | 1999 | 2002 |
|---|---|---|---|---|---|
| Cocaine | 4,424 | 4,277 | 4,556 | 4,816 | 4,024 |
| Heroin | 3,525 | 3,953 | 4,021 | 4,434 | 3,264 |
| Alcohol | 3,376 | 3,473 | 3,701 | 3,903 | 3,200 |
| Total ME Mentions | 22,539 | 23,466 | 24,917 | 28,427 | 28,846 |
| Total ME Deaths | 9,306 | 9,584 | 9,750 | 11,464 | 10,002 |

*Source:* DAWN, ME data, 2003.

| TABLE 6-4 | Drug Mentioned in Top-Five Drugs Reported in "Drug Misuse/Abuse" Deaths, Medical Examiner (ME) Reports, 2003 |
|---|---|

| | Percent* |
|---|---|
| Opiates | 70 |
| Cocaine | 43 |
| Alcohol | 30 |
| Benzodiazepines | 17 |
| Antidepressants | 17 |
| Stimulants | 4 |

*Percent is drugs or drug types appearing in the top-five drugs mentioned in each of 32 participating metropolitan areas reporting.

*Note:* Opiates include heroin, morphine, methadone, hydrocodone, and oxycodone; benzodiazepines include Xanax, Ativan, Dalmane, Valium, Librium, Halcion, and Rohypnol; alcohol includes alcohol-in-combination only for persons 21 and older but any alcohol for persons under 21; antidepressants include Prozac, Paxil, Tofranil, Zoloft, Wellbutrin, Nardil, Effexor, and others; stimulants include amphetamines and methamphetamine; all other drugs less than 0.5 percent. Percentages add up to more than 100 percent because more than one drug can be mentioned in a given death.

*Source:* DAWN, ME data, 2005.

for patients and decedents under age 21). Both the ED and ME figures for alcohol would be *vastly* higher if alcohol-only episodes were tallied for all patients and decedents. One expert estimates that alcohol consumed by itself causes *six times* as many ED admissions than when it is used in conjunction with another drug (Goldstein, 2001, p. 11). This does not mean that it is more dangerous to use alcohol only than in combination with other drugs; it is just that a lot more people use alcohol only than use it with other drugs. Hence, alcohol's role in overdoses is hugely minimized by DAWN.

The second story contained in Tables 6-2, 6-3, and 6-4 is that marijuana ranks third in DAWN's ED data, surpassing heroin in this respect. (Marijuana appears in an extremely small percentage of DAWN's ME figures—almost always in combination with another drug—indicating that the drug is not terribly toxic.) As with alcohol, marijuana is a frequently used drug, and hence its appearance in DAWN's ED figures should not be surprising. On a dose-for-dose basis, it rarely causes complications, although a small minority of users do experience untoward reactions. A surprisingly large percentage of ED patients mentioning marijuana (13%) do so because they are "seeking detoxification," not usually from marijuana but from some other drug they are taking.

The third story that these tables tell is overwhelmingly the main point: There are three drugs—DAWN's "Big Three"—that appear consistently in both ED and ME figures: cocaine, heroin, and alcohol. These are the three most dangerous drugs consumed in America in the sense that they are associated with the greatest number of untoward reactions, both lethal and nonlethal. More specifically, given that heroin is used roughly one-twentieth as often as cocaine and less than one-hundredth as often as alcohol, the fact that it appears so often in DAWN's data is clear and unambiguous evidence that it is an extremely dangerous, toxic drug. It bears an extremely high risk of damage on an episode-by-episode, user-by-user, gram-by-gram basis. Of course, in DAWN's 2003 ME data, heroin is lumped with the other opiates and opioids, and hence, in that report, the specific role of heroin cannot be separated from that of the other narcotics.

And lastly, many drugs and drug types that have received a great deal of media attention in recent years (methamphetamine and the club drugs most notably) appear rarely or not at all in DAWN's ED and ME reports. In other words, the media have exaggerated their dangers, and the public has come to believe that they are more harmful than they really are. Amphetamines and methamphetamine are mentioned in only 5 percent of drug-related ED episodes, far behind alcohol, cocaine, sedatives/hypnotics, Valium-type benzodiazepines, and even marijuana. And they appear among the top-five "drug misuse/abuse" mortalities in only 5 out of 32 metropolitan areas, lagging far behind not only opiates, cocaine, and alcohol, but also benzodiazepines and antidepressants. Club drugs (Ecstasy, GHB, Rohypnol, and ketamine) rank near the bottom of drugs causing or associated with ED episodes, and never appear in the top five of **ME mentions.** (Since Rohypnol is a benzodiazepine, it is included in that category for ME reports.) The interested observer suspects that hype has as much to do with media stories on these drugs as with their potential dangers.

In spite of the drawbacks of DAWN's data, they do provide an approximate picture of the acute consequences of drug abuse in the United States—more specifically, the relative contribution each drug makes to ED episodes and ME reports, that is, nonlethal and lethal untoward effects. By any reasonable calculation, a drug that is mentioned frequently in both the ED and ME lists can be said to be commonly abused. DAWN gives us a fairly accurate glimpse at one aspect of drug abuse. Together with other sources, DAWN's data help us to understand the entire drug picture.

## MONITORING THE FUTURE (MTF)

Each year since 1975, the Institute on Survey Research at the University of Michigan has surveyed a nationally representative sample of 15,000 or so high school seniors about their use of and attitudes toward legal and illegal drugs. In addition, beginning in 1977, adults, both college educated and noncollege educated, who completed high school one or more years earlier were also questioned. The adult sample is divided into college students and noncollege respondents, whose answers are tabulated separately. In 1991, samples of eighth- and tenth-graders were included. In 2005, its survey of drug use among eighth-, tenth-, and twelfth-graders drew a sample of 50,000 students in 400 secondary schools around the country. This ongoing survey is referred to as the **Monitoring the Future (MTF)** survey.

The MTF's surveys are conducted in the classroom, and its questionnaires are self-administered by each respondent. For each drug, four levels of use are asked about: (1) lifetime prevalence, that is, whether the respondent ever used the drug in question; (2) annual prevalence, or use during the past year; (3) 30-day prevalence, or use during the past month; and (4) daily use, or use on 20 or more of the past 30 days. Respondents are also asked about perceived risk, their disapproval of drug use, and perceived availability of specific drugs.

Table 6-5 has some interesting things to say about the drug use of eighth-, tenth-, and twelfth-graders. Clearly, it is alcohol that attracts the greatest percentage of school-age users—and by a considerable margin. (Remember that alcohol cannot be legally purchased by anyone under age 21; hence, all teenagers who use it are in violation of the law.) Nearly half (47%) of MTF's high school seniors drank alcohol at least once in the past month—which is about the same as the average for the population as a whole. And close to a fifth of the sample's eighth-graders (most of whom are only 13 years old!) did so. Among the illicit

| TABLE 6-5 | Annual and 30-Day Prevalence of Various Drugs by Eighth-, Tenth-, and Twelfth-Graders, 2005 |
|---|---|

|  | Annual | | | 30-Day | | |
|---|---|---|---|---|---|---|
|  | Eighth | Tenth | Twelfth | Eighth | Tenth | Twelfth |
| Any illicit drug other than marijuana | 8.1% | 12.9% | 19.7% | 4.1% | 6.4% | 10.3% |
| Marijuana/hashish | 12.2 | 26.6 | 33.6 | 6.6 | 15.2 | 19.8 |
| LSD | 1.2 | 1.5 | 1.8 | 0.5 | 0.6 | 0.7 |
| MDMA (Ecstasy) | 1.7 | 2.6 | 3.0 | 0.6 | 1.0 | 1.0 |
| Cocaine | 2.2 | 3.5 | 5.1 | 1.0 | 1.5 | 2.3 |
| Crack | 1.4 | 1.7 | 1.9 | 0.6 | 0.7 | 1.0 |
| Heroin | 0.8 | 0.9 | 0.8 | 0.5 | 0.5 | 0.5 |
| Amphetamines | 4.9 | 7.8 | 8.6 | 2.3 | 3.7 | 3.9 |
| Methamphetamine | 1.8 | 2.9 | 2.5 | 0.7 | 1.1 | 0.9 |
| Any illicit drug | 15.5 | 29.8 | 38.4 | 8.5 | 17.3 | 23.1 |
| Alcohol | 33.9 | 56.7 | 68.6 | 17.1 | 33.2 | 47.0 |
| Been drunk | 15.0 | 35.4 | 50.4 | 6.0 | 17.6 | 30.2 |

*Source:* Adapted from University of Michigan news release, December 19, 2005.

drugs, marijuana stands out as the most popular—again, by a considerable margin. Indeed, it is possible that half of all episodes of illegal drug use involve marijuana only. One-fifth of seniors (19.8%) said that they had used marijuana in the past month. The drugs that the media tend to focus on, the ones with the greatest potential for harm—crack cocaine, heroin, methamphetamine, and Rohypnol—are for the most part exotic, marginal, and very rarely used. GHB and ketamine, two widely publicized "date rape" drugs, were so rarely used at the 30-day prevalence level that their rates could not even be calculated. The MTF survey reminds us that frequency of use and media attention are two entirely separate matters.

There are some limitations to the MTF survey. Two obvious limitations involve absentees from school and dropouts. The drug use of students who are absent the day a survey is conducted, and those who have dropped out by their senior year of high school (the latter, nearly 20% nationwide), is not studied by MTF. It is almost certain that the drug use of absentees and dropouts is higher than that of students who attend regularly and graduate with their class. Hence, MTF's estimates of drug use among students in the eighth, tenth, and (especially) twelfth grades must be regarded as an underestimation. The dropout rate is especially high by the senior year; hence, twelfth-graders form a less representative segment of the appropriate age category than is true of tenth- and, especially, eighth-graders. It is also not clear whether and to what extent answering questions in a school setting about an illicit activity (drug use) reflects real-world behavior. As we've seen, reason dictates that respondents are likely to understate their drug use to a certain, but unknown, degree.

All reservations to the side, however, it must be emphasized that MTF's yearly survey on the use of and attitudes toward legal and illegal drugs is the best available study on the subject. Its sample is huge and reasonably representative of its target population; its questions are standardized and permit comparison on a year-by-year, drug-by-drug, region-by-region, and social category-by-category basis; and the data tabulations in MTF's publication are detailed and informative. The Institute for Social Research's survey on drug use sheds a clear light on a significant area of human behavior.

## THE NATIONAL SURVEY ON DRUG USE AND HEALTH (NSDUH)

In 1972, the first systematic survey of drug use among a randomized sample of Americans was conducted. Sponsored by the National Commission on Marihuana and Drug Abuse, this survey gave us our first accurate look at patterns of drug consumption in the United States. Between 1975 and 1991, nine similar surveys were sponsored by the National Institute on Drug Abuse (NIDA). Beginning in 1992, yearly surveys of drug use in the American population have been sponsored by the Substance Abuse and Mental Health Services Administration (SAMHSA), a division of the U.S. Department of Health and Human Services. In 2002, the survey's name was changed from the National Household Survey on Drug Abuse to the **National Survey on Drug Use and Health (NSDUH).** The 2005 NSDUH survey was based on a sample of 67,500 respondents. The resultant report, released in 2006 provides, in the words of the SAMHSA, national estimates of rates of use, number of users, and other measures related to the use of illicit drugs, alcohol, cigarettes, and other forms of tobacco by persons ages 12 and older.

As in the MTF study, the NSDUH asks about lifetime prevalence, yearly prevalence, 30-day prevalence, and daily prevalence for each drug. SAMHSA's national household survey divides its sample into youths ages 12–17, young adults ages 18–25, and adults ages 26 and older. Beginning in 1999, the sample has been large enough to provide reliable estimates of drug use in each state. Although a state-by-state breakdown is unlikely to be useful theoretically (for instance, to help explain why people use drugs), it may produce information that has important policy implications—such as where to deploy law enforcement personnel or build treatment facilities.

Table 6-6 tells basically the same story for the population at large that the MTF survey revealed for drug use among school children. Alcohol is by far the drug used by the largest percentage of the American population, followed by tobacco. And, again, marijuana is America's most popular illicit drug, likewise by a considerably margin. No other illegal drug is used by remotely as many people as is true of marijuana. In the month prior to the survey, only for cocaine is the proportion of the population who used any illicit drug other than marijuana as much as 1 percent. Drugs such as heroin, crack cocaine, methamphetamine, and PCP were used during the previous month, at most, by 0.2 percent of the population.

Large as its sample is, even the NSDUH is less than useful for subsamples in the population that are statistically rare. For instance, estimating heroin or crack addicts from the NSDUH's data is extremely problematic. Not only do they turn up fairly infrequently in its sample (since they make up a tiny number even in a sample of 67,000), they are also difficult to locate. Most addicts do not live at a fixed address, and so a sample based on a household survey will not be able to locate them. Many are homeless, many avoid responding to surveys, and relatives often refuse to acknowledge their existence. Hence, as with surveys

**TABLE 6-6**   Use of Various Drugs, Lifetime, Past Year, and Past Month, Persons Ages 12 and Older, 2005

|  | Lifetime | Past Year | Past Month |
|---|---|---|---|
| Marijuana/hashish | 40.1% | 10.4% | 6.0% |
| Cocaine | 13.8 | 2.3 | 1.0 |
| Crack | 3.3 | 0.6 | 0.3 |
| Heroin | 1.5 | 0.2 | 0.1 |
| LSD | 9.2 | 0.2 | 0.0 |
| PCP | 2.7 | 0.1 | 0.0 |
| MDMA (Ecstasy) | ˙ 4.7 | 0.8 | 0.2 |
| Methamphetamine | 4.3 | 0.5 | 0.2 |
| Nonmedical use of pharmaceuticals |  |  |  |
| Pain relievers | 13.4 | 4.9 | 1.9 |
| Tranquilizers | 8.7 | 2.2 | 0.7 |
| Stimulants | 7.8 | 1.1 | 0.4 |
| Sedatives | 3.7 | 0.3 | 0.1 |
| Total | 20.0 | 6.2 | 2.6 |
| Any illicit drug other than marijuana | 29.5 | 8.3 | 3.7 |
| Any illicit drug | 46.1 | 14.4 | 8.1 |
| Cigarettes | 66.6 | 29.1 | 24.9 |
| Alcohol | 82.9 | 66.5 | 51.8 |

*Note:* Percentages cannot be added up because they overlap. Pain relievers are mainly narcotics such as OxyContin, hydrocodone, and Percodan; tranquilizers are banzodiazepam-type drugs such as lorazepam (Ativan), Valium, Rohypnol, and Xanax; stimulants include the amphetamines, Ritalin, and Adderall; sedatives include the barbiturates, methaqualone (Quäälude), and GHB.
*Source:* 2005 National Survey on Drug Use and Health, SAMHSA, 2006b.

on serious crime, self-report drug surveys are increasingly inadequate the more serious—and therefore, the less common—a particular form of drug use is.

In spite of its limitations, the NSDUH is probably the best survey on the consumption of psychoactive substances that has ever been conducted among the American population as a whole. And future surveys will be improved, year by year.

## SUMMARY

Without a grounding in research methodology, we have no idea whether the estimates of prevalence figures of drug use we hear or read in the media, or the "guesstimates" of our friends, relatives and acquaintances, are accurate. Knowing how data are gathered is a first step in developing a critical perspective toward any social phenomenon. Of course, all data sources are flawed or incomplete, which means that we have to examine them more carefully, and critically, rather than simply dismiss them outright.

Researchers try to put together a variety of sources of information to give them a complete picture of drug use. This is called "triangulation," a term borrowed from land surveying to refer to pinpointing an exact location, or distances to a location, by observation from two other locations. When two or more data sources agree, we call this "multiple confirmation." The drug researcher is primarily interested in "incidence" figures, that is, the occurrence of drug use within a specific period of time, whether in the form of a rate or percentage or in the form of an absolute number. For instance, in 2005, 19.7 million Americans, or 8.1 percent of the population ages 12 and older, used one or more illegal drugs at least once during the previous month. Fortunately, drug researchers have multiple sources of data to determine such things as incidence and prevalence of drug use, drug use in different demographic categories, drug use over time, and drug use in various geographic locales. One data source is, of course, the survey.

Lying occurs—many people consciously underestimate the extent of their consumption of psychoactive substances—but it is less of a problem than you might think. We can get a roughly (although not completely) accurate picture of drug use from the answers people give in surveys. Lying influences the absolute size of figures more than the relative rank of categories of users. Sample size and representativeness are a more serious problem than respondent lying. For instance, with small samples, it is impossible to accurately estimate the size of rare forms of drug use. In addition, in drawing a sample, it is difficult to locate homeless people, and most surveys do not include prison populations—two segments of the population most likely to use drugs. Hence, we must always be skeptical about the percentages that surveys produce for the use of various drugs.

Many statements about the incidence of drug use are made in the form of statistics, which present information in a condensed and precise fashion. It is not difficult to understand "descriptive" statistics, which describe what something is in quantitative terms, that is, in the form of numbers. "Inferential" statistics are more complicated, and measure cause-and-effect relationships. They hold constant or control for a variety of factors to reach an explanation for why things happen. For instance, does drug use cause criminal behavior? Inferential statistics attempt to answer this question.

To answer the question of the how many people use which drugs, who does so, with what frequency, and with what consequences, we rely on a variety of sources. For legal drugs, we have sales records. For illicit drugs, we have ADAM (Arrestee Drug Abuse Monitoring), DAWN (Drug Abuse Warning Network), the MTF (Monitoring the Future) survey, and the National Survey on Drug Use and Health (NSDUH).

Each year, ADAM (formerly referred to as DUF—Drug Use Forecasting) gathers a sample of adult male and adult female arrestees in more than 30 metropolitan counties and asks them if they would agree to be interviewed (85% agree) and drug tested (94% of interviewees do so). ADAM also gathers information on much smaller samples of juveniles in a much smaller number of areas. Although ADAM's data are limited, they tell us a great deal about drug use and trends in different metropolitan counties. For instance, we know that heroin and PCP use is relatively rare among arrestees, that cocaine use has declined and marijuana use increased since 1990, and that methamphetamine use is confined to a limited number of jurisdictions around the country.

DAWN collects data in hospitals around the country. Two sources of data are gathered: untoward drug effects requiring emergency department (ED) intervention, and medical examiner (ME) reports on drug "overdoses" or drug-related deaths. In ED visits often, and in

ME reports usually, more than one drug is involved. Except for drug users presenting themselves for treatment, all of DAWN's data are based on acute effects. The important news in DAWN's data is that three specific drugs appear frequently both in ED and ME reports—alcohol (in combination with one or more other drugs), heroin, and cocaine.

Since 1975, every year, MTF has drawn a huge sample of twelfth-graders, college students, and young adults not in college, and, since 1991, eighth- and tenth-graders, and asked them about their drug use and their attitudes toward drug use. More than 15,000 respondents are in each category—a total of 50,000 schoolchildren and about 35,000 post–high schoolers. The school surveys are conducted in schools; in 2005, about 400 schools participated in the study. Questions about lifetime, yearly, monthly, and daily prevalence are asked. Obviously, for the school samples, dropouts and absentees are not included, and they are segments of the population most likely to use drugs; this represents a limitation of MTF's data. Overall, however, MTF is probably the best ongoing survey on drug use.

National household surveys on drug use were first conducted in 1972. Between 1975 and 1991, nine surveys were conducted under the auspices of the National Institute of Drug Abuse (NIDA). Since 1992, these surveys, now conducted yearly, have been sponsored by the Substance Abuse and Mental Health Administration (SAMHSA), a division of the federal Department of Health and Human Services. The NSDUH sample is huge (67,000 respondents in 2005). Its results are not to be trusted, however, for the rarer forms of drug use (such as heroin and crack consumption), and they are questionable in adolescent drug use (adults are present a third of the time in adolescent interviews). But for most forms of drug use for the adult segment of the population, we can have a great deal of confidence in the results of the NSDUH. Overall, the NSDUH is the best survey on the drug use of the general population.

One point must be emphasized before we turn to other matters: Chronic or more frequent drug users have characteristics or experiences that are much more likely to influence year-to-year tallies of their numbers than is true of occasional or infrequent users. For instance, the chronic user is more likely to be arrested and incarcerated than is the occasional user, and hence more likely to be removed from the street (where the likelihood of drug use is much higher) and incarcerated (where the likelihood of drug use is much lower). Thus, the number and proportion of chronic users in the population at large is strongly influenced by arrest patterns. In addition, chronic users are more likely to be infected with AIDS than are more occasional users, and so, as the disease progresses, the chronic user becomes increasingly enfeebled, and thereby less capable of paying for and using drugs such as cocaine and heroin. In addition, older (and typically, chronic) users tend to show up more often in DAWN's ME statistics, that is, to die directly or secondarily as a result of drug use. Given these and other factors, the number of chronic users of cocaine and heroin may manifest year-to-year variations that do not characterize occasional users. This is not because the actual use patterns of the same users vary from year to year—for instance, they decide to give up the drug habit—but because the choice of whether to use drugs is no longer up to them, as a result of being incarcerated, sick, or dead. This is an important point, because officials often misread downturns in chronic use, claiming that they indicate that "we have turned the corner on drug abuse," when all it indicates is that a substantial number of chronic users are now no longer able to use drugs because they are incapacitated—or dead.

## KEY TERMS

# HISTORICAL TRENDS IN DRUG CONSUMPTION

## From Past to Current Use

Did alcohol consumption increase during Prohibition? No, actually, it decreased (though when I ask this question in a true-false quiz, most of my students think otherwise). Is alcohol consumption in the United States at an all-time high? In fact, it is at a fairly low point compared with most other periods of history. Did drug use increase during the 1980s? No, it decreased rather dramatically during that decade. Was LSD consumption at an all-time high during the 1960s?

No, data show that it was quite low during the first half of the 1960s. When you spend a lifetime studying and writing about a topic, it's discouraging to discover that most people hold an extremely inaccurate picture of what you have spent so much time trying to understand. As it turns out, aside from simple ignorance, there are psychological and cognitive reasons why people reason about the world in mistaken and inaccurate ways. Many people have a difficult time thinking clearly and accurately about drug use. In their thinking, they exhibit a great many sources of error, and it would require a virtual library to discuss them all.

More generally, there are at least four distinct but interconnected social categories whose members often make incorrect inferences about social phenomena (Best, 2001), including rates of drug use and criminal behavior: the media, politicians, social activists and advocates, and the general public. In Chapter 5, we looked at how the media report on the drug beat. And I discuss the mistaken views of the public, politicians, and activists throughout this book. It's important at this point to emphasize that certain constructions of the reality of drugs are mistaken.

Most people hold an extremely erroneous idea of rates of nearly every activity. The public bases its notion of the frequency of behavior not on logic or systematic evidence but on "rules of thumb" that are both commonsensical and illusory. Cognitive psychologists, who study how people think, refer to these rules of thumb as **judgmental heuristics.** They have located and documented several distinctly different sources of bias in the way most of us reason about rates. For the sociologist of drug use and the criminologist, perhaps the most relevant of the judgmental heuristics that distort our reasoning ability is the **availability heuristic** (Kahneman, Slovic, and Tversky, 1982, pp. 163ff).

"Availability" is a mental process that mistakenly tells us that what sticks in our minds is more common than something that takes more effort to recall. In other words, we tend to exaggerate the frequency of phenomena that come readily to mind. Since those things that do not pop into our heads are readily forgotten, most of us underestimate their frequency. Ironically, our minds work in almost precisely the opposite way from the way the world works. The mundane, the everyday, the ordinary—in other words, what is usually very common—is taken for granted and, hence, conveniently forgotten, while the spectacular, the vivid, the unusual—because it is so easily recalled—frequently is mistakenly thought of as more common than it actually is.

*Vividness* is an especially powerful factor in the availability heuristic: People tend to recall what's vivid and dramatic, and they usually mistakenly believe that what they can recall is more common than it actually is. For instance, in study after study, people tend to overestimate the likelihood of dramatic, memorable events, such as a shark attack (versus drowning); contamination from a nuclear power plant (versus natural radon contamination from the soil); interracial crime, or crime that crosses racial categories (versus intraracial crime, or crime in which the offender and the victim share the same race); violent crime (as opposed to property crime); murder (versus more ordinary causes of death, such as pneumonia); and drug overdose (as opposed to death by tobacco- or alcohol-related causes). In each case, the principle is the same: Events that are dramatic and vivid tend to stick in one's mind and thus be "available" for recall, and hence their frequency or likelihood tends to be exaggerated. Whenever we think about vivid, dramatic phenomena such as drug use and crime, we should keep the availability heuristic in mind. Avoiding it will help keep our observations on track.

# RATES AND PATTERNS OF DRUG USE: THE BASICS

There are four concepts you must know to understand rates and patterns of drug use. They are overall prevalence, continuance or "loyalty" rates, consumption levels, and life cycle rates.

## Overall Prevalence Rates

It is important to distinguish between and among rates of the use of different drugs and drug types. Many commentators discuss illicit drugs as if the use of each and every one were precisely equivalent. The fact is, the number of users that different drugs attract varies considerably. The **prevalence rate,** or the number and percentage of people in the population who use a given drug during a designated period, is crucial; we must never lose sight of the *size* of a given drug's user population. Hence, when the 2005 National Survey on Drug Use and Health (NSDUH) reports that 10.4 percent of the population used marijuana at least once during the past year, while 2.3 percent did so for cocaine, these are *prevalence* rates for that year for these two drugs. Prevalence rates can be measured by lifetime, past-year, or past-month use.

This point is important because journalists have been known to exaggerate the shifts from one decade to another, implying that a particular substance is the "drug of choice" during each period. For instance, supposedly, LSD was *the* drug of the 1960s—the implication being that it was the most frequently used drug during that decade. The same is often said of cocaine during the 1980s (the so-called me or greed decade). Let's make a clear distinction between the drug that commentators say is typical, characteristic, or paradigmatic of a period and the drug that evidence says is actually used most frequently.

The first observation about overall prevalence rates of drug use in America—one that hits like an onrushing avalanche—is the huge difference in the prevalence of the use of *legal* versus *illegal* drugs. In 2004, only 19.7 million Americans ages 12 and older were "current" users of any illicit drug, that is, took one or more illegal drugs one or more times in the 30 days prior to the survey. But in that same year, there were 126 million users of alcohol and 60 million cigarette smokers. Alcohol and cigarettes—the legal drugs—are used by vastly more people than all the illicit drugs added together.

Alcohol, then, is by far the most popular of all psychoactive substances. This has been true for at least a century, it is true now, and, in all likelihood, it will remain true a century from today. Half the American population age 12 or older (52%) took at least one alcoholic drink in the past month; more than 8 in 10 (83%) have consumed alcohol one or more times during their lives. Given alcohol's effects, the sheer number and percentage of people who use alcohol means that this drug's entanglement in activities of all kinds, including criminal behavior, is likely to be considerable.

Of all *illicit* drugs, marijuana is the one used by the greatest number of people—and by a considerable margin. In 2005, 4 out of 10 Americans (40.1%) said that they had used marijuana at least once in their lives; 1 in 10 (10.4%) did so in the previous year; and 1 in 16 (6.0%) did so during the prior month. In contrast, cocaine, the illicit drug with the *next*-highest incidence rate, racked up figures of only 13.8, 2.3, and 1.0 percent, respectively. In short, marijuana is the illicit drug that attracts the largest number of users—by far. There is no close competitor. This has been true for decades, and in all likelihood, it will remain true for a number of decades to come.

However, let's keep in mind the fact that some drugs that are used by relatively few people can generate an enormous volume of social and personal disruption, including a great deal of criminal behavior. Two such drugs are heroin and crack cocaine. In the NSDUH, heroin ranks dead last in popularity, having ever been used by only 1.5 percent of the population and, during the past month, by a minuscule 0.1 percent. Crack cocaine is also used by a very small proportion of respondents—3.3 percent ever and 0.3 percent during the past month. Of course, if the NSDUH had access to prison and homeless populations, and if we had a sure-fire way of obtaining completely honest answers, the heroin and cocaine figures would likely double, triple, or increase even more. But no matter what information we manage to obtain, the fact is, compared with other drugs, some substances are used by relatively few people, yet have huge repercussions for crime and the criminal justice system—and heroin and crack cocaine are two such drugs. In any examination of drugs and crime, we have to make a sharp distinction between patterns of use and social impact.

## Continuance or "Loyalty" Rates

The number of people who have used a given drug is less important than the number and proportion who use it *regularly*. **Continuance rate** is one of the most important features of a drug's pattern of use. Drugs vary with respect to user "loyalty," as users stick with some drugs longer than others. Some people tend to give the drug up after experimental use; others used the drug over a long period of time but episodically, sporadically, on a once-in-a-while basis; still others use the drug more regularly, even frequently.

Of all drugs, alcohol generates the strongest user loyalty. Of all illegal drugs, marijuana generates the strongest user loyalty. Of the many factors that determine a drug's continuance rate, perhaps the legal-illegal distinction is most influential. As a general rule, *legal drugs have higher continuance rates than illegal drugs*. In spite of some observers' claims, illegal drugs are not as easy to obtain as alcohol and cigarettes. There is a certain "hassle factor" involved with obtaining them; they are considerably more expensive, and obtaining them entails the risk of arrest. As a result of the hassle—coming up with the money, locating a dealer, and risking arrest—illegal drugs are much more likely to be given up or used much more infrequently and sporadically than are legal drugs.

How are drug use continuance rates measured? One way is to compare lifetime use with use in the past month. Picture a large circle representing all the people who have ever used a given drug, even once, during their lifetimes. Then picture a smaller circle within the larger one that represents the number of people who have used that drug within the past month. If the smaller circle is a substantial proportion of the larger circle—that is, if most of the people who ever used a given drug are still using it—then that drug generates a *high* continuance rate; in other words, its users are relatively loyal to it. On the other hand, if the inner circle is much smaller than the outer circle—if most of the people who ever used a given drug are no longer using it, or last used it a long time ago—then the drug's continuance rate is low; that is, its users are not very loyal to it.

As we have seen, of all psychoactive substances, alcohol generates the highest loyalty or continuance rates. In the 2005 NSDUH, summarized in Table 7-1, of all at-least one-time users of alcohol, 6 in 10 (62%) drank in the past month. Just under 4 in 10 people who

| TABLE 7-1 | Continuance or "Loyalty" Rates for Selected Drugs, 2005 | | |
|---|---|---|---|
| | **Past-Month to Lifetime<br>Continuance Rates** | | **Past-Month to Past-Year<br>Continuance Rates** |
| Alcohol | 62.5% | Cigarettes | 84.1% |
| Cigarettes | 37.4 | Alcohol | 78.0 |
| Marijuana | 15.0 | Marijuana | 62.6 |
| Pain relievers | 14.2 | Crack | 49.4 |
| Tranquilizers | 8.6 | Cocaine | 43.4 |
| Crack | 8.6 | Pain relievers | 39.4 |
| Cocaine | 7.1 | Methamphetamine | 39.5 |
| Stimulants | 5.6 | Stimulants | 38.5 |
| Methamphetamine | 4.9 | Sedatives | 36.3 |
| Ecstasy | 4.4 | Heroin | 35.9 |
| Heroin | 3.8 | Tranquilizers | 34.6 |
| Sedatives | 3.0 | PCP | 29.3 |
| PCP | 0.7 | Ecstasy | 25.6 |
| LSD | 0.5 | LSD | 18.5 |

*Source:* 2005 National Survey on Drug Use and Health, SAMHSA, 2006b.

smoked cigarettes once or more in their lives (37%) smoked them within the past month. In this study, marijuana—considered the least illicit of the illegal drugs—generated a 15 percent continuance rate. (Keep in mind not only the drug but also the route of administration: Cigarettes and marijuana are smoked, while alcohol is taken orally.) Heroin and cocaine, the most serious and the least popular—although in principle the most dependency-producing—of the illegal drugs, manifested continuance rates of 5 percent and 6 percent, respectively. LSD, a drug of very sporadic or episodic use, generated a continuance rate of less than 1 percent. This same pattern—that is, the legal drugs displaying much higher continuance rates than illicit substances—prevails in the Netherlands (Sandwijk, Cohen, and Musterd, 1991, pp. 20–21, 25) and, as far as drug researchers are able to determine, everywhere else as well.

A somewhat different continuance rate can be obtained by comparing the use of a given drug in the past *year* with use in the past *month* (see Figure 7-1). As measured by this particular indicator, the drug with the highest continuance rate is the nicotine in tobacco cigarettes; in 2005, 84 percent of all people who smoked during the past year also smoked during the past month. Measured this way, only 78 percent of alcohol drinkers continued to take their drug of choice, as did 63 percent of marijuana users; for LSD, the comparable figure was 19 percent. Clearly, while many more people use alcohol than smoke cigarettes, people smoke cigarettes a great deal more often than they drink alcohol. In fact, the typical pattern of cigarette smoking is *chronic* use. For illicit drugs, lifetime users divide into quitters, sporadic or less-than-monthly, and monthly-or-more users. For most illicit drugs, daily use tends to be extremely atypical. But for cigarettes, it is the rule; for alcohol, it is common. (See also Table 7-1.)

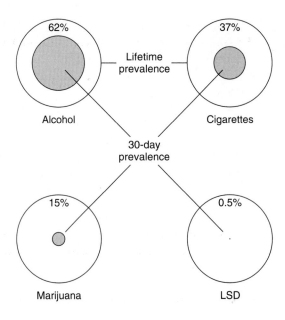

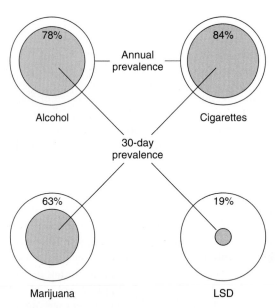

**Figure 7-1** **Continuance rates, 2005.**
Lifetime vs. 30-Day Prevalence Rates and Annual
vs. 30-Day Prevalence Rates.

*Source:* National Survey on Drug Use and Health, 2006.

## Consumption Levels

Continuance rates lead us into another measure of use: **consumption levels.** A given drug may be widely used (prevalence rate) but not necessarily heavily used by those who take it (consumption level). During a particular year, there may be many casual, recreational users (prevalence rate) and very few heavy, chronic users (consumption levels). For instance, from the late 1970s to the early 1990s, prevalence rates declined sharply but consumption levels remained high, because the number of heavy, chronic users remained fairly stable during this period, and most of the total quantity of drugs that is consumed is taken by the small minority of the very heaviest users. It is important to make this distinction because many observers who comment on policy changes (such as legalization) confuse prevalence rates with consumption levels. As we'll see, legalization is more likely to influence consumption levels (that is, the quantity of drugs consumed, mostly by the heaviest users) than prevalence rates (that is, the number of individuals who use drugs).

Here's a good example of the difference between prevalence rates and consumption levels. In the United States, as we've seen, far more people drink alcohol than smoke cigarettes; the 30-day prevalence rate for alcohol is 25 percentage points higher than it is for cigarettes—63 percent versus 37 percent. But the total consumption level of cigarettes is much higher than it is for alcohol. The fact is, more individual cigarettes (or "doses") are consumed than are alcoholic drinks. The U.S. Department of Agriculture estimates that in 2005, the 70 million smokers in the United States consumed 15 cigarettes per day for a total consumption level of 378 billion cigarettes (or doses). In contrast, over 150 million drinkers consumed an average of 1.5 alcoholic drinks per day for a total consumption level of only 82 billion drinks (or doses). In other words, while alcohol is the drug that is consumed by the greatest number of people, tobacco (which contains nicotine) is the drug that is used the greatest number of times.

Consider, too, the difference between cocaine and heroin in prevalence rates versus consumption levels. Cocaine is a widely used intoxicant; during 2005, according to the NSDUH, over 5 million Americans used cocaine. In contrast, only 400,000 used heroin during that year. However, again, remember that the NSDUH does not include the homeless or the prison population. A research organization, Abt Associates, in an attempt to get around the homeless and prison population problem, estimates 900,000 chronic heroin

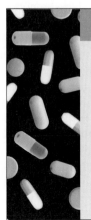

## True-False Quiz

The statement my students were most in agreement with was "Of all drugs (legal or illegal), the one that is used *the greatest number of times* is tobacco, in cigarettes"; 95 percent said that it is a true statement, while only 5 percent said that it is false. In point of fact, as we see in this chapter, this is a true statement. The modal or typical smoker uses tobacco over 20 times a day, while drinkers consume alcohol only once or twice a day, on average. Of all drugs, the nicotine in tobacco cigarettes generates the most compulsive patterns of use; very, very few smokers are casual in their use. In contrast, most users of the illegal drugs do not become compulsive, chronic abusers.

users in the United States. Either way, cocaine has significantly higher prevalence rates than heroin. But far more striking is the difference between the consumption levels of cocaine versus heroin. In terms of the total amount consumed, according to the Abt Associates' report, *What America's Users Spend on Illegal Drugs,* cocaine is used *19 times* more than heroin—in 2000, 259 tons versus 13.3 tons. In other words, the regular cocaine user consumes a greater volume of his or her drug than the regular heroin user does. Hence, an understanding of total consumption levels is crucial to getting a sense of levels of drug use. *How much* of a given drug is used is not the same thing as *how many* people use it.

## Life Cycle Rates

From time to time, the media report that drug use has become uncharacteristically high among an age segment of the population not typically given to high rates of use. For example, we read or hear that drug use is "common," "rampant," or "epidemic" among 11- or 12-year-olds, the middle-aged, or even the elderly. If this were true, it would be news. Apparently, even when it is not true, it becomes news.

The fact is, in spite of slight variations, wrinkles, and wiggles in this picture, for at least three decades, drug use has been, and remains, relatively low among youths (ages 12–17), extremely high among young adults (ages 18–25), lower in the older adult years (ages 26–34), and lower still after age 35. Practically no study has found a higher rate of drug use among young adolescents or older adults than among older adolescents and young adults. In all likelihood, this will remain true for a number of decades to come. (An obvious exception: During the 1990s, older categories, for instance, the 26- to 34-year-old age group, had higher rates of lifetime drug use than slightly younger ones, such as the 18- to 25-year-old age group, simply because their lifetime rates reflected use when they were younger. But their current rates of use—that is, use in the last year and month—remained significantly lower.) The fact is, drug use is an expression of lifestyle, and lifestyle is a reflection of age-related life cycle patterns—and these **life cycle rates** are not likely to change on a whim.

As we can see from Table 7-2, in 2005, only 2.5 percent of 12-year-olds had used at least one illicit drug, any illicit drug, during the previous month. This percentage rose fairly rapidly into the early, middle, and late teen years; reached a peak at age 20 (24%) and, with a few tiny wrinkles, declined year by year and decade by decade after that. Only 9.6 percent of people in their early thirties and 7.6 percent in their late thirties used one or more illegal drugs during the past 30 days; for the early and late forties, this was 7.2 percent and 6.6 percent, respectively; for the fifties, it was 5.2 percent and 3.4 percent, respectively; and for the late sixties, it fell below 1 percent (0.8%). In other words, illegal drug use is strongly related to one's age or position in the life cycle. Drug use begins at a low point, rises in early adulthood, and declines fairly steeply after that. After age 35, drug use falls to a level only a quarter to a fifth of what it was during the peak years. Very roughly the same pattern prevails for alcohol consumption; however, for alcohol use, there is a rise after the teenage years, and the decline after its peak year is extremely gradual—almost flat until the fifties. For instance, in 2005, alcohol use in the past month was 58 percent for 20-year-olds, 69 percent for 21-year-olds, 67 percent for 25-year-olds, 62 percent for 35- to 39-year-olds, 60 percent for 45- to 49-year-olds, and 51 percent for 55- to 59-year-olds. Unlike illicit drug use, which plummets in the older adult years, alcohol consumption is almost flat between its peak and later middle age; it does not decline sharply until the late fifties and again in the late sixties.

| TABLE 7-2 | Past-Month Use of Illicit Drugs and Alcohol, by Age, 2005 | |
| --- | --- | --- |
| **Age** | **Any Illicit Drug** | **Alcohol** |
| 12 | 2.5% | 2.5% |
| 13 | 4.9 | 5.8 |
| 14 | 6.7 | 10.6 |
| 15 | 11.1 | 19.6 |
| 16 | 15.8 | 27.0 |
| 17 | 18.2 | 33.2 |
| 18 | 20.5 | 44.4 |
| 19 | 22.6 | 52.1 |
| 20 | 24.1 | 57.6 |
| 21 | 20.7 | 69.4 |
| 22 | 20.0 | 66.2 |
| 23 | 19.5 | 69.5 |
| 24 | 16.6 | 64.8 |
| 25 | 16.4 | 67.0 |
| 26–29 | 12.9 | 63.7 |
| 30–34 | 9.6 | 61.6 |
| 35–39 | 7.6 | 62.4 |
| 40–44 | 7.2 | 60.1 |
| 45–49 | 6.6 | 60.2 |
| 50–54 | 5.2 | 58.3 |
| 55–59 | 3.4 | 50.8 |
| 60–64 | 1.8 | 47.5 |
| 65+ | 0.8 | 40.0 |
| Total | 8.1 | 51.8 |

*Source:* 2005 National Survey on Drug Use and Health, 2006.

## TRENDS OVER TIME: AN INTRODUCTION

One of the most interesting issues a sociologist or criminologist addresses is *trends* in drug use over time. The media are concerned about trends when television news and newspaper headlines announce that drug use is "up" or "down" over the past year or decade, that it has "risen" or "declined."

In order to make statements about changes in any human behavior over time, not only do we need data, we need valid, reliable, and systematic data on the behavior we're interested in. "Systematic" means that the data were gathered in a planned fashion, that they represent an accurate, cross-sectional view of the phenomenon under study. If the data are truly systematic, we have confidence that what's being described during a given year can be meaningfully compared with what's being described during another year. What systematic, valid, and reliable evidence do we have that bears on the matter of changes in drug use over historical time?

## ALCOHOL CONSUMPTION: 1700S–1919

Because the sale of alcohol was legal from colonial times to 1919—the year before Prohibition—historians have an excellent and uninterrupted record of trends in consumption over a stretch of several centuries. Of course, alcohol *sales* are not exactly the same thing as alcohol *consumption*. That's why researchers who investigate the matter refer to alcohol sales during a given period as "apparent" consumption. Most experts feel that the discrepancy between sales and consumption is likely to be small and that, for all practical purposes, the sale of alcohol can be used to measure its consumption. In addition, researchers feel that the total production—and therefore consumption—of homebrew and "moonshine," or illegal alcohol, does not alter the picture a great deal. In any case, the total volume of unrecorded alcohol production (and, presumably, consumption) diminishes the closer we move toward the present time.

Before we look at the historical record, it's necessary to explain that alcohol consumption is measured in a variety of ways, but one major way is the *volume* of alcohol purchased. Volume is expressed in the total number of gallons of absolute alcohol consumed per person (usually tabulated in the population over the age of 12, or 14, or 15, depending on the study) per year. "Absolute" alcohol refers to the volume of alcohol that is contained in a given alcoholic beverage. The alcohol a beverage contains varies considerably from one beverage to another.

Beer contains about 5 percent alcohol, wine contains 13 percent, and distilled spirits such as whiskey, vodka, gin, and tequila contain 40–50 percent. Thus, if 100 ounces of each of these beverages were poured into a separate bucket, the one containing the beer would hold only 5 ounces of absolute alcohol, the one with the wine about 13 ounces, and the one with the distilled spirits about 40–50 ounces. Therefore, sale amounts for each of these beverages has to be converted into the total amount of alcohol each contains to make comparisons meaningful. For instance, the per capita consumption of 2 gallons of alcohol for the nation during a given year would represent drinking more than 40 gallons of beer, or 15 gallons of wine, or nearly 4.5 gallons of distilled spirits.

What about alcohol consumption in the past? To put the matter plainly, during colonial times, drinking "constituted a central fact of . . . life"; most people "drank often and abundantly" (Lender and Martin, 1987, p. 9). Beer and cider were common at mealtime, with children often partaking. Collective tasks, such as clearing a field, were usually accompanied by the tapping of a cask of brew, and farmers typically took a jug with them into the fields each morning. Employers often gave their workers liquor on the job. Political candidates usually "treated" the voters to alcoholic beverages—including at polling places on election day. And the Continental Army supplied its troops with a daily ration of 4 ounces of rum or whiskey. In short, drinking was extremely common in seventeenth- and eighteenth-century America—strikingly more so than it is today (Lender and Martin, 1987, pp. 2–3). Estimates put per capita alcohol consumption for all Americans ages 15 and older in 1790 (the year of the first U.S. Census) at 5.8 gallons of absolute alcohol per year, more than twice its current level (pp. 9–10, 20, 205).

As high as the rate of consumption of alcohol was in the 1700s, it actually rose in the early 1800s—from 5.8 gallons in 1790 to 7.1 gallons in 1830. Moreover, over time, a high proportion of Americans shifted from beer and wine, which were roughly 5 percent and 13 percent alcohol, respectively, to the vastly more potent distilled spirits, which were

40–50 percent alcohol. In 1790, 40 percent of the alcohol consumed in America was in the form of distilled spirits; by 1830, this figure had climbed to 60 percent. Hence, not only were more people drinking from the late 1700s to the early 1800s, but they were drinking more potent beverages.

Said one observer, in 1814, "the quantity of ardent spirits" consumed in the United States at that time "surpasses belief." Drinking "had reached unparalleled levels." The notion that alcohol "was necessary for health remained firmly fixed. It was common to down a glass of whiskey or other spirits before breakfast . . . instead of taking coffee or tea breaks." Americans customarily took work breaks at 11 A.M. and 4 P.M. for a few pulls at the jug. "Even school children took their sip of whiskey, the morning and afternoon glasses being considered 'absolutely indispensable to man and boy.'" Distilled spirits "were a basic part of the diet—most people thought that whiskey was as essential as bread" (Lender and Martin, 1987, pp. 205, 47).

Records indicate that 1830 was the high point in the nation's alcohol consumption; after that, drinking declined. The cause? In a nutshell, the impact of the temperance movement. Actually, the seeds of temperance were planted nearly a half century before with the publication of Benjamin Rush's treatise *An Inquiry into the Effects of Ardent Spirits on the Human Mind and Body* in 1784. At the time, Rush, a prominent physician, was something of a voice in the wilderness. He did not condemn drinking per se; his target was the heavy, uncontrolled consumption of distilled spirits. "Consumed in quantity over the years," he wrote, distilled spirits "could destroy a person's health and even cause death." Rush was the first medical figure or scientist to argue that what we now refer to as alcoholism is a disease and an addiction.

Rush had friends who were influential in religious affairs and who heeded his call. The first local temperance society was founded in 1808, and in 1826, a national organization, the American Temperance Society, was founded. Following Rush's example, it preached the gospel of moderation rather than prohibition. It "helped organize local units, sent lecturers into the field, distributed literature (including Rush's *Inquiry*), and served as a clearinghouse for movement information." By 1830, more than 200 local anti-liquor chapters had been formed, and temperance had become "a burgeoning national movement." By the 1830s, the movement boasted more than 1.5 million members, and its efforts began to have a real-world impact.

Employers stopped supplying liquor on the job, politicians ceased "treating" their constituents with alcohol, and local taverns—notorious locales for heavy, uncontrolled drinking—were denied licenses (Lender and Martin, 1987, p. 68). As a result of these and other efforts, alcohol consumption in the United States plummeted between 1830 (7.1 gallons of alcohol per person per year) and 1840 (3.1 gallons). In 1867, the Prohibition Party was formed, which ran political candidates on an anti-liquor platform. Interestingly, many of the party's planks were extremely progressive for their time; they included women's rights, prison reform, and universal public education.

With minor fluctuations, rates of drinking remained fairly stable between 1850 and the dawn of Prohibition, at just over 2 gallons per person ages 15 and older per year. Between 1916 and 1919, alcohol consumption actually declined significantly, to below 2 gallons, in large part because, even before national alcohol prohibition took effect, roughly two-thirds of the American population lived in "dry" states, that is, states with their own alcohol prohibition laws. Between 1908 and 1917, over 100,000 licensed bars closed down nationwide.

## ALCOHOL CONSUMPTION DURING PROHIBITION

In 1920, the Eighteenth Amendment to the Constitution, or Volstead Act, went into effect, making it illegal to manufacture or sell alcoholic beverages anywhere in the United States (see Chapter 4). Everyone agrees that enforcement of Prohibition was difficult and problematic. But what impact, if any, did it have? Did drinking rise, decline, or remain the same when it was prohibited? What other effects did Prohibition have?

What is your mental image of drinking during Prohibition? If you are like most people, chances are, you imagine that Americans drank *more* alcohol during Prohibition than when its sale was legal. As I said, I've distributed questionnaires asking the students in my classes whether they thought that alcohol consumption *increased* or *decreased* during Prohibition. The majority—the last time I asked this question in this way, roughly 85 percent!—said they thought it increased. In the public imagination, making alcohol illegal actually stimulated its consumption. (The percentage agreeing with the question varies according to its wording.)

Images of bathtub gin, silver hip flasks, speakeasies, out-of-the-way and hole-in-the-wall jazz clubs, gang warfare, night convoys of trucks crossing the border, weighed down with loads of Canadian whiskey—all are part of American historical lore. *Of course* the consumption of alcohol increased during Prohibition, most of us think. It makes a good story, doesn't it? It's dramatic and vivid, and it sticks in the mind. Imagining most Americans staying home and sipping Coca-Cola, root beer, or Dr. Pepper is just too boring for words.

The fact is, alcohol consumption *declined* during Prohibition—and by quite a bit. True, many Americans did drink alcohol—but how many? Saying that "many" Americans drank says nothing about the *number* or the *proportion*. It's a very vague and highly impressionistic statement. Compared with the decade or so before and after Prohibition, was the consumption of alcohol higher—or lower? How much higher or lower? And how do we know?

Scholars estimate that alcohol consumption was more than twice as high in the decade or so before Prohibition as during (Lender and Martin, 1987, pp. 205–206). And in the years after Prohibition, it began at a low point—largely because it took a few years for most

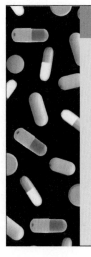

### True-False Quiz

Is the statement "In the sense of reducing alcohol consumption, Prohibition was a success; during the period of national alcohol prohibition (1920–1933), when it was illegal to sell alcoholic beverages, the use of alcohol actually *decreased*" true or false? Only a quarter of my students (25%) thought it is true; three-quarters (75%) said they believed it to be false. As we learn in this section, the statement is true. Piecing together a number of indicators tells us that *fewer* people drank during Prohibition than during both the pre- and post-Prohibition eras. The myth of heavy drinking during the 1920s is widespread—and memorable (after all, these were the Roaring Twenties). It appeals to the rebel in us, and to our opposition to overly restrictive laws. But the fact is, most people stopped drinking during Prohibition, and only very slowly began drinking again after 1933.

people to get back into the habit of drinking—but climbed during the 1940s. The per capita consumption of absolute alcohol for all Americans ages 15 and older plummeted in the years immediately before Prohibition (1916–1919–1.96 gallons), stayed low during Prohibition (1920–1930—0.90 gallons), and rose slowly in the year following Prohibition (1934—0.97 gallons), a bit more quickly the year after that (1935—1.20 gallons), and more substantially during the late 1930s. By the 1940s (1942–1946), it stood at 2.06 gallons.

The consumption figures for the pre- and post-Prohibition eras are robust, "hard," or incontrovertible data, based on the taxable sales of beer, wine, and distilled spirits. In contrast, consumption during the Prohibition years is based on *indirect* alcohol-related indicators such as rates of cirrhosis of the liver, hospital admissions for alcohol-related dementia, drunk driving citations, automobile fatalities, and arrests for drunk and disorderly conduct. For instance, the death rate from cirrhosis of the liver declined from the 1900–1919 era, when it was 12–17 persons per 100,000 population, to the 1920s and early 1930s, when it was 7–9 per 100,000 (Grant, Noble, and Malin, 1986). Epidemiologists regard cirrhosis as a very reliable measure of the percentage of heavy drinkers in the population. Although the history of Prohibition is indeed very vivid and colorful, it does not point to an increase in drinking during that era. The picture is a great deal more mundane and less dramatic than flappers, hip flasks, and jazz clubs, which existed but were not as common as the stereotype has it. The truth is that most Americans who drank *before* Prohibition stopped drinking *during* Prohibition. Boring as it may seem, Prohibition actually discouraged alcohol consumption.

## Repeal: Alcohol Consumption, 1933–Present

As we saw, the first year of the repeal of the Eighteenth Amendment witnessed a slight increase in alcohol consumption, to just under a gallon per person ages 15 and older—about half the pre-Prohibition level. The use of alcoholic beverages climbed throughout the 1930s and early 1940s, jumped significantly during the World War II years, and leveled off, with slight year-to-year fluctuations, until the late 1960s, when it began to rise again. As we'll see, during the second half of the 1960s, illicit drug use increased as well, suggesting that the use of legal and illegal psychoactive substances are related to one another.

Alcohol consumption reached a post-Prohibition peak sometime between the late 1970s and the early 1980s (as it did for illicit drug use as well), and (except for a few one- or

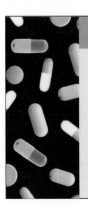

### True-False Quiz

"In the past 20–25 years, alcohol consumption in the United States has *decreased*"—true or false? Alcohol consumption, as based on sales, a very reliable figure, reached something of a twentieth-century peak 20–25 years ago and has been declining since then. Hence, that statement is true, but only 19 percent of my students thought so; 81 percent said that it is false. People often think that contemporary problems are more serious than those in the past, that the country's social problems are getting worse and worse. This is not necessarily the case, as the data on alcohol consumption show.

| TABLE 7-3 | Per-Year, Per-Capita Consumption of Absolute Alcohol, 1790–2003 |
|---|---|

| Selected Years | Gallons |
|---|---|
| 1790 | 5.80 |
| 1830 | 7.10 |
| 1840 | 3.10 |
| 1850 | 2.10 |
| 1860 | 2.53 |
| 1870 | 2.07 |
| 1911–1915 | 2.56 |
| 1916–1919 | 1.96 |
| 1920–1930 | 0.90* |
| 1934 | 0.97 |
| 1935 | 1.20 |
| 1936–1941 | 1.54 |
| 1942–1946 | 2.06 |
| 1951–1955 | 2.00 |
| 1961–1965 | 2.16 |
| 1966–1970 | 2.45 |
| 1971 | 2.69 |
| 1978 | 2.71 |
| 1980 | 2.76 |
| 1985 | 2.62 |
| 1990 | 2.45 |
| 1993 | 2.23 |
| 1998 | 2.14 |
| 1999 | 2.16 |
| 2000 | 2.18 |
| 2003 | 2.22 |

*Estimate, based on rates of cirrhosis of the liver, admissions to mental hospitals for alcohol-induced dementia, and so on.
*Note:* Population ages 15 and older, 1790–1970; 14 and older, 1971–2003.
*Source:* Lender and Martin, 1987, pp. 205–206; Nephew et al., 2003; Lakins et al., 2005.

two-year wrinkles) declined steadily throughout the 1980s and 1990s. Interestingly, as we'll find out in more detail momentarily, property crime victimization also reached a peak in the late 1970s and declined after that, and violent crime declined throughout the 1990s. It is entirely possible that in important ways, these three developments—the decline of alcohol consumption, illicit drug use, and criminal behavior, including property and violent crime, are interrelated. Just as interesting: After 1998 and into the twenty-first century, the consumption of alcohol began to inch upward. In 1998, Americans consumed 2.14 gallons of absolute alcohol; in 2003, this figure was 2.22. In any case, the historical corelationships between alcohol use and crime, and alcohol and illicit drug use, are well documented. Per capita rates of alcohol consumption for selected years are depicted in Table 7-3.

## DRUG USE TRENDS OVER TIME: 1960S–1979

As we have seen, systematic surveys on drug use were not conducted until the early 1970s. Any statements about illicit use before that time are, for the most part, based on guesses, anecdotes, fragmentary information, and, as with alcohol consumption during Prohibition, indirect indicators and measures. Hence, it makes a great deal of sense to begin our discussion of illicit drug use with the early 1970s—with one qualification.

The 1979 national household survey made use of **retrospective estimates,** that is, projections backwards in time, based on the respondent's age and the age at which he or she began using one or more drugs, to estimate drug use patterns as far back as 1960 (Miller and Cisin, 1980). Hence, rates of drug use during the 1960–1971 era can be "reconstructed" from the 1979 survey data. Rates of drug use during 1972 and afterwards can be calculated from the data in household surveys that were conducted in the appropriate years.

The dominant stereotype of the 1960s is that it was a decade of extremely high rates of drug use. Nowadays, when the 1960s are depicted, no representation is complete without portrayals of long-haired young people smoking marijuana, "dropping acid," wearing clothes with the appropriate psychedelic designs, and engaging in political demonstrations. In addition, aside from marijuana, LSD is often depicted as the drug of choice in the "psychedelic sixties." The idea that LSD use was widespread during the 1960s is even enshrined in some drug textbooks. Say three psychopharmacologists (without supplying evidence), "LSD seems to have peaked in 1967 and 1968, after which it tapered off" (Ksir, Hart, and Ray, 2006, p. 343). All these "psychedelic sixties" elements tell a colorful story, they stick in the mind, and they seem to belong together.

The fact is, during the 1960s, the stereotype of extraordinarily broad use of drugs generally, and LSD specifically, is one of those vivid, colorful stories that remains lodged in our minds (remember our old friend the "availability heuristic"?) but has very little basis in fact. The true story of drug use during the 1960s, as told by the 1979 national household survey's retrospective estimates, is quite different. In actual fact, LSD use was at an extremely low level in 1960, rose slowly during the early to mid-1960s, and rose more rapidly in the late 1960s and 1970s.

The 1960 estimates for lifetime use (a measure that obviously encompasses the largest number of users) for young adults, a segment of the population that is most likely to use illicit drugs, are extremely low. In 1960, according to the 1979 national household survey's retrospective estimates, only 4 percent of young adults ages 18–25 had ever used marijuana, even once. By 1967, this had risen to 14 percent. For the "stronger" drugs—cocaine and the hallucinogens—a category that includes LSD, these figures were much, much lower. In 1960, the "ever used" statistic was 1 percent for cocaine and 1 percent for the hallucinogens; by 1967, these figures had risen to 2 percent for cocaine and 3 percent for the hallucinogens. These figures do not paint a picture consistent with widespread drug use during the 1960s. The available evidence suggests that the 1960s were psychedelic only for a very small proportion of the population (Miller and Cisin, 1980, pp. 13–18).

What *is* true, however, is that the 1960s initiated the modern era of drug use. In a significant sense, the decade provided the launching pad for the patterns of illicit drug use in today's society. As we can see from Table 7-4, illicit drug use—as measured by lifetime use among young adults ages 18–25, for three representative drugs or drug types—rose

**TABLE 7-4**    **Lifetime Use of Selected Drugs by Young Adults (18–25), 1960–1979**

|  | 1960 | 1967 | 1974 | 1979 |
|---|---|---|---|---|
| Marijuana | 4% | 14% | 53% | 68% |
| Cocaine | 1 | 2 | 13 | 28 |
| Hallucinogens | 1 | 3 | 17 | 25 |

*Note:* 1960 and 1967 figures based on retrospective estimates.
*Source:* Fishburne, Abelson, and Cisin, 1980, pp. 26–32; Miller and Cisin, 1980, pp. 13–18.

significantly from the early to the late 1960s, *skyrocketed* from the late 1960s to the mid-1970s, and continued to rise into the late 1970s. The 1967–1974 increase is especially striking. It was the 1970s—and not the 1960s—in which the recreational use of illicit drugs was most widespread.

As we learned in Chapter 6, multiple confirmation is one method of generating confidence that a given observation is true. Unfortunately, the Monitoring the Future (MTF) survey on high school seniors did not begin until 1975, so it can't confirm the national household survey's report of a huge increase in drug use from the 1960s to the 1970s. But it does document that 1979 (or 1980, or 1981, depending on the specific drug or measure) was the high point in recreational drug use in the United States.

Attitudes and behavior are not always perfectly correlated with one another. Often, what people *say* and what they *do* are very different (Deutscher, Pestello, and Pestello, 1993). Nonetheless, if attitudes and behavior are in agreement with one another, the researcher can feel more confident that the observed tendency is actually taking place. And the fact is, according to the MTF study of high school seniors, trends in illicit drug use during the 1970s were almost perfectly paralleled by attitudes toward drug use during that period. Between the mid-to-late 1970s, when drug use *increased,* the percentage of high school seniors saying that drug use is harmful *decreased*—two observations that are consistent with one another. For instance, between 1975 and 1979, the percentage of high school seniors saying that taking LSD "once or twice" is harmful decreased from 49 percent to 42 percent. The comparable figures for cocaine were 43 percent and 32 percent.

The MTF survey also asked high school seniors about whether they "disapprove of people" age 18 or older engaging in illicit drug use. For smoking marijuana "once or twice," the percentage declined between 1975 (43%) and 1979 (34%). For nearly every drug category and level of use, the percentage of twelfth-graders disapproving of the consumption of the illicit substance declined.

In addition, over the course of the 1970s, high school seniors' attitudes regarding the legality of the use of illicit drugs also became more relaxed, tolerant, and laissez-faire. Correspondingly, the proportion supporting the current criminalization of drugs shrank. Between 1975 and 1979, the percentage saying that marijuana use "should be a crime" declined from 31 percent to 24 percent. In these same years, rates of approval for legalizing the sale of marijuana to adults increased from a bit more than a third (37%) to a majority (53%). Clearly, then, during the course of the 1970s, attitudes toward illicit drug use—as measured by perception of harmfulness, degree of disapproval, and support for legalization—became increasingly tolerant.

In nearly all respects, the 1970s represented a high point of tolerance toward use, an attitude that was translated into legal policy. During the decade, 12 states decriminalized the possession of small quantities of marijuana, indicating that legislators sensed a more accepting public attitude toward at least one illicit drug and implemented that sense into legal policy. We will look at the criminalization and decriminalization of marijuana and the other currently illicit drugs in more detail in Chapter 15.

## DRUG USE: 1980S–PRESENT

Two remarkable things happened in the world of drug use on its way to the twenty-first century: First, in the decade or so after its high point, which occurred roughly 1978–1980, drug use experienced a dramatic decline; and second, during the early 1990s, it looked very much as if it were on the rise again.

When we compare the figures for illicit drug use for 1979 with those for 1991, the decline of the 1980s seems more than simply remarkable—it is almost astounding. In many ways, the 1970s represented the fulfillment of the hedonistic 1960s. By the end of the 1970s, America was using illicit drugs in unprecedented numbers. For instance, among 18- to 25-year-olds, between 1960 and 1979, lifetime marijuana use shot up more than 15 times and cocaine use more than 25 times (see Table 7-4). But the decline of the 1980s seemed to usher in the dawn of an age of moderation, a turnaround in use that can be compared with the sharp decline in alcohol consumption nationwide after 1830 (or, for that matter, during Prohibition). For the first time for many decades, we seemed to be doing something right.

But along came the 1990s, and everything changed. The rise in illicit drug use during the last decade of the twentieth century seems surprising because the nation seemed to have its drug use under control. Things were going right, but then suddenly, they weren't. The increase was problematic, troubling, very much in need of an explanation. But the rise in illicit drug use in the first half of the 1990s was peculiar, because it was extremely selective, partial, and piecemeal.

Let's look at the 1979–1991 national household figures, as depicted in Table 7-5. In 1979, 17 percent of youths ages 12–17 said that they had used marijuana once or more in the past month; in 1991, only 4 percent had—a decline of four-fifths. In 1979, an almost astounding one-third of young adults ages 18–25 (35%) had used marijuana in the past 30 days; by 1991, this figure had been cut by two-thirds to 13 percent. In 1979, an astonishing 1 young adult in 10 had used cocaine in the past month (9%); by 1991, only 1 in 50 had done so (2%). Clearly, over the course of the 1980s, young people became much more moderate in their use of illegal drugs. For all drugs, for all age categories, and for all categories of use, the consumption of illicit drugs declined between the late 1970s and the early 1990s. Even the use of alcohol declined during this period. In 1979, over a third of youths had consumed an alcoholic beverage during the previous month (37%); in 1991, only a fifth (20%) had. For young adults, the comparable figures were 76 percent and 64 percent. Table 7-5 details these findings. (See also Figure 7-2.)

The drug use trends for high school seniors from 1979 to 1991, as documented by the MTF survey, were nearly as impressive as those the national household survey turned up.

| TABLE 7-5 | Drug Use in America, 1974–2005 | | | | | | | |
|---|---|---|---|---|---|---|---|---|
| | | **Youths (12–17)** | | | | **Young Adults (18–25)** | | | |
| | | **1974** | **1979** | **1991** | **2005** | **1974** | **1979** | **1991** | **2005** |
| Marijuana | Life | 23% | 31% | 13% | 17% | 53% | 68% | 51% | 52% |
| | Year | 19 | 24 | 10 | 13 | 34 | 47 | 25 | 28 |
| | Month | 12 | 17 | 4 | 7 | 25 | 35 | 13 | 17 |
| Cocaine | Life | 4 | 5 | 2 | 2 | 13 | 28 | 18 | 15 |
| | Year | 3 | 4 | 2 | 2 | 8 | 20 | 8 | 7 |
| | Month | 1 | 1 | * | 1 | 3 | 9 | 2 | 3 |
| Stimulants | Life | 5 | 3 | 3 | 3 | 17 | 18 | 9 | 11 |
| | Year | 3 | 3 | 2 | 2 | 8 | 10 | 3 | 4 |
| | Month | 1 | 1 | 1 | 1 | 4 | 4 | 1 | 1 |
| Hallucogens | Life | 6 | 7 | 3 | 4 | 17 | 25 | 13 | 21 |
| | Year | 4 | 5 | 2 | 3 | 6 | 10 | 5 | 6 |
| | Month | 1 | 2 | 1 | 1 | 3 | 4 | 1 | 2 |
| Alcohol | Life | 54 | 70 | 46 | 41 | 82 | 95 | 90 | 86 |
| | Year | 51 | 54 | 40 | 33 | 77 | 87 | 83 | 78 |
| | Month | 34 | 37 | 20 | 17 | 69 | 76 | 64 | 61 |

*Indicates less than 0.5 percent. All figures rounded off to whole numbers, except for 0.5.

*Source:* Fishburne, Abelson, and Cisin, 1980, pp. 26–32; NIDA, 1991; SAMHSA, 2002, 2003, 2006a.

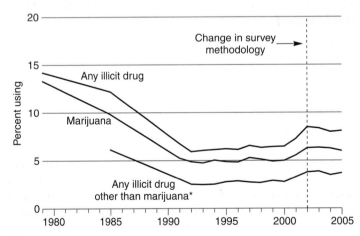

**Figure 7-2** **Percentage of U.S. household residents (ages 12 and older) reporting past-month use of any illicit drug, marijuana, or any illicit drug other than marijuana, 1979–2005.**

*No data are available for "Any illicit drug other than marijuana" for 1979.

*Source:* Adapted by CESAR from the Substance Abuse and Mental Health Services Administration (SAMHSA), National Household Survey on Drug Abuse (NHSDA) and National Survey on Drug Use and Health (NSDUH). CESAR is the Center for Substance Abuse Research at the University of Maryland at College Park.

**TABLE 7-6**   **30-Day Prevalence in Use of Selected Drugs by High School Seniors, Selected Years, 1975–2005**

|  | 1975 | 1979 | 1985 | 1991 | 1996 | 2002 | 2005 |
|---|---|---|---|---|---|---|---|
| Marijuana | 27% | 37% | 26% | 14% | 22% | 22% | 20% |
| Cocaine | 2 | 6 | 7 | 1 | 2 | 2 | 2 |
| Amphetamines | 9 | 10 | 7 | 3 | 4 | 6 | 4 |
| LSD | 2 | 2 | 2 | 2 | 4 | 1 | 1 |
| Barbiturates | 5 | 3 | 2 | 1 | 2 | 3 | 3 |
| Any illicit drug | 31 | 39 | 30 | 16 | 25 | 25 | 23 |
| Alcohol | 68 | 72 | 66 | 54 | 51 | 49 | 47 |
| Cigarettes | 37 | 31 | 30 | 28 | 34 | 27 | 23 |

*Note:* These drugs were selected because there is a continuous time line for them from 1975 to the present.
*Source:* University of Michigan, News Service, December 19, 2005.

As we can see from Table 7-6, the use of any illegal drug during the past month declined from nearly 4 seniors in 10 in 1979 (39%) to only 16 percent in 1991. For marijuana, the decline was just as steep—from 37 percent to 14 percent. In 1991, only one-fourth as many high school seniors had used cocaine in the past month (1.4%) as had done so in 1979 (5.7%). Once again, even the use of alcohol had become more moderate during this period; monthly use declined by almost a fifth.

Many observers saw extremely good news in these figures. Although the country's drug use was still extremely high—drug use in the early 1990s was vastly higher than it was in the early 1960s—it seemed to be moving in the right direction. But 1991 represented another turning point in the country's drug use trends: After the early 1990s, a significant rise in illicit drug consumption was in the works. Indeed, the increases in drug use after 1991 in some population categories were quite dramatic.

The biggest increases in drug use after the early 1990s took place among the very young—segments of the population whose use began to be recorded for the first time in that year. In 1991, the MTF survey began to include eighth- and tenth-graders in its sample. And, for the first time, a substantial proportion of the students in those grades began using illegal drugs. Initiation into the use of illicit substance was beginning to take place at earlier and earlier ages. And these increases were not only substantial but practically unprecedented.

Let's look at the 1991–2005 period in two chunks—between 1991 and 1996, and between 1996 and 2005. As we can see in Table 7-7, in 1991, 5.7 percent of eight-graders and 11.6 percent of tenth-graders said that they had used any illicit drug during the past 30 days. By 1996, 14.6 percent of eighth-graders and 23.2 percent of tenth-graders had used marijuana in the previous 30 days. In other words, in the brief span of just five years in the early-to-mid-1990s, recent or current illicit drug use more than *doubled* among an extremely vulnerable adolescent segment of the population. (Correspondingly, among high school seniors, this figure increased from 16.4 percent to 24.6 percent, a substantial increase—but much less than a doubling.) Clearly, after the early 1990s, a disturbing trend in drug use among the young was in the works, and no one knew what to do about it.

| TABLE 7-7 | Trends in 30-Day Prevalence of Use of Various Drugs, 1991–2005 | | | | |
|---|---|---|---|---|---|
| | **1991** | **1996** | **1997** | **2002** | **2005** |
| Marijuana | | | | | |
| 8th grade | 3.2% | 11.3% | 10.2% | 8.3% | 6.6% |
| 10th grade | 8.7 | 20.4 | 20.5 | 17.8 | 15.2 |
| 12th grade | 13.8 | 21.9 | 23.7 | 21.5 | 19.8 |
| Cocaine | | | | | |
| 8th grade | 0.5 | 1.3 | 1.1 | 1.1 | 1.0 |
| 10th grade | 0.7 | 1.7 | 2.0 | 1.6 | 1.5 |
| 12th grade | 1.4 | 2.0 | 2.3 | 2.3 | 2.3 |
| Amphetamines | | | | | |
| 8th grade | 2.6 | 4.6 | 3.8 | 2.8 | 2.3 |
| 10th grade | 3.3 | 5.5 | 5.1 | 5.2 | 3.7 |
| 12th grade | 3.2 | 4.1 | 4.8 | 5.5 | 3.9 |
| LSD | | | | | |
| 8th grade | 0.6 | 1.5 | 1.5 | 0.7 | 0.5 |
| 10th grade | 1.5 | 2.4 | 2.8 | 0.7 | 0.6 |
| 12th grade | 1.9 | 2.5 | 3.1 | 0.7 | 0.6 |
| Any illicit drug | | | | | |
| 8th grade | 5.7 | 14.6 | 12.9 | 10.4 | 8.5 |
| 10th grade | 11.6 | 23.2 | 23.0 | 20.8 | 17.3 |
| 12th grade | 16.4 | 24.6 | 26.2 | 25.4 | 23.1 |
| Any illicit drug other than marijuana | | | | | |
| 8th grade | 3.8 | 6.9 | 6.0 | 4.7 | 4.1 |
| 10th grade | 5.5 | 8.9 | 8.8 | 8.1 | 6.4 |
| 12th grade | 7.1 | 9.5 | 10.7 | 11.3 | 10.3 |
| Alcohol | | | | | |
| 8th grade | 25.1 | 26.2 | 24.5 | 19.6 | 17.1 |
| 10th grade | 42.8 | 40.4 | 40.1 | 35.4 | 33.2 |
| 12th grade | 54.0 | 50.8 | 52.7 | 48.6 | 47.0 |
| Cigarettes | | | | | |
| 8th grade | 14.3 | 21.0 | 19.4 | 10.7 | 9.3 |
| 10th grade | 20.8 | 30.4 | 29.8 | 17.7 | 14.9 |
| 12th grade | 28.3 | 34.0 | 36.5 | 26.7 | 23.2 |

*Source:* University of Michigan news release, December 19, 2005.

Interestingly, most of this increase in illegal drug use was with marijuana only. While the 1991–1996 eighth- and tenth-grade increases for illicit drugs *other than* marijuana represented substantially less than a doubling, those for marijuana were substantially more than double. In 1991, 3.8 percent of eighth-graders and 5.5 percent of tenth-graders used any illicit drug other than marijuana during the past month; in 1996, these figures were 6.9 percent and 8.9

percent, respectively—less than a doubling. But for marijuana specifically, in 1991, this was true of 3.2 percent of eighth-graders and 8.7 percent of tenth-graders, and in 1996, it was 11.3 percent and 20.4 percent, respectively—more than a doubling. Clearly, the bulk of the eighth- and tenth-grade increases in illicit drug use that took place during the 1990s came about as a result of expanded marijuana use.

However, as with nearly all the time trends we've examined so far, there is no uni-directional pattern. The drug use, especially marijuana, that began to skyrocket during the early-to-mid-1990s fizzled out in the late 1990s and early twenty-first century. Between 1997 and 2005, illegal drug use among schoolchildren remained flat—indeed, even dipped slightly. In 1997, 12.9 percent of eighth-graders and 23.0 percent of tenth-graders had used one or more illicit drugs in the past 30 days; in 2005, the figures were 8.5 percent and 17.3 percent, respectively. Even for marijuana, the percentage dropped: In 1997, it was 10.2 per-cent for eighth-graders and 20.5 percent for tenth-graders; in 2005, the comparable figures were 6.6 percent and 15.2 percent, respectively. Clearly, the young adolescent drug use "boom" that began in the early 1990s was incapable of sustaining itself; the explosion in adolescent drug use that some had feared had fizzled out. Between 2001 and 2005, past-month illicit drug use for eighth-, tenth-, and twelfth-graders combined dropped from 19.4 to 15.8 percent. While the percentage decline might seem small, it represents abstinence for a half million more schoolchildren who five years before had been using one or more illegal drugs—encouraging news for public health experts. (See Figure 7-3.)

There is a category of chemically and pharmacologically miscellaneous substances whose use boomed late in the twentieth century but declined early in the twenty-first. In the short run, consumption of these substances grew from nearly zero to significant levels. In 1996, the MTF survey began asking respondents about their use of MDMA (or Ecstasy) and Rohypnol, and in 2000, GHB and ketamine were added to the list. These drugs are used with a fair degree of frequency among teenagers and young adults in clubs and "raves" where all-night dancing to throbbing, hypnotic music takes place. In 2002, among high

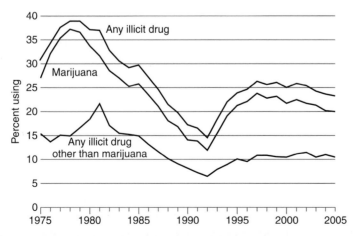

**Figure 7-3**  **Percentage of U.S. high school seniors reporting past-month use of any illicit drug, marijuana, or any illicit drug other than marijuana, 1975–2005.**

*Source:* Adapted by CESAR from the National Institute on Drug Abuse (NIDA), monitoring the future survey. CESAR is the Center for Substance Abuse Research at the University of Maryland at College Park.

school seniors, lifetime Ecstasy use was just over 1 in 10 (10.5%), and the figure for use in the previous month was roughly 1 in 40 (2.4%). But by 2005, these figures had declined to 5.4 percent and 1.0 percent, respectively. And use rates for the other "club" drugs was considerably lower, in the 1.0–2.5 percent range for annual use and less than 0.5 percent for 30-day use. Hence, as compared with several of the more traditional drugs, such as marijuana and cocaine, at the dawn of the twenty-first century, the use of these club drugs remains fairly limited. In the 2005 press release that reported that year's schoolchildren drug use, the MTF survey results did not even include ketamine or GHB.

## SUMMARY

When we examine prevalence rates, that is, the percentage of the population who use specific drugs during a specific time period—whether during their lifetimes, in the past year, or in the past month—we see that the *legal* drugs (alcohol and cigarettes) are used by many more people than the *illegal* drugs. According to the National Survey on Drug Use and Health (NSDUH), in 2005, while only 8.1 percent of the American public, or 20 million people, used one or more illicit drugs at least once during the past month, for alcohol, this was true of 52 percent, or 126 million people, and for cigarettes, 24.9 percent, or 60 million people. Thus, alcohol and cigarettes are used by *vastly* more people than are the illicit drugs. Heroin and crack cocaine are used monthly or more by a very small proportion of the population—considerably less than 1 percent. (But keep in mind that the NSDUH cannot locate homeless people, whose use of heroin and crack is likely to be much higher than that of people who live in households.) Nonetheless, a small number of people can commit a great deal of crime and cost society an enormous amount of money in social services.

Sociologists and criminologists of drug use are also interested in continuance or "loyalty" rates. Users tend to "stick with" legal drugs more than illicit drugs, which are more likely to be given up or used infrequently. If we compare lifetime with monthly prevalence rates, drinkers are more loyal to alcohol than users are to any other drug. On the other hand, if we compare yearly with monthly prevalence rates, cigarettes—which contain the drug nicotine—generate the highest user loyalty. Tobacco is actually used vastly *more often* than alcohol, since, on average, each of those 60 million smokers takes 15 "doses" of their drug (over a billion cigarettes) per day, whereas consumers of alcohol average only one or two drinks per day (one if a "double," two if a regular drink)—only about 150 million daily "doses" of this drug.

Drugs tend to be used over the life cycle in specific and identifiable patterns. Illicit use is very low among 11- and 12-year-olds; it rises sharply into the mid-to-late teens, reaches a peak at 19 or 20, and declines, at first slowly and then more sharply. Illicit drug use is very rare after the age of 35. Some observers believe that this pattern is closely related to similar rises and declines in criminal and deviant behavior (Gottfredson and Hirschi, 1990). In contrast, alcohol consumption plateaus at its peak, then declines fairly slowly in the fifties and sixties.

Drug use trends over time are important to any understanding of historical and cultural changes. Alcohol consumption was extremely high in colonial, eighteenth-, and early-nineteenth-century America; in 1790, Americans above age 15 drank a yearly average of 5.8 gallons per person; in 1830, this figure had reached an all-time high of 7.1 gallons. But beginning early in the nineteenth century, the temperance movement began exerting an influence, and drinking declined after 1830, reaching an average of just over two gallons per person per year in the years before Prohibition. Between 1900 and 1919, alcohol consumption began to decline again as a result of state alcohol prohibitions. During Prohibition (1920–1933), according to indirect measures such as cirrhosis of the liver, drunk driving citations, and alcohol dementia mental hospital intakes, alcohol consumption declined sharply, to roughly half of its pre-Prohibition level, that is, just under a gallon per person per year. After 1934, the first year of national legal alcohol distribution, it began to rise, from roughly a gallon to a post-Prohibition level high of 2.8 gallons in 1978. Since that year, it has declined more or less yearly, to just a shade over two gallons per year (2.14 in 1998), but rose again after that (2.22 in 2003).

In the second half of the twentieth century, illicit drug use both reflected and departed from rates of alcohol consumption. Retrospective estimates indicate that illegal drug use was extremely low in the early 1960s, rose throughout that decade, and continued to rise in the 1970s, reaching a late-twentieth-century high in 1979. During this decade, liberal, tolerant attitudes toward drug use grew as well. Trends in drug use during the 1980s were consistently down. But beginning in 1991, though adult rates were more or less stable, use among eighth-graders (especially) and tenth- and twelfth-graders began to rise sharply, especially for marijuana. Although this rise stalled sometime between the mid-1990s and the present, an extremely high proportion of young adolescents still use illegal drugs.

In addition, in the 1990s, a number of club drugs were either introduced or revived and became at least modestly popular among young people—Ecstasy, ketamine, Rohypnol, and GHB. Since the late 1990s, however, use of these drugs has declined.

## KEY TERMS

| | | |
|---|---|---|
| availability heuristic 170 | judgmental heuristics 170 | retrospective estimates 183 |
| consumption levels 175 | life cycle rates 176 | |
| continuance rate 172 | prevalence rate 171 | |

## ACCOUNTS

*This chapter discusses historical changes in rates and patterns of drug use, mainly illicit drug use, over the past three or four decades. Accordingly, the personal accounts that follow were gathered by me (or, in one case, another researcher, Marsha Rosenbaum) between the 1960s and the early twenty-first century.*

## Marijuana Use (1967)

Things start striking me funny—I mean, somebody would say something and I'd keep hearing it. Or I'd look at something, and I'd find myself looking at it for an overly long period of time, and all of a sudden I'd wake up and say, what the hell am I doing, looking at this for so long? When I'm high, I always listen to music. Music would begin to sound extraordinarily good. And then, after four or five minutes more, I would realize that I was high, and I'd get very happy. I spend most of my time high listening to music. I'd listen to the music, and I'd always concentrate on one instrument, it didn't matter which one. I could never listen to all at the same time, which is the only drawback I see to being high and listening to music, as opposed to being straight. But I could listen to what I consider good rock and roll and just love it. It would be just about the most pleasing thing I've ever done in my life.

I play the guitar. I prefer to play casually, informally, high. I will not play before an audience high, because it's too uncomfortable. I know that I have to perform, and I get scared. I start to think, what if I pass out, what if I don't have enough wind for the next song, 'cause I do get short-winded. I almost blew the whole thing at a nightclub last summer. But rehearsing, or getting together with the rest of the group when you're high, it's a great experience. I sit there and play and play and play. I play much better. I'm quite convinced that this is not a high fantasy. I *know* I'm playing better. 'Cause I don't make any mistakes, like I usually do. And I can anticipate what's coming. And throw phrases back and forth between guys, if somebody else is high. We had a job once at Bryn Mawr, where I played. We all smoked in the afternoon and came back to this room where we were going to play, and we sat down and played one song, one instrumental song, for 45 minutes without stopping, and it was the best thing I've ever done.

I used to play games, I used to do things with my eyes, great things. Nothing that really ever scared me, because I could always be cautious not to get too high, so that I wouldn't have, you know, a bad time. I could always know where I was, what I was doing, unless I made myself forget. Sometimes I'd listen to the Byrds. I could lie down on the bed, and pick myself up, and throw myself down, sort of float down one of those concentric-ring, manhole type things. Or there was one experience I had recently, where I was listening to them [the Byrds]. And the notes were coming out, it's a very strident, shrill, crisp 12-string electric guitar, and it's beautiful. He [Roger McGuinn, leader of the group, who plays a 12-string electric guitar] does Indian-type stuff on it. And the notes sounded to me as they came into my ears, it sounded is if I were a million miles away. I had a picture in my mind of sitting out in space and watching the notes come flying by. They were very sharp, coming by. I said to myself, the machine is making these notes, and these notes will be free from now on, they're coming out in a certain order to make a tune, and I saw them coming out from the earth into space, and they could always be heard if you had sensitive enough ears. It was great when I was out there, for about ten seconds I was sitting out there, in space, looking at the earth, watching the notes come by. And it was all black around me. And then all of a sudden, I realized that everything, my whole world, was back there, several million miles away. And I got clutched for a minute. So I opened my eyes and I came back. I like to do stuff like that.

I have changed colors on some of those psychedelic posters. I've made them flash from red and white to black, then changed it to blue. Very often I can place myself inside a concert hall when I'm listening to records. I can see the performance taking place in front of me. This happened the first time I got high, I saw the band, and they were dancing, and the drummer's feet, and all the performers' heads, came to a sharp point, because the music was very shrill, and the notes were sharp and pointed. And then, during the solo, I remember the drummer got up and danced around his drums while he was playing them—on his points, the points of his toes.

Simultaneously, I thought of the guy I was with in the room. I realized I was sitting on the floor with my ear next to the speaker, and I said, this must look very foolish. And then I said, well, it looks foolish, and if it looks foolish, I'll have to get up. But I don't want to get up. So I'll just pretend that it doesn't look foolish. You'll do almost anything to rationalize away something that gets in the way of your enjoyment.

There's always sex. If you don't want it, you get turned off. If a girl repulses you, you definitely wouldn't think of going near her. But once you get the idea into your head that you want to get your hands on her, there's very little that can stop you. And you don't care. The easiest thing to do is to walk up to a girl, if you're at a party or something, and to let her know you're high, so she'll understand if you try to con her into bed in one minute. There's definitely a heightening of all the physical impulses high. They are much, much stronger, in every way. Pain, too. If you concentrate on pain, you'll really start to hurt. Sex is more purely physical high, that's the only problem. It's a lust orgy. When you are involved in it, you don't think of the girl at all, you just think about the physical pleasure. But the physical pleasure is immense. However, it doesn't detract from my normal, straight sex life. I don't say, "Gee whiz, I wish I were high." But when you want it to, marijuana acts as a frighteningly powerful aphrodisiac. At least for me it does.

I get very, very thirsty when I'm high. My mouth dries out. In fact, the last time I smoked, my mouth dried out so much that I actually thought I was going to do some physical damage to it, because it got to the point where I couldn't speak, because my lips were sticking to the insides of my gums, and it was totally dry.

Just walking around feels good, nice, you know. You can groove on your own movements. In some cases I became pretty uncoordinated. I tried playing tennis once high, and it was a complete disaster. Whereas I can sit in my room with an imaginary set of drums and coordinate my two feet and two hands to different beats, which I could never do straight.

My eyes get very heavy. Hot.

## Heroin Abuse (1971)

I'll . . . talk about what happened to me in the heroin scene I was in. It may be typical, but I don't really think it is. It started for me in the summer of 1968. There are no intricate sociological or psychological explanations needed for my involvement. . . . I didn't even think twice about the dangers or morality of turning on to heroin. . . . At the time, all of us were deeply involved in the underground post–high school drug subculture in an affluent suburban community. . . . Most of the primary group was in college, and ranged from 18 to around 21 years of

age. . . . I didn't know much more about heroin at the time than the average ignorant law enforcement officer, and I think I shared at least partially the conventional negative stereotype of the junkie— not putting heroin down completely because of my own drug orientation, but saying things like, "I can't see myself *injecting* something into my body," or "I'm afraid of needles," and so on. As long as all the others felt the same way, this was not considered a cowardly position. Anyway, around the beginning of July, I took my hash-filled body away on a trip with my family, returning three weeks later.

When I got back, my boyfriend, Edward, . . . said he had shot heroin. . . . Heroin was not only accepted, it was cool . . . I was taken over to the house of a friend who had recently dived head first into heroin without a backward glance, after a youth of similar experiences with alcohol. . . . I went to his house, and he cooked up shots for Edward, himself, and me. I've since been told that we were either very brave or very foolish to put ourselves in his hands like that, and since it was only my first shot, I know it wasn't bravery. Eddie got his shot first. His previous experience had been very pleasant, a mild, warm feeling, and probably a pretty weak shot. This one was not so weak. . . . [Then] our friend . . . gave me my shot.

The needle went in quickly, with one light tap and no pain. That boy gave me a better injection than I've had from doctors! I watched, fascinated, as he squeezed the clear solution out of the dropper and then gave me a "boot"—letting blood run back into the dropper and then shooting it back into my arm. I doubt there was any greater physiological effect as a result of booting, but it prolonged the shot. My "doctor" enjoyed booting so much that he often did it as many as ten or more times on each shot, but that night I said a couple would be plenty, thanks.

I've had better and more powerful rushes than the one I got that first night, but maybe I don't remember it as the best because I didn't know what to expect. . . . And so it began. I am extremely fortunate for the many circumstances which intervened to keep me from setting off on the junkie trait right from the start. There were almost as many circumstances militating in just that direction.... Soon, heroin became the only thing [in my life] to look forward to. The weekend became synonymous with "getting off." Eddie was living with me at the time, and his psychological need for the escape and deadening of pain which heroin provided was the major reason for our continuing use. I can't say what my individual reaction to heroin would have been [without Eddie's taking the initiative], because I was simply following his lead. The winter was long and cold, Eddie was depressed constantly, only occasionally holding a job. Heroin was the only warm spot in the week. We were careful to avoid shooting up more than four days in a row because we knew that addiction would destroy all of the great "therapeutic" value which we attributed to heroin. Also, we just couldn't afford it....

Eddie and I continued shooting up until April 1969 without getting a habit. We were always aware of how much we were doing and marked an "X" on the calendar for each shot. While we managed to avoid physical dependence, psychologically we were hooked good. We turned to heroin whenever we were depressed, or when we wanted to reward ourselves. Because of its capacity for alleviating tension and depression, because it enabled us both to overcome our anxiety in social interactions, and because it seemed to fill up the holes in our empty lives (something we couldn't do for each other), heroin acquired a great deal of power [over us]. I think this psychological addiction is far more enduring and resistant to cure than any physiological addiction, and it is for this reason addicts will usually relapse. It took a near-fatal overdose for Eddie (and three days of waiting to hear if he was alive or dead for me) to make us realize where we were at. Death was a price we were not willing to pay, even for all the benefits we thought we had been receiving. We went completely straight, not even smoking grass, for three months....

It was not until later in June, just before we were about to split on a camping trip ..., that we began dropping in on our [heroin-using] friends again

to say good-bye. Naturally we were offered hash and grass ..., and we accepted. But the memory of the O.D. was too clear for us to be tempted by the smack they were doing, and we told them were off [heroin] for good.... The power that heroin had over us, however, did not dissipate. We returned from our camping trip only to experience a massive post-vacation let-down. We were home. The trip had only changed our lives for a little while. School didn't start for another month, and same with Eddie's new job.... To make matters worse, our friends had developed real, honest-to-goodness habits over the summer and now when we went to see them there wasn't any grass or hash. All they were interested in was heroin and morphine, a new discovery they had made. I guess it was inevitable, wasn't it? The brush with death had been so long ago, and if we just had a little bit ... and we *had* to try that morphine ... and we'll only do it till school and the job start ... and we *deserve* some fun before getting back to the rat race ... and God am I bored....

We began to shoot more dope than ever before. This time no "X" marks went on the calendar, though we still tried to control it and avoid getting hooked. We did, but it was harder now because everyone else was hooked.... I was shooting several times a week, sometimes daily for four or five days, waiting for school to begin. I really liked morphine, which was much cheaper than heroin and seemed to give a better rush.... The quality of the morphine was much more consistent than that of heroin.... I still wasn't addicted, not physically anyway, but something else was beginning to happen. I began to get nauseous after I shot up, not immediately ..., but much later, sometimes as much as several hours.... It was a weird kind of sickness, too, because I didn't even mind throwing up....

It got to the point where I wasn't even enjoying my shots that much because I would already be feeling nauseous before the needle was in my arm.... The rush coming on top of that just made me feel worse. Eddie was displaying similar sensitivity which also seemed to be getting progressively more pronounced. We didn't like what was happening. We were spending good money for a bag of dope and then getting sick from it! We might as well have been buying bottles of Ipecac, that stuff that makes you throw up. Who needs that? Friction was also springing up between us. Getting sick made Eddie afraid that he would O.D. again, so he would say, no more dope. But as soon as he became depressed, which was often, I would sooner or later suggest getting some. In the past this had always worked, at least for a while. But now it didn't help any more. It only made us both sick as well as depressed, and made Eddie's fears of overdosing return. Then he would turn on me and condemn me for suggesting it. He felt that since he was so unable to resist, I should be the strong one and keep us off dope. When he began to realize that I was pretty weak myself, he really got scared.

Finally, just a day or two before school was to start, we reached the turning point. . . . I decided to treat myself to a really big shot. . . . I got what I wanted: a super rush. But then it went beyond my control and I fell back on the bed . . . , my eyes wide open. Eddie was slapping me, trying to get me to talk, do anything! But I couldn't move my lips and I just lay there, mouth hanging open, eyes staring, hearing him and not being able to answer. I couldn't believe what was happening to me. . . . Eddie . . . just kept shaking me until at last I had become able to speak. We were both *really* scared—we had never been that stoned before and we thought we might die. I had always prided myself on being able to control myself on drugs. . . . But not that night. . . . We went outside and staggered up and down the driveway . . . , retching and hanging onto each other like a couple of drunks. Somehow, I made coffee but we couldn't drink it. We put ice cubes on our faces and wrists, trying to keep ourselves from passing out. . . .

Somehow, we came out of it. But the real hell was just beginning. We began to argue violently, blaming each other. Eddie said he would leave me if I ever got dope again. . . . I realized that many of Eddie's accusations were true, and many of my proud illusions were false. I continued to retch my insides out halfway through the next day . . . in a state of total self-disgust. I never wanted to see another needle again. That afternoon, I called the mental health clinic and asked for psychiatric help.

So, you say to yourself, after all *that,* she finally got off drugs. Well, yes . . . , for another three months. . . . I continued smoking marijuana every day, but only when I was alone. . . . Eddie and I . . . didn't see our friends for months. Then Eddie lost his job just before Christmas, and there we were again. It was winter again. The exuberance and gaiety of the holiday season seemed mocking and artificial. Like all good American, we made holiday visits to our friends, and what were they doing? You know. . . . We got on the merry-go-round again, only the music wasn't quite the way we remembered it. The expense was still a problem, and the hassles involved in copping had seemed to increase until they were almost intolerable. Luckily, it was no longer feeling good enough to us to make it worth waiting hours for, like our junkie friends did, or to risk getting busted for, as many were.

Even worse, we discovered that when a person becomes a junkie, he often ceases to be a person. There was so much ugliness, lying, cheating, and stealing, even among guys who were supposed to be the best of friends, that we finally decided it wasn't worth it. At least the power of the group was broken, but what about that other power? It drove us to the city, looking for a better connection. It almost turned out to be Eddie's connection to the Great Beyond, because after shooting only a relatively small amount of heroin, IT HAPPENED AGAIN. An overdose isn't pretty, especially if it's someone who you don't want to die. And all the poor guy wanted was just a little relief, a little time out from misery. A friend and I managed to bring him out of the coma without sending him to the hospital, but it was many minutes before he could breathe on his own. I knew it was the end of heroin for Eddie, because he wouldn't come back a third time. He knew it too, and was glad it had happened to let him know where heroin was at for him.

And what about me? As soon as I got Eddie home and in bed, I shot one of the two remaining bags we had. Insane? Probably, but I could tell from the rush I got (weak) and the time I stayed high (short) that heroin had lost its immense power over me, too. I shot the last bag with the same results. It simply wasn't worth it. The hassle to get it, the money it costs, the risk of dying—which in Eddie's case was now almost a certainty—it's all not worth some weak little sensation in your head and a high that lasts ten minutes. Maybe those last two bags were just extra-weak, maybe it would have been different with good dope, but I chose to think not. The weakness of the dope served perfectly to point up the absurdity of trying to fool oneself.

You see, for a lot of people, it *is* worth the tremendous price because of the power to do magic, even if, in my case, the magic ceased to happen long ago. There's only the memory, and the hope to get it back again like it was. For me, other things like my plans for graduate school and my growing self-awareness have helped me to start filling in a lot of the empty holes in my life that heroin only appeared to fill. I still think about it [heroin], especially when things are going badly for me. But then I think of how much I would be gambling for ten minutes of an uneasy peace which is no peace at all. I finally have something to lose! That makes all the difference in the world. When I think about the reward I've promised myself for graduation, right now I'd rather go out for a good dinner than shoot a bag of heroin. And even if I ever do shoot again, I don't think heroin will ever exert the power over me that it once did.

# Ecstasy Use (1988)

*The following interview was conducted by Marsha Rosenbaum. The interviewee is a physician; at the time of the interview, she was in her early forties.*

**Q:**  Do you remember the first time you heard about it [MDMA]?

**A:**  No, not clearly. Not directly. I have a vague memory of getting this description of a drug, the way that I describe it, a designer drug, that is not psychedelic and very, very light and enjoyable and great to do in a beautiful place. . . .

**Q:**  Do you remember the first trip?

**A:**  I think so. I could be wrong, but what I remember of the first trip was one of the times [when we went on vacation]. . . . It was

a whole group of people, good people, dear people. And we took it after breakfast and went down to the . . . creek. And you come to a place where there's natural rocks at the waterside. And people don't have to wear clothes there, so we just sort of hung out on a rock facing the water. Oh, and it was beautiful! It is just incredibly beautiful and [we] took the stuff.

**Q:**  So tell me about it.

**A:**  I always get this little nervous thing. But once you come down to it, it was—there may have been 10 or 15 minutes where the drug effect was more than I would have wanted, where I felt a little bit like, "Which way do you go?" with it. And then after that, then I also felt confident because I was around people who were pretty well obviously interested in doing it. . . . What I remember about that first trip was, first of all, just being so physically in tune . . . , where everything is so crystalline . . . , everything being made sharper . . . , visual, not hallucinogenic whatsoever, but contrasts are greater, getting in and out of the water . . . , on the rocks. . . . I didn't sit still. . . . I would go from one group of people . . . and I'd sit and hug and talk to them. And I'd get in the water and swim to another group and get involved with them for a while and then take off and go to another one. I really flitted around like a butterfly. . . . It was a perfect drug for that day.

**Q:**  OK, and it was all very positive, and everything that you had been told kind of happened for you. . . . It mean, do you remember what they told you to do, not to do, how it was gonna be?

**A:**  Yeah. Yeah. [It] was definitely a . . . very comfortable, nice drug. And I remember a lovely situation. . . .

**Q:**  OK, and what about sensually? Any body things? Did you and [your husband] have sex while you were on it the first time?

**A:**  Every time. Every time, yeah. It's definitely a sensual drug. It didn't make me erotic the way coke does. But that's also part of it.

That's also the setting. . . . It is a very sensuous drug for me, but it's not erotic. It doesn't make me want to have sex. . . .

**Q:** What about the people that you were with? Did you feel that you were bonding with them? I mean, was your relationship with them different after you all did Ecstasy together?

**A:** No, but they were all very, very close friends.

**Q:** To begin with?

**A:** Yeah.

**Q:** All right, and so it didn't make any difference one way or the other. It was pretty much the same?

**A:** Yes.

**Q:** OK, some people talk about getting into subjects that are difficult. . . .

**A:** I haven't. It would be interesting to try and do that, but I think that it just hasn't been that situational. When [my husband] and I have done Ecstasy, we haven't had issues that needed to be talked about.

**Q:** [Is] the M.O. [modus operandi, way of doing things] pretty much always the same?

**A:** It's always important to be away from the kids. That's real important. . . . I feel like I want to reserve it somewhat, to make it special. . . . [With taking Ecstasy], it just fits into my realm of playing, really playing, playing and not having the responsibility of taking care of my children.

**Q:** I mean, how often can that happen for a person like you?

**A:** Yeah, away from work, away from the kids. . . .

**Q:** So it takes a considerable amount of planning.

**A:** True.

**Q:** And organization.

**A:** Mm . . . , hmmm.

**Q:** In order to really cut loose.

**A:** Mm hmmm. It has to be planned. It's always planned. It's never come out of the blue [for me]. . . .

**Q:** And what about dosage? Is it always the same?

**A:** I don't know. It's what everybody gives me. . . .

**Q:** OK, so basically, has MDMA made an impact on your life, positive, negative? Has it been an impact, or was it more like a gift every once in a while?

**A:** The latter.

**Q:** Yeah, no major significance.

**A:** Hm mm.

**Q:** All right. And how about, would you recommend it to other people?

**A:** Sure.

**Q:** OK, I mean, you were talking about how you thought it would facilitate working through some stuff. . . . So you must see some potential there, right?

**A:** Oh, absolutely.

**Q:** But you don't use it that way?

**A:** No.

**Q:** That's interesting, don't you think?

**A:** I could use it that way. I mean, I just never—it never has happened.

# Multiple Drug Use (1996)

I grew up in the perfect family. Dad came to every soccer game. When I stepped off the bus each day, Mom was always waiting for me with cookies and milk. I went to church every Sunday; I was in the Girl Scouts; I was an honor student. My friends were described as "a nice group of girls," and everyone in town thought I was a sweet, innocent girl. Growing up, the person I was closest with was my grandmother. In 1988, she was diagnosed with cancer, and two years later, she was dead. I was devastated. My perfect world suddenly turned upside down.

The night my grandmother died, I met a guy named Rick. He was one of the "bad seeds" at my school. I was so angry at everyone (God, the doctors, my parents) for taking my grandmother away from me, I did the unthinkable: I got drunk, smoked pot, and had sex. It was truly a night of firsts for me. If she hadn't died, who knows, I'd probably still be a Girl Scout and go to church every Sunday. Her death made me question the way I was living my life for the first time. After that night, I did a complete turn-around. No longer was I dressed in Gap jeans and J. Crew sweaters. I turned into one of those freak alternative people, dressed in strange clothes, hanging out with bad kids, and rejecting any and all authority figures.

I started smoking pot on a regular basis, every night, seven to ten times a week. I often smoked before, during, and after high school. I lived in a small town, so there's rarely something fun for us to do there. One night, my friends and I heard about a "rave" that was happening in our area. In case you don't know it, a "rave" is an all-night dance party with loud techno music on records by DJs from all over the world. At raves, you'll find certain types of drugs, mostly acid [LSD] and Ecstasy. You can go to a rave wearing anything from a chicken costume to jeans and a T-shirt, and the people there will welcome you with open arms. Raves are held at locations which change every week. We hopped into my car and headed upstate. Even though I didn't do any drugs that night, the experience changed the next four years of my life. I loved every minute of that party, and from then on, I began to go to raves every weekend.

I had to lie to my parents every weekend so that I could go. At the time, I was a sophomore in high school, and I had a very restrictive midnight curfew. Even though my parents noticed changes in who my friends were and the way I dressed, they trusted me and naively believed I wouldn't lie to them. Every weekend I told them I was sleeping at a different friend's house. One night at the parking lot behind where the party was being held, a friend gave me a hit of acid. That night, I danced as never before. On acid, I was able to actually *feel* the music flowing through my body. The music became a part of me. The visuals were so intense, it was amazing. I felt as if I had been blind my whole life; suddenly, I was able to see the world for the first time.

For the next year or so, I took acid a couple of times a month. It didn't seem to be much of a big deal. At the time, raves weren't about drugs, they were about dancing, music, peace, love, and happiness. Drugs were just taken to bring the dancing, music, peace, love, and happiness to new heights.

Some nights, I went to a rave, there would be acid there, and so I'd take it; other nights, there was no acid, and I had a great time anyway.

The summer of 1994, I went to a rave they called Camp Earth in Providence. It was a huge amusement park. I had been thinking about doing Ecstasy for a long time, but I was afraid of it. I had heard that the drug makes you love everything you see. It makes you feel good about yourself and it gives you a sense of self-esteem. I didn't believe it was possible for a drug to do these things. Besides, a hit of Ecstasy sold for $25, and my job at Burger King didn't pay very well. But I decided to try it anyway and find out for myself, so I found a dealer who had some. She told me that "Brooklyn Bombs" were the best, so I bought one from her for $25, and I took it. After a half-hour, all the friends I was taking it with were feeling the effects; I was the only one who still felt nothing. We decided to go on some of the park rides, so we headed for the Cannonball Express. The ride started. All of a sudden, I felt my hands start to tingle. I walked off that ride with a big, cheesy grin that I just couldn't wipe off my face. I never felt so good in my life. All my problems seemed to disappear in a matter of seconds.

I went inside the building to dance, and I didn't stop for the next five hours. I looked at my image in the mirror on the wall and realized that I was the most beautiful girl in the world. Normally, I have very little self-esteem; I even look at the mirror in disgust. But that night, I couldn't stop feeling how beautiful I was. The Brooklyn Bomb made me feel beautiful, popular, smart—GREAT! I loved Ecstasy because it didn't make you hallucinate. It doesn't even make you feel as if you're high on drugs. It just makes you feel great. After that night, Ecstasy became my drug of choice. One way or another, I was able to scrape together $25 each week.

I told myself I would never do cocaine. Commercials on TV made it out to be really horrible. I really thought I would never do it. One night, I drove to Baltimore for a party they called the Emerald Forest. The guy who threw the party was able to rent a state park, so the party was being held outdoors. I bought a hit of Ecstasy, but it didn't seem to be working. I began dancing near the DJ booth; suddenly, I felt a tremendous pain in my leg. My whole right leg had become paralyzed and I was frozen in midair. My friends saw there was something wrong with me and came over to help. They sat me on the ground and called a park ranger. He thought I should be taken to the emergency room; if anything was really wrong, he said, my parents had to be notified. If he did that, I'd be grounded; I definitely didn't want that. My friends told him not to worry, they had something to make the pain go away, and so he left. They gave me a "bump" (a hit) of coke. My pain went away, and suddenly my spirits felt lifted. In small amounts, coke doesn't make you feel screwed up, it just makes you feel good; it wakes you up and makes everything feel better. After I took it and felt better, I kept waiting for all the effects I had heard about to kick in, but they never did. I couldn't believe that there were so many anti-coke campaigns when the high doesn't really mess you up.

By this time, I was in my second year of community college. My relationship with my parents had deteriorated to the point where they kicked me out. They didn't accept that I wasn't their good little girl any more, and I didn't accept the fact that they just wanted the best for me. I had saved a couple thousand dollars. I moved in with a couple friends and we shared a two-bedroom apartment. The money didn't last very long, but I was working at two jobs to support myself. Since my pay was so low and the money was so tight, I ran some drugs for a dealer friend. He gave me six hits of Ecstasy for $100, and I'd sell them for $25 or $30. One night, I sold 100 hits for him, and I made over $1,000.

Living on my own was great, but I was completely without parental control. Nobody told me what to do. I went to raves Wednesday nights in Albany, Friday nights in Manhattan, and Saturdays wherever the biggest rave was being held. To do this without getting tired and sleepy, I began doing crystal. Crystal is speed—methamphetamine. It wakes you up and keeps you up for a long time. If I did a bump of crystal when the party started, 11

o'clock one night, I'd stay up until seven the next night.

My biggest problem was tolerance. One hit of Ecstasy was no longer enough. Neither was a bump of crystal. Some weekends I'd do six or eight different drugs. I even felt proud of how many drugs I was doing. My friends were all doing the same quantity of drugs. It almost turned into a contest; we tried to outdo one another. If Jim did one bag of crystal, I did two, then Sally would do three. Afterwards, we sat around and compared how many different drugs we had done.

Most people who end up doing a lot of drugs begin dropping out of society. They quit school or don't work. Not me. Deep down, all along, I knew that the things I was doing weren't really me, so I tried to hang onto the other areas of life which, I felt, were the real me. I went to all my classes. I was in the honors program and maintained a 3.25 GPA. I babysat after school. I worked in a video store, in Burger King, and a movie theater when I had the time. I liked to keep busy because I knew that if I had too much free time, I would start thinking about some of the things I had been doing a little too much.

At some point, I realized I'd have to get away from my circle of friends. I figured that if I moved away, I'd get a fresh start. My aunt and uncle own a clothing boutique in the Hamptons; because of their business, they had a lot of contact with gay men. It happens that, one day, they called and offered me a job in the store and a place to live. After I left home, my relationship with my parents improved considerably; we realized that we love each other but we just have different notions about how I ought to live my life. Before I lived in Southampton, I believed that gay men didn't really do drugs. I've never been more wrong in my life! Not only do they do drugs, they even give out free samples. I began doing a lot of coke. I frequented the clubs out there, and many nights, the customers gave me free coke.

A guy who worked for my aunt and uncle was really cute. He was into heroin, I was into coke; we were perfect for one another. Every day, we'd work all day, and at night, we'd go to Manhattan to cop drugs. We did this almost every day all summer. One day, he asked me if I wanted to try heroin. He told me that he does four bags at a time, so I'd better do just one. I snorted a $20 bag and collapsed onto the couch. For the next 24 hours, I threw up. Anytime I moved, I threw up. Whenever I talked, I threw up. If I did anything at all, I threw up. It was the most horrible experience of my entire life. I didn't feel any of the euphoria a lot of people talk about. All I felt was horrible.

After that, I pretty much stuck to coke. I really cut back on the amount I did, though; I only did it a couple of times a week. Then in the fall, I moved into the dorms at the university, once again believing that I had been given a chance to start all over again. But once again, I was wrong. The friends I made were doing drugs. For some reason, I always seemed to gravitate to a circle of friends who are doing drugs. I met a guy, Bill, who seemed perfect for me. He smoked pot once in a while; other than that, he really wasn't into drugs. One day, I got a bad cold; I couldn't seem to shake it. It eventually developed into bronchitis. I was determined to go to a really big rave that weekend. Bill tried to talk me out of it, but he was unsuccessful. We went to a club in the City, the Ritz. I did a couple bumps of crystal. Before long, I realized I had gotten sicker; my bronchitis had developed into pneumonia, and I had to be hospitalized. Lying on my hospital bed, I thought about how foolish I had been; my judgment was so messed up that, even though I was sick, I had to go out and party and do some crystal, which made me sicker. I swore I would never do drugs again. And I haven't.

I can't give you a one-sentence of why I did drugs. At first, it helped me escape the pain of losing my grandmother. Once you begin hanging out with people who do drugs, you change, your attitudes, your beliefs, your behavior all change. You start holding the same positive attitudes they have about drugs. And once you're done things you like doing, it's hard after that not to do it. I liked the way I felt when I was high, so I did it. And in a friend's apartment, with everyone bumping, doing something you've done before, and like, it's hard to "just say no." You just do it.

To be honest, I don't regret anything I've done. I consider these experiences another chapter in my book of life. I feel that my experiences have turned me into a much more knowledgeable person. I feel I am able to have a better understanding of a great deal of life because I've been to some of the places I've been. I have a more critical capacity to evaluate many of the issues facing the society today as a result of how I lived until recently. I hear people talking about certain topics and think how fortunate I've been to have done what I've done.

I wonder if I was every actually a drug addict. I was able to stop using when I decided that the time had come without having to go into a treatment program. I did cocaine to the point of everyday use, yet when I decided to call it quits, I was able to stop, no problem. Not once did I ever experience any form of withdrawal. There's no doubt in my mind that I was psychologically dependent on drugs. It had gotten to the point that I was dependent on drugs to create happiness for me.

I sincerely doubt that I will ever do drugs again. I am at a point in my life where I am happy without drugs, and happy with the way things have worked out for me. Bill has made that possible. Before, it was Ecstasy that made me feel beautiful; now it's Bill. A lot of the people I thought were my friends are long gone. I've gone straight, and they just disappeared. Once, I would have done anything for these people. I thought they were true friends. When I used to do acid, I felt as if the drug made me able to see the world in a better, clearer way. Now that I've stopped doing drugs, I feel the same way: Now I am able to see the world in a clearer way.

## Multiple Drug Use (2003)

About a year ago, my younger brother threw a party at the house where we and our parents were on vacation. That day, my parents, who happen to ride motorcycles, went out to a motorcycle rally. My brother invited a friend of his whom we nicknamed "Horse." He's big and strong, 20 years old, and he uses his size to get what he wants. The absence of my parents allowed my brother, Horse, and me to have the house for ourselves for the day. My parents had bought lots of beer for us so by the time breakfast was over, at 10 in the morning, we started drinking. We also had a large supply of liquor which enabled us to mix drinks and do shots of various flavors. By noon, my brother called me upstairs to smoke marijuana with him and Horse. I decided to join them because I was curious. After I got high, I became paranoid, which happens to some people when they smoke marijuana, and I climbed into a wardrobe for no apparent reason.

This experience, however, did not deter me from joining my brother and Horse when they chopped up some "E" [Ecstasy] pills they brought with them. So that each person got the right amount, my brother and Horse chopped the pills into a fine powder on a mirror using a razor blade. We did it in the kitchen, which is the first room you enter from the outside. At about two in the afternoon, we were very tired so we went to the bedroom for a nap, expecting our parents to come home late at night. At 4:30, I heard a noise from downstairs and remembered that the E was still on the kitchen table, chopped up into lines on a mirror with a razor blade still on it.

I knew that if my parents saw the lines, they'd think we were doing cocaine, which to them would be much worse than if they had found a pile of marijuana. My first reaction was to jump off the top bunk of the bunkbed, run out of the room, and run down the stairs to the kitchen. When I got there, I saw my mother stepping into the house with an armful of trinkets from the motorcycle rally. I instantly realized that if I didn't do something there would be big trouble. Without stopping, I ran square into my mother, knocking her with great force back into the porch area. Angrily, she yelled, "What the hell's going on?" I jumped back in the house and covered the mirror with my arm and replied, "Nothing's going on—I was just startled when the porch door slammed." Still angry, my mother reentered the house, putting her bags down on a counter. "I don't know what's going on here," she said, "but I want it stopped." I moved a cutting board that was resting on the table onto the mirror and took them down to the basement for proper hiding and disposed of the evidence. We only lost about a pill and a half, or the equivalent of $30 in street value. Small price to pay for not getting caught.

The next night, the three of us went into the resort village where our family vacations to walk around the strip of shops and flirt with girls. Stopping along the way, I picked up a pint and a half-pint of Southern Comfort and two bottles of Coke. After we finished the liquor, we walked around, coming upon another liquor store. We decided to buy another bottle. This time, we went to a small park and Horse drank from a bottle wrapped in a brown paper bag. Two police officers walked up to us and began questioning us. Drunk and very scared, I cooperated with the police. They asked for my license, which had expired. I told them that I had just renewed it and the new one hadn't yet arrived in the mail. I showed them the interim license the DMV had given me, but they took that as punishment for drinking so that I couldn't buy any more liquor.

As a result of my experiences with Horse, I became friendly with his group of friends. A couple of weekends ago, Horse, my brother, and I went to a "rave," a party where the main purpose is doing various drugs at the same time. The party was being held at "Chef's" house. Chef is so named because of the way that "K" (short for ketamine) is prepared. Ketamine is an animal tranquilizer that is used by veterinarians. Ketamine is prepared by heating it until it solidifies, then it's scraped off the surface with a knfe. The result is a fine powder that allows the user to sniff it into one or both nostrils. The person who obtained the K is called "Chemist," who is known for having many different kinds of drugs readily available. At the party most of the people were also taking E pills and K at the same time. Horse took E and K within 10 minutes of each other. E does not take effect right away— there is usually a 30- to 40-minute waiting period. Depending on the dose, if it's snorted, K takes effect right away and lasts about 30 to 45 minutes. The effect of K is simply detachment. The user feels as if he is weightless. Everything that happens, like walking, is extremely smooth. This feeling of detachment begins to intensify and eventually, the user feels that nothing is real. Everything takes place in a dreamlike state. The two major drawbacks of K are the "K drip" and the "K hole."

The K drip is post-nasal drip. The K hole occurs when one drinks a lot before snorting K, or does too much K, at which point, the brain shuts down all functions except the operation of life-sustaining organs. This can last for hours, putting the user into a comatose state.

Once E takes effect, it can last for three or four hours. The effect it has is similar to euphoria. K and E do not mix. At this party, Horse started to "bug out." Bugging out is when reality no longer seems feasible. While bugging out, the user does things he or she would not ordinarily do, like yelling and screaming gibberish. It seems that partying, drinking, and smoking marijuana are the main pastimes of this group at the party. Colleen, one of the girls who was present, told me about a rave that took place the previous weekend. Colleen was disgusted by the use of drugs at that party. Chef had done too much K and fell into a K hole. After Chef recovered, he went right back to the K and cooked up more to snort. Several people there tried to stop him before he did extensive damage to his body, but to no avail. I felt sick and decided to go home and sleep it off, but the rest of the group there partied and drank into the early hours of the morning.

The next night, my brother and I ran into Horse and two girls. We hung out for a while, sitting in a car on a dead-end street, drinking and smoking. Horse rolled some blunts [large marijuana joints] and polished off a bottle of liquor I had gotten him. Then he drank another. After he had finished the second bottle, he asked me to get him a 40 [a 40-ounce bottle of beer]. His speech was slurred and he became very aggressive. I told him he didn't need another drink, so he punched me in the chest. He recognized through his drunken haze that I meant business and so he apologized. But he kept begging me about the 40. We took off, and whenever my brother stopped the car, Horse got out so that he could walk to a 7-Eleven and steal a 40. At one light, we had to stop, so Horse jumped out of the car and I grabbed him by the collar, but he wrestled free and ran off, but came back and jumped in the car when the light turned green. Finally, my brother told me to get a 40. I bought a 22-ounce bottle of beer instead, figuring he wouldn't know the differ-

ence. After I handed him the beer, he became more docile. He never figured it out. At some point, he said he felt cold and tried to put on his jacket. While he was struggling to do this, he knocked the head of my cigarette onto the seat of my brother's car. Then Horse began to pass out. The beer slipped from his hands and spilled all over the floor. My brother got very angry and pulled the car over to the side of the road so the beer would stop spilling. We finally dropped Horse off at his house. This experience taught me that Horse will drink just about anything just because it's there.

There is an entire subsociety that thrives on mischief and deviant activities. Most of these actions are done under the noses of their parents. That an entire subsociety exists just out of reach of parents seems hard to believe. One would think that if a person has good parents growing up they will be good kids and obey the law. When asked if their parents would allow them to use drugs, each member of this group I asked said "No." Even though these kids are aware of the bad effects drugs have on them, they continue to use. It all comes back to having a good time. It doesn't matter if one of them gets sick or has to show up at work the next day, they still partake in the huge party atmosphere.

## QUESTIONS

Can you find clues to when these accounts were written? In what way does each bear the stamp of the era in which the behavior being described took place? What is your reaction to the type of drug use each account depicts? To the people engaging in the drug use? What do these accounts tell us about how historical changes influence the use of psychoactive substances? What do you think happened to the people who contributed these accounts? Do you think their fates differed from their nonusing peers? How would you characterize the dominant or modal drug use in each decade since the 1960s? What is it like today? How do past events influence current events?

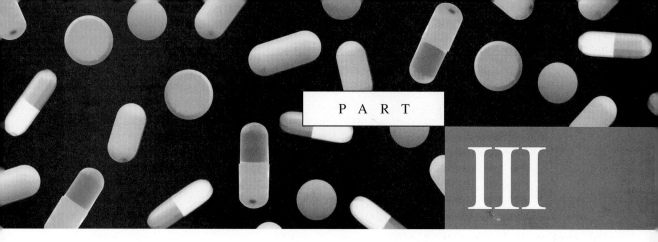

# III

# DRUGS AND THEIR USE

# 8

# LEGAL DRUGS

*Alcohol, Tobacco,
and Psychotherapeutic Drugs*

**W**hat's the difference between alcohol and tobacco and the substances we usually refer to as drugs—for example, LSD, heroin, and cocaine? We've already seen that alcohol is a depressant,

LSD a hallucinogen, heroin a narcotic, and cocaine a stimulant—but are alcohol and tobacco *drugs* in the same sense that the illicit substances are? Do alcohol and tobacco belong in their company? What about the psychoactive medicines prescribed by physicians—such as Prozac, lorazepam, or Stelazine? Do they deserve to be referred to as "drugs" in the same breath as the illicit substances? Clearly, the answer centers around the *psychoactive* properties of these legal substances.

If we drink enough alcohol, we become drunk, high, or intoxicated. In other words, alcohol influences how our mind works. Likewise, nicotine, a substance that is in all tobacco cigarettes, generates an arousal state. Like alcohol, nicotine is psychoactive. And, because alcohol and nicotine are psychoactive, they have come to be used mainly for the effects they have on their users; in other words, they are *recreational* drugs. And they are drugs for a third reason as well: Alcohol and tobacco can induce an "addiction" or dependence; that is, heavy, long-term drinkers or smokers engage in extraordinary measures to continue using in spite of the day-to-day or potential harm they experience, or know they will experience, by using. Our two most common addictions or dependencies involve alcohol and tobacco. There are roughly 10 million alcoholics who continue to drink heavily in spite of the social cost to themselves and others, and nearly 60 million Americans who smoke daily or more—for whom, as we saw, the median level of tobacco consumption is approximately 15 cigarettes (or "doses") a day. The toll this drug consumption takes on them is enormous, but they seem to be powerless to stop it. In a nutshell, in the pharmacological sense, then, *all drinkers and smokers are drug users.* Physically—that is, in the essentialistic sense—alcohol and tobacco are drugs, no different from LSD, heroin, or cocaine.

And the **psychopharmacological revolution,** wherein the administration of psychoactive chemicals has replaced "talking" therapies for mental disorders, represents perhaps the most significant change in the history of psychiatry. It is a development to which any student of drug use must pay attention. Moreover, a substantial number of psychotherapeutic substances have "escaped" into recreational street use, and hence have become interesting to the criminologist and drug researcher. Barbiturates, the Valium-type (or benzodiazepine) tranquilizers, and methaqualone (Quäälude) began as psychotherapeutic agents but fairly quickly were used for recreational purposes. A substantial number of the drugs discussed elsewhere in this book, such as amphetamines, Ecstasy, and even LSD, were used by licensed psychiatrists and psychologists as a means of healing or treating the troubled psyches of their patients.

If we refer to their psychoactive properties, the question of whether alcohol, or tobacco, or the psychotherapeutics, are drugs can be answered in a straightforward fashion. In the essentialistic or objectivistic sense, *yes,* alcohol, tobacco, and psychoactive medications are drugs: They influence the workings of the mind. When introduced into the body, they produce physiological changes that are not qualitatively different from the category of substances we refer to as drugs.

But, according to the framework spelled out in Chapter 1, it is also true that in the subjectivistic or constructionist sense, *no,* alcohol, cigarettes, and the psychotherapeutics are not drugs. Most people do not regard or classify them as drugs and do not treat or interact with their users in the same way as they do the users of the illegal drugs. Moreover, their use is not stigmatized, and adults cannot be arrested for possessing or purchasing them. This dual nature of legal drugs, their use, and their users means that there will be both similarities and differences between alcohol, cigarettes, and legally prescribed medicines, and "street" drugs, that is, the substances universally regarded as "drugs."

Let's not imagine, however, that these two types of substances, legal and illegal, exist in separate and distinct behavioral realms. An interesting clue to the linkage between alcohol and the illegal drugs is that there is a remarkable and powerful correlation between them. The 2003 National Survey on Drug Use and Health (NSDUH) revealed that, among 12- to 17-year-olds, over 6 in 10 (65%) of the "heavy" drinkers (that is, respondents who said they had consumed five or more alcoholic drinks on the same occasion five or more times during the past month) had also used an illicit drug within the past 30 days. In contrast, only 5.1 percent of respondents who had not used alcohol at all during the past month had also used an illegal drug at least once. The same correlation prevails for all drugs and all levels of alcohol consumption (SAMHSA, 2004, p. 21). In the 2005 NSDUH survey, smokers were five times as likely to use illicit drugs as nonsmokers.

If the NSDUH had tabulated substance consumption for the other age categories, no doubt much the same correlation would prevail. The fact is, the recreational consumption of psychoactive substances, taken as a whole, tends to reflect, in degrees, a drug-taking lifestyle. People who drink, especially heavily, are more likely to use controlled substances, and, to turn the equation around, people who use controlled substances overwhelmingly drink alcohol.

The same relationship applies between smoking cigarettes and using illicit drug use. In the 2003 NSDUH, among 12- to 17-year-olds, eight times as many smokers as nonsmokers had used an illegal drug in the past month (48.4% versus 6.1%). The same relationship with smoking prevails for all the illicit drugs. Among arrestees in the Drug Use Forecasting/Arrestee Drug Abuse Monitoring (DUF/ADAM) program, likewise, cigarette use was strongly correlated with the use of illicit drugs (Durrah and Rosenberg, 2002). Clearly, illicit and legal drug use do not exist in separate realms; actually, they heavily overlap. The impulse to alter one's consciousness with *one* substance—whether legal or illegal—is strongly related to the desire to alter it with *other* substances, again, legal or illegal.

Here is one last point to consider in this introduction. An interesting statistic, one that relates directly to the dual themes that have run throughout this book, is the essentialistic versus the social constructionist approaches to drug use and its effects. More than 100 epidemiologists and biostatisticians from the World Health Organization surveyed the available data and isolated roughly 20 leading risk factors for premature death in countries around the world. The risk factors were considerably different for developing (that is, less industrialized) countries as compared with developed (more industrialized, more affluent countries). In developing countries such as Nigeria, Indonesia, and Bolivia, factors such as malnutrition and poor sanitation were the leading causes of premature death. But in developed countries such as France, the United States, and Japan, among all risk factors, tobacco consumption accounted for 12.2 percent of the years of life lost, while excessive alcohol consumption accounted for 9.2 percent. Tobacco and alcohol were the number-one and number-three factors in this respect. In contrast, illicit drugs accounted for only 1.8 percent of years of life lost. In other words, in the industrialized world, the legal drugs, taken together, contribute more than five times as much to premature death as do the illegal drugs (Brown, 2002; Krug et al., 2002). Clearly, then, objectively speaking, legal drug use is a far more serious social problem than is illegal drug use. At the same time, illegal drug use is socially constructed. That is, it is subjectively—the way the public regards it and the government deals with it—the more serious social problem. We will have to grapple with dilemmas such as these throughout the rest of this book.

## ALCOHOL: AN INTRODUCTION

Alcohol has an ancient and checkered history, as touched on in Chapters 4 and 7. Fermentation was one of the earliest of human discoveries, dating back to the Stone Age. Alcohol emerges spontaneously from the fermented sugar in overripe fruit; the starch in grains and other food substances also readily converts to sugar and from there to alcohol. Because this process is so simple and basic, the discovery of alcohol by humans was bound to occur early on. Alcohol consumption, in all probability, began when a prehistoric human consumed fermented fruit and experienced its effect. Alcohol can induce pleasure, euphoria, intoxication, a sense of well-being, a state of relaxation, relief from tension, a feeling of goodwill toward others, the alleviation of pain, drowsiness, and sleep. As a result, it is an almost universally acceptable beverage. Consequently, as paleontology tells us, humans have been ingesting beverages containing alcohol for at least 10,000 years. In fact, coffee excepted, alcohol is the most widely used drug in existence—ubiquitous, almost omnipresent the world over.

Societies differ vastly in their average levels of alcohol consumption. Every society that has some acquaintance with alcohol has devised and institutionalized rules for the proper and improper consumption of alcohol. These vary systematically from society to society and from one social group or category to another. Although alcohol does have objective or biochemical effects, both short- and long-term, most of them can be influenced, mitigated, or drastically altered by the belief in and observance of cultural rules. The extent to which intoxication leads to troublesome, harmful, or deviant behavior varies considerably from society to society. In many places, alcohol use poses no problem to the society according to almost anyone's definition; the drug is consumed in moderation and is associated with little or no untoward behavior. In other places, alcohol use has been catastrophic by any conceivable standard. The overall impact of alcohol, then, is determined not solely by its biochemical effects, but by its relationship to the characteristics of the people drinking it. This is not to say that alcohol can have *any* effect the members of a society expect it to have. There is a great deal of latitude in alcohol's effects, but these lie within certain boundaries.

### Acute Effects of Alcohol

The potency of alcoholic beverages is measured by the percentage of alcohol (sometimes referred to as "absolute" or pure alcohol) they contain. Pure ethyl alcohol or ethanol is 100 percent absolute alcohol. Beer contains about 4–5 percent alcohol. Wine is about 10–13 percent alcohol; it is the most potent drink we can concoct through the natural fermentation process. "Fortified" wine, in which alcohol is added to the wine, is legally set at no higher than 20 percent alcohol. (The wines skid-row alcoholics drink are usually fortified.) Sherry is a wine fortified with brandy. Most wine coolers contain about the same level of alcohol as beer, that is, 4–5 percent. The process of distillation (boiling, condensing, and recovering the more volatile, alcohol-potent vapor from the original fluid, and adding an appropriate quantity of water) produces beverages like Scotch, vodka, gin, rum, and tequila, which are about 40–50 percent alcohol, or 80–100 proof. Consequently, in order to consume roughly an ounce of absolute alcohol, someone would have to drink two 12-ounce cans of beer, or one 6-ounce glass of wine, or a mixed drink containing 2–2.5 ounces of Scotch or gin.

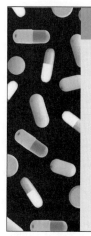

## True-False Quiz

"At the same weight, it takes *less* alcohol to intoxicate a woman than a man." True or false? This is a true statement; women tend to be more susceptible to the effects of alcohol than men are. In part, it has to do with body fat; on average, by weight, women's bodies are 28 percent fat, while men's average 14 percent. The fact is, alcohol does not have an affinity for fat, and so it circulates through the remainder of body tissue, which, for a man, is more voluminous than it is for a woman of the same weight. This means that alcohol tends to be more concentrated, and less diluted, in woman's bodies than in men's—and hence, usually has a more potent effect. Most of my students recognized this difference; 58 percent said that this statement is true.

According to the **rule of equivalency**—which states that the effects of alcohol are determined principally by the volume of pure alcohol that is drunk, rather than the type of drink itself—these drinks would be roughly equal in strength and would have approximately the same physical effects. The rule of equivalency denies that different drinks—separate and independent of their alcohol content—have different levels of potency, as well as the assertion that mixing different types of drinks is more potent than consuming the same drink. Other things being equal, alcohol is alcohol is alcohol; nothing else makes a significant difference.

Alcohol, it has been said, is "the only addictive drug that dangerously alters behavior yet at the same time is freely and legally available without a prescription" (Goldstein, 2001, p. 137). When it enters the body, alcohol translates into what pharmacologists call **blood alcohol concentration (BAC)** or **blood alcohol level (BAL).** This corresponds fairly closely to the percentage of the volume of one's blood that is made up of alcohol after it is ingested. A given BAC or BAL level has been described as "bathing the brain" in a given alcohol concentration (p. 137). There is a relationship between BAC and behavior. The effects of alcohol are, to a large degree, dose related: With some variation, the more that is drunk, the greater the effect.

The effects of alcohol are, however, influenced or mitigated by many factors in addition to the total volume of alcohol in the drinker's body. Some of these factors are directly physiological. For example, because alcohol registers its impact via the bloodstream, the size of the drinker influences BAC. Other factors that mitigate the effects of alcohol include the presence of food and water in the stomach, the speed with which one drinks, and one's sex or gender. As noted previously, women seem to be more sensitive to the effects of alcohol, and manifest effects at lower doses, or greater effects at the same dosage, than do men. In addition, as with practically all drugs, alcohol builds up pharmacological tolerance: It takes more alcohol to achieve a given effect in a heavy or regular drinker than in an abstainer or infrequent drinker.

As we've already seen, alcohol is a depressant, much like sedatives such as barbiturates. Alcohol depresses, slows down, retards, or obtunds many functions and activities of organs of the body, especially the central nervous system. In other words, organs become more sluggish, slower to respond to stimuli. If the dose is too high, the body's organs will shut down altogether, and death will ensue. Alcohol also disorganizes and impairs the ability of the brain to process and use information, and hence impairs many perceptual, cognitive, and motor skills needed for coordination and decision making. One ounce of alcohol, or roughly two mixed drinks, consumed in less than an hour will result in a BAC of roughly 0.05 percent in an average-size person. This produces in most people a mild euphoria; a diminution of anxiety, fear, and tension; a corresponding increase in self-confidence; and, usually, what is called a release of inhibitions. Decreased fear also typically results in a greater willingness to take risks; this effect has been demonstrated in laboratory animals. For most people, alcohol at low doses is a mild sedative, an anti-anxiety agent, and tranquilizer. This is by no means universally the case, however. For many people, alcohol ingestion results in paranoia, distrust, heightened anxiety, and even hostility. When these effects do occur, they do so at moderate to high doses.

Alcohol's effects on motor performance are familiar to us all: clumsiness, an unsteady gait, an inability to stand or walk straight, slurred speech. One's accuracy and consistency in performing mechanical activities decline dramatically as BAC increases. And the more complex, abstract, and unfamiliar the task, the steeper the decline in accuracy and consistency. The most noteworthy example is the ability to drive an automobile. It is crystal clear that drinking, even moderately, reduces the ability to drive and contributes to highway fatalities. How intoxicated does one have to be to lose the ability to perform mechanical tasks? What does one's BAC have to be to cause a significant decline in motor coordination? And how many drinks does this represent?

The answers depend on a number of factors. All drinkers experience a loss of motor skills at a certain point, and this occurs at a fairly low BAC. There is a kind of "zone" within which alcohol impairment takes place. At about the 0.03 percent BAC—that is, after finishing a single fairly weak alcoholic drink—some very inexperienced and particularly susceptible individuals will display a significant decline in the ability to perform a wide range of tasks. At the 0.10 level, even the most experienced drinker will exhibit some impairment in coordination; this represents roughly four drinks, each containing an ounce of 50 percent alcohol. However, many drivers are quite willing to get behind the wheel while intoxicated: According to the FBI's *Uniform Crime Reports,* in the United States in 2004, there were over 1.7 million arrests for drunk driving.

## Alcohol Consumption: Accidents, Disease, and Social Cost

The fact that alcohol causes discoordination leads us to emphasize the subject of one of this drug's more harmful consequences: its role in causing automobile accidents, especially on the highway. Zador (1991) estimates that, compared with someone who is sober, a driver with a BAC between 0.02 and 0.04 has a 1.4 greater chance of having a fatal single-vehicle crash. This risk increases to 11 times for a driver with a BAC between 0.05 and 0.09, 48 times at the 0.10–0.14 level, and 385 times for a BAC over 0.15. The risk increases even more sharply among younger drivers. For instance, the increased risk of being killed in a single-vehicle crash at the 0.15 BAC level for 16- to 20-year-old males is over 15,000 (Hingson and Winter, 2003, p. 66).

But there is a ray of hope: In the United States, over the long run, alcohol-related automobile fatalities have been declining. Each year, the National Highway Traffic Safety Administration compiles, tabulates, and publishes data on motor vehicle accidents.

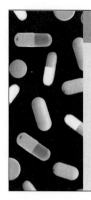

## True-False Quiz

Most of my students (69%) thought that the statement "In the past 20–25 years, the number of alcohol-related automobile fatalities has actually *decreased*" is false; only a bit more than a quarter (27%) thought it to be true. But the fact is, alcohol-related automobile fatalities decreased between the 1980s and the early twenty-first century—in spite of the fact that, during that time, the number of miles driven in the United States has doubled. Experts believe that the reason for this decline is heightened public awareness of the seriousness of and increased vigilance against drunk driving.

In 1982, 53 percent of all automobile fatalities involved one or more drivers who had a BAC of 0.08 or higher—a total of 23,246 deaths. This figure continued to decline through the 1980s and mid-to-late 1990s, reaching a low of 34 percent and 14,421 deaths in 1997. However, during the late 1990s and early 2000s, the numbers plateaued, even creeping up slightly; in 2001, of all fatal crashes, 35 percent or 14,953 involved an alcohol-impaired driver. (It must be kept in mind that twice as many miles are driven on America's roadways today as compared with two decades ago; hence, the number of fatal alcohol-related accidents per 100 million miles has consistently declined over time.) In roughly half of all fatal crashes, the driver had a BAC of 0.16 or higher. The overall decline is partly due to the fact that, as we saw in Chapter 7, U.S. alcohol consumption has been declining since its twentieth-century high in 1980 (though it began to creep up early in this century), and also because today, law enforcement in particular and society in general are significanctly less tolerant of and more punitive toward drunk driving. Despite the long-term decline, alcohol's effects remain distinctly discoordinating, and at the legal level of driving while impaired (0.08% in two-thirds of the states), drivers are most decidedly a danger to themselves and others.

Motor vehicle accidents are not the only source of alcohol-related death. In Chapter 12, we'll see that alcohol consumption is causally related to violent crime; both offenders and victims are highly likely to have been drinking before incidents of criminal violence. In addition, compulsive alcohol consumption, if it takes place over a long period, is medically harmful and typically results in premature death. Since 1971, the U.S. **National Institute on Alcohol Abuse and Alcoholism (NIAAA),** a division of the Department of Health and Human Services, has periodically issued summary reports assessing alcohol's impact on health. As of this writing, the most recent volume was released in 2000. To put its findings in perspective, keep in mind that just under half of the American population consumes a dozen or more alcoholic drinks a year, and approximately 7 percent of the population drinks abusively, according to NIAAA criteria. Alcohol is used by more people than any other drug (caffeine excepted), although tobacco is consumed more often. Alcohol is consumed five to ten times as often as is true of all the illicit drugs combined. According to the NIAAA's summary of the available data:

- The total cost of alcohol abuse in the United States is $185 billion.
- Alcohol alone is involved in substance-related violence in one-quarter of all incidents, a total of 2.7 million acts of violence per year; in a substantial proportion

of the remainder of incidents, alcohol is used in conjunction with one or more illicit drugs.

- About 900,000 residents of the United States suffer from cirrhosis of the liver, mainly caused by the heavy use of alcohol, and 26,000 die of the disease each year.
- Excess alcohol consumption is related to immune deficiencies, causing a susceptibility to certain infectious diseases, such as tuberculosis, pneumonia, HIV/AIDS, and hepatitis.
- Heavy drinkers (those who consume 29 or more drinks per week) have twice the risk of mental disorder as compared with abstainers.

These highlights do not exhaust the NIAAA's list of harms caused by alcohol. In 2004, the federal **Centers for Disease Control (CDC)** estimated that roughly 85,000 people perished due to alcohol-related causes, two-thirds of which involved accidents, suicide, homicide, and other nondisease-related elements (NIAAA, 2000; Ravenholt, 1984). As we've noted, alcohol is one of the "Big Three" drugs, along with heroin and cocaine, that causes or is implicated in overdose deaths, as tabulated by the Drug Abuse Warning Network (DAWN). Many experts believe that in the United States roughly 10 percent of all deaths can be attributed to alcohol consumption. In comparison with that of a moderate drinker, an alcoholic's life is shortened by roughly 15 years. To be succinct, human life is undermined, threatened, corrupted, and destroyed by alcohol abuse.

However, the NIAAA does point out that moderate alcohol consumption is not only *not* harmful but may actually confer distinct and measurable health benefits on the drinker. All studies on the same subject say more or less the same thing (Zuger, 2002): For some diseases, the morbidity of moderate drinkers is actually *lower* than that of abstainers—and moderate drinking is vastly far more common than heavy drinking. It is entirely possible that, taken as a whole, from a public health standpoint, the positives of alcohol consumption outweigh the negatives. Nonetheless, as a psychoactive substance, alcohol stands below only tobacco as a major source of death and disease, and stands virtually alone as a source of violence and accidents.

## Alcohol Consumption Today

In 2003, Americans age 14 or older consumed an average of 2.2 gallons of absolute alcohol per person per year, according to the NIAAA. This is a fairly "hard" or reliable statistic because it is based on sales and not simply self-reports. This figure is called "apparent" alcohol consumption, because not every drop of the alcohol purchased is actually drunk during a given year. Still, the possible sources of error are small, mere blips on the radar screen; they do not change the big picture at all. The fact is, the figures on alcohol sales are very close to actual consumption levels. In any case, 2.2 gallons of absolute alcohol per year works out to just under 1 ounce of absolute alcohol per person per day. Of course, some people drink a lot more than this, some less, and some not at all. Roughly one-third of all Americans are more or less total abstainers—that is, they did not consume a single drop of alcohol during the previous year. As a consequence, it makes sense to tabulate the quantity of alcohol consumed specifically for drinkers, leaving abstainers out of the picture altogether. On average, adult drinkers (ages 18 and older) consume roughly 1.5 ounces of absolute alcohol per day. This represents two and a half 12-ounce bottles or cans of beer, or one and a half 6-ounce glasses of wine, or three 1-ounce drinks of hard liquor per day for every drinking adult in the country.

Recorded yearly alcohol sales (a "hard" statistic) can be backed up with information on the proportion of the American population who say they drink (a "soft" statistic). Every year or so, the Gallup poll asks a sample of Americans ages 18 and older the following question: "Do you have occasion to use alcoholic beverages such as liquor, wine, or beer, or are you a total abstainer?" This question was first asked in 1939, when 58 percent defined themselves as drinkers and 42 percent as abstainers. In 1947, 63 percent said that they drank. The percentage rose steadily throughout the 1950s and 1960s, reaching a peak of 71 percent in 1976–1978. After that, the figure declined slightly. In Gallup's latest poll as of this writing (2003), just over 6 Americans in 10 (62%) said that they "have occasion to use alcoholic beverages." Three out of 10 respondents (31%) said that they had drunk an alcoholic beverage within the past 24 hours.

The 2005 NSDUH (SAMHSA, 2006) I've cited questioned respondents on their alcohol consumption in addition to their drug use. The questions this survey asks are a bit different from Gallup's; they are more specific about the time periods in which the alcohol consumption took place—that is, has the respondent ever drunk alcohol, drunk it within the past year, and drunk it within the past month. In 2005, as we saw, half (52%) of the population ages 12 and older had consumed one or more alcoholic drinks in the past month. This was two-thirds (67%) for use in the past year, and eight in ten (83%) for lifetime use. The comparable figures for 1991 were 51 percent, 68 percent, and 85 percent (NIDA, 1991, p. 85), indicating stability in the consumption of alcohol over the past decade or so. For youths ages 12–17, between 1979 and 1991, the proportion who had ever taken a drink dropped from 70 percent to 46 percent; in 2005, it was 41 percent. The figure for use in the past 30 days for 12- to 17-year-olds was 37 percent in 1979, 20 percent in 1991, and 17 percent in 2005. For young adults ages 18–25, the corresponding 30-day figures declined from 76 percent in 1979, but remained stable between 1991 (67%) and 2005 (66%) (Fishburne, Abelson, and Cisin, 1980, p. 91; NIDA, 1991, p. 85; SAMHSA, 2006). In other words, the NSDUH data, like the sales figures, shows a significant decline in alcohol consumption among the young during the 1980s but stability after that into the early 2000s. Given what we said about triangulation in Chapter 6, and given that the sales figures back up survey data, this trend must be regarded as real and not the artifact of one particular study or measuring device.

The claim that youths under 21 are drinking at least as much as, if not more than, they did since the legal drinking-age was raised to 21 (Mooney, Grambling, and Forsyth, 1992; Ravo, 1987) is not born out by the evidence. The MTF survey verifies what other systematic studies tell us. The annual prevalence for alcohol use among high school seniors stood at 88 percent in 1979; in 2005, it was 69 percent. The 30-day prevalence was 72 percent in 1979 and 47 percent by 2005. For the study's full-time college subsample, the annual prevalence dropped 10 percentage points between 1980 (when the first survey of college students was conducted) and 2004—91 percent versus 81 percent—and the decline in the 30-day prevalence was 14 percentage points, from 82 percent to 68 percent (Johnston et al., 2005, pp. 246–247). Given the weight of the evidence, it seems difficult to deny the decline in alcohol consumption by adolescents and young adults—indeed, for the population as a whole—in the past generation or so. Some critics have pointed out that, though teenagers' overall level of alcohol consumption may have declined, binge drinking among the young has increased (Hoover, 2002)—a distinct possibility, although the figures for 12- to 17-year-olds and 18- to 25-year-olds do not bear this out.

| TABLE 8-1 | Traffic Fatalities and Alcohol Consumption |
|---|---|

**Alcohol-Related Traffic Fatalities per 100 Million Vehicle Miles Traveled, United States, 1977–2003**

| | |
|---|---|
| 1977 | 1.19 |
| 2003 | 0.46 |
| Percent change | −63.0 |

**Alcohol-Related Fatalities per 100,000 Registered Vehicles, United States, 1977–2003**

| | |
|---|---|
| 1977 | 11.71 |
| 2003 | 5.39 |
| Percent change | −54.0 |

**Alcohol-Related Fatalities per 100,000 Licensed Drivers, United States, 1977–2003**

| | |
|---|---|
| 1977 | 12.61 |
| 2003 | 6.51 |
| Percent change | −48.4 |

**Decreases in Alcohol-Related Crashes by Age of Drivers, United States, 1982–2001**

| | |
|---|---|
| 16–17 | 60% |
| 18–20 | 55 |
| 21–24 | 41 |
| 25 and older | 39 |

**Per Capita Alcohol Consumption, United States, 1977–2003 (expressed in gallons of absolute alcohol consumed)**

| | |
|---|---|
| 1977 | 2.64 |
| 2003 | 2.20 |
| Percent change | −16.7 |

*Source:* http://www.niaa.nih.gov/databases; MMWR Weekly, December 6, 2002; Lakins et al., 2005.

One beneficial consequence of the nationwide prohibition on the sale of alcohol to persons under the age of 21 has been a decline in alcohol-related highway fatalities among drivers in the 16- to 20-year-old age range. As we can see from Table 8-1, between 1982 and 2001, the percentage of alcohol-related fatal crashes among 16- and 17-year-olds declined 60 percent, and for 18- to 20-year-olds by 55 percent; the number of such fatalities declined from just under 4,000 in 1977 to just over 1,500 in 2003. The rate of decline in alcohol involvement in fatal crashes among the youngest young drivers (60%) is substantially below the rate among drivers ages 25 and older (39%)—a clear indication that something positive has happened on the teenage drinking-and-driving front. It is possible that the American public is aware of this development. In a 2002 Gallup poll, the vast majority of the respondents questioned (77%) said that they opposed lowering the drinking age to 18; only 18 percent were in favor. When asked whether penalties for underage drinking should be more strict or less strict, or should remain as they are now, 60 percent said more strict, 6 percent said less strict, and 33 percent said they should remain as they are now. Clearly, the laws are doing some good, and the majority of the public supports them.

# Who Drinks? Who Doesn't?

Just as interesting as the overall figures on alcohol consumption and their changes over time is group-to-group variations in drinking. Who drinks and who doesn't? Are certain groups or categories significantly and consistently more likely to drink than others?

There are at least two crucial measures of alcohol consumption: drinking at all and drinking to excess. Drinking varies dramatically from one category in the population to another; likewise, drinking heavily, compulsively, and abusively—that is, to excess—varies along sociological lines. We might expect that categories or groups in the population that have a high proportion of drinkers (and, contrarily, a low proportion of abstainers) would also rank high in the likelihood that their members are alcoholics, that is, those who drink to excess. The opposite side of the coin should be expected as well: The lower the proportion of drinkers in a social category, the lower the likelihood that the members of that category will be abusive drinkers. This is not always the case, however; some groups in the population have extraordinarily high proportions of drinkers but low proportions of alcoholics, while other groups are more likely to abstain, but their drinkers are more likely to drink compulsively and abusively (Armor, Polich, and Stambul, 1976). For instance, persons of Jewish and Italian ancestry are highly likely to drink, but their rates of alcoholism are extremely low. In contrast, men over age 60 have higher-than-average rates of alcohol abstention but also higher than average rates of alcoholism.

Social class or socioeconomic status (SES), which is usually measured by income, occupation, and/or education, correlates strongly and consistently with the consumption of alcohol. As a general rule, in the Western world, including the United States, the higher the social class or SES, the greater the likelihood of drinking at all. This generalization is confirmed by the 2001 national household survey, which found a remarkably strong correlation between education and drinking during the previous year. Among respondents ages 26 and older, only 46 percent with less than a completed high school education had drunk during the prior year; 54 percent of high school grads had done so; 64 percent of respondents with some college had; and a whopping 77 percent of college graduates had drunk an alcoholic beverage once or more during the past year. The same finding consistently turns up in the annual Gallup poll in its question about whether respondents "have occasion" to use alcoholic beverages: the higher the income, education, and SES of the respondent, the greater the likelihood that he or she drinks alcohol.

Gender, too, correlates strongly with drinking. Of all variables (except age), perhaps gender correlates most strongly with alcohol consumption. Men are consistently more likely to drink than are women, and they consume more when they do drink. The 2003 NSDUH found a sizeable male-female difference in drinking: 57 percent of the males but only 43 percent of the females in the study had drunk alcohol during the past month; 31 percent of the men said that they were "binge" drinkers, or drank five or more times on at least one occasion over the past month, while only 15 percent of the women did; and 10 percent of the men but only 3 percent of the women were, according to the criteria of the survey, "heavy" drinkers.

As we've seen, age is also strongly correlated with drinking. Drinking tends to be extremely low in early adolescence, shoots up in the middle-to-late teenage years, reaches a peak between age 19 and the early twenties, and declines slowly after that. In the 2005 national household survey, drinking in the past month increased from 2.5 percent among

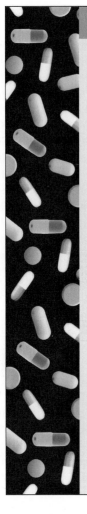

### True-False Quiz

In my true-false quiz, I asked my students a number of epidemiological questions, that is, questions about the social and demographic characteristics of drinkers versus nondrinkers. They were asked to agree or disagree with the following statements: (1) "The higher the social class—as measured by education, income, and occupational prestige—the *higher* the likelihood that someone will drink alcohol; people at or near the top of the social class hierarchy are *unlikely* to be abstainers from the use of alcohol"; (2) "Persons of Irish descent, as compared with the population as a whole, have a *higher*-than-average likelihood of becoming alcoholic"; and (3) "African Americans are statistically more likely than the national average to be *abstainers* from alcohol; that is, during a given period of time (for instance, the past year), they have a greater than average likelihood of *not* consuming any alcohol at all." All three of these statements are true, but the majority of my students thought that they are all false—43 percent for the first statement, 40 percent for the second, and 30 percent for the third. The idea that higher-SES individuals are more likely to drink contradicts the notion that alcohol consumption is most common in the lower social class rungs of the society. (Higher-SES persons are more likely to drink, but the vast majority drink moderately.) Saying that Irish-Americans are more likely to drink heavily contradicts the impulse of most of us to avoid ethnic stereotypes, but a few stereotypes contain a grain of truth, and this is one of them. And it is possible that a substantial proportion of white college students do not believe that Black Americans are more likely than whites to be alcohol abstainers because, again, of the SES factor. According to the national household surveys, about two-thirds of African-Americans abstained from drinking during the prior month, while about half of whites did so.

12-year-olds to a peak of 69.5 percent among 23-year-olds, remained at something of a plateau after that, diminishing only very slightly into middle age: 58 percent among 50- to 54-year-olds, then 51 percent at ages 55–59, then 40 percent at ages 65 and older. This is a very different pattern from drug use, and very different from that hypothesized for a wide range of criminal and "deviant" behaviors (Gottfredson and Hirschi, 1990, pp. 124–144). Of course, drinking during the past month is not as "deviant" as illicit drug use; in American society, it is conventional, very much in the mainstream.

## TOBACCO: AN INTRODUCTION

Is tobacco a drug? Like marijuana, tobacco is a plant product that contains a number of naturally occurring ingredients—chemicals—that have psychoactive properties. The principal psychoactive drug in tobacco is nicotine; the tobacco leaf contains roughly 1 percent nicotine by weight. In the dosages normally taken, nicotine does not produce a profoundly psychoactive effect on users. The short-term or **acute effects** of small doses of nicotine are fairly mild and transient; Avram Goldstein refers to the effects of nicotine as "a low-key high" (2001, p. 121).

Of course, as we've seen so many times before, the route of administration is crucial here: Smoking is such an efficient means of taking a drug that, by this factor alone, nicotine's impact is heightened over and above that obtained with other methods of use, such as chewing tobacco or inhaling snuff (pulverized tobacco). In addition, keep in mind the fact that cigarette smokers almost always inhale—and inhalation is an extremely effective method of use—while pipe and cigar smokers almost never do. So, the consequences of tobacco use will vary markedly according to *how* it is used. Also keep in mind that smoke is air-borne, which means that nonsmokers may have to inhale the tobacco smoke generated by the people in their presence (this is referred to as **passive smoke,** or sidestream or secondhand smoke), and as a consequence, in a very real sense, they are forced to use the drug nicotine.

## Tobacco: Medical Harm

Nicotine is a poison; if injected directly into the bloodstream, roughly 60 milligrams is the lethal dose, that is, the amount sufficient to kill a human being. Since cigarettes are smoked, a substantial proportion of nicotine's strength is dissipated into the air. A cigar contains about 100–120 milligrams of nicotine, but its smoke is not inhaled. Nicotine kills as a result of muscular, and hence respiratory, paralysis. Fortunately, not enough of the drug is ab-sorbed in a brief period of time for it to be lethal. Perhaps the most noticeable acute effect of cigarette smoking is that it releases carbon monoxide, which reduces the body's supply of oxygen to the blood, causing shortness of breath and, in more substantial doses, dizziness. (Over the long run, this chronic oxygen deficit will damage the heart and the blood vessels of smokers.) The same effect in expectant mothers can damage the fetus and increase the likelihood of birth defects (Goldstein, 2001, pp. 126–127).

Nicotine is a vasoconstrictor; that is, it constricts the blood vessels, causing the heart to work harder to maintain a sufficient supply of blood and oxygen. It also inhibits the stom-ach contractions that are associated with hunger; hence, the belief that if one stops smok-ing, one may gain weight has some validity. More broadly, the drug does not produce profound behavioral changes or impairment; nicotine (along with caffeine) is the only drug passengers do not have to fear if their pilot is using it (Goldstein, 2001, p. 122). Intellectual and motor ability do not decline significantly under the influence; indeed, at certain doses, they may even improve slightly.

Is nicotine addicting? In the 1980s, Philip Morris, a major cigarette manufacturer, com-missioned a study on whether tobacco produces an addiction in rats. The results of this research showed that, indeed, nicotine is an addicting drug. Was this study published? No; when the company reviewed the findings, the researchers were fired and the lab was closed down (Ksir, Hart, and Ray, 2006, p. 255). And in 1994, tobacco executives testified before Congress to the effect that nicotine is *not* addicting. Today, however, most pharmacologists agree that nicotine is indeed addicting and the main, and very possibly the only, addicting sub-stance in tobacco. However, as Goldstein (2001, p. 121) points out, the addictive properties of nicotine were difficult to establish in the laboratory since animals found the drug so unpleas-ant that it was difficult to induce them to self-administer it. It took researchers many years to

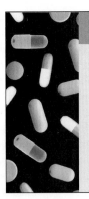

## True-False Quiz

My students were not fooled by the statement "More people die as a result of using tobacco than all other drugs—legal and illegal—combined." The vast majority (88%) agreed with it, and as we see in this section, it is true. According to the Centers for Disease Control, smoking kills roughly 440,000 Americans a year—and millions more in other countries. This *vastly* outweighs deaths from alcohol consumption (85,000) and illicit drugs (20,000–30,000), added together. Today, the public has become much more aware of the dangers of smoking than was true in decades past.

figure out a way of getting laboratory animals to become tolerant enough to the effects of nicotine to take it regularly; this was possible only through a slow and gradual process. Years of research with both humans and animals have shown that nicotine does produce a physical dependency, and its strength depends on the size of the tobacco "habit," that is, the quantity of nicotine consumed per day. What evidence do we have for this generalization?

Specifically, with respect to nicotine, there are at least six indications of nicotine's addicting or dependency-producing properties. First, as we've already seen, of all drugs, tobacco is the one that is used *most frequently*. In the United States, smokers take their drug, on average, 15 times a day, indicating that the drug has a strong hold over its users. In addition, of all drugs, users of tobacco cigarettes display the strongest yearly-to-monthly ratio or "loyalty" rate—they use it most regularly. Second, if we were to plot use during the day with levels of nicotine in the blood, their correspondence would resemble a thermostat. That is, the nicotine level in the smoker's body rises during and immediately after smoking, and declines soon afterward. When it falls below a certain level, the smoker lights up again, elevating that level once again (Goldstein, 2001, pp. 118–121). A line depicting the presence of nicotine in the smoker's body during the course of a day would resemble a sawtooth pattern, rising and falling over time. Third, once laboratory animals have been induced to take nicotine regularly, they work extremely hard to continue self-administering it. If smokers switch to a low-nicotine cigarette, they inhale more deeply and/or smoke more cigarettes to obtain the same level of nicotine in their body. Fourth, smokers who quit describe feeling a strong craving for cigarettes that persists even years after the onset of abstention. Fifth, the statistics on relapse show that, although many smokers do quit, they do so only with great difficulty and as a result of repeated efforts; as many heroin addicts return to their drug of choice as smokers do. And last, there are the physical effects produced by nicotine abstention: headaches, fatigue and drowsiness, shortened attention span, irritability, anxiety, insomnia, hunger, heart palpitations, and tremors.

Smokers are much, much more likely to die a premature death than nonsmokers are. The federal Department of Health and Human Services estimates, a nonsmoker is more likely to live to the age of 75 than a smoker is to live to 65. A two-pack-a-day smoker is 23 times more likely to die of lung cancer than a nonsmoker is. In what was no doubt a carefully crafted public relations move, in 1999, Philip Morris executives publicly admitted that medical research indicates that smoking causes cancer. The fact is, long before this date, scientists had accepted the fact that cigarettes cause disease and death. The latest estimate issued (in 2002) by the federal Centers for Disease Control (CDC) estimates that tobacco causes roughly 440,000 premature deaths in the United States each year. This means that tobacco causes more deaths *than all other drugs combined,* and by a wide margin. The death toll from alcohol is in the 85,000 range; the death toll for illegal drugs plus the illegal use of prescription drugs may be in the realm of 20,000 or so. Moreover, tobacco kills more than its smokers. The Environmental Protection Agency estimates that 50,000 Americans die as a result of passive smoke, that is, smoke inhaled by a nonsmoker from a smoker's cigarette. And, according to an extensive review of the literature, over 5,000 infants die as a result of their mother's smoking habit; this does not include an estimated 19,000–141,000 spontaneous abortions (or miscarriages) directly or indirectly induced by tobacco smoke (DiFranza and Lew, 1995).

The CDC estimates that, in the United States, *one out of five* of all deaths can be traced to smoking. And medical experts affiliated with the United Nations estimate that in the industrialized countries of the world, 12 percent of all premature deaths (before age 65) are caused by the consumption of tobacco. The CDC estimates that, while cigarettes cost about $3 a pack nationwide, because of the multiple harms they cause—an immense loss of life, health, and productivity, and huge medical costs—they actually cost society about $7 per pack. (But as we'll see below, some economists calculate that society *saves* money by the premature deaths of smokers, since they tend not to live long enough to collect retirement benefits! See Viscusi, 2002.) In short, tobacco is by far the country's number-one drug menace. Smoking shaves an entire decade off one's life. Moreover, it reduces the quality of life, since the last few years of the smoker's life are likely to be marred by diseases such as lung cancer, stroke, emphysema, heart disease, and bronchitis. The harmful effects of cigarettes have been known for some time.

## Tobacco: A Brief History

The tobacco plant is indigenous to the Western Hemisphere; prior to the 1490s, its use was completely unknown in Europe and Asia. The native inhabitants of San Salvador, an island in the Caribbean, presented Columbus with a sheaf of tobacco leaves. When first introduced into Europe, the practice of tobacco consumption generated a great deal of hostility, as well as legislation outlawing the sale and use of this plant product. Some of these laws even called for the death penalty for offenders. In 1604, King James issued a "Counterblaste" condemning the consumption of tobacco; he referred to smoking as "a custom loathsome to the eye, hateful to the nose, harmful to the brain, [and] dangerous to the lung." Nonetheless, within a decade, the English decided to live with the "stinking weede." Tobacco's story was essentially the same everywhere the plant was introduced—the Ottoman Empire, Russia, China, Japan, Hindustan: condemnation, followed by legislation, and eventually, legal and public acceptance.

Today, cigarette smoking is such an overwhelmingly favorite method of tobacco consumption, it is difficult to imagine that, just a bit more than a century ago, cigarettes were smoked hardly at all. The earliest recreational use of tobacco involved inhaling the fumes of the combusted leaf through a tube or a straw. By the 1700s, sniffing or snorting powdered or shredded tobacco (snuff) came to be far more popular. In the United States in the 1800s, the most popular method of tobacco consumption was chewing, but as the society became more urban, more middle class, more fashionable, and more sophisticated, this unsightly and unaesthetic habit declined in popularity. Still, as late as 1920, three out of four pounds of tobacco were devoted to cigar and pipe smoking, snuff, and chewing.

Smoking tobacco in the form of cigarettes did not become popular until well into the first half of the twentieth century. The change was partly cultural and partly technological.

In 1880, according to the U.S. Department of Agriculture, the total American sale of cigarettes was only half a billion; on a per population basis, consumption was only one-three-hundredths of what it is now. In 1881, the cigarette-rolling machine was patented. It could manufacture 120,000 cigarettes a day—the work of 40 hand rollers. By 1900, 2.5 billion cigarettes were being sold annually in the United States, an average of 54 cigarettes per adult. A dozen years later, the total number manufactured shot up by more than five times, to 13.2 billion, and the per capita average increased by three times, to 223 cigarettes. By the end of the decade, the consumption of cigarettes had tripled, to 44.6 billion. And between 1920 and 1930, the number of cigarettes consumed in the United States more than doubled, to 119.3 billion. Between 1900 and 1963, the number of cigarettes sold in the United States increased from 2.5 to 523.9 billion, and the per capita consumption jumped from 54 to 4,345. (See Figure 8-1.) Today, about six out of seven pounds of tobacco consumed in the United States are devoted specifically to cigarette smoking.

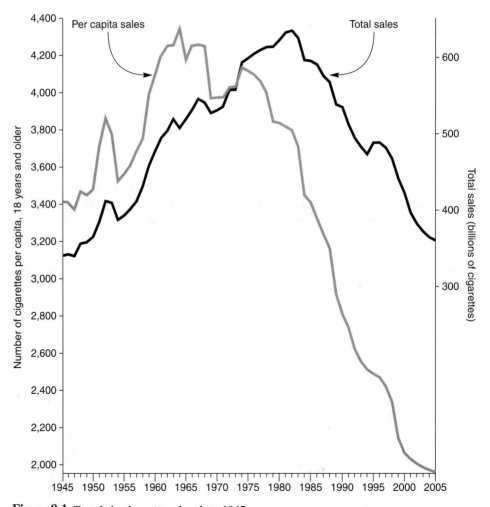

**Figure 8-1** Trends in cigarette sales since 1945.

| TABLE 8-2 | Cigarette Consumption, Ages 18 and Older, United States, 1963–2005 | | |
|---|---|---|---|
| | **Selected Years** | **Billions Consumed (Estimate)** | **Per Capita Sales** |
| | 1963 | 523.9 | 4,286 |
| | 1964 | 511.2 | 4,143 |
| | 1970 | 536.4 | 3,969 |
| | 1975 | 607.2 | 4,123 |
| | 1980 | 631.5 | 3,858 |
| | 1985 | 594.0 | 3,400 |
| | 1990 | 525.0 | 2,827 |
| | 1995 | 487.0 | 2,483 |
| | 2000 | 430.0 | 1,977 |
| | 2005 | 378.0 | 1,689 |

*Source:* U.S. Department of Agriculture, 2006.

## The Decline of Smoking

In 1964, the U.S. government published what is probably the most influential document in the history of the tobacco industry—the Surgeon General's Report, titled *Smoking and Health*. Summarizing the research current at that time, this report argued that the use of tobacco products represents a serious health hazard to smokers. The impact of this report was immediate; in 1964, the per capita consumption of cigarettes declined slightly, and it continued to fall throughout the remainder of the twentieth century and into the twenty-first. From its 1963 high of 4,345, by 2005, America's per adult tobacco consumption for the population ages 18 and older had declined to 1,740. The total number of cigarettes sold continued to rise decades after 1964, of course, since the American population continues to grow; 1981 represents the peak year for total tobacco sales, when 640 billion cigarettes were sold. By 2005, the total had fallen to 378 billion. (See Table 8-2.)

Perhaps the factor most closely tied into the cessation of smoking is education. According to the information supplied on the Internet by the Epidemiology and Statistics Unit, today, high school dropouts are more than two and a half times more likely to smoke (36%) than are college graduates (14%); persons with at least three years of college are more likely to be ex-smokers (65%) than are persons without a high school diploma (45%). Between the 1970s and the late 1990s, smoking declined 51 percent among college graduates but only 19 percent among persons with less than 12 years of education. Educated people are much less likely to smokes and, if they do smoke, much more likely to give up the habit, than is true of less well-educated persons.

It is important to recognize that tobacco is a multibillion-dollar-a-year industry, still one of the largest in the country; executives, employees, communities, stockholders—and governments—profit from the sale of tobacco products. Indeed, since, economically speaking, tobacco is an industry just like any other product, it generates wealth that indirectly benefits the entire country, not just persons directly involved with it. In 2001, according to the Federal Trade Commission, the industry spent over $11 billion on advertising and promotion, a figure that rises as sales decline. While most agricultural products yield about $4,000 per acre cultivated, the annual gross for tobacco is over $200,000 per acre (Torregrossa, 1996). Factor in, too, a bizarre and grim statistic: State and federal governments save about 33 cents per pack on Medicaid and Social Security benefits that don't have to be paid out because smokers generally die before they are able to collect them (Gravelle and Zimmerman, 1994; Viscusi, 2002). All in all, the incentives to protect tobacco from legal, political, and economic assault are massive. In 1996 alone, the tobacco industry spent $600 million, employing 350 separate law firms, to protect their business from lawsuits (Feder, 1997). On the basis of these facts alone, you might predict that tobacco was an impregnable fortress.

The crack in the fortress was caused by a variety of factors, perhaps none so powerful as a growing concern for the fate of teenage smokers. Over 90 percent of all adult smokers began their habit before the age of 18; some experts argue that, if people do not begin smoking as teenagers, they are unlikely to begin at all. Consider, too, the fact that the earlier the smoking habit begins, the greater the likelihood that tobacco will kill the smoker. Experts estimate that, today, roughly 3,000 American teenagers will take up the habit *every day;* of these, one third will eventually die of a tobacco-related illness (*The New York Times,* August 18, 1996, p. E14). The CDC estimates that roughly 5 million American teenagers age 17 or younger who currently smoke will die of one or more diseases caused by cigarette smoking; if the downward trend that began in the late 1980s had continued, perhaps as many as 4 million of them would have survived (Feder, 1997). Contemplating the horrific loss of life in the decades to come has led many policy analysts to seek drastic measures to curtail the consumption of tobacco. Fortunately, a decline in smoking among adolescents took place during the early 2000s. For 1995–1999, Monitoring the Future's 30-day prevalence figures for high school seniors were in the 33.5–36.5 percent range. In 2000, this declined to 31.4 percent, and in 2005, it stood at 23.2 percent. In other words, in spite of the rise in smoking during the 1990s among secondary school students, the current level is lower than it has been since MTF began conducting its surveys. If present trends continue, the decline that took place between the late 1990s and the early 2000s will translate into several million lives saved. Public health officials hope for a continuation of the recent decline well into the remainder of this century.

## PSYCHOTHERAPEUTIC DRUGS: AN INTRODUCTION

Some psychoactive drugs are used for medical and psychiatric purposes; their action is such that, physicians believe, by taking them, troubled individuals are able to lead more comfortable, less anguished lives. These drugs are prescribed by physicians for patients for what is defined as legitimate medical use. Some are used for common and not especially severe psychiatric ailments, such as anxiety, irritability, nervousness, and insomnia. Others are used to suppress the less common and far more serious symptoms of mental disorder, such as schizophrenia and clinical depression. Although, traditionally, the term **psychotherapeutics** has been used to refer only to antipsychotics and antidepressants, I have chosen to broaden this category to include sedatives and tranquilizers as well, since they are used for or in the treatment of psychological and psychiatric problems and disorders. The psychotherapeutic drugs I'll discuss in this chapter include the sedatives and tranquilizers, the antipsychotics, and the antidepressants. Elsewhere, I will discuss the use of other drugs, such as the amphetamines and the narcotics, which have also been used for therapeutic purposes; they are interesting for other reasons. Thousands of Americans die from ingesting substantial quantities of psychotherapeutic drugs. According to the Drug Abuse Warning Network (DAWN), in the United States, there have been 1,800 lethal overdoses each year as a result of taking tranquilizers (or benzodiazepines) and 2,300 as a result of taking antidepressants (such as Prozac, Paxil, and Zoloft). Almost none of these deaths come from recreational use; such overdoses tend to occur as a result of suicide.

For our purposes, the most important thing to keep in mind with two of the principle categories of psychotherapeutics—antipsychotics and antidepressants—is that, though they are psychoactive drugs, their effects on non–mentally disordered individuals are not pleasurable; hence, there is almost no recreational use of them. This generalization does not apply, however, to sedatives (such as GHB and barbiturates) and tranquilizers (such as Valium and Rohypnol), which are used recreationally on a widespread basis. And it most certainly does not apply to any of the stimulants, such as Adderall and Ritalin, which are also use therapeutically—and recreationally.

## Sedative/Hypnotics

**Sedatives** are **general depressants;** they retard signals passing through the central nervous system. As such, then, their effects are contrary or antagonistic to the stimulant drugs. Sedatives also slow down a number of functions and actions of a wide range of organs of the body, as well as general activity, or "behavioral output." Sedatives also decrease anxiety. At higher doses, sedatives are hypnotics—that is, they induce sleep. The term **"sedative-hypnotic"** can be used synonymously with "general depressant." In this text, I'll use the term "sedative" to cover drugs that act as general depressants. (By extension, this includes the tranquilizers, which sedate in moderate-to-medium doses.)

Alcohol is the most widely used of all sedatives, although for the most part, today, it is not used in medical therapy. Two sedatives that have been widely used both legally and illegally are the barbiturates and methaqualone. **Barbiturates** are defined as central nervous system depressants that are derived from barbituric acid. The first barbiturate, Veronal, was marketed commercially in 1903. Since then, medical chemists have synthesized some 2,500 different derivatives of barbituric acid, but only a dozen of these are widely sold and used in the United States. Barbiturates are classified according to the speed of their action. The *short-acting* barbiturates include Amytal ("ammies," in street parlance), Tuinal ("tooies," or "Christmas trees"), Seconal ("sekkies," "seggies," "reds," or "red devils"), and Nembutal ("yellow jackets," "nimmies," or "nimbies"). They all induce an intoxication or high if taken in sufficient doses, and they all have been used recreationally on the street. *Long-acting* barbiturates include phenobarbitol and mephobarbital, which do not produce a high, are rarely used on the street, and need not be discussed here.

The barbiturates represent a formerly widely psychotherapeutically used sedative; they were used at one time mainly as an anti-anxiety agent and sleep aid. As a result of harmful recreational use in the 1960s and 1970s, medical use of the barbiturates declined sharply; currently, roughly one-twentieth as many prescriptions are written for the barbiturate drugs as was true 30 years ago. From 1966 to 1986, the number of prescriptions written for Amytal, Seconal, Nembutal, and Tuinal dropped by 90 percent; between 1987 and 1990, it declined another 50 percent; and in 1996, the number of prescriptions written for all barbiturates was less than half that in 1992. The current prescription use of barbiturates is insignificant. In 2004 and 2005, none of the fast-acting barbiturates were in the list of the 200 top-selling prescription drugs.

**Methaqualone** is another sedative with effects similar to the barbiturates. Once commonly prescribed, it has since been classified as a Schedule I drug, and hence is no longer legally prescribed in the United States. Originally, sedatives were distinguished from tranquilizers, mainly the benzodiazepines, by the fact that, at doses only slightly higher than therapeutic, over a period of continued use, sedatives induced mental clouding, intoxication, discoordination, and physical dependence, whereas physicians thought that tranquilizers did not. Later research showed the two drug types to more similar than different in these respects; the most important factor determining whether these drugs induce the specified effects seems to be the dose rather than the drugs type taken. Nonetheless, these differences are a matter of degree, and barbiturates and methaqualone are still regarded as more dangerous and abusable than the tranquilizers.

Methaqualone was marketed under a number of different trade names, including Quāālude ("ludes"), Sopor ("soaps"), Parest, and Optimil. At one time, the medical profession regarded methaqualone as safe and nonaddicting. Now, the drug is considered to be capable of producing death by overdose, extreme mental clouding, drowsiness, discoordination, disorientation, and a true physical dependence. Methaqualone has not been legally prescribed in the United States since 1985.

In terms of their effects, the barbiturates are remarkably like alcohol; alcohol is sometimes referred to by pharmacologists as a "liquid barbiturate." Goldstein (2001, p. 6) classifies barbiturates, the other sedatives, and tranquilizers in a category he refers to as "alcohol and related drugs." Barbiturates are, in many ways, even more dangerous than heroin. The classic withdrawal syndrome appears upon discontinuation of "chronic" use of barbiturates: symptoms include nausea, muscular twitching, aches and pains in the head and body, anxiety and nervousness, trembling, profuse sweating, dizziness, cramps, feelings of feebleness, and finally, in the later stages, convulsions and sometimes coma, occasionally resulting in death. Naturally, the heavier the dependence, the more extreme the reactions.

Death from an overdose of a barbiturate can occur at ten times the therapeutic dose. Death is caused by respiratory failure, an inhibition of the breathing mechanism. Since the two drugs are so similar in their actions, barbiturates demonstrate a cross-tolerance with alcohol. The effects of the two taken together are **synergistic,** that is, more toxic than the sum of their separate effects. Since the two drugs are commonly taken in conjunction, this synergistic or multiplier function is especially problematic. In other words, it is easier to die of a drug overdose when taking alcohol and barbiturates in combination than it is when taking twice as much of either substance alone. In addition, when taking both together, users become discoordinated at far lower doses than is true when taking either separately.

In contrast to the drastic decline in legal medical use after the 1970s, the decline in street or recreational use of barbiturates has been much more gradual. In 1975, 17 percent of twelfth-graders said that they had taken barbiturates to get high at least once in their lifetimes; 5 percent said that they had done so in the past 30 days. In 2005, these figures were 10.5 and 3.3 percent, respectively (University of Michigan press release, December

19, 2005). In spite of their nearly total discreditation in the medical profession, barbiturates are still at least modestly popular as a recreational drug among high school students.

In contrast, the decline in the recreational use of methaqualone, which lagged a few years behind its spectacular decline in prescription use, was much more drastic. In 1972, Quāālude, a trade name of methaqualone, ranked 112th among the nation's most commonly prescribed drugs (up from 153rd in 1971). In 1973, the federal government reclassified it as a Schedule II drug, and in a few short years, it dropped out of the circle of the top 200 drugs, never to return. More than ten times as many prescriptions for the methaqualone drugs were written in 1971 and 1976 as in 1966; in 1981, only one-third as many were written as in these peak 1970s years. By late 1985, no prescriptions were written for methaqualone in the United States at all. Its heyday of popularity on the street as a recreational drug was from 1980 to 1984. Today, methaqualone is one of the drugs least likely to be used by high school students. In 1981 and 1982, roughly one high school senior in ten (11%) had even tried methaqualone; in 2005, this was just over 1 percent (1.3%).

## Tranquilizers

In large doses, **tranquilizers** act as sedative-hypnotics, that is, they produce drowsiness; in small-to-moderate doses, they are calming agents and are effective in combating anxiety and tension. Tranquilizers include Valium (whose generic or chemical name is diazepam), Librium (chlordiazepoxide), Equanil and Miltown (meprobamate), Xanax (alprazolam), Ativan (lorazepam), and Rohypnol. The pharmaceutical use of the tranquilizers that were immensely popular in the 1960s and 1970s dropped sharply in the late 1970s and early 1980s. Valium, once the most popular of all prescription drugs, lost almost half of its sales between 1975 and 1980, and its use is still declining. In 1995, it ranked only 192nd in popularity among all prescription drugs; in 1996, it dropped off the list of the 200 most popular pharmaceuticals. In 2004, its generic equivalent, diazepam, ranked 64th in sales. Equanil ranked as the 50th most popular prescription drug in the United States in 1972 and 90th in 1976; by 1981, it had slipped off the list of the top 200 pharmaceuticals. Librium, which dropped during that same period from 3rd to 44th, Placidyl (120th in 1972), and Miltown (155th in 1972) are now not represented among the 200 most-prescribed drugs in the country. However, a number of related substances, such as alprazolam or Xanax (12th), lorazepam (33rd), and clonazepam (43rd), are extremely widely prescribed as tranquilizers. The anxiety business, it seems, will always be brisk. (See Table 8-3.)

There are several reasons for the decline of the original or "flagship" tranquilizers and the rise of related substances. The first is that the patent held by a pharmaceutical company that initially markets a prescription drug is valid for only 28 years; after that, barring legal wrangles, any company can sell it under its generic name. Physicians soon realize that it is more economical to prescribe to their patients what is exactly the same drug (that is, the generic brand) instead of a substance that costs far more (the trade or specific brand). Today, the generic diazepam outsells the specific Valium by a factor of ten to one; since 1992, the sale of Xanax, a specific drug, decreased by over 75 percent while, during that same period, the sale of its generic version, alprazolam, increased by ten times. When the patent a drug company holds runs out, the sales of once-popular trade products decline sharply.

A second reason why nearly all psychoactive prescription drugs decline in popularity over the long run is that physicians become aware of some of their undesirable side effects

**TABLE 8-3    The 54 Top Prescription Drugs by Number of Prescriptions Written, 2004**

| Drug Name | Number of Prescriptions Written | Drug Type |
|---|---|---|
| 1. Hydrocodone | 92,719,975 | Painkiller/analgesic |
| 2. Lipitor | 69,766,431 | Anti-cholesterol agent |
| 3. Lisinopril | 46,206,563 | Anti-hypertension agent |
| 4. Atenolol | 44,162,229 | Anti-hypertension agent |
| 5. Synthroid | 44,056,176 | Thyroid therapeutic |
| 6. Amoxicillin | 41,393,538 | Antibacterial agent |
| 7. Hydrochlorothiazide | 41,345,733 | Anti-hypertensive |
| 8. Zithromax | 37,171,754 | Antibacterial agent |
| 9. Furosemide | 36,508,251 | Anti-hypertensive |
| 10. Norvasic | 34,729,004 | Anti-hypertensive |
| 11. Toprol | 32,794,562 | Blood pressure agent |
| 12. Alprazolam | 32,404,743 | Antianxiety/panic disorder agent |
| 13. Albuterol | 31,219,862 | Anti-asthma agent |
| 14. Zoloft | 29,877,707 | Antidepressant |
| 15. Zocor | 27,234,005 | Anti-cholesterol agent |
| 16. Metformin | 25,472,580 | Anti-diabetic agent |
| 17. Ibuprofen | 25,188,051 | Painkiller |
| 18. Triamterene | 24,616,014 | Anti-edema agent |
| 19. Ambien | 24,494,669 | Anti-insomnia agent |
| 20. Cephalexin | 23,665,172 | Antibacterial agent |
| 21. Nexium | 23,641,811 | Treatment for GI disorders |
| 22. Prevacid | 23,628,587 | Treatment for ulcers/acid reflux |
| 23. Lexapro | 22,597,383 | Antidepressant |
| 24. Prednasone | 22,506,888 | Anti-asthma/inflammation agent |
| 25. Zyrtec | 22,382,823 | Anti-allergy agent |
| 26. Singulair | 22,020,478 | Anti-asthma agent |
| 27. Celebrex | 21,916,220 | Anti-arthritis agent |
| 28. Fluoxetine | 21,752,487 | Antidepressant |
| 29. Fosomax | 20,972,548 | Anti-osteoporosis agent |
| 30. Metoprolol | 20,840,044 | Anti-blood pressure/angina agent |
| 31. Premarin | 20,324,619 | Hormone replacement |
| 32. Levoxyl | 19,760,520 | Hormone replacement |
| 33. Lorazepam | 18,873,635 | Anti-anxiety agent |
| 34. Allegra | 18,772,070 | Anti-allergy agent |
| 35. Plavix | 18,721,885 | Anti-coagulant agent |
| 36. Effexor | 18,574,507 | Antidepressant |
| 37. Potassium chloride | 18,523,548 | Electrolyte balance agent |
| 38. Protonix | 18,359,740 | Gastrointestinal agent |
| 39. Propoxyphene | 17,931,369 | Narcotic analgesic |
| 40. Advair diskus | 17,400,826 | Bronchodilator |
| 41. Warfarin sodium | 16,581,657 | Blood thinner/anticoagulant |

## TABLE 8-3

| Drug Name | Number of Prescriptions Written | Drug Type |
|---|---|---|
| 42. Acetaminophen w/codeine | 16,079,867 | Painkiller/analgesic |
| 43. Clonozepam | 15,968,529 | Anti-anxiety agent |
| 44. Neurontin | 15,476,692 | Anti-convulsant |
| 45. Flonase | 15,136,691 | Anti-inflammatory |
| 46. Amitriptyline | 15,086,803 | Antidepressant |
| 47. Ranitidine | 14,884,810 | Gastrointestinal agent |
| 48. Trazodone | 14,450,339 | Antidepressant |
| 49. Naproxen | 13,918,496 | Analgesic |
| 50. Amox tri-potassium clavulanate | 13,810,927 | Anti-infection agent |
| 51. Enalapril maleate | 13,732,556 | Cardiovascular agent |
| 52. Paroxetine | 13,731,071 | Antidepressant |
| 53. Pravachol | 13,662,403 | Cardiovascular agent |
| 54. Viagra | 13,539,272 | Erectile dysfunction agent |

and search for less toxic substances. The pharmaceutical corporations—which stand to earn a profit by marketing it—submit initial reports on a drug's supposed safety and effectiveness to the Food and Drug Administration. Hence, these corporations may understate a drug's dangerous side effects or overstate its therapeutic effectiveness. When a drug becomes widely used in medical practice, many more types of patients take it than was true initially. These side effects, even though they may be atypical, become publicized within the profession, and sometimes (as with Prozac and Halcion), the publicity becomes so intense that it reaches the mass media. Although the substitutes that are found for these drugs may be no safer than the originals, their side effects are not yet known in detail. In this game of "musical drugs," substances introduced early are knocked out of the market or suffer sharp declines, and newer ones enter the arena. Hence, in this shifting-around process, the *total volume* of prescriptions written for a given drug category may remain stable or even rise, while *particular* drug products (whether brand names or generics) will rise and fall precipitously. For minor tranquilizers as a whole, between 1992 and 2004 (adjusting for a slight population increase), sales have either risen slightly or remained more or less flat.

With respect to the recreational use of tranquilizers, the trend line shows a decline, then an increase. The Monitoring the Future (MTF) survey showed that the recreational use of tranquilizers by high school seniors declined fairly steeply between 1975 (10.6% annual prevalence) and 1992 (2.8%), but in the past decade, there was an upturn—to 6.8 percent in 2005. Since tranquilizers are so hugely prescribed to large numbers of patients who have problems in coping with life, it should come as no surprise that some of those patients—a tiny proportion—decide to commit suicide by taking an overdose of the very drug that is so readily available in their medicine chest. To the extent that tranquilizers continue to be prescribed to large numbers of patients who experience difficulty in coping with life's many problems and who are not infrequently depressed, they will be used by some to take their life. Keep in mind that in 2000, the **benzodiazepines** (Valium-like tranquilizers), taken as a whole, caused or were associated with 1,800 deaths in the areas tabulated by DAWN. This was only slightly less than half the number racked up by each of the "Big Three" DAWN drugs—cocaine, heroin, and alcohol.

Tranquilizers are sold on the street (at several times the pharmacy price) and are used for both recreational (when taken in sufficiently large doses) and quasi-therapeutic purposes. Taken in large enough doses over a long enough time, all the minor tranquilizers can produce a physical addiction or dependency. With the cessation of such heavy, long-term use, the patient will experience withdrawal symptoms consisting of convulsions, tremors, cramps, and sweating. The vast majority of users take nowhere near enough of a quantity to become addicted, and such reactions are therefore relatively rare. However, remember that Rohypnol, one of several "date rape" drugs, and a substance associated with hundreds of untoward medical and psychiatric reactions per year, is a tranquilizer or benzodiazepine.

## Antipsychotics

The antipsychotics were once referred to as "major" tranquilizers, to distinguish them from the "minor" tranquilizers. Major tranquilizers pacified mental patients, or psychotics, that is, individuals with a major psychiatric problem, while minor tranquilizers pacified ordinary neurotics, that is, individuals with minor psychiatric ailments. The similarities between these two drug types are superficial; they are in most ways strikingly different in their effects. Today, the antipsychotic drugs are hardly ever referred to as "major" tranquilizers. The **antipsychotics** (or "narcoleptics") are used in the treatment of psychosis; they do not produce a high or intoxication, are almost never used recreationally, and are not sold in the underground market. Nearly all antipsychotic use is legal, licit prescription use for the purpose of controlling mental illness, especially schizophrenia. The antipsychotics have had an extremely important impact on the field of psychiatry.

The effect of the antipsychotics can be measured by examining the changes in the number of the resident patients in mental hospitals in the United States from the 1950s onward. In 1955, there were almost 560,000 mental patients in residence on a given day in nonfederal mental hospitals across the country; that year, Thorazine, an antipsychotic drug, was introduced to treat psychosis. The number of resident patients dropped every year since then; today, there are fewer than 50,000 resident patients in publicly funded mental hospitals on any given day. It is possible that this is an "irreducible minimum," that is, that the number of mentally ill patients who are unresponsive to current drug treatment modalities will remain more or less stable over time. The change in the number of mental patients in the United States is certainly not due to a mentally healthier population. And it is not due to a decline in new admissions to mental hospitals, because these actually more than doubled between the 1950s and the 1970s. Rather, the change was a result of the drastic decline in the average length of stay in mental hospitals. In 1955, the average period of hospitalization was six months; today, it is two to three weeks. The decline in the number of mental patients living in hospital facilities at a given time, and the reduction in their average length of stay in those facilities, is due almost entirely to the use of the antipsychotics. About 85 percent of all patients in local, state, and federal mental hospitals receive some form of antipsychotic medication.

One of the antipsychotics, Thorazine (whose chemical name is chlorpromazine) is described as having the following effects on agitated, manic, and schizophrenic patients: The drug "produces marked quieting of the motor manifestations. Patients cease to be loud and profane, the tendency to hyperbolic associations is diminished, and the patients can sit still long enough to eat and to take care of normal physiological needs" (Goldman, 1955). The emotional withdrawal, hallucinations, delusions and other disturbed thinking, paranoia, belligerence, hostility, and "blunted affect" of patients are all significantly reduced.

As a result of the use of the antipsychotics, patients exhibit fewer symptoms of psychosis and have become more manageable, which has permitted mental hospitals to cut back or discontinue such ineffective or dangerous practices as hydrotherapy and lobotomy. And, as a result of the administration of these drugs, the hospitals have, in the words of one observer, been transformed from "zoo-smelling, dangerous bedlams into places fit for human beings to live and, at times, to recover from psychosis" (Callaway, 1958, p. 82). And, by inducing a more "normal" psychological state in patients, it has been possible to release them into the community as outpatients, with only minimal treatment and care in aftercare facilities. Studies have shown that about three-quarters of all acute schizophrenics demonstrate significant improvement following the administration of antipsychotic drugs, and 75–95 percent of all patients relapse if their medication is discontinued. The antipsychotic drugs not only are regarded as effective for most mental patients but are the least expensive of all treatment modalities. It should be added that, though these drugs do reduce the most bizarre symptoms of schizophrenia and other mental illnesses, very few mental patients are able to live what are regarded as completely "normal" lives; an early estimate by the Veteran's Administration places this figure at only 15 percent.

The antipsychotics are not addictive and rarely result in lethal overdoses. There are some side effects of a category of these drugs—the **phenothiazines**—however, including abnormal, involuntary, and sometimes bizarre movements of the tongue, lips, and cheeks; facial tics; tremors; rigidity; and a shuffling walk. These symptoms are treated with a separate type of drug, the anti-Parkinsonian drugs. Some observers are optimistic about a new antipsychotic drug, Risperdal, that was announced in 1994 in the journal *Drug Topics* as being more effective in improving the condition of schizophrenics and having fewer and less serious side effects. Some critics also argue that the phenothiazines reduce the mental acuity and intelligence of patients. The effects of these drugs are not experienced as euphoria-inducing, and they are not used recreationally on the street.

## Antidepressants

Schizophrenia, for which the antipsychotics are effective, is classified as a **thought disorder;** the patient's perception of reality is judged to be bizarre and delusional. In contrast, **mood** (or affect) **disorders** influence the emotions rather than the intellect. The principal mood disorder is depression. Serious clinical depression is marked by feelings of "sadness and despair," an "inability to experience joy or pleasure" in almost all activities, pessimism and helplessness, worthlessness, and, in about 15 percent of all cases, suicidal thoughts or acts (Julien, 1995, p. 187). Patients who evidence only depressive symptoms are classified as suffering from a unipolar depressive disorder, while those who experience depressive symptoms alternated with mania—feeling abnormally grandiose, expansive, agitated, delusional, hyperkinetic, and easily distracted and wildly erratic in behavior and judgment—are said to be suffering from a **bipolar** or **manic-depressive disorder.**

Although anxiety usually accompanies clinical depression, it is not its primary symptomology; hence, anti-anxiety or tranquilizing agents (such as Valium or Xanax) are ineffective as treatment. The stimulants cocaine and the amphetamines, both euphoriants for non-depressed individuals, are not effective as antidepressants, since the pharmacological mechanisms of the two drug types, stimulants and antidepressants, are radically different. In the past, electroconvulsive or shock therapy (ECT) was commonly used as therapy for the clinically depressed. Although effective in a high proportion of cases, it remains controversial. Moreover, although many mental health professionals swear by the procedure, its image in the general public is largely negative: Much of the public regards it as barbaric and inhumane. In the United States, ECT is used mainly on depressed patients who are suicidal (since its effects are immediate rather than long-term) or unresponsive to drug treatment. In the United Kingdom, with a population one-quarter the size that of the United States, ECT treatments are administered twice as frequently—200,000 versus 100,000 per year in the United States.

Today, a majority of mental health professionals regard clinical depression (in the absence of external reasons for depression) as having a neurochemical basis; moreover, it is often transmitted genetically. While the precise etiology of the disorder has not been traced out, it is clear that certain classes of psychoactive drugs are effective in the treatment of depression. **Antidepressants** (or mood elevators) are classified by pharmacologists according to their chemical structure and mechanism of action, but what unites them is that they have been used in the treatment of affective disorders. Prozac, Tofranil, Zoloft, and Elavil are trade names for several widely used antidepressants. In addition, lithium, or lithium chloride, although technically not an antidepressant, is often used for the treatment of bipolar or manic-depressive disorders.

Antidepressants do not induce a euphoric state. In nondepressed individuals, the effects of the antidepressants are experienced as unpleasant; they produce drowsiness and lethargy. Hence, these drugs have no recreational value and so are therefore not used in an illicit context. Most of the antidepressant effects of mood elevators appear only after two to three weeks of continued use. In 60–70 percent of clinically depressed patients, they do elevate mood, increase physical activity, enhance mental alertness, improve appetite and sleep patterns, and reduce morbid preoccupation (Julien, 1995, Chs. 8 and 9). However, roughly 1 in 20 depressed patients who are being administered mood elevators will suffer from serious side effects, including disorientation and hallucinations. Large doses of the antidepressants can be fatal. Antidepressants show up with a fair degree of frequency in DAWN's tabulations. Throughout the 1990s and into the early 2000s, the number of emergency department mentions of antidepressants remained more or less stable at between 30,000 and 40,000, and each year in the early 2000s, over 2,000 persons in DAWN's catchment area died as a result of having taken one or more of the antidepressants, often, although not always, in conjunction with another drug.

Prozac was introduced by Eli Lilly as a prescription drug in 1987. From its first full year of sale, 1988, to 1990, the number of prescriptions written for Prozac jumped five times; in 1996, it was the seventh-best-selling prescription drug overall in America. Practically overnight, Prozac became the most popular and successful antidepressant in history. For years, Prozac was the most widely prescribed of this drug category. But since the late 1990s, it dropped out of the top ten, and today, its generic, fluoxetine, ranks 28th among the most often prescribed drugs in the country. Zoloft was the most popular prescription antidepressant in 2004, ranking 14th among all prescription drugs and selling just under 30 million prescriptions that year. Paxil, another antidepressant, ranked 79th.

In the 1990s, a large number of physicians swore by Prozac for their depressed patients. In Eli Lilly's own clinical trials with the drug, over 3,000 depressed patients were randomly assigned to one of six antidepressants; a seventh group was assigned to take a placebo. At the end of the trials, the Prozac group was least likely to be prone to suicidal thoughts. Says physician Jerrold Rosenbaum, who conducted a study of his clinically depressed Prozac patients, "This drug is transporting a lot of people from misery to well-being" (Cowley et al., 1991, p. 64). Peter Kramer, a physician and author of the best-selling book *Listening to Prozac* (1993), argued that the drug permitts patients to *remake* their depressed personality from one that is depressed, suicidal, and lacking in confidence and a will to seek pleasure, into one that is strong, positive, sensual, and active. Prozac, says Kramer, is not a "mood brightener" but a *personality transformer*.

But Prozac also had a darker side. Beginning in the early 1990s, a small number of Prozac patients began to engage in bizarre, violent, self-destructive behavior, including murder, suicide attempts, and self-mutilation. Said one patient, "You sit down and every nerve in your body has to move. . . . You feel like you're going to jump right out of your skin." This patient also had an "unaccountable longing for pain, which she satisfied by tearing at the flesh on her thighs, arms and torso." When her physician took her off Prozac, she "promptly stopped mutilating herself" (Cowley et al., 1991, p. 65). Psychiatrist Martin Teicher claimed that six of his patients, "depressed but not suicidal," suddenly developed an "intense, violent suicidal preoccupation" after taking Prozac for two to seven weeks.

A certain proportion of clinically depressed patients have suicidal thoughts anyway—in spite of, not because of, an antidepressant drug they might be taking—and some are also violent and self-destructive. If there is such a syndrome, unique to and caused by Prozac, it is too rare to be detected in ordinary studies, which usually have at most a few dozen, occasionally a few hundred, and rarely a few thousand subjects. Even Dr. Teicher continued to prescribe Prozac to his clinically depressed patients. Still, it is conceivable that, among a tiny minority, idiosyncratic effects may stimulate an impulse to violence and self-destructiveness. In any case, the negative publicity surrounding Prozac caused many physicians to switch to other, less notorious antidepressants. Whether this made a difference in their treatment is difficult to say.

## SUMMARY

Objectively speaking, alcohol is a drug; it is psychoactive, it is taken for its effects on the mind, it is physically and psychologically addictive, and it can cause a lethal overdose. Again, judging strictly on the basis of objective criteria, alcohol (along with tobacco cigarettes) represents society's most serious drug problem. In addition, many of the same people who use alcohol also use illicit drugs, indicating that the alteration of consciousness characterizes both drinkers and users of controlled substances. But subjectively, or in the constructionist sense, alcohol is not a drug at all—that is, its possession and sale are legal—and it is not regarded, or socially or mentally "constructed," as a drug by much of the public.

The use of alcohol dates back thousands, possibly tens of thousands, of years; humans have been drinking alcohol longer than they have been fashioning metals. The members of nearly every society on earth consume alcohol. At the same time, the way it is used varies from one society to another. In some societies, its use has become a serious problem; in most, moderation is typically the rule.

Alcohol's effects are closely related to the concentration of alcohol in the bloodstream. Perhaps its most well-known effect is discoordination, which results in a substantial increase in the likelihood of accidents and death while engaged in a wide range of activities. Violence, too, is associated with intoxication, although the causal dynamics here are not altogether clear. In addition, alcohol consumption causes or is associated with a wide range of medical pathologies.

Since 1980, the use of alcohol has been declining on a year-by-year basis (though it has crept up slightly in the early 2000s). It now stands at slightly above two gallons of "absolute" alcohol per year per teenager or adult, or roughly an ounce and a half per drinker per day. Though some observers claim that the 21-and-older law has stimulated drinking among teenagers, the evidence points to lower teenage alcohol use since the law was passed. (Binge drinking may have increased since the law was passed, however.) Drunk driving and alcohol-related automobile fatalities have decreased as well, especially for teenagers but also for the population as a whole.

Alcohol use is distributed unevenly in the population, with some groups and categories drinking significantly more than others. As a general rule, drinking is *positively* related to social class or socioeconomic status (SES)—the higher the income, education, and occupational prestige, the greater the likelihood that someone will drink. However, though upper-SES persons tend to drink, they are highly likely to do so moderately. The lower the SES, the lower the likelihood that someone will drink—but, among those who drink, the higher the likelihood that he or she will drink heavily and abusively. Men are more likely to drink than women, and the men who do drink have a higher likelihood of doing so in greater volume. Of all age groups, young adults under the age of 35 are most likely to drink; the likelihood of drinking declines with age, although slowly.

As is the case with alcohol, whether the nicotine in tobacco can be regarded as a drug depends on our definition of "drug." By objectivistic criteria, nicotine most decidedly is a drug; it is psychoactive, and it can generate a serious dependency. In the past, however, nicotine was not regarded as a drug either by the law or by the public. In the 1990s, the awareness that smoking cigarettes is a form of drug-taking behavior began to grow; in addition, legal restrictions on the sale and use of cigarettes have multiplied as well. Objectively speaking, among all psychoactive substances, tobacco causes the most damage; experts at the federal Centers for Disease Control estimate that roughly 440,000 Americans die prematurely as a result of cigarette smoking; the heavy consumption of tobacco cuts an average of ten years off the life of the smoker.

Some psychoactive drugs are used for medical and psychiatric purposes. As we saw earlier, the prescription drug industry is big business; according to *Pharmacy Times,* in 2004, roughly $235 billion was spent at the retail level in the United States on prescription pharmaceuticals. That same year, between 3 and 4 billion prescriptions were written for Schedule II–V drugs. Most prescription drugs are not psychoactive; they work more or less exclusively on the body. Nonpsychoactive prescription drugs include antihistamines, anti-cholesterol agents, antibiotics, and bronchodilators. One prescription in five or so influences the workings of the human mind. Although many of the drugs discussed throughout this book were, or are still, used for medical purposes (the narcotic analgesics, stimulants, and several of the currently used "club" drugs), this chapter discusses only the sedatives, the tranquilizers, the antipsychotics, and the antidepressants.

Sedatives are general depressants; they retard signals passing through the central nervous system and dull the activity of the brain. Sedatives are extremely dangerous drugs, with a fairly narrow ED-LD (effective dose to lethal dose) ratio; they kill by inhibiting the breathing and heartbeat commands transmitted by the brain. Barbiturates and methaqualone are sedatives (as is alcohol); the first is prescribed at less than one-tenth the level at which it was used medically in the 1970s, and methaqualone (which had the trade name of Quāālude in the United States) is no longer legally prescribed at all. Since the 1970s, the recreational use of barbiturates has declined to half of what it was, while that of methaqualone has plummeted to insignificance.

Tranquilizers or benzodiazepines are drugs that are taken in response to anxiety, for sedation, or as sleeping pills. Once thought to be safe and nonaddicting, we now know that tranquilizers can be as dangerous as the sedatives if taken in a sufficiently large dose. Valium, once the nation's number-one drug, has outlived the patent for its manufacturer, Roche; it is no longer on the list of the 200 most-often prescribed prescription drugs. In contrast, its generic and related benzodiazepines, lorazepam and diazepam, rank 33rd and 64th, respectively. Today, the generic diazepam outsells the specific Valium by a ratio of more than ten to one. In addition, newer competing (and supposedly safer and more effective) tranquilizers are entering the prescription drug market and becoming extremely successful.

Antipsychotics are drugs that suppress the symptoms of mental illness, especially schizophrenia. In the mid-1950s, on any given day, 560,000 patients were inmates in publicly funded mental hospitals; today, this figure is under 50,000. Where are the majority of mental patients now? Today, overwhelmingly, mental patients are being administered antipsychotic drugs, mainly phenothiazines, such as risperidone (Risperdal), Haldol (haloperidol), and Clozaril (clozapine). Antipsychotic drugs do not produce a "high" and are not used recreationally; there is no street usage of the phenothiazine drugs. Some untoward symptoms are produced by antipsychotic drugs, however, such as a dulling of intelligence, a shuffling gait, and slurred speech.

Schizophrenia is a thought disorder; an altogether different mental disorder is depression, a mood disorder. Since severe clinical depression is currently regarded as being caused by a chemical imbalance, it is usually treated with prescription antidepression drugs. A small minority of depressed patients reacts very negatively to antidepressants, including Prozac. Some researchers believe that there is a Prozac "syndrome," while others argue that no drug can be 100 percent successful in treating persons with a clinical depression. Very possibly as a result of the unfavorable publicity surrounding Prozac, its popularity has declined to the point at which two more recent antidepressants, Zoloft (14th) and Paxil (79th), have surpassed its sales.

## KEY TERMS

acute effects   217

antidepressant drugs   230

antipsychotic drugs   228

barbiturates   223

benzodiazepines   227

bipolar disorder   229

blood alcohol
   concentration/level
   (BAC/BAL)   209

Centers for Disease Control
   (CDC)   212

general depressants   223

manic-depressive
   disorder   229

methaqualone   224

mood disorder   229

National Institute for
   Alcohol Abuse and
   Alcoholism
   (NIAAA)   211

passive smoke   217

phenothiazines   229

psychopharmacological
   revolution   206

psychotherapeutics   222

rule of equivalency   209

sedative drugs   223

sedative-hypnotics   223

synergy   224

thought disorder   229

tranquilizers   225

# ACCOUNT:   MY EXPERIENCES WITH ALCOHOL

*When the author, Jane, wrote this account, she was a 19-year-old college sophomore.*

The first time I drank alcohol, I was a high school freshman. I was part of a group of friends who were always together. One night, collectively, we all decided to drink. Our plan was to meet at my cousin's house and drink in her cellar. Her mother, my aunt, was either very naive or very liberal. If something was going on in her house, like under-age drinking, she would pretend to be oblivious to it. In a way, it seemed as if she condoned the activity by staying upstairs where, presumably, she did not know what was going on. On weekends, her oldest son, my cousin, frequently hung out in the cellar with several of his friends. It became such a habit to get together at my cousin's house that it became known as the "Speak Easy."

My friend Donna had an older sister who bought us a case of beer. We were all really excited and anxious to try beer; we all began drinking immediately. I recall how guilty I felt holding the bottle in my hand; I knew that it was wrong for someone that young to drink, but that didn't stop me. Everyone else was drinking, so it seemed all right.

At first, beer tasted unpleasant to me. Still, even though I didn't like the taste, I continued to drink it. All of us watched the others to see if we had any reactions to the alcohol. We had two or three beers that night, and that was about it. We started acting silly by laughing and joking. We thought we were pretty cool because we felt what seemed like a "buzz." We all liked out first experience and agreed to do it again the following weekend.

Drinking in my cousin's basement became routine for us; eventually, these meetings turned into parties. The more people showed up, the more beer we bought. My tolerance built up to the point where I could drink and handle about six beers. In other words, I could consume this amount and still stand up. We began hanging out in the "Speak Easy" with some of the older and more popular

kids. We thought we were the coolest freshmen in our school. We'd get alcohol from older siblings or by "tapping shoulders." (That's hanging outside a liquor store and asking a stranger to purchase beer for us.) We called getting beer going on a "packee run," and whoever came through for us that partic-ular weekend was in the limelight.

Eventually, we started combining our money with the other kids so we could get more beer. We began buying party balls, pony kegs, then full kegs. Drinking from kegs led to drinking games. We tried to get drunk as quickly as possible, then we'd play all kinds of card games. One game, "Circle of Death," involved drinking a cup of beer in the center of a circle of cards every time a king is drawn. Another, "Quarters," is a game of skill; if a quarter lands in your cup, you have to drink it up. The object of all these games was to drink more; they allowed us to get drunk faster. We liked the feeling of being a little out of control.

Most of my friends lived in the neighborhood, so after a night of drinking, we simply walked home. Most of us had curfews, so we gave our-selves about an hour to sober up before we went home to our parents. I began carrying mouthwash and Visine in my pocket to prepare myself for my parents. Usually, I had to lie about where I was going because they knew my cousin's house was trouble. They weren't the only ones who knew, though; pretty soon, rumors began to circulate about my aunt allowing underage drinking at her house. Before long, most of my friends were not allowed to go there any more.

Being forbidden to go to the "Speak Easy" turned out to be a small obstacle. If we wanted to drink, we would just find a new place to hang out. We decided to move our parties to the woods; we found open areas back in the woods where we could get together. Usually, it was a long trek, but once we got there, it was worth it. We made a fire and listened to a radio someone brought. It was cold, but we didn't care—we were having fun. We were away from our parents and with our friends. If we needed to relieve ourselves, we did it right in the woods. For the guys, no problem; for the girls, it was a different story. We brought tissues in anticipation that they would be needed.

We began to drink other beverages in addition to beer. Mad Dog, a cheap wine, was the first of the other drinks. A bottle cost about three bucks, and that one bottle would get you completely wrecked. My cousin and I shared a bottle of Mad Dog; usually, we spent the rest of the night puking our guts out. Even before we drank, we knew we'd probably end up getting sick, but we continued to do it because it was a cheap way to get drunk.

Hanging out in the woods lasted about two years, until the cops found out about it. Neighbors complained, so the cops eventually found out where we partied and broke it up. We developed a system, though. If the cops broke up a party one weekend, we'd hold it somewhere else the next weekend. We kept changing the spot in an effort to outsmart them. We continued hanging out in the woods until the end of my sophomore year. By then, most of my friends got their drivers license, so we had a lot more options as to where to go. Some of them included places we called the wharf, the circle, the tracks, fork road, and the warehouse. . . .

My drinking continued throughout my senior year of high school. We had many parties at our hangout places, and sometimes we would even rent a hotel room to have a warmer place to drink. When my friends and I turned 18, we started going to clubs on weekends. We either drank before we left or on the way there. If we did the latter, that meant the driver also drank. We all brought something—cups, ice, alcohol, and juice. Even though what we were doing was illegal and dangerous, we rationalized it by reminding each other that the club was only 20 minutes away. Anyway, we only got a little buzzed, not really drunk. In our eyes, it was almost all right to drink and drive. Luckily, none of us ever got into an accident.

Drinking in high school was just an excuse to have fun. We knew it was wrong, but we did it anyway. After all, our parents did the same thing, so it was almost as if we were *supposed* to do it.

Alcohol was easy to get, and, though we were underage, it was always available at parties. I do admit, however, that for all the good times I have had with alcohol, I have probably had just as many bad times.

Which brings me up to the present. I am now in my sophomore year of college. When I first came here, I really didn't think I had anything to worry about with alcohol. I assumed I wouldn't be out of control because I had already had experiences with alcohol in high school. I knew I would drink, but I thought I'd keep it down to a minimum. Well, college is a whole new world, with no parents. In a way, it is as if we have our own society. We decide when to eat, sleep, go to class, mingle, and work. Nobody tells us what to do; we are free to make our own decisions. This freedom allows us to do and experience anything, including alcohol.

In high school, I only drank on weekends; in college, many students also drink on week nights. At most bars, there is a theme for each night, like, "Monday Night Football," "Lady's Night," or "College Night." There's always a frat party, a dorm party, an open bar, a beer blast, an open keg, or other drinking events that go on even during the week. When I first came to college, I said I would never go out drinking during the week; that ended in short order. My new friends were always going out, so I eventually decided to join them. My friends and I especially made use of "Lady's Night." My roommate and I usually kept some beer in the refrigerator. First we'd drink a few beers in our room, then head for a bar across campus.

Getting into the bar was the tricky part, because we were still underage. Most of my friends have a fake ID; if someone doesn't, we just passed one back to each other while we were standing in line. Girls usually have an easier time than guys; we almost always got admitted. Once we were admitted, we had about two hours until "Lady's Night" ended. We always took full advantage of this and we'd usually be drunk after the first hour. Then we'd dance, sing, and drink until all hours of the night. Getting home really late usually led to missing Thursday classes. For me, this practice usually took place every week. I started looking forward to the middle of the week so that I could drink. . . .

I'm still not legally allowed to drink. This year, I tried to set my priorities straight and limit my drinking. I drink every Saturday night, usually at a party in my room. I go out every once in a while during the week, but I don't overdo it. I admit I like drinking alcohol. It leaves me with a good feeling, and I usually have a good time with the people I drink with. I wouldn't say I am an alcoholic, but I definitely like the effects of alcohol. I have probably already had more experience with drinking than most people my age, but I do not regret it. As long as I drink alcohol in moderation and keep a focus on college, I do not really see it as a serious problem.

## QUESTIONS

Given Jane's earlier episodes of uncontrolled use, do you accept her explanation that from now on, she'll drink "in moderation"? Do you believe her when she says she is not an alcoholic? Is Jane atypical? What sets her apart from other teenagers who are able to drink less compulsively? Do Jane's experiences with alcohol differ in any major respect from those of heavy, compulsive users of marijuana, Ecstasy, or methamphetamines? If so, in what ways? If not, why not? Should law enforcement crack down on underage drinking? What do you think the consequences of such a policy would be? Should the drinking age be lowered to 18? Why or why not?

# MARIJUANA, LSD, AND CLUB DRUGS

T he chemically miscellaneous substances marijuana, LSD, and "club drugs"—Ecstasy (MDMA), Rohypnol, ketamine, and GHB—all share important qualities. For one thing, all are more likely to be used by persons with a more or less middle-class background than by persons at the bottom of the socioeconomic hierarchy. For another, all tend to be used in conjunction with and as an adjunct to recreational activities, such as dancing, partying, and going to concerts. And all of them are, statistically speaking, less associated with the chronic, day-to-day abuse practiced by the heroin or crack or methamphetamine addict, the alcoholic, and the cigarette smoker. Socially—that is, how they are used, who uses them, and what degree of stigma is attached to their use—these drugs stand somewhere in between the legal drugs (alcohol and tobacco) and the so-called hard drugs (cocaine, methamphetamine, and heroin). Because they share these similarities, I'll group them together in this chapter.

## MARIJUANA: AN INTRODUCTION

Jim and Janie, both 35, are happily married, ambitious, successful professionals with two young children. They are also marijuana smokers. They light up only on weekends, only at night, and only when their kids are asleep. Marijuana plays a recreational and fairly minor role in their lives, much as going to the movies and drinking wine with dinner do. There are many weeks when they do not indulge, and when they do, they share just one joint.

Tim is 15, a high school student doing so poorly academically that he is on the verge of dropping out. This year, he has missed nearly half his classes, and he snoozes through many of those he does attend. He lights up a joint as soon as he is awake, and he smokes four or five more joints during the day and just before he goes to bed. Tim is high just about all his waking hours: He is obsessed with weed.

Jim and Janie, and Tim illustrate points along the spectrum of marijuana use. And they demonstrate what is the central point of this book: Although drugs do have objective, pharmacological properties, exactly *how* drugs are used and *what role* they play in users' lives depend as much on the user as the drug. The properties of a drug do not dictate use patterns or even effects; it is how those properties intersect with the lives of the people taking them that determines how a drug is used and with what consequences.

### Marijuana: A Unique Substance

Technically, marijuana is not so much a drug as a vegetable substance that contains a wide array of chemicals, at least one of which is strongly psychoactive. What is sold on the street as marijuana in the United States is made up of the dried leaves and flowering tops of the plant and, increasingly less commonly, the leaves, of the plant *Cannabis sativa* or *Cannabis indica*. The cannabis plant is also referred to as the **hemp** plant. However, today, this term tends to be reserved for plants with low-potency leaves whose fiber is used for non-psychoactive purposes, such as rope, paper, and clothing. The cannabis plant contains some 400 chemicals; 61 of them, called cannabinoids, are found nowhere else. Moreover, different marijuana plants contain a different mix of this complex brew of chemicals, and, or so some users claim, different mixes produce different highs. Since so many chemicals are found in marijuana, its effects, as you might expect, are complex. The drug has been classified at different times by different observers as a hallucinogen, a sedative or depressant, a narcotic, a stimulant, and even a psychomimetic (a drug that can drive the user insane). One pharmacologist refers to marijuana as "a unique sedative-euphoriant-psychedelic drug" (Julien, 1995, p. 330). Usually, marijuana does produce sedation, but that is not among its most noteworthy or interesting effects. At higher levels of potency, the user may experience some hallucination-like effects, but these are practically nonexistent at lower, and more frequently taken, doses. The fact is that, properly speaking, marijuana belongs in none of the usual drug categories. Today, most expert observers put marijuana alone, in its own, unique category.

The most prominent and most common psychoactive agent in marijuana among the cannabinoids is Δ-9-tetrahydrocannabinol, or THC for short. It is generally agreed that it is THC that gets the user high. Different batches of marijuana contain varying proportions of THC. Marijuana from a wild or uncultivated plant growing in a field might yield marijuana that is less than 1 percent THC. A batch of average-potency marijuana bought on the street will come in at about 3 percent. Batches from Colombia or Hawaii might be 4–6 percent THC. Varieties specially grown without seeds, from California and Hawaii, called *sinsemilla* (meaning "without seeds" in Spanish), may contain as much as 8 percent THC. Hashish, which contains the resin of the marijuana flower with no leaves, usually has a higher THC content than marijuana; 8–14 percent THC is common. Hashish usually comes from South or Central Asia and the Middle East; currently, in the United States, it is far less frequently sold than leaf marijuana, although it is common in Europe. "Hash oil," a product produced by boiling hashish in alcohol, can be as potent as 50 percent THC. Most users argue that more potent pot does not necessarily make them correspondingly higher so much as get them high with less marijuana. Many authorities are not convinced, however, believing that more potent marijuana automatically translates into "higher" highs.

It is crucial here to recall our discussion from Chapter 2 on the route of administration. In the United States, the most common route of administration for marijuana use is smoking. This basic fact has a number of important consequences. As we learned, smoking is an extremely rapid and efficient means of using a drug; the same principle applies whether we are discussing tobacco, crack cocaine, or marijuana. Inhaled smoke enters the lung sacs, quickly passes to their surrounding capillaries, and enters the brain, undiluted. In contrast to oral ingestion, when a drug is combusted, it releases chemicals that are more readily "bioavailable" in the body. Moreover, taking the fumes of a burning chemical into the lungs can have toxic effects that occur with no other mode of use. These implications take on even more significance as levels of use rise and length of use is prolonged.

One crucial fact to consider when it comes to smoking marijuana: The drug contains at least two **carcinogens** that are also found in tobacco: tar and benzopyrene. If these chemicals contribute to the high cancer rate of cigarette smokers, what might they do to marijuana smokers? Of course, consider another crucial fact: Marijuana tends to be used roughly 1–5 percent as frequently as tobacco by the typical smoker. On the other hand, marijuana is inhaled more deeply and held in the lungs for a longer time than is true of cigarette smoke. Surprisingly, however, a study of over 2,000 subjects found no association between marijuana use—or frequency of marijuana use—and lung, neck, or head cancer; even the heaviest users did not have elevated rates of any of these forms of cancer. (The research, directed by Donald Tashkin, was presented at the 2006 meeting of the American Thoracic Society International and reported in *The Washington Post,* May 26, 2006, p. A3.) In contrast, two-pack-a-day smokers have a 20-fold increase in lung cancer as compared with nonsmokers.

One feature of marijuana that makes it different from alcohol as a recreational substance is that, whereas alcohol is metabolized and passes through the body fairly quickly, THC is stored in the body—specifically, in the fatty tissue—for long periods of time. The half-life (the period of time after use when half the chemical is still in the body) of THC in the blood is 19 hours, and its metabolites have a half-life of 50 or more hours. After one week, 25 percent of THC's metabolites remain in the body; complete elimination may take two or three weeks (Lemberger et al., 1970, 1971). The slow rate of the elimination of THC and its by-products suggests that if used regularly, some storage or accumulation takes place, which may be medically harmful to the user.

Moreover, these lingering traces may have effects on human behavior, including coordination and the capacity to remember and learn. For instance, in one experiment (Yesavage et al., 1985) researchers tested pilots 1, 4, 10, and 24 hours after smoking one marijuana cigarette. Under all four conditions, their ability to perform a landing maneuver in an airplane simulator deteriorated to significantly below normal levels. Interestingly, these pilots did not feel high 24 hours after smoking, and when taking the test at that time, they felt confident that they could fly a plane as well as they could normally—but the fact is, they couldn't. As a result of experiments such as these, many experts feel that marijuana's extremely slow rate of elimination could be harmful to users in a variety of ways. This is especially the case for frequent users since, for them, the drug *never* disappears from their body. On the other hand, there is a positive side to marijuana's slow absorption: Because it is released into active receptor sites very slowly, and traces of the drug remain over long periods of time, abrupt discontinuance of the use of marijuana does not produce classic withdrawal symptoms. In contrast, heroin and alcohol, which disappear from the body more quickly, do generate clear-cut withdrawal effects.

## Rates and Patterns of Usage

Worldwide, as well as in the United States, marijuana is the most commonly used illegal substance. Overall, it is the fourth most widely used drug in the world, after caffeine, nicotine, and alcohol. In the United States, it is found practically everywhere. Although users are not in the majority in any major social category, nearly all young people have to come to terms with the drug; 85 percent of high school seniors say that marijuana is either "fairly" or "very" easy to obtain (University of Michigan news release, December 19, 2005). Thus, regardless of whether they use, just about all American teenagers have to "confront choices and decisions about whether, when, and how to use" this nearly ubiquitous drug (Jessor, 1983, p. 22).

Marijuana is *by far* the most commonly used illicit drug in the United States; no other drug comes even close. The 2005 National Survey on Drug Use and Health (NSDUH), (SAMHSA, 2006) reported that more than 4 out of 10 Americans ages 12 and older have at least tried marijuana once or more in their lifetime, a total of 97 million people; about 10 percent, or 25 million people, said that they had used once or more during the past year; and about 1 in 16 used during the past month—more than 14 million persons. Worldwide, too, marijuana is by far the most popular illicit drug. In its 2005 *World Drug Report,* the United Nations estimated that during 2004, 200 million people used one or more illegal drugs; of that total, 160 million used marijuana. The European Monitoring Centre for Drugs and Drug Addiction estimated that in 2003, about 20 percent of persons over the age of 15 living in the European Union (EU) had used marijuana once or more during their lives. For amphetamines, Ecstasy, and cocaine, the comparable figure was 3 percent, and for heroin, less than 1 percent (http://annualreport.emcdda.ed.int).

The most remarkable fact about recent patterns of marijuana use may be the massive increases in teenage use during the 1990s. The numbers fairly leap from the page when we view the results of the annual Monitoring the Future surveys. In 1991, eighth- and tenth-graders

TABLE 9-1    **Percentage of Marijuana Use, 1991–2005**

| NSDUH | 1991 | | | | 2005 | | |
|---|---|---|---|---|---|---|---|
| | Ever | Past Year | Past Month | | Ever | Past Year | Past Month |
| Age | | | | Age | | | |
| 12–17 | 13 | 10 | 4 | 12–17 | 17 | 13 | 7 |
| 18–25 | 51 | 25 | 13 | 18–25 | 52 | 28 | 17 |
| 26–34 | 60 | 15 | 7 | 26+ | 41 | 7 | 4 |
| 35+ | 24 | 4 | 2 | | | | |
| Total | 33 | 10 | 5 | | 40 | 10 | 6 |

| MTF | 1991 | | | 1996 | | | 2005 | | |
|---|---|---|---|---|---|---|---|---|---|
| | Ever | Past Year | Past Month | Ever | Past Year | Past Month | Ever | Past Year | Past Month |
| Grade | | | | | | | | | |
| Eighth | 10 | 6 | 3 | 23 | 18 | 11 | 21 | 12 | 7 |
| Tenth | 23 | 17 | 9 | 40 | 34 | 20 | 34 | 27 | 15 |
| Twelfth | 37 | 24 | 14 | 45 | 36 | 22 | 45 | 34 | 20 |

*Source:* NIDA, 1991, p. 25; SAMHSA, 2006; University of Michigan news release, December 19, 2005.

were added to the survey, which began studying high school seniors in 1975. Between 1991 and 1996, marijuana use increased for *all* grades. (Between 1996 and 2005, the numbers flattened out.) Table 9-1 spells out these increases in detail. In contrast, according to the NSDUH, teenage marijuana use—that is, use for 12- to 17-year-olds—has increased although the rates are somewhat less steep.

The story told in Table 9-1 is remarkable. As you can see from the last line in the national household data, marijuana use in the general population increased only slightly in the past decade; the differences between 1991 and 2005 are fairly small. However, the increases in use among 12- to 17-year olds during this period was more substantial—from 13 to 17 percent for lifetime use, from 10 to 13 percent for use in the past year; and from 4 to 7 percent for use in the past month.

Monitoring the Future's survey reveals more striking, even startling, increases during the 1990s. In comparison with 1991, more than twice as many eighth-graders in 1996 had used marijuana at least once in their lives; for use in the past year and past month, the figure was *three times* as many. For tenth-graders, the increases were not quite so substantial; still, roughly twice as many used marijuana recently in comparison with a decade ago. And for twelfth-graders, the increases, again, were substantial but not quite as impressive. Interestingly, after 1996, the use curve has been flat; indeed, it has dropped off a bit. What Table 9-1 reveals is that young people are beginning marijuana use, and incorporating it into their lives, at an increasingly early age. Whereas a decade ago, it was the modal or most common pattern for users to initiate marijuana consumption by the tenth grade, or roughly at age 15, the modal pattern now seems to be a year or two years earlier than that. During the 1990s, marijuana use was ratcheted up a notch. And even though use has slipped a bit since then, it has not yet reverted to early 1990s levels.

One possible explanation for the upsurge in marijuana use among the young is that it may be a baby boom "echo." That is, a substantial proportion of the children of the baby boomers, who were an extremely large population cohort born between 1946 and 1957, began their teenage years in the early 1990s. One characteristic of the baby boomers is that the percentage who used drugs, at least on an experimental basis, was unprecedented; in addition, many of them held attitudes that seemed to accept or tolerate their use. Hence, it should come as no surprise that an increasing percentage of their children began to use marijuana in the 1990s. One study found that a surprisingly high proportion of the baby boomers who are now parents not only retained more accepting attitudes than their older peers but also were resigned to the fact that their own children would use illegal drugs (Morrow et al., 1996).

## Acute Effects of Marijuana

While the acute effects of marijuana were emphasized in the media in the 1930s, today, the chronic effects are the center of researchers'—and the media's—attention. (See "Chronic Effects" below.) Of course, it is the *acute* effects that the user seeks. Some of the more superficial of marijuana's acute physical effects include a reddening of the eyes, a slight increase in the heartbeat rate, and a dryness of the mouth. Blood sugar levels, which regulate hunger, are curiously unchanged by the drug, despite the fact that many users report becoming ravenous under the influence. As we saw in Chapter 2, the ratio between effective dose and lethal dose is extremely wide; in other words, when it comes to death by overdose, there is an enormous "safety factor" with marijuana. Marijuana is one of the least toxic drugs known to humans. One pharmacologist states flatly, "No overdose deaths due to marijuana have been reported" (Goldstein, 2001, p. 202). In many cities, marijuana is mentioned with a certain amount of frequency in DAWN's medical examiner (ME) reports, but these are not, for the most part, single-drug episodes. Within the real-world limitations of actual use patterns, it is all but impossible to die of a marijuana "overdose." As we saw in Chapter 2, there is a biochemical reason for this: There are no receptor sites (the "locks") in the brain that regulate breathing or heartbeat rate into which marijuana chemicals fit (the "keys").

Contemporary research suggests that marijuana's effects are detrimental to motor coordination. The earliest systematic scientific report on this question, interestingly, indicated that marijuana does not deteriorate simulated driving skills (Crancer et al., 1969). Later research, however, demonstrated beyond any doubt that the drug does deteriorate motor coordination and impairs performance on driving tests. The more complex and unfamiliar the task, the more inexperienced the subject is with marijuana, and the more intoxicated the subject is on the drug, the greater the degree of discoordination (Canadian Commission into the Non-Medical Use of Drugs, 1972, pp. 62–63, 131–144).

One study (Barnett, Licko, and Thompson, 1985) found that levels of THC in the blood correlate significantly with lower performances on the motor tasks that are necessary for driving. In a posthumous sample of more than 400 male drivers in California ages 15–34 who had been killed in an auto accident, 81 percent were found to have one or more drugs in their blood samples (Williams, Peat, and Crouch, 1985); alcohol was present in 70 percent of the cases, THC in 37 percent, and cocaine in 11 percent. THC alone was found in one of eight of these drivers. Clearly, then, marijuana users are significantly overrepresented in fatal automobile accidents in terms of their numbers in the population; just as clearly, marijuana use seems to contribute to a greater number of deaths and accidents on the highway. As we saw, marijuana consumed a day before engaging in a complex motor task still exerts a detrimental effect on coordination (Yesavage et al., 1985). Once again, the discussion in Chapter 2 supplies the answer as to why marijuana impairs coordination: It binds to receptor sites in the cerebellum, which controls motor coordination. Of course, alcohol is still by far the number-one drug in this regard, although the additive effects of alcohol and marijuana should give anyone cause for concern.

What about the drug's *psychic* effects? What does it feel like to be high on marijuana? What do users describe as the subjective effects of this drug?

The many interview studies and summaries that have been published over the past three decades and more (for instance, Goode, 1970; Hochman, 1972; McKim, 2007; Tart, 1971; www.hyperreal.org) have produced a more or less consistent picture of marijuana's subjective effects. For instance, in my interview study, the most common response was that the user felt more peaceful and more relaxed under the influence of marijuana; 46 percent mentioned this effect spontaneously—that is, without direct prompting or formal questioning on my part. Thirty-six percent said that they felt their senses were more "turned on"—that they were more sensitive in almost every way than was true normally. Thirty-one percent said that they felt their thoughts were more profound, deeper—that their thoughts ran in a more philosophical and cosmic vein. Twenty-nine percent said that everything seemed much funnier than usual—that they laughed much more than they did when they were straight. More recent studies report very much the same findings.

What is the general impression conveyed by this and other studies of marijuana intoxication? What effects stand out as most common? Probably the most obvious and dominant impression is that *users overwhelmingly describe their marijuana experience in favorable and pleasurable terms;* in short, they like what they feel. This is not to say that they never experience unpleasant effects; for instance, studies indicate occasional feelings of paranoia under the influence in a minority of users. (Of course, fear of arrest is based on a very real possibility.) But the pleasant effects are by far the most common. *Most users, most of the time, enjoy their marijuana experiences.*

A second impression conveyed by these descriptions is that marijuana use is largely a recreational activity. The vast majority of effects reported by users are whimsical in nature: happy, silly, euphoric, relaxed, hedonistic, sensual, foolish, and decidedly unserious. Moreover, marijuana use is commonly associated with highly pleasurable activities such as eating, having sexual intercourse, listening to music, watching a film, and attending a party. The most common periods of use for most marijuana smokers are specifically during these recreational moments. The high is deliberately sought as a means of intensifying enjoyable experiences. The drug tends not to be used—or is used far less—during more serious periods, such as studying or reading. Moreover, these serious activities are felt to be impaired while under the influence of the drug, in contrast to the recreational activities, which are felt to be improved by the drug's effects. For instance, in my sample, only a third said that they had ever read anything while high, and of this group, two-thirds said that the experience was worsened by the drug. But 85 percent had listened to music while high, 75 percent had had sexual relations, and 75 percent had eaten food; about 90 percent of those who reported these experiences said that the drug made them more enjoyable. In short, marijuana is used as a means of enhancing pleasurable activities but not in conjunction with activities which require intellectual effort or precision and motor coordination.

## Chronic Effects of Marijuana

Today, the *chronic* effects of marijuana are more worrisome to the drug's critics than are its acute effects. This fear dates back to the 1960s, when it was thought that marijuana use was largely confined to high school and college dropouts. Later, specific and concrete medical damage was added to a growing list of chronic harms. In 1974, fearing a growing "epidemic" of marijuana users in the nation, Senator James Eastland conducted a series of Senate subcommittee hearings. Two dozen "experts" presented data showing that marijuana is a dangerous, damaging drug. Eastland assembled witnesses specifically known for their anti-marijuana stance; any researcher who had reported that marijuana was not harmful was not invited to deliver testimony. "We make no apology," Eastland stated, "for the one-sided nature of our hearings—they were deliberately planned that way" (Eastland, 1974, p. xv). Some of marijuana's ravages, these witnesses claimed, were brain damage and "massive damage to the entire cellular process," including chromosomal abnormalities. The drug "adversely affects the reproductive process," causing sterility and impotence. In addition, it causes cancer and (the only nonorganic item in the list) will lead to a life of lethargy and sloth, called the "anti-motivational syndrome." Eastland concluded from this testimony that if the "cannabis epidemic continues to spread . . . we may find ourselves saddled with a large population of semi-zombies." Were Eastland's expert witnesses correct in viewing marijuana as medically dangerous and damaging? What is the consensus in the scientific and medical community on marijuana's long-term effects?

### Contradictory Research Findings

Such studies are fraught with complications. There may be an empirical relationship between the use of marijuana and a certain medical pathology, but a cause-and-effect relationship may not exist at all; marijuana use may be related to a third factor that, in turn, actually causes the medical pathology. Some studies tracing the medical impact of marijuana have been shown to be faulty specifically because of this complication; the results obtained were based on experimental or measurement error. For instance, one study suggested that marijuana use may damage the liver (Kew et al., 1969). However, a later study attempted to replicate this finding but failed to do so (Hochman and Brill, 1971); its findings refuted those of the original liver damage study. It turns out that the original study had not controlled for the marijuana users' alcohol consumption. When the subjects were asked to refrain from drinking alcohol, their liver functioning reverted to normal. So the abnormal livers the researchers saw in their subjects were related not to the subjects' marijuana use, but to the fact that many of them also drank alcohol, a number of them heavily. One major difficulty in tracing marijuana's medical effects is that there are very few marijuana-exclusive drug users. Many also smoke cigarettes, most drink, and a substantial percentage have had experience with other illicit drugs as well.

One study purported to demonstrate that marijuana causes "cerebral atrophy"—a shrinking and shriveling of the brain (Campbell et al., 1971). However, its research methodology turned out to be flawed: Its sample consisted of mental patients, all of whom were also users of more dangerous drugs. Two more carefully conducted studies found no evidence of cerebral atrophy in marijuana users (Co et al., 1977; Kuehnle, 1977). A somewhat notorious study conducted by Tulane medical researcher Robert Heath entailed strapping Rhesus monkeys to chairs and attaching gas masks to their heads; the smoke from marijuana joints was passed into the gas masks of each monkey. The monkeys were forced to inhale the smoke; none was lost to the air. Brain damage was characteristic of the animals when they were dissected, and Heath claimed that this proved that marijuana damages the brain. An equally plausible explanation, however, is that the monkeys suffered from asphyxia and carbon monoxide poisoning. This study was widely criticized by the medical fraternity and is not often cited in the scientific literature. At the same time, the American Council on Marijuana, an anti-marijuana propaganda organization, on whose scientific advisory board Heath sits, distributes a pamphlet by Heath titled "Marijuana and the Brain" (1981), which summarizes the monkey study.

One study purported to find that chronic marijuana users manifested a significantly lower testosterone level. Testosterone is the major male sex hormone, and insufficient levels can lead to impotence and sterility (Kolodny et al., 1974). However, soon after this study was published, another one reported that marijuana has no connection to testosterone levels in the male (Mendelson et al., 1974). One study revealed extensive chromosomal damage as a consequence of marijuana use (Stenchever et al., 1974). This study, one propagandist claimed, demonstrated that marijuana users exhibited "roughly the same type and degree of damage as in persons surviving atom bombing with a heavy level of radiation" (Jones, 1974, p. 210). However, another study did not bear out the original result; the chromosomes of users and nonusers turned out to be almost identical (Nichols et al., 1974). One research team produced laboratory results indicating that marijuana users' white blood cells demonstrated a lower capacity to fight disease; their "cellular immunity" was distinctly diminished (Nahas et al., 1974). However, this finding was challenged by later research showing no difference between users and nonusers in the resistance of their blood cells to disease (Hollister, 1988; Lau et al., 1976; White et al., 1975).

The only finding that seems not to have been refuted or seriously qualified elsewhere is the one indicating that heavy, chronic cannabis use is related to an impairment in the functioning of the lungs (Morris, 1985; Tashkin et al., 1976). This makes a certain amount of sense. After all, marijuana is smoked just as cigarettes are smoked, and it is inhaled more deeply and held in the lungs for a longer period of time. When cannabis and tobacco are smoked in the same way, marijuana produces more than twice as much tar as tobacco does (Rickert, Robinson, and Rogers, 1982). Avram Goldstein says that marijuana smoke "contains more carcinogens than tobacco smoke, so lung damage and cancer are real risks for heavy smokers" (2001, p. 201). Impaired pulmonary functioning is one finding that remains fairly "robust" among different researchers.

The reason for the contradictory findings that have turned up in most of the studies conducted should be fairly clear. Except for the liver and the brain damage studies, in which the drug seems to have no effect at all, and the studies in pulmonary functioning, in which its effect is fairly clear-cut, marijuana's effect on all other organs and functions of the body seems fairly weak. When there is a weak effect, some studies will produces positive results and some will turn up negative ones—especially if different measures or instruments are used. For instance, cannabis causes only minor chromosome breakage, and it is likely to be detected only in extremely sensitive tests (Morishima, 1984). Marijuana may lower testosterone functioning in males, but even the lowered rate is typically within normal limits (Harclerode, 1984). Marijuana administered to pregnant animals decreases the birth weight in some offspring, but in humans, the amount of fetal birth weight loss is insignificant (Abel, 1985), if not nonexistent (Tennes et al., 1985); moreover, young children born to marijuana-smoking mothers do not display poorer functioning on various intellectual and motor tests. And the evidence that marijuana smoking lowers the body's resistance to disease and infection "remains inconclusive" (Cohen, 1987, p. 82).

### Is Marijuana Dangerous?

Is marijuana a dangerous drug? Some experts believe that evidence gathered as recently as the 1990s suggests that the effects of the drug are not as innocuous as was previously believed. We know that marijuana is one of the least toxic drugs known to humanity; it is virtually impossible to die of a cannabis overdose. We know that it does not produce the kinds of withdrawal symptoms that heroin and the barbiturates do; it is not "addicting" in the classic sense of the word. We know that many of the chronic effects that have been claimed for the drug (such as most of those discussed above) have not been confirmed by subsequent researchers. Nevertheless, could it be harmful in some way that is still under investigation? Some researchers believe so. During the past decade and a half, several studies have been conducted that have led researchers to the conclusion that, if used frequently, the effects of marijuana may be not altogether harmless. Several news stories have picked up on this "dangerousness" theme, confirming the conviction among most lawmakers and a majority of the public that this drug should not be legalized or decriminalized (Anonymous, 1996; Blakeslee, 1997). Here are a few of the findings of this new and still-evolving line of research.

As we saw in Chapter 2, the effects of drugs depend on the match or "fit" between the chemical structure of a given drug and the location and function of certain receptor sites. While marijuana's chemicals do not fit with receptors in the brain stem, which is the location of sites that regulate breathing and heartbeat, the cerebellum and the hypocampus, in contrast, are rich in marijuana receptor sites. Hence, marijuana use is highly likely to impair thinking, learning, and memory, as well as other crucial cognitive processes. (Permanently? Researchers are still working on the issue.) Says Miles Herkenham, "It's completely different from all the other drugs" (Anonymous, 1996; Deadwyler et al., 1990).

One team of researchers discovered that a specific chemical compound that blocks the binding of THC to the body's receptors, when injected into rats regularly administered THC, will cause those rats to undergo withdrawal symptoms (Tsou, Patrick, and Walker, 1995). Another team of researchers discovered that the dopamine levels in rats injected with chemically active marijuana surged to a level as high as that of another group that was given heroin. The capacity of the brain to produce dopamine diminishes over time, and hence potentiates the mechanism that is referred to as tolerance. Since dopamine is the chemical that regulates feelings of reward, and hence reinforcement, some researchers believe that these findings suggest that marijuana may generate a dependence not essentially different from that of heroin and cocaine (Tanda, Pontieri, and Di Chiara, 1997). Yet another team of researchers injected rats with a synthetic form of cannabis once a day for two weeks, then administered another drug that nullified the effect of marijuana's principal active ingredient. This threw the rats into withdrawal; they exhibited teeth chattering and compulsive grooming behavior, and the levels of a particular drug in the brain, which is commonly found when addictive drugs are withdrawn, were two to three times a normal level (Rodriguez de Fonseca,

1997). It is entirely possible, these researchers suggest, that not only does marijuana produce a dependence that is far higher than is currently believed, but the drug may also "prime" the brain's pathways for harder drugs.

These recent research lines are still in the process of development. They concentrate almost entirely on laboratory animals, not humans. They rely for the most part on forced administration of marijuana rather than free choice by these animals, and they administer extremely large doses of the drug rather than those that correspond with realistic doses—that is, those taken in real life. Keep in mind that studies of long-term marijuana smokers do not produce gross or major clinical, psychiatric, psychological, or social difference between users and nonusers, or between heavier and lighter users (Gruber, Pope, and Oliva, 1997). And except for the fact that users are *statistically* more likely to contract HIV/AIDS—owing to the fact that male smokers are more likely to engage in unconventional sex—nonusers, experimenters, and current users have the same mortality rates (Sidney et al., 1997). The lack of correspondence between animal experiments and human epidemiological studies probably indicates that, for some purposes, the results of lab research on nonhumans should not hastily be extrapolated to effects among users.

## Who Uses Marijuana?

What factors and forces lead someone to "turn on" to marijuana? More importantly, what causes someone who tries the drug to become a regular user? It is fallacious to assume that any behavior as complex as the use of drugs, or any one drug, can be explained completely by one factor or variable, or even a single integrated theory. Many factors, forces, and mechanisms contribute to the use of drugs in general, to the use of a single drug, and even to drug use by a specific individual. We have a number of empirical regularities associated with illegal psychoactive drug use generally and marijuana use specifically. These correlations apply to each and every drug discussed in this chapter and, in all likelihood, even more broadly, to recreational, psychoactive drug use in general. They are not in doubt; they are, as statisticians are fond of saying, "robust" relationships, solidly documented, independently confirmed by different researchers in a variety of locales, and constant over time. The validity of the various explanations that account for these regularities, however, is still being debated.

A team of researchers (Radosevich et al., 1980) distinguished three interrelated sets of variables that are causally related to marijuana use: (1) structural variables, which include sociodemographic factors such as age, sex, social class, race, and community or region of residence; (2) social-interactional variables, which pertain to interpersonal relationships, or the likelihood of associating with and relating to individuals with varying degrees of involvement with marijuana, or its correlates and accompaniments (an example would be one's friends' use of marijuana, or use patterns in one's peer group); and (3) attitudinal variables, including behavioral factors, which point to individuals' views of both the drug itself and the behavior associated with its use (beliefs about whether the drug is harmful and about the user's willingness to break the law are two examples of this dimension). Of course, these three sets of variables overlap a great deal; they cannot be cleanly separated.

## Age

The structural variable most strongly correlated with the use of marijuana is age. If we had to select one major characteristic to predict whether a given individual uses or has used marijuana, we could not make a better selection than age. The use of marijuana is low in the early teenage years, rises throughout the teen years, peaks in the late teens to early twenties, and declines steadily after that; it is unlikely after the forties. (See Figure 9-1.) The data gathered by the 2005 NSDUH verify this picture. The likelihood that someone has smoked marijuana at least once during the past month increases fivefold from age 13 (1.5%) to 15 (7.9%), then almost doubles by age 17 (15.2%), and increases again among 20-year-olds (20.8%). But it decreases after that, from 16.5 percent among 21-year-olds to 9.9 in the

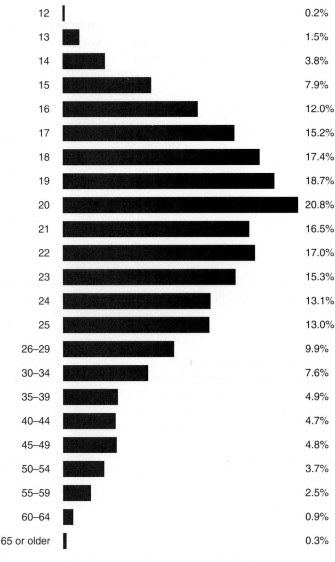

| Age | Percent |
|------|---------|
| 12 | 0.2% |
| 13 | 1.5% |
| 14 | 3.8% |
| 15 | 7.9% |
| 16 | 12.0% |
| 17 | 15.2% |
| 18 | 17.4% |
| 19 | 18.7% |
| 20 | 20.8% |
| 21 | 16.5% |
| 22 | 17.0% |
| 23 | 15.3% |
| 24 | 13.1% |
| 25 | 13.0% |
| 26–29 | 9.9% |
| 30–34 | 7.6% |
| 35–39 | 4.9% |
| 40–44 | 4.7% |
| 45–49 | 4.8% |
| 50–54 | 3.7% |
| 55–59 | 2.5% |
| 60–64 | 0.9% |
| 65 or older | 0.3% |

**Figure 9-1** **Marijuana Use in Past Month by Age, 2005.**

*Source:* National Survey on Drug Use and Health, 2006.

26- to 29-year-old bracket, and decreases again among 35- to 39-year-olds; and after age 35, use declines steadily, to under 1 percent for 60- to 64-year-olds, and to 0.3 percent for the 65-and-older set. Again, this same strongly age-graded pattern seems to prevail for a wide range of criminal and "deviant" activities. So robust is this pattern that some observers regard it as *invariant* across time and among societies everywhere (Gottfredson and Hirschi, 1990, pp. 124–144).

Two life circumstances associated with those in the adolescent-to-young-adult age range (the midteens to early twenties) relate to unconventional behavior: a growing independence from adult supervision, and relative freedom from adult responsibilities. Older teenagers are in the process of discovering what it means not to be supervised by their parents as closely as before, but at the same time, they have not yet assumed the responsibility of supporting a household or raising children. A team of researchers summarized a number of variables that are related to the use of drugs of all kinds, especially marijuana, and concluded that these variables have one thing in common: They all "have to do with the degree to which a young person is under the direct influence and/or supervision of adult-run institutions. . . . Those who most avoid such influence are also the most likely to be involved in all forms of substance use," marijuana included (Bachman, Johnston, and O'Malley, 1981, p. 67). The same explanation applies to the decline in use after the age of 20 or so. That is, while individuals in the 18- to 20-year-old age range maximize freedoms and minimize responsibilities, as they move into their twenties, conventional responsibilities increase: marriage, children, full-time work. As a consequence, their marijuana use, and the use of other illicit substances, as well as their involvement in other illegal and "deviant" activities, tends to decline as well (Bachman et al., 1997, 2002).

### Sex

Although there are many exceptions to this rule, in general, males are significantly more likely to use marijuana than are females; this disparity becomes increasingly pronounced as level of use increases. For instance, in the Monitoring the Future study of secondary, college, and noncollege youth, the male-female ratio grows from 1.2 for lifetime use to 2.7 for daily use, that is, use 20 or more times in the past month. In sum, then, males are *slightly* more likely than females to use marijuana at all, *considerably* more likely to use it regularly, and *much, much* more likely to use it heavily and frequently. As a general rule, the greater the level or frequency of use, the greater the male edge (Johnston et al., 2005, pp. 90–91). The fact is, males are significantly more likely to take risks and to engage in more deviant, criminal, and unconventional behavior than females are, regardless of the specific activity in question. Certainly, the male-female involvement in criminal behavior, especially violent crime, bears out this generalization. Differences in risk taking and a willingness to engage in rule breaking (from the point of view of the mainstream adult world) and crime could help explain the male-female differences in marijuana use we observe, especially at the higher or more frequent levels.

### Peer Influences

It has become a cliché, in searching for the causes of drug use, to point a finger at "peer pressure." The term seems to imply that youngsters are forced to engage in activities they find distasteful and would otherwise not have engaged in, in the absence of this pressure.

Peer *influence* is not the same thing as peer *pressure*. Peer influence implies a *reciprocal* or two-way relationship between a youngster and his or her friends, rather than a one-way pressuring. (It is interesting that the term "peer pressure" is almost always used to apply to activities someone who uses the term doesn't approve of.) The use of marijuana by an individual's own friends is massively and overwhelmingly correlated with his or her own use of the drug. Adolescents report more similarity with their friends in marijuana use than in any other activity. Of all things that friends have in common—except for obvious demographic characteristics such as age, sex, and race—they are more likely to have the use of marijuana in common than anything else (Kandel, 1973, 1974). Youngsters whose best friends have never tried marijuana are extremely unlikely to have tried the drug themselves. On the other hand, young people whose best friends smoke marijuana are extremely likely to do so themselves. Almost no one becomes involved in marijuana use who does not have marijuana-using friends. As I said, although this influence is sometimes called peer pressure, it clearly operates in all other aspects of a person's life, both favorable and unfavorable; it is not unique to drug use. A more neutral term is "peer *influence.*"

The fact that marijuana use flows from friend to friend, within and among social intimates, demonstrates the fallaciousness of two classic but clearly outdated beliefs concerning the drug: the "peddler" myth that young people use drugs mainly because they are induced to do so by drug sellers, and the "outcast" myth that someone uses marijuana because he or she is frightened, lonely, isolated, or forlorn. Neither assumption is borne out by the facts. Young people are turned on by their friends, specifically because they value the opinions and activities of their friends. In countless studies on the subject, the principal motivating force underlying turning on is that the person's friends use marijuana. Young recreational drug users tend to have more intimate friends than do nonusers (Kandel and Davies, 1991).

In short, marijuana users tend to be "heavily involved in social networks" in which marijuana use "is prevalent and tolerated." The marijuana use of someone's friends (and spouse or partner) increases "dramatically" with his or her own use. In one study, 85 percent of men ages 24–25 who used marijuana four or more times a week said that most or all of their friends were also users, as opposed to 60 percent of those who used the drug between two or three times a month and two or three times a week; 23 percent of those who used less than once a month; 16 percent of those who used, but not in the past year; and only 7 percent of those who had never used marijuana. For women the same age, the comparable figures were 96, 68, 36, 14, and 6 percent (Kandel, 1984, pp. 205, 206). The association between friends' use of marijuana and one's own use is remarkably strong.

### Unconventionality

Researchers have identified a number of attitudinal and behavioral correlates and antecedents of marijuana use. One such commonsensical variable is the perception or belief that the drug is relatively harmless. Individuals who believe that the effects of marijuana are benign, that the drug is not likely to harm them, are significantly more likely to try and use it than are those who believe that it is harmful (Kandel, Kessler, and Margulies, 1978, pp. 12, 28).

Marijuana users have also been found to be more politically liberal than nonusers. The more politically conservative the individual, the lower the likelihood of his or her smoking marijuana; the more politically liberal or left-leaning his or her ideological views, the higher is this likelihood (Johnson, 1973, pp. 54, 60; Kandel, Kessler, and Margulies, 1978). However, over time—that is, as we move further and further away from the 1960s and 1970s—this relationship may be gradually breaking down. Certainly, a powerful and enduring relationship exists between alienation from traditional religious expression and the use of marijuana. The stronger the religious belief and the more frequent the religious observance, the lower the chances of smoking marijuana; the less traditionally religious and the less religiously observant, the greater the likelihood of marijuana use (Jessor, 1998; Johnson, 1973, pp. 54, 56–57; Kandel, Kessler, and Margulies, 1978). Finally, marijuana users tend to be less traditional in the realm of sexual beliefs and practices. They are more likely to engage in sexual intercourse earlier in their lives, to have had intercourse with a greater number of partners, and to approve of more unconventional, unorthodox sexual practices. Nonusers, in contrast, tend to be more traditional in the sexual arena and have sex later in their lives and with fewer partners (Goode, 1972a; Hochman, 1972, p. 104; Hochman and Brill, 1973; Johnson, 1973, p. 153f). But marijuana use does not "cause" this greater sexual activity, since it frequently takes place even before the individual uses the drug for the first time.

What seems to be common to all these attitudinal and behavioral correlates of marijuana use is a broader "lifestyle" dimension made up of several components. For example, marijuana users tend to differ from nonusers "on a cluster of attributes reflecting unconventionality, nontraditionality, or non-conformity." They display "a more tolerant attitude toward deviance, morality, and transgression"; greater rebelliousness toward rules and regulations, especially those issuing from the parental generation; and a higher "expectation for independence or autonomy" (Jessor, 1979, pp. 343–344). Marijuana users, in short, tend to be more willing to break with the norms of the society, to deviate from cultural prescriptions more frequently in a wide range of ways. They also tend to be risk takers in comparison with nonusers. They have a greater receptivity to new experience, "to uncertainty and change as against an emphasis on familiarity and inflexibility"; they are somewhat less likely to say "I shouldn't do that" when faced with an alternative that appears tempting but a bit risky or laden with danger (Jessor, 1998).

In short, the use of recreational drugs generally, and of marijuana specifically, is strongly related to **psychosocial unconventionality.** Not only do these generalizations hold when comparing users with nonusers, but they also hold when comparing heavy and light users with nonusers; unconventionality is a continuum, not an either-or proposition. This dimension covers many different areas of life; "the use of marijuana is not an isolated behavior but is part of a larger constellation of behaviors" (Jessor, Donovan, and Costa, 1986, p. 35). This includes, as we have seen, precocious and unconventional sexual behavior, heavier involvement with other drugs, increased aggression and delinquency, and greater tolerance for unconventional and "deviant" behaviors. It also includes a lesser degree of involvement with traditional institutions. This manifests itself in a more critical attitude toward conventional social norms, a lower level of academic achievement, and a weaker link with—indeed, indifference to—conventional religious beliefs and practices (Jessor, 1983, pp. 24–25). This pattern "has been shown to be relatively invariant over time" (Jessor, Donovan, and Costa, 1986, p. 37). In all likelihood, the connection between marijuana use and unconventionality will remain in force for the foreseeable future.

# THE "GATEWAY" HYPOTHESIS: THE PROGRESSION TO MORE DANGEROUS DRUGS

Mitch Earleywine (2002, pp. 49–52) draws a distinction between marijuana as a "stepping-stone" and as a "gateway" to more dangerous drugs. Referred to as a "stepping stone," he argues, the ingestion of marijuana is regarded as a cause of the use of drugs such as heroin and crack cocaine; referred to as a **"gateway,"** marijuana use is simply a precursor, or one of many factors that, statistics demonstrate, "lead to" the harder drugs. The problem, Earleywine says, is that most observers and even experts are unable to tell the difference between causality and "simple precursors."

As we saw above, the recreational use of every psychoactive drug (both legal and illegal) is correlated with use of every other psychoactive drug (again, both legal and illegal). Individuals who take or use any given drug for pleasure are statistically more likely to take or use any other drug than are those who do not take or use that given drug. Adolescents who smoke cigarettes and drink alcoholic beverages are more likely to go on to use marijuana in the future than are those who have not and never will use tobacco or alcohol. Marijuana users, in short, are disproportionately drawn from the ranks of individuals who use legal drugs. When we ask who uses marijuana, our answer must include drinkers and cigarette smokers (Kandel, 1980b). The same applies to the users of marijuana: They are statistically more likely than nonusers of marijuana to use the more dangerous drugs.

The correlation between the use of marijuana and the use of all other drugs is an extremely robust one. Every researcher who has investigated the issue systematically and empirically, myself included (Goode, 1969), has found a strong positive relationship. There is no question about its existence: Marijuana users are more likely to use any and all illegal dangerous drugs than are nonusers; and the more they use, the greater the likelihood. Moreover, the earlier in life that a person uses marijuana, the greater the probability that that individual will try and use a wide range of illegal drugs, including cocaine, heroin, and the hallucinogens. In addition, the more that he or she uses marijuana, and the earlier in life, the greater the likelihood of using and becoming seriously involved with other illegal drugs.

The evidence supporting these relationships is overwhelming, persuasive, and incontrovertible. No one in the field of drug studies questions the validity of the strong, positive, and significant correlations between the use of marijuana and the use of other illegal, dangerous drugs. The only question that exists is the casual mechanism underlying the relationship. Why does it prevail? Why are marijuana users significantly more likely to use other drugs than nonusers, heavy users more likely than light users, and early users more likely than later ones? What impels more of them to progress to other illegal psychoactive substances?

There are three schools of thought on these questions. The first could be called the pharmacological school, the second the sociocultural school, and the third the predisposition school.

## The Pharmacological School

The proponents of the **pharmacological school** (Jones, 1974, pp. 236–237, 249; Jones and Jones, 1977; Nahas, 1990) argue that there is something inherent in marijuana use itself—the experience of getting high on the drug, which is caused by its pharmacology—that leads to the use of and dependence on more dangerous drugs. The causal mechanism here lies within the drug itself—or, more properly, in the interaction between marijuana and the human brain. This mechanism does not rely on the intervention of any outside factors or variables. Rather, the relationship between marijuana and the use of more dangerous drugs is a constant, and it occurs in all social groups at a more or less uniform rate. A given number of marijuana smokers translates into another specific number of heroin or cocaine addicts after a given period of time. The correlation between marijuana use and the use of more potent psychoactive substances is, in effect, a process resembling a biochemical or pharmacological reaction.

Artificial, drug-induced pleasure, the argument goes, is temporary. When drugs are taken for pleasure over a period of time, the user becomes more tolerant and therefore desensitized to the pleasurable sensations the drug normally delivers. Thus, the drug must be taken more often. The experimental, episodic user must increase his or her frequency of drug use until he or she takes the drug daily and becomes physically and psychically dependent. Still, desensitization continues, and the pleasure continues to diminish. Consequently, a drug with a more potent effect must be taken. "The demand for pleasurable sensations caused by *Cannabis* will require in time larger and larger amounts of the drug. A biological urge will develop to substitute more potent drugs for *Cannabis,* in order to reach a similar feeling of detachment from the world" (Nahas, 1973, p. 276). One anti-marijuana propagandist, Hardin Jones, claims that his "statistical computation" demonstrates that 10 percent of all daily marijuana users become heroin addicts within three years (Jones, 1974, p. 236). The mechanism? He claims that "cross-tolerance" is to blame, pointing to "some similarity in chemical action," which is to be expected "because of the marked similarity in chemical structure between opiates and cannabinols. . . . In my studies," Jones states, "daily users who have transferred to heroin use do not show withdraw symptoms," which is, he claims, "an indication of crosstolerance. Crosstolerance enables cannabis users to have increased sensual effects from heroin without the unpleasant withdrawal symptoms of cannabis" (p. 237). Interestingly, Jones does not present concrete evidence either in this publication or in any other; his "studies" seem not to extend beyond his assertions.

On a more evidentiary level, two sociologists (O'Donnell and Clayton, 1982), arguing for the pharmacological or **intrinsic school,** claim that their evidence shows that "marijuana is a cause of heroin use in the United States." They make this claim on the basis of a rule dictating that if (1) two variables are statistically associated, (2) one variable is prior to the other at the relevant time, and (3) the association does not disappear when the effect of a third variable is removed, then the relationship between the two variables is causal in nature. They hold that this is the case with marijuana use and heroin addiction, that the association between these two variables meets these three criteria. The metaphor used by the pharmacological school is that of a conveyor belt. Heroin addiction, and the heavy, dependent use of all dangerous drugs, is seen as the later stage in a process that begins with experimental marijuana use. If marijuana use is halted, slowed down, or diminished, fewer users of hard drugs will be produced at the other end.

Laboratory evidence does not support the pharmacological, physiological, or "conveyor belt" theory of marijuana as a gateway drug. For one thing, "If marijuana created physiological changes that increased the desire for other drugs, animals exposed to cannabis would ingest other intoxicants when given the opportunity." The fact is, "No animal experiments have found that exposure to THC increases the likelihood of using other drugs" (Earleywine, 2002, p. 51). For another, the likelihood of a marijuana user progressing to harder drugs is quite small. Tabulating the data from the National Household Survey on Drug Abuse, Earleywine came up with the following statistics (p. 55).

The percentage of persons who have tried marijuana at least once in their lives who have:

Used marijuana in the past year: 1 in 4 (25.5%)

Used marijuana in the past month: 1 in 7 (14.7%)

Tried cocaine at least once in their lives: 1 in 3 (33.0%)

Used cocaine in the past year: 1 in 20 (4.8%)

Used cocaine in the past month: 1 in 50 (2.0%)

Tried crack cocaine: 1 in 13 (7.7%)

Used crack in the past year: 1 in 100 (1.3%)

Used crack in the past month: 1 in 200 (0.5%)

Tried heroin at least once in their lives: 1 in 26 (3.9%)

Used heroin in the past year: 1 in 200 (0.5%)

Used heroin in the past month: 1 in 333 (0.3%)

In short, the statistical odds of what the pharmacological school argues is commonplace are actually extremely rare. If the marijuana experience impels users to experiment with and become involved with harder drugs, why doesn't the epidemiological evidence bear out this claim? As we saw in Chapter 3, the sequence of steps leading up to "hard" drugs such as cocaine, methamphetamine, and heroin begins with the *legal* drugs—not with marijuana. Just as youngsters who smoke marijuana are more likely to "progress" to the use of hard drugs than those who do not, those who drink beer and wine and smoke cigarettes, especially at an early age and especially if they do so frequently, are more likely to use marijuana. Just as marijuana is a kind of "gateway" for harder drugs, the legal drugs are, even earlier in their lives, a gateway for marijuana. (Remember, for the vast majority of beginning smokers and drinkers, cigarettes and alcohol are *illegal* drugs; that is, they began using them when they were minors, and so not legally permitted to purchase, obtain, or consume them.) Drug use takes place in stages; those stages are patterned, not random; and the legal drugs alcohol and cigarettes are a crucial ingredient in that pattern.

Setting aside alcohol and tobacco, not all people who use more dangerous drugs "began" with the use of marijuana. Studies on drug progression show that between 1 and 39 percent of hard-drug users started that use without having used marijuana first (Earleywine, 2002, p. 56).

## The Sociocultural School

In contrast to the claims presented by the intrinsic or pharmacological school, the **sociocultural school** holds that the progression from marijuana to other drugs takes place, when it does, not because of the physiological action of the drug itself, but because of the activities, friends, and acquaintances users are involved with during the course of use (Goode, 1969, 1970, 1972b, pp. 237–250, 1974; Johnson, 1973). Users tend to make friends who have attitudes toward drug use that are more favorable than those of nonusers; the more a person uses marijuana, the higher the proportion of his or her friends who use not only marijuana but other drugs as well. Also, the more positive their attitudes toward use are, the more opportunities they offer the user to try other drugs. It is not the *physical experience* of marijuana use itself—that is, getting high on the drug—but the *activity* of use, and all of its surrounding social features, that is the major factor influencing this drug progression. Associating with peers who also use marijuana alters the individual's identity as a drug user, which, in turn, leads her or him to view opportunities to use other, harder, drugs in a more positive light. Taking advantage of such an opportunity is more likely *not* to happen than it is to happen, but it is more likely to happen for someone with marijuana-using peers than for someone without them. The sociocultural school argues that the drug use by friends influences the progression from marijuana to more dangerous drugs. And it is the youngster's peers in each progressive social circle that, for a minority, socialize him or her into the next drug that provides the "progression" to harder drugs. In addition to altering values and identity, peers also provide opportunities to use harder drugs in the form of buying and selling drugs other than and in addition to marijuana.

As you might expect from the selective interaction/socialization theory discussed in Chapter 3, the predisposition hypothesis (see "The Predisposition School" below) merges with subcultural theory, since youngsters who are predisposed to engage in unconventional behavior gravitate toward unconventional peers who, in turn, socialize one another into further unconventionality. The two theories are separable more in principle than in practice. And both regard the pharmacological theory as incorrect. It is not the experience of getting high on marijuana that provides the causal mechanism for drug progression, when and if it occurs, but who the user is and what his or her friends are doing.

Would the magical removal of marijuana from the picture eliminate a major causal mechanism impelling (a minority) of young people down the path toward the use of cocaine and heroin? This is unlikely, since the use of addicting drugs in China, Southeast Asia, and the Middle and Near East has been widespread in the absence of marijuana use. More importantly, would the magical removal of alcohol and cigarettes result in vastly less hard drug use? Interestingly, few who endorse the stepping-stone theory consider this earlier and absolutely crucial process. Says one drug prevention expert: "In my view, tobacco is the gateway drug. . . . [It] teaches kids how to get illegal drugs, it teaches them how to hide their behavior, how to inhale drugs to get a mood swing, how to deny what they've been taught since kindergarten . . . , and how to disrespect laws" (Haddad, 1996, p. 1B).

## The Predisposition School

Another problem with the stepping-stone theory involves the "common syndrome" factor: The kinds of people who engage in *one* type of behavior are highly likely to be the kinds of people who engage in *another*. Hence, the **predisposition** model or school of thinking: It is not so much that behavior A (using marijuana) causes behavior B (hard drug use), but that factor X (a certain personality syndrome, lifestyle, or orientation to life) causes them both. As discussed earlier in this chapter and also in Chapter 3, a specific theory or explanation of drug use is unconventionality or problem behavior proneness. Some youngsters, even at an extremely early age, begin to engage in unconventional behavior that is predictive of later unconventional behavior.

Youngsters who smoke cigarettes and drink wine and/or beer at an early age increase their odds of smoking marijuana at a slightly later age not so much because of the biochemical action of these drugs but because they are unconventional: They are risk takers, adventure seekers, and rule breakers. They are also more likely to be alienated from parents, school, traditional religion, and conventional rules, and to be drawn to a variety of parallel behaviors, including early sex, delinquency, and rebelliousness. The use of drugs is simply part of a whole syndrome of behaviors that includes the use of legal drugs as a minor, the use of marijuana a bit later on, and the use of harder drugs at a slightly later age. Once again, this is a statistical process, and the likelihood that it takes place is maximized the earlier each process takes place and to the extent that the drug use at each stage is frequent. The drug use itself is secondary in this process; what counts is the general orientation to life that this syndrome expresses.

Andrew Morral and his colleagues subjected the data from the National Household Survey on Drug Abuse to a precise mathematical model, which predicted the likelihood, given a variety of background factors, of whether marijuana users would be more likely to progress to the harder drugs. "We've shown that the marijuana gateway effect is not the best explanation for the link between marijuana use and the use of harder drugs," Morral explains. The statistical associations that are observed, he says, are a product not of marijuana use per se but of the age at which users take marijuana versus harder drugs and of differences among individuals with respect to their willingness to alter their consciousness, that is, to take any drug. "The people who are predisposed to use drugs and have the opportunity to use drugs are more likely than others to use both marijuana and harder drugs," Morral says. "Marijuana typically comes first because it is more available. Once we incorporated these facts into our mathematical model of adolescent drug use, we could explain all of the drug use associations that have been cited as evidence of marijuana's gateway effect" (Morral, McCaffery, and Paddock, 2002). Morral believes that the results of his study demonstrate that reducing marijuana consumption will have no impact whatsoever on reducing hard drug use, since persons who use the harder drugs are *already* predisposed to do so—whether or not they use marijuana. In short, argues Morral, the gateway hypothesis is a myth.

In September 2002, after surveying the available literature, the Canadian Senate issued a report on marijuana titled *Cannabis: Our Position for a Canadian Public Policy*. On the issue of the gateway hypothesis, the report concludes:

> We feel that the available data show that it is *not cannabis itself that leads to other drug use* but the combination of the following factors: Factors related to personal and family history that predispose to early entry on the trajectory of use of psychoactive substances starting with alcohol; Early introduction to cannabis, earlier than the average for experimenters, and more rapid progress towards a trajectory of regular use; Frequenting of a marginal or deviant environment; Availability of various substances from the same dealers.

The Canadian Senate Special Committee on Illegal Drugs rejected the gateway theory that the use of marijuana per se "leads to" or causes the use of harder drugs.

In short, the available evidence suggests that the claim that marijuana use *causes* the progression to harder, more dangerous drugs—the so-called **stepping-stone hypothesis**—is false.

## MARIJUANA AS MEDICINE

One morning in September 2002, 30 agents from the federal Drug Enforcement Agency (DEA), wearing military fatigues and carrying automatic weapons, swooped down on a small farm in northern Santa Cruz County in California run by the Wo/Men's Alliance for Medical Marijuana. They yanked 130 marijuana plants out of the ground and arrested the founders of the collective, Valerie and Mike Corral. The Corrals had been growing the marijuana for patients who had been given prescriptions for marijuana, legal in the state of California, "to help them with chronic pain brought on cancer, diabetes and other illnesses." In 1996, California voters had approved marijuana as medicine—that is, under state law, as a Schedule II drug. Ten other states have since followed suit. Two weeks later, the mayor of Santa Cruz stood in front of City Hall, distributing marijuana to "the sick and dying" (Krohn, 2002). Why was an elected official in the state of California handing out marijuana? Why are state and federal laws on a collision course with one another?

By federal law, marijuana is classified as a Schedule I drug, which means that, officially, the government regards it as having both great abuse potential and no accepted medical use. Under federal law, it is legally available only under extremely rare, almost nonexistent, experimental conditions. The basis of this classification is not accepted by a substantial number of researchers and clinicians, however; these mavericks believe that marijuana's abuse potential is low and its utility as medicine is great. And herein lies one of the most controversial of all marijuana-related issues.

The earliest psychoactive use of marijuana was medicinal; the drug was used in ancient times in a variety of medical applications, including as a painkiller, a hypnotic (sleep-inducer), an appetite stimulant, and an antidepressant. Stationed in India in the 1830s and observing its medical uses there, W.B. O'Shaughnessey, a British physician, conducted research on the medical effects of cannabis; he administered it to patients who suffered from a wide range of ills, including tetanus, rabies, and rheumatism. When he returned to England in 1842, O'Shaughnessey brought a quantity of cannabis with him, providing it to pharmacists. It became such a popular medication that it was administered to Queen Victoria by her court physician (Grinspoon and Bakalar, 1993, p. 4). Between 1840 and 1900, more than 100 articles were published in European and North American medical journals on marijuana's role as a medicinal agent (Mikuriya, 1973). However, with the discovery of more potent, reliable, and stable drugs, as well as the widespread use of the hypodermic needle, which delivers only water-soluble drugs, the use of marijuana as medicine was in decline by the end of the nineteenth century.

In 1972, research demonstrated that marijuana is effective in reducing the nausea induced by the drugs that are administered to cancer patients; later research found the same effect in treating the side effects of AIDS-related medication (Grinspoon and Bakalar, 1993, pp. 24–40). The use of marijuana as medicine was back on the map. Since the 1970s, the federal government's classification of marijuana as having no medical utility has come under vigorous challenge from a variety of quarters. A survey of oncologists (physicians who diagnose and treat cancer) found that nearly half (48%) said that they would prescribe marijuana as therapy for their patients if it were legal; more than half (54%) felt that marijuana should be available by prescription; and a remarkable 44 percent said that they had recommended the drug to a patient, even though it is illegal (Doblin and Kleiman, 1991). The Physician's Association for AIDS Care and the National Lymphoma Foundation sued the DEA to reclassify marijuana as a Schedule II drug. In 1993, Lester Grinspoon, associate professor of psychiatry at the Harvard Medical School and author of more than a half dozen volumes on drugs, published a book that vigorously, and to some, persuasively, advocated the use of marijuana as medicine (Grinspoon and Bakalar, 1993, 1997). Dozens of published medical works cited in the book refer to studies supporting the author's position. And the voters in nine states (Alaska, Arizona, California, Colorado, Maine, Montana, Nevada,

Oregon, and Washington), in margins ranging from 54 to 65 percent, passed medical marijuana initiatives; the legislatures of two more (Hawaii and Vermont) legalized marijuana as medicine. It's not clear what the legal impact of these changes in the marijuana laws will be, because medical marijuana is still against the law at the federal level. Nonetheless, the outcome of these initiatives and laws carries a great deal of symbolic weight in the fight to reschedule the drug. Moreover, in all probability, the laws and initiatives presage future changes in a number of other states. In addition, since 2000, several dozen public opinion polls have been conducted on medical marijuana and all of them say the same thing: The overwhelming majority of the American public favors legalizing marijuana as medicine. A Gallup poll, sponsored by CNN and *Time* magazine, shows that roughly 80 percent of respondents endorse legal medical marijuana.

In 2002, the federal government's General Accounting Office (GAO) released the results of a study on how medical marijuana is working in four states: Alaska, California, Hawaii, and Oregon. Law enforcement officers told GAO researchers that access to medical marijuana seemed to be working well. The system had not been abused, adolescents were not taking advantage of the medical "foot in the door," and the majority of patients using the drug were males over age 40 with legitimate medical ailments for which, in their physicians' judgment, marijuana was a viable treatment. The GAO found that most patients prescribed to use medical marijuana under state laws used the drug to treat chronic pain and/or multiple sclerosis. In October 2002, a San Francisco federal appeals court ruled that the federal government may not revoke the licenses of physicians who prescribe marijuana to their patients—a huge victory for the proponents of marijuana as medicine and a corresponding defeat for the anti-marijuana forces.

In an exhaustive summary of the literature, the Institute of Medicine (Joy et al., 1999) concluded that the available scientific data "indicate the potential therapeutic value of the cannabinoid drugs, primarily THC, for pain relief, control of nausea and vomiting, and appetite stimulation" (p. 179). At the same time, the Institute warned, smoked marijuana "also delivers harmful substances." Its recommendation was that clinical trials on the use of marijuana for medical purposes be conducted under specific, delimited circumstances, including the failure of other medications, with review boards in place to protect the rights of experimental subjects, close supervision and assessment, and documentation of results (p. 179). Given that such alternatives have been exhausted, there may be no option other than to administer smoked marijuana, the Institute of Medicine's Advisory Panel concluded.

These developments do not demonstrate conclusively and definitively that marijuana is useful in medical and therapeutic contexts; what they show is that many physicians *believe* this to be the case. Other physicians and scientific researchers disagree, however. In 1992, Robert Bonner, head of the DEA, issued a 46-page clarification of the federal government's policy. Dismissing studies that found the drug useful, Bonner stated: "Lay testimonials, impressions of physicians, isolated case studies, random clinical experience, reports so lacking in details that they cannot be scientifically evaluated and all other forms of anecdotal proof are entirely irrelevant" (Treaster, 1992). In January 1997, Janet Reno, at that time attorney general of the United States, declared that the federal government would prosecute physicians who prescribed marijuana for their patients. In 1997, Barry McCaffrey, then director of the Office of National Drug Control Policy (the federal drug "czar"), echoed the sentiment of the National Institutes of Health in stating that "there is no proof that smoked marijuana is the most effective available treatment for anything."

Government representatives believe that the Schedule III substance Marinol, which has many of marijuana's medical benefits without its psychoactive properties, should be used to combat ailments such as glaucoma and extreme discomfort from cancer medication. The "marijuana as medicine" advocates disagree. Many observers feel that the government's opposition to prescription marijuana has nothing to do with the drug's medical efficacy— or supposed lack thereof. Rather, they maintain, federal authorities fear that legal *medical* marijuana will represent a "foot in the door" to legalizing *recreational* marijuana. As we saw, both the GAO and the Institute of Medicine (Joy et al., 1999, pp. 101–104) reject this and related claims. Given the federal government's adamance, and the efforts of state governments to legalize of medical marijuana, it is likely that this collision course trajectory will be maintained for the foreseeable future.

## LSD AND THE HALLUCINOGENS: AN INTRODUCTION

LSD is another drug, like marijuana, that according to popular mythology was hugely popular during the 1960s and declined in popularity thereafter. As we saw in Chapter 7, this myth is even enshrined in a popular textbook on drugs (Ksir, Hart, and Ray, 2006, p. 343), which claims that the use of LSD "peaked" in 1967 and 1968 and declined after that. As we've seen, precisely the reverse is true; LSD use was extremely low in the 1960s, and it increased from the late 1960s into the 1970s. A Gallup poll indicated that in 1967, only 1 percent of college students, one of the segments of the population most likely to use the drug, had taken LSD even once. A study of "retrospective estimates" found that only 3 percent of 18- to 25-year-olds, again, a segment of the population highly likely to have taken LSD, had ever tried the drug (Miller and Cisin, 1980, p. 17). The use of LSD skyrocketed after that and has remained remarkably stable for more than a quarter century, that is, since Monitoring the Future began its surveys of drug use among high school seniors in 1975. What did reach a peak in the 1960s was media attention, which is an altogether different matter from actual use.

Some observers believe that LSD and the psychedelics are making a comeback. In point of fact, as other observers argue, LSD and the psychedelics "never really went away." Says psychopharmacologist Ronald Siegel, "It's like the Disney films. . . . Every seven years they re-release them so a new generation gets exposed to them" (Seligman et al., 1992, p. 67). What has changed, however, is the motive for use. In the 1960s, many individuals took LSD for what they described as mind expansion and "inner exploration." Today, "it's just another chemical in the stew" (p. 67). In 2001, about 1 high school senior in 10 (11%) took LSD at least once in their lifetimes, and a shade over 2 percent took it once or more during the past month. But by 2005, these figures had declined sharply, to 3.5 and 0.7 percent. Clearly, the early 2000s witnessed a waning of teenage interest in the use of LSD.

The hallucinogens (or psychedelics) produce profound, even spectacular effects on the consciousness, mainly in perceptions of reality. This category includes LSD, psilocybin (a substance naturally contained in the so-called magic mushroom), mescaline (the main psychoactive ingredient in the peyote cactus), a few less-often-used substances such as DMT and DET, and morning glory seeds. PCP, once used as an animal tranquilizer and anesthetic, is often classified as a hallucinogen, but it produces practically none of the psychic

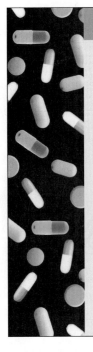

## True-False Quiz

Most (61%) of my students believed this statement: "The use of LSD reached its peak in the 1960s; after that decade, the use of this drug *declined*." As I explain in this chapter, it is part of the mythology of American culture that the 1960s were the "psychedelic" decade, and that included widespread use of LSD. In fact, the recreational use of LSD, which did begin in the 1960s, was extremely newsworthy; media attention to LSD use *exploded* during that decade. In reality, the use of this drug was *extremely* low in the early 1960s and rose throughout the decade, but it did not reach a plateau until the mid-1970s. After that, its use never really fluctuated very much; between 1975 and the 1990s, the lifetime prevalence rate of LSD use among high school seniors remained in the 8–11 percent range—making it consistently one of the half-dozen of America's recreational drugs; its peak was not until 1997 (14%). Since 2000, however, the use of LSD has declined; in 2005, for high school seniors, its lifetime prevalence rate was only 3.5 percent. As we see in this chapter, in 1967, the "ever used" statistic for hallucinogens among young adults—a segment of the population *highly* likely to use illicit drugs—was only 3 percent.

effects associated with the psychedelics. MDMA, or Ecstasy, likewise, does not generate the spectacular psychic effects of the LSD-type drugs. LSD (or "acid") is by far the best known of all hallucinogens or psychedelics.

LSD was synthesized and named by the Swiss chemist Albert Hofmann in 1938, but its potent psychoactive properties were not discovered until 1943, when Hofmann accidentally inhaled a minute quantity of the drug. Describing his experiences, Hofmann wrote: "I had to leave my work in the laboratory and go home because I felt strangely restless and dizzy. Once there, I lay down and sank into a not unpleasant delirium which was marked by an extreme degree of fantasy. In a sort of trance with closed eyes . . . fantastic visions of extraordinary vividness accompanied by a kaleidoscopic play of intense coloration continuously swirled around me. After two hours this condition subsided." Later, after discovering it was the LSD that had caused these reactions, and after some additional self-experimentation, Hofmann wrote: "This drug makes normal people psychotic." The Swiss chemist had inadvertently taken the first LSD "trip" in history.

LSD is taken via a capsule or tablet, or by means of swallowing squares of blotter paper impregnated with the drug. Even as minute a quantity as 25 micrograms of LSD is psychoactive for most people. (An ordinary headache tablet contains more than 300,000 micrograms of aspirin.) In the 1960s, the usual dose of LSD was purported to be between 200 and 500 micrograms; contemporary doses contain perhaps a quarter of this amount. However, since black-market LSD is both frequently contaminated (most often with an amphetamine) and unstandardized as to potency, very few users of street LSD can be even remotely sure of the dosages they take. An LSD trip lasts from 4 to 8, or even 12, hours, depending on the dose.

## Subjective Effects of Hallucinogenic Drugs

In one study I conducted (Goode, 1970), about half the respondents had used at least one hallucinogenic drug, mainly LSD, and I elicited from them descriptions of their experiences. Other studies and summaries of the subjective effects of LSD substantially agree with this description. One of the most commonly reported effects was what is referred to as **eidetic imagery,** or "eyeball movies." Under the influence of the psychedelic drugs, the subject, with his or her eyes closed, "sees" physical objects, usually in motion, as sharply as if watching a film. Often, these images are abstract and lacking in dramatic form. They frequently represent almost interminable repetitions of a pattern or design, much like moving wallpaper. One interviewee described his vision of eidetic imagery as follows: "Closing my eyes, I saw millions of color droplets, like rain, like a shower of stars, all different colors." Another said he saw "hundreds of fleurs-de-lis, repeating themselves, moving in several lines."

Another psychedelic experience commonly reported was **synesthesia**—the "mixing" of the senses or the simultaneous perception of the stimulation of several senses. Users reported "hearing" color or "seeing" sounds. The subjective meaning attached to a stimulus perceived by one sense is felt to mean something in other senses as well—that is, to be translatable from one sense to another. One researcher describes synesthesia's most common form as occurring "when auditory stimuli produce changes in visual" sensations; for example, he stated, "the experimenter claps his hands and the subject sees flashes of color in time to the clapping" (Klee, 1963, p. 463). An early researcher who took mescaline himself wrote: "I felt, saw, tasted, and smelled the tone. I was the tone myself. . . . I thought, saw, felt, tasted my hands" (Guttman, 1936, pp. 209, 210). A woman I interviewed put it this way: "I really got into music on my trip. I was traveling on the notes. I felt as if I was on an arc of fireworks—a quiet explosion. I felt as if the music was inside me, I felt as it was making love to me. It was beautiful."

A third effect of the psychedelics reported by my respondents was what might be called the perception of a multilevel reality. Sometimes these levels related to perspective perceptions. One subject told me: "You just see things from seven different ways at once." Another young woman said: "I looked at any object, and it would breathe and move and also appear from all angles in one instant." Occasionally, this multilevel perspective invades scientific realms; the diverse levels are those that a scientist might explore one at a time. A young artist put it this way: "I was sitting on a chair, and I could see the molecules, I could see right through things to the molecules." A young woman had this experience: "I stared at my dog—his face kept changing. I could see the veins in his face, under his skin."

Another perception beyond the range of "normal" reality was that the world was continually fluid. This perceived dynamic quality of the universe was perhaps the most commonly mentioned of any of the varied aspects of the psychedelic trip. The static universe seems to explode into a shimmering, pulsating cosmos, a world in continual flux. "Things were oozing as if they were made of jelly," one interviewee said. Others reported: "A brick wall wobbled and moved," "Paint ran off the walls," "Every physical thing seemed to be swimming in a fluid as if a whole wall had been set in liquid and was standing there before me, shimmering slightly," "I saw wriggling, writhing images," and "I saw flowers on the window sill, blowing in the breeze. I went to touch them, but there was no breeze, and the flowers were dead."

A fifth commonly reported psychedelic experience was subjective exaggeration, of practically anything—an object, an event, a mood, a person, a situation—a kind of baroque rendering of the world outside. The exaggeration may be in sheer number—perceiving more things than are there—or it may be the dramatization of a single characteristic of the stimulus, or an allegory on the nature of its essence. This type of experience ranges from modest exaggerations, some within the range of normal imaginative minds, to extravagant and detailed visions. A female college student told me: "One pillow turned into 50 million pillows—all the pillows in the world." Another said: "The mind is very suggestible. Sudden appearances of things take on strange forms. A towel falling off the edge of my tub looked like a giant lizard crawling down. The mind works faster, and is more suggestible." A young man had this experience: "When my girlfriend was peeling an orange for me, it sounded like she was ripping a small animal apart. I examined it carefully. It seemed to be made up of tiny golden droplets stuck together. I'd never seen an orange before. My girlfriend was eating scrambled eggs, and it was as if I was watching a pig with its face in a trough of garbage. A few bits of egg clung to her teeth, and it seemed as if globs of garbage were oozing down her face and out of her mouth. But I knew I was imagining it."

This experience of subjective exaggeration of the things around shades over into what some clinicians call the "eureka experience," the feeling that what is usually seen and thought to be quite ordinary takes on extraordinary and even epic proportions.

The full-blown, authentic hallucination—the perception of a materially nonexistent physical object created out of whole cloth and felt by the subject to be actually there—is a rarity under the influence of LSD. Usually, trippers know that the things they are seeing do not really exist. And often some sort of "actual" stimulus touches off the sensation. Perhaps **pseudohallucination** or **virtual hallucination** would be a more appropriate term for these sensations. One very common variety is the perception of one's own body in various unusual and never-before-seen states. Sometimes this occurs before a mirror; often a dynamic element is introduced into the perception—the individual sees him- or herself over time or repeated in space. A college student said: "I saw myself, my face in the mirror, developing from 5 years old to 40 years old." Another said: "In the mirror, I saw my clothes change into costumes from different periods of history." A young man had a similar sensation: "I could see 10 images of myself on each side of me, like a tuning fork." Sometimes the body appears transmuted into a state that is at once horrible and fascinating. A bizarre beauty clung to many of my respondents' descriptions of the self-metamorphosis. An artist reported: "The first thing I noticed was that my arm was made of gold. This held my attention for a long time. It was beautiful." A young woman said: "I saw myself in the mirror with one eye. It was disturbing, but not horrible." Another subject exclaimed: "My eyelashes grew and became like snakes."

Unlike marijuana, which most users describe as being pleasurable most of the time, LSD seems to elicit a formidable sense of ambivalence. Users experience both good and bad sensations during the same episode of use, and sometimes at the very same moment in time. A given trip may be described as horrifying, ecstatic, depressing, rapturous, frightening, and uplifting. Sensations of every conceivable sort seem to rush in on the user, pulling him or her in contrary directions. Emotional inhibitions are lowered with LSD. Everything is sensed as much more extreme than normally. This means that what is felt as pleasant will seem to be ecstatic, a magic voyage of the gods. And what is normally experienced as simply unpleasant will become dreadful—the absolute pit of hell. One of Aldous Huxley's books describing his mescaline experiences was titled *Heaven and Hell*—testimony to the very powerful ambivalence most users experience during a trip on a hallucinogenic drug. Most of us do not find such extremes to our liking. Extreme mood swings can be unsettling. Nearly everyone who emerges from a strong psychedelic experience, whether he or she likes it or not, is struck by this basic characteristic. After a given LSD trip is over, users are rarely able to describe their feelings about it in unambiguous terms; typically, these descriptions are shot through with feelings of ambivalence.

Another commonly described effect of LSD-type drugs is **sensory overload.** Hallucinogens do not necessarily sharpen the senses, but they do open up the psyche to sensations. Our normal psychological inhibitions enable us to limit what we see around us, to "attend" to a very narrow range of sensations. There is a particular structure in the brain referred to as the "reticular formation." It governs our ability to filter out the many sensations bombarding us every moment and allows us to focus on a small number of relevant stimuli. Without it, minute-to-minute existence would be fraught with overwhelming complications. LSD interferes with the functioning of the reticular formation. Under psychedelics, the mind is overloaded with sensory input, including the many irrelevant impressions and sensations we normally filter out. One individual I interviewed, a lawyer in his twenties, was under the influence of LSD and received a call from someone who said he was in Queens. He answered by muttering the word, "Queens . . . , Queens . . . ," over and over again. The many associations of the word crowded in on his mind—the borough of New York, female monarchs, effeminate homosexuals, a spectacularly desirable woman—and he was unable to formulate a single coherent thought in response to the caller. Finally, he handed the phone to his companion and said, "Here, you take the phone; I just can't deal with it right now."

The issue of the generation of psychotic episodes, panic reactions, or extreme emotional disturbances by LSD and the other hallucinogens was a major media theme in the 1960s. Some observers went so far as to say that all experiences with the drug were, by their very nature, a temporary psychosis or psychosis-like state. Although the temporary psychosis was rare, it did occur in a certain proportion of episodes with the drug.

According to DAWN's data, in the year 2004, only 1,953 out of roughly 2 million untoward drug episodes resulting in a visit to the emergency departments of the country's hospitals involved the use of LSD. The 2005 NSDUH estimates that 563,000 Americans took LSD during the previous year; of these, 104,000 took it during the last month. Working with an extremely conservative figure of nearly 5 million LSD "trips" (that is, assuming that the 563,000 Americans took the drug only three times during the past year, and 104,000 took it twice a month), roughly 1 in 2,500 results in an experience sufficiently serious as to require emergency department intervention. Whether this represents a great many or very few depends on your perspective, but it is clear that the drug is vastly safer than suggested by the biased media stories of the 1960s. Moreover, the fact that emergency department episodes involving LSD declined substantially between 1994 (about 5,200) and 2004 (1,953) is encouraging news. And the fact that the 2004 DAWN data are much more comprehensive and representative than the 1990s data also indicates that a decline took place in LSD-related untoward effects.

## LSD and Genetic Damage

### The Hype

In March 1967, the prestigious journal *Science* published an article by Maimon Cohen, a physician and geneticist, and two associates, reporting that when human blood cells were placed in a culture containing LSD, the cells underwent some chromosome breakage.

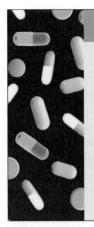

## True-False Quiz

One of the strongest agreements was generated by the following statement: "All other things being equal, women who take LSD during pregnancy have a significantly higher likelihood of bearing children with one or more anatomical, neurological, and behavioral disorders and abnormalities." In fact, 92 percent of my students agreed with this statement. As we see in this section, the statement is false; in the doses typically taken, LSD has no power to cause birth defects or any other congenital abnormalities. But this belief is so compelling that it is part of the ineradicable mythology of the drug. And, even though it is false, it is possible that belief in it will never disappear.

In addition, one schizophrenic mental patient who was treated with LSD 15 times in a therapeutic setting was found to have a higher degree of chromosome damage than was typical or normal (Cohen, Marinello, and Back, 1967). As we saw in Chapter 5, these rather flimsy findings touched off a huge, nationwide panic. These findings from an inadequately controlled study immediately became translated into the inescapable "fact" that LSD would damage one's offspring. The public was led to believe that generations of infants would be born deformed if their parents took LSD. What are the facts on LSD and chromosomes?

### The Reality

An enormous range of factors influences the outcome of chromosome and fetal studies; controls are extremely important because when one variable is changed, the results of an entire experiment may be altered. In any study on drug effects, it is absolutely crucial to be aware of the "identity" of the drugs involved. Much street LSD contains impurities; thus, it is important to know (1) whether any given subject whose chromosomes are examined took pure (rare) or contaminated (common) LSD and (2) how many times, at what dosage levels, and how recently the subject did so. Low doses of a drug may produce no measurable effect on chromosomes, but high doses may generate a significant effect. In addition, many users of LSD ingest other drugs as well. It then becomes necessary to sort out which of the various drugs ingested has an effect, if any; in most cases, this is impossible to determine. Effects in animals do not demonstrate effects in humans, and effects *in vitro* (cells in a solution or culture) do not imply effects *in vivo* (cells taken from a living being). Furthermore, chromosome breakage does not necessarily mean fetal damage. Even the occurrence of birth defects by itself may not be significant. About 4 percent, or 140,000, of the infants born in the United States each year have some significant defect, irrespective of the factor of LSD use (Lyons, 1983). Thus, the fact that a mother who has taken LSD gives birth to a child with certain congenital aberrations is not automatic evidence of LSD's **mutagenic effect,** that is, its capacity to alter chromosomes; the significant question is whether the birth defect rate among all mothers who have taken LSD is any different from that among non-LSD-taking mothers—assuming that all factors are controlled, which they rarely are.

In an exhaustive study of the available findings reported in nearly 100 scientific papers, four researchers concluded that in moderate, or "trip," doses, LSD does not appear to induce genetic damage, and that only in massive dosages (never ingested by humans) do any mutagenic effects occur: "We believe that LSD is, in fact, a weak mutagen, effective only in extremely high doses; it is unlikely to be mutagenic in any concentration used by human subjects." The researchers conclude that "there is no evidence that pure LSD is teratogenic in man [and woman]" (Dishotsky et al., 1971, p. 439). In short, LSD does not appear to damage chromosomes or produce birth defects. That erroneous view was disseminated and accepted because there is a strong tendency to believe that a drug with such powerful effects must inevitably harm the body in a wide range of ways. If the same mistaken research findings had been published (if, indeed, they would ever have been published) concerning the effects of a commonly used and widely accepted substance, this would not have been accepted as true by the public. Clearly, our prejudices and preconceptions shape our view of reality and truth. The hysteria that exploded in the 1960s over LSD's supposed harmful effects on human chromosomes illustrates the principle that, during moral panics, the media, the public, agencies of social control, and even scientists are sensitized to the potential harm that an agent seen to be threatening can cause.

The same evidence that is used to convict agents of the moral panic will acquit more familiar agents. If the same lab results that sparked the LSD–chromosome stories in 1967 had been produced by alcohol, hardly anyone would have paid attention. The fact that it was LSD that, supposedly, caused chromosomal breakage made the story newsworthy, threatening, and believable. Even today, many people still believe that LSD is a mutagenic agent. On the first day of a course on alcoholism and drug abuse that I teach, 9 out of 10 of the students in the class (91 percent) erroneously agreed that the statement "Women who take LSD during pregnancy, even once, have a significantly higher likelihood of bearing children with birth defects than women who do not take LSD," is true. Some myths, it seems, never die. The lesson of the hysteria surrounding LSD's supposed role in generating birth defects illustrates the importance of the contrast between drug use as an essentialistic phenomenon, with concrete, materially real properties, and a constructed phenomenon whose reality exists on the airwaves, on pages, and in the minds of observers. LSD was constructed in a certain way by the culture of the 1960s; to some extent, some elements of this social construction have survived to this day. As careful students of the world of drug use, we must be careful to distinguish these two ways of looking at drugs so that we do not confuse one with the other.

## LSD: Continuance Rates and Frequencies of Use

Users of LSD hardly ever take it frequently, chronically, or compulsively. It tends to be used episodically, on a once-in-a-while basis. "The most important fact about chronic or long-term psychedelic drug use is that there is very little of it" (Grinspoon and Bakalar, 1979, p. 176). As we saw earlier, of all drugs, alcohol attracts the greatest user loyalty; roughly two-thirds of all individuals who have used alcohol at least once in their lives have also used it within the past month. In this respect, hallucinogens rank very low in user loyalty. Only one-half of one percent of all at-least one-time users of LSD in the general public said that they took the drug within the past month. LSD is not even remotely addicting in the physical sense, nor does the drug produce psychological dependence. Judging by their behavior, laboratory animals dislike being high on LSD; they avoid taking it if they can. The drug thus does not have the "immediate sensual appeal" of cocaine, heroin, and the amphetamines. Among humans, LSD is very rarely a drug of frequent use, no matter what sort of myth may be used to explain its use. In fact, the concept of psychological dependence has less relevance to a discussion of the hallucinogens than it does for *any other* drug or drug type. It is extremely difficult to have a psychedelic drug "habit." And the users of LSD seem to have learned from the experiences of earlier users; today, LSD is taken in much smaller doses than was once true—50, 80, or 100 micrograms versus 200, 250, or 300 micrograms, which was typical in the 1960s. Consequently, the effects of the drug they take are less extreme and less florid than was the case in the 1960s and 1970s.

There are at least three reasons why the hallucinogens almost never produce a dependency in users. First, the body builds up a tolerance or resistance to hallucinogens extremely rapidly—faster than for any other drug or drug type. Unlike all the other drugs under consideration, LSD does not allow users to be high all of their waking hours, day after day, for a long period of time. And cross-tolerance sets in for the various psychedelics, so getting high on one will diminish the ability to get high on another.

Second, the LSD experience requires a monumental effort. To get through eight hours of an LSD high—including sensory bombardment, psychic turmoil, emotional insecurity, alternations of despair and bliss, one exploding insight on the heels of another, images hurtling through the mind as fast as the spinning fruit in a slot machine—is draining in the extreme. Most experienced marijuana users claim to be able to "get straight" during the marijuana high in the event of an emergency. They say they would be able to go to work or to classes stoned without being detected, and to function in a reasonable manner. Perhaps this is possible; it may depend on the individual. But almost no one claims to be able to do this with LSD. Users report that it is impossible to function normally, to "come down" at will. "You really are in another world," explained one heavy marijuana smoker of the psychedelic experience.

A third reason why LSD-type drugs are rarely taken on a frequent, compulsive basis is that, more than any other drug used on the street, LSD has extremely inconsistent effects; the experience varies markedly from trip to trip. One trip might be ecstatic, another horrifying, and a third relatively uneventful. Most drugs are taken for some aspect of intoxication, to achieve a certain kind of high. A drug as unreliable as LSD would not be used on a day-to-day basis by someone seeking a specific drug experience.

## CLUB DRUGS

**Club drugs** is an informal name given to a group of illicit substances that are commonly consumed in nightclubs, at parties and raves and concerts, and at other gatherings where teenagers and young adults gather to have a good time and alter their consciousnesses. The term is not scientific, but the drugs that are most commonly included in the category include Ecstasy, Rohypnol, ketamine, and GHB. All became at least modestly popular in the 1990s; Monitoring the Future added Ecstasy and Rohypnol to its questionnaire in the 1990s, and ketamine and GHB were added in 2000. These four drugs make up a chemically and pharmacologically diverse lot: Rohypnol is a sedative-hypnotic similar to lorazepam; GHB is analogous to an extremely concentrated form of alcohol; ketamine is most similar to PCP, although with milder effects; and Ecstasy is an "empathogen," in a category by itself. All are synthetic chemicals.

During the 1990s, the use of club drugs increased substantially. Fearful that the use of what he referred to as "designer drugs" would become epidemic in his state, Florida

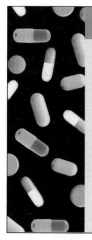

True-False Quiz

When a new drug bursts on the scene, its use becomes widespread, and media attention is focused on it; consequently, the public tends to exaggerate how widely and frequently it is used. Newness equals memorability, and memorability equals an exaggerated sense of how common it is. The statement "In recent years, Ecstasy (MDMD) has become the illegal drug that is used by the *highest* percentage of people under the age of 25" is false, of course; marijuana remains youth's most widely used drug, and by a considerable margin: According to Monitoring the Future, in 2005, 20 percent of high school seniors had used marijuana in the past 30 days, while only 1 percent had used MDMA, or Ecstasy— a margin of 20 to 1.

governor Jeb Bush gathered a team of drug "experts" to search for proof that these deadly drugs were "stalking nightclubs and the rave scene." In 2000, in the state capitol, Jim McDonough, the state's chief of the Office of Drug Control, announced the team's report, "a very thorough, autopsy-by-autopsy review" of club-drug-caused deaths. Club drugs, they said, "were killing many more youngsters than anyone had suspected." The report's tally of rave drug deaths in the state of Florida since 1994 was given as 254.

The claim, it turns out, was bogus. A few months after the report's unveiling, *The Orlando Sentinel* ran a story by reporter Henry Pierson Curtis (2000) that examined each of the 254 supposed club- or designer-drug-related deaths. The reporter found that at least half the claims of a club drug connection were completely unfounded. The flaws in the report were myriad. To begin with, the study included a remarkably broad total of 20 drugs in its definition of "club drugs," including fentanyl, a narcotic; nitrous oxide, or "laughing gas"; and amphetamine, a stimulant. And many of the deaths had little or no connection to what the research team referred to as designer drugs. Rose Pope, age 82, of St. Petersburg, died eight days after being hit by a car; she was included among the club drug deaths. A 74-year-old cancer patient in Miami–Dade County Hospital was given an overdose of morphine; he too was included in the tally. A 41-year-old Orlando man who shot himself after losing his job tested positive for amphetamine; he was included as well. Tavani Smith, a 4-year-old, had a day-long headache, so his mother took him to the hospital; he stopped breathing after being administered a dose of sodium brevital, an ultra-fast-acting sedative, and ketamine. Sodium brevital is used to euthanize dogs and execute prisoners in some states. Ketamine does happen to be a club drug, and so Smith's death was included.

When the flaws of this study were revealed by the press, McDonough, Florida's "drug-fighting chief," asked "why a reporter would question shortcomings in the research instead of helping his staff fight drug abuse. . . . We are trying to get the facts," he added. "We've discovered that we have a club-drug problem in this state that is immense, and we want to do something about it" (Curtis, 2000).

Synthesized by a biochemist working for a chemical company, MDMA (Ecstasy), an analogue of the amphetamines, was never manufactured or officially approved for medical use. Though it was originally used in psychotherapy, in 1985, the FDA provisionally classified it as a Schedule I drug; in 1988, this classification was finalized. MDMA's dominant effect is empathy; that is, it generates a feeling of identification with others. "I love the world and the world loves me," said one user (Gahlinger, 2001, p. 340). Scientists worry about the drug's depletion of the brain's serotonin.

GHB, a sedative, once prescribed as a sleep aid and an anti-anxiety agent, produces a state of relaxation and drunkenness without the hangover. It is also used by some body-builders to help increase muscle mass. At higher doses, like alcohol, it inhibits breathing and heartbeat, and can starve the body of oxygen. In 2000, the federal government classi-fied GHB as a Schedule I drug.

Ketamine (trade names Ketelar, Ketajet, Ketaset, and Vetelar) is, like PCP, a "disasso-ciative anesthetic" that, like PCP, began its career as a drug for both humans and animals. It works as a painkiller without inhibiting breathing. During the Vietnam War, ketamine was used as a battlefield medicine, but patients complained of hallucinations and "bizarre thoughts"—the very qualities that make it popular as a recreational drug (Gahlinger, 2001, p. 187).

Rohypnol (generic name, flunitrazepam) is a sedative drug, a benzodiazepine like Valium, Librium, and Xanax. Benzodiazepines are anti-anxiety agents and muscle relaxants, but Rohypnol is roughly 10 times as potent as Valium and, in high doses, can cause uncon-sciousness and short-term paralysis and amnesia—all effects that make it an attractive "date rape" drug.

Not only is the use of club drugs a recent phenomenon, it is confined to a fairly small—and declining—minority of teenagers and young adults. In 2001, 9 percent of high school seniors used Ecstasy during the past year, while only 3 percent did so in 2005; the percent-age using it in the past month was 3 percent in 2001 and 1 percent in 2005. For Rohypnol, in 2005, the number was too small to calculate; ketamine and GHB did not even appear in the 2005 Monitoring the Future's tables, indicating that rates of use of these drugs had dropped below 0.5 percent. In other words, the latest indication is that club drugs, which became popular in the 1990s, had faded from prominence by the first half of the first decade of the twenty-first century.

DAWN, the Drug Abuse Warning Network, has tallied club drugs over the past decade and has found that for several of them, their untoward, nonlethal emergency department (ED) mentions have substantially increased during this period. Keep in mind that when numbers are very small to begin with, even a tiny *numerical* increase produces a huge *per-centage* increase. Still, the numbers seemed to be alarming. Between 1994 and 2001, ED mentions for ketamine increased 36 times, for Royhpnol 36 times, for MDMA 22 times, and for GHB an astounding 60 times! These numbers did not consistently increase, how-ever, into the 2000s, as we can see from Table 9-2: For two of the club drugs (Rohypnol and ketamine), between 2001 and 2004, ED visits leveled off; for one (MDMA), they increased by over a third; and for a fourth (GHB), they declined by half. The numbers are quite small, especially in proportion to the media attention paid to these drugs.

As noted previously, MDMA was synthesized early in the twentieth century and patented by Merck as a possible appetite suppressant, and sat on a shelf for decades. Then the army tested it in 1953. In large doses, it turns out, MDMA kills animals. Because of its mind-altering properties—most notably, its capacity to induce empathy and a sense of "newness" in subjects—quietly, during the 1970s, psychiatrists began using it on their pa-tients as an adjunct to therapy; according to one estimate, at that time, some 30,000 doses

| TABLE 9-2 | Club Drug Emergency Department Visits, 1994, 2001, and 2004 | | | |
|---|---|---|---|---|
| Year | MDMA | Rohypnol | GHB | Ketamine |
| 1994 | 253 | 13 | 56 | 19 |
| 2001 | 5,542 | 469 | 4,969 | 263 |
| 2004 | 8,621 | 473 | 2,340 | 227 |

*Source:* DAWN, 2002; SAMHSA, 2006.

were being administered per month (Klein, 1985, p. 42). By then, it had attracted the attention of authorities. In 1985, the DEA temporarily classified it as a Schedule I drug, indicating that authorities believed it had a high abuse potential and no medical utility; in 1988, this classification became permanent. Anyone selling the drug could face a 15-year prison term. Classifying MDMA as a Schedule I drug, says one observer, "may well have been one of the most criminal acts of our recent U.S. government" (Stafford, 1989, p. xxii). As we'll see, not all experts agree.

Ecstasy, also referred to as "XTC," "Adam," or simply "E," is MDMA, a synthetic analogue of the amphetamines. While it has some effects that are similar to those of the amphetamines, such as jaw clenching and tooth grinding, most observers classify Ecstasy as a psychedelic or hallucinogen. Actually, this designation is misleading, since the drug has none of the major effects of the hallucinogens. However, as a mind transformer, a drug that powerfully alters the user's consciousness, it can be regarded as a psychedelic. Some observers prefer the term "empathogen" (Eisner, 1989, pp. 3, 33ff) to refer to Ecstasy—that is, a drug that facilitates empathy or a close emotional bonding with others. Several experts object to the term "Ecstasy" to refer to MDMA, arguing that the drug produces not ecstasy in users, but empathy, "an ability to feel trust, a lowering of psychological barriers" (Seymour, 1986, p. 9), serenity, a feeling that all is well with the world, openness, self-awareness, peacefulness, euphoria, and a "noetic feeling—the experience of seeing the world in a fresh way, as if for the first time" (Eisner, 1989, p. 3).

In a series of experiments on rats and guinea pigs, psychopharmacologists Lewis Seiden and Charles Schuster discovered that Ecstasy may cause long-term, possibly irreversible, damage to the brain. A neurotransmitter, **serotonin,** which helps to send signals to various organs of the body and regulates sleep, sex, aggression, and mood, was found to be at "alarmingly low levels." The brain had been depleted of its supply of serotonin, and eight weeks after the conclusion of the experiment, the researchers saw no indication of its return. Based on their animal experiments, Seiden and Schuster conclude that doses harmful to the brain are only two to three times those taken on the street (Roberts, 1986, p. 14).

In another set of experiments, doses of Ecstasy were administered to monkeys and baboons, and the primates suffered damage to the cells that produce **dopamine,** a neurotransmitter that regulates coordination, pleasure, and emotion; 2 of the 10 monkeys and baboons died of heatstroke (Ricaurte et al. 2002). Critics charged that the dosages of Ecstasy that were administered to the primates were many times higher than the doses that are taken by users on a recreational basis. Una McCann, a co-author of the study, denied the charge, claiming that their doses were "actually slightly less" than a human would take (McNeil, 2002). But a year later, *Science* magazine, where the findings of this study were reported, made a shocking admission: Somehow, the samples of Ecstasy administered to the primates in the experiment had been switched with methamphetamine, making the conclusions of the study completely invalid. *Science* retracted the results of the study, forcing Ricaurte, its senior author, to withdraw four other papers reporting on studies in which drug samples were also switched. As of this writing, there is no scientific evidence that Ecstasy causes brain damage in humans (Avalania, 2003; McNeil, 2002). Still, the controversy is likely to be with us for decades to come.

## SUMMARY

Marijuana is highly variable with respect to potency; hence, its effects are likely to be very different according to the strength of the batch that is used. Marijuana is usually smoked, so its effects are tied in with this particular route of administration. The principal psychoactive ingredient in marijuana is THC, which is an extremely slowly metabolized chemical; the half-life of its metabolites is more than 48 hours, and traces remain in the body for several weeks after use. This crucial fact has important consequences; for instance, these traces may have lingering effects on motor coordination and intellectual competence.

Marijuana is by far the most widely used illicit psychoactive drug in the United States and, in all likelihood, in the world as well. A third of the American population age 12 or older has at least tried the drug, and roughly 1 American in 20 used it in the past month. The use of marijuana increased dramatically among teenagers between the mid-1990s and 2000—by some measures, a doubling or a tripling. Although the figures have leveled off and even dropped slightly since then, they remain higher than they were in the early 1990s. Many experts fear that this increase could translate into a wide range of harms, such as increased fatalities on the highway and increased use of more dangerous drugs, a few years down the road.

All observers agree that cannabis is one of the least toxic drugs known; it is practically impossible to die of a marijuana overdose, and it is possible that none have ever occurred. Marijuana does, however, impair motor coordination and cognitive performance. The subjective effects of marijuana are more interesting than its objective effects. Under the influence, users report feeling more peaceful, more "turned on," and more sensitive and perceptive; having more "profound" thoughts; being more amused by many more things than normally; feeling more emotionally open or sensitive; sensing that time is slower, more stretched out; and feeling more incapable of concentrating, more lethargic, and less able of remembering things that are happening. Clearly, marijuana use is a euphoric, pleasurable, unserious, hedonistic, somewhat foolish activity, compatible with recreation and incompatible with precise movements and serious, sustained intellectual effort.

It is the long-term or chronic effects of marijuana that have preoccupied much of the medical research on the drug in recent decades. A number of findings that were reported by the earliest researchers—that marijuana caused a wide range of pathologies, including brain damage, liver damage, and a diminished testosterone level, chromosomal damage, and a diminished capacity of the white blood cells to fight disease—were not confirmed by later researchers. It is possible that marijuana does have an impact on the organs or functions that were studied, although an extremely weak one. One pathological finding that has been sustained independently by several researchers, however, is impaired pulmonary functioning. It should come as no surprise that a drug whose principal route of administration is smoking should cause some damage to the lungs of users.

Marijuana use is patterned by a number of sociological variables. Of these, age may be the most potent; use is low in the early teens, rises, reaches a peak during the late teens to the early twenties, and declines thereafter, sharply so after the age of 35. It is likely that two factors influence this pattern: simultaneous freedom from adult supervision and adult responsibilities. Males are significantly more likely to use marijuana than females; as marijuana use increases, so does male overrepresentation in use. This pattern is parallel to most (but not all) deviant and/or criminal activities, in which males are more likely to participate.

Peer influences are strong and pervasive; the more the individual's friends use, the greater is his or her own use of marijuana. Marijuana is also part of a pattern of psychoactive drug use generally; users are more likely to be drawn from circles of young people who have had experience with alcohol, and are more likely to "go on" to the use of more dangerous drugs, such as cocaine, amphetamines, and even heroin. This does not mean that all marijuana users progress in this way—actually, very few do—but only that smoking marijuana increases the statistical likelihood of doing so. Marijuana use is also related to unconventionality; the greater the tolerance for and participation in deviance and nonconformity prior to use, the greater the likelihood that some will eventually use marijuana. And the more risks a youngster accepts and takes, the greater the likelihood of using marijuana.

No researcher questions the correlation between the use of marijuana and the use of more dangerous drugs; it is a robust relationship that every study ever conducted has turned up. But what is the causal mechanism here? *Why* this strong and consistent relationship? Three schools of thought attempt to explain it.

The first is the pharmacological school, which argues that drug use is much like a conveyor belt, with users moving almost inevitably to increasingly dangerous drugs. The cause, its adherents argue, can be found in marijuana itself and in the brain's neurological pathways, in the experience of getting high, more or less unmodified by social and personality factors. Several lines of evidence, however, suggest that this school of thinking is incorrect in its conclusions.

The sociocultural school, in contrast, argues that it is not getting high, in and of itself, that causes a higher proportion of users to "go on" to stronger drugs. Instead, it is influenced by the personal associations the user forms when using. That is, the very fact of use entails forming friendships with other users, who are more likely both to endorse the use of other drugs and to provide opportunities to use them. The fact that persons who use marijuana but who have very few marijuana-using friends are unlikely to progress to the use of more dangerous drugs suggests that the sociocultural model may be more valid than the pharmacological model.

The predisposition school argues that the kinds of people who use marijuana have a higher statistical likelihood of using harder drugs than do the kinds of people who do not use marijuana. They tend to be unconventional in a variety of ways, more likely to take risks and engage in "deviant" activities. Marijuana use is merely a stand-in for a certain type of predisposition. Of course, since taking harder drugs is a more extreme activity than smoking marijuana, only a minority of marijuana users will "progress" to the harder drugs, but the statistical relationship holds nonetheless. It is not the experience of getting high that counts here, but the type of person who has the impulse to engage in such an experience.

Is marijuana useful as medicine? This issue has become extremely controversial in the past decade. Representatives of the federal government and many traditional physicians insist that cannabis should not be used medically, that its status as a Schedule I drug should remain intact. They maintain that acceptable, efficacious, and nondangerous substitutes exist, and that its use as medicine will function as a foot in the door toward tolerating its recreational use. In contrast, many observers argue that the drug is effective as medicine and that for some patients it is the *only* substance that works. These observers hold that if the government will not permit its legal use, illegal channels of supply should be sought out. Presently, 11 states have approved marijuana's medical use, and several others will soon put the proposal on the ballot for voters to decide. This controversy is likely to remain with us for some time to come. Still, federal law supersedes state law, and purveyors and users of marijuana as medicine remain liable to prosecution by the federal government.

A common myth about LSD is that it was widely used in the 1960s but its use declined thereafter. Actually, the use of LSD was quite low during the 1960s, although it grew explosively during that decade, and it continued to grow throughout the 1970s. The fact is, in 2000, the recreational use of LSD was about where it was in 1975, when the Monitoring the Future survey began research on high school seniors. The use of LSD declined during the 2000s, however, and today is less than half of what it was a half decade age.

Some common effects of LSD and other psychedelic or hallucinogenic drugs include seeing eidetic imagery (bold, stark visions with one's eyes closed), experiencing synesthesia (the feeling that one of the five senses translates into another, such as "seeing" sounds or "feeling" colors), sensing phenomena to exist on a variety of dimensions or levels of reality, seeing the world as eternally fluid or in motion, sensing an emotional exaggeration of phenomena, and experiencing a sense of timelessness. "True" hallucinations, or seeing things the user thinks are real but aren't, are relatively rare. More common is the "virtual" hallucination, the vision the user knows isn't really there but is caused by the drug.

The incidence of psychotic episodes associated with LSD was hugely exaggerated by the media; in the 1960s, it was erroneously depicted as commonplace. In any case, relatively rare as "freaking out" was in the 1960s, its incidence declined in the 1970s and 1980s. Some observers believe that panic reactions and other untoward effects of the LSD-type drugs were strongly influenced by cultural interpretations of the unusual psychic states generated by them, and not by the intrinsic effects of these substances.

Like psychotic episodes, genetic damage was a supposed effect of LSD seized upon by the media that turned out to be completely untrue. LSD is an extremely weak agent of genetic alteration; subsequent research demonstrated that the alleged "monster-producing" impact of LSD simply did not exist. The hysteria generated by the use of LSD demonstrates the importance of sensitization during a drug panic: The media exaggerated the harmful effects of a new and different drug, the public came to believe the exaggeration, and any and all manner of evidence was used to "prove" the harms that were believed to occur in the first place. By the 1970s, the fear and hysteria associated with LSD only a half dozen years earlier had dissipated. Eventually, the psychedelics simply became yet another illegal substance that was added to the recreational drug stew.

Perhaps the most important fact about LSD and the LSD-type drugs is that they are used extremely infrequently and episodically. They are not drugs of chronic or compulsive use. Among recreational drugs, their user loyalty is among the weakest; not only are those who use them unlikely to take LSD-type drugs more than once in a while, a very high percentage use them experimentally once or twice, then discontinue their use altogether. There are at least three reasons for this: (1) Tolerance builds up rapidly; (2) the effects of these drugs are powerful and disruptive enough to discourage frequent use; and (3) the effects are inconsistent and variable. There is no such thing as an LSD addict, unlike for alcohol, tobacco, heroin, and cocaine.

The so-called club drugs—for our purposes, Ecstasy, ketamine, Rohypnol, and GHB— are a chemically and pharmacologically miscellaneous group of substances that have attained at least moderate popularity as recreational or street drugs only within the past decade or so. It is feared that Ecstasy (MDMA), chemically related to the amphetamines and regarded by some experts as an "empathogen" or generator of close bonding with others, permanently depletes serotonin, a crucial neurotransmitter that regulates emotion, anger, mood, impulsivity, the sex drive, hunger, and other crucial functions of the body. More recent research suggests that the supply of dopamine, another crucial neurotransmitter, may also be a victim of Ecstasy use. Ketamine ("special K"), a close relative of PCP, which was previously a popular street drug, is a "disassociative anesthetic"—a sedative that induces a hypnotic state sometimes accompanied by hallucinations. Along with Rohpynol and GHB, ketamine has been accused of having been used as a "date rape" drug, that is, of rendering women incapable of resisting or unconscious. These four drugs are used, in addition to methamphetamine, LSD, and others, by young people in clubs and at parties, raves, and concerts to enhance good times. Considering its relative recentness and rarity, GHB has generated a sizable number of untoward acute effects. Since 2000, both the use and the untoward effects of club drugs have declined.

## KEY TERMS

carcinogen   239

club drugs   267

dopamine   270

eidetic imagery   261

gateway hypothesis   252

hemp   238

intrinsic school   253

mutagen   265

pharmacological
  school   252

predisposition school   255

pseudohallucination   262

psychosocial
  unconventionality   251

sensory overload   263

seratonin   270

sociocultural school   254

stepping-stone
  hypothesis   256

synesthesia   261

virtual hallucination   262

## ACCOUNT:   Raving

*Jim is a 20-year-old college junior. Here, he explains the subculture of raving, which is usually accompanied by the use of club drugs, most prominently Ecstasy.*

A modern-day Woodstock, called a "rave," is the outlet for today's youth of America. A rave is basically a huge, usually outdoor, illegal party where hundreds, thousands, and in some cases, as many as

10,000, ravers gather to not only enjoy each other but to bathe in the music throughout the night and well into the next day—with the help of some psychedelic substances, of course. No folk rock or Birkenstocks here. It's techno, the underground club music that sends ravers to the hills, beaches, stadiums, warehouses, and even vacant airplane hangars. Some of these kids may even look like hippies. A real rave is like Woodstock gone techno with lots of lasers, enormous sound systems, and thousands of people coming together with one thing in mind—to have fun. . . . People of all races and colors join together as friends to dance and party for days on end, tripping out on acid and Ecstasy. A nation's youth culture has come together to create a scene so strong that authorities can do nothing about it. The atmosphere created by special people is enhanced by mind-blowing visuals and lasers; mind, body, and soul ascend into a state of bliss.

Because of the illegal, underground nature of these parties, a strong sense of unity and loyalty develops among those present. Kids willingly drive hundreds of miles to attend raves set in remote locations. Often, busses are hired to bring in those who have purchased combination bus-rave tickets. People want to be there. They are drawn to others who simply want to have fun together. The vibe is entirely positive, and at times almost overwhelming. There is enormous energy created by the music, energy, and setting. . . . The music is at the heart of any rave—hardcore techno—a form of music that can be matched by no other in creating the energetic atmosphere and mind trip to make the scene work.

Ravers have to put up with a lot. The anti-rave hysteria created by the press years back—about Ecstasy-crazed kids, mass orgies, and total chaos—nearly killed off the rave scene altogether. The police have closed down many raves due to pressure from the tabloid-reading public. In LA there is even a special police force assigned to seeking out and dispersing raves. . . . Some rave organizers have begun to work with the police, but they complain that they can't have their sound systems loud enough for the audience to feel the pressure of the music—which is the key. Other ravers have stated that the police simply hate seeing anyone

having a good time, so they keep seeking out new sites, thus maintaining the standards of raving their crowds have set. . . .

I consider myself lucky to have experienced this incredible feeling. Having used mescaline, acid, and Ecstasy, I personally, as well as do most other ravers, prefer to take Ecstasy at raves because of the calm high it gives you, the sensitivity and insight. It's a lot better than taking acid, which typically produces much more disassociation and disorientation, as well as more anxiety reactions. Ecstasy has been called the "love drug" and even the "sex drug" among ravers because it produces a sensual euphoria that goes perfectly with the rave scene. Having had experiences with the drug, including, once, with my two brothers (age 19 and 21) and my girlfriend, a sense of insight and bonding with others seems to take place that one wouldn't feel unless they take the drug themselves. I hate to say that a drug could actually open your eyes to life but that is what it does. People who have never taken Ecstasy will never know this "sixth sense" one feels when taking it. If you tell them that, they'll just ridicule you, just as people who have never raved will do if you tell them about how great raves are.

Drugs give you the energy to rave all night and not get tired. Any real raver will tell you that. The people who condemn it are ignorant about what it is and what it's like. There's a sensation, a sixth sense you get when you rave. . . . I only use acid and Ecstasy moderately, and then only if the time and place are appropriate. I never do it just for the hell of it. If you are at a rave, you will see people with dilated pupils, hugging each other. Raving is a state of mind. People don't go to them to show off their fashionable clothes or fancy dance steps. Raving takes over your life. It's not something you go to on a weekend to forget your boring life. It's not somewhere you go to look down on someone who's not wearing the same clothes as you. Everyone is on a trip and that trip is trance-dancing. If we can't have world peace, what's wrong with going to a rave where there is love, peace, and unity, even if it doesn't last? I consider ravers to be the luckiest people around because we can escape from a cruel world and enjoy the friendliest gathering in the country in a way only we know how to do.

## QUESTIONS

Do you accept Jim's rationale for drug use at raves? Are Ecstasy and the other club drugs as safe as he says? Are ravers "the luckiest people around"? Are raves as peaceful and loving as Jim claims? Are nonravers missing out on a wonderful experience, as Jim argues? If we accept Jim's statements as true, shouldn't we all be taking Ecstasy and attending raves? Is the rave culture unfairly persecuted? How would you characterize the social composition of ravers? How does it differ from that of drug users of other drugs, in other scenes? What is it about the characteristics of users of certain drugs that attracts them to those particular substances? More than a dozen years ago, the typical user of Ecstasy was a youngish middle-aged professional (Beck and Rosenbaum, 1994); why do you think the age composition of the users of this drug has changed?

**D**oug is 38; he makes his living as a writer. "When I snort cocaine," he told me, "I feel powerful. Smart, sharp, suave, articulate—and *unbelievably* sexy. I feel I can do anything I want, including make love to every woman on Earth. There's really nothing I've had any experience with that's anything like it. It's very hard for me to limit my use of this seductive, alluring drug to just once in a while. Maybe I have a habit," Doug wondered, "I'm not sure."

Mike, 27, a university instructor, told me about an experience he had with amphetamines. He spent most of the evening engaged in a heated argument with his on-again, off-again girlfriend. By the time he managed to convince her to go to bed, at three in the morning, he realized he hadn't prepared the lecture he had to give just a few hours later, concerning a subject about which he knew virtually nothing. Taking two 10-milligram capsules of Dexedrine and staying up the rest of the night, Doug read what he could on the topic, took notes, and typed up an outline of what he wanted to say. Swallowing two more capsules just before his class at nine, he walked in and began lecturing. "I was masterful, knowledgeable, articulate, charismatic, clever, and charming," he told me. When the class was over, half a dozen students surged forward and congratulated him on his wonderful lecture. "Amphetamine is just great," Mike told me. "I wonder if maybe I ought to lecture that way more often," he mused.

Pharmacologist Avram Goldstein refers to the use of cocaine and the amphetamines (including methamphetamine), the two principal and strongest stimulants, as "the wild addictions" (1994, p. 155). The immediate subjective effect of these drugs is euphoria and a sense of confidence and well-being. As I pointed out in Chapter 2, of all known drugs or drug types, cocaine and the amphetamines are the two with the greatest **immediate sensual appeal** (Grinspoon and Bakalar, 1976, pp. 191–194; Lasagna, von Felsinger, and Beecher, 1955). This means that if they, along with other drugs, are administered in an experiment, to subjects who do not know what drug they have been given, in comparison with the other drugs, the subjects enjoy their effects the most and are most likely to say that they want to take them again. In short, humans find these stimulants pleasurable to take. Of all drugs, cocaine and the amphetamines also produce the most powerful psychological dependence.

In laboratory experiments, rats, mice, and monkeys will self-administer cocaine in preference to food, and they will even starve to death self-administering cocaine. If experimental animals receive cocaine as a result of engaging in a certain activity, like pushing a bar, and the researchers then discontinue administering the drug, these animals will go on engaging in that previously rewarded activity—thousands of times an hour—at a higher rate and for a longer time than will animals deprived of any other drug (Grinspoon and Bakalar, 1976, p. 193; Johanson, 1984). In psychological terms, then, cocaine and the amphetamines are powerfully *reinforcing;* taking them produces the impulse to take them over and over again, regardless of the obstacles, pain, or cost. In popular or lay terms, they are pleasurable. It should come as no surprise, therefore, that these two drugs are widely used for recreational purposes—that is, to get high.

Stimulants speed up signals passing through the central nervous system; they activate organs and functions of the body, heighten arousal, increase overall behavioral activity, and suppress fatigue. In low doses, stimulants can heighten the body's sensitivity and improve mental and physical performance. At high doses, however, many of these functions seem to go haywire. Behavior becomes unfocused, hypersensitivity easily translates into paranoia, and mental and intellectual performance becomes uncontrollable, ineffective, counterproductive, and often compulsively repetitive. Among the many famous chronic stimulant abusers, we may include Adolf Hitler, whose deranged behavior, especially toward the end of World War II, may have been due in part to immoderate amphetamine consumption (Robson, 1994, p. 59); Sigmund Freud, whose peculiar theories, some argue, could owe something to his early cocaine abuse (Streatfeild, 2001, pp. 105–116; Thornton, 1984); and Robert Louis Stevenson, who wrote his famous (and bizarre) novel, *The Strange Case of*

*Dr. Jekyll and Mr. Hyde,* in three days under the influence of cocaine. Arthur Conan Doyle made his famous detective Sherlock Holmes a cocaine addict.

## THE AMPHETAMINES

The amphetamines and amphetamine-like drugs include Benzedrine, Dexedrine, Methedrine, methamphetamine, Desoxyn, Biphetamine, and Dexamyl. Over the years, they have gone by the street names of "speed," "ups," "uppers," "crank," "splash," "pep pills," "meth," "crystal," "bennies," "dexies," and, most recently, "ice." Amphetamine was first synthesized in a laboratory in 1887; the first commercial product from the drug was marketed over the counter in the United States in 1932, as an inhalant for nasal decongestion. (The Food and Drug Administration banned its use for this purpose in 1959, but, because of loopholes, the ban did not become effective until 1971.) During World War II, substantial numbers of American, Japanese, and German soldiers were issued Benzedrine to make them more effective and alert fighting machines. Amphetamines have been used to treat narcolepsy (compulsive and involuntary sleep), depression, alcoholism, schizophrenia, obesity, hyperkinesis (amphetamine, like Ritalin, seems to have the paradoxical effect of calming down hyperactive children), Parkinson's disease, fatigue, nicotine and caffeine addiction, sea sickness, and bed-wetting. It became known fairly quickly that amphetamine drugs have a number of side effects, including euphoria, that make them attractive for recreational use. Throughout the 1940s and 1950s, prescription amphetamines were increasingly diverted into illegal channels. By the 1960s, amphetamines had become one of the half dozen most popular street drugs. In addition, amphetamines were used extramedically for instrumental purposes—to combat fatigue and drowsiness.

Amphetamines are used instrumentally and quasi-therapeutically in tablet or capsule form; between 2.5 and 10 milligrams constitute a typical dose. In such low doses, the typical bodily and mental effects of the amphetamines are (1) a heightened competence in motor skills and mental acuity; (2) an increased alertness, a feeling of arousal or wakefulness, and a diminution of drowsiness and fatigue; (3) a feeling of increased energy; (4) a stimulation of the need for motor activity, particularly walking about and talking; (5) a feeling of euphoria and an inhibition of depression in normal persons (it does not work on clinically depressed patients); (6) increased heartbeat; (7) an inhibition of appetite; (8) constriction of the blood vessels; (9) dryness of the mouth; and (10) a feeling of confidence and even grandeur.

### Trends in Use

Amphetamines were popular in the 1950s and 1960s and into the mid-1970s as prescription diet pills. The drug does inhibit the appetite, but studies have shown that weight loss tends to be modest and temporary; physicians concluded that amphetamine is an ineffective means of losing weight. In addition, there was a growing awareness that the immoderate use of amphetamines can be dangerous. Because of these restrictions, far fewer physicians prescribed the drug for weight loss. As a result, many overweight (and not-so overweight) patients, mainly women, sought out amphetamines through underground channels, either on the street or in the offices of unscrupulous physicians. The nonprescription use of amphetamines for weight loss represents only one of a great number of illegal instrumental uses of the drug. Other familiar uses include truck drivers staying up all night for several nights running to transport cargo cross-country, students pulling an "all-nighter" to cram for an exam (as we saw at the end of Chapter 1), athletes seeking alertness and quickness on the playing field, and a wide variety of ordinary people using the drug so that they can face life in a less depressed, more positive mood. These users are taking the drug not to get high but to achieve certain goals of which society approves, such as working at a job, doing well in school, and socializing with others. For the most part, such illegal instrumental users tend to restrict their use to specific occasions and to limit the amount they take when they do use (usually 2.5 to 10 or 20 milligrams). The instrumental use of the amphetamines still takes place, but stringent controls on these drugs have diminished the frequency and extent of their use.

From 1971 to 1986, the number of prescriptions written for the amphetamines declined by 90 percent, and this decline continued throughout the 1980s and into the 1990s. For two typical amphetamines, Desoxyn and Biphetamine, the number of prescriptions in 1990 was roughly one-third of what it was in 1986. The popularity of prescribing amphetamines continued to decline throughout the 1990s and into the twenty-first century. Today, the amphetamines have very few widely accepted medical uses. Reference guides such as the *Physician's Desk Reference* usually list two of them, amphetamine sulfate and dextroamphetamine sulfate, as having medical and psychiatric utility only for narcolepsy (involuntarily falling asleep during inappropriate moments), a short-term treatment for obesity, and hyperactivity with attention deficit disorder. However, the first of these conditions is rare, and most physicians seek means other than amphetamine for the other two. No amphetamine derivative has appeared on the list of the country's top 200 prescription drugs for more than 20 years. (The generic equivalent of Ritalin, methylphenidate, which is a stimulant, dropped from 178th in sales in 2001 to 285th in 2004; it is prescribed for attention deficit disorder.)

A type of illicit amphetamine use, which has existed for decades, is practiced by recreational multiple drug users, who take speed in combination with other drugs, especially alcohol, marijuana, barbiturates, or Quāālude. Amphetamines are simply one of a variety of psychoactive drugs taken by users to get high. A recreational multiple drug user might take two to four 10- or 20-milligram tablets or capsules at a time. The data from the Monitoring the Future study indicate a peak for the recreational use of amphetamines during the early 1980s, with annual prevalence rates for high school seniors of 21 percent (for 1980), 26 percent (1981), and 20 percent (1982); a decline into the early 1990s, with annual rates of 7 percent (for 1992), 8 percent (1993), and 9 percent (1994); and 9–11 percent throughout the late 1990s and into the twenty-first century (1996–2005). Clearly, amphetamine use among the young does not seem to be disappearing: Between 2000 and 2005, roughly twice as many high school seniors took amphetamines as took cocaine—annual rates of 9–11 percent versus 5 percent. On the other hand, the nation's youth does not seem to be "swamped" by the use of stimulants. The national household surveys show lifetime figures for the nonmedical use of stimulants for the population as a whole of 9 percent for 1979 (Fishburne, Abelson, and Cisin, 1980, pp. 85–87), 9 percent for 1982 (Miller et al., 1983, pp. 59–61), 9 percent for 1985 (NIDA, 1986), 7 percent for 1991 (NIDA, 1991, p. 61), 7 percent for 2000 (SAMHSA, 2001, p. 132), and 8 percent for 2005 (SAMHSA, 2006b). The use of the drug persists, but in comparison with marijuana, on average, it is used at a much more moderate level.

## Physical and Psychological Effects

Is amphetamine harmful? A pattern of heavy, compulsive amphetamine abuse inevitably has a dramatic impact on the user's life, mind, and body. (Keep in mind that route of administration plays a role in medical harm, independent of the specific drug that is taken; both injecting and smoking—of *any* drug—carry with them potential hazards not encountered in safer methods, such as oral ingestion.) Taking substantial quantities of a strong stimulant, combined with chronic sleeplessness, produces a state of hyperactivity and hyperexcitement. Amphetamine is a vasoconstrictor, which means it shrinks the diameter of blood vessels. Hence, blood pressure is elevated, and the heart has to work harder to maintain a constant supply of blood to the body. Researchers also believe that the "amphetamine psychosis" is an *inevitable* accompaniment of high-dose amphetamine abuse. Its features include paranoia, fearfulness, a tendency toward violence, a schizophrenia-like psychosis, hallucinations, delusions, disordered thinking, mania, and wild mood swings. One medical observer has noted that "anyone given a large enough dose" of amphetamine "for a long enough period of time will become psychotic" (Kramer, 1969, p. 10). Contemporary experts agree (McKim, 2007).

Another feature of heavy amphetamine use is the development of certain behavioral fixations, which are repeated over and over again, such as picking at bits of dust in a rug or spending a whole night counting the cornflakes in a cereal box. This repetitive activity is called **punding** (users refer to it as "getting hung up" on something); it can be induced in laboratory animals. One "speed freak" (as compulsive, high-dose users of amphetamines have been called) I interviewed told me of a fellow user who had spent two years engaged in covering an entire wall with heads of George Washington, carefully cut out from cancelled postage stamps; supposedly, he had pasted 60,000 of these figures on the wall. Punding is also related to compulsive jaw and teeth grinding, which can result in extensive dental damage if use is prolonged. In addition, some chronic, compulsive users feel the sensation of bugs crawling under their skin; some feel so disturbed by this that they tear open their skin to get at the nonexistent bugs.

Is amphetamine addicting? Does it produce a physical dependence in the same way as the narcotics and the sedatives and alcohol? Discontinuing the use of amphetamine after taking it in quantity over a period of time does produce **withdrawal symptoms,** but they do not closely resemble those associated with withdrawal distress from using heroin or the barbiturates. Amphetamine withdrawal consists of severe depression—often to the point of becoming obsessed with suicide—as well as anxiety, fatigue, lethargy, lassitude, sleeplessness, nightmares, irritability, fear, and even terror (Grinspoon and Hedblom, 1975, pp. 153–160).

If addiction is defined by or equated with the "classic" withdrawal syndrome described in Chapter 1, then amphetamine is not addicting; that is, it does not—typically—produce muscular spasms, vomiting, or (as with alcohol and barbiturates, at least) the possibility of cardiac arrest and death. On the other hand, the withdrawal symptoms that are produced by amphetamine are serious, and many of them occur reliably. It is possible that what we refer to as addicting or physically dependency producing is characteristic only of the narcotics and the general depressants, and that other drugs produce a somewhat different set of withdrawal symptoms—and so a somewhat different type of physical dependency (Grinspoon and Hedblom, 1975, p. 153). Thus, whether a given drug such as amphetamine, which does not produce a classic withdrawal syndrome, is addicting seems in part a matter of semantics. Moreover, amphetamine, especially if smoked or taken intravenously is *strongly* reinforcing, and thus causes a powerful psychological dependence that is nearly as strong as cocaine's. Consequently, the question of whether amphetamine is literally physically addicting may be somewhat irrelevant, since heavy, chronic users display a pattern of behavioral dependence that seems to be identical to that of persons who are physically addicted to drugs such as heroin or the barbiturates. Clearly, it makes little difference whether users are technically physically addicted in the classic sense or not.

## METHAMPHETAMINE

Methamphetamine is a more potent sister of the amphetamines. Unlike the amphetamines, however, since it is more reinforcing, methamphetamine use tends to escalate—far more rapidly—to high-dose, compulsive abuse. This is less a function of the direct action of these two drugs than of their route of administration: The amphetamines are usually taken orally via capsule or sniffed in powder form, while methamphetamine, in powder form, is injected, snorted, or smoked. At one time, a type of methamphetamine was prescribed under the brand name Methedrine; it is no longer legally manufactured in the United States. (Another methamphetamine is currently marketed in pill form under the brand name Desoxyn.) In the 1960s, the Methedrine found on the street was manufactured mainly in illicit, clandestine laboratories, often in Mexico, although some was stolen from legal labs. At that time, Methedrine was injected intravenously in high doses; a sizable "speed scene" developed, which involved tens of thousands of youths taking huge doses day in and day out. Use peaked around 1967 and declined sharply after that. Many speed freaks at the time eventually became heroin addicts because they alternated the use of methamphetamine (a stimulant) with heroin (a depressant), so that they could "come down" from their Methedrine high. They began to use more and more heroin and less and less methamphetamine, and eventually, the heroin took over. Considering the way that Methedrine was used by speed freaks, heroin turned out to be a safer, easier drug to take, and it had a less deleterious impact on their lives.

Although the street speed scene did not last very long, it had a tremendous impact on its participants' lives. What was it like? The speed freak of the late 1960s took Methedrine or amphetamine to get high. More specifically, the drug was injected intravenously (IV) to achieve a "flash" or "rush," whose sensation was likened to a "full-body orgasm" or a jolt of electricity. Extremely large quantities of the drug were taken. While 5–10 milligrams of Dexedrine or Dexamyl taken orally via tablet or capsule would represent a typical thera-peutic or instrumental dose, the speed freak would inject as much as a half or even full gram (500–1,000 milligrams!) in one dose. Such massive doses of speed would cause uncon-sciousness or even death in a nonhabituated person but a pleasurable rush in the experienced user. Since amphetamine inhibits sleep, IV administration causes extended periods of wakefulness, often two to five days at a stretch (called a "run"), if the drug is injected into the user's system every four hours or so. This would be followed by long periods of sleep ("crashing"), often lasting up to 24 hours.

In the late 1980s, methamphetamine (now nicknamed "ice") made a comeback, beginning in Hawaii and spreading to California. The current form of methamphetamine is considerably

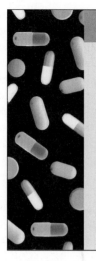

## True-False Quiz

In my quiz, I asked whether the following statement is true or false: "The use of methamphetamine (crystal, crank, speed, or ice) is evenly spread across the country; people are just as likely to use it in Washington and New York as they are in Los Angeles and Honolulu." That statement is false, as we see in this section; in fact, methamphetamine is used almost not at all in East Coast cities and a great deal in cities in the West. Only 41 percent of my students thought that this statement is true, while 58 percent said that it was false. In short, judging by my students' responses, it is a myth that does not seem to have much credibility. Still, in the 1980s, when the alleged popularity of methamphetamine was extolled in the media, that "nationwide scourge" image was widely disseminated; it seems, however, that the myth did not catch on.

more potent than its older version. (Its manufacture involves an additional chemical process in which ephedrine, a heart and central nervous system stimulant, is used.) Its effects are fairly long, lasting up to 12 hours; its half-life is at least as long; and it takes two days to be totally eliminated from the body. Its relatively slow breakdown rate means that if taken daily, accumulation can occur. This both boosts the effect of each subsequent dose and potentiates serious organic harm. Unlike the 1960s version, which was injected IV, in the late 1980s and beyond, methamphetamine has most often been smoked.

## Is There an "Ice" Epidemic?

As we saw in Chapter 5, every decade or two, a particular drug or drug type is designated by the media as, in the words of criminologist Ronald Akers, the "scary drug of the year." A panic is generated about its use: A tidal wave of abuse has hit or is about to hit our shores, these stories assert, and we should be prepared. In the 1930s, that drug was marijuana; in the 1960s, it was LSD; in the late 1970s, it was PCP; in 1985–1990, it was crack cocaine. Just as the crack scare had begun to die down, a terrifying "demon" emerged: methamphetamine. In every case, the headlines were exaggerated. Experts do not doubt the dangers attendant upon compulsive drug use, but they do argue that the "scary drugs" are not nearly as harmful, nor are they likely to be used as compulsively or as widely, as most of these headlines claimed. Sober, systematic evidence eventually revealed that the vast majority of episodes of PCP use did not result in self-destructive or violent behavior, that neither LSD nor crack use by expectant mothers produced birth defects in their babies, and that very few crack users engaged in the "inferno of addiction" described by the press. And now, the proclamations that smoking marijuana causes, as was claimed in the 1930s, a frenzy of violence and insanity, are regarded as laughable.

What of methamphetamine? *Is* the country awash in "ice"? Has "crystal meth" become the drug of choice for our younger generation? Is it as dependency producing as the headlines proclaimed? What evidence do criminologists, epidemiologists, and sociologists have of the use of this powerfully reinforcing drug?

As we saw from the ADAM (Arrestee Drug Abuse Monitoring) figures in Chapter 6, the use of ice is highly regionalized, *much* more so than for any other drug. Arrestees in Hawaii and California (and a few cities in other states where dealers have begun distributing the drug) frequently test positive for methamphetamine, but its use is extremely rare, and even nonexistent, in most other locales around the country. In 2003, in Oahu County, in which Honolulu is located, 4 out of 10 arrestees tested positive for the presence of meth; and in the counties in which Phoenix, Sacramento, San Diego, and San Jose are located, over 3 in 10 tested positive. For a substantial number of other western urban counties, roughly 1 in 5 of arrestees did as well. In other words, methamphetamine abuse is an enormous problem in much of the West and in some parts of the Midwest (in Missouri and Nebraska, for example). However, that year, the figure was between 0 and 1 percent for arrestees in nearly all the urban counties along the eastern seaboard.

In addition, the Monitoring the Future (MTF) survey does not show widespread use of methamphetamine. The *lifetime* prevalence figures for "ice" for high school seniors in 1990, when the MTF began asking questions about "ice," was 2.7 percent; in 2005, this figure was 4.0 percent. For *annual* prevalence, the figures were 1.3 and 2.3 percent, respectively. The percentage of high school seniors who took "ice" during the previous month ("current" use) was 0.6 percent in 1990 and 0.9 percent in 2005. (The figures are slightly different if MTF researchers ask about methamphetamine instead of "ice." MTF only began asking about "methamphetamine" in 1999.) Only 4.3 percent of SAMHSA's 2004 National Survey on Drug Use and Health said that they had used methamphetamine once or more during their lives; only 0.6 said that they had done so in the past year, and only 0.2 percent in the past month. The last of these figures represents a bit more than half a million people. It is entirely possible, however, that heavy, chronic methamphetamine abusers did not fall into SAMHSA's sample.

In addition, in 2003, DAWN failed to come up with strikingly high medical examiners' (ME, or death by "overdose") statistics for methamphetamine. Even in the communities that recorded high ADAM positives for arrestees, methamphetamine mentions were significantly below those for heroin, cocaine, and alcohol-in-combination. In Phoenix, meth was mentioned in 132 drug-related deaths; the figures for cocaine in that same city were 209; for alcohol, 190; and for heroin, 169. In San Francisco, meth garnered 38 mentions versus 95 for heroin, 90 for cocaine, and 52 for alcohol. Only in San Diego was meth (81 mentions) ahead of even one of the "Big Three" drugs. In addition, in nearly 9 out of 10 (88%) ME cases in which methamphetamine was mentioned as a factor in the drug-related overdose, at least one other drug was mentioned as well. In no urban county that appeared in DAWN's program for 2003 was methamphetamine the leading cause or even a contributing factor in overdose deaths. In contrast, DAWN's data for methamphetamine-related emergency department (ED) visits showed a spectacular increase between 2001 (14,923) and 2004 (73,400). It's possible that DAWN's more complete system of reporting is responsible for this change: In 2001, its catchment area for ED visits was mainly urban, while in 2004, its data were more representative of the country as a whole—and meth's users tend to live in smaller communities than do users of drugs such as cocaine and heroin.

In short, systematic evidence does not suggest that the nationwide epidemic predicted for methamphetamine abuse (Labianca, 1992; Lerner, 1989; Young, 1989) has yet materialized. There is no indication that the country as a whole is "awash" in meth, although clearly the abuse of "ice" is the most serious drug problem in many communities and in certain regions of the country. Let's be clear about this point: Methamphetamine is an extremely dangerous drug. Many users become dependent on it, and its use causes or is associated with a wide range of medical pathologies. But most regions of the United States are not experiencing a methamphetamine epidemic, most social categories in the population have little or no experience with drug, nowhere is it causing as many deaths as the "Big Three" drugs, and its use is not increasing over time. (Only one indicator points to a sharp rise in use: emergency room visits.) In looking at the phenomenon of drug abuse, it is important not to fall victim to media hype. Basing drug policy on mistaken information can all too often do more harm than good.

## COCAINE

Of all drugs, cocaine's acute or immediate effects are most similar to those of amphetamine; actually, in laboratory studies, injected experimental subjects cannot tell the difference between the two (Goldstein, 2001, p. 180; McKee, 2007; Van Dyke and Byck, 1982, p. 128). Cocaine's effects, however, are more transient; they last no more than a half hour, whereas the effects of a sufficiently large dose of amphetamine will last several hours. It should come as no surprise, therefore, that cocaine is broken down in the body much more swiftly than amphetamine; its half-life is roughly an hour. Cocaine's effects are also said by users to be more subtle; it is more of a "head" drug, whereas amphetamine is described as more of a "body" drug. Unlike amphetamine, however, cocaine is a local or topical anesthetic. This means that it kills pain upon contact with organic tissue. It can be useful in conjunction with operations on organs with extremely delicate, sensitive nerves, such as the human eye. Since cocaine's role as a recreational drug has become clear to physicians, another drug, usually lidocaine, which has cocaine's anesthetic but not its psychoactive property, has been used for this purpose. For its potential as a topical anesthetic, in spite of its extensive abuse, cocaine remains a Schedule II drug.

### A Brief History

The use of cocaine, at least in its natural form of coca leaves, dates back at least 2,000 years, and possibly as much as 5,000 years (Van Dyke and Byck, 1982, p. 128). The coca (not cocoa) plant grows in the Andes Mountains of South America, and its leaves contain from less than 1 percent to as much as 1.8 percent cocaine (p. 130). Indians living in the region chew the leaves of the coca bush to offset fatigue and hunger, and they can work long hours without stopping as a result of the drug's effects. The ancient Incan civilization regarded the coca plant as divine; one of the gods they worshipped was "Mama Coca."

Because the drug was taken in a natural and extremely low-potency form, its effects were largely beneficial. There is no archaeological or anthropological evidence that this practice did any harm to the indigenous Andean peoples who engaged in it. The Catholic Church regarded coca's worship, and even its use as an abomination, and tried to stamp out both. However, beginning in the mid-1500s, the Spanish crown recognized that Indians refused to work in the silver mines unless they were paid in coca leaves. In order for the king to earn his fifth share from the silver mine profits, the use of coca had to be tolerated. Hence, the church's appeal to ban the drug fell on deaf ears (Streatfeild, 2001, pp. 28–36). Coca leaves made their way to Europe, where scientists and physicians studied their effects.

Cocaine was extracted from coca leaves in about 1860. (The exact date and the scientist who first achieved this feat are in dispute.) Cocaine was hailed as a wonder drug by much of the medical profession, including Sigmund Freud, who recommended it as a cure for digestive disorders, anemia, typhoid fever, narcotic addiction, alcoholism, asthma, and sexual unresponsiveness. He soon regretted his endorsement of the drug, however: His close friend Ernst von Fleischl-Marxow became a cocaine addict as a result of Freud's medical care. "Unwittingly, Freud had created the first cocaine addict" (Streatfeild, 2001, p. 85).

Cocaine, in the form of coca leaves, was a major ingredient in many popular beverages sold in the late nineteenth and early twentieth centuries. Mariani's Coca Wine was one of the most popular of these; its manufacturer published 13 *volumes* of testimonials by prominent users (including President William McKinley, Thomas Edison, Pope Leo XIII, Pope Pius X, King Oscar II of Sweden and Norway, and writers Jules Verne and H.G. Wells) singing the praises of this concoction (Andrews and Solomon, 1975, pp. 243–246). Coca-Cola, too, contained the extract of coca leaves until the early twentieth century, when it was removed because of pressure applied "by Southerners who feared blacks' getting cocaine in any form" (Ashley, 1975, p. 46). Extracts of coca leaves still make up one of Coca-Cola's many ingredients—but only after the cocaine has been removed.

Indeed, a major reason for cocaine's legal downfall in the United States, some observers argue, was racism. Although there is *no* reliable information documenting that African-Americans were more likely to use cocaine than whites were at the turn of the century, some whites feared that this was so—and that Blacks were especially dangerous and violent while under the influence. The fact that this myth was believed by certain elements in the white majority brought the drug under state and federal control. Numerous articles were written just after the turn of the century claiming that cocaine stimulated violent behavior in African-Americans. In 1903, *The New York Tribune* quoted on Col. J.W. Watson of Georgia as saying that "many of the horrible crimes committed in the Southern States by the colored people can be traced directly to the cocaine habit." Dr. Christopher Koch asserted, in an article published in the *Literary Digest* in 1914, that "most of the attacks upon white women of the South are a direct result of a cocaine-crazed Negro brain." Even the staid *New York Times* published an article on February 8, 1914, titled "Negro Cocaine Fiends Are a New Southern Menace," which detailed the "race menace," "cocaine orgies," and "wholesale murders," by "hitherto inoffensive" Blacks, "running amuck in a cocaine frenzy." (These articles are summarized in Ashley, 1975; Grinspoon and Bakalar, 1976; and Musto, 1999.) These articles were based on no more than racist fantasy, of course, but they reflected the wave of panic, fear, and racial hostility that led to the inclusion of cocaine as a narcotic in the Harrison Act of 1914.

"All the elements needed to insure cocaine's outlaw status were present by the first years of the twentieth century: It had become widely used as a pleasure drug . . . ; it had become identified with despised or poorly regarded groups—blacks, lower-class whites, and criminals; it had not been long enough established in the culture to insure its survival; and it had not . . . become identified with the elite, thus losing what little chance it had of weathering the storm" (Ashley, 1975, p. 74). By the time of the Harrison Act, 46 states had already passed laws attempting to control cocaine (only 29 had done so with the opiates). This indicates that cocaine was seen by many legislators as the major drug problem at that time. It seems almost inconceivable that a major force behind this legislation was not at least in part related to racial hostility toward African-Americans on the part of the white majority. Such images as were expressed in the newspaper articles published at the time could not have taken root had racial prejudice not already been ingrained among a substantial pro-portion of American whites.

It is impossible to know with any degree of certainty or accuracy just how frequently cocaine was used in the years following its criminalization. We have anecdotes and often-hysterical newspaper stories, but no reliable information. Cocaine is frequently mentioned as the drug of choice (after alcohol, of course) among rarified, elite social circles in the 1920s. But after that came "The Great Drought." "Virtually every source I have consulted," wrote Richard Ashley, "agrees that cocaine use was insignificant during the 1930s" (p. 105). Most other observers agree; Dominic Streatfeild (2001, pp. 174ff) titled his chapter on cocaine's use in the 1930s "Down . . . But Not Out." Its use remained confined to a very tiny number of Americans more or less into the 1960s.

Historian Paul Gootenberg claims that the federal government "created" the contemporary cocaine problem by simultaneously driving cocaine labs out of business yet supporting the Stepan chemical works, the firm that extracts the cocaine from coca leaves (Gootenberg, 2004; Streatfeild, 2001, pp. 188–194). How the behavior of a few officials could have deterred the drug-taking behavior of millions of users or what driving cocaine labs out of business had to do with having "eradicated" cocaine "altogether" (p. 192) is not clear. (Illicit drug operations can crop up with any twist and turn in the demand for an illegal product.)

In any case, during the 1960s, as we've seen, the cocaine explosion occurred—paralleling the marijuana explosion, though, of course, on a much smaller scale. Use rose from 1960, when there was a 1 percent lifetime figure for young adults ages 18–25, to a 28 percent lifetime figure. The 30-day prevalence figure for young adults in 1974, the first year that that statistic was tabulated and published, was 3 percent; by 1979, it had tripled to 9 percent, but in the 1990s, it declined to between 1 and 2 percent. Tables 10-1 and 10-2 detail the rise,

**TABLE 10-1**    **Use of Cocaine among Young Adults (18–25), Selected Years, 1960–2004**

|  | Lifetime | Past Year | Past Month |
|---|---|---|---|
| 1960 | 1% | * | * |
| 1967 | 2 | * | * |
| 1972 | 9 | * | * |
| 1974 | 13 | 8% | 3% |
| 1977 | 19 | 10 | 4 |
| 1979 | 28 | 20 | 9 |
| 1982 | 28 | 19 | 7 |
| 1985 | 25 | 16 | 8 |
| 1991 | 18 | 8 | 2 |
| 1995 | 10 | 4 | 1 |
| 1998 | 10 | 5 | 2 |
| 2000 | 11 | 4 | 1 |
| 2005 | 15 | 7 | 3 |

*Figure not tabulated.

*Source:* National Household Survey on Drug Abuse and National Survey on Drug Use and Health for the relevant year; 1960 and 1967 figures, Miller and Cisin, 1980, p. 17. Note that in 2002, the National Survey on Drug Abuse and Health changed its survey methodology; hence, the figures after that year are slightly higher than in prior surveys.

| TABLE 10-2 | Use of Cocaine among High School Seniors, Selected Years, 1975–2005 | | |
|---|---|---|---|
| | **Lifetime** | **Past Year** | **Past Month** |
| 1975 | 9% | 9% | 2% |
| 1980 | 16 | 12 | 5 |
| 1985 | 17 | 13 | 7 |
| 1990 | 9 | 5 | 2 |
| 1995 | 6 | 4 | 2 |
| 2000 | 9 | 5 | 2 |
| 2005 | 8 | 5 | 2 |

*Source:* Johnston et al., 2006.

decline, and stabilization of cocaine use among 18- to 25-year-olds and high school seniors. As the data show, there was something of a cocaine "epidemic" between the late 1970s and the mid-to-late 1980s, but it had subsided by the early 1990s.

## Route of Administration and Resulting Effects

Most users of powdered cocaine sniff or "snort" the drug. Often, they chop the drug into fine lines with a razor blade on a smooth surface and sharply inhale each line, usually one to a nostril, often through a straw or a rolled-up bill. Another method is scooping up the powder with tiny "coke spoon," placing it directly under the nostril, and snorting the powder up out of the spoon. Occasionally, users with at least one long fingernail will scoop up the powder on that nail, convey it to a nostril, and snort it off the nail. Or users might snort cocaine off the crook of their hand, between the thumb and the index finger.

In the 1980s, two other methods became more common—freebasing and injecting— although, even then, they were atypical when compared with snorting. Freebase is a substance that is the product of dissolving cocaine in an alkaline solution and boiling it; a volatile chemical such as ether is also used. What remains is a purer, more potent form of the drug. More specifically, what is referred to as "pure" cocaine is really cocaine hydrochloride; freebase is actually pure cocaine, with the hydrochloride salt removed, which is 90 percent pure cocaine. (Cocaine hydrochloride is more stable, and hence has a longer shelf life; freebase is more volatile and unstable.) Freebase cocaine is smoked or, more properly, heated and the vapors then inhaled. Freebase declined in popularity after 1985, when the use of "crack" became widespread. As we'll see, chemically, crack is very different from freebase, although both are smoked. Cocaine hydrochloride can be smoked, but the temperature required for its vaporization is higher than it is for crack cocaine, and so the practice is less common.

At this point, it is necessary to refer back to our old friend, route of administration. The Indians who chew coca leaves have a vastly different (and far safer) experience with cocaine than the Americans who snort cocaine; likewise, persons who inject or smoke the drug, again, are having a very different drug experience. Both injecting and smoking cocaine, as we already know, are far more efficient and effective means of delivering a drug to the bloodstream than is snorting. With smoking, the high hits 6–8 seconds after inhaling; with injecting, the time lag is 12–15 seconds. Both produce an intense "rush," a flash of extreme, orgasmlike pleasure that is even more powerful than the rush from cocaine taken intranasally. Injecting and freebasing cocaine are not only dangerous in themselves but are associated with and more likely to generate frequent, heavy, chronic use. Two experts argue that snorting cocaine results in "a pattern of continued use while supplies are available and in simple abstention when supplies are lacking. . . . It may interfere with other activities but it may a source of enjoyment as well." In stark contrast, injecting or smoking coke can often lead to "almost continual consumption and drug-seeking behavior, destructive to personal competence and productivity" (Van Dyke and Byck, 1982, p. 140).

What is the appeal of cocaine? Four researchers (Erickson et al., 1987, p. 79) assert that cocaine's appeal is greater than that of any other drug, licit or illicit; most users would probably agree. There is a feeling toward cocaine among many recreational drug users that borders on reverence and awe; cocaine has been referred to as "the champagne of drugs" and the "caviar among drugs." Poet Michael McClure dubbed it "The Ace of Sunlight." As we already know, the cocaine intoxication is extremely pleasurable; behavioral psychologists refer to it as reinforcing, more so than for any other known drug, including heroin. As I've noted, laboratory animals will give up food, sex, and water for self-administered doses of cocaine, and they will even starve themselves to death to continue receiving cocaine instead of food (Brady and Lucas, 1984; Clouet, Asghar, and Brown, 1988; Johanson, 1984). Of course, these experiments were conducted on laboratory animals and not humans, who, presumably, are governed by a more conscious will than are other species. We should not, in other words, adhere rigidly to the **monkey model of addiction** to understand drug-related behavior among humans (Wilbanks, 1992). Moreover, humans do not necessarily take cocaine via the same route of administration as that forced upon laboratory animals—that is, intravenously—and, as we know, route of administration strongly influences a drug's effects. The responses of lab rats to cocaine notwithstanding, we do not know that humans will necessarily do the same thing. However, from these studies, we do have a clue that, even among humans, cocaine has the *potential* to generate a strong psychological dependency—in all likelihood, more so than for any other drug. (Remember, laboratory animals generally refuse to become intoxicated on alcohol, and yet this experience is extremely popular among humans.) When all is said and done, cocaine is extremely reinforcing for both humans and animals. Cocaine's principal effects are exhilaration, elation, and euphoria—voluptuous, joyous feelings accompanied by a sense of grandiosity. William Burroughs, a novelist who was once addicted to heroin and who has tried just about every drug known to humankind, described taking cocaine as "electricity to the brain."

Another common effect of the drug is confidence—a sense of mastery of and competence in what one does and is. Yet another effect is increased energy and a suppression of fatigue, causing a stimulation of the ability to continue physical and mental activity more intensely and for a longer time. As we saw, Indian workers in South America can endure ordinarily exhausting conditions without food or rest for days on end because of the effects of the coca leaves they chew. We've also seen that Robert Louis Stevenson, a sickly man, wrote *The Strange Case of Dr. Jekyll and Mr. Hyde,* a 60,000-word novel, in just three days under the influence of cocaine. (To be more exact, he wrote one version in three days, was dissatisfied with it, tore it up, and wrote another version in three days.) And users frequently assert that in small doses, cocaine is an aphrodisiac for them; however, research shows that if it is taken in large doses or used frequently over long periods of time, the sexual urge is inhibited, not stimulated (Siegel, 1982).

## Quality, Availability, Price, and Usage

Today, cocaine is far more abundant and cheaper, and its purity is greater, than was true a decade ago. In 2001, the Abt Associates, a research group under contract with the federal Office of National Drug Control Policy, estimated that the average price of a gram of cocaine, at the less-than-gram-level purchase, declined from $423 nationwide in 1981 to $212 in 2000 (in 2000 dollars). In that same 20-year period, the purity of that gram increased from 36 percent cocaine to 61 percent. In other words, while the purchase price of a gram of cocaine in 2000 was one-half of what it was in 1981, its purity increased by about 70 percent (Rhodes, Johnston, and Kling, 2001, p. 43). Clearly, the government's interdiction efforts have been a failure; cocaine is cheaper, purer, and more abundant than it has been for quite some time—perhaps since the drug was criminalized more than eight decades ago. What impact has this lower cost, greater purity, and greater availability had on actual use patterns?

According to the data collected by the Monitoring the Future survey, the peak year for among cocaine use among high school seniors was 1985, when lifetime prevalence reached 17 percent, annual prevalence was 13 percent, and 30-day prevalence was a remarkable 7 percent. In the past two decades, these figures have diminished considerably—to 8 percent, 5 percent, and 2 percent, respectively. The National Survey on Drug Use and Health shows a decline for all categories in the population in cocaine use between the 1980s and the early twenty-first century. In 1985, there were an estimated 5.7 million current users (those who used within the past month); by 2005, this figure had declined to 2 million. (In a study for the Office of National Drug Control Policy, an agency of the White House, the Abt Associates estimated that there are 2.8 million chronic cocaine users in the United States.) Clearly, then, there has been a significant decline in the recreational use of cocaine in the American population since 1985. Interestingly, the national survey also warns that, since 1985, the frequent use of cocaine (use on more than 50 occasions over the past year) has remained stable or even increased somewhat. And as we've seen, the national survey is likely to underestimate the number of heavy, chronic users of cocaine (and heroin), since they often do not live in households.

We're already familiar with DAWN, the Drug Abuse Warning Network, which tracks both nonlethal and lethal drug-related episodes over time; specifically, the two types of episodes on which data are gathered are emergency department (ED) episodes (such as suicide attempts and untoward psychic effects) and medical examiner (ME) reports (that is, deaths in which drugs are a direct causal or contributing factor). We learned that DAWN's data are unstandardized with respect to a number of factors, and hence should be used with great caution (Caulkins, Ebener, and McCaffrey, 1995; Ungerleider et al., 1980). In 1996, DAWN issued a report on ED episodes that standardized its databases, which means that we can be fairly confident that the yearly trends it reports are valid. From 1978 to 1994, cocaine-related ED episodes increased almost astronomically, from 3,400 to 142,900. At latest tally (2004), this figure was 383,350, an increase of two and a half. (But remember, as we saw in Chapter 6, DAWN's 2004 ED data are much more complete than for any other year, so the increase is probably an artifact of improved data collection.) The trend during this period has continued to be almost uniformly and sharply upward. Although DAWN has not as of this writing performed this same data standardization for this entire period for lethal overdoses (or ME reports), it did provide these figures for 1991–1995. In the areas studied, in 1991, 2,938 dead bodies were found in which cocaine was believed to be a cause of or a contributing factor in the death; in 2002, in DAWN's catchment area, 4,024 people died directly or indirectly as a result of ingesting cocaine. No other drug (or even major drug type) produced as many "overdoses" as this alluring, seductive substance.

## Is Cocaine Addicting?

Cocaine is similar to the amphetamines in that it does not produce what is referred to as "classic" **drug addiction;** that is, there are no heroinlike physical withdrawal symptoms—nausea, vomiting, severe aches and pains, muscular twitching and spasms, and so on—upon discontinuation of heavy, long-term use. However, psychological consequences, including depression, irritability, restlessness, agitation, fatigue, and, of course, craving, often follow discontinuing the use of this drug. Some observers suggest a biochemical basis for this syndrome (Wesson and Smith, 1977). Many users claim that cocaine is a safe, extremely nontoxic drug; this is partly true and partly false. Cocaine, if taken occasionally (say, less than weekly), in moderate doses, causes little if any physical or mental damage (Van Dyke and Byck, 1982). However, this pattern of use, and its attendant relative safety, has mainly to do with the drug's cost, according to many contemporary experts. Even today, the regular use of cocaine represents a substantial financial investment. Some heavy users can go through an ounce or more of powder cocaine in a week; they find its effects so pleasurable that taking cocaine once in a while is not enough—they want to take it again and again. Using it more than occasionally is prohibitively expensive for the average recreational drug user, and thus its cost, in all likelihood, keeps its heavy use down. At the same time, remember that the price of cocaine has declined considerably in the past decade or so, yet the drug's use has also declined. Clearly, cost is not the only factor here.

In sum, when we consider cocaine's addicting or dependency-producing properties, we should not get hung up on semantics—that is, on what words mean—rather than focusing on what is happening in the real world. What do we mean when we ask whether cocaine is addicting? Are we asking if cocaine produces the same withdrawal symptoms as heroin? The answer would have to be *no,* cocaine is not addicting. On the other hand, if we ask whether it is possible for a sizable proportion of users to develop a craving so intense that they will give up many of the things they value—money, possessions, relationships, jobs, and careers—in order to continue taking the drug, then the answer is an emphatic *yes,* cocaine is addicting. To put it in more precise current terminology: Many users develop a **behavioral dependence** on cocaine that is as strong as for drugs that are clearly physically addicting, such as heroin and alcohol. This does not mean, however, that it is cocaine's biochemistry, and that alone, that determines the user's patterns of use. Pharmacology alone does not determine how a drug is used. The social and personal characteristics of the user also make a great deal of difference.

As David Smith, a physician and founder of the Haight-Ashbury Free Medical Clinic, says: "What you're taking does not matter as much as who you are. Some people will take the drug—any drug—and not get addicted. Others will take it once and be inexorably drawn to it. The drug is the same, the people are different. . . . Interestingly," Smith adds, "the person who is addicted to cocaine responds differently the very first time he [or she] uses it. Later he'll [or she'll] use terms that are qualitatively different from those that others use to describe the experience of taking cocaine the first time: 'This is the greatest thing that's ever happened to me,' or words to that effect." Smith estimates that the proportion of more or less regular users of powdered cocaine who become behaviorally dependent on the drug is roughly 1 in 10, the same as with alcohol. In addition, Smith estimates that 30–40 percent will experience at least one episode of dysfunction—a seizure, a coke binge that makes them sick, or some other adverse reaction. All of this means that some people "can experiment with the drug and not abuse it." Smith is quick to add, however, that this is an extremely dangerous experiment, and certainly not worth the odds (Gonzales, 1984, p. 114).

Ronald Siegel, a psychologist who conducted an eight-year study of cocaine users, agrees, but with one crucial qualification. He distinguishes between cocaine that is taken in powdered form intranasally, or snorted, and cocaine that is smoked. One of Siegel's most remarkable findings was how closely method of consumption and quantity of use were related. It would be naive to say that the way a drug is used determines how much is used; after all, the quantity an individual uses may influence his or her choice of what method to use. Still, it's possible that it works both ways. Intranasal users averaged 20 milligrams per administration if a coke spoon was used and 50 milligrams if "lines" were used; taken together, users who employed one or both of these methods averaged between 1 and 3 grams per week. In contrast, smokers averaged 100 milligrams per administration (or "hit") and 1.5 grams per day, nearly seven times as much. The temporal spacing of hits, the total duration of a smoking episode, and hence the total quantity of use varied enormously for smokers. For some, hits were taken every five minutes for periods ranging from a half-hour to four days straight. Consumption ranged from 1 gram to 30 grams during a 24-hour period; one subject in the study consumed 150 grams (roughly a third of a *pound*) in a 72-hour period! For compulsive users, smoking continued until supplies of the drug were depleted or the user simply fell asleep from exhaustion (Siegel, 1984, p. 100). In spite of smoker variability in use, however, smokers nearly always consumed more cocaine than snorters.

For social-recreational users, negative effects of use were reported in 40 percent of episodes; these included restlessness, irritability, perceptual disturbances, an inability to concentrate, fatigue, lassitude, and nasal problems. Smokers reported one or more of these reactions in 71 percent of their episodes of use. None of these social-recreational users reported the more serious physical or psychological reactions. On the other hand, in roughly 10 percent of the intoxications, smokers experienced severe toxic reactions, including chest pains, nausea or vomiting, difficulty in breathing, seizures, convulsions, a loss of consciousness, and hallucinations with "violent loss of impulse control." In addition, psychomotor agitation, depression, paranoia, and even attempted suicide were extremely common (p. 102). In short: "Many of the social-recreational cocaine users do not change their long-term pattern of use and do not appear to develop toxic crisis reactions." Social-recreational users tended to maintain "relatively stable patterns of use [even] when supplies were available." The hypothesis that "long-term use of cocaine is inevitably associated with an escalating dependency marked by more frequent patterns of use is not supported by these findings" (pp. 105, 106). If the drug were less expensive, however, it is possible that it would be used with considerably greater frequency.

A study of 111 Canadian users (Erickson et al., 1987, p. 86) confirms Siegel's findings; users mentioned the drug's cost as its least appealing aspect, even before the risk of addiction, negative social consequences, or adverse physical or psychological effects. In contrast to nonabusive social-recreational users, the minority of subjects whose use did escalate and whose use became compulsive were invariably smokers. They became incapable of controlling their use, became dependent on cocaine, and experienced a wide range of physical and psychological reactions, some of which were life-threatening and required treatment. Extreme paranoia and depression were exceedingly common in this minority (Siegel, 1984).

In another study (Waldorf, Reinarman, and Murphy, 1991), the researchers interviewed 19 cocaine users in 1975 and again 11 years later, in 1986. (The original study included 27 users, but not all of them could be located for the follow-up.) They had been using the drug for an average of three years when the study began; all were social-recreational—in the words of the researchers, "controlled"—users at that time. What happened to their use of cocaine in the intervening 11 years? All began by snorting cocaine and, for the most part, stuck with this route of administration. Five of them injected cocaine less than a half dozen times, and three freebased, but they returned to snorting because, by freebasing, they recognized that they could fall into compulsive, uncontrolled use patterns. Six were controlled users throughout the 1975–1986 period. Seven were heavy users during most of the time between the two interviews, but they had eased into a controlled pattern by 1986. Two were controlled users through most of that time but ended up abstainers, and three were heavy users who also became abstainers. Only one was a heavy user throughout (Waldorf et al., 1991). While the study's sample was small, its findings are suggestive.

We cannot know if these findings reflect cocaine use generally. However, while the proportion of users among the public at large who are in the categories occupied by the researchers' interviewees (heavy, controlled, snorting, injecting, freebasing, and so on) is likely to be quite different from those in this study, the study does point out the inescapable fact that cocaine use does not always or inevitably lead to addiction. "Despite what the popular press would have us believe, there is not *one* inevitable result of beginning to use cocaine—that of inevitable 'addiction' or dependence. . . . Continued and uncontrolled cocaine use is, however, a possible outcome, but so is controlled use" (Murphy, Reinarman, and Waldorf, 1986, p. 17). The authors use the findings of their study to question what they call "pharmaco-economic determinism"—and what I referred to as the **chemicalistic fallacy**—that is, the assumption that "users become powerless before or lose control over their use of a consciousness altering drug" (p. 27).

A very different perspective is presented by research based on treatment populations or callers to cocaine hot lines (Chatlos, 1987; Gold, 1984), which includes mainly or almost exclusively people who are experiencing or have experienced difficulty as a result of their drug use. Consequently, they are unlikely to be typical of users generally. This type of study supports the "inevitability" model that the Waldorf-Reinarman-Murphy team is arguing against. Rather than claiming that drug use sets in motion a kind of inevitable progression in which all experimenters become regular users, who, in turn, become heavy, chronic, and dependent abusers, what makes more sense to these authors is to view the process as a *tendency:* For some users, there is a tendency to escalate to heavier use and to more dangerous drugs; for most users, in contrast, this tendency does not exist. Seeing addiction as an inevitable outcome of use, they add, denies the existence of the power of human free will (Waldorf et al., 1991).

Whereas today it is necessary to warn the public about exaggerations of cocaine's harm and addictive potential, interestingly, two decades ago, something of the reverse was the case. In the 1970s and early 1980s, the dangers of cocaine were hugely *underplayed* by many observers, including some medical experts. Notes Richard Ashley: "No lethal reactions have been reported among illicit users in modern times"; he adds, "There appears no good reason and even less evidence to suggest that cocaine is an especially dangerous drug" (1975, pp. 165, 173). As for dependence, he claims, when the "typical" user discontinues taking cocaine, there is no more "discomfort . . . beyond that which everyone feels when something they like is no longer available"; they take it "on special occasions—in much the same way as those who regularly drink wine with their meals will occasionally treat themselves and their guests to a fine vintage Bordeaux" (p. 173). In a review of the literature at the time (1982) in a prestigious scientific journal, while warning against use by "naive people," Craig Van Dyke and Robert Byck declare: "Medically cocaine is a relatively safe drug" (p. 141). The pattern of using powder cocaine intranasally when it is available, and abstaining when it is not, they say, "is comparable to that experienced by many people with peanuts and potato chips" (p. 140).

Contemporary research shows that cocaine is both far more dangerous (in DAWN's most recent tally, cocaine was implicated in more deaths than any other illicit drug) and more dependency producing (it may rank first in this respect) than these decades-old judgments claimed. There is an object lesson to be learned from all this: While it is rash to declare a drug dangerous before the evidence is in, it is equally inadvisable to claim that a drug is safe before we know the full story of its effects.

## CRACK

In the United States, the widespread use of crack emerged in 1985. Like freebase, crack is a crystalline form of cocaine. Also like freebase, crack is smoked. (Or, as I said earlier, it is heated and the vapors are inhaled into the lungs.) But crack is not freebase. As we saw, what is sold on the street as cocaine is actually cocaine hydrochloride; freebase is pure cocaine—more volatile, more combustible, more dangerous. Between 1970 and 1985, as many as 1 regular cocaine user in 10 smoked freebase, and as frequency of use increased, so did the likelihood of using freebase (and vice versa). With the appearance of crack in 1985, the availability of freebase cocaine declined along with the number of users. In contrast to freebase, crack cocaine is made by soaking cocaine hydrochloride and baking soda and then applying heat. The crystals that are precipitated from this solution are what is called crack or crack cocaine. (Baking soda causes a crackling sound when heated and smoked; presumably, this is the origin of the name.) Unlike freebase, which (without adulterants) is pure cocaine, or cocaine "freed" from its adulterants, crack is impure by its very nature, containing only 30–40 percent cocaine. Most of what's in crack cocaine is baking soda (sodium bicarbonate).

In New York in the 1980s, a $50 gram of powdered cocaine yielded enough crystals for 15 vials, which could be sold for $3–10 each (and up to $40 in small cities); this was a substantial incentive for a dealer to sell crack instead of powder cocaine. Since crack is smoked—that is, it enters the lungs as a vapor—it is used by means of a highly efficient route of administration. Thus, using crack is highly reinforcing in comparison with sniffing powder cocaine. There is no special magic in crack as opposed to powder cocaine that makes it vastly more addicting; pharmacologists cannot distinguish between the two drugs once inside the body. With respect to the intrinsic psychoactive properties of these two forms of cocaine, they are one and the same drug. The difference between them lies not in their biochemistry but in their route of administration. Taking powder cocaine intranasally produces a high that takes roughly three minutes to occur and lasts perhaps a half hour; there is no real rush. As we've seen, injecting the drug produces a high that takes only 12–15 seconds to appear, and the rush is a major attraction of IV administration. However, when cocaine is smoked either in the form of freebase or crack, the onset of the rush is even faster, some 6–8 seconds, and produces an intense, orgasmlike high. This rush lasts for perhaps two minutes, followed by an afterglow that lasts 10–20 minutes. The euphoria achieved is extreme and intense, and it impels many users to want to take the drug over and over again. Many resist its blandishments; some do not. As I said earlier, the reason why the rush is quicker and more intense via smoking is physiological: The drug enters the lung sacs, which are surrounded by capillaries, which convey the drug immediately, and undiluted, to the brain. In contrast, when a drug is injected IV, it enters the bloodstream and is conveyed to the heart, where it is mixed with fresh blood that does not contain the drug; from there, it travels, diluted, to the rest of the body, including the brain. As a consequence, while both methods are efficient and effective means of getting high, smoking has a slight edge over IV administration.

Although crack has been used on a small scale on the West Coast since the early 1980s, and freebase has been smoked at least as far back as the early 1970s, the large-scale, widespread use of crack is more recent. As of mid-1985, its use was still extremely rare. One indication of that fact is that the national hot line for cocaine information and help (1-800-COCAINE) received no calls whatsoever about crack cocaine from its founding until mid-1985, out of a total of one million calls reporting problems with powder cocaine. Just a year later, *half* of all its calls involved crack (Chatlos, 1987, p. 12).

## Myth versus Reality

In spite of the fact that the drug's use virtually exploded within an extremely short period of time, even when its use was growing, the extent of its use was hugely exaggerated by the media. This pattern, as we saw in Chapter 5, is typical when new drugs burst on the national scene; the same thing took place in the 1930s with marijuana, in the 1960s with LSD, in the 1970s with PCP, and in the late 1980s and beyond with methamphetamine. Some of the more sensationalistic newspaper headlines and television news programs implied that all teenagers in the country either used crack or were in imminent danger of doing so, and that every community in the nation was "saturated" by the drug. This is, of course, a gross overstatement. While crack is, indeed, a frightening drug, the facts on the scope of its use are considerably less unsettling than the news media would have us believe.

The Monitoring the Future (MTF) study verifies that, among eighth-, tenth-, and twelfth-graders at least, the national incidence of crack use remains at a fairly low level. (But keep in mind that MTF cannot study dropouts or absentees, whose drug use is likely to be higher than that of students currently enrolled in and attending school. Moreover, drug use is always higher in some communities than others; the MTF survey looks at averages, not extremes.) In 1987, 5.3 percent of all high school seniors had tried crack; by 1991, this

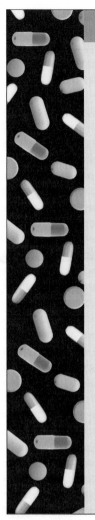

## True-False Quiz

Relevant to the material discussed in this section, I offered three statements about crack cocaine in my true-false quiz: "All other things being equal, women who use crack cocaine during pregnancy have a significantly higher than average likelihood of bearing children with one or more anatomical, neurological, and behavioral disorders and abnormalities"; "It is not possible to take crack cocaine recreationally; anyone who uses crack more than a few times will become addicted to or dependent on it"; and "During the crack epidemic (1985 to 1990), crack cocaine was the most widely used illegal drug in the country." All three of these statements are false, of course, as we see in this section. Taken together, the average rate of agreement for these statements among my students was two-thirds, or 66 percent; however, agreement varied from one statement to another. Nearly all students (93%) agreed that crack cocaine causes congenital abnormalities; just under half (47%) agreed that recreational crack use is impossible; and just over half (57%) agreed with the astoundingly wrong statement that in the late 1980s, crack became the country's most popular illicit drug. We see a parallel between the "crack babies" phenomenon in the 1980s and the supposed birth defect–producing effects of LSD in the 1960s, but both are equally false, although equally memorable. The fact that no one could experiment with or use cocaine recreationally was part of the drug's mythology; the notion that the drug caused an "inferno of desire" was part of its early media mythology and demonology. And, as with Ecstasy, when crack burst on the scene, its very newsworthiness led much of the public into the illusion that its use was far more common than it was. Even at its peak, only 5 percent of youth had *ever* used crack, and less than 2 percent had done so in the prior 30 days; in contrast, marijuana was used 10 times as frequently, and more than a half dozen drugs were more widely used.

lifetime prevalence figure had declined slightly to 3.1 percent; and in 2005, it stood at 3.5 percent. The comparable figures for annual prevalence, or use once or more during the past year, were 3.9 percent for 1987, 1.5 for 1991, and 1.9 in 2005. And the 30-day prevalence figures—use once or more during the past month—were 1.3, 0.7, and 1.0 percent, respectively. As with most other drugs, there was a slight rise between the early and mid-to-late 1990s; still, the numbers for crack use remain minuscule. And they are lower today than they were at their height in the mid-to-late 1980s. Only a small minority of American youth has even tried crack, and an extremely small minority does so regularly. Of course, this is not to deny that its use has been a serious problem in some communities.

"Try it once and you're hooked for life!" "Once you start you can't stop!" Slogans such as these are repeated about crack so often that they take on a kind of reality of their own. If we look at the actual patterns of use among crack users, however, these messages are immediately revealed as serious distortions of the truth. One Miami study of 308 heavily involved juvenile drug users ages 12–17 (obviously, an extremely narrow and skewed sample of the teenage population as a whole) found that 96 percent had used crack once or more, and 87 percent used it on a regular basis. Yet, of those who used crack, only a minority (30%) used it daily, and half used it once or more a week but not daily. A majority of even the daily users limited their consumption to one or two "hits"—"hardly an indication of compulsive and uncontrollable use. Although there were compulsive users of crack in the Miami sample, they represented an extremely small minority" (Inciardi, 1987). Inexpensive as crack was at the time of this study—$5–10 a vial—it is highly likely that, if the drug had been more freely available, it might well have been used with more frequency. Keep in mind, however, that the inexpensiveness of crack is deceptive, since each high lasts for a very short period of time. Dose for dose and dollar for dollar—ignoring the fact that crack smokers achieve an intense rush, while the cocaine high is less intense and more subdued—the high from snorting cocaine is a longer-lasting bargain than that achieved by smoking crack.

In spite of the fact that the crack cocaine "problem" is not nearly as horrifying as the media depict, the drug is far from innocuous. During the late 1980s, overdoses requiring ED treatment as a result of crack use became increasingly common, and fatal reactions took place. Chronic, compulsive use was not uncommon, and the shorter the time between episodes of use, the greater the chance that the user would have moved toward destructive, uncontrollable use. And as we saw, with the more immediate, intense, and reinforcing effect of the drug that results from a combination of the pharmacology of cocaine and smoking as a chosen route of administration, there was a substantial likelihood of behavioral dependence. Moreover, many of the same medical, psychiatric, and social consequences of the heavy use of powder cocaine also resulted from an immoderate use of crack cocaine: paranoia, violence, heart problems, impotence among men, sexual unresponsiveness among women, blackouts, dizziness, insomnia, tremors, convulsions, and depression (Chatlos, 1987, p. 55).

Still, much of the public fear that arose in the mid-to-late 1980s concerning crack cocaine proved to be baseless. The majority of crack users remained (so far) once-in-a-while users, avoided compulsive abuse, and did not experience these undesirable medical complications. As I explained above, once in the body, crack breaks down into precisely the same drug as powder cocaine; the only difference between them is route of administration. It is important to stress the fact that crack is not a magical, demonic substance with a unique hold over the user, or with uniquely destructive powers. To say, as *Newsweek* did at the height of the crack hysteria (June 16, 1986, p. 18), that using crack immediately hurls the user into "an inferno of craving and despair" is the kind of hysterical sensationalism that can only contribute to the drug problem.

All the indicators for crack consumption among young recreational drug users have declined since the late 1980s. Said ethnographer Terry Williams in the early 1990s: "I'm seeing . . . a movement away from crack. . . . Right now, it's certainly clear that that's happening at the street level. . . . The average crack addict is now in the mid-to-late 20s. . . . At the beginning of the epidemic [in the mid-1980s], the average age was 18." Reported Ansley Hamid, another anthropological researcher studying street-level drug use: "Young people are ridiculing crack-heads in their neighborhoods." Recently, Hamid visited a crack house where sex was exchanged for crack. "All these girls were coming out of the woodwork, looking like the brides of Dracula," he said. "Not a single one of them had started using crack later than . . . 1985." Summarized Philippe Bourgois, another drug ethnographer: "There is most definitely a strong awareness in the youngest generation that crack is a loser's drug" (Kolata, 1990, p. B4). These conclusions are backed up by observations made by researchers and the police indicating that there is a decline in the crack traffic, again, especially in New York City. Said the state's Division of Substance Abuse Services, in an early 1990s report (1990): "The six- or seven-person crews, which had been common in medium and heavy drug-copping locations, have largely disappeared." Said Ansley Hamid: "Where you had maybe 15 to 25 people selling [crack] on a block [in New York City in 1989], now you have three" (Treaster, 1990).

## Does the CIA Peddle Crack?

For years, a story has circulated, mainly among African-Americans, to the effect that the government (variously, the "white power structure," the "higher ups," "the powers that be," the CIA—sometimes in complicity with "big business") "places," "plants," or "distributes" drugs, most commonly crack, in the Black community. The motive? To "destroy the black race with drugs." Is the story true? Until very recently, it had been classified as an urban or contemporary legend—a modern myth (Turner, 1993, pp. 180–201). In 1990, a poll was conducted in New York concerning the validity of the claim that the government was involved in distributing drugs in the minority community. Fully a quarter of New Yorkers of color believed that the American government "deliberately makes sure that drugs are easily available in poor black neighborhoods in order to harm black people" (Golden, 1996).

On the face of it, the tale makes no sense whatsoever. This does not automatically mean that it is false, only that it is implausible. Simply on a statistical basis, however, some assertions that don't seem likely actually turn out to be true, just as some that seem almost certainly true are eventually shown to factually false.

To begin, *no* shred of evidence has ever been produced to document the assertion. To put the matter another way, the evidence that has been used to verify the story has ranged from merely speculative to outlandish. Patricia Turner, an African-American folklorist, collected over 200 versions of this conspiracy tale (1993, pp. 180–201). Some of the evidence her informants cite include the following: Ronald Reagan (president of the United States 1981 to 1989), supposedly one of the key authors of this conspiracy, is the devil (there are six letters in each of his names, and 666 is the mark of the devil); the FBI "tried to get rid of" Marion Barry (mayor of Washington DC, who was convicted and jailed briefly for crack possession); television has always depicted drug abusers as Black, even though most are white (and if TV attempts to harm Blacks, then why not the government?); "someone's getting rich off of drugs, and it sure isn't us"; and "we don't have the resources to bring drugs into the community, somebody else must be doing it; therefore, it must be the government."

Second, the story makes no acknowledgment that by peddling crack political leaders would be creating a more disharmonious, more unstable society. They would be fostering a society that is far more difficult to govern, by "infesting" any community with a drug known to be a catalyst for violent behavior. It shows an extremely naive, zero-sum notion of how society works: What is thought to be good for whites is bad for Blacks; what is supposedly good for "the power structure" is bad for the poor; and so on. In actual fact, spreading crack around in a minority community makes the job of "the powers that be" more difficult, not less; their constituents, no less than residents of the inner city, complain about the drug crisis and evaluate them on the basis of what they are doing about it. Even if we view representatives of the government as the most cynical humans on Earth, it is hard to imagine that they would go along with a scheme that hurts their own interests. And if the story were to leak out, as have revelations of President Nixon's complicity with Watergate, President Reagan's with Iran-Contra, and President Clinton's with Whitewater—not to mention Paula Jones accusing Clinton of sexual harassment—their careers would be compromised and, in all likelihood, ruined. What major politician would be stupid enough to take the risk of being implicated in a charge that is far more explosive than any of these past scandals? (True, some politicians have taken such risks and made such foolish decisions; the drug charge, however, would represent several steps beyond the already documented foolish decisions we know they have made.) The charge, if true and documentable, might very well be the major domestic news story of the century; if the evidence were available, what journalist could resist writing that story? This does not mean that the claim is impossible. Consider the fact that, during the presidential campaign of 1972, President Richard Nixon (whose administration ended in scandal and disgrace in 1974) not only ordered his assistants to engage in a number of illegal acts but also authorized millions of dollars in "hush money" to keep everything quiet. Implausible? To be sure. Impossible? Of course not; the evidence supporting these assertions is incontrovertible. However, as I pointed out above, we have no such evidence for the claim that the government distributes drugs in the Black community.

A third problem is its maddening vagueness. To begin with, "the government" or "the powers that be" do not act in unison; who, exactly, makes up these entities? Do "they," for example, include Black members of the House of Representatives such as Charles Rangel and David Dellums? (And if they are not involved, they must know about this widely circulated story; why aren't they speaking out? Would they be killed because "they know too much," a common defense in conspiracy tales to explain the silence of sympathetic figures?) *Who is doing what?* is never quite answered. It's hard to picture what the actors are *doing* in this plot. It's never explained; somehow, shadowy figures are moving around in the dark, doing evil things. To any skeptic, the story lacks the ring of verisimilitude because it never quite gets around to explaining the exact mechanism by which the drugs got from their point of origin to their ultimate destination.

The tale is also implausible because, ironically, it is extremely contemptuous of Black people. That is, it assumes that large numbers of African-Americans lack the agency or willpower to refuse to use drugs; once faced with the opportunity to use psychoactive substances, they are uncontrollably driven by the impulse to consume them. The image this tale projects of a substantial portion of Blacks is that they are automatons, obediently following unspoken orders from "the white power structure." The tellers of this tale consider African-Americans to have even less independence than horses, judging by the maxim "You can lead a horse to water but you can't make him drink." They believe that when you lead Blacks to drugs, they will automatically use them. I find this assertion not only untrue but racist as well. I have the same problem with Gootenberg's assertion that the U.S. government "created" the cocaine epidemic as I have with the one that the CIA peddles crack, namely, neither addresses the issue of how the behavior of a few officials or operatives of officials translates into the behavior of millions of potential users.

As researchers of contemporary legends point out (Fine and Turner, 2001; Turner, 1993), many absurd beliefs, even if they lack historical or literal, concrete truth, do contain a grain of *narrative* truth. This means that these beliefs reflect strongly held values among persons who hold them. The beliefs seem to resemble events they know to be true, that have in fact taken place; the line between "resembling" something that is true and being literally and concretely true becomes fuzzy. The belief that the government is "delivering" drugs to the ghetto is also an atrocity tale, taken as a metaphor or exaggeration for racist mistreatment. Blacks *have* been the victims of a long history of racist practices in which the government has either looked the other way or has been an active perpetrator. In the United States, persons of African descent suffered 250 years of slavery and 100 years of lynching, and were treated by the government throughout the twentieth century as legal and political second-class citizens. For 40 years, the Public Health Service (PHS) conducted an experiment on 400 Black males who had contracted syphilis. These men were observed by PHS physicians, but they were not told that they had the disease; the researchers studied the progress of the disease, withholding treatment from them as if they were laboratory rats. And many of these men ultimately infected their wives and, through them, their children (Jones, 1981). The point is, given that all these dreadful things actually did happen, a tale about the involvement of government higher-ups in supplying crack to the Black community is likely to seem extremely *plausible* to many of its residents. However, keep in mind an important difference here: Slavery entailed involuntary servitude of millions of human beings because of their race; the PHS experiments withheld information from infected patients. In both cases, there was no action *by* the victims that had anything to do with their victimization. In the tale in which the government provided drugs to the Black community, presumably, African-Americans collude in their victimization by voluntarily choosing to use drugs, a significantly different category of oppression and victimization. Again, the story only makes sense if we imagine that substantial numbers of Blacks have no willpower whatsoever.

Until very recently, no substantial evidence existed that the story was true; it was based on speculation, conjecture, and a great deal of resentment. In August 1996, however, a newspaper story was published that seemed to verify what was previously thought to be a legend. Under the byline of Gary Webb, a three-part series titled "Dark Alliance" appeared in the *San Jose Mercury News* that suggested a strong CIA–crack connection. The articles asserted that a Los Angeles drug dealer, Rick Donnell Ross, was supplied cocaine by two Nicaraguan Contra leaders, Danilo Blandon and Norwin Meneses, who had close ties to the CIA. (The Contras were an armed opposition force, supported by the CIA, that attempted to overthrow the socialist Nicaraguan regime.) Webb asserted that the operations Ross conducted, assisted by Blandon and Meneses, helped "spark a crack explosion in urban America." In exchange for its help, the drug ring had funneled "millions" of dollars in drug profits back to the Contras. The article implied that CIA operatives, and very possibly its leadership, were aware of these developments and either did nothing or actively encouraged them. To some of "the more extreme voices among African-Americans, the articles validated a belief that the crack epidemic was part of a shadowy genocidal plot involving the Federal Government" (Holmes, 1997).

Within a week or two after the story was published, the computer website the *San Jose Mercury News* devoted to the story began receiving 100,000 hits *a day* on the series (White, 1996). A couple of years after the newspaper articles appeared, Webb's book *Dark Alliance:*

*The CIA, the Contras, and the Crack Cocaine Explosion* (1998) appeared. The fact that a minor publisher (Seven Stories Press) rather than a major one published the book is significant.

The *San Jose Mercury News* articles raised four entirely different questions or sets of questions that demand answers. The first, of course, is, Are these assertions factually true? More specifically, is there evidence that CIA operatives were actively involved in drug operations? The second: What did higher-ups in the CIA know, and what did they do about it? It is one thing to say that low-level agents or operatives became inadvertently entangled in drug operations to foster U.S. interests abroad; it is quite another to say that a high-level official ordered, encouraged, or condoned an ongoing, CIA-sponsored, drug-related operation.

The third question that might be asked is: What were the motives or intentions of the participants in these operations? Did the CIA intend to commit harm (in its most extreme form, genocide) against the African-American people? Or was the drug use a *by-product,* in this case, of a struggle to overthrow a socialist regime?

And the fourth question is: What role did the cocaine supplied by Ross play in the crack explosion that took place in the mid-1980s? How was it possible for a single drug operation to create a massive historical trend toward widespread crack use throughout the country? To answer all four of these questions would necessitate four entirely different sets of evidence; answering one does not necessarily follow inevitably from the other.

Nine months after the "Dark Alliance" series appeared, the editor of the *San Jose Mercury News,* Jerry Cepos, issued a qualification; the articles were flawed, Cepos stated, "marred by serious shortcomings" because their "most sensational implications . . . were not supported by the facts" (Purdum, 1997, p. A1). It is entirely possible that members of the Ross–Meneses drug ring met with CIA operatives; it is entirely possible that money and other resources did change hands. However, it should be emphasized that Webb's claims are based on inferences from a number of court documents and several interviews, most notably with Ross himself, who is currently facing a life sentence on a drug trafficking conviction. Independent investigation undertaken by *The New York Times, The Washington Post,* and *The Los Angeles Times,* did not unearth any clear-cut evidence of a direct connection between the CIA and the drug dealers mentioned in the articles; moreover, the financial connection between the dealers and the Contras could not be established factually. Once again, this does not mean that the relationships never existed, only that Webb's claims are based on evidence that most journalists do not consider adequate; they lack independent corroboration, which most reporters consider the bedrock of journalistic documentation.

Even if these links could be established, exactly what they *mean* is a far more crucial issue. Does a connection between one or more CIA operatives and one or more drug dealers mean that "the government" (or even the CIA) intends to inflict harm on the African-American people? Or that the operations described in the news stories, if they existed, were instrumental in launching the crack epidemic in America?

The CIA historically has been involved in a substantial number of extremely unsavory activities. It has assisted in the overthrow of a number of popular or democratically elected governments and has helped replace them with more repressive regimes. A few examples: the nationalist Mussadegh regime in Iran in 1953, replaced by the repressive monarchy of the Shah of Iran; the democratic Arbenz government in Guatemala in 1954, replaced by a military dictatorship; the socialist Allende administration in Chile in the 1973, replaced by a military dictatorship. The Contras of Nicaragua (funded roughly from 1981 to 1990), supported by the CIA with the objective of overthrowing the leftist Sandinista government, headed by Daniel Ortega, were a particularly unsavory bunch. (The Sandinistas were voted out of office in 1990, and the Contras were disbanded.)

Moreover, in its opposition to communism and support of anticommunist forces, the CIA has been implicated in several operations that entailed the production and/or distribution of drugs. During the Vietnam War, several generals of ARVN, the South Vietnam forces, America's allies, were actively involved in transporting and selling heroin. After the invasion by the then-Soviet Union of Afghanistan in 1976, the CIA supported the pro-Muslim, anti-Soviet guerrilla movement, the *muhajadin,* whose other source of support was selling opium; its contemporary counterpart, al-Qaeda, still sells opium. For years, the CIA assisted Panama's president, General Manuel Noriega, who was well known throughout Latin America as a drug kingpin; in 1989, when he seemed expendable, the United States government fought a small war to kidnap and convict him (in 1992) of the very drug dealing it had known about when he was useful. The fact is, drugs are almost instant cash; practically any regime or opposition force with few scruples will be tempted to sell them to advance its own interests (or, in the case of regimes in power, to enhance the bank statement of their leaders). At the very least, on-the-ground support of forces in Vietnam, Afghanistan, and Panama certainly involved supplying resources and materiel to known drug dealers. To imagine that the CIA, or any government agency involved in the dirty operation of protecting its own interests on the ground, has never aided and abetted drug transactions in any way is naive. At every level, there are so many possible connections and interactions between and among so many personnel that drug dealing almost inevitably enters into the picture.

I would emphasize, however, that being implicated in the drug operations of others is not the same thing as dealing drugs oneself. "Being implicated" is a vague, slippery term; we'd have to know more about exactly what this means before we can make sense of any claim to a drugs–government connection. Likewise, being implicated is not the same thing as operating for the purpose of harming the ultimate customer or the category of persons who are supposedly most likely to become customers. Untangling motives or intentions is a notoriously tricky enterprise; an entire library of books and articles, indeed, a whole subfield of social psychology, attribution theory, is devoted to the study of the process by which people devise explanations of what others are up to when they do what they do. The huge body of research that has been conducted on the attribution of motives shows that people tend to be extremely inaccurate in making these judgments. Most of us overattribute; we tend to see intentionality in the actions of others where there is none and to underplay contextual constraints and motives we consider irrelevant, especially if someone else is engaging in behavior of which we disapprove. The fact that someone who is affiliated in some way with a government agency may have links to a drug operation does not demonstrate that anyone in the government, or the government itself, intends to harm anyone. In order to document that a given motive exists, we would need to have far more definitive evidence to that effect.

The fact is, not a shred of hard, credible evidence exists (that is, evidence that most journalists accept as valid) suggesting that higher-level officials in the CIA ordered, authorized, or condoned the alleged operations charged in the Webb articles; not a shred of such evidence exists that indicates that anyone in the CIA or the federal government has launched a genocidal campaign of any kind against African-Americans; and no evidence exists indicating that the Ross shipments of cocaine, which were sold in Los Angeles, launched or started the crack epidemic. It is not clear what conceivable evidence could be presented to refute these charges that would convince persons who now believe them. (In contrast, it is a very easy matter to imagine what evidence would convince current skeptics that the conspiracy charges are true; after all, a mountain of tape recordings convinced Nixon admirers that he authorized the Watergate break-in, even though he denied it at the time and tried to cover it up.) It is not enough to say that the government has done evil things to African-Americans in the past; by itself, this does not constitute evidence. It is unlikely that a careful review of the evidence is going to change very many observers' minds. On the other hand, a truly sober assessment of the facts is likely to lead to the conclusion that the available evidence does not support the charge of a plot to commit genocide against, or even harm, the African-American community. If substantial evidence were to be produced documenting this claim (for instance, a memo, a tape recording, a physical document of some kind), then the skeptics among us, myself included, would become convinced that it is true. Until that time, those of us who have great respect for evidence will simply have to withhold judgment.

## SUMMARY

Stimulants speed up signals passing through the central nervous system, that is, the brain and the spinal column. The two major stimulants are amphetamine (and its sister drug, methamphetamine) and cocaine, along with crack cocaine. Of all drug types, the stimulants possess the greatest immediate sensual appeal: In comparison with other drugs or drug types, persons administered them for the first time enjoy their effects most and are most likely to say they want to take them again. In small doses, stimulants increase concentration, mental acuity, and physical performance. In moderate to high doses, however, mental processes go haywire and physical activity becomes counterproductive and compulsive.

Amphetamines and their sister drug, methamphetamine, are called "speed," "ups," "pep pills," "crystal," "glass," and, most recently, "ice." The amphetamines stimulate arousal, enhance alertness, cause a diminution of fatigue, and inhibit sleep. They have been used for a variety of medical and psychiatric ills; overprescribed in the 1960s, today, the pharmaceutical use of the amphetamines is approved for only an extremely narrow range of ailments. Although amphetamine use among the young outstrips that of cocaine, it remains vastly below marijuana with respect to the number who use and its total volume of use. Its peak years were in the early 1980s.

There are several somewhat different street or illicit amphetamine "scenes." One is the illegal instrumental use of speed—for instance, staying up all night to study for an exam. Another is recreational multiple drug use—that is, using amphetamine along with other drugs, such as alcohol, the club drugs (including Ecstasy), LSD, and marijuana. And the third is the high-dose use of methamphetamine. In the 1960s, "meth" was injected; from the late 1980s into the 2000s, it tends to be smoked. Today, the use of methamphetamine remains regionalized; evidence suggests that it is extremely rare in most large cities of the eastern United States. It is not a major drug of use among schoolchildren, including high school seniors. Although its use represents a serious drug problem in much of the West and Midwest, the predicted nationwide epidemic of "ice" abuse has not yet come to pass. The heavy, compulsive use of the amphetamines and methamphetamine leads to paranoia, psychosis, behavioral fixations, and behavioral dependence, in addition to the medical harm that results from the lifestyle in which speed freaks indulge.

The amphetamines and cocaine have similar effects; cocaine is a much faster-acting drug, however, and its effects are more transient. Cocaine in its natural form has been used for thousands of years; the Inca worshipped it as a god. Cocaine was extracted from the coca leaf in the 1860s. For a time, the drug's effects were thought to be entirely beneficial; cocaine in one form or another could be found in a variety of tonics, concoctions, and pseudo-medicines. It is believed that public sentiment favoring the earliest laws against cocaine, passed in the United States in the early twentieth century, resulted from the fear among many whites that African-Americans became violent under the influence and committed crimes against whites, especially white women. These fears were completely groundless, of course, but they were instrumental in the passage of anticocaine laws nearly a century ago.

Cocaine is either sniffed or snorted, in its powdered form, or smoked, in its crystalline form. (Some users also inject cocaine IV.) Smoking is an extremely efficient and effective form of using cocaine, and produces a rapid, intense "rush" that is highly reinforcing and often leads to behavioral dependence.

The use of cocaine rose sharply between the 1960s and the late 1970s, declined in the 1980s, and may have increased slightly into the 1990s and the 2000s. However, the figures supplied by DAWN indicate that emergency department episodes and medical examiner reports involving cocaine have increased sharply since records were kept. (These figures have not, however, increased into the 2000s.) This may indicate a stable or possibly increasing population of heavy users (as opposed to more typical, less compulsive recreational users), purer and therefore more dangerous cocaine on the streets over time, and/or the fact that cocaine users are aging, and hence becoming more vulnerable to the ravages of the drug.

Although cocaine does not produce the "classic" picture of addiction, and hence withdrawal, the abstinence syndrome associated with cocaine use indicates a dependency nonetheless. In any case, the drug clearly generates behavioral dependence, that is, the desire to take it over and over again regardless of personal and financial cost. However, most users do not become behaviorally dependent; who an individual is determines dependence far more than does the nature of the drug he or she is taking. Patterns of use among a broad spectrum of users indicate there is no single or stereotypical cocaine user and no inevitable result of using the drug.

In the 1970s, expert judgments about cocaine's effects tended to underplay its harmful potential; today, almost without exception, experts see it as far more harmful.

Crack is a crystalline and impure form of cocaine that is smoked. The difference between powder cocaine and crack is not so much the composition of these two substances but the route of administration. Crack became extremely popular in mid-1985. Hysteria was generated about the use of this drug in extremely short order. Crack never became widely used on a national basis, and its dangers were greatly exaggerated. By about 1990, the crack "epidemic" had begun to abate. Although the drug is less dangerous than the public believes, it is a far from safe drug; its use left harm in its wake that will continue to be felt well into the twenty-first century.

For decades, an urban legend circulated to the effect that the government and/or big business had "planted," "sold," or "distributed" harmful, addicting drugs—variously, heroin, cocaine, or crack—in the Black community to commit genocide against African-Americans. No evidence has been found to support this claim. In 1996, Gary Webb wrote a series of articles for the *San Jose Mercury News* that later became a book, *Dark Alliance,* which presumably documented the assertion that the CIA, through two Nicaraguan Contra leaders, supplied cocaine to a Los Angeles drug dealer, igniting the crack epidemic. Though Webb's story received an enormous measure of attention, it was based largely on interviews with a drug dealer who faced a life sentence for dealing; no documentary evidence backs up the claims. Nine months after Webb's articles appeared, his newspaper published a warning that they were "flawed," "not supported by the facts." Several newspapers, including *The New York Times* and *The Washington Post*, could not verify Webb's assertions.

## KEY TERMS

behavioral dependence   290

chemicalistic fallacy   292

drug addiction   290

immediate sensual appeal   277

monkey model of addiction   288

punding   280

withdrawal symptoms   280

## ACCOUNT: Crack Cocaine

*Winston is "knocking on the door of 50." He served in the military for five years, was married twice, and has five children. Currently, he lives with his mother and sleeps on her living room couch. Although a high school graduate, trained in computer technology, and previously stably employed, these days, Winston is unemployed or casually employed.*

Running the street and getting high was my thing. But in the '70s, I stopped for a minute. I had a wife and three children to support. At this point, I only had my high school diploma, so I enrolled in computer school and graduated. In the '80s, I was a bookkeeper for a major chemical plant. Then I moved on and became senior technician for a check distribution company. I worked there 14 years. I was making 52K. Still frequenting the marijuana and heroin until freebase came along. Mid-'80s, freebase would become my drug of choice and my means of destruction.

Today, I smoke crack. I would spend my last dime on it. I don't drink beer—sometimes hard liquor—and I don't smoke marijuana any more.

Those drugs don't do what crack does [for me]. The sensation is like no other, rating right up there next to an orgasm. Even the taste is appealing. It's my escape from reality, the struggle, the pain, and life. I don't feel the pressure when I'm high. See, I have always considered myself a loner by nature. I don't like to talk to people about my problems. I don't want anyone to hear me whine. If someone sees me or calls the house, I may be down, if they pick up on it, I change. I put more pep in my step and in my voice, and a smile is always on my face. If I'm around other people, I always try to make them laugh. I'm the jokester with no worry in the world. That's how I want others to perceive me.

When I worked for the check distribution company, I used my intelligence and conniving ways to my advantage. I started my little operation on the side. It was '93, and I was remarried with two more children and this scheme provided me with more than enough money to keep my wives happy and my habit happy. Check this out. A get-high buddy of mine and I had an idea. The checks I wrote courtesy of my job, whose clients' names I used as the companies that would issue the checks, would be deposited in accounts, then withdrawn. The banks wouldn't dispense all the funds at once because the checks were at least $10,000 a pop. So every three days after the checks sat for a week, my partner would write out a check for cash and cash it at the bank. The operation was going smoothly for over six months. Every time we opened a different account, we would cash the checks at different banks.

But one afternoon, my partner was supposed to take out $8,000, but instead, he wrote a check for $800. So the teller asked him, how would you like your $800, in big or small bills? He realized he had forgotten a zero, so he asked the teller for the check back to do it over, and the teller got suspicious. Three days later, next time he tried to make a withdrawal, the cops were waiting for him. Operation fell apart at this point in time. I think that even before they could get the handcuffs on my partner, the police were walking through the door where I was staying. My second wife and I had been separated, and I had my own little apartment around the way. This white chick I was frequenting had just left the apartment, and I had told her to leave the door open so that when my partner came back from the bank, he could let himself in. Before I knew it, three police officers had let themselves in and were standing, guns drawn, one on either side of the bed and one at the doorway. All I saw was the guns, really, and I remember saying to them, "Are you going to shoot me?"

My partner sang like a bird. There was no way I was getting out of it. I had to cop to a plea of five years on 14 counts of fraud, theft by deception, and embezzlement. During the six months of [our little caper], we went through a little over $100,000. All that went to buying crack and partying. The judge saw that I had a clean record and that I was capable of holding a job for 14 years in a white-dominated profession. I represented myself well during the plea arraignment, and so she lowered my sentence to three years. I was paroled after serving only six months of that behind bars.

After this melting point in my life, it was hard for me to get a job. It was so much easier to do nothing. But I had a habit to feed, plus five children who

are being raised by their mothers. I never got back in the [employment] game after that hit. I just couldn't get a job. Shit, I'm a Black man with intelligence and numerous skills, but I have a record for embezzlement and a $100-a-day [crack] habit. All things said and done, hard as it was, I did go out and I found a legitimate job. I couldn't find a job that paid more than $12 an hour, though, and what I did make went to my children and crack. Then, slowly but surely, it was all going on crack. I lost my job because I got high late at night and didn't make it to work in the morning. They weren't paying me enough anyway. It's easier to get high late at night because I don't have to worry about anybody having to go to the bathroom and interrupting me. [Winston lives with his mother and sleeps on the living room couch. His sister and her three children live there as well.] I get high in my house, in the bathroom, or even in the living room if everyone's asleep. [Also], the dealers are easier to get at night because there's less traffic and not as many people outside watching. You beep your dealer and they come over. Or you go there and pick it up. On some occasions [your dealer] may be hanging out by the corner store or in the building, so you walk right up to him and make your transaction. The 'hood has cameras and nosey people who call the cops, but you try to avoid areas in which you know the camera is pointing or [where there are] people who would rat.

I support my habit by doing things for people around the 'hood—family and friends. I paint houses, fix and program computers, fix television sets. Hell, I could lay down wood. I could build you a deck if you wanted me to. I cook for people and bake cakes. Anything, really. I'm the go-to guy when something needs to be done, from moving furniture around the house to helping you pack to move. . . . I never stole or robbed from anybody or anything, that isn't my thing. . . . I borrow from my family, with the hope to pay them back. But basically, it's begging for money whenever I need it. . . .

The life I live now is the life I choose to live. I only regret not being able to live two lives at once. I love getting high and I wouldn't trade it for the world. I would just like for there to be some balance and stability in my life. I know I'm not able to hold down a job and continue to do the things I do. It's hard having your cake and eating it too, and I guess I had to find that out the hard way.

## QUESTIONS

What do Winston's experiences tell us about using crack? More generally, about using any and all illicit drugs? Do you think that Winston's difficulties with crack are related to the sort of person he is—or with getting high on this seductive drug? Could he have used less compulsively and achieved more in his life? If given the chance, would most people prefer to get high and fail to achieve most of life's more conventional goals—or abstain and take the path of mainstream success? Are compulsive drug use and success incompatible? Are some people able to achieve both? Are Winston's compulsive drug use, his failure as a husband and father, and his inability to hold a good job all related to the same factor—a lack of self-control? How much control did he have in making life choices—or was his path in life preordained?

# HEROIN AND THE NARCOTICS

F or decades, it was the most feared, the most dreaded, the "hardest" drug (Kaplan, 1983); heroin has virtually defined the drug problem. In spite of being somewhat overshadowed since the mid-1980s by cocaine, and specifically crack, heroin probably remains the single substance the American public is most likely to point to as an example of a dangerous drug. Until recently, disapproval of any level of heroin use was greater than for any other drug. And, until recently, heroin addicts were the most stigmatized of all drug users. Heroin is the epitome of the illicit street drug. Its association in the public mind with street crime, even today, is probably stronger than for any other drug. The stereotype of the junkie is that he or she is by nature a lowlife, an outcast, a "deviant," a dweller in the underworld, an unsavory, untrustworthy character to be avoided at any cost. And to top it all off, even though heroin ranks nearly dead last in use among well-known illicit drugs—its volume of use is one-tenth that of cocaine—it remains in the "Big Three" drugs with respect to causing overdose deaths. These facts alone make heroin a fascinating drug to study.

## NARCOTIC DRUGS: AN INTRODUCTION

Heroin is chemically derived from morphine. In volume, five units of morphine produce one of heroin. Morphine, in turn, is extracted from opium, which is roughly 10 percent morphine by weight. The Abt Associates, a research group, estimate that two-thirds (67%) of the heroin consumed in the United States comes from South America; a quarter (25%) from Mexico; 6 percent from Southwest Asia, mainly Afghanistan and Pakistan; and 2 percent from Southeast Asia, mainly Myanmar, formerly Burma (Bruen et al., 2002, p. 1). The United Nation's 2005 *World Drug Report* places 85 percent of the world's production of opium in Afghanistan, but most of that is destined for Europe and other points around the Eastern Hemisphere. All the various alkaloid products of opium are **opiates,** and they include, aside from opium itself, morphine, heroin, codeine, Dilaudid (a semisynthetic derivative of opium), laudanum (a 10% alcohol-based tincture of opium), and paregoric (a 4% tincture of opium). There are also several synthetic narcotics with many of the same effects as heroin, usually called **opioids** (or opiate-like drugs); these include Demerol (meperidine), Dolophine (methadone), Percodan, Darvon, fentanyl, and oxycodone (one of its trade names, OxyContin).

Properly speaking, narcotics are painkillers or **analgesics.** These drugs reduce sensory feeling and sensitivity of all kinds, to pleasure as well as pain. There are several widely used over-the-counter (OTC) painkillers that are not classified as narcotics, of which aspirin, acetaminophen, and ibuprofen are the best known; they do not produce a high, mental clouding, or dependence, and they are far safer in terms of overdosing. Still, thousands of Americans do overdose on these OTC painkillers each year; for instance, in 2000, there were 33,000 nonlethal emergency department (ED) acetaminophen-related episodes in the United States, 18,000 such episodes involving ibuprofen, and over 15,000 as a result of taking aspirin. (Most of these episodes were failed suicide attempts.) At the same time, on a user-for-user, dose-for-dose basis, the non-narcotic analgesics are extremely safe. In contrast, the recreational use of the narcotics, especially heroin, is clearly extremely dangerous. The problem is, as analgesics, narcotics are completely without peer; they are quite simply vastly more effective and efficient painkillers than the non-narcotic varieties, and they are therefore of immense therapeutic value. Hence, for many purposes, aspirin, acetaminophen, or ibuprofen simply will not do. The physician must reach for morphine, oxycodone, Darvon, Percodan, or Demerol.

Aside from their analgesic property, narcotics also generate euphoria. After the IV injection of a narcotic, the user feels a flash, a rush, which has been described as an intense, voluptuous, orgasmlike sensation. Following this is the feeling of well-being, tranquility, ease, and calm, the sensation that everything in the user's life is just fine. Tensions, worries, problems, the rough edges of life—all seem simply to melt away. Few drugs or drug types generate this feeling of well-being as effectively as narcotics, and of the more commonly used narcotics, heroin seems to do the job best of all.

A third characteristic of narcotics is that they tend to be soporific—that is, in sufficiently large doses, they induce drowsiness, mental clouding, lethargy, even sleep. (Morphine is named after Morpheus, the Greek god of dreams, and the scientific name for the opium poppy is *Papaver somniferum*, named for its quality of inducing somnolence or sleepiness.) It is this dreamy, sleeplike state that addicts seek and inject narcotics to achieve.

The narcotic analgesics are also—and this is their fourth characteristic or property— without exception, physically addicting. In the terms I introduced in Chapter 2, they generate a physical dependence. They are also highly reinforcing; that is, they generate a very strong psychic or **psychological dependence,** possibly second only to that of cocaine and the amphetamines. And they are capable of generating an overwhelming behavioral dependence. (However, the belief "One shot and you're hooked for life" is completely false; of the total universe of all people who have used heroin at least once, the vast majority are not even currently using the drug, and of those who are, most are sporadic, occasional, infrequent users rather than addicts.)

One thing that makes heroin and the other narcotics dangerous is, as we've seen, that the range between their effective dose (ED) and lethal dose (LD) is fairly narrow: The quantity that can kill a user is only 10–15 times the amount that can get him or her high. Thus, it is extremely easy to die of an overdose on any of the narcotics, and especially heroin. Although the mechanism of death by a narcotic overdose is not completely understood, taking huge doses of a narcotic is an almost certain way to kill oneself. As do alcohol and barbiturates, an overdose of heroin causes respiratory paralysis, resulting in oxygen starvation of the brain.

## THE USE AND ABUSE OF NARCOTICS TODAY

### Rates and Patterns of Use

It is remarkable that heroin is such a well-known and almost universally dreaded drug, since it attracts far fewer users than almost any other major illegal drug or drug type. The fact is, however, the small number of heavy heroin users that we do have inflict a great deal of damage on the rest of society—and in turn, the rest of society inflicts a great deal of damage on them.

There are two fundamental facts you need to know about heroin use. First, as I said, it is one of the least often used drugs in the United States; in most surveys, it ranks dead last in popularity. Second, in spite of its extreme infrequency in use, it shows up with remarkable frequency in the Drug Abuse Warning Network's (DAWN's) overdose statistics, indicating that, on a dose-for-dose, person-for-person basis, it is an extremely dangerous drug. (As we saw, in 2003, DAWN's medical examiner (ME) reports combined heroin with all other narcotics into a single category, "opiates," so that after that date, it became impossible to draw any conclusions on heroin's lethality versus that of the other narcotics.) In the high school survey I've cited a number of times, heroin ranks dead last in popularity among all drugs asked about. In 2005, only 1.5 percent of the high school seniors surveyed said that they had *ever* tried heroin, and only 0.8 percent had used it in the past year. In the latest National Survey on Drug Use and Health, conducted in 2005, just over 1 percent of all Americans (1.5%) said that they had tried heroin at least once in their lives—0.2 percent for youth ages 12–17, 1.5 percent for young adults ages 18–25, and 1.6 percent for persons ages 26 and older. (Males are three times more likely to have used heroin once or more in their lifetimes as females.) Only 0.2 percent of the population as a whole reported use of heroin during the past year. Of all persons who had used at least one illegal drug once or more in their lives, fewer than 2 percent had tried or used heroin. Only a small fraction of 1 percent of all episodes of illegal drug use involves heroin. Clearly, then, heroin is one of the least widely used of all the well-known drugs or drug types.

Consider, however, the methodological warning I issued in Chapter 6: Surveys are a very poor method of calculating the total number of heroin users because they fail to capture a substantial proportion of this population. Students who use heroin are highly likely to drop out of school, and hence are unlikely to appear in a survey based on the student body. In addition, many heroin users do not live at a fixed address, and hence are disproportionately unlikely to appear in a survey based on a sample of American households. The Abt Associates, basing their figures on a wide range of different indicators, estimated the number of "hard core" users of heroin in the United States in 2000 at 900,000. In contrast, based on its sample of households, the 2005 National Survey on Drug Use and Health (NSDUH) estimated that only 136,000 persons used heroin in the previous month. The disparity between these two figures forces us to consider the fallibility of the data on which these two estimates are based. Still, both Abt's estimate and the NSDUH's figure, however wide apart they are (and I'm inclined to believe Abt's estimate rather than the NSDUH's) are both fairly small compared with the figures for most other drugs. For example, as we saw in Chapter 6, Abt Associates estimated that in the United States during 2000, 13 tons of heroin were consumed; in contrast, 259 tons of cocaine were used—20 times as much. Hence, Abt Associates suggest that the total volume of heroin used in the United States is extremely small relative to several other well-known drugs, cocaine most notably.

Nevertheless, heroin shows up with remarkable frequency in drug abuse statistics. According to DAWN's figures for 2002, nearly one in six of all emergency department (ED) episodes (14%), entailed the use of heroin, and in that same year, heroin was involved in 33 percent of all lethal drug-related episodes. Note that not every time a drug is mentioned or reported in DAWN's figures is it the sole or causal mechanism in the overdose. Nonetheless, when a given drug shows up extremely frequently in overdose episodes, we can presume that it plays a significant role in lethal or life-threatening reactions. Given how infrequently heroin is used in comparison with all of the other well-known drugs, its contribution to nonlethal and especially lethal overdoses is nothing short of spectacular. Compared with cocaine—which is used, by volume, 20 times as frequently—heroin is a *very* dangerous drug, indeed.

Heroin is not the only narcotic that is used for recreational or nonmedical purposes. In the survey of high school seniors cited above, all the other narcotics, added together, were used by *six times* as many individuals as heroin was. In its 2005 NSDUH, the Substance Abuse and Mental Health Administration Services Administration (SAMHSA) estimated that, while only 3.5 million Americans had used heroin at least once during their lives (1.5% of the population), 32.6 million (13.4%) had used one or more of the narcotic analgesics (or "pain relievers") for nonmedical purposes. In 2005, the lifetime use of OxyContin, a narcotic whose use has recently attracted considerable media attention, was almost as great as that of heroin (SAMHSA, 2006).

And, as we saw with DAWN's figures, in 2000, for the first time, all the nonheroin and nonmorphine narcotics, taken as a whole, surpassed heroin (and alcohol-in-combination) in the number of mentions to which they contributed in ME reports of a lethal drug overdose—4,624 versus 4,398. Narcotics aside from heroin (and morphine) are widely used and abused, and they result in a substantial number of overdoses. Nonetheless, even though they are used so much more frequently than heroin, they contribute about the same number of lethal overdoses.

Clearly, then, on a dose-by-dose basis, heroin remains by far the most dangerous among the circle of the six or eight recreationally used narcotics. And the fact is, among street users and abusers of narcotics, heroin is their drug of choice. Street addicts will ingest any narcotic that is available at a particular time. Although they may prefer heroin, it may not be as readily available as some of the other narcotics, such as codeine, methadone, Dilaudid, Percodan, or Darvon. Consequently, they will use other narcotics until heroin becomes available. In some communities, oxycodone (OxyContin) is beginning to be used even in preference to heroin.

## A New Heroin Epidemic?

Beginning in the mid-1990s, media sources began reporting that a new heroin "epidemic" was gripping America, that this drug, which had become unfashionable in the 1985–1995 period, was coming back into frequent use. Did it happen? What evidence do we have of a fresh resurgence in heroin use at that time? First, we already know that heroin is a relatively rare drug of abuse; it is a drug that ranks near the bottom in illicit use in America. Thus, if only, say, 0.1 percent of the population begins using heroin in a given year, this would represent a massive increase in heroin use. Second, the "hard core" comprising the heroin addict population has not changed much over the past decade or two; as we just saw, it now stands at roughly 900,000. (Remember that the criteria defining who a heroin addict is could change, and thus the number of addicts would magically "grow" or "shrink" accordingly.) Third, to know how much heroin use exists in a given year, we must rely on concrete indicators, reliable measures of use that point to the extent of use in a given year. What indicators or measures do we have?

We've already seen that the data supplied by ADAM (Arrestee Drug Abuse Monitoring) point to a surprisingly low percentage of positive drug tests for heroin among arrestees in the United States. In 2003, this figure was an all-city median of only 5.8 percent for men and 6.6 percent for women, a very slight decline over the past decade. In short, ADAM's figures show no real increase in heroin use, at least among urban arrestees. At one time, the drug of choice of inner-city criminals was heroin; today, that is no longer true. Bruce Johnson and colleagues (2000; Golub and Johnson, 2001), relying on interview data from Drug Use Forecasting (DUF) and ADAM, argue that drug use among arrestees can be divided into three more or less distinct "eras." The first is the heroin injection era, which peaked between 1960 and 1973; its members were born between 1945 and 1954—that is, they were 15–28 years old when this era was at its height. The second era, the crack/cocaine era, peaked between 1984 and 1989, when its members, born between 1955 and 1969, were between the ages of 15 and 34. And lastly, there is the marijuana/blunt era, which began in

1990 and is still ongoing, and the members of which were born beginning in 1970. (A "blunt" is a large, fat marijuana joint.)

For each generation, there are huge clusters of respondents who used during each specific era. Among persons born between 1945 and 1953, a huge majority of arrestees said that they had used heroin. But among those born after 1953, the percentage saying that they had used heroin declined sharply. Likewise, for arrestees born after 1954 but before 1970, a huge cluster said that they had used crack cocaine—but very few born after 1970 had done so. Apparently, each succeeding generation "burns itself out." Each generation doesn't so much stop using their drug of choice as its members age and recede into the background. They are no longer members of the most prominent drug-using generation, nor are they the most active among criminal populations; as they age, their criminal behavior declines, and they begin to die out. Those who are left are part of an ever-diminishing community that, because of higher mortality rates among older users, harbors a dwindling number of members. The same persons do not switch from one drug to another. Instead, a new drug comes along, luring new (and younger) members into its ranks of use (Johnson, Golub, and Dunlap, 2000). In short, heroin is used by a shrinking percentage of arrestees and, presumably, street criminals as their ranks age.

In contrast, our second measure of use over time, DAWN's overdose statistics, shows indicators of a consistent increase in heroin abuse in recent years. Between the late 1970s and the late 1980s, the number of heroin overdoses grew alarmingly. As we know from our discussion of DAWN data in Chapter 6, trends in drug complications over time could involve a number of factors—an increase in the purity of the drug, an increase in the frequency of use among the same number of users, the greater tendency for users to take the drug in combination with other drugs, potentially lethal routes of administration (injecting, for instance, instead of snorting), and so on. It is entirely possible that the increase in lethal and nonlethal heroin overdoses between 1979 and the late 1980s came about even as the number of heroin abusers was actually declining. In addition, there are serious methodological problems with DAWN's data collection, among them the lack of standardized procedures by which data are collected from year to year and from one jurisdiction to another, and the fact that some jurisdictions inexplicably float into and out of the total tallies from one year to the next. However, from time to time, DAWN issues a report that standardizes its data. Two reports (Adams et al., 1989; DAWN, 1987) indicate that, roughly between the late 1970s and the mid-to-late 1980s, depending on the exact years tallied, heroin-related ED visits increased between 50 percent and 300 percent, while ME reports increased between 25 percent and 200 percent. In 1991, there were just over 63,000 heroin-related ED visits; in 2002, the number was a shade over 93,000, an increase of less than one-and-one-half times. In 1991, there were slightly fewer than 3,900 heroin-related mentions in lethal ME reports; in 2003, as we saw, there were only 3,264, which represent a decline during the 1990s and into the 2000s.

Once again, the increases in heroin use in the 1980s shown by DAWN statistics could stem from the fact that the purity of heroin purchased on the street increased over time. Between the 1970s and the 1990s, the potency of street heroin increased dramatically. For decades, the heroin available at the retail or user level was 3–5 percent pure, with the rest of the substance purchased made up of adulterants and fillers, such as mannitol, lactose, and quinine. According to Abt Associates, in 1981, the average purity of street heroin purchased at the level of less than one-tenth of a gram was 4 percent; during 2000, it increased to 25 percent—a huge increase. Clearly, in spite of the efforts of law enforcement, the street user is purchasing purer heroin now as compared with a generation ago. Moreover, the price of a gram of heroin in 1981 was $4,393; in 2000, it was only $316—less than one-tenth the earlier price (Rhodes, Johnston, and Kling, 2001, p. 43). The reality is, the streets are awash with inexpensive, relatively pure heroin. The most likely explanation for the high number of heroin mentions in DAWN's figures, especially given the extremely low percentage of heroin users among ADAM arrestees, is that, combined with lower price and higher purity, there is a differential rate of mortality among heroin's aging users. Compared with other drug users, heroin addicts seem to be dying off, although at levels that have been slowing down in recent years.

What of the survey data? Do they indicate an increase in heroin use in recent years—specifically, between the early 1990s and today? Keep in mind the warning I issued at the beginning of this section: Surveys are a questionable method for estimating the number of heroin users, since so many of them are *not* to be found in the two locales surveys are most likely to use to contact interviewees—that is, in schools and stable households. Still, what do the surveys say about heroin use in the past decade or so? Comparing 1991 with 2005, among eighth-, tenth-, and twelfth-graders, for lifetime, annual, and 30-day prevalence, these figures increased 1.5–2 times. (Remember, heroin use figures are extremely small, and so the increase in tiny numbers will seem huge when translated into percentage increases.) For these three grades, the average lifetime prevalence figure for 1991 was 1 percent; again, taking all three grades together, in 2005, it was 1.5 percent. For annual prevalence, the three grades averaged 0.5 percent in 1991 and 0.8 percent in 2005. As for 30-day prevalence, the proportion grew from 0.2 percent in 1991 to 0.5 percent in 2005. Clearly, the Monitoring the Future study indicates a substantial increase in heroin use among schoolchildren nationally during the 1990s and into the twenty-first century. Though the numbers are small, the percentage increases are fairly large. Does this indicate that the aging addict population will eventually be replaced with today's schoolchildren heroin experimenters? It is too early to tell, but the increases in heroin use among eighth-, tenth-, and twelfth-graders is a disturbing development.

## WHY TURN ON? THE USER'S PERSPECTIVE

Given the obvious social and medical pathologies associated with heroin use and addiction, the question that immediately comes to mind is, Why should anyone want to become involved with narcotics? Why should a young person—with the facts staring him or her in the face—wish to experiment with heroin? It is extremely easy for the more conventional members of society to apply their own standards of morality to an activity. They offer commonsense explanations in an attempt to justify their views by attributing a negative cause to something that is socially condemned. Thus, heroin addiction—"evil" in the public mind—has to have an evil or negative cause. Yet commonsense explanations are often wide of the mark; common sense, after all, is what tells us the world must be flat. Most explanations of drug experimentation are little more than an effort to inform the public that it is bad, and they nearly always ignore the most important source of information—users themselves. Typically, theories about drug use and addiction are based on virtually no firsthand acquaintance with the addict, the user, or the experimenter. Such theories are necessarily cut off from the drug *experience*—which only the user is capable of conveying. It is an easy matter for us, removed from the drug scene, to declare what the user "should" feel, what he or she inevitably "must" experience. Yet how can we possibly know unless we go directly to the source?

In the past, the great majority of the works on addiction adopted an externalistic and objective posture toward the addict. (There were a few outstanding exceptions to this rule, however.) Obviously, the method selected to study the addict influences what is seen. Many studies relied on addicts in prison or on those who came to the attention of psychiatrists, a highly skewed segment of the addict world. But the prison is not the street, and by relying on prison addict populations, researchers distort the reality of the drug scene. Data collected from caught criminals are biased as well as suspect. Any reliable and valid study of drug use should utilize information secured outside an institutional context. Fortunately, some researchers have attempted to understand addicts by getting out into the street with them, into their world, their natural habitat (Gould et al., 1974; Hanson et al., 1985; Johnson et al., 1985).

A 22-year-old college senior wrote a detailed account of her involvement with heroin. Although her experiences apply to a generation ago, most of the main features of what she said have not changed a great deal. And naturally, her experiences are at once unique and representative; no one else has undergone quite the same experiences, yet many of the broad features of what she did and felt are shared by many middle-class heroin users. Although she never became addicted and stopped using heroin about a month before she wrote her account, she was a weekly user for almost two years. Heroin use, especially the initial experience, and particularly for women, is almost exclusively a group phenomenon. "I did it because my boyfriend did it," she explains. "He did it because his two closest friends did it." Coming back from a vacation with her family, my informant writes: "My boyfriend had a surprise for me. He said he had shot heroin. Suddenly, all of the conventional stereotypes were forgotten. I was more mad about not being there when the first shots were fired than anything else. Instantly, I said I wanted to try it too."

It should be reiterated that most people are first "turned on" to a drug, whether it is heroin or marijuana, by friends rather than drug dealers. It is precisely because drugs are initiated, used, and circulated among intimates that their spread appears almost impossible to stop. Friendship networks are far more difficult to penetrate than those of the drug peddlers.

A kind of bizarre ranking system seems to have emerged among many drug-oriented youths today. My young heroin informant writes that there was in her group

> an unofficial competition, usually unverbalized, concerning who could do [take] the most drugs. . . . I was taken over to the house of a friend who . . . was given to stating that he intended to be the most outrageous drug addict in town, no matter what the drug was. (He was one of the few who talked openly about the competition.) As an example, the best show I ever saw him put on was the night he swallowed some LSD, and shot a couple of bags of dope [heroin], after which he *shot* several more LSD trips, shot at least four more bags of dope, smoked hash [hashish] all night, and took some amphetamines as a nightcap.

This case is obviously extreme, but there seems to be no question that, among a certain proportion of today's youth, experience with, and the ability to handle, various types of drugs has formed a new ranking system, partially replacing athletics, schoolwork, sex, or the ability to "hold your liquor" among some young men who require affirmations of their masculinity. Thus, daring and bravado play some part in the lure of many drugs, although certainly not all.

It is a cruel irony that many of the values of the drug subculture appear to be almost a mirror image—somewhat distorted, to be sure—of some of the most sacred tenets of mainstream America. Thus, the values of success and competition, evidenced by these quotations, can be poured into molds of many different shapes. A country that urges its adolescents to get ahead, to do better than their classmates, and to attend a prestigious college is going to be a country with a competitive drug subculture, with such exotic specimens as these.

Often the user will explain his or her use of a drug by contrasting the excitement of the drug world with the banality of the "straight" world—particularly that of his or her parents. My informant writes:

> I tend to think that the primary target of my striving for deviance is possibly the sterility and blandness of the life I had always been exposed to. . . . My parents . . . gave me a life devoid of real, deep, feeling. I wanted to feel! I wanted to play in the dirt. I wanted to transgress those lily-white norms, break those rules designed to make me a good little Doris Day. And when the first transgression was followed not by the wrath of God . . . but by feeling of being alive, and free, and different, that I had never known before, then I guess after that, all rules and norms lost their meaning and power over me. . . . I knew that there was a way for me to declare my independence from the straight, conventional, and BORING! life my mother wanted me to lead. . . . When I shot up, I felt so superior, so wicked, so unique . . . I thought I had found the ultimate rebellion, the most deviant act possible. I was drawn to it because it set us apart from, and above, everyone even the other drug users, the "soft" drug users. . . . I was . . . irresistibly attracted to and proud of the deviance and antisociability of the act. . . . The "badness" of shooting heroin was precisely why I did not hesitate to do it.

It has been conventional wisdom among drug experts for some time that drug effects are not inherently pleasurable, that users do not experience euphoria the first time they take a given drug, that they have to learn to enjoy the effects that they do experience. As a generalization, this is fairly sound, but it is far from universally true. It is true that many marijuana smokers do not even become high the first time they smoke. On the other hand, when novices do experience the effects of the drug for the first time, they have already been socialized to know what to expect and to define what they do experience as pleasurable. Certainly, alcohol's effects are not always pleasurable to all drinkers, and animals tend to avoid taking it in laboratory settings. However, as we've seen, the amphetamines and cocaine seem to be a different matter; without knowing what they are taking, human subjects usually enjoy the effects of these drugs and want to take them again. Animals seem to enjoy these two stimulants, too, and will do almost anything to continue taking them, over and over again; they possess, in short, an intrinsic, immediate sensuous appeal.

What about the narcotics, especially heroin? Many individuals who take heroin for the first time do not enjoy its effects. This is not, however, always the case. A summary of a number of studies of individuals' first experience with heroin found that about two-thirds of future addicts felt euphoria on their first trial; among nonaddicts, the comparable figure was 31 percent (McAuliffe, 1975, p. 379). Thus, what is often stated in the form of a universal truth should be qualified: Many individuals, including some future addicts, do not feel euphoria the first time they take heroin. Not a few describe the experience in extremely negative terms, as distasteful and unappealing. But often the negative aspects are explained away. Part of the potential addict's learning experience is an arsenal of rationalizations and justifications. My informant described to me her first shot, taken with her boyfriend, who had tried the drug before. When her boyfriend took his shot first, "the rush was so powerful that he almost fell down. He turned white and began to sweat profusely." After her injection, she writes:

> I, too, began to sweat and tremble. If anyone had seen . . . us walking out of the house, he would have called an ambulance. . . . We could barely walk. For some insane reason, we had decided to drive home immediately after shooting up. . . . I had to keep pulling over to throw up on the side of the road. . . . I am truly surprised that we both didn't die that very first night. I was more physically miserable than I had ever been before. The whole night was spent vomiting. The thing that surprises me is that we didn't forget about heroin right then and there. It was horrible! *But we later decided that our dear friend had given us too much. So I decided to give it another chance.* . . . My friends were all doing it, and it had become a question of prestige within our small group [italics added].

Heroin users and addicts paint the pleasure and pain of the drug experience as the most exaggerated that life has to offer. Because of the black-or-white, either-or nature of the drug controversy, antidrug propagandists feel obligated to denounce what might be considered positive traits in illicit drug use: Even so primrose an experience as euphoria becomes reinterpreted as something insidious and artificial. As Philip Slater points out, by conceding favorable characteristics, "we thereby admit their seductive appeal." With drugs, as with all phenomena about which there is considerable controversy, we wish to "devise a conceptual system in which all things one likes fall into one category and all those things one dislikes into another. But good and bad are always orthogonal to [at a right angle or askew from] important distinctions" (Slater, 1970, pp. 2, 154).

Extreme pleasure, then, is a self-reported feature of a large proportion of heroin experiences. My informant describes her first few experiences, after the first shot, in these terms: "I can't describe the rush to you. . . . At the time, *it was better than orgasm*" (italics added). Sexual imagery and analogies are prominent in the descriptions by junkies of their drug experiences. The stiff, rigid needle being inserted into the soft, yielding flesh; the wave of ecstasy flooding the body just after the injection; the feelings of serenity, satisfaction, and well-being after the initial period of euphoria—all these have sexual overtones; indeed, for many junkies, heroin becomes a substitute for sex. (Addiction to heroin produces a reduced interest in sex and often temporary impotence in men.) In evaluating the appeals of heroin, therefore, we cannot omit its hedonistic component. I have been told by heroin addicts and experimenters that the euphoria occurring upon injecting heroin into the vein is far more glorious and pleasurable than anything the nonaddict could possibly experience.

## HEROIN ADDICTION

The linguistic categories used in a particular subculture to typify various forms of behavior and conditions often capture the flavor of the attitudes that participants have about them. Both heroin addicts and marijuana smokers employ the term "straight" to describe pharmacological states (as well as to describe someone who does not use drugs), but the term refers to precisely the opposite states for these two drug users. Heroin addicts say that they are straight when they have just averted withdrawal sickness and are back on an even keel, under the influence of the drug. Marijuana users say that they are straight when they are not under the influence of the drug. This linguistic distinction reveals the radical contrast between addiction, which—when the addicting agent is illicit—becomes an entire way of life (the drug state being a state of "normalcy" toward which all other aspects of life are directed), and the occasional use of a recreational drug, which is typically little more than a hobby, an amusement that is somewhat outside the routine of the everyday. For the heroin addict, heroin is precisely "the everyday."

Evaluations of heroin vary according to individual attitudes and social location. Addicts attribute magical powers to the drug. Far from viewing continued administration of heroin as stupid and senseless, the addict sees abstention as stupid and senseless. In abstention, there is pain and misery; in taking the drug, there is well-being, comfort, and security. The addict's view of heroin as a magic potion arises from both the euphoric rush achieved upon administration and its wondrous ability to allay withdrawal sickness. "We are in the realm of myth," Seymour Fiddle writes, "with heroin as a divine or heroic substance" (1967, p. 66). This mythic attitude extends even to the nonuser, who describes the drug in quite similar terms but evaluates it in precisely the opposite terms. Nonusers often credit heroin with demonic powers, with a kind of black magic hold on the addict.

It is difficult for a nonaddict to understand the almost religious quality of addiction; to someone enmeshed in the narcotics addict subcommunity, heroin is an absolute, something that transcends utilitarian calculation. Every conceivable aspect of life becomes translated into the heroin equation. It is beyond rational cost accounting. Something becomes relevant only insofar as it is related to the acquisition and use of dope. Everything else must be subordinated to it. A choice between heroin and anything else is no choice at all. A journalist quotes an addict on the value of heroin versus the value of money: "A good stash is a lot better than money. Money is phony stuff. . . . It's not a commodity. But heroin's a real commodity. Get a couple of kilos of clean, pure heroin and you've got lifetime security. Better than gold. You've got gold, you've got to spend it to get dope—if you can get it. You've got dope, you've got everything you need. Gold you can always get if you've got dope" (Keating, 1970, p. 30).

Another aspect of addiction often distorted by public stereotypes and misunderstood by nonusers is the role of the heroin seller, or dealer. Public wrath is reserved for the peddler who profits from human misery by selling heroin to the junkie. Sentences ranging up to death have been designed for the pusher. He is, it seems, one of the most insidious characters in the current popular demonology. But the problem is that the addict does not view the dealer in this light. Far from viewing the dealer as a source of misery and pain, the junkie sees him as a kind of savior—a faith healer, a medicine man. Without his supply, the addict would undergo the agonies of withdrawal. The peddler is his lifeline. (To be even more precise, the addict has an ambivalent, love-hate relationship with the dealer, who has something the addict desperately wants but is often unreliable about supplying it.) From this limited—and obviously distorted—perspective, it is possible to view the dealer in positive terms.

## Kicking Heroin

Not all individuals who are referred to as addicts or junkies are literally physically dependent on heroin. Most find this drug so immensely *psychologically* reinforcing that they want and try to take it again and again. For them, discontinuing the use of the drug would be painful not so much as it might entail withdrawal symptoms but because they would be deprived of an experience that has been so euphoric for them in the past. At the same time, the narcotic user or addict is enmeshed in a social network of other users, and kicking the habit is extremely difficult for that very reason. If "turning on" is a group phenomenon, so is turning off—or failing to do so. My college informant writes:

> Whenever I saw my friends, they were shooting up too. . . . The problem with kicking heroin . . . is that all of your friends aren't kicking at the same time. . . . A three months' abstention was accomplished only by almost total isolation from friends in the drug world. . . . One guy . . . sat there praising my boyfriend for being the only one who managed to avoid getting a habit, telling him to "keep it up." My boyfriend said something like, "We couldn't shoot up if we wanted to, we haven't got a spike." Immediately this guy gets a brand new needle and says, as he hands it to my boyfriend, "I hate to think I'm knocking down one of the barriers that keeps you away from dope." He then proceeded to offer my boyfriend a free shot.

In her autobiography *The Fantastic Lodge,* published under the pseudonym Janet Clark, a young woman heroin addict (who later died of an overdose of barbiturates) explains the pressure that others place on the user to continue taking heroin:

> When you hear about them kicking, how does the junkie friend feel about his junkie friend who's kicked, supposedly, and is really cool, making some steps toward improvement in a hopeful manner? He hates his guts. For one thing, he's envious, deeply envious that the friend can get out of the morass, and not him. . . . But for another thing, it gives him a feeling of panic, like, are they fleeing the scene? Am I going to be left here alone? I have to have these people. (Hughes, 1961, pp. 143–144)

Lest we become unduly pessimistic about the addict's chances of getting off heroin, we need only remind ourselves of the remarkable success rate of returning Vietnam veterans who were addicted to heroin. Of all the Army enlisted men who returned to the United States in September 1971, more than 1 in 10 tested positive for narcotics, amphetamines, or barbiturates. Almost 9 out of 10 who tested positive for narcotics were actually addicted—that is, had one or more signs of physical dependence: They designated themselves as addicted, used a narcotic regularly for more than a month, experienced withdrawal lasting two days or more, experienced two or more of the "classic" symptoms of withdrawal, and preferred injecting or sniffing narcotics to smoking them. Three out of four of the narcotics-positive men had three or more of these signs of dependence.

These men were interviewed 8–12 months after their return to the United States. Only 2 percent of the total sample told the interviewers that they were currently using narcotics; urine samples collected at the interview were positive for only 1 percent of the sample. Half of the men who were dependent on narcotics stopped use entirely on their return, only 14 percent became readdicted, and the rest used sporadically. Entering a treatment program had nothing to do with the remarkable success rate—only 5 percent had enrolled in such a program since their return. Clearly, a high proportion of the men who used drugs, and even became heroin addicts, did not continue their habit upon their return to the United States. In spite of the extraordinarily high rate of narcotics use and addiction in this population during their service in Vietnam, a year or so after their return to the States, these men reverted to their pre-Vietnam levels of drug use—as if they had never used drugs in Vietnam in the first place! Simply being an addict does not force the individual to continue using (Robins, 1973). Instead of the cliché "Once an addict, always an addict," what seems to be true in this case is "Once an addict, seldom an addict" (Johnson, 1978).

## Addiction: Myth and Reality

It is a simple matter to apply conventional judgments and evaluations to the world of the addict. Thus, psychiatrists will proclaim that the addict is immature and irrational, and that he or she has a compulsion to avoid responsibility. An earlier tradition of sociologists also built an entire theoretical edifice on the assumption that addiction (this is often stretched to include all illegal drug use) is a **retreatist** adaptation to the problem of social adjustment and that addicts are attracted to their drug because they are "double failures" (Cloward and Ohlin, 1960, pp. 178–184). These views have built into them the biased assumption that to conform to society's expectations is "normal" and that to do otherwise requires an explanation invoking a pathology or a dysfunction of some kind.

To look at the behavior of the addict from the perspective of the addict subculture is to judge the behavior radically differently. Indeed, from conventional society's point of view, addict behavior is irresponsible, because addicts generally do not act in ways that society defines as responsible. Thus, the validity of the retreatist conception of the addict is based on the value assumption that he or she should want the things that society (as well as the researcher) has decided are appropriate for him or her. However, the addict will have a different definition of what constitutes responsible behavior. From the addict's point of view, responsibility rests in being able to hustle the money necessary to maintain a heroin habit. Admiration is reserved for those addicts who are able to succeed gracefully at these demanding requirements: "Prestige in the hierarchy of a dope fiend's world is allocated by the size of a person's habit and his success as a hustler" (Sutter, 1969, p. 195). Addicts are acutely aware that they are masters of forms of behavior at which the "square" would be a hopeless failure. The difficulty of treating heroin addiction, as with all other forms of drug abuse, is rooted precisely in these alternative definitions of reality. To the extent that compulsive dug users define the reality of drug use in positive terms, it will be difficult for a treatment program to convince them to stop; to the extent that a treatment program does not understand such an alternative definition of reality, it will be a failure.

The public image of the addict derives in part from the Chinese opium smoker of a century ago. He is seen as existing in, or retreating into, a state of dreamy idleness, a euphoric temporary death. This state of oblivion does, indeed, typify a certain slice of the addict's day; it is known as "going on the nod." (Its occurrence is, however, dependent on the quality of the heroin administered.) But it is only a small portion of the addict's daily life—the climax, so to speak—and the hectic hustle and bustle of the day is oriented toward this brief moment of transcendence. Far from taking the addict out of contact with the world, addiction "plunges the newly recruited addict into abrasive contact with the world" (Lindesmith and Gagnon, 1964, p. 179). Fiddle calls the kind of life the typical street addict lives a "pressure cooker universe" (Fiddle, 1967, pp. 55–63). Paraphrasing the addict's views on rejecting the retreatist theory of drug addiction, Fiddle writes: "Could a square survive . . . in the kind of jungle we live in? It takes brains, man, to keep up a habit that costs $35 to $40 a day—every day in the year" (Fiddle, 1967, p. 82).

A sensitive and informative account of addiction written by an anthropologist and an economist, titled "Taking Care of Business—The Heroin Addict's Life on the Street" (Preble and Casey, 1969), neatly summarizes the aggressive, rather than retreatist, orientation of addicts' lives:

> Their behavior is anything but an escape from life. They are actively engaged in meaningful activities and relationships seven days a week. The brief moments of euphoria after each

administration of a small amount of heroin constitute a small fraction of their daily lives. The rest of the time they are actively, aggressively pursuing a career that is exacting, challenging, adventurous, and rewarding. They are always on the move and must be alert, flexible, and resourceful. The surest way to identify heroin users in a slum neighborhood is to observe the way people walk. The heroin user walks with a fast purposeful stride, as if he is late for an important appointment—indeed, he is. He is hustling (robbing, or stealing), trying to sell stolen goods, avoiding the police, looking for a heroin dealer with a good bag . . . coming back from copping . . . , looking for a safe place to take the drug, or looking for someone who beat (cheated) him—among other things. He is, in short, *taking care of business.* (Preble and Casey, 1969, p. 2)

## CONTROLLED OPIATE USE

As we've seen, many—indeed most—heroin abusers take their drug of choice on less than a daily basis and are not literally physically dependent on it. However, most street opiate abusers would also become addicted if given the opportunity. They simply cannot sustain the daily grind of raising the cash, locating the seller, dealing with the consequences, or running the risk of arrest that several-times-a-day use entails. At the same time, a high proportion of opiate users take their drug on a *controlled basis*. Until fairly recently, it was not realized that controlled opiate use is possible; it was thought that one was either an addict or an abstainer. However, it is entirely possible that the occasional yet regular controlled user of narcotic drugs is more common than the addict. The term that is used in the world of narcotic drug use to describe this limited use is **chipping** (or "chippying"), which means to fool around or play around with heroin, to use it once in a while or somewhat more often without getting hooked. How common is opiate chipping?

We all recognize that the controlled use of alcohol is not only possible—it is the majority pattern. Most drinkers are moderate in their consumption and do not become alcoholics. Yes, you might object, but narcotics are, well, *addicting*; they produce a physical dependence. Fair enough, but so does alcohol. As we saw in Chapter 7, during much of the history of the United States, alcohol was consumed at levels far greater than it is now; in the period roughly from 1790 to 1830, for instance, in terms of quantity consumed, there were proportionally many more alcoholics than there are today. The fact is, patterns and styles of drug use are not a simple function of the properties of the drugs themselves. To think that they are is to fall victim to what I call the chemicalistic or pharmacological fallacy, or what Jerome Himmelstein calls "the fetishism of drugs" (1979). It is people who choose to take drugs, not drugs that control people. What they take, how they take them, how often, and under what circumstances—all are under the control of the actor, the individual deciding to take (or not to take) a given drug or set of drugs. All drug use is surrounded by values and rules of conduct; these values and rules spell out sanctions—penalties for misuse and rewards for proper use—and these values, rules, and sanctions have an impact on how drugs are actually used.

These rules (sociologists call them *norms*) may be widely accepted and operate on the societywide level, as with alcohol, or they may be characteristic of only small groups or subcultures, whose attitudes and values differ from those of society at large. But when the important people in someone's life believe in a rule, act on it, and enforce it, her or his own behavior will be influenced by that fact. Of course, some will follow their society's or subculture's rules on drug use, and others will not. Norms set limits or establish guidelines that form the framework within which use takes place; they influence people's behavior, but they do not dictate it.

According to Norman Zinberg, who has written a book titled *Drugs, Set and Setting: The Basis for Controlled Intoxicant Use*, values, rules, and sanctions promoting controlled or moderate drug use "function in four basic and overlapping ways." First, they "define moderate use and condemn compulsive use." For instance, controlled opiate users "have sanctions limiting frequency of use to levels far below that required for addiction." Second, such sanctions "limit use to physical and social settings that are conducive to a positive or 'safe' drug experience." Third, sanctions "identify potentially untoward drug effects," and precautions must be taken before and during use. For instance, opiate users may "minimize the risk of overdose by using only a portion of the drug and waiting to gauge its effect before using more." And fourth, sanctions and rituals "operate to compartmentalize drug use and support the users' nondrug-related obligations and relationships." For instance, users may budget the amount of money they spend on drugs and limit use to evenings or weekends to avoid interfering with work and other obligations (Zinberg, 1984, pp. 17–18).

Is it really possible to use heroin or the other opiates on a moderate or controlled basis? One study (Zinberg, 1984) located a number of controlled opiate users and examined their patterns of use, including what made them distinctive and how they accomplished this seemingly impossible feat. They had been using opiate drugs for an average of more than seven years; for four and a half years, they had been using them on a controlled basis. (Some controlled users had used opiates compulsively, and some on a marginal basis, for part of the time they had been using opiates overall.) For the year preceding the study, about a quarter (23%) used opiates sporadically, or less than once a month; a third (36%) used one to three times a month; and two-fifths (41%) used twice a week. None used them daily or more. Their pattern of use, and the length of time that they sustained this pattern, showed "without question that controlled use can be stable" (Zinberg, 1984, p. 69).

Some observers have objected that opiate users who are not yet addicted simply have not reached the stage in their drug "careers" when use inevitably becomes uncontrolled or compulsive (Robins, 1979). But the length of time of opiate use in this sample was not only substantial (more than seven years), it was not significantly different from that of compulsive users in the sample. Moreover, most compulsive users had never had a period of controlled use. And the length of time controlled users had been taking opiates on a moderate basis (four and a half years) was ample time for them to have become compulsive users (Zinberg, 1984, pp. 69–70). Clearly, controlled use is a stable pattern for a significant proportion of narcotic users; moderate use does not necessarily or inevitably turn into compulsive use or addiction. It is a phenomenon that must be understood in its own right.

This same study compared and contrasted the patterns of use that characterized controlled users with those of the compulsive users and found interesting differences. They did *not* differ in type of opiate used—say, sticking with "soft" narcotics, such as Darvon or codeine, versus using heroin. They did *not* differ in route of administration—snorting versus IV injection. And they did *not* differ in personal acquaintance with other users who suffered extremely negative consequences as a result of opiate use—for instance, death from an overdose.

However, the controlled users *did* differ from the compulsive users in a number of crucial ways. In contrast to compulsive users, controlled users (1) rarely used more than once a day, (2) often kept opiates on hand for a period of time without immediately using them, (3) tended to avoid using opiates in the company of known addicts, (4) tended not to use opiates to alleviate depression, (5) usually knew their opiate source or dealer personally, (6) usually used opiates for recreation or relaxation, and (7) tended not use opiates to "escape" from the difficulties of everyday life (Zinberg, 1984, pp. 69–81).

While the controlled use of narcotics, including heroin, is clearly a stable, long-term pattern for many users, it is not clear just what makes it possible for some to avoid physical dependence—how, for instance, they manage to stick to the practices spelled out above—while, for others, this seems to be an impossibility. And, while survey data suggest that recreational nonaddicted users of narcotics are more common than addicts, it would be rewarding to know with a bit more precision just how numerous the representatives of each category are. Clearly, controlled opiate users are worthy of far more study than they have attracted so far.

## Heroin and AIDS

AIDS was first recognized only in 1981 and was not widely publicized until 1983; it has since spread among heroin users like wildfire. The disease is caused by a virus that is spread through bodily fluids—mainly semen and blood. During anal intercourse, infected semen can enter the body through a break, a tear, or a sore or infection. Vaginal intercourse can also spread the virus, but much less effectively than anal intercourse. IV injection itself represents a rupture of the skin; an infected needle can transmit the virus from a fluid, the drug dissolved in water, into the bloodstream of the individual shooting up.

According to the latest (2006) United Nations/World Health Organization estimate, 38.6 million people worldwide are infected with HIV, the virus that causes AIDS. In 2005, 2.7 million people in Africa alone died of AIDS. Globally, roughly 13.2 million HIV infections came about as a result of needle drug use; the rest mainly come from heterosexual and homosexual contact and tainted blood transfusions. According to the latest estimates provided by the federal Centers for Disease Control (CDC), 944,000 cases of HIV/AIDS have been diagnosed in the United States, of whom 529,000 have died; the remainder are still alive and living with the disease.

At the beginning of the AIDS epidemic, almost all of the AIDS cases in the United States involved men who had engaged in anal sex with a male partner. Today, the picture is much more complicated. As Table 11-1 shows, among adolescents and adults, *cumulatively*, as the CDC reports, just over 8 in 10 AIDS sufferers have been male (83%). For persons diagnosed and reported between the second half of 2000 and the first half of 2001, 3 out of 4 (75%) were men. In other words, women have become a substantial minority of AIDS cases in the United States. It should be said that many narcotics-related deaths have not been recognized as caused by HIV. When addicts die of pneumonia, hepatitis, or another, related by-product of addiction, the fact that they have AIDS has often been overlooked. It has been estimated by the CDC that roughly half of the heroin addicts in the United States are infected with HIV, and a quarter of the regular (weekly or more) needle-using cocaine users are likewise infected; most have neither been diagnosed nor have yet contracted AIDS itself.

**TABLE 11-1** **AIDS Cases in the United States by Sex, Adolescent and Adult Only New Cases, 2000–2001, versus Total Cases ("Cumulative")**

| | Males | | Females | |
|---|---|---|---|---|
| | 2000–2001 | Cumulative | 2000–2001 | Cumulative |
| Homosexual Sex | 58% | 61% | — | — |
| Injecting Drugs | 23 | 24 | 36 | 48 |
| HS *and* ID | 6 | 8 | — | — |
| Heterosexual Sex | 11 | 5 | 62 | 48 |
| Medical | 1 | 2 | 2 | 4 |
| Total | 22,919 | 595,757 | 6,350 | 113,103 |

**AIDS Cases in the United States by Race, Adolescent and Adult Males Only**

| | White | | Black | | Hispanic | |
|---|---|---|---|---|---|---|
| | 2000–2001 | Cumulative | 2000–2001 | Cumulative | 2000–2001 | Cumulative |
| Homosexual Sex | 75% | 77% | 44% | 43% | 51% | 47% |
| Injecting Drugs | 12 | 10 | 32 | 39 | 32 | 38 |
| HS *and* ID | 8 | 9 | 6 | 9 | 5 | 7 |
| Heterosexual Sex | 4 | 2 | 18 | 9 | 12 | 7 |
| Medical | 1 | 2 | 1 | 1 | 1 | 1 |
| Total | 9,201 | 293,583 | 8,819 | 189,546 | 4,542 | 105,875 |

*Note:* Table excludes other, unknown, and unreported risks. 2000–2001 is new cases diagnosed between July 2000 and June 2001. "Cumulative" includes all known, reported cases as of June 2001. "Medical" includes cases of hemophilia, blood transfusion, and tissue transplants. "HS *and* ID" refers to cases in which the person engaged in both male-to-male sexual behavior and injecting drugs. All pediatric cases are excluded.
*Source:* Adapted from Department of Health and Human Services, Centers for Disease Control, 2001.

In a sense, there are three distinct AIDS epidemics in the United States. To begin with, women tend to be infected through very different routes than men. Male infections have come about via two main routes. Roughly 6 out of 10 are exclusively a result of male-male anal sexual contact; only a quarter came about as a result of injecting drugs. Today, only 1 out of 10 men (11%) are infected with HIV/AIDS as a result of heterosexual contact. In contrast, for all cases cumulatively, women were evenly divided between IV drug injection and heterosexual sexual contact (48%). However, the majority of recent (that is, the 2000–2001 period) female cases are a result of heterosexual contact (62%) as opposed to drug injection (36%)—and a majority in the former category were infected by lovers who were needle-injecting drug users.

A second AIDS epidemic is among white males, for whom HIV is mainly transmitted through homosexual contact. As we can also see from Table 11-1, about three-quarters of both 2000–2001 and cumulative cases among white men resulted exclusively from homosexual sex, and slightly less than 1 in 10 were infected by homosexual contact and/or IV use of drugs; only 1 in 10 came about exclusively from drug injection. For white men, heterosexual sex is a fairly rare source of HIV infection.

A third epidemic is among Black males, for whom homosexual contact is a bit more than half as likely, drug injection three times more likely, and heterosexual sex is four times more likely, to be the source of infection in comparison with whites. Hispanic patterns of acquiring the disease resemble those of African-Americans more than they do those of whites. In short, among minorities, homosexual sex is a somewhat less substantial source, while IV drug use and heterosexual contact are a more substantial source, of HIV infection in comparison with whites.

To sum up: Women are infected mainly through heterosexual contact; white men are infected mainly through homosexual contact; and Black males (and to some extent, Hispanics) are also infected primarily through homosexual contact—less so than for whites, however—but nonetheless significantly, though secondarily, through drug injection and heterosexual sex.

Some jurisdictions have launched needle-exchange programs in which addicts receive clean syringes in exchange for used ones; the programs also distribute condoms. Critics of these programs object, claiming that they only encourage drug use. However, no evidence has ever been presented that backs up that claim, and the evidence that needle-exchange programs reduce the rate of HIV infection is strong. A two-year study of 2,500 needle-using drug abusers conducted at New York's Beth Israel hospital found that the rate of HIV infection was cut from 4–7 percent per year to only 2 percent. Injection with (possibly tainted) syringes "rented" from other addicts declined 75 percent, and injection with (again, possibly tainted) borrowed needles declined 63 percent, while the use of alcohol swabs before injecting, distributed by the program, increased 150 percent. Interestingly, participants in this program used drugs slightly less often per day, the opposite of what common sense would suggest (Lee, 1994). To the informed eye, needle-exchange programs clearly do help to reduce the incidence of AIDS. Such programs have been adopted in Liverpool and other British locales, and in the Netherlands, a country devoted to a thoroughgoing program of harm reduction. The fact that they are so uncommon in the United States means that the death rate from AIDS, other things being equal, will continue to climb in the needle-using drug community.

## SUMMARY

The public stereotype of heroin addicts may be more negative than for any other drug user. Heroin represents the stereotypical or archetypical street drug; the junkie is seen as a lowlife, an outcast, a deviant. To the sociologist and the criminologist, these images make the use of this drug worth studying.

Heroin is derived from morphine (when consumed, heroin is broken down into morphine in the body), which, in turn, is derived from opium. Heroin is a narcotic, a drug category that also includes (aside from morphine and opium) codeine, Dilaudid, laudanum, paregoric, methadone, Demerol, Percodan, Darvon, oxycodone (OxyContin), hydrocodone, and fentanyl. Narcotics are excellent and effective painkillers, and are used extensively in medicine for that purpose; they are also, without exception, physically addicting. In addition, all are reinforcing; that is, they produce euphoria—a "high." This, in turn, means that they generate a psychological as well as a physical dependence. And, since their lethal dose is only a few times higher than their effective dose, they can kill, principally by paralyzing respiration and the heart.

It is remarkable that heroin is discussed in conjunction with other drugs such as marijuana, cocaine, and amphetamine, since it is one of the least often used drugs both in the United States and worldwide. Only 2 percent of high school seniors and 1 percent of the population as a whole have even tried heroin, and use during the past month is only a small fraction of this small percentage. (Keep in mind, however, that dropouts, absentees, the homeless, and prisoners do not get into conventional samples of the population.) The Abt Associates, using a variety of factors, estimate the size of the chronic heroin population in the country at just under a million. However small its user population is, heroin can cause a great deal of harm; in DAWN's overdose statistics, heroin appears with great frequency: Heroin figures in 1 emergency department mention out of 6, and in over 4 out of 10 medical examiner reports. Given its relative infrequency of use, heroin must be regarded as an extremely dangerous drug.

There is some evidence that the recreational use of heroin rose during the 1990s, and it is possible that this increase continued into the early years of the twenty-first century. The Monitoring the Future survey of secondary school children indicated a substantial increase in most measures of heroin use in eighth grade through the senior year of high school between 1991 and 2005. Still, ADAM's arrestee figures do not indicate an increase in heroin use among the criminal population. Will today's schoolchildren drift into ADAM's future samples? I suspect not, but the possibility should cause concern in any apprehensive observer.

Given the fact that heroin and the other narcotics are powerfully physically dependency producing, it is surprising that many (possibly most) regular users are not actually physically addicted; most are *controlled* opiate users. They regulate their habit by using small amounts, not escalating the amount they use, taking their drugs on special occasions, not hanging out with addicts, using it strictly for recreational purposes, and not getting hooked. Although the junkie is certainly the most well-known type of narcotics user, he or she may very well not be the most *typical* one.

Talking to heroin addicts and users gives us a very different slant on the reality of their use of this drug from that which is promulgated in the media. To begin with, the use of the drug is described in extremely pleasurable terms; one of my informants told me that, for her, shooting heroin was "better than orgasm." Euphoria has to be counted as a major motive for use, especially continued use. As we saw in Chapter 3, reinforcement is almost certainly a stronger motivator for continued use than physical addiction itself. Most of the public wants to attribute dependence to "enslavement" or physical addiction, but the fact is, the jolt of orgasmlike pleasure certainly accounts for far more behavioral dependence than does the avoidance of withdrawal.

The difficulty of kicking heroin stems more from the fact that most of the addict's friends are also addicted than from the drug's supposed magical or demonic hold. Still, many addicts—the majority—do kick, most on their own rather than as a result of a treatment program. Studies of returning Vietnam War veterans who were addicted to narcotics demonstrated that the majority gave up their use of heroin, and of these, the majority did so, again, on their own, without benefit of a formal treatment program. However, what was distinctive about them is the fact that most of their close relationships were with nonaddicts, which indicates that the addict is not "enslaved" to heroin as is popularly thought.

A very high percentage of needle-using heroin addicts, possibly as many as half, either have AIDS or are either infected with HIV and will eventually contract full-blown AIDS.

It is possible that the majority are unaware of being infected. AIDS is an extremely recent disease in the United States; it was not discovered until 1981 and not diagnosed until 1983, the year it became widely publicized. HIV is difficult to contract; for the most part, the only way of becoming infected is through an exchange of bodily fluid (semen and blood, for example) from an infected person to a noninfected person. Anal intercourse and the use of an infected needle are the two most common modes of infection. About 6 out of 10 AIDS patients contracted HIV through anal intercourse, and about 1 in 4 through IV drug use; less than 1 in 10 engaged in both high-risk activities. Women's patterns of contracting HIV are very different from men's; for women, roughly half were infected as a result of drug injection, and half from heterosexual contact. Among white men, homosexual contact is a more substantial source of HIV infection than it is among Blacks and Hispanics, for whom injection and heterosexual sex loom comparatively larger.

## KEY TERMS

analgesics   308

chipping, chippying   320

opiates   308

opioids   308

psychological
   dependence   309

retreatism   319

## ACCOUNT:   OxyContin Addiction

*The author of this account is a 20-year-old female college student who suffers from chronic pain. Although she took (and was addicted to) OxyContin for medical reasons, I include her account in this chapter because it describes an experience with addiction and withdrawal, a major theme in the use of narcotics.*

I have suffered from a chronic pain syndrome my whole life. When I reached the age of 15, the pain became much worse. From that point on, I suffered from a pain that has taken over almost every aspect of my life. After trying injections, surgeries, medications, and several other torturous treatments with no success, my doctor prescribed OxyContin to me. He said that some preliminary research had shown that the painkiller may help me live a normal, pain-free life. At this I was ecstatic. It sounded like, for the first time, there was a possibility for me to be pain-free. Little did I know I was starting down a path that would lead me on a hellish journey for the next four months of my life.

I had my last surgery in May 2002, and I was put on the OxyContin afterwards for pain management. The plan was for me to use the OxyContin to deal with the pain from the surgery and then remain on it as a permanent treatment for my everyday pain. My doctor assured me that I would be fine on the medication. When I asked about addiction, he said that I would not have to worry about it. I felt horrible after the surgery and naturally assumed that my discomfort was mainly from the operation. I soon found out that the surgery had nothing to do with the side effects I experienced. While on the OxyContin, I was unable to eat. Food, even the very thought of food, made me extremely nauseated. If I did attempt to eat anything, I threw up. When I first started the medication I was unable to ride in a car or be exposed to light or noise because my head would pound constantly. That was just the beginning of my suffering.

After I healed from the surgery I started working at a local grocery store for a temporary summer job. At that point, OxyContin was successfully taking away the majority of my pain, but causing me a tremendous amount of distress because of the side effects. I constantly felt miserable while on OxyContin, but there were times when I simply was unable to function. One night at the end of July I was working at the store and I became extremely ill. I had not been feeling well all day, but the store was shorthanded. I became very weak. I suffered from dizziness, confusion, lightheadedness, nausea, and severe stomach upset. I didn't know what to do. I felt as if I couldn't even walk, let alone wait on customers. After a few minutes I ended up going to the back of the grocery store and lying down on the floor. The floor was nasty. It was in the back where all of the shipments came in and out. There I lay. I couldn't even move. I didn't care that I was on that disgusting floor. I stayed there for about 20 minutes. When I got up the strength to walk to the front of the store I asked to go home. My supervisor took one look at me and quickly complied. I was white as a ghost and so weak I could barely stand. I thought that was as bad as it could get. I was wrong.

The next day I was back to my "normal" self. I felt very bad, but I was able to go to work and put on a happy face. I was constantly miserable. Not a minute went by that I didn't feel nauseated or dizzy. Sometimes it was hard for me to stand, and I often worried about my ability to drive a car. This way of life continued on until the middle of August. My body was drained. I was absolutely miserable. I had lost about 25 pounds from being so ill. Every day I woke up and told myself that day would be better but it never was. One morning I woke up extremely ill. I couldn't get out of bed. My legs felt like jelly and I could not support myself just to walk down the stairs. I called out of work and my boss was extremely upset. He yelled at me and told me I was letting him down. This hurt my feelings more than anyone could have ever known. I have always prided myself on being responsible and reliable, and OxyContin took that away from me. It got to the point where I was always letting someone down. I made promises and wasn't able to follow through on them because I was too sick to do what I was asked to do. That was the final straw for me; I decided then and there that the medication was not worth it.

That evening I called my doctor and asked him how I should go about withdrawing from OxyContin. At that point I was getting the medication through patches that I put on my stomach every three days, so I thought going off the medication gradually would be tricky. My doctor disagreed. He said I would have no problem. I had two sets of packages and he told me to simply remove the stronger patch and apply the weaker patch for one week and then just stop using the patches altogether. It sounded simple enough, so I followed his directions. That was on August 20, 2002. I did not stop taking OxyContin until September 24, 2002. The month in between was absolutely horrible for me. The withdrawal was unbearable. I was even more nauseated trying to go off the medication than I was while I was on it. I suffered from diarrhea, upset stomach, dizziness, confusion, trouble with my vision, and worst of all, insomnia. I got into bed at night and lay there tossing and turning until the next morning. I know it doesn't seem possible for a person to suffer from insomnia for an entire month, but it is true. During that month of my life I probably slept a total of 24 hours.

Nighttime was the worst. When I was lying in my bed unable to sleep I shook and twitched. It drove me crazy. As the night went on, I became more agitated. . . . In the beginning of the withdrawal I would give up around 5 o'clock in the morning and put a patch on. Instantly, I got relief and I fell asleep right away. The next day I removed the patch and the battle started all over again. After a couple days that no longer worked. I put the patch on, but I got no relief from it. At that point things became really bad. When I lay in my bed, unable to sleep, I began thinking about killing myself. I just couldn't handle what I was going through. I wanted to die. During the day I could handle the withdrawal, but when I was alone at night I felt I was going crazy. At that point I decided I needed help before I did something to hurt myself.

I called [a pain relief treatment program] and begged to get admitted. . . . After three days of constant phone calls I was admitted into the program. It was a five-day out-patient program. My mother flew in to support me and take care of me throughout the five days. The first morning I went to the center,

I sat in a waiting room for over three hours filled with addicts of all kinds. It just so happened that I was the only person in the pain relief program. The rest of the patients were admitted because of their recreational addiction. This made things very hard for me. I saw one man get admitted while I was in the waiting room. He was so messed up he could not stand on his own. He was yelling at his mother and staring at me. I was scared. This was truly a nightmare for me. I felt ashamed. I wondered what the other people were thinking of me. I wanted to wear a tag on my shirt that told everyone that I was addicted because of my doctor, that it wasn't my fault.

A nurse finally took me into the main part of the facility and explained to me what the next five days would be like. The first three days I would come morning and night to get shots of morphine to help get the OxyContin out of my system as well as help me with the withdrawal symptoms. I would also be given a variety of pills that would help with symptoms and allow me to get some sleep. After I got my first shot of morphine, I was extremely ill. My mother carried me out to the car in the parking lot, and we stayed there for seven hours. If she tried to drive somewhere I got ill, so I slept and she sat by my side in the car all day long. That evening I felt a little better, and she helped me out of the car and back into the center for my second shot of the day. After I got my shot, they gave me medication to help me sleep that night. I was still very ill and I was unable to withstand the long drive home, so we stayed in a hotel across the street. That night was one of the hardest, yet most wonderful nights ever. I felt extremely weird and disoriented from the morphine, but for the first night in a month I slept the whole night through.

The next morning I got up and went for my second day of shots. The shots were administered on the floor where the in-patient addicts were staying. This made me feel very uncomfortable. The patients would walk by and stare at me. Some were even blatantly rude to me. Several of the patients were very upset because I got to go home. They just couldn't figure out why I was able to leave during the day and at night. One person sat next to me and asked how long I had been using heroin for. She told me that the other patients had told her that is what I was "in" for. The rumors got stronger and stronger each day. I dreaded having to go there every day. When I went each day I was drug tested. This offended me because I was there for medical addiction. It made me feel like I was a bad person and I couldn't be trusted. After day three I was no longer given shots. I went morning and night to get drug-tested and they gave me pills for the day. I got some medication to deal with any of the symptoms that I still had and I also continued to get the pills that helped me sleep. After those five days I was finally free of the OxyContin. For the following month I had slight problems here and there, but nothing compared to what I had suffered previously. My experience was hell, but I would not change it if I could. It has made me a stronger person and I am also much more aware of the dangers of drug use, whether recreational or prescription.

## QUESTIONS

Why do you think this woman's experiences with OxyContin (generic name: oxycodone) were so terrible? Were they an effect of the drug alone? Or a combination of the drug and her idiosyncratic biochemical makeup? If the drug's effects are as painful as this, why is it becoming popular with so many recreational drug users? Why is it currently being prescribed for pain? Do you think that there's any relationship between the medical use of psychoactive drugs and their recreational use? That is, are often-prescribed, psychoactive, Schedule II drugs more likely to be used recreationally than Schedule I drugs? Should oxycodone be reclassified as a Schedule I substance?

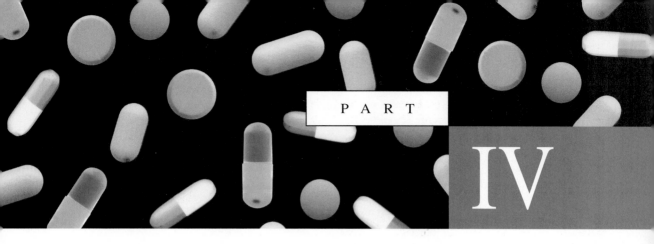

# DRUGS, CRIME, AND DRUG CONTROL

# DRUGS AND CRIME

## What's the Connection?

In the 1930s, a flood of articles, books, and films proclaimed that marijuana caused crime and violence. The drug "is as dangerous as a coiled rattlesnake," proclaimed the then commissioner of the Federal Bureau of Narcotics. "How many murders, suicides, robberies, criminal assaults, holdups, burglaries, and deeds of maniacal insanity it causes each year," Harry Anslinger stated, "especially among the young, can only be conjectured." The commissioner cited the case of a young man who, under the influence of "reefer," murdered a harmless old man. "Something just told me to kill him!" the young man was quoted as saying. "That's marijuana!" the commissioner declared (Anslinger, with Cooper, 1937, pp. 18, 153).

Today, we recognize such claims as fanciful propaganda. Hardly any expert observers conducting research nowadays argue that the effects of marijuana *cause* violent, criminal behavior. This media-fabricated linkage should warn us that all claims about the **criminogenic,** or crime-causing, effects of drugs should be examined with a certain degree of healthy skepticism and a strong dose of empirical evidence.

## WHAT'S THE NATURE OF THE DRUGS–CRIME LINK?

And yet, there *is* a connection between these two universes of human behavior—drug use and sale on the one hand, and criminal behavior on the other. This connection is empirical. By that I mean that, factually speaking, the users of illicit drugs, taken as a whole, are more likely to engage in criminal behavior than are persons who abstain from the use of illegal psychoactive substances. This is also true of people who sell illegal drugs: Setting their illicit drug selling aside, their rate of criminal behavior is higher than average—a great deal higher. Interestingly, people who drink alcoholic beverages are also more likely to commit criminal behavior than people who do not. There are myriad ways in which these two areas of behavior (that is, using, and selling psychoactive substances on the one hand, and committing crime on the other) overlap and intertwine. In this chapter, we'll look at some of them. But before we do, I have to make several absolutely crucial points; otherwise, our subject will be meaningless and incomprehensible.

The first point is the following: When we ask what the exact nature of the connection between drugs and crime is, we are most interested in spelling out their causal (cause-and-effect) relationship. As we saw in Chapter 6, many relationships exist in which two or more things are *statistically* but not *causally* related. Remember that rape and the consumption of ice cream are connected, but not directly or causally; eating ice cream does not cause men to rape women. The connection is *indirect* in that ice cream consumption is higher in the summer, as is the rate of rape. In contrast to the ice cream and rape example, a cause-and-effect relationship is one that is *direct,* in which one factor has an impact on another. Do drugs have that cause-and-effect connection with crime? If so, exactly what is its nature?

A second point: In a discussion of any cause-and-effect connection, we have to be clear on the *direction* of the relationship. Does factor A cause factor B—or is it the other way around? If I bang my thumb with a hammer, it hurts. Hitting my thumb (A) caused the pain (B). In contrast, in a given relationship, two things could both be caused by a third factor—factor C. This is the ice cream and rape connection.

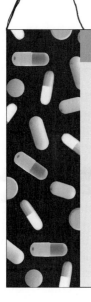

## True-False Quiz

I asked my students to give me an idea of their notion of the crime rate over time, that is, whether it has been rising or declining. The statements tapping this question read: "Between the 1970s and the early twenty-first century, the rate of *property* crime decreased significantly" and "Between the 1990s and the early twenty-first century, the rate of *violent* crime decreased significantly." As we see in this section, these two statements are true; in fact, the decline in the crime rate over the past several decades is one of the most remarkable developments in the field of criminological statistics. Researchers are still debating *why* it occurred, but all agree that it is a fact. My students did not seem to be aware of this development; 63 percent thought the statement about property crime's decline is false, and 52 percent thought the one on violent crime is false.

The question then becomes: Does drug use—getting high—*directly* cause the user to commit criminal behavior (A causes B)? Or does a certain factor (C) cause someone both to use drugs (A) *and* to engage in criminal behavior (B)—thereby creating an *indirect* relationship between our two variables? In the latter case, both drug use and crime are effects of a common cause. For instance, do certain kinds of people like to engage in risky behavior and so both use illegal drugs and engage in criminal behavior? Here, having a predilection for risky behavior (C) causes both drug use (A) and crime (B).

Researchers refer to one factor or variable that causes another as the **independent variable,** and the factor or thing that is caused, on which an effect may be observed, as the **dependent variable**. For instance, as noted previously, young people are more likely to use drugs than older people. Hence, in the relationship between age and drug use, age is the independent variable and drug use is the dependent variable. That is, age causes drug use— drug use does not cause age. With drugs and crime, which one is the independent and which is the dependent variable? Or, alternatively, are both effects of a common cause, which is the true independent variable? This is the central question here, the issue that forms the foundation of this chapter.

The third point is that, since the possession and sale of illegal substances is *by definition* criminal behavior, we have to distinguish between drug crimes and nondrug crimes. Of course drug use causes users to engage in drug crime, since the possession and transfer of illegal substances are themselves a violation of the law. The ways in which drug use and drug selling influence one another, and the ways that each influences the commission of criminal behavior, are likely to be somewhat different; each connection deserves a separate discussion. In this chapter, we are interested in how drug use and nondrug crimes, mainly the FBI's Index Crimes—murder, rape, robbery, aggravated or serious assault, burglary, motor vehicle theft, and a miscellaneous category called larceny-theft—influence one another.

The fourth point is that, since alcohol is a legal drug, its role in causing criminal behavior is likely to be somewhat different from the role played by the controlled substances. For instance, consuming alcohol does not as often place someone in contact with persons who are willing to break the law as is true with the use of illicit substances. Using drugs is more likely than using alcohol to entail interacting in social circles in which illegal behavior is taken for granted and routinely practiced. As a result, the consequences for criminal behavior of consuming alcohol are likely to be a bit different from those entailed by the consumption of illicit drugs. To put the matter a bit differently, statistically speaking, predicting solely on the basis of your companions, lifting a glass of beer in your neighborhood tavern is less likely to lead to an assault than is true of smoking a pipeful of crack cocaine.

A fifth point is related to the previous two: We have to clarify *whether* and *to what extent* the connection of illicit drugs with crime is a consequence of their criminal status or their pharmacological properties. Do users commit crime more often than nonusers because of the illicit status of the substances they use? Or because of the direct effects of those substances? Does the very fact of prohibition actually encourage or stimulate criminal behavior? Untangling the causal role of the law from the causal role of chemicals acting on the human body is an essential goal of any discussion in the drugs–crime connection.

A final key point is that there is a close link between *committing* crime—especially violence—and *being a victim* of crime. This is not in the definitional sense that predatory crimes need a victim to occur. Rather, it is in the sense that many of the same social and personal characteristics that correlate with engaging in crime also correlate with being victimized by crime. Criminals and victims of criminals tend to be alike in many crucial ways, including being in one another's presence a great deal more often than randomly selected individuals. Hence, many of the same dynamics that produce one also produce the other. When researchers say that the world of drugs is more criminal than worlds that are free of drugs, they mean that users are more likely to be both offenders *and* victims. Using and being under the influence of psychoactive drugs is as closely related to committing crime as is being victimized by crime. Because of the way most crimes take place, the second can be predicted from the first. Some observers have argued that this line of reasoning "blames the victim" (Ryan, 1976), but the fact is, "blame" is a moral concept, whereas "cause" is a scientific concept (Felson, 1991). And both empirically and causally, drug users are more vulnerable to crime victimization than is true of persons who do not use drugs.

All this being said, some drugs are vastly more criminogenic than others. Their connection with criminal behavior is extremely strong and does not weaken or disappear when other factors are controlled or held constant. Every time we look at a cross section of offenses, certain drugs stand out as both empirically and causally implicated. These drugs are frequently in evidence wherever crime is committed, and they are part of the reason why crime is committed. In addition, crime frequently follows in the wake of drug use. And if there can be said to be a "Big Three" in the drugs–crime connection, they would almost certainly be the same "Big Three" that appear in DAWN's data—alcohol, cocaine, and heroin. Their contribution to the crime picture is huge, on a crime-by-crime, use-episode by use-episode basis, and hence their place in the discussion that follows will be correspondingly large.

But why? Why are these drugs connected to crime, and more specifically, why are they hugely implicated in the drugs–crime equation? To repeat, what's the *reason* behind the drugs–crime connection?

James Inciardi refers to this as "The Riddle of the Sphinx"—a riddle that seems fiendishly difficult, that demands an answer upon pain of death, yet whose answer may be simpler than we realize (2002, p. 182). The relationship between drug use and criminal behavior has been debated among drug researchers at least as far back as the 1920s. The questions that these researchers have asked are these: Does drug use cause criminal behavior? Does crime cause drug use? Or are they both effects of a common cause? Drug researchers offer different explanations, depending on the theorist articulating the explanation and whether the offense is a violent or a property crime. What are these explanations, what evidence supports them, and which ones seem to make the most sense?

## Drugs and Crime: Three Models

Researchers most often argue three explanations or models of the connection between drug use and crime: the enslavement, the predisposition, and the intensification models. In one way or another, over the years, these three have dominated the discussion on the issue. The enslavement and the intensification model focus mainly on economic crime, whereas the predisposition model addresses crime in general, whether property or otherwise. In addition, the enslavement and the intensification models focus mainly on addicting drugs—specifically, the narcotics—whereas the predisposition model applies to the consumption of any and all illicit substances.

### The Enslavement Model

The **enslavement model** argues that basically law-abiding citizens, more or less as a result of accident or happenstance—a mental defect, medical addiction, poverty, unemployment, or temporary life problems—become trapped into the use of addicting drugs. The illicit nature of the narcotics market forces these citizens to resort to a life of crime to support their habits. If authorities regarded drug abuse as a medical problem, and if narcotics were legal and dispensed inexpensively at clinics, addicts would not have to resort to moneymaking crimes. Under a regime of legal, medically supervised narcotics, there would be virtually no connection between drug use and criminal behavior. Heroin users commit crimes only because narcotics are illegal—and therefore expensive—and addicting—thereby "enslaving" themselves to both a life of addiction and a life of crime (Lindesmith, 1965; Schur, 1962). This perspective is also referred to as the "medical model."

### The Predisposition Model

The **predisposition model** argues against and opposes the enslavement or medical model. According to proponents of this model, addicts do not engage in criminal behavior because they are forced into a life of crime by their drug use, and they were not law-abiding people before they became involved in the use of narcotics. In fact, most of the people who become addicted were *already* engaged in a life of crime, even before they became involved with drugs. The drugs–crime connection exists because criminals are deviant, antisocial people who have a predisposition to both crime and drug use, and because criminals and users of illicit drugs are the same people. This predisposition is reinforced by the fact that in the social circles in which criminals move about, drug use is accepted, encouraged, and widespread. As a result of this predisposition, legalizing drugs would be futile. Under legalization, criminal behavior would remain high among the people who might eventually become addicts—whether or not they do become addicts—because they engaged in a life of crime even before they began using drugs. This predisposition hypothesis was promulgated in the 1950s and early 1960s by representatives of the Federal Bureau of Narcotics and the FBI. Currently, it is supported by Michael Gottfredson and Travis Hirschi's "general theory of crime" (1990). This perspective is also referred to as the "criminal model."

## The Intensification Model

The **intensification model** offers both a synthesis and a reformulation of the enslavement and the predisposition models. This model argues that both contain a grain of truth, yet as complete explanations both are fatally flawed in that they are based on an unarguably false empirical premise. Neither is entirely consistent with the facts, which is where the intensification model comes in.

Contrary to what the enslavement model argues, juvenile crime frequently precedes drug use. More than half the people who eventually become addicts began committing crime *before* they became addicted (Anglin and Speckart, 1988, p. 223). But there is no consistent pattern here: Property crime may occur before addiction, or addiction before property crime. Their temporal sequence is almost irrelevant. Both alcohol and illicit drug use are extremely common among delinquents, and engaging in substance abuse and committing criminal offenses typically go hand in hand. Drug addiction does not take place at random; only certain types of people use and become heavily involved with narcotics—and these tend to be precisely the type who are also highly likely to commit criminal behavior. This would seem to support the predisposition model.

On the other hand, contrary to what advocates of the predisposition model might predict, when addicts *abstain* from the use of narcotics, their crime rate plummets. Researchers John Ball and David Nurco conducted a study of 350 narcotic addicts in Baltimore. They found that during their first addicted period, these addicts committed criminal offenses, on average, on 255 days per year; for their first nonaddicted period, they averaged only 82 crime-days per year. The same difference between periods prevailed during their second and subsequent addicted and nonaddicted periods (Ball et al., 1981; Ball, Shaffer, and Nurco, 1983). When narcotics addicts are enrolled in a maintenance program and are taking their prescribed methadone, they commit roughly *one-half to one-third* the volume of moneymaking crimes as when they are off the program, not taking methadone, and using or addicted to narcotics (Hubbard et al., 1989).

While it is true that criminal behavior does not disappear during periods of abstention, nor does it decline to the average for people who do not use illicit drugs, it is massively lower than during periods of addiction. There is a linear relationship here. There are "strong, monotonic increases in property crime activities with increasing narcotics use levels" (Anglin and Speckart, 1988, p. 198). The greater the use of narcotics, the higher the rate of property crime; the lower the use of narcotics, the lower the rate of property crime.

Though drug use does not create or generate criminal behavior from a law-abiding way of life, the use of and addiction to narcotics *intensifies* and *perpetuates* criminal behavior and criminal careers. "In that sense, it might be said that drug use freezes its devotees into patterns of criminality that are more acute, dynamic, unremitting, and enduring than those of other [that is, nonusing] offenders" (Inciardi, 1992, p. 158). In short, "drug use *drives* crime," that is, it intensifies "already existing criminal careers" (p. 163).

Although each contains a grain of truth, as complete explanations, both the enslavement and predisposition models are fatally flawed. The only explanation that adequately accounts for the connection between heavy, continued, and especially addictive drug use, and criminal behavior, especially property crime, is the intensification model.

## THE DRUGS–VIOLENCE NEXUS: THREE MODELS

Violence is a major type of crime. The FBI includes four violent offenses among its Index Crimes—criminal homicide or murder, aggravated (or serious) assault, forcible rape, and robbery. Just as property crime is connected with drug use, so is violent crime: Drug users are more likely to engage in more, and more serious, violent offenses than nonusers, and as use escalates, so does the likelihood of engaging in violence.

The most serious of all forms of violence, of course, is murder. The evidence says that drug users are much more likely to both kill and be killed than people who do not use drugs. But this link—or at least, the *strength* of this link—is fairly recent. For example, between 1974 and 1986, only one person in Los Angeles County died with detectable levels of cocaine in his or her body. In 1988 alone, this figure was 1,160. Of the victims with cocaine in their systems, 6 out of 10 died a violent death; of these, two-thirds were either shot or stabbed. And 1 in 5 were committing violence against another person when they met their demise (Budd, 1989).

Or consider the following: There were about 16,000 murders in the United States in the most recent year tabulated (2004), for a rate of 5.5 per 100,000 in the population. Over a 15-year period, given the current rate, the odds of a randomly selected person being murdered is less than 1 in 1,000. In the 1960s, Edward Preble interviewed a sample of 78 heroin addicts; then, 15 years later, he tried to locate them for a reinterview. Out of the sample, 11 had been the victims of homicide, which represents a rate of homicide victimization more than 100 times that of the general population. Of course, heroin addicts are not a cross section of the population at large, and the homicide rate was much higher in 1970s and 1980s than it is today. Still, the lesson should be clear: Drug use is *heavily* implicated in the world of violence, and in interesting and complicated ways.

As with crime generally, what causes or makes for the relationship between drugs and violence? Paul Goldstein proposed three possible models to explain the **drugs–violence nexus:** the psychopharmacological, the economic-compulsive, and the systemic models.

### The Psychopharmacological Model

The most commonsensical and traditional model or explanation of why drugs and violence are connected is the **psychopharmacological model.** Proponents of this line of thought hold that it is the psychological and physical effects of psychoactive substances that cause users to become violent toward others. As a result of ingesting one or more substances, users "may become excitable, irrational, and may exhibit violent behavior" (Goldstein, 1985, p. 494). As we saw in the opening to this chapter, this is what the Federal Bureau of Narcotics of the 1930s thought happened under the influence of marijuana (Anslinger and Cooper, 1937)—a view that has been thoroughly discredited. However, although the effects of opiates tend to be soothing and soporific, the "irritability associated with the withdrawal syndrome . . . may indeed lead to violence" (Goldstein,

1985, p. 495). In addition, as we saw, someone is more likely to be victimized when under the influence of one or more psychoactive substances, and hence, in that sense, the effects of drugs may lead, albeit more indirectly, to violence.

### The Economic-Compulsive Model

Another explanation or model for drug use often leading to violence is the **economic-compulsive model.** Here it is thought that because addicts need to raise large sums of money quickly, they engage in high-risk crimes, including theft, robbery, and burglary, that often escalate into acts of physical harm against the victims. For instance, in a given robbery, both the perpetrator and the victim may be nervous; the victim may resist, struggle, or attempt to retaliate against the offender, and may be accidentally stabbed or shot. In a burglary, the offender may be confronted by the resident and may attempt to flee, resulting in a struggle; suddenly, a crime of stealth becomes assault or even murder. Economic crimes undertaken to support a drug habit don't always remain simple property crimes; inadvertently, a certain proportion turn into crimes of violence.

### The Systemic Model

The world of drug dealing is thoroughly saturated with violence. Not having recourse to the protection of the law, dealers often resort to taking the law into their own hands. Drug sellers carry or stash drugs—a commodity more valuable on the streets than gold—and handle large sums of cash. The temptation for all manner of street people is to rob dealers of both the cash and the drugs. Drug sellers are vulnerable to arrest, and informers often turn them in to avoid long prison sentences; violent retaliation is a common response to such betrayal. Drug sales may result in disputes over the quality and quantity of the goods sold. One gang may decide to "muscle into" the turf or territory of an already established gang, resulting in a shooting war. Buyers may receive a shipment of drugs, use most of it themselves, and be unable to pay for what they consumed.

Systemic violence, then, refers to "the traditionally aggressive patterns of interaction within the system of drug distribution and use." In the **systemic model,** systemic violence is "normatively embedded in the social and economic networks of drug users and sellers. Drug use, the drug business, and the violence connected to both of these phenomena, are all part of the same general lifestyle. Individuals caught in this lifestyle value the experience of substance use, recognize the risks involved, and struggle for survival on a daily basis. That struggle is clearly a major contributor to the total volume of crime and violence in American society" (Goldstein, 1985, pp. 497, 503).

### Which Model Makes the Most Sense?

The question of which of these three models best explains the strong relationship between drug use and violence was tackled by a team of researchers who examined the dynamics of criminal homicide in New York City during the height of the crack crisis in the late 1980s (Goldstein et al., 1989). A homicide was classified as "drug-related" if it was decided by both the researchers and the police that drugs contributed to the killing "in an important and causal manner" (p. 662). A sample of roughly a quarter of all criminal homicides that took place in 1988 was selected. It was made up of 414 "homicide events," (some of these events

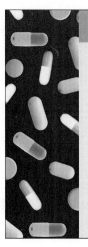

## True-False Quiz

When I offered the statement "The majority of crack cocaine-related murders took place in the late 1980s occurred because the user was under the influence and, as a consequence, became irritated, excited, angry, disturbed—and thus, committed violence," just under half of my students (45%) agreed and just over half (54%) did not. This is interesting, because clearly, a substantial proportion rejected the psychopharmacological model of crack-related violence, a key ingredient in the drug's mythology. Perhaps the notion that in the 1980s, crack dealers settled scores with one another through violence—a far more accurate image than the one that emphasized crack's effects as the culprit—has seeped into the public's consciousness.

involved more than one perpetrator and more than one victim). Just over half (53%) of these events were classified as primarily drug related; just under half (47%) were deemed not to be drug related. Studying each event on a case-by-case basis, the researchers and the police determined that 60 percent of the drug-related homicides involved crack cocaine; an additional 22 percent involved powder cocaine.

The question that dominated the focus of this research team was: Which of the three models best explains the connection between drugs and criminal homicide? The psychopharmacological model, which during the crack epidemic in the late 1980s attracted so much media attention and is so intuitively appealing to much of the public, does not offer an adequate guide to reality. Of the 118 crack-related homicides, only 3 (3%) were deemed to have been caused by the psychoactive effects of the drug. Only 8 (7%) were judged to have been economic-compulsive in origin. Except for a few "multidimensionally" caused homicides, all of the remainder (100 out of 118, or 85%) could be explained by the systemic model. The circumstances of systemic homicides included territorial disputes, the robbery of a drug dealer, efforts to collect a drug debt, disputes over a drug theft, and reactions to a dealer selling poor-quality drugs. In other words, typically, killings connected to crack (and powder cocaine as well) were caused *not* by the effects of the drug but by the violent and conflictual nature of the crack *business.*

What makes the crack business an especially disputational enterprise? Why was the crack trade, for example, in comparison with the heroin business, an arena in which murder took place with special frequency? The authors trace the volatile nature of the crack trade to its unstable, disorganized distribution system. Since cocaine hydrochloride can be extremely easily converted into crack, there is no hierarchy or organizational structure to hold dealing networks together. The marketplace is made up of many small-scale entrepreneurs, independents who are able to start up a business for themselves and compete in the same territory for a clientele. Hence, boundary disputes are plentiful, and there are no higher-ups—indeed, no organization at all—capable of controlling violence when it does threaten to erupt.

Moreover, in addition to the simplicity of the cocaine-to-crack conversion process, since crack is so inexpensive on a dose-by-dose basis, anyone with a modest cash investment can set up shop. As a result, extremely young dealers entered the crack trade, many of whom were fearless, reckless, and lacking in judgment. As Robert Stutman, a former Drug Enforcement Administration (DEA) agent (1985–1990) notes in the 1998 PBS broadcast *Drug Wars,* the DEA was frustrated in its efforts to disrupt the crack trade because they couldn't find anyone who controlled it. There was no organization, he explains. "The organization," Stutman says, emphasizing his point, "was a 20-year-old guy and three 10-year-old kids." Hence, the extremely frequent resort to violence—*systemic* violence.

## COCAINE USE AND VIOLENT BEHAVIOR

Several of the same researchers who were involved in the study on the connection between drugs and criminal homicide (Goldstein et al., 1989) became curious about how cocaine use more generally influenced violent behavior. It is one thing to determine that in 1988, at the height of the crack epidemic, the nature of the drug trade was responsible for a majority of New York City's drug-related homicides. It is quite another to ask about the role of crack and powder cocaine use in accelerating violent behavior in general.

The researchers interviewed a sample of cocaine users weekly, for a period of eight weeks, about their day-to-day drug use, drug dealing, drug treatment, sources of income, expenditures, and criminal and violent behavior (Goldstein et al., 1991). Then they divided their sample into "big" and "small" users—the dividing line being the expenditure of $34 worth of cocaine on days when they used. "Big" male users averaged $76 per use-days, "small" male users $19, "big" female users $55, and "small" female users $18. (To keep prices in perspective, between 1990 and 2004, the consumer price index increased by about 50 percent; however, over the past two decades, cocaine's price declined by half and its purity increased by 70 percent.)

The most important finding of this study was that, among males, as the volume of cocaine use increased, their likelihood of being a *perpetrator* of violence increased, whereas among females, as cocaine use increased, their likelihood of being a *victim* of violence crime increased.

For male small users, the violent events that most often took place were more or less evenly divided among robbery, non-drug-related disputes, and drug-related disputes. In contrast, nearly half of the male big users' violent events entailed robbery alone. For women, however, consistently across the board, violent victimization represented the largest category of violent events; a substantial proportion of these were "domestic disputes involving spouses, boyfriends, and lovers" (p. 359). During the 56 days of the period investigated, nearly one out of eight (12%) of the big female users were sexually assaulted. Clearly, then, the important finding of the study is this: For men, increased use of cocaine escalated violent behavior; for women, increased use escalated violent victimization.

In contrast with their previous study on drug-related homicide, the Goldstein team found that psychopharmacological violence was most prevalent in the violent events that took place among their sample of users. Among all users groups, they say, for both males and females, "there was a greater proportion of violent events with a psychopharmacological dimension than with a systemic dimension" (p. 361). This is not to say that cocaine was the only factor involved in the violence. Males committed a great deal of violence that was not related to cocaine at all. For instance, most of the male psychopharmacological violent events entailed the consumption of alcohol. In addition, most of the systemic violence that took place was related to the sample's use and sale of heroin, not cocaine.

These researchers trace the violence in which their sample was involved, either as a perpetrator or a victim, to their "mode of living," to a "subculture of violence" in which cocaine use "may be a correlate, but not a cause, of violence" (p. 365). Clearly, the regular use of cocaine often situates the user in a milieu in which violence is a frequent accompaniment. While it is certainly possible to find social circles of cocaine users who do not readily and routinely engage in or subject others to violence, statistically speaking, those odds diminish the more that the drug is used and is a fixture or accompaniment of the social life of a group or social circle in question. This study does not settle the issue of what causes the cocaine–violence link, but it does provide powerful evidence that it is strong and unlikely to disappear as a result of any conceivable policy change. The fact is, heavy cocaine use tends to take place in social settings in which violence is a common accompaniment, among social circles that readily and almost routinely engage in violent behavior. The cocaine itself almost certainly escalates the frequency and level of violence, but the people who use the drug engage in violence far more than is true of the population at large, and this would remain the case, cocaine or no cocaine. And equally clearly, the legalization, and hence greater availability, of cocaine would not diminish the cocaine–violence link but might very well magnify it. If greater cocaine use results from legalization, a greater volume of violence would almost inevitably result as well.

## HEROIN ADDICTION AND VIOLENCE

During the 1950s and 1960s, the image of the narcotic addict held by most experts was of a person underrepresented in crimes of violence (Finestone, 1957a, 1957b; Lindesmith, 1965; Preble and Casey, 1969; Schur, 1962). In that era, a majority of researchers believed that, for the most part, heroin addicts rarely engaged in violence. Instead, they engaged in crime rationally and in pursuit of a specific end: to obtain money so that they could purchase heroin to support a habit over which they had no control. (This approach is tied to enslavement theory, discussed previously.) To the extent that the addict was engaged in a life of crime at that time, it was a product of the artificially high prices of the drug. The compulsive nature of continued heroin use impelled users into addiction; the heroin laws and their enforcement drove up the price of the drug and made it profitable to sell on a large, organized scale. If some violence did take place in the world of heroin use—for instance, in robberies in which the victim resisted—it was an artifact of the criminalization of the drug.

In other words, these early researchers argued, heroin-related violence was overwhelmingly economic-compulsive rather than psychopharmacological or systemic. Remove the economic motive by supplying addicts with cheap, pure heroin, and you sever the connection between addiction and crime and, as a consequence, between addiction and violence. Clearly, these early researchers' position was closely coupled with a policy agenda—the legalization of heroin.

During the 1970s, drug researchers began to realize that the dominant image of the narcotic addict as nonviolent was inaccurate (McBride and Swartz, 1990). As Michael Agar pointed out (1973), buying and selling heroin take place in a climate of fear, suspicion, mistrust, and paranoia, with each party attempting to take advantage of the other. Aggression and violence are never remote from the enterprise of street heroin dealing. Joseph Fitzpatrick (1974) found that criminal homicide was the leading cause of death among the clients of drug treatment programs. (Being murdered grows out of many of the same dynamics as committing murder.) J. R. Monteforte and W. U. Spitz (1975) found that two-thirds of homicide victims in Detroit were involved in illegal drug use or dealing. Certainly, by the mid-1970s, the view that the heroin addict was less violent than other criminals was no longer tenable. If anything, the world of narcotic addiction was shown to be every bit as violent as most other sectors of the criminal world and, in all likelihood, significantly more so.

How could these early researchers have been so wrong about a major aspect of the addict's life? Duane McBride and James Swartz (1990) suggest that the reasons are a mixture of misperception and an actual historical shift in the addict subculture. No doubt, some of these early researchers saw addiction in a somewhat distorted light. To begin with, they relied far too much on the pharmacological model, emphasizing heroin's contrasts with cocaine. Heroin, they argued, soothes, sedates, and tranquilizes; its effects incline the user away from aggressive, violent acts. Under the influence, all the addict wants to do is to relax, nod out, and doze off. Vigorous activity is undertaken only when the addict is searching for money and drugs. What these early researchers failed to take into account was that the frequent periods of withdrawal the addict endures are marked by irritability, discomfort, and the strong craving for a fix (McBride and Swartz, 1990, p. 149)—conditions that make violence a potentiality. In any case, the pharmacological effects of drugs do not explain all facets of the user's life; indeed, factors other than these effects may explain far more of the addict's criminal and violent behavior.

Another source of confusion among these early researchers lay in their classification of robbery as a nonviolent property crime. Robbery—entailing, as it does, victim confrontation and force or the threat of force—is itself a crime of violence. Addicts commit robbery at a significantly higher rate than most major categories of criminals. Moreover, robbery often sparks other crimes of violence, such as assault and homicide, as when the victim resists, struggles, or attempts to escape, or when the robber misreads the victim's intentions. We can't so easily discount this avenue of violence.

It is also true that after the early 1970s, the world of narcotic addiction *became* more violent than it had been previously (McBride and Swartz, 1990, pp. 149–150). Evidence suggests that the subculture of addiction experienced a dramatic shift in 1970 or so. Individuals initiated into heroin use after that time were socialized into a subculture that was far more willing to use violence than was true of those initiated prior to that date (Stephens and Ellis, 1975; Zahn and Bencivengo, 1974).

In addition, before 1970 or so, most addicts used heroin more or less exclusively. After that time, heroin addicts became **polydrug users.** And polydrug users are more prone to resort to violence than are individuals who use heroin and only heroin. This is especially true when cocaine is combined with heroin, as is so often currently the case. In short, by the early 1970s, "a new and different breed of heroin user was living on the streets of American cities" (Inciardi, 2002, p. 191)—a far more violent breed.

Obviously, the earlier image of the narcotic addict as less violent than other offenders is false and has been for more than a generation. In one study of state prisoners in 1979, twice as many said that they had been under the influence of heroin (8%) as cocaine (4%) when they were arrested for the violent crime for which they were incarcerated. And 12 percent of those convicted of robbery said that they had been under the influence of heroin at the time of committing the crime, whereas only 6 percent mentioned cocaine (Kalish and Matsamura, 1983). One study of the drug use habits of inmates in three states—Michigan, California, and Texas—found that half of the most violent criminals were heroin users, most of whom were daily users with high-cost habits. Three-fifths of the violent predators in this study (that is, those who had committed robbery and assault) were heroin users, and a third were high-cost, daily heroin users. And over half of those with high-cost heroin habits were violent predators or robber-dealers (Chaiken, 1986). Heroin abusers and addicts have rates of aggravated assault, sexual assault, and criminal homicide that are as high as or higher than those of drug users who do not abuse heroin (Johnson and Kaplan, 1989, p. 528). It is true that, as a cohort of the population, heroin addicts and abusers are aging and are not being replaced by younger recruits (Johnson, Golub, and Dunlap, 2000). And it is also true, as we saw in Chapter 6, that the ADAM program has demonstrated that arrestees are more likely to test positive for marijuana (between 30% and 45%) and cocaine (between 30% and 35%) than for heroin (about 6%). Still, on a user-by-user basis, heroin users, abusers, and addicts are far from the nonviolent criminals they were made out to be over a generation ago. Most are violent, and most are predators; and for most, violence is one out of a large repertory of criminal behavior in which they frequently engage. The use of heroin substantially increases the likelihood of committing violent crime.

## ALCOHOL AND VIOLENCE

The majority of adult Americans drink alcohol. More than half the respondents in the national household survey ages 12 and older said they had consumed at least one alcoholic beverage in the past 30 days, and 50 percent of high school seniors (all of whom are seriously underage) said that they had done so. Wine, beer, and liquor are very much an established fixture of mainstream American culture. Hence, the assertion that alcohol is related to violence is likely to sound exceedingly strange. Such a statement might seem equivalent to saying that consuming tea, chocolate, or Pepperidge Farm cookies is related to violence. Common sense rejects the idea that alcohol has anything to do with violent behavior. What could possibly be wrong with drinking a glass of wine with dinner, a beer while watching the ballgame, or a nightcap of sherry before retiring? Most people drink, and the vast majority do so with no untoward consequences whatsoever.

However, let's keep in mind what criminologists and drug and alcohol researchers mean when they say that alcohol is "related" to violence. They do *not* mean that alcohol— and alcohol alone—arouses the impulse to inflict harm upon others. They do *not* mean that most episodes of drinking lead to violence. They do *not* mean that most people who drink have committed one or more criminally violent acts during the past year, month, or week. Of the many millions of daily instances of alcohol consumption, very, very few have anything to do with violence. Violence is *extremely rarely* an accompaniment of alcohol consumption.

Criminologists mean two things when they say that alcohol and violence are related: (1) Drinkers have higher rates of violence than nondrinkers, and (2) the more someone drinks, the greater the likelihood that he or she will inflict violence on another person. Moreover, alcohol is related to being a victim of violence; that is, drinkers are more likely to be victimized by violence than are nondrinkers, and the more they drink, the greater this likelihood is.

These statements are statistical, not absolute; they refer to likelihoods, not certain outcomes. They are based on a comparison of the rate of violence of drinkers versus nondrinkers, and heavy versus light drinkers. Even granting that violence is an extremely rare event, the fact that it is more common among drinkers than nondrinkers, and more common among heavy than light drinkers, means that the statement "Alcohol is related to violence" is true. While most of the time alcohol is consumed, violence does not take place, it is also true that, with respect to the absolute number of episodes, alcohol consumption is an *extremely frequent* accompaniment of violence when it does take place. *Most* cases of criminal violence are accompanied by the consumption of alcohol. It's just that alcohol consumption is a great deal more common than are acts of criminal violence.

Remember, for a relationship to exist, it is not necessary to always or usually find the two things together. What is necessary is that when the first thing is present, the second is *more likely* to be found than is the case when the first is absent. Even if alcohol were associated with violence in only 1 out of 10,000 cases of drinking, if that frequency were *higher* than when alcohol is *absent*, we could say that a relationship between alcohol and violence exists.

The generalization that alcohol and violence are associated is so well established in the research literature that it seems almost redundant to document it. Still, since it contradicts common sense, establishing this relationship empirically seems to be in order. In the reviews of the worldwide research literature conducted by the U.S. Department of Health and Human Services, published every few years in its volume *Alcohol and Health*, consistently, an average of 50–60 percent of the perpetrators of criminal homicide were under the influence of alcohol when they killed their victims. True, government-sponsored, authorized killings—in warfare, for instance—rarely involve alcohol intoxication (although if armies were under the influence in battle, the carnage would almost certainly be even higher than it is). But alcohol is implicated in the majority of criminal killings, and criminologists regard this fact as causally significant.

Interestingly, the proportion of homicide *victims* who were intoxicated at the time of their demise is usually very similar to that for the perpetrators. Intoxication interferes with judgment and self-protection, increases the likelihood of risky behavior, and places interacting parties in a position of profound vulnerability—hence its causal connection with violent victimization. Also interesting is the fact that the role of alcohol varies according to the sex of the perpetrator and the victim. According to one study, alcohol was present in 62 percent of cases involving a male assailant and victim, in 53 percent of those involving a male assailant and a female victim, but in only 27 percent of those involving a female assailant and a male victim (Pernanen, 1991). This study indicates that norms play a role in the contexts within which alcohol-related violence occurs. The role of alcohol in episodes of violence generally and homicide specifically is one of the most robust, well-established, and empirically grounded generalizations in the entire criminological literature. Any challenge to it would be a fool's errand.

Once again, now that we've established the empirical regularity, the question becomes, Why? What *causes* higher rates of violence among drinkers versus nondrinkers, and among heavy versus lighter drinkers?

For centuries, folk wisdom held that alcohol caused violence because drinking releases inhibitions. When someone asked what alcohol's role was in causing violence, the commonsensical answer was that the inhibitions that normally keep most of us from striking out at others are freed. It seemed a reasonable explanation for such a long time that few questioned its validity. The proposition that alcohol more or less automatically released inhibitions and caused violent behavior in the violently inclined is referred to as the **disinhibition** (or pharmacological) **model.** This theory assumes that it is the effects of alcohol, and that factor alone, that causes what drinkers do under the influence, violence included. Describing the effects of alcohol, one expert writes: "Progressively the centers of basic emotional control are depressed, and the inhibitory functions of the centers are lost with an alteration in the conduct of the individual moving towards [being] 'miserable, mean, nasty and brutish'" (Paul, 1975, p. 16).

A different perspective is presented by anthropologists Craig MacAndrew and Robert Edgerton in their book *Drunken Comportment*, whose central thesis directly challenges the "release of inhibitions" claim (1969). Alcohol does not act on the human animal in a standardized fashion, they argue. Instead, alcohol's effects are influenced or mediated by cultural norms that dictate that specific forms of behavior are appropriate under the influence, while other forms are completely unacceptable. In other words, drinkers are not under the influence of alcohol; instead, the effects of alcohol are under the influence of the culture in which drinkers live and grow up. Alcohol alone cannot account for the variation in alcohol-related behavior since alcohol is the same everywhere it is consumed. In short, **drunken comportment**—behavior under the influence—is a cultural, not a pharmacological, product. Drinking does not simply release inhibitions and stimulate the drinker's assaultive and homicidal tendencies. Rather, the alcohol–violence link is culturally determined and usually takes place within circumscribed, normatively governed limits.

This perspective is referred to as the **cognitive guidedness model.** So marginal are alcohol's effects to this approach that one researcher was led to comment with reference to two anthropological studies of barroom behavior, "as far as one can judge from their description, the patrons might as well have been drinking orange juice." In such studies, says this researcher, "the role of the physiological and psychological effects of alcohol is downplayed almost to the vanishing point" (Pernanen, 1991, pp. 18, 211).

Which perspective is correct—the pharmacological (disinhibition) or the guidedness perspective? Is it the effects of the alcohol or the norms of society that create the link between drinking and engaging in violent behavior? Which of these two "explanatory master frames" (Pernanen, 1991, p. 215) offers the best explanation of why heavy consumption of alcohol so often leads to assault, rape, and homicide? As is frequently the case, the best explanation borrows a bit of both "frames."

Clearly, norms do not provide a ready justification for the most seriously untoward behavior that takes place under the influence of alcohol and *that would not happen when the actors are sober.* Pernanen (1991, p. 211) cites the case of drunken passengers of jet planes who attempt to enter the cockpit to convince the pilot that they should fly the plane. Examples could be multiplied endlessly. Such extremely dangerous behavior is fairly rare under the influence—but it is also vastly rarer sober. "Why is alcohol used in this way and not coffee, tea, or milk?" Pernanen asks (p. 212). The obvious answer is that alcohol has certain "natural" effects that these other substances do not.

Arguing that alcohol has natural or pharmacological effects does not deny the fact that, in being socialized into the rules and norms of drinking, drinkers learn culturally approved behavior under the influence. In learning the appropriate norms of drinking, they also learn that drinking puts them in a position where they can do things they would not ordinarily do.

Part of learning the drinking process involves learning *what the effects of alcohol are*—which is itself largely a product of the natural, pharmacological effects of this drug (p. 213).

For instance, the social setting in which drinking takes place influences how much a person drinks—the amount consumed in one sitting, the speed of drinking, and the length of drinking occasions (Pernanen, 1991, p. 193). Of course, once the drinking begins—socially occasioned though it may be—the effects of the alcohol begin kicking in. In other words, the pharmacology of alcohol *does* disinhibit behavior, and this disinhibition sometimes *does* result in violent behavior. But that violence clearly has limits, at least statistically speaking; it is selective as to time, place, and target.

Yes, there are other "causal agents" in violent behavior aside from alcohol (Parker, 1995, p. 28). But given the fact that violence is such a statistically rare event, some situations involving heavy alcohol consumption are much more likely to result in violence than other situations, identical except for the presence of alcohol. Acknowledging that alcohol is "selective" in producing disinhibition, we are nonetheless forced to accept the fact that alcohol disinhibits, that this disinhibition is a product of the drug's pharmacological effects, and that one consequence of disinhibition is the hugely higher incidence of violent behavior. Does alcohol *cause* violence? Stripped of qualifications and reservations, most contemporary researchers would answer this question in the affirmative. In Paul Goldstein's vocabulary (1985), the alcohol–violence link seems—in large part—to be psychopharmacological in origin.

##  SUMMARY

What is the connection between drug use and crime? All researchers know there is a statistical relationship—people who use drugs are much more likely to commit nondrug crime than are nonusers, and people who commit crime are much more likely to use drugs than are people who do not commit crime. And the connection between certain drugs, such as heroin and crack cocaine, is vastly stronger than that between others, such as LSD and Ecstasy. But what's the causal relationship between drug use and criminal behavior? Establishing a descriptive relationship between drugs and crime is fairly easy; establishing an analytic or inferential relationship is much more difficult.

Numerous researchers have proposed different models for the drugs-crime link. (See Table 12-1 for a summary.) The enslavement model, strongly linked with a legalization, medical, or treatment approach to the problem of addiction, argues that more or less noncriminal citizens more or less inadvertently become addicted to drugs, and hence become "enslaved" to a drug habit. Not having the money to pay for the habit, they are forced into a life of crime. If addicting drugs were dispensed in clinics, the link between drug addiction and a life of crime would be severed. This model was dominant among drug researchers until the 1970s.

The predisposition model argues that it is not drug users who turn to a life of crime but delinquents and criminals who take up the use of drugs. Most of the people who eventually become addicted were already committing delinquent and criminal acts in their teens. The drugs–crime link is strong not because addicts are enslaved to a life of crime but because both addicts and criminals are deviant, antisocial personalities. Drugs and crime are two sides of the same behavioral coin. They are manifestations of exactly the same tendency or predisposition.

| TABLE 12-1 | A Summary of Models of the Drugs–Crime Connection |
| --- | --- |

**Drugs and Crime**

| Model | Empirical Support |
| --- | --- |
| Enslavement model | Partial |
| Predisposition model | Partial |
| Intensification model | Complete (Inciardi, 2002) |

**The Drugs–Violence Nexus**

| Model | Proportion of Cases |
| --- | --- |
| Psychopharmacological model | Minority of cases |
| Economic-compulsive model | Minority of cases |
| Systemic model | Majority of cases (Goldstein et al., 1989) |

**Heroin and Addiction and Violence**

| Model | Studies |
| --- | --- |
| Before 1970: economic-compulsive/enslavement model | Many |
| After 1970: predisposition and systemic model | Many |

**Alcohol Consumption and Violence**

| Model | Studies |
| --- | --- |
| Cognitive-guidedness model | MacAndrew and Edgerton, 1968 |
| Disinhibition/psychopharmacological model | Pernanen, 1991 |

Researcher James Inciardi argues that a third model, the intensification model, explains the drugs–crime connection. This model agrees that illicit drug use and criminal behavior grow out of the same tendency to engage in illegal, hedonistic, risky behavior. And it also agrees that becoming addicted, even though it does not create criminal behavior from scratch, at least escalates or intensifies the number and seriousness of criminal acts. The same person, when addicted to heroin, commits many more, and more serious, crimes than he or she does when not addicted. Neither the enslavement nor the predisposition model is completely faithful to the facts; only the intensification model, which is something of a synthesis between the two, accounts for the observed relationship between drug use and criminal behavior.

What's the connection between drugs and violence? The connection (or nexus) between the world of drugs and the world of violence has also been subjected to a three-part framework. The psychopharmacological model argues that when high, in their agitated condition, users become excitable, belligerent, hostile, and violent, striking out and even killing others as a result. The economic-compulsive model, much like the enslavement model of the drugs–crime link, argues that drug use and violence are connected because in committing economic crimes, addicts may inadvertently lash out against their victims—for instance, if the victim struggles or resists. It is not the drug that made the addict commit violence but the need to earn money to support the drug habit. And the systemic model argues that the world of drug, especially cocaine, dealing is inherently competitive, aggressive, and conflictual—and hence, violent. It is drug dealing—and specifically, drug dealing in the context of the drug laws and law enforcement—and not drug use that forges the link between the world of drugs and the world of crime.

Researcher Paul Goldstein and his colleagues argue that the systemic model best explains the facts. Looking at a sample of criminal homicides in the city of New York during the late 1980s, that is, at the height of the crack epidemic, these researchers found that half were drug related, and of the ones that were drug related, 60 percent were crack related. Using judgments made independently by the police and the researchers, it became clear that very few of the crack-related homicides (3%) were psychopharmacological in origin and relatively few (7%) were economic-compulsive in origin. The vast majority were systemic. The crack trade is inherently disputational; killings arose as a result of conflicts between and among dealers and customers, rival dealers, and dealers and their employees.

However, the fact remains that cocaine and violence are frequent companions—and the greater the amount of cocaine someone uses, the greater the likelihood, and the seriousness, of violent behavior. Paul Goldstein and his colleagues also examined cocaine use and routine (less than lethal) violence. At the upper reaches of use, psychopharmacological violence is extremely common, even routine; violence is an inextricable fact of life, a part of the subculture of cocaine abuse. But this violence tends to be gender-related. As men's cocaine abuse increases, their likelihood of being the perpetrator of violence increases; as women's cocaine abuse increases, their likelihood of being the victim of crime increases.

What about heroin? Prior to the 1970s, most researchers viewed the heroin addict as a basically peaceful person who committed almost exclusively property crimes. Violence was considered rare. (This view is consistent with the enslavement model mentioned earlier.) But beginning in the early 1970s, a new view of heroin addicts emerged: Their tendency to commit violence was significantly greater than that of the ordinary criminal or property offender. It is possible that these early researchers misunderstood the world of heroin addiction. Just as likely, the world of heroin addiction became more violent—a world of younger users, who took many drugs, including alcohol and cocaine, in addition to heroin, and who were more likely to confront their victims in robberies rather than relying on stealth. The 1970s marked the coming of a "new breed" of heroin addicts.

What about alcohol? What's the connection between alcohol consumption and criminal behavior? Alcohol is a legal drug, but statistically, drinkers have higher rates of violence than nondrinkers. Is it the effects of the drug or the type of person who drinks that generate this difference? Some researchers believe that alcohol is the culprit, arguing that alcohol disinhibits behavior, neutralizing the centers of our brains that force us to think twice about striking out at those around us. Other researchers believe that our behavior is cognitively guided by cultural norms, not pharmacologically guided by alcohol. Most of us know what the norms say about acceptable behavior, and when it comes to drinking and committing untoward acts against others, we follow them. Hardly any of us transforms from a "Dr. Jekyll" when sober to a "Mr. Hyde" when under the influence; still, untoward, violent behavior is not only more common under the influence but would not have taken place if the actor had not been under the influence. For the most part, we do not act more violently after drinking coffee or tea; had we not drunk coffee or tea, we would have acted the same way. The fact is, alcohol has certain natural or pharmacological effects that coffee and tea lack. Even though cultural norms do influence and limit our behavior, alcohol disinhibits us, and this disinhibition sometimes—more often than when we are sober—results in violent behavior. In a phrase, a substantial slice of the alcohol–violence link is psychopharmacological in nature.

## KEY TERMS

cognitive guidedness model   345

criminogenic   332

dependent variable   333

disinhibition model   345

drugs–violence nexus   337

drunken comportment   345

economic-compulsive model   338

enslavement model   335

independent variable   333

intensification model   336

polydrug use   342

predisposition model   335

psychopharmacological model   337

systemic model   338

## ACCOUNT: Drugs and Crime

*"**Bob**," the interviewee, is a former heroin addict and substance abuser. He served in the military, was in an automobile accident, was seriously injured, and picked up a narcotics habit in the hospital. I am the interviewer. He describes his life from the late 1960s until 1986, when he took his last shot of heroin.*

**A:** The girl I was with and I both had habits. We went through all our savings, went through all our resources. At one point, I broke a leg. And she got hepatitis, she couldn't work, I couldn't work. I started doing stickups. Our habits were fairly big. In the beginning, I was wild and crazy with it. The first year of my addiction, like I said, I was trying to test the limits. I was shooting a lot of dope. And when the money dried up, I had no idea what to do. I wasn't a street kid, I wasn't a hustler. I knew the military, I knew guns, I knew violence. And I just, uh, that's what I did. The first one was scary—the first time, I got this guy around closing time, at a drugstore. I said, this is a stickup, give me your money. I had a gun, and he gave me the money. It was easy. But it was scary. The obsession wasn't with the stickup itself, it was with what I'm going to get. I'm going to get this bag of dope. It was great. You get a bag full of money. You go into the City [New York City]. You get a whole pile of dope.

**Q:** Do you have any idea how many times you did this?

**A:** Over a couple of years, probably 60, 70 times. A lot. The first time was in February. I was arrested for 21 robberies.

**Q:** Did you do all of them?

**A:** Yeah.

**Q:** You copped to [admitted] doing them.

**A:** Well, I didn't cop to doing them all at the time. As part of the sentencing arrangement, they indicted me for that many, to clear the books. I was promised a lenient sentence, and they sat down with my lawyer and the DA and said, OK, now, what did you do? And I told them. This was so, later on, at the sentencing, it wouldn't be brought up. The first couple times I was arrested, they sentenced me to the Rockefeller program, the five-year clinical commitment to the Narcotic Addiction Control Commission. It was a joke. There was no treatment. It was the same uniform, same cell block, same everything, as the next guy [that is, other nondrug offenders].

**Q:** It was just detox and incarceration.

**A:** Yeah. You were supposed to go to therapy three times a week and the therapist was a corrections officer. There was some kind of baloney going on at that time. Addicts who had been arrested were sitting in county jails for a year, year and a half, waiting for room in the narcotics program, and somebody brought suit about this, and the court said, place these people in a program within 90 days or cut them loose. So, what they did was, they went down the list from the top of people in the program. Before they were going to let these guys loose they were going to let us loose. I had only 90 days in the program, and they let me go. So I said, the stickup business is not going to work. Because I could see how crazy I'm getting. Sometimes I did three in a night. I'd say, let's get a whole *pile* of money so we won't have to do this again for a while. I'd go out and do three, four in a night. So I said, Oh, well, I'll deal drugs. So I started dealing. I had a connection in Harlem. A Cuban. I was buying ounces and quarter-pounds of heroin, bringing it out here, cutting it, bagging it, and selling it. And I got busted. [Laughs.] So they gave me another go-around with the Narcotic Addiction Control Commission. I only served two months this time. And they let me go. So I said, well, that didn't work, let me try stickups again. And I got popped [arrested] for another, oh, I don't know, 10, 15 more. [That is, he was arrested for one armed robbery and admitted to having committed the others.] I had pretty good lawyers at the time, cost me a lot of money. That time, they gave me seven years. They said, next time, you're getting life, so think about this. That was the fourth or fifth felony conviction. So I did the seven in 34 months. I went to Sing-Sing. I went to Auburn, I went to Clinton. I served 30 months in Clinton. And it was rough. I didn't like that business at all. Sometimes,

before, I got arrested and it was an adventure. But I didn't like being in a state penitentiary at all. It was tough. People there were crazy. You lived in constant fear. The only time I felt safe was when the cell doors slammed at night and even then, I didn't feel safe. . . . Anyway, I got out of prison. I said, That's it, never again. Look at what it's done to my life. Moved upstate New York, almost 200 miles from the City. I decided to take the geographical cure, moved to a place I figured there would be no dope. I got a place, I was working. I had a pretty nice apartment, but I couldn't afford it, so I met this guy in a bar, I had an extra bedroom, rented this guy the room. Turned out, there couldn't have been more than six dope fiends in the whole town—he was one of them! Now, I didn't know that when I rented him the place. So now, instead of driving from Huntington to Harlem, about 40 miles, I'm driving four hours each way, five times a week.

**Q:** So you started up again.

**A:** Yeah, I started up again. I'm on parole, too. I still owe 40-something months to the department of parole. It was just a matter of time before I got busted. So, I went down to Albany, I got on the methadone clinic there. . . . I was on the methadone clinic up there for a while. Two years. And it helped. Pretty much all I had was methadone, smoked a little pot. That was it. But I got busted. A *stupid* thing. I was out of work. And I was doing volunteer work at the VA hospital, working for the Red Cross. I had nothing to do, I lived right by the VA. And some guy in the hospital says, Can you get me some pot? I said, Sure, there's pot all over, I'll bring you half an ounce or so, and he says, Great. So I brought it to the hospital, I'm giving it to him in the men's room, and a cop walks out of the stall. So I says, Aw, shit! I was always armed. I had a knife. He said, Come here, and tried to grab me. I pulled a knife on him, I ran, they caught me, I got busted. I did six months in the county jail. Possession [of a controlled substance] and assaulting a police officer. That was the last time I went to jail. That was in '75.

**Q:** Surprisingly lenient sentence. You were very lucky.

**A:** Yeah, yeah, I was. But six months in Albany County jail was no picnic, I'll tell you!

**Q:** I imagine. But it's better than being sent back to prison.

**A:** Yeah, well, that was the thing. I thought that when the six months was up, I was going to go back [to prison] and do the 40 months I owed to the parole board. I had a parole officer who was a decent guy. And he got me reinstated on the methadone program on the condition that the day I left the jail, they brought me down to the clinic—he drove me down himself. And I got on methadone.

**Q:** But you were detoxed at the time.

**A:** Yeah, I was detoxed.

**Q:** But they put you on methadone.

**A:** First day out—40 milligrams. I was flying. They didn't want me to be able to use heroin. When I started using heroin, I was a nut. So they didn't want the possibility of me using heroin to occur. So they took me directly from the jail to the methadone clinic. I spent another year on methadone. I said, I gotta get out of this. I applied to a nearby community college. And I started detoxing. I came down from methadone five milligrams at a time. From 100 milligrams to nothing in about four months. Because I remember, the first day of class at the community college was my last dose of methadone. It was great. And I had never been to college before. It was interesting. It was exciting. And I did well. Fairly well. And I thought it was great. I had always felt *less than* everybody else. I didn't think I could do this stuff [college work]. And I could. So that was great. During that two

years, I drank, smoked a lot of pot, on a daily basis. But I didn't really do much of anything else [that is, he used no other drugs]. I came back down to the Island [Long Island] after that, '78, and I started clamming again. I drank every day, smoked a lot of pot. I said, well, I can't shoot heroin [so] once in a while, I would bang some cocaine. Actually, I never really liked cocaine. But for a guy who didn't like it, I would use an awful lot of it.

**Q:** Why didn't you like it?

**A:** Because it made me alert, up. What I wanted was, like, put me to sleep, I don't want to feel this. That's what I wanted. Something soporific. I didn't want this jangly business—mainlining cocaine, a gram, half a gram, quarter of a gram, whatever, you get this tremendous rush and five minutes later, you're looking for more. I couldn't *believe* the amount of cocaine you could use. I wound up with this girl. Topless dancer. She was something. The only thing we had in common was we liked needles. And we started a run. It lasted six years. Drinking. Smoking. And then going on these runs [that is, nonstop periods of cocaine use]. It started out two, three, four days, once a month, and the runs got closer and closer together. I married her at some point. She says, to make her mother happy.

**Q:** How did you pay for this?

**A:** I was working. She was working. We had some credit cards. We were running a boarding kennel, 150 dogs. We could plan some "creative book work." And dealing a little bit. Not much.

**Q:** Weren't you afraid of getting popped again?

**A:** I was but, you know, we were fairly discreet with it. Like I said, it started out as, maybe a weekend a month. Towards the end, it was, like, we'd blow everything, spend everything we had, borrow everything we could, and then, pay the credit cards. This is crazy—we were going on cocaine runs at 19 percent interest, because we were running the credit cards out. So, pay the credit cards back, pay this back, fix the books, pay the creditors, do all right for a week or so, and then, boom! Go again. So, towards the end, it just got crazy. I couldn't stand it. Some people drink to come down from coke. I used to shoot Dilaudid and then my Dilaudid connection got busted. So I went back to Harlem and picked up some dope [heroin] and I said, well, I'll come down from the cocaine with the dope. And then, when I got the dope, I said, what am I even doing this other stuff for in the first place? Something I gotta shoot *dope* to come down from? So I said, to hell with the cocaine, I'm just going to shoot heroin. . . . [So I] went back on methadone, because that worked once. . . . I did this for about nine months. Methadone. Drank all day. Actually, I was drinking around the clock. Beer. One of these controls: I'll only drink beer. You're not an alcoholic if all you drink is beer. I'd get up in the morning, drink a couple of beers, go to the methadone clinic, pick up my methadone, go to this sleazy little bar downtown, drink till about 10 o'clock, grab a six-pack, go out on the boat, dig enough clams to keep me going. Come in, hit another bar near my apartment, drink till I was passed out, go home. And that's what I did for nine months. . . . So I went to the VA hospital, I detoxed from about 80 milligrams of methadone and a couple of cases of beer a day. . . . I was drinking constantly around the clock. I was drinking three or four cans in the morning, I was drinking between five and ten beers before I went to work, I was drinking a six-pack of half-quarts after work. And I was drinking from four [in the afternoon] till 11–12 o'clock at night. Straight through. And bringing a six-pack home with me, usually. So a couple of cases a day, it had to be. I had the DT's [delirium tremens, alcohol withdrawal reactions] from beer. Never had the DTs in my life. And I had the DTs in that detox. . . . So I detoxed. I went on a 90-day program. . . . I was alone and miserable. So I went on one more run with heroin. One day, January '86. Tough day. Froze my ass off. Took about six bags of clams. I got $300–400 for the clams. I went in, saw a friend of mine, for the money, I had a whole pocketful of money. He says, You want a ride home? Then he says, You want to take a ride to Harlem to cop some dope? I says, Let's go. They talk about diseases of addiction. And I could hear my disease talking to me. Believe me, I could *hear* it talking to me. I remember getting off that time, because I had been away from needles a couple years. Between methadone and dibbing and dabbing, I wasn't abstinent, but I had been away from needles a couple years. And I remember getting off, sitting in a shooting gallery in Harlem, and getting this *tremendous* high. I remember this thing in my ear saying, Whatever you gotta do, whatever lies you gotta tell to keep feeling this, do it. I said, right. I did. For six months, I did. Weekends and then every other day. Then the guy I originally went with said, You're crazy, and didn't go with me any more. Worked back up to a habit. Took a couple overdoses. Woke up in Harlem Hospital. I was digging clams, making $500–600 a day, and it was all going into my arm. . . . I had a habit, I got high that night—[my brother] gave me the money. The next day, I threw my stuff in the boat, I was going to pull the boat down the [Long Island] Sound, I was going to detox, all that stuff. So I said, aw, just one more time. Took the boat, under the Throgg's Neck Bridge, under the Whitestone, up through Hell's Gate, up the Harlem River, tied my clam boat up in Harlem [laughs], and I tried to get high one more time. I couldn't get high. Spent about 400 bucks. Couldn't even get high. It just didn't work any more. Some guy that was with me—I went to three or four different shooting galleries—some old Black guy I picked up at one of the shooting galleries, he was *falling down,* so I knew it wasn't the dope was bad. For me, it just didn't work any more. So then, I got in the boat, I came down the Sound. That was the second of July. The third, I woke up, I got high that morning, then I went to detox. So July 4th, 1986, that was the first full day clean.

## QUESTIONS

Which theories or models of the drugs–crime nexus does Bob's case best illustrate? What was the cause of his criminal career? What do you think was the cause of his drug addiction? It is true that he was a substance abuser from an early age; still, most alcoholics do not become heroin addicts. Why did he? In his life of crime, Bob received fairly lenient sentences. Is this a comment on the harsher sentences addicts and drug abusers receive today? Bob got his life straightened out, but only after a substantial number of attempts. Does this mean that his treatment was ineffective—or that addiction is very difficult to overcome? Some observers argue that self-help organizations such as Narcotics Anonymous and Alcoholics Anonymous become a kind of dependency that replaces members' dependence on drugs. What do you think about this claim? NA and AA do not keep records on their rates of success, so it's difficult to compare their effectiveness with other treatment programs. Should they violate their pledge to anonymity and tabulate what happens to their members?

# 13

# THE ILLICIT DRUG INDUSTRY

In Chapter 3, I explained that there are two absolutely necessary preconditions for use—**predisposition** and **availability**. These are theoretically, but not practically speaking, independent of one another, since the predisposition to use drugs stimulates their trafficking, and the availability of drugs may stimulate the tendency or predisposition to use them. They are two side of the same coin. Each is necessary; neither is sufficient.

Alfred McCoy argues that theories of predisposition, which focus on poverty, unemployment, subculture, and so on, miss the point; they leave out of the picture the marketing and trafficking of drugs. Heroin, he says, "is a mass-market commodity with salesmen and distributors just like cigarettes, alcohol, or aspirin. . . . Without global distribution systems, there can be no mass addiction to cocaine or heroin" (1991, pp. 389–390). McCoy is less than half right, since the existence of "global distribution systems" is only one way that drugs become available to users. The fact is, folk societies have been using drugs for millennia in the absence of such distribution systems—they simply harvested them from plants. Likewise, using home-grown marijuana does not require a global network of traffickers. Moreover, what McCoy neglects is predisposition; in its absence, distribution is futile. Still, half of what is necessary (but again, not sufficient) for use is availability, and that is the result of getting drugs into the hands of users, whether potential or actual. Not all drug trafficking is global, of course; trafficking varies from drug to drug with respect to how global it is. Marijuana and methamphetamine are usually either home-grown or manufactured in the United States, or cross only one border to get into the user's hands. But whether local, national, international, or global, nearly the entire drug trade entails economic transactions—buying and selling illicit psychoactive substances. Still, availability is half the drug use equation, and the availability of drugs comes about as a result of socially, economically, and politically patterned systems of distribution. How drugs are distributed is crucial to any understanding of their use.

How do users get ahold of the drugs they take? What are the distribution patterns for psychoactive substances? How are they manufactured and by whom? Where do they come from? Where do they go? In short, how are they produced and transported from there to here? And what does this mean for the flow of money, not only from there to here, but everywhere? Who gains? Who loses?

As with all economic products, drug transactions are part of a web or network that can be described and analyzed. This chapter examines how drugs are manufactured and get from their origin to their destination, and what impact the particular routes along which they travel have for the economy of the country of origin, the country of destination, and the world as a whole. The process is extremely complex and differs according to a number of key factors, the most important of which is the legal/illegal dimension.

While prohibition may not have stamped out the availability and use of illicit drugs, it certainly has put its distinctive coloration on where and how they are produced, how they make their way through the distribution chain—and, perhaps most importantly, how expensive they are. Most illicit drugs could be produced as cheaply as aspirin; instead, they are among the most expensive products on Earth. Cocaine costs 30 times as much as gold, and heroin is nearly 10 times as expensive as cocaine. At the very least, criminalization has increased the price of illicit drugs—and by many times over. Legal and illegal drugs share at least one commonality: They are both products whose distribution contributes to the size and shape of the overall economy. But their differences are far greater than their commonalities. In this chapter, I will deal only with the buying and selling of illicit drugs. The distribution of prescription drugs, alcohol, and tobacco demands a separate, and very detailed, discussion.

There are three commonly believed myths about illicit drug trafficking. The first is that it is the biggest economic enterprise on Earth. The second is that it is highly centralized, with a "boss of all bosses" in the United States who controls the entire enterprise. And the third is that illicit drugs represent a drain on or a clear-cut, unambiguous cost to the nation's economy. Let's address these three myths in turn.

## THE MYTH OF THE SIZE OF THE DRUG TRADE

The illegal drug trade is a huge enterprise, rivaling many legal industries. Its scope, however, has been hugely exaggerated. In the United States in the 1980s, the total retail value of drug sales was estimated to be $100 billion—more, said one seemingly authoritative source, "than the total net sales of General Motors, more than American farmers take in from all crops" (Lang, 1986, p. 48). The American market, everyone seemed to agree, accounted for roughly half the world's total illicit drug sales. Said another commentator, even more grandly: "There is more money in illegal drug traffic than in any other business on earth" (Gonzales, 1985, p. 104). A third observer weighed in, growing expansive on the subject:

> The inhabitants on earth spend more money on illegal drugs than they spend on food. More than they spend on housing, clothes, education, medical care, or any other product or service. The international narcotics industry is the largest growth industry in the world. Its annual revenues exceed half a trillion dollars—three times the value of all United States currency in

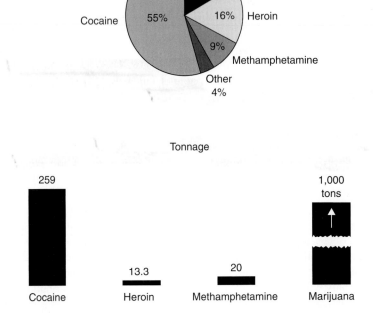

**Figure 13-1** Total expenditures and tonnage of illicit drugs, United States, 2000.

circulation, more than the gross national products of all but a half-dozen of the major industrialized nations. To imagine the immensity of such wealth, consider this: a million dollars in gold would weigh as much as a large man. A half-trillion dollars would weigh more than the entire population of Washington, D.C. (Mills, 1987, p. 3)

It is true that in the 1980s, $100 billion in retail sales (in today's dollars) for the illicit drug trade in the United States was a reasonable estimate. Still, granting the fact that drug use has declined since then (and taking inflation into account), the economic reality of the drug trade, while admittedly enormous, is a great deal more modest than the most expansive of these estimates.

The Abt Associates have conducted several data-based research studies for the federal Office of Drug Control Policy on the size of the drug trade and the cost of cocaine and heroin. And the information gathered by this research outfit is based on ADAM (Arrestee Drug Abuse Monitoring) interviews with arrestees, the National Household Survey on Drug Abuse, DAWN (Drug Abuse Warning Network) emergency department reports, and Uniform Crime Report data supplied by the National Institute on Justice. Abt estimated that in the year 2000, Americans spent $35 billion on cocaine, $10 billion on heroin, $5.4 billion on methamphetamine, $10.5 billion on marijuana, and $2.4 billion on all other illicit drugs—for a total of just under $65 billion (see Figure 13-1). The total volume of these drugs consumed was 259 tons of cocaine, 13 tons of heroin, 20 tons of methamphetamine, and 1,000 tons of marijuana. Tables 13-1 and 13-2 provides detailed figures for expenditures and, for cocaine and heroin, for the total tonnage consumed since 1988.

**TABLE 13-1**   **Total Expenditures on Illicit Drugs, United States, 1988–2000, in Billions (in 2000 dollars)**

|  | 1988 | 1992 | 1996 | 2000 |
|---|---|---|---|---|
| Cocaine | 107.0 | 49.9 | 39.2 | 35.2 |
| Heroin | 26.1 | 17.2 | 12.8 | 10.0 |
| Methamphetamine | 5.8 | 4.8 | 10.1 | 5.4 |
| Marijuana | 12.1 | 14.6 | 9.5 | 10.5 |
| Other drugs | 3.3 | 1.5 | 2.7 | 2.4 |
| Total | 154.3 | 88.0 | 74.3 | 63.5 |

*Source:* Rhodes, Layne, et al., 2001, p. 3.

**TABLE 13-2**   **Total Tonnage of Cocaine and Heroin Consumed, United States, 1988–2000**

|  | 1988 | 1992 | 1996 | 2000 |
|---|---|---|---|---|
| Cocaine | 660.0 | 346.0 | 301.0 | 259.0 |
| Heroin | 14.6 | 11.7 | 12.8 | 13.3 |

*Source:* Rhodes, Layne, et al., 2001, p. 4.

## True-False Quiz

As we will see in this chapter, more money is spent on cocaine than on all other drugs combined, and less money is spent on drugs today than was true a dozen or more years ago. But when I presented my students with two statements relevant to these facts, they said that they believed them to be false. Only 43 percent agreed with the statement "More money is spent on cocaine than all other drugs combined," and only 15 percent agreed with the statement "Over the past 10–20 years, the amount of money spent on illegal drugs has *decreased* significantly." As we've seen in reactions to other statements, agreement with the second of these statements seems to reflect the tendency to think that certain social problems are getting worse and worse. It is true that chronic cocaine and heroin use remain serious problems in this society, and it is also true that these drugs are more potent than they were in the past. But they are also cheaper, which means that less money is being spent on them. Most of the public is not aware, however, of cocaine's dominance in the drug industry; the volume of its sales outweighs that of all other illicit drugs combined.

Several additional estimates made by Abt Associates describing the distribution and trafficking of illicit drugs are worth mentioning. First, the information provided by ADAM interviewees made it possible for researchers to estimate the average weekly cocaine and heroin expenditures by chronic users, defined as use of cocaine once or more times a week for a year or use of heroin on at least 10 days for a month prior to the survey. The average weekly amount spent by the chronic cocaine user in 1988 was (in constant 2000 dollars) $440; in 2000, the average was $212. For the chronic heroin user, the comparable figures were $365 and $201 (Rhodes, Layne, et al., 2001, p. 14). Second, the average retail price (that is, purchased in quantities of less than a gram) for a gram of cocaine in 1981 was $423; in 2000, it was $212. For heroin, the figures were $3,295 and $2,088 (p. 43). And third, as we've seen, the Abt Associates also found that just as prices have dropped, purity has gone up. These researchers found that between 1981 and 2000, the purity of cocaine, purchased at the less-than-one-gram level, rose from 36 percent to 61 percent, and for heroin, the purity of one-tenth of a gram rose from 4 percent to 25 percent.[1] In short, since the 1980s, the price of cocaine and heroin has declined, their purity has increased, and the average amount of money that chronic users spend on their drug habit has declined (Rhodes, Johnson, and Kling, 2001, pp. 43, 44).

---

[1]The most recent *National Drug Control Strategy* (2006) issued by the White House displays a bar graph indicating that between 2001 and 2004, the purity of Colombian heroin declined from 50 to 33 percent. However, the White House refuses to release the full report on which the data in that graph are based. (Titled *What America's Users Spend on Illegal Drugs, 1988–2003,* the report was prepared by Abt Associates.) One possible explanation of why the White House will not release the full report is that some of the data in this report may contradict this finding, which shows that the administration is winning the war on drugs. In any case, if researchers cannot assess the range of data from the full report, a single statistic from the study that generated this datum is suspect.

Keep in mind, however, these figures are *very* rough estimates. Some observers question the methods used by analysts in estimating the volume and sales of illegal drugs (Reuter, 1996), and hence believe that all such estimates are suspect at best. Still, rough and possibly unreliable as these figures may be, the fact is, illicit drugs are bought and sold on a large scale. The information on which we can have confidence generates the following, almost certainly valid, generalizations. First, with respect to both the total amount of money spent and the total tonnage, cocaine is the country's number-one drug, dwarfing heroin by a factor of nearly 20 to 1. Second, with respect to both money spent and total tonnage, cocaine is used less today than it was a dozen or so years ago. Third, although considerably less is spent on heroin than in the past, since it is so much cheaper today, roughly the same quantity of heroin is brought into the country as was true previously. Fourth, in spite of its regionalized use, methamphetamine is a major player in the illicit drug market. And fifth, marijuana, being a very bulky substance, is the illicit drug whose trafficked weight is the greatest; however, the economy of the cannabis market barely exceeds that of heroin, a drug used by vastly fewer consumers and in a much smaller quantity. These generalizations, however valid, harbor a swarming host of particulars. They raise questions that demand answers: Where do these 259 tons of cocaine come from? The 13 tons of heroin? The 1,000 tons of marijuana? The 10 tons of methamphetamine? How do they get from there to here? Who's involved in the enterprise? What are the consequences of the trafficking of these drugs? Later in the chapter, we'll find out.

## THE MYTH OF MARKET CENTRALIZATION IN THE DRUG TRADE

Just as we have to address myths about the size of the illicit drug trade, we also have to address the myth about how hierarchical, centralized, and organized it is. Most people imagine that illicit drugs are sold by a highly structured organization like the Mafia, with a single "Mr. Big" or "Boss of all Bosses." Yes, the drug trade is highly organized, or at least some sectors of it are. (It may not be as organized as General Motors or IBM, but as in GM and IBM, the roles and actions of participants in major sectors of it are closely coordinated with one another.) A great deal of organizational coordination is necessary to grow an agricultural product, extract a chemical from it, ship it to the United States (not to mention dozens of other locales), evade detection, cross borders, get it into the hands of higher- and middle-level dealers, and sell it to the ultimate consumer. But just as country of origin varies according to the drug in question, degree of hierarchy and organization varies according to what drug it is and how it is produced and distributed. But even for the more highly hierarchical, centralized drug enterprises, today, there is no Mr. Big, no boss of all bosses. The fact is, the drug trade is quite decentralized, and is becoming more so over time.

If it weren't for the fact that many Americans still believe in the myth of a boss of all bosses, it might not seem necessary to refute it. A surprising number of my students still believe that the illegal drug trade is highly centralized, that a single, shadowy figure in the United States directs the sale of all illicit drugs nationwide. Their Mr. Big is swarthy in all probability (Latin or Mediterranean), wears dark sunglasses, sits at a large desk, and speaks into a telephone with a deep, gravelly voice. And if he were arrested and incarcerated, drug sales in the country would come to a screeching halt. But—the myth continues—he is protected by corrupt law enforcement officials and politicians at the highest levels of power,

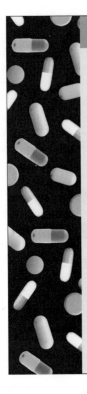

## True-False Quiz

"Illegal drug trafficking is highly centralized; the great bulk of the illicit substances consumed in the United States was sold by organized crime with a very small number of 'Boss of all Bosses' at the top of the hierarchy of power"—true or false? It certainly is a widespread belief, as my students indicate; 57 percent agreed with the statement. On the face of it, however, the statement should be implausible. Think of the many drugs that are consumed—and bought and sold. Is it even conceivable that the same organized drug mob, with a small number of 'bosses' at the top, would sell marijuana, cocaine, heroin, Ecstasy, LSD, *and* methamphetamine? Or that the mob that brings heroin into the country from Southeast Asia would be the same one that brings heroin from Mexico? Or that the same cast of characters would distribute drugs that have very different sources? Or that, somehow, the Belgian chemists who produce MDMA are in cahoots with the Canadians who import "BC Bud"? Not to mention that, by now, everyone must be aware of the fact that more than half the marijuana consumed in the United States is home grown. But the sinister nature of the "Boss of all Bosses" image is so strong that, to convince ourselves that the drug trade is evil, we must attach a single face to it—another feature of demonizing that which is considered bad.

possibly even up to the presidency. If only we could clean up the corruption and arrest Mr. Big, we could wipe out drug abuse in the country overnight!

This belief would be amusing if it weren't so pervasive. The fact is, drug dealing in this country is highly decentralized, and has become increasingly so in the past generation; different dealers operate in hundreds, possibly thousands, of independent enterprises. Illegal drugs are smuggled into the United States from several dozen countries, and they are sold by dealers of almost every national, racial, and ethnic background. Certainly, there are one or several Mr. Bigs in various countries or regions. Indeed, a number of them have been arrested or killed—such as Carlos Lehder and the Ochoa brothers in Colombia, and Kung Sah in Burma—and yet the drug trade continues unabated. And in the United States, there are, again, one or several *local* Mr. Bigs with respect to cartels and monopolies that operate at the community or neighborhood level. Still, to imagine that any single figure, or even a small number of players, could run the whole show in the United States even for a single drug, let alone for all drugs, demonstrates an almost unbelievable naiveté.

The fact is, over the past 30 years, the illicit drug market has become extremely decentralized. Each drug has its own distribution patterns, including sources, routes, price structure, and cast of characters. And for each drug, there are anywhere from a dozen or so to thousands of separate but overlapping distribution chains, hierarchies, and networks. Depending on the drug in question, dealers at every level of the distribution chain could be Cuban, Haitian, Dominican, Canadian, Puerto Rican, Jamaican, Chinese, Nigerian, Israeli, Russian, Colombian, Mexican, Dutch, Belgian, African-American,

Italian, Italian-American, Pakistani, Iranian, Lebanese, Syrian, or the members of a California biker gang, who could be from almost any racial, ethnic, or national background. It is true that, for specific drugs, there is patterning to the ethnic backgrounds of drug sellers at all points along the distribution hierarchy, but a single formula cannot even remotely paint a portrait of the illicit drug market as a whole. With several drugs, the ethnic composition changes as the drug moves up—or down—the distribution ladder. Organizations composed of members from one ethnic or national background are continually attempting to muscle into the turf or territory dominated by members of another ethnic or national group; sometimes, they succeed. What was once a more or less monopolistic, monolithic market structure has become fluid, decentralized, diverse, and adaptable. Mr. Big—if he ever existed—is a phenomenon of a dim, distant decade.

## THE MYTH OF THE DRUG TRADE AS AN ECONOMIC LIABILITY

The White House, in its 2002 report *National Drug Control Strategy,* estimated that in 2000, the economic cost of illicit drug use to American society was $160 billion. This total included health care costs ($15 billion), losses in economic productivity ($110 billion), and all other costs ($35 billion), such as goods and services "lost to crime," the increased cost of the criminal justice system, and "social welfare." Interestingly, although economists do consider them, the White House did not calculate the same sorts of costs to society as a consequence of alcohol and tobacco consumption. And equally as interesting, when the Gross Domestic Product (GDP)—the sum total of the nation's economic productivity for a given year—is calculated, the amount of money spent on health care, the criminal justice system, and so on is typically *added* to the figure, not *subtracted* from it. Herein lies perhaps the most significant fact about the drug trade.

The fact is, in strictly economic terms, the illegal drug trade is an industry exactly like every other industry. The money spent on illicit substances contributes to the economy in exactly the same way as the purchase of legal products. Just as with alcohol and tobacco, illegal drug use can produce undesired costs, including medical care, the loss of an income to a family, and, in the case of alcohol, substance-related crimes. Some of these losses take place in one sector, but they may also benefit another; others take place in all sectors. But in principle, there is no difference between legal and illegal economic enterprises with respect to contributing to the economy.

Clearly, not all crime is economically productive. Gunning down a father or mother of four small children is likely to benefit only the funeral industry. Even in strictly economic terms, a rape and an assault involve no generation of wealth, no transfer of assets from one party to another. All crime is *not* economically productive, and much of it can be sterile—even detrimental to society as well as the victims. In other ways—such as undermining the victim's sense of psychological well-being—many crimes can be extremely negative in their consequences.

In contrast, when an illegal enterprise provides goods or a service to a clientele that willingly pays for it, calculating economic gain is in principle no different from doing so for a legal enterprise that provides goods or a service to a clientele that willingly pays for it. Looked at strictly as an economic transaction, is there such a distinction between purchasing Ecstasy and purchasing candy? Between purchasing marijuana and purchasing cigarettes? If a 20-year-old is not carded and buys a mug of beer in a bar, is that purchase *subtracted* from the country's GDP—or added to it? On his or her twenty-first birthday, does that mug of beer magically cross from the minus to the plus column? The economy knows no *moral* or *legal* distinctions between and among products or between and among laws. The sale and purchase of *all* products—whether alcohol, cigarettes, pornography, candy bars, cars, video games, Bibles, or cocaine—entail plusses and minuses for the economy and for different sectors of the economy.

Clearly, demand is the number-one factor that permits the drug trade to flourish. Without the desire or impulse to take drugs, there would be no drug market. It is demand that makes the drug industry profitable (demand, it should be said, along with the illegal status of the product). And the enterprise is profitable not only for higher-level drug dealers. A very large number of people earn a living from the trade—even people who are working to stamp it out. (For them, it provides jobs.) Once we recognize that the drug trade is a component of a society's, and the world's, total economy, we must consider its *economic* contribution to a region or an entire nation—up and down the hierarchy, from the grower to the importer to the lowliest worker. It isn't only those at the top of the drug trade who profit; it is anyone who derives employment from it, both directly and indirectly. All workers who earn a wage from the drug trade spend much of that money in the legal sector, on food, clothing, shelter, and other necessities, as well as luxuries. Hence, we have to consider the influence of the drug trade in spreading the money around—what is sometimes referred to as the economic "ripple" effect. Again, considered strictly from an economic point of view, eliminating an illegal industry would be no different from eliminating any legal industry. Wiping out the drug trade worldwide would devastate the economies of a large number of countries.

In Colombia, the cocaine trade is as profitable as the coffee business. Try to picture Colombia's coffee industry wiped out overnight; the result would be economic catastrophe for the country as a whole. In principle, this is no different for the cocaine trade. The marijuana crop in the United States is more profitable than the corn crop (Pollan, 1995). Picture the entire corn industry being obliterated: Again, this would affect not only growers and sellers but everyone who is dependent on their business, and everyone who does business with them, and so on down the line—that is, the entire country. One reason why the drug trade is so deeply entrenched at the supplier level is that entire regions and even nations are economically dependent on it, including citizens who have no idea that they are. Half of Bolivia's foreign trade derives from the coca business (Gonzales, 1985, p. 242). Bolivia is a poor country; what would replace this revenue in the event of the loss of the cocaine trade? (The illicit drug trade also contributes to a country's death toll and, in many nations, to the corruption of its law enforcement, but that is separate from its impact on the economy, which is calculated only in terms of profit and loss.) The Drug Enforcement Administration estimates that Jamaica earns more from exporting marijuana than from all other exports combined; if this source of income were obliterated, how would it be replaced? What industry would contribute as much to these and other countries' GNP? The fact is, the drug trade produces an endless supply of entrepreneurs willing to take risks in order to earn huge sums of money and to employ any number of laborers to work at jobs that pay them many times what they would earn producing a legal crop (Gonzales, 1985, p. 238). In many regions of the world where drugs are grown, no legal agricultural product is even viable; either it cannot be grown under local conditions or, since most are perishable, it cannot reach a market soon enough to make the enterprise profitable.

# WHERE DO DRUGS COME FROM?

Each illicit drug has its own unique source, and each reaches the ultimate customer in a different way. Moreover, patterns of distribution are extremely volatile, shifting from year to year, according to law enforcement practices, climate changes, competition, and innovations by growers, traffickers, and sellers. As a result of this enormous variability in country of origin, making valid generalizations that apply to all illegal drugs is all but impossible. What applies to affluent chemists in Belgium is not likely to apply to poor peasants in Mexico.

We can delineate three models of drug trafficking: the pure agricultural model, the pure chemical model, and the mixed model.

- The **pure agricultural model** refers to systems of trafficking that harvest a product requiring little or nothing (aside from drying and separating parts of the plant) in converting it into the ultimate product; it is consumed more or less as grown. Theoretically, the consumer could walk up to the farmer and purchase the usable drug. The reasons this transaction does not usually take place are social and economic, not technological. Clearly, marijuana offers the best example here. Raw opium—rarely consumed in the United States—also fits the pure agricultural model.
- The **pure chemical model** refers to a completely synthetic substance that does not have its origin as an agricultural product at all, but is developed exclusively in the lab. The user needs a manufacturer with technical expertise to turn precursor chemicals into the finished product—a usable drug. Ecstasy, LSD, methamphetmine, and the club drugs fit this model.
- The **mixed model** refers to a substance that began as agricultural produce whose principal psychoactive agent is then synthesized from the plant or converted into a chemical, eventually becoming what is consumed by the user. The mixed model can be depicted by an hourglass shape; it requires funneling the produce of many farms to a fairly small number of labs, through high-level trafficking and smuggling, fanning out once again, from higher-level to lower-level dealers. Hence, the user relies on both the grower and the manufacturer with chemical know-how to obtain a usable drug. Heroin (which began as the Oriental poppy or opium plant) and cocaine (which began as the coca plant) provide paramount examples here.

Each of these models harbors some variation, of course, depending, in the case of agricultural products, on the hardiness of the plant and whether it can be grown locally or must be imported, and, in the case of synthetic products, on the complexity of the chemical process. It is economically feasible to grow certain plants both indoors and outdoors, and hence, they can be cultivated in the United States. Marijuana provides an excellent example. In contrast, given the market, the ubiquity of law enforcement, and the nature of the plant, it is not economically feasible to grow coca bushes or Oriental poppies indoors in areas where they would not thrive outdoors. Hence, cocaine and heroin must be imported from source countries.

The question that should dominate our thinking about the illicit drug trade is this: Why do the existing distribution patterns prevail? That is, why is this drug produced in a given source country and brought to a destination country through a certain route, while that drug is produced in different locations and shipped through different routes to the same final destination? Could distribution patterns be different? Drug distribution patterns are far from preordained; in fact, many have changed over time, due to a variety of factors. There is, however, both stability and volatility. Because of competition and the dismantling of distribution networks, trade routes have shifted enormously for some drugs—but interestingly, not for others. For instance, the sources of marijuana and heroin have been transformed markedly in the past three decades, while the broad outlines of cocaine distribution have remained more or less stable.

With these qualifications in mind, let's look at the origins of illicit drugs that are distributed and consumed in the United States.[2]

## Heroin

The breakup of the French Connection in 1972 brought about a vacuum in heroin distribution in America. (We'll read more about this development later in this chapter.) Within fairly short order, a substantial proportion of the heroin that had been circulated within Asia or had been shipped to Europe began to be rerouted to the United States. For the better part of two decades, most of the heroin consumed by addicts in this country originated from either the so-called **Golden Triangle** of Southeast Asia (that is, mainly Burma but also Laos, Cambodia, and Thailand) or the **Golden Crescent** (mainly Afghanistan but also Pakistan, Iran, and eastern Turkey). But in the United States, in the past decade or two, the primary source for heroin has shifted to Latin America. The Abt Associates estimate that 67 percent of the heroin consumed in the United States comes from South America, principally Colombia; 23 percent from Mexico; 6 percent from Southwest Asia (mainly Pakistan and Afghanistan); and 2 percent from Southeast Asia (Bruen et al., 2002, p. 1). In contrast, the United Nations estimates that most of the heroin consumed *worldwide* originates in Afghanistan.

According to the DEA, Colombian heroin traffickers bring small-to-medium loads (between a half and one kilo) by individual couriers flying in from Costa Rica, the Dominican Republic, Ecuador, Panama, Mexico, Argentina, and Venezuela. Since 2000, however, Colombian heroin has been moved by ship in much larger loads. Once it arrives in the United States, on the East Coast, Dominicans play the primary role in moving the drug from the wholesale to the retail levels. Mexican heroin is primarily destined for the West Coast, often in the form of "black tar." In addition, the majority of the Colombian heroin sold in the western United States is moved by Mexican nationals. Again, most loads are in the small-to-medium range (up to three kilos) and come into the country via individual couriers; however, recently, larger loads of dozens of kilos have been seized on vehicles at the border. A still-important source of American heroin is Southwest Asia, mainly Afghanistan. Careful and cautious, the personnel distributing this heroin at the smuggling and wholesale levels is almost entirely composed of national and ethnic Southwest Asians. Although Southeast Asia has diminished in importance in the past decade and a half as a source for American-bound heroin, the area remains a substantial point of origin for the drug. It is sent via container ships from China, Japan, Malaysia, the Philippines, Taiwan,

---

[2]The following account is based on the Drug Enforcement Agency's Internet publication "Drug Trafficking in the United States," and on Bruen et al., 2002; Layne, Johnston, and Rhodes, 2002; Rhodes et al., 2001; Rhodes, Johnston, and Kling, 2001; and the United Nations' *Global Illicit Drug Trends* for 2005, published in 2006.

South Korea, and Singapore in large loads. Interestingly, Nigerians play a not-insignificant role in smuggling and distributing in American cities with well-established Nigerian populations. These figures could change over time, depending on the transformation of a variety of economic, political, and legal factors.

Heroin is an example of a drug whose production and distribution conform to the mixed model. It begins its life embedded in the chemical structure of millions of poppy plants whose opium gum is harvested by tens of thousands of peasants and farmers who sell their product, after a step or two, to a much smaller number of wholesalers who, in turn, sell to an even smaller number of processors who convert the raw opium first into morphine and then, higher up, into heroin. The first half of heroin's journey, from cultivation to processing, is pyramidal or fan-shaped, wide at the bottom and tapering narrowly toward the top. The second half of the journey, distribution (after adulteration), is also fan-shaped, moving from a small number of high-level traffickers to a very large number of sellers at the street level.

## Cocaine

Virtually all of the cocaine consumed in the United States has its origin in Colombia, Peru, or Bolivia, with Colombia contributing the lion's share, possibly as much as 90 percent. However, roughly two-thirds of the cocaine entering the United States today, according to the DEA, crosses into the country over the border with Mexico. In the past decade or two, Mexican traffickers have played a growing and now major role in the cocaine trade. Until the late 1980s, Colombians dominated the business of smuggling cocaine into the United States, even when it passed through Mexico. But huge seizures convinced Colombian traffickers that it would be advantageous to relinquish major portions of the business to Mexican nationals. By the mid-1990s, half of all cocaine entering the United States, most of it of Colombian origin, was controlled by Mexican transport groups. Cocaine sold on the eastern seaboard tends to be distributed at the wholesale level by Dominicans or brought from the Southwest by Mexicans. Cocaine sold in the Midwest and West is usually distributed by Mexican organizations. Cocaine also comes into the United States by ship from the Caribbean.

Cocaine shares with heroin the shape of its distribution system—two fans, laid end to end, the narrow end of the top one pointing down, meeting the narrow end of the bottom one pointing up. It is this funneling effect that provides huge profits to a very small number of high-level wholesalers—which, in certain economic and political settings (discussed below), also generates extremely high levels of violence and repression, and much smaller profits to the peasant farmer and petty street seller.

## Marijuana

Cannabis production and distribution is extremely decentralized. Of all the marijuana consumed in the United States, more than half is grown domestically. About half of the remainder comes from Mexico, a quarter from Colombia, and a quarter from other countries. A small but growing percentage comes in from Canada. "BC Bud," grown in British Columbia, has shown up recently in West Coast locations, selling for $5,000–$8,000 a pound in major metropolitan areas. The five leading states for indoor growing, according to the DEA, are California, Florida, Oregon, Washington, and Wisconsin; the four leading outdoor growing states are California, Hawaii, Kentucky, and Tennessee. Authorities do not detect any particular ethnic pattern among sellers, though growers are overwhelmingly white. With the government crackdown on marijuana growing in the United States, cultivation has become increasingly sophisticated. Today, enough plants to generate profits of nearly $200,000 a year can be grown in an indoor area the size of a pool table. Within a very few years, some claim, "virtual" marijuana gardens will be self-regulating; their ownership will be almost untraceable, the grower appearing only to harvest the product, replant some seeds, and, once again, disappear into anonymity (Pollan, 1995). Authorities have been busting indoor operations by monitoring electricity usage, tracing the purchase of grow-lights, and using thermal imaging of rooftops for excessive sources of heat. Most of the marijuana smuggled into the United States from Mexico is concealed in vehicles, though individual couriers will bring across small loads on foot, and sometimes, substantial shipments of the drug brought in by large ships will be offloaded onto smaller boats, brought into coastal locations, and distributed from there.

Of all drugs, the marijuana business most closely conforms to the pure agricultural model previously outlined. It is a decentralized, comparatively nonhierarchical, and scattered industry. It is the drug most likely to be—and it is uniquely—produced directly by consumers. It is the drug for which the step from producer to consumer is most likely to be local rather than global. No single seller or wholesaler is likely to wield much power; hence, violence and political repression are—although far from unknown—fairly infrequent and not a major factor in the drug's distribution system. Hence, many of the issues discussed below (globalization, for instance) are least likely to apply to marijuana. Hashish, the resin of the marijuana plant, is a bit more difficult to produce than what is generally referred to as marijuana, which includes the plant's buds, flowering tops, and some leaves. Hashish is produced in North Africa, largely in Morocco, but the bulk of this form of cannabis makes its way to Western Europe, not the United States (United Nations, 2006, pp. 235–239).

## Methamphetamine

Because the chemical process is relatively simple, nearly all production of and trafficking in methamphetamine is either domestic or crosses only one border—that is, is brought from Mexico into the United States. Prior to the mid-1990s, the majority of the methamphetamine sold in the United States was manufactured and distributed by members of motorcycle gangs operating small, clandestine labs in the Southwest, mainly California. But about ten years ago, Mexican gangs began muscling into the bikers' turf and managed to wrest a major portion of the business away from them. Independent labs continue to operate in the United States, but they tend to be smaller and have a much lower production capacity than the Mexican labs, which are not only larger but also tend to be part of an organized criminal cartel.

In 1994, a total of only 263 methamphetamine labs were seized by law enforcement authorities; in 2000, 1,800 were seized by the DEA alone, and 4,600 by state and local police. But in its latest (2006) report, the *National Drug Control Strategy,* the White House claims that in 2004 and 2005, the number of meth lab seizures decreased nationwide because the manufacture of the drug is being stamped out by law enforcement. In addition, in the 2000s, the federal government seized hundreds of thousands of tablets containing ephedrine and pseudoephedrine, the chemical precursors necessary in the manufacture of methamphetamine. But the DEA also reported that the number of methamphetamine seizures at the Mexican border doubled between 2001 (1,173) and 2004 (2,300)—also, claims the White House, a sign of the federal government's law enforcement and deterrence effectiveness.

## Ecstasy

Western Europe, mainly Belgium and the Netherlands, remains the country's principal source for MDMA; the DEA estimates that 80 percent of the Ecstasy sold in the United States originates from these two countries. The remainder, says the DEA, is produced in various other countries and distributed by either Russian or Israeli organized crime syndicates. In 2000, seven labs were seized in the United States, and in 2003 another ten labs were seized, suggesting that in the future, domestic production, while small, may become a significant source of the drug. According to the DEA, in 1997, 400,000 tablets of Ecstasy were seized by authorities; in 2000, the figure was over 9 million, but in 2001, the figure dropped to 7 million, and in 2003 and 2004, to 1.5 million. The White House argues that the decline in Ecstasy seizures indicates that the war against this drug is being won. In 2002, the United States and the Netherlands entered into an agreement, called "Operation Double Dutch," which calls for customs officials to target "suspicious cargo" from the Amsterdam airport. Dutch seizures increased from 3.6 million tablets in 2001 to 5.5 million in 2004. In 2002 and 2003, 30 of the 46 European labs seized were located in the Netherlands. The White House credits this and coordinated operations with the decline in Ecstasy use discussed in Chapter 9.

## LSD

Although the process for manufacturing LSD has been published in a number of books and articles and posted on the Internet, it is an extremely difficult, time-consuming, and complex process, requiring a great deal of chemical sophistication. The number of labs that manufacture the drug is small; perhaps as few as a dozen or two supply the bulk of the country's LSD. Most of these labs are located in California and the Pacific Northwest, and the bulk of their product is destined for domestic consumption (or use in Canada). According to the DEA, the chemists who manufacture the drug tend not to distribute it, but sell the crystal form of the drug to a few "trusted associates, insulating themselves from the wholesale distributors." Because of the secretive nature of the business at this level of the distribution chain, clandestine LSD labs are only rarely seized by authorities. Traffickers convert the crystal into liquid form and usually soak blotter paper with droplets of LSD. Less often it is sold in liquid form in vials or breath mint bottles; occasionally, it appears in gelatin tablets.

## Purely Synthetic Drugs: A Summary

Methamphetamine, Ecstasy, and LSD are all chemicals, and hence conform to the pure chemical model. Yet, interestingly, each has its own distinctive distribution pattern. Methamphetamine, which is comparatively easy to manufacture (given one of its precursor chemicals, ephedrine or pseudoephedrine), is fairly decentralized, making only one border crossing (from Mexico into the United States) or is entirely domestic in origin. Ecstasy, which is not as easy to manufacture, manifests a more centralized distribution system. But it originates not in countries with corrupt, authoritarian, repressive political regimes, but largely in liberal Western European democracies. And LSD, much more difficult to manufacture, is likewise centralized and hierarchical, originating in a very small number of locales. But, unlike Colombian drug lords, LSD manufacturers and distributors are practically invisible, having little or no impact on the political landscape. Hence, not all of the factors discussed below (such as poverty, a weak or corrupt political regime, economic privatization, and the collapse of the Soviet Union) have any relevance for the sale of Ecstasy or LSD. These examples should remind us that the relationship between a given social, political, and economic system, and the manufacture and distribution of drugs is far from preordained.

## FACTORS THAT FACILITATE THE ILLICIT DRUG TRADE

Drug-trafficking patterns have evolved into their present form, and continue to develop along certain lines, for a complex mix of reasons. Some of these factors are local, such as climate and indigenous cultural patterns, while others can be generalized to settings all over the world. Without question, the most fundamental, crucial factor that is the very engine of the illicit drug trade, without which it would either not exist at all or exist in radically different form, is so obvious that it may be overlooked—**prohibition.** If all psychoactive substances were legal, by definition, there would be no such thing as an illegal or illicit drug. But the buying and selling of drugs would look very different as well. If the possession and sale of cocaine and heroin were legal, coca bushes and Oriental poppy plants would be grown in the United States, and Ecstasy and methamphetamine "superlabs" would be located here as well. It's also likely that the drug trade would be substantially bigger than it is now, and an immense number of ancillary services (such as drug treatment centers) would spring up in response to the greater use. Just as importantly, if legal, the currently illicit drugs would be incredibly cheap, costing no more than aspirin or Rolaids. Whatever impact drug prohibition may have had, it has increased the price of illicit substances; this is perhaps its most significant by-product. The fact is, the drugs in which we are interested are illegal, and their patterns of distribution, as well as the reasons for those patterns, are what we have to examine at this point.

One principle that has influenced the sale of illicit substances all over the world is the emergence of worldwide networks that link the source of drugs with their ultimate customer. International and intersocietal commerce has existed for thousands of years. However, it was not until the late twentieth century that the distribution of the currently illicit drugs took on a truly global complexion. Prior to the early 1970s, international drug linkages tended to be fairly simple: Marijuana was imported into the United States from Mexico; opium, grown in Turkey, was processed into heroin in Marseilles, and smuggled into New York; cocaine, produced in labs in Colombia from coca leaves gathered in Peru and Bolivia, was brought into the United States and Western Europe.

Perhaps the watershed event that transformed drug distribution to its present global form was the dismantling in 1972 of the French Connection heroin-trafficking network by the French police, U.S. federal agents, and the New York City Police Department. The cartel had previously supplied 80 percent of the heroin sold in the United States, and its demise generated a drug "panic" among users, creating an enormous, importunate demand for the drug. This opened up an economic opportunity that many daring, unscrupulous entrepreneurs around the world could not pass up. In the past three or so decades, the routes through which heroin specifically—and perhaps as a by-product, illegal drugs generally—travel, the number of source countries and the number of countries through which drugs move, and the national and ethnic groups involved in drug trafficking have virtually exploded (Stares, 1996, pp. 25, 27–28). Since the 1970s, the international drug trade has been transformed from a cottage industry to a global enterprise whose profits are greater than three-quarters of the national economies of the world, estimated at between $180 and $300 billion annually (p. 2). While some of the preconditions for this development existed previously, the conjunction of several key factors made this development possible specifically during the last quarter of the twentieth century. Some of these developments include the following.

## The Collapse of the Soviet Union

Authoritarian regimes (such as the former Soviet Union) "have generally fared better than open democratic countries in suppressing drug market activity because the state plays a more intrusive and repressive role in almost all aspects of daily life. By contrast, the capacity of liberal democratic states to reduce the availability of drugs is clearly limited by their commitment to the very principles and values upon which they are based" (Stares, 1996, p. 74). While the Soviet Union, its constituent republics, and the Eastern Bloc nations were never completely successful in suppressing crime and, more specifically, illicit drug trafficking, the collapse of the Soviet Union produced a power vacuum into which has stepped an array of unscrupulous, ruthless actors willing to violate the law to earn a substantial profit.

   In the Central Asian republics, for instance, "thousands of acres have been given over to the cultivation of opium poppies and cannabis. . . . Hungary and [the former] Czechoslovakia have become major transit countries for Asian heroin destined for West Europe. . . . Polish health officials warned that a dramatic rise in intravenous drug abuse in Warsaw has unleashed criminal networks engaged in drug trafficking" (Flynn, 1993, p. 6). The "unraveling of socialism and the move toward freer trade among industrialized countries has created a fertile environment for international business"—including, perhaps especially, illicit ones. The collapse of the Iron Curtain has produced "torrents of people, goods, and services . . . pouring across borders. In their midst, drug shipments . . . move with little risk of detection by customs authorities" (pp. 6–7). The Central Asian republics, especially Turkmenistan, Uzbekistan, and Tajikistan, have become major opium-growing areas for heroin bound for Eastern Europe. Georgia and Kazakhstan have become major leaf cannabis–growing areas. And Russia as well as its former republics and satellite countries, especially Poland and the Czech Republic, have become major amphetamine- and methamphetamine-producing and -distributing countries (United Nations, 2006).

## Economic Privatization

Since the collapse of the Soviet Union and the end of the Cold War, economies all over the world have becoming increasingly privatized, liberalized, and deregulated (Flynn, 1993). China has opened free trade zones in a number of port cities, in which state control and even monitoring of commerce have been lifted, and an extreme version of laissez-faire capitalism now operates. In 1989, Mexico deregulated the trucking industry, liberalizing barriers to entry into the country and permitting free movement into every city, port, and railroad station. Within two years, the number of registered trucks had increased by 62 percent. Soon after, Chile and Argentina followed suit. In 1991, Mexico allowed private companies to construct and operate their own ports (Stares, 1996, p. 56). The creation of the European Union in 2002 resulted in a single currency for most of Western Europe and enabled free and open trade across national boundaries. In the 1990s, the North American Free Trade Agreement (NAFTA) removed thousands of trade barriers between the United States and Mexico and the United States and Canada. Worldwide economic deregulation has expedited the flow of goods, both licit and illicit, across national borders. It has proved to be a major shot in the arm for the global drug trade.

## Money Laundering

Banking is a major worldwide industry. In some countries, banks operate under a principal of extreme secrecy. "Don't ask, don't tell" is their watchword. Clients may deposit bundles of cash totaling millions of dollars, and the bank maintains no record of the transaction and releases none to the government. Offshore banks, such as those in Aruba and the Cayman Islands, and banks located in tiny European countries such as Liechtenstein and Luxembourg, as well as in Hong Kong, Cyprus, and Panama, offer "financial secrecy and client confidentiality" (Stares, 1996, p. 58). Liechtenstein has more post office box corporations (72,000)—a high percentage of them banks—than people (23,000). The emergence, indeed, the immense expansion, of such banks has permitted traffickers to launder money earned in the illicit drug trade back into the legitimate economy, thereby avoiding official detection, in effect, nullifying a major arm of law enforcement.

## Globalization

Globalization is both a relatively recent product of political, economic, technological, cultural, and social changes taking place nearly everywhere on Earth and an umbrella concept whose manifestations have enormously accelerated the illicit drug trade during the past quarter century or so. During that time, international commerce, travel, and communication have grown exponentially; the huge increase in the worldwide illicit drug trade is one consequence of globalization.

In 1970, according to the U.S. Department of Commerce, the value of exports from the United States to foreign countries totaled $42 billion; its imports from other countries were valued at $40 billion. In 2004, these figures were $818 billion and $1.5 trillion, an increase of roughly 20 and 35 times, respectively; adjusting for inflation, this represents an increase of roughly four to five times. Each year, the number of persons simply crossing the border into the United States (over 400 million) is greater than the number of its residents (280 million). In 1991, the first Internet browser was released. By 1994, there were 3 million users of the Internet, nearly all of them in the United States; in 2004, there were 85 million DSL broadband subscribers and 820 million Internet users. According to the International Telecommunication Union, international phone traffic, as measured in minutes, increased from 33 billion in 1990 to 130 billion in 2002. In the United States, cell phone subscribers increased from 340,000 in 1985, to 34 million in 1995, to 159 million in 2003; worldwide, the figure is nearly a billion. In trade, travel, and communication, the world has become a global village. We have become, in effect, a "borderless" world (Stares, 1996, p. 5).

The movement of persons, goods, information, and messages across national borders has created a superhighway for traffickers to transport drugs from source to using countries. The sheer volume of bodies and freight coming into every country in the world from every other makes it impossible for officials to monitor and stem the tide of illicit products. Instant communication to and from every point on the globe enables traffickers to convey information on transactions practically without detection. As a result, the drug trade "has increasingly become a transnational phenomenon, driven and fashioned in critical ways by transnational forces and transnational actors. Thus the global diffusion of technical expertise and the internationalization of manufacturing have made it possible to cultivate and refine drugs in remote places of the world and still be within reach of distant markets" (Stares, 1996, pp. 5–6). The huge global expansion in trade, transportation, and tourism has facilitated trafficking in established drug-using areas and "opened up new areas of the world to exploit" (p. 6). Huge increases in international travel, the mass media, and telecommunications "have undoubtedly increased the global awareness of drug fashions around the world" (p. 6).

Globalization permits enormous flexibility with respect to where illicit drugs may be grown or manufactured and how they may be delivered to their ultimate markets. If law enforcement shuts down an operation in a given region or country, entrepreneurs in another region or country quickly move into the economic vacuum. As we saw, the dismantling of the French Connection in 1972 created opportunities for growers and traffickers in other areas of the world to provide the opium and heroin necessary to supply American addicts. Whereas in 1972, Turkey accounted for 80 percent of the botanical source of the heroin used in the United States, today, that source is mainly Colombia (67%), secondarily Mexico (23%), and, far less importantly, Southwest Asia (6%) and Southeast Asia (2%). After "Operation Intercept," when the U.S. border patrol guards searched every car and person entering the country for drugs (1969), the cultivation of home-grown American marijuana increased dramatically (Inciardi, 2002, pp. 54–55; Pollan, 1995). Today, it represents well over half the volume of the marijuana consumed in the United States. (Recently, marijuana grown in and imported from Canada has begun to be distributed in the United States.) Observers refer to this phenomenon as the "balloon" effect or the "push down/pop up" factor (Nadelmann, 1988, p. 9); that is, whenever drug trafficking is "pushed down" in one area, it "pops up" in another. The reason for this is, of course, the enormous profits to be made in the drug trade and the unlimited supply of people willing to take the legal risk to earn those profits. It is possible that globalization is the single factor most responsible for the enormous expansion in the illicit drug trade during the past three decades. If it were much more burdensome and problematic to move drugs and money across borders, traffickers would not have the same degree of flexibility to adapt to changing legal, political, and economic circumstances around the world.

## Poverty

While upper-level drug dealers tend to be wealthy, almost beyond comprehension, the foot soldiers of the drug trade at either end of the distribution spectrum tend to be poor. As the worldwide economic crisis deepens, exacerbating the enormous gap in wealth between the industrialized, developed countries of Western Europe, North America, Australia, and New Zealand; the Asian "tigers," that is, industrialized East Asian countries—like Japan, Taiwan, Hong Kong, Singapore, and Malaysia; and a few oil-rich Persian Gulf states, on the one hand, and the poorer, developing nations of the world, on the other, poverty assumes an increasingly greater role in drug trafficking. At the source end, the opium poppy, from which heroin is derived, and the coca plant, which yields cocaine, tend to be grown by peasant farmers cultivating small plots of land, whose livelihood depends on the illicit crop. (Most of the world's opium and coca, it should be noted, are grown for the production of *legal* substances.) Very few substitute crops are capable of being grown on most of such land, and practically no other crop can get to a sufficiently nearby market to support the peasant's family at subsistence earnings.

This generalization about the poverty of the majority of hands-on growers does not apply to the leaf cannabis or marijuana grown in North America and Europe, since that industry is extremely decentralized, but it does apply to the resin cannabis or hashish that comes from North Africa and Western Asia. These farmers are more affluent than their peers who do not grow a drug crop, but poverty is an enormous incentive to move from a licit to an illicit product—or not to move from an illicit to a licit product. Toward the middle of the distribution chain, likewise, many (though almost certainly not most) of the illicit drugs smuggled into a country where they are sold are brought across the border by poor couriers ("mules" or "smurfs") who carry them on their person, often by swallowing drug-filled condoms. And at the low-level, seller-to-consumer end, especially in poor neighborhoods, are petty street dealers; typically, they are addicts themselves, barely earning enough on their transactions to pay for their own drug habits. As we'll see in more detail below, there are middle-class drug dealers who sell directly to consumers, but they tend to take fewer risks because they usually sell to persons they know, in fairly substantial quantities a small number of times, indoors, in places of residence, and in settings in which violence rarely takes place (Dunlap, Johnson, and Manwar, 1994, pp. 5–6).

To put the matter another way, the poorer an area, society, or community, the greater the incentive to produce, traffic, and sell illegal drugs. This is because, although the affluent are willing to take moderate risks to earn a great deal of money, the poverty-stricken are willing to take much greater risks to earn relatively little money. A small fraction of 1 percent of the wholesale price of heroin and cocaine goes to the grower, and, refined, once they cross the border into a destination country, their wholesale value increases ten times (Stares, 1996, pp. 53–54). It is the major trafficker and wholesaler who earn the lion's share of the illicit drug profits. The industry's foot soldiers take the most risk and earn the least profit. The poor, with little in the way of economic wherewithal or prospects, are most likely to take such risks. Hence, poverty must be counted as a major factor in the production, distribution, and sale of illicit drugs.

## Weak or Corrupt Local and Federal Governments

When the central government does not control major areas of a country, when the police and the military cannot enter an area for fear of being shot, they cannot control illegal activity within that country's borders, and drug lords are free to grow botanicals from which drugs are extracted, distributed, and sold at will. Major territories of Burma (Myanmar) have been under the control of private drug armies for decades. In Colombia, the army cannot enter major territories that are controlled by rebels, who use drug revenues to finance their operations. In Afghanistan, likewise, it is local tribes, not the federal government, that control the extremely rugged, mountainous terrain where most of the world's opium is grown. (The White House claims that since the U.S. invasion of Afghanistan, poppy production has declined.) In Mexico, until the election of the Vicente Fox regime, the corruption of the police and the army was vast and extensive, reaching up to the president's family. Border assignments were bought and sold with the expectation that an officer would earn substantial sums from bribes by drug dealers in exchange for immunity from arrest. In such weak or corrupt regimes, honest law enforcement is a virtual impossibility and drug trafficking is able to flourish.

## THE STREET SELLER-TO-USER TRANSACTION: FOUR VIEWS

The ultimate transaction in the illicit drug trade is the step that delivers illicit substances into the hands of the user. This process, as with all the others, is enshrouded in myth and misconception. One widely believed myth is that there is a yawning gulf between the dealer, who is a ruthless exploiter and victimizer, and the user, who is the unfortunate victim of a bad habit. The dealer makes enormous sums of money while the user, poverty-stricken, down and out, desperate and at the end of his or her rope, must resort to a life of money-making crimes to support the habit. As usual, the reality is considerably more complicated than this popular misconception.

In the sections that follow, we examine four views on the final step in this process. The first gives us a detailed look at the economics of the heroin abuser. The second tells us about drug sales by delinquent gangs. The third offers an interpretation of crack selling in a predominantly Puerto Rican neighborhood in Manhattan. And the fourth, by examining racial and ethnic styles of selling, may help explain racial disparities in arrest and incarceration.

### The Street-Level Economics of Heroin Abuse

A team of researchers led by sociologist Bruce Johnson gathered respondents in the East and Central Harlem communities of Manhattan, in New York City (Johnson et al., 1985). Respondents who met three criteria were recruited. First, they used heroin (or methadone) during the period under investigation; more specifically, they administered the heroin they took via injection. Second, they lived on the street; they spent little time in conventional settings, such as in a home or at school or work. And third, they engaged in criminal activity. Subjects who failed to meet any of these criteria were excluded from the study. Respondents were recruited by ex-addict, ex-offender staff members sent into the community to locate stranger users or to interview acquaintances, who would then introduce them to potential interviewees. For the most part, respondents were interviewed in a storefront setting, rented for this purpose. The eventual sample size was 201.

The study produced a number of findings that contradicted commonly held stereotypes about heroin abusers. Several of these were not specifically related to drug buying and selling—for instance, the myth that heroin abusers stick to heroin (most use several other drugs in addition to heroin, including alcohol, often at abusive levels) and that all or most heroin abusers are physically addicted (most are not). But perhaps the most interesting—and surprising—of this study's findings relate specifically to the buying and selling of drugs.

In the 1980s, commonly cited figures for the dollar value of the heroin consumed by addicts per day ranged from $100 to $150. (That $100 in 1982 was worth $188 in 2004; $150 then was worth $280 twenty-two years later. However, keep in mind that heroin was much cheaper in 2004 than in 1982.) The image often projected of the addict with respect to money-making crimes resembles a voracious blast furnace that requires incessant feeding, consuming everything hurled into its maw. The Johnson team found such an addict to be highly atypical. The total income that was derived from criminal activity averaged $12,000 annually for their sample as a whole. For the daily users, the figure was $19,000. (Again, adjusting for 2004 dollars, these figures come out to roughly $22,668 and $35,891.) While these are substantial sums, they fall far short of the $100–150 per day attributed to the heroin addict in the early 1980s; these sums average out to only $33 and $52 per day (or $62 and $98 per day in today's dollar). What accounts for this discrepancy?

In the past, the dollar value of the heroin consumed by addicts and abusers, and along with it, their rate of criminal activity, usually were calculated in an extremely slipshod fashion. One way was to calculate the number of shots of heroin necessary to remain addicted and then to calculate the cost of those shots. Another way was to ask users to estimate the cost and size of their drug habits. As the Johnson team discovered, neither of these calculations produces even a remotely accurate estimate of habit size. The sample's irregular users were asked to provide an estimate of the average cost of heroin used per day during the previous year; their global, overall estimate averaged out to $25. The drawback of relying on such estimates was underscored when the Johnson team asked their respondents about their detailed, day-by-day usage, which came to an astoundingly low dollar amount of $4 per day—one-sixth of their initial response! The higher their actual use, the more accurate their estimates were of the dollar value of their heroin habits. Still, even the daily users were off by 50 percent—$53 estimated versus $36 actually used. The sample as a whole roughly doubled their rough estimates of what they actually used, as measured by their more rigorous, detailed, day-by-day accounts—$43 versus $18.

Again, why the discrepancy? It seems that respondents made their rough estimates on the basis of their self-image as heroin abusers or addicts. They tended to forget about those days when they used little or no heroin. When they were asked to average use across long periods of time, such as a year, they usually recalled only those days when they were successful in obtaining heroin. It is easy to understand how journalists—and sloppy researchers—could have arrived at $100–150 a day habits for the typical abuser or addict.

Another important and unexpected finding was that the heroin abuser does not purchase all the heroin he or she consumes. The more frequently users consume heroin, the lower the proportion of the heroin that they use actually is purchased. In this study, daily users purchased only 58 percent of the heroin they consumed with hard cash. For the next-lower level of use—regular but not daily users—this figure was 62 percent, and for irregular users, it was 71 percent. Heroin abusers receive a substantial proportion of their heroin by serving as the "day laborers" of the heroin distribution industry. They cut (dilute), bag, and sell heroin, and they "steer, tout, and cop" customers on the street; that is, they act as go-betweens for sellers slightly higher on the distribution chain and customers, or next-to-customer sellers. And most of what they receive for such work is not cash but heroin. The Johnson research team also calculated a category of "income" representing value received for the heroin abuser in the form of "avoided drug expenditures." This came to an average of $2,000 for the sample as a whole and $3,400 for the daily users. In other words, heroin abusers are masters at mooching free drugs from others.

In addition, abusers often steal drugs from others; the dollar value of this economic activity came to $1,700 worth on a yearly basis; clearly, this is not the sort of crime cited in the media or feared by the public at large. Heroin abusers also sell drugs to others, but to judge from the dollar value sold—a $2,400 annual average for the sample as a whole and $3,400 for the daily user—they are as low on the distribution chain as it is possible to get, short of their own catch-as-catch-can customers. In addition, they don't sell that often, at least not as a regular source of income. And their revenue from prostitution and pimping accounts for more than 40 percent of their average criminal income—and more than half for the irregular users. In short, the classic stereotype of heroin addicts as earning all, the overwhelming bulk, or even most of their drug money from robbery, theft, and other predatory criminal activity is erroneous.

Of course, heroin users, abusers, and addicts do regularly victimize others by committing classic predatory crimes against them. Robbery, burglary, and shoplifting accounted for nearly two-thirds (63%) of the sample's criminal income and between one-third and one-half (44%) of its total income overall. The authors (Johnson et al., 1985) argue that this does not represent a total loss to the community or the society as a whole. Instead, thievery represents a loss for some parties and a gain for others. The victim loses from an instance of theft, of course, but the thief gains, as does the purchaser of the stolen item—who receives, in the authors' words, a "deep discount"—as does the retail merchant who sells a replacement item to the victim, and the dealer who sells heroin to the thief-addict. That's four winners and only one loser. According to the authors, thievery may be looked upon as "involuntary transfer payments," and stolen goods are "a major component of the ghetto" economy. The fact that many people benefit from drug-related economic crime, the authors argue, "while fewer individuals have identifiable [economic] losses is likely to be sobering." With ghetto crime, "the economic results are good for some persons and bad for others. Little can be done or is likely to be done to stop heroin-abuser theft and the vigorous demand for stolen goods in ghetto communities." In sum, the economic functions of drug-related crime are not simple; since so many parties gain in the many transactions it entails, it is unlikely to be eliminated with simplistic solutions.

## Delinquent Gangs

More than four decades ago, Richard Cloward and Lloyd Ohlin (1960) published what is considered a classic work on the origins and dynamics of delinquent gangs. In it, the authors posited three distinctly different types of gangs—the criminal gang, the conflict gang, and the retreatist gang. The criminal gang was primarily involved in theft and other money-making crimes; the conflict gang was primarily involved in violent behavior; and the retreatist gang was primarily involved in drug-related behavior. If this distinction ever had any relevance for real-world urban street gangs, it is certainly meaningless today. Today, urban delinquent gangs do not specialize in any one of the three activities; most tend to participate in all three. Moreover, "retreatist" is an extremely inaccurate label for the drug-related activity that gangs actually participate in. The fact is, a very high proportion of urban delinquent gangs—in all likelihood, a majority—are involved in the business of selling illicit drugs. And their participation is anything but a retreatist activity. It is a business, a ruthless business, and it involves not a "retreat" from this-worldly activity but a direct, face-to-face confrontation with it.

Steven Levitt and Sudhir Venkatesh (1998) were granted access to the financial records of a drug-dealing gang in an almost exclusively Black inner-city neighborhood. They examined the gang's records monthly for a four-year period. The gang's books included detailed information on revenues, such as drug sales, extortion, and member dues, and expenses, such as wages and the cost of the drugs and weapons that were purchased, as well as tribute paid to the gang's higher-ups. The drug that put the gang on the map, economically speaking, was crack, and that is the drug that brought in the organization's principal revenues.

Gang drug dealing is not as lucrative as is widely believed. For the gang as a whole, the average wage at the beginning of the study period was $6 an hour; four years later, it stood at $11 an hour. (Both are expressed in 1995 dollars, which were worth about 20 percent more than a decade later.) Wages were, however, highly skewed toward the top of the gang's organizational structure. During this four-year period, the wages of the gang's leader tripled, from $32 to $97 an hour. The wages of the gang's foot soldiers also tripled, or almost so, but were less than one-tenth of those at the top—from $2.50 an hour in year 1 to $7.10 an hour in year 4. In addition, say the authors, the risk of death for occupants of all positions in the organization was extremely high—a factor that seemed to carry very little weight among gang members.

Keep in mind that economic factors, as well as the consideration of life-and-death risks, are not the sole issues here, at least for gang members. The symbolic value of gang membership and participation, the authors argue, was formidable for these young men. Taking over leadership positions in the organization resembled a contest or tournament in which a struggle for power produced clear-cut winners and losers. Leaders lorded it over foot soldiers and the rank-and-file in ways that are not possible in "civilian" life. The seductive allure of gang life, and more specifically, of drug selling, is a major inducement to young men whose life options are relatively limited (Katz, 1988). Such instances should convince us that even economic transactions cannot be reduced to economic considerations alone.

At the same time, the authors argue that given the low-level gang member's extremely low pay, the legitimate wage sector can offer inducements that could entice them away from and be a viable substitute for drug selling. Still, their conclusions are qualified:

> [A] large fraction of the low-level gang members in our data already have at least intermittent contact with the [legitimate] job market. When gang wages rose in the latter part of our sample, participation in the legitimate labor market decreased. To the extent that attractiveness of legitimate sector jobs can be improved, either through increased wages or more attractive jobs, youths may reduce gang involvement. The symbolic aspects of gang membership, however, remain attractive. (Levitt and Venkatesh, 1998, p. 31)

## Selling Crack in El Barrio

A more emphatic statement that the denial of access to legitimate and fulfilling jobs has an impact on drug dealing can be found in Philippe Bourgois' now-classic *In Search of Respect: Selling Crack in El Barrio* (1995). Crack is a drug whose sale represents the fanning-out of a distribution system, from wholesale to retail, that conforms to the mixed model—but with an interesting twist. Crack is produced by heating cocaine hydrochloride with baking soda. The process is so simple that anyone who can purchase a few rocks of cocaine can set up shop selling crack. During the heyday of the crack epidemic (1985–1990), many thousands of enterprising adolescents and young adults in the nation's inner cities began selling crack on their own—thousands of daring, reckless, independent entrepreneurs who were bound by no structure, no organization, no ties, and no obligations to anyone. The result, as we saw in Chapter 12, was competition for territory or turf, conflict, violence, and a sharp rise in the country's homicide rate. Interestingly, while marijuana's decentralized economic structure seems to have generated a less conflictual, less violent distribution system, with crack, much the same structure spawned precisely the opposite—a far more violent distribution system than would otherwise have been the case. The findings from Bourgois' field research bears out this generalization.

According to Bourgois, substance abuse and petty dealing are both symptoms and symbols of "deeper dynamics of social marginalization and alienation" (p. 2). Consider the neighborhood Bourgois studied—East Harlem or, to the Latino residents, "El Barrio." During the period when he studied this neighborhood (which coincided precisely with the crack epidemic, 1985–1990), 5 out of 10 residents were Puerto Rican; 4 out of 10 were African-American. Four out of 10 were living below the poverty line, 4 out of 10 received welfare assistance, and 4 out of 10 declared no wages at all to the Census Bureau. (These are separate but overlapping categories, of course.) Yet very few were homeless, hardly anyone starved, and no one on the street was dressed in rags. What was their secret?

A substantial proportion of every urban community on Earth is supported by an "enormous, uncensused, untaxed underground economy"—that is, an income-generating structure that represents an alternative to the formal economy, which is recorded, taxed, monitored, controlled, and licensed by the state. There is no worker's compensation or hospitalization in the informal economy, and there are no safeguards to protect workers from harm or exploitation. At the same time, the informal economy is capable of providing pay to workers who would be unacceptable in the formal economy. Many of Bourgois' informants, especially the males, were—or believed they were—"locked out of the legal labor market" (p. 123). When they did work in the legal sector, it seemed a "foreign, hostile" workplace, a world in which they experienced "racially charged cultural miscommunication" (p. 143). For instance, the sexual banter, sexual come-ons, and "sexually aggressive behavior" that were acceptable on the street in El Barrio were offensive in the legal sector. Based on their lack of education and their style of dress, they were looked down upon and were made to "look like idiotic buffoons to the men and women for whom they work[ed]" (p. 143).

Bourgois sees these experiences as "structural victimization." By "embroiling themselves in the underground economy"—by selling crack, for instance—"and proudly embracing street culture," his informants "are seeking an alternative to their social marginalization." However, therein lies the dilemma, says Bourgois. In embracing Latino street culture, along with its values, norms, and behavior—not only radically different from but antagonistic to dominant, white, middle-class culture—they further marginalize themselves and make it all but impossible to achieve a modicum of success. And in engaging in economic transactions that represent an "alternative" to a demeaning office job—that is, by dealing crack—"they become the actual agents administering their own destruction and their community's suffering" (p. 143).

Substance abuse, says Bourgois, is not the problem; instead, drug abuse is "the epiphenomenal expression of [a] deeper, structural" problem—which is economic and racial inequality. It is class and race victimization and polarization "that generate self-destructive and criminal activity." Clearly, Bourgois falls into the camp I referred to in Chapter 3 as conflict theorists. The answer to the drug abuse problem? asks Bourgois. His solution is twofold:

(1) "recognize and dismantle the class- and ethnic-based apartheids that riddle the U.S. land-scape" (p. 319), and (2) "destroy the profitability of narcotic trafficking by decriminalizing drugs." In so doing, he says, drugs would be made less accessible "because it would no longer be profitable" for inner-city youths to sell once-illicit, now-legal drugs; addicts would not have to "pay exorbitant sums for their daily doses"; and dealers would not have to resort to violence in the streets because they would "no longer have such high profits to fight over" (p. 321).

Bourgois does not explain the vastly greater availability, sales, profitability, addictive use, and harmful effects of alcohol and tobacco, which are legal. He seems to think that le-galizing crack and heroin will make their sales unprofitable, but it is enormously profitable to sell the *legal* drugs, and they are widely used and cause enormous harm to society as a whole, including residents of the inner city. Why would the currently illicit drugs, if legal-ized, not follow the same pattern? And as we saw in Chapter 12, there is vastly more total violence—mainly psychopharmacological—associated with alcohol abuse (again, a legal drug) than currently exists with crack or heroin. Would greater availability produce higher levels of psychopharmacological violence for these currently illegal drugs? We'll examine some of the major legalization issues in Chapter 15. Bourgois also does not explain why most residents of El Barrio, whether "locked out" of the legal job sector or not, do not re-sort to violence, serious crime, or drug dealing. But his analysis of the underground econ-omy as an alternative to the legal economy is remarkably insightful.

## Racial Disparities in Arrest and Incarceration, and Class and Ethnic Styles of Dealing

As we've seen, in 1988, Congress approved a 100-to-1 ratio for the quantity of powder cocaine (500 grams) versus crack (5 grams) that can draw the same five-year federal sentence. Although not immediately recognized at the time (11 out of 21 African-American members of the House of Representatives, nearly all of them Democrats, voted in favor of the bill), the disparity became the target of the critics of the war on drugs. Either the intention (Tonry, 1995, pp. 81ff) or the consequence (Duster, 1995) of the bill was racist, its critics said. Why? Roughly 85 percent of crack cocaine defendants who appear in court are Black, while only 30 percent of powder cocaine defendants are Black; the rest are Hispanic (50%) or white (20%). This disparity is fueling the rising percentage of African-American prison in-mates who have been convicted of a drug crime. The mean time served by federal drug of-fenders *released* at the beginning of the twenty-first century was nearly a year longer for Blacks than for whites; the mean time served by offenders *sentenced* in 2000 and 2001 was roughly three years longer for Blacks than for whites. Clearly, these critics say, we have a racist criminal justice system when it comes to the drug laws.

Racial differences in drug use, as indicated by surveys, are practically nonexistent. Ac-cording to the National Survey on Drug Use and Health, for 2004, practically identical pro-portions of whites (8.1%) and African-Americans (8.7%) said that they had used one or more illicit drugs once or more in the past month; for respondents ages 12–17, these figures were 11.1 and 9.3 percent, respectively. If Blacks and whites use drugs in the same proportion, how is it possible that more than half of all incarcerated drug offenders are Black? African-Americans are overrepresented as drug offenders relative to their numbers in the population by a factor of four or five. The criminal justice system *must* be racist in its application for such disparities to exist. It begins, critics of the drug war contend, with racial profiling, with police differentially monitoring Black neighborhoods and differentially following, stopping, frisking, and arresting Black suspects. It continues with racist laws that target activities in which Blacks are more likely to engage, as reflected in the crack cocaine–powder cocaine disparity. And it culminates with a racist court system that is more likely to convict and incarcerate Black defendants, and to harsher, longer terms of imprisonment. Or so some critics of law enforcement claim.

The American criminal justice system may very well be racist, although the literature on the subject is far from clear-cut. The same facts can be read in different ways (Cole, 1999; Kennedy, 1997; Russell, 1998; Wilbanks, 1987); moreover, it seems to operate somewhat differently at different *levels* of the system (Walker, Spohn, and DeLonc, 1996). In any case, one possible reason for the racial disparities independent of (and very likely in addition to) the workings of a criminal justice system that may discriminate against African-Americans is what has been referred to as racial and ethnic *styles* of seller-to-user drug dealing. The fact is, the police are more likely to apprehend low-level street dealers and couriers than higher-level dealers, in part because they are so much more numerous and in part because their illicit activities are more visible. As the United States Sentencing Commission observed in 1995, roughly two-thirds of crack defendants were considered by the police to be street-level dealers or couriers, only 3 in 10 were regarded as midlevel dealers, and only 1 in 20 was a high-level dealer. Given the fact that parties lower down on the distribution chain are more likely to be Black than white, while those higher up are more likely to be white than Black, racial disparities in arrest figures seem to be almost preordained.

The work of Eloise Dunlap, Bruce Johnson, and their colleagues (1994) suggests a strong linkage between routine police practices and racial disparities in police scrutiny. There are two "distinctively different" types or styles of drug selling, say Dunlap and colleagues: the "inner-city" (mainly Black) and the "middle-class" (mainly white) career types. In each type, seller-to-user dealers are primarily male youths and young adults, and are characteristically users themselves. But these two types differ radically in styles of dealing.

Middle-class dealers "almost always sell to steady customers [known to the dealers] in private settings." Quantities tend to be fairly substantial, sales to each customer are intermittent, and violence is rare. As the Office of National Drug Control Policy observed, powder cocaine is most likely to be bought and sold indoors—away from the open observation of the police.

In contrast, inner-city dealers "often lack access to private settings for sales and typically sell in public [or semipublic locations—such as crack houses—which are likely to be known by and accessible to undercover officers] to buyers they do not know." They sell much more often and in smaller quantities, and high customer turnover is common. Crack cocaine is most likely to be visible on the street, and hence to the police. In such settings, violence is a frequent accompaniment, and so arrest in such venues is much more likely.

None of these "point of contact" factors address the very real and, for Blacks, palpable fact that, in the inner city, they are subject to intense and unequal police scrutiny and, all too often, interrogation (Anderson, 1999). The offense "walking down the street while Black" is practically a daily routine for the young, urban, African-American male. Nonetheless, police tactics and the daily routine of drug use and dealing explain a major chunk of the racial differences in arrests and incarceration. They cannot be ascribed to racist motives alone, and they will not disappear when the police no longer practice racial profiling.[3]

---

[3]Much of the preceding discussion on racial differences in arrest and incarceration is adapted from Goode, 2002.

## SUMMARY

The sale of illicit drugs is enshrouded in myth. While the drug trade is large, it is much smaller than numerous inflated estimates would have it. It is certainly not true, as more than one observer has claimed, that people spend more money on illicit drugs than on any other consumer product in existence. The White House sponsors ongoing research to determine how much money Americans spend on illicit drugs. In 2000, an estimated $65 billion was spent in the United States at the retail level, more than half of that specifically on cocaine. However, the figure has declined since its peak in the 1970s and 1980s; the 2000 sum is only 40 percent of the amount spent in 1988, expressed in constant dollars. With respect to total tonnage, in 2000, nearly 20 times as much cocaine was purchased (259 tons) as heroin (13 tons). On a gram-by-gram basis, however, heroin is roughly 10 times as expensive as cocaine.

The second myth about the illicit drug business is that the industry is highly hierarchical, centralized, and organized, much like the Mafia, with one Mr. Big (or a small number of Mr. Bigs) at the helm. Any coordinated action must entail some degree of organization, of course, and the distribution of some drugs requires a great deal more organization—and centralization—than others. But the truth is that, since the 1970s, the illegal drug trade has been highly decentralized, and is becoming increasingly so over time. Traffickers from practically every nation on Earth are involved in the drug trade, though, of course, for some drugs, ethnicity clusters around specific rungs of the distribution ladder.

The third myth centers around the economic harm to the nation from illicit drug use—more specifically, the fact that Schedule I drugs represent nothing but a deficit to the economy. In 2002, the White House estimated the economic cost of illicit drug use to the country at $160 billion. The fact is, drug sales support an industry more or less identical to all other industries, regardless of whether they are legal or illegal. When an illegal enterprise provides goods or services to a clientele who willingly pay for them, the transfer of money from one party to another is infused into the economic stream in precisely the same way as with the sale of legal products. The drug trade supports not only the people who work for it but also those who work for the legal sector of the economy that drug workers patronize, that is, workers in practically every industry on Earth. Consequently, the obliteration of the drug industry would wipe out these jobs in exactly the same way that the demise of the corn, coffee, automobile, or computer industry would.

Numerous agencies carefully monitor indicators bearing on how drugs are produced, where they go, where they are sold, and how. Whether a drug is a pure agricultural, a pure chemical, or a mixed product determines in part its system of distribution. In the United States, heroin originates mainly in Colombia, secondarily in Mexico, and to a much lesser extent in Southwest and Southeast Asia.

Nearly all the cocaine consumed in the United States comes from South America, and perhaps 90 percent of that specifically from Colombia. However, as a result of recent restructuring of the system of cocaine distribution, half or more of the Colombian cocaine entering the country is smuggled from Mexico.

At least half of America's marijuana is grown domestically, a quarter comes from Mexico, and the remainder originates from Colombia or other countries. Recently, Canadian marijuana has been entering the United States. Of all the illicit drug enterprises, the marijuana market is the most decentralized, and the cannabis used in this country is most likely to have been obtained from local or regional sources.

Methamphetamine consumed in the United States is likely to come from one of two sources—large labs in Mexico run by centralized organizations, or small, scattered labs in the United States run mainly by biker gangs in the Southwest. Very recently, Canada and Southeast Asia have entered the picture as a minor but potentially significant source of the drug. In the early 2000s, the number of methamphetamine labs seized by the authorities increased by almost 20 times, but after 2003, that number declined, one indication, says the White House, of the effectiveness of the DEA in wiping out the meth trade. Border authorities seized twice as much methamphetamine coming into the United States in 2004 as in 2001, another indication, the White House argues, that law enforcement is stamping out meth consumption.

Ecstasy is manufactured mainly in Belgium and the Netherlands. Judging from the fact that a few labs were seized early in the 2000s, MDMA production seems to have been launched in the United States. Overall, the number of Ecstasy tablets seized in the United States increased nearly 20 times between 1997 and 2000 but declined after that. But "Operation Double Dutch," inaugurated in 2002, targeted suspicious cargo slated for transport from the Amsterdam airport, resulting in a growing number of Ecstasy tablets bound for the United States being seized.

LSD is difficult to manufacture; perhaps as few as a dozen labs in the United States supply nearly all of the LSD consumed in this country. Manufacturers tend not to involve themselves in distributing the drug, but rather sell to a very small number of trusted associates.

In the past three decades, the illegal drug trade has become a worldwide business, with social and economic links that extend all over the globe. A number of factors have contributed to this explosion of the globalization of the drug trade, including the collapse of the Soviet Union; a growing worldwide trend away from government control of the economy and toward economic privatization; the global movement toward becoming a borderless world; poverty at the two ends of the distribution chain (that is, growing and street-level dealing), at least for our two mixed products, heroin and cocaine; and weak or corrupt local and federal governments.

The ultimate economic transaction is that which takes place between the street seller and the user. As with all other aspects of the drug trade, this step is enshrouded in myth and misconception. One is that the dealer is a wealthy exploiter and the user is a poverty-stricken victim. The matter is not quite this simple, as our four views of the low-level sale of illicit drugs demonstrate.

Transactions made by heroin abusers provide a look at how drug sales actually take place. Journalists, the public, and even some researchers often have an inflated notion of how much money heroin users, abusers, and addicts spend on their drug. Addicts spend considerably less than the $100–150 per day (or, since these estimates were made in the 1980s, $188–280 today) typically attributed to them. And the predatory crime they commit to pay for their drug habit likewise generates far less money than is generally believed. Most of what they earn is derived from a variety of nonpredatory crimes.

While it is true that most juvenile gangs sell illegal drugs, the rank-and-file members earn relatively little from such sales—barely minimum wage. Symbolic values probably play a substantial role in their gang participation. Still, some believe that improved economic opportunities would draw a high percentage of young male residents in the inner cities away from engaging in gang-related drug sales.

Crack cocaine is widely available and sold in the inner city. Participation in the drug trade is, for many of its residents, a symptom of marginalization and alienation. The drug trade represents an alternative to the mainstream economy from which many minority residents feel excluded.

Street styles of drug dealing may help explain at least a portion of racial disparities in drug-related arrests and incarceration. The middle-class style entails dealing in private to customers known to the seller, dealing in larger quantities a smaller number of times, and dealing in locales in which violence rarely or never takes place. The inner-city style entails dealing typically to strangers, dealing smaller quantities, dealing in public and semipublic places, and dealing in locations in which violence often takes place. Arrest is obviously far more likely to take place under the latter conditions than the former. Since the middle-class style is characterized overwhelmingly by white users, and the inner-city style overwhelmingly by Black and Hispanic users, based on this factor alone, racial disparities in arrest are extremely likely to exist.

## KEY TERMS

| | | |
|---|---|---|
| availability  354 | mixed model  363 | pure agricultural model  363 |
| globalization  370 | predisposition  354 | |
| Golden Crescent  364 | prohibition  368 | pure chemical model  363 |
| Golden Triangle  364 | | |

## ACCOUNT: Dealing Cocaine

*At the time of this interview, Billy was a 22-year-old college senior. He dealt drugs, mainly cocaine, for his last year or two in high school and his first three years in college. Quitting before his senior year, he had to move away from his former dealing associates to be removed from the temptation to sell; a few months later, they were all arrested. Billy was never indicted or arrested for his drug-selling activities.*

It began in high school. I used to hang out and party with my friends a lot. We would cut class, sit around the park, and smoke joints. Occasionally, we would chip in whatever money we had to buy some cocaine. We didn't buy that much, maybe a quarter of a gram, which we'd split three or four ways. We didn't get a lot, but we loved it.

As time went on, we bought more and more. We would use whatever money our parents had given us for lunch or new sneakers to buy cocaine. We sat in Greg's car for hours doing lines on the rear-view mirror, which we had taken off for that purpose. All of us went to class with our heads somewhere in outer space. I couldn't pay attention or do work in class. Sometimes I would just get up and walk around, not being able to take the paranoid feeling that surged through my head. Yet I didn't stop. I bought more and more coke until it was impossible to make excuses to my parents for more money. I had to figure out how I could snort cocaine without having to pay for it. A friend told me that if I dealt cocaine, I would be able to snort for free plus make really good money. The idea of having all that cocaine and money excited me. So I went to the friend who sold it to me and told him I wanted to sell it. I asked him if he would teach me what I needed to know to be able to sell cocaine. He said yes, and I was in business.

I began selling quarter- and half-grams to friends. On a transaction, I would make a quarter gram for myself and 50 bucks. At the time, I thought that was a lot. I continued selling for the rest of the year and through the summer. I never even thought about what my parents would do if they found out, or what would happen to me if they did. All I thought about was having the power because I was the man with the cocaine.

I knew that, when I went away to college and lived on my own, I could do whatever I wanted. I didn't have to hide paraphernalia any more or worry about what I said to friends because of the fear of my parents being on another phone. But there was a problem: No one would front me the cocaine. If I wanted it, I had to pay for it up front. If I wanted to continue dealing cocaine with my friend, I'd have to drive 50 miles to pick it up. So I began selling marijuana. It was cheap and I could sell enough to save some money to begin my cocaine business.

During the first semester of my sophomore year, I met Alfonso in one of my classes. He told me that he was looking to buy some good weed, so I told him I had some he could buy. After a few weeks of ongoing sales between us, Alfonso wanted to make a deal: He would trade $50 worth of cocaine for $50 worth of marijuana. I told him that I wanted to deal but I needed him to front the cocaine for me. He said he could trust me, all I had to do was to go to the City once a week to pick up whatever I needed.

At first, I was scared. I would go to this old, rundown building at night and speak to one of Alfonso's friends. Alfonso was always there, but I really didn't know him all that well. At the time, I was so infatuated with the idea of having so much money, I really didn't think. I picked up three and a half grams for $350. Then I'd cut three and a half grams and make it five grams. . . . I sold that for $700, and in one deal, I made $350 profit.

Things were going well, but I wanted more. I asked a friend I knew was interested if he wanted to go into the business with me. He knew a lot of people and could help the business grow rapidly. He anxiously agreed. Our trips to the City were no longer for 3½ grams, but for 10 and sometimes 20 grams. The ride back was always wild because we

opened the bag and snorted as much as we wanted. We blasted the music in my new partner's car and laughed the whole ride back to State. When we got back, we cut up the coke, then we'd package it. When all this was happening, our friends from the hall hung out and enjoyed the drug that was now ours at will.

My partner and I were on top of the world. At State, we were the elite. We had hundreds of friends and more money than we knew what to do with. We were now buying an ounce of cocaine (28 grams) for $1600. We would turn it into 40 grams by cutting it and earn $1200 a week profit. At this point, we started partying more than ever. We would stay up all night and blow five grams of coke a day. Anybody who was our friend could come and party. It was always lying around on a desk, and anybody could stick a spoon into the pile and help themselves. . . .

A few months later, three other friends let me know that they wanted to get involved with the business. I set them up and soon, they were making a lot of money. The thrill of it all was unbelievable. We felt like a corporation. We had meetings about our business in fancy restaurants; we drank $100 bottles of wine. We felt as if we were an organized business with the potential for unbelievable growth. Among the five of us, we were selling four or five ounces of cocaine a week and earning more than $5,000. And we were partying—a lot. We knew that if we cut down on our personal consumption, we could make much more money. Everyone agreed that one of the reasons we were dealing was so we could snort cocaine whenever we pleased, with no questions asked.

Things started getting out of hand. By our junior year, two guys were dealing marijuana, one was dealing Ecstasy, five of us were dealing coke. One guy was even dealing mescaline. Our floor was like a drug haven, with constant traffic of people, night and day. There was never any privacy because people always came by to buy drugs. Day in and day out, cocaine was being snorted. Sometimes, at five in the morning, we would try to rationalize what we were doing. Everyone looked like a wreck. The sun was coming up and still we'd want more. It was a sickness I knew I had to get away from, otherwise

I would ruin my life. I finally realized that things were starting to get crazy and maybe I should get out. I couldn't, though. I couldn't give up the power I had worked so hard for.

Everyone knew where they could buy drugs—especially cocaine. Our popularity was incredible. I had visions of being caught. I thought about my parents. I realized I could break away from this empire which I had started three years ago. I spoke to my roommate, who never wanted to sell it even though he too enjoyed the rewards which it had brought me. He decided that the best thing to do was to move across campus and just get away from it all. Don't sell it, don't snort it, don't even look at it.

In the fall of my senior year, we moved across campus. It was a different scene altogether. There were no blasting stereos, no kegs of beer, no garbage lying around. It was quiet and clean. I stayed away from drugs for about a month, experiencing a new side to campus. As time went on, people would approach me and ask if I would sell them cocaine. At first, I said no. Then I said, "Well, hold on." I went to a good friend who had also moved from our old haunt, and asked him for some cocaine. He had some, and I sold it. Still, things remained quiet for me. It wasn't like the scene I had left, the three years of dealing and partying. Not many people knew where I was, so I figured things would be okay. On the other side of the campus, though, things were still going strong. They were still selling an immense amount of cocaine without me being there. They weren't about to stop. I had warned my former partners that things were getting out of control, but they just laughed. They'd say to me, "You enjoyed it—why can't we?"

One night at the end of the semester, I got a phone call. The person on the other end of the line was a friend who still lived on our old hall where our "corporation" was located. This is the conversation we had:

**He:** "The boys have been arrested."
**Me:** "Oh, my God! How?"
**He:** "They were set up. They sold an ounce to a police officer. They're in big trouble."

**Me:** "Do the police know anything else?"
**He:** "I don't know. Just get rid of everything."

Within five minutes, everyone else who had been involved in dealing was called and told what had happened. They were all given instructions about what to do and say if they were picked up and questioned. We were all connected. It had become one giant monopoly, with every dealer on campus being a part of it.

I sat down and began to think. All those times we talked about what would happen to us if we ever went to prison. Now I pictured all those things actually happening to my friends. I saw them being locked up in a cell, sexually abused, being ruined for the rest of their lives. I was scared and didn't know what to do. I wished I could go back and erase what I had done, but I knew it was too late. I must have known that this day eventually had to come.

My roommate who moved across campus with me came down to talk. He nearly began crying when I told him what had happened. He was as scared as I was. Neither one of us knew what to do. We felt like criminals just waiting to be arrested and thrown in a cell with the rest of the slime.

Someone must have been watching over us because nothing happened after that. It seems we were okay. We promised to each other that we would never go near cocaine again. It took the arrests of our close friends to finally show us how sick we had become. If we wanted to go on living our lives, it was really time to get out and stay out.

## QUESTIONS

What does this dealing operation tell you about selling drugs on the college campus? What do you think accounts for Billy's decision to sell drugs? Is he different from other students who didn't and don't sell? Or would everyone, given the opportunity, succumb to the allure of being a drug dealer? Do you wish that Billy had gotten caught? Why or why not? Do you think he will go back to dealing, or was that a phase of his life he won't revisit?

# DRUG CONTROL

## *Law Enforcement, Drug Courts, and Drug Treatment*

As we saw in Chapter 7's discussion of drug use and drug control in America, although matters had been brewing for some time, with the election of Ronald Reagan as president in 1980, the United States entered an era of minimum tolerance and maximum enforcement. Hence, a consideration of contemporary patterns of drug enforcement in contemporary America is necessary. In 1986, Reagan declared a "war on drugs," a war that, indicators say, remains ongoing. How is this war carried out?

| TABLE 14-1 | Percentage Use of Illicit Drugs in Past Month, Ages 12 and Older, 1979–2005 | | | | | | | | | | | | | |
|---|---|---|---|---|---|---|---|---|---|---|---|---|---|---|
| | 1979 | 1985 | 1991 | 1992 | 1993 | 1994 | 1995 | 1996 | 1997 | 1998 | 1999 | 2000 | 2001 | 2005 |
| Any illicit | 14.1 | 12.1 | 6.6 | 5.8 | 5.9 | 6.0 | 6.1 | 6.1 | 6.4 | 6.2 | 6.3 | 6.3 | 7.1 | 8.1 |
| Cocaine | 2.6 | 3.0 | 1.0 | 0.7 | 0.7 | 0.7 | 0.7 | 0.8 | 0.7 | 0.8 | 0.7 | 0.5 | 0.7 | 1.0 |

*Source:* National Household Survey on Drug Abuse and National Survey on Drug Abuse and Health.

What are its basic foundations, outlines, patterns, dynamics, and trends? And what about the "cracks" in the law enforcement armor—that is, drug courts and drug treatment? Might alternatives to strict enforcement and incarceration be more effective in reducing our currently high levels of drug abuse?

## DRUG USE AND THE CRIME RATE VERSUS ARRESTS AND INCARCERATION

When we look at the sweep of time over the past three decades, we witness an enormous disconnect between the incidence of drug use and the number of drug arrests and incarcerations. Drug use declined between the late 1970s and 1980s and the 1990s, and has remained more or less stable since then. In sharp contrast, during that period, drug arrests and imprisonments skyrocketed. According to the National Household Survey on Drug Abuse and the National Survey on Drug Use and Health, between 1979 and 1991, the percentage of the American population ages 12 and older who used at least one illicit drug in the past month (defined as "current" use) declined from 14.1 percent to 6.6 percent, and between 1992 and the early 2000s, that percentage remained more or less stable at 6–8 percent; in 2005, the figure was 8.1 percent. The percentage taking cocaine in the past month was 2.6 percent in 1979, 3.0 percent in 1985, and 1.6 percent in 1988. Between 1992 and 2005, again, that figure remained more or less stable, at 0.5–1.0 percent; in 2005, the figure was 1.0 percent. (See Table 14-1.)

During that same time, the total number of adult drug arrests tripled; for instance, between 1980 and 2004, it rose from 580,900 to 1.745 million (see Figure 14-1). During that period, the number of defendants who appeared in federal courts on drug charges grew

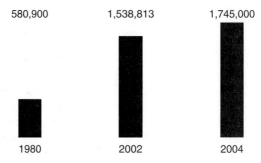

**Figure 14-1** Drug arrests, 1980–2004.

*Source:* U.S. Department of Justice, *Crime in the United States,* Uniform Crime Reports for relevant years.

| TABLE 14-2 | Selected Data on Prison Population |
| --- | --- |

*Number of Persons in Prison and Jail, 1980–2004*

| | State and Federal Prison | Jail |
| --- | --- | --- |
| 1980 | 319,598 | 183,988 |
| 2004 | 1,421,911 | 713,990 |

*Number of Persons in Custody in State Prisons by Most Serious Offense, 1980–2002*

| | Violent | Property | Drug | Public Order |
| --- | --- | --- | --- | --- |
| 1980 | 173,300 | 89,300 | 19,000 | 12,400 |
| 1990 | 313,600 | 173,700 | 148,600 | 45,500 |
| 2002 | 624,900 | 253,000 | 265,100 | 87,500 |

*Characteristics of Federal Prisoners, 2006*

**Total Federal Prison Population: 190,565**

**Types of Offenses**

Drug offenses: 54%

Weapons, explosives, arson: 14

Immigration: 11

Robbery:  6

Property offenses:  4

Extortion, fraud, bribery:  4

Violent offenses:  3

Sex offenses:  2

Miscellaneous and other:  3

| Inmates by Race and Ethnicity | Inmates by Gender |
| --- | --- |
| White:  56% | Male: 93% |
| Black:  40 | Female:   7 |
| Native American:   2 | |
| Asian:   2 | |
| Hispanic*:  32 | |

*Hispanics may be of any race.

*Source:* www.ojp.usdoj.gov/bjs (U.S. Department of Justice) and www.bop.gov (Bureau of Prisons).

from 7,000 to roughly 30,000; and the percentage of all prisoners in federal penitentiaries who were convicted of drug offenses increased from 20 percent to 54 percent. In 1980, there were 19,000 prisoners incarcerated in state penal institutions for drug crimes (6% of all state inmates); today, there are 265,000 (22%). Currently, the average time served by an inmate convicted of a drug offense, about 42 months, is only slightly less than the length of sentence for arson and for explosives, weapons, and racketeering and extortion offenses. Drug offenders released from federal prisons today served only a year and a half less than violent offenders, taken as a whole. (See Table 14-2.)

In short, the scare over drug abuse that was brewing in the 1970s and that exploded in the 1980s has borne fruit in the 1990s and early 2000s in the form of strikingly stricter law enforcement. Today, we arrest more drug suspects, convict more drug defendants, and incarcerate more drug offenders than ever before in the nation's history—and for longer sentences. This striking fact demands a close look at the part the law, the police, and the courts play in our drugs-as-crime drama.

It is important to stress that the increases in drug arrests and sentences that took place after the 1980s were not unique to drug offenses. In the last quarter of the twentieth century and into the twenty-first, the country was seized with an almost evangelical fervor to punish offenders of nearly all stripes. Between 1980 and 2004, the number of prisoners in federal and state penitentiaries overall increased from 319,000 to over 1.4 million (see Figure 14-2). In addition, over 700,000 are in jail, awaiting trial or serving brief sentences for misdemeanors. In 1980, our total rate of incarceration (prisons and jails) was 139 per 100,000 population; by 2004, this figure had grown to 486, an increase of over two and a half times. And, most importantly, the rise in the prison population over the past generation or so is not due to a rising crime rate. Indeed, while incarceration rates have increased, the crime rate has actually declined—and dramatically. Between 1994 and 2004 alone, the violent crime victimization rate dropped by

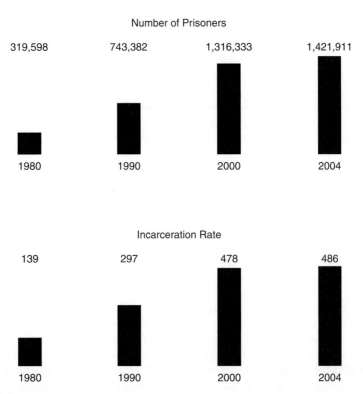

**Figure 14-2** **Numbers of state and federal prisoners and incarceration rates, 1980–2000.**

*Source:* U.S. Bureau of Prisons.

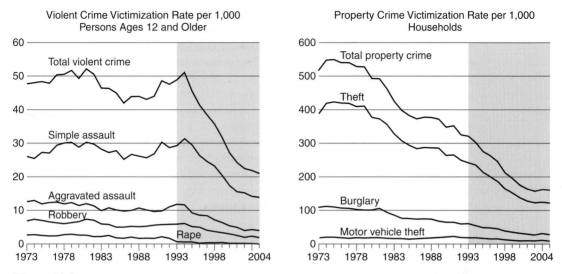

**Figure 14-3** Crime victimization rates, 1973–2003/2004.

*Source:* U.S. Department of Justice, "Criminal Victimization, 2004, 2005."

more than half, from 51.2 to 22.0 per 1,000 population. The decline in rates of property crime began much earlier. Between 1977 and 2004, the total property crime victimization rate per 1,000 households declined by two-thirds—from 544.1 to 162.2, an unprecedented decline (see Figure 14-3). And even as our crime rate has been declining, our prison population has been rising sharply.

Three factors account for the increases in the prison population in the face of a declining crime rate. First, parole is being denied more often than in the past; in some states, it has been eliminated altogether. Today, prisoners serve a longer stretch of their mandated sentence than was true in the past. Second, parole is more often revoked than it was in the past; parolees are being sent back to prison for infractions that previously were ignored. Third, and most importantly, not only are drug arrests more likely to result in incarceration than was true in decades past, the increase is greater than it has been for property and violent offenses. (It's not clear how a fourth possible factor, the "three strikes and you're out" laws, influence the increase in the prison population, since the proportion of prisoners who are subject to them nationally is fairly small.) Clearly, the enforcement of the drug laws is absolutely central to our mission of understanding drug use in the United States.

## PROHIBITION: THE PUNITIVE MODEL

The word "prohibition" has both a specific and a general meaning. In its most specific meaning, **Prohibition** refers to the legal ban on the manufacture and sale of alcohol beverages that was in effect in the United States between 1920 and 1933. In its more general sense, **prohibition** refers to banning any activity, service, or product through the criminal law. Prohibition may be referred to as a punitive approach; the **punitive model** calls for punishing persons who ignore the law and purvey or partake in the relevant activity, service, or product.

Clearly, as it applies to drugs, "prohibition" can refer to a ban on any psychoactive substance. With a punitive policy, someone who is engaged in a drug transaction or who is in possession of a quantity of an illegal substance may be arrested, prosecuted, convicted, and imprisoned. Under a punitive policy, drug possession and sale are crimes, much like rape, murder, and armed robbery; a criminal penalty is provided in the penal code. This penalty could entail a fine, a jail or prison sentence, or probation instead of imprisonment; in some jurisdictions (outside the United States), this may even entail execution. When laws are passed providing penalties for a given offense, this is referred to as **criminalization.**

Currently, advocates of the punitive or prohibitionist position urge that the possession and sale of the currently illegal psychoactive substances remain a crime—or even be more harshly criminalized than they are—because, its supporters feel, use will decline as a result. (Or because they feel that such penalties symbolize society's opposition to such use.) Since staunch or strict prohibitionists support a war on drugs, advocates of the punitive policy may be referred to as **hawks,** a term that is usually used to refer to the more warlike factions in a society. In contrast, legalizers may be referred to as **doves,** since they oppose this war on drugs and believe we should "lay down our weapons" and "declare peace" (Reuter, 1992, p. 16).

The more extreme versions of the punitive approach that are used elsewhere are not legally possible in a society such as the United States, which values civil liberties, the right of due process, and freedom from unreasonable punishment. For instance, very few commentators support the death penalty for drug violations. (A few do, and have so stated in public.) In China, executions of drug dealers is routine; they number in the thousands per year. While lecturing at Beijing's Medical University, psychopharmacologist Avram Goldstein (2001, p. 296) watched television coverage of the public hanging of 52 convicted heroin dealers. With a crowd of thousands watching, the governor of the province declared: "This is how we deal with drug traffickers!" Such a draconian penalty is simply not a viable option in the United States. However, some advocates of the punitive policy call for execution of the most serious offenders. In testimony before the Senate Judiciary Committee, Daryl Gates, former chief of the Los Angeles Police Department, testified that casual marijuana smokers "ought to be taken out and shot," because, he said, "we're in a war" (Beers, 1991, p. 38). Speculated William Bennett, former federal drug "czar," on a nationwide radio talk show, perhaps anyone who sells illegal drugs to a child should be beheaded. "Morally," he said, "I don't have any problem with that at all" (Lazare, 1990, p. 25). These are minority opinions, however, even among criminalizers.

The reasoning behind the passage and enforcement of drug laws is, presumably, that substance use has become a problem for society that can and should be eliminated, or at least reduced, by arresting and imprisoning violators. While lawmakers may have noble intentions in mind when drafting and enacting a given piece of legislation, as Robert Burns, Scottish poet (1759–1796) reminds us (rendered in modern English), "The best laid plans of mice and men often go astray." The fact is, lawmakers do not always achieve their desired goals, and a variety of unintended, unanticipated, and undesired consequences often result even with the best of intentions. Some legislation has caused a great deal more harm than good, as we learned from the lesson of national alcohol prohibition (1920–1933). However, this should not condemn all legislation, for surely some laws have had beneficial results. Hardly anyone would vote to repeal laws against serious crimes such as rape, robbery, and murder, simply because they fail to eliminate the behavior they criminalize, or because such criminalization may sometimes have unanticipated consequences.

## Two Punitive Arguments

It should also be noted that there are two entirely different punitive arguments, and many observers confuse the two. Let's call them the hard or strict and the soft or moderate versions. The strict punitive version makes use of the logic of **absolute deterrence,** while the moderate punitive version makes use of the logic of **relative deterrence.**

According to the hard or strict punitive argument, a given activity can be significantly reduced or eliminated by law enforcement; that is, crime is deterred or discouraged in some absolute or abstract sense by law enforcement. This is the rationale for the government's war on drugs: Escalate the number of arrests of users, addicts, dealers, and producers; impose longer prison sentences on them; fill the jails and prisons; and eventually, drug use will be "defeated." The advocates of the hard punitive argument quite literally assume that drug use can be wiped out, or at least drastically curtailed, by an escalation in arrests and sentencing. Arrest and imprison enough drug users and sellers, and use will drop to nearly zero, or at least to tolerable, minimal levels.

In contrast, according to the soft or moderate punitive position, law enforcement cannot bring about a defeat of or even a drastic reduction in drug use or abuse. This argument is quite different from the hard or strict criminalizer's position. It says, in effect, that in the absence of law enforcement, a given activity will be much more common than it is with law enforcement. It relies on the logic of relative deterrence because it asserts that with law enforcement—as compared with no law enforcement—certain kinds of crime less often take place. If there were no laws or penalties against, say, robbing or assaulting others, more people would engage in such behavior. (Not most people—*more* people.) Law enforcement does not reduce the incidence of these acts so much as contain them. Same thing with drug use: Punishing the drug violator is not, and under most circumstances cannot be, a means of drastically reducing or eliminating drug use. But if there were no drug laws, and no penalties for the production, importation, possession, and sale of the presently illegal substances, use would be significantly higher than it is now.

Thus, the soft or moderate criminalizers do not see the inability of law enforcement to "stamp out" drug abuse as a failure of the punitive policy. They view stamping out drug abuse as a futile task, and an absurd measure of the ineffectiveness of the laws against drugs. Unlike the legalizers, who argue that "everyone knows" that the drug laws have failed (Best, 1990; Hyse, 1994; Yett, 1990), the proponents of the soft punitive position base their argument on relative deterrence. Do a mental experiment, they say. Imagine removing any and all penalties for any and all drug manufacture, cultivation, possession, distribution, and sale. Anyone claiming that drug use would not rise under such circumstances—contrary to every known currently prohibited pleasurable action—risks absurdity. In looking at the drug legalization debate, the difference between these two versions of the punitive argument should be kept in mind. It will assume central importance in several future discussions.

## Drug Control: The Current System

In the United States at the present time, a range of psychoactive substances are regulated by the criminal law; they are controlled substances. The **Controlled Substances Act**—also referred to as the **Drug Control Act**—provides for schedules or categories of drugs with varying controls and penalties for violations. To simplify a complex situation, three categories of psychoactive substances or drugs are controlled by the law.

### Three Categories of Drugs

The first category of drugs may be referred to as the legal drugs. They are not included in the Controlled Substances Act at all; in effect, the government does not consider them to be drugs. These psychoactive substances are available to anyone over a certain age. A variety of laws, rules, and regulations stipulate the conditions of sale and consumption—where, when, and by whom they may be purchased and consumed. Violation of these laws may result in arrest and/or a criminal fine. Still, these substances may be obtained and consumed under a wide range of circumstances without violating the law. Alcoholic beverages and tobacco cigarettes provide examples of legal drugs. Their sale and use are controlled by law, but they are not mentioned anywhere in the Controlled Substances Act. In addition, some other substances, not strongly psychoactive, are commonly referred to as drugs because they are used for medicinal and quasi-medicinal purposes, but they do not appear in the Controlled Substances Act. These are the **over-the-counter (OTC) drugs,** such as aspirin, Tylenol (acetaminophen), No-Doz, Dexatrim, and Compoz. Since OTC drugs are not psychoactive and are not used recreationally, we will not consider them here.

The second category of substances is the **prescription drugs;** these are the Schedule II–V drugs in the Controlled Substances Act. Thousands of drugs that are psychoactive are available by prescription, which are written by physicians for their patients' medical and psychiatric problems, illnesses, or maladies. These drugs are controlled more tightly than alcohol and tobacco, which are completely legal. These drugs are available only by prescription, and only within the context of medical and psychiatric therapy. The schedules define the degree of control over the dispensing of prescription drugs and spell out the penalties for violating the law. Schedule II drugs (such as cocaine, amphetamines, and short-acting barbiturates) are tightly controlled; Schedule III–V drugs are less tightly controlled. The sale of any of these drugs for nonmedical purposes—for instance, to get high—can result in the arrest and imprisonment of the physician and the user. In addition to their legally prescribed use, as we saw, a number of prescription drugs mentioned in the Controlled Substances Act that are psychoactive are also widely used illegally for the purpose of intoxication; some are manufactured illegally in clandestine labs rather than by legitimate pharmaceutical companies.

In addition to individual patients with specific ailments, prescription drugs are widely used for two other populations: (1) the mentally disordered, both as inmates of mental hospitals and as outpatients, and (2) narcotic addicts who are clients or patients of methadone maintenance programs or (less commonly) drug therapy programs. The administration of antipsychotic medication to mental patients and methadone to narcotic addicts provides a partial exception to the rule that American society pursues a punitive approach to drug use. As a general rule, doves advocate an expansion of methadone programs, while hawks either wish to hold the line on maintenance programs or call for a serious cuts in their funding.

The third category of drugs is made up of those whose possession and sale is *completely* illegal; they are not available even by prescription. The Controlled Substances Act regards these drugs as having no medical utility and a high potential for abuse; they are classified as Schedule I drugs. (The "no medical utility" is, of course, largely a legal fiction, since some medical experts regard marijuana and heroin, two Schedule I drugs, as being medically useful.) They cannot be legally purchased or obtained for any reason whatsoever (except under extremely rare experimental conditions). Anyone who possesses, transfers, or sells them automatically violates the law, is subject to arrest, and, if convicted, may have to serve a jail or prison sentence and/or pay a fine. Examples of the Schedule I drugs include marijuana, heroin, MDMA (or Ecstasy), LSD, and GHB; they are always (or almost always) obtained illegally and are widely used, illegally, for the purpose of intoxication.

## A Punitive Approach

For the completely legal drugs, the use of a given substance is not in question; possession and sale for the purpose of just about any and all use—including intoxication—is legal. For the completely illegal drugs, it is the exactly the opposite—no possession and sale for any use whatsoever is legal. In the United States, it doesn't much matter why someone wishes to use heroin; even medical uses are against the law.

In sharp contrast to these two, things are quite different for the prescription drugs: It is the *use* of the drug (and the way it is obtained) that defines its legal status. If used in a manner the government deems medically acceptable and obtained by means of a legal prescription, their possession and sale are legal; if used for what are regarded as illicit or disapproved purposes (say, getting high), or obtained without benefit of a prescription, their possession and sale are illegal. Notice, too, that, technically, drug use is not a crime; it is possession and sale that are against the law. (A partial exception: The public use of illicit drugs is illegal.) When observers refer to the illegal use of prescription drugs, this is shorthand for nonprescription possession and sale for the purpose of illicit use. For Schedule I drugs, likewise, although it is possession and sale that are technically illegal—and not use—it is ultimately the use of these substances the law is presumably intended to control.

Marijuana provides two partial exceptions to the punitive policy toward Schedule I drugs. First, under their state laws, 10 states have elected to permit marijuana as medicine; still, it remains completely illegal under the federal Controlled Substances Act. And second, 12 states have partially decriminalized the possession of small quantities of marijuana. (In 1989 and 1990, the electorate of two states, Oregon and Alaska, voted to *re*criminalize small-quantity marijuana possession.) In these states, possession of a small quantity of marijuana (the amount varies) is not a crime but a civil offense, a "violation." If individuals are apprehended with less than the stipulated amount, they cannot be arrested—although their stash will be confiscated—convicted, or sentenced to jail or prison time, unless they have a criminal record. For such an offense, they will receive a citation much like a traffic ticket and pay a small fine. The sale or transfer and the cultivation of marijuana, and the possession of more than the stipulated amount, remain on the books as crimes in these states; only the possession of small quantities is exempt.

Currently, the predominant legal stance in the United States is punitive toward a wide range of drugs. Many drugs are completely illegal; their possession and sale is controlled through the criminal law in every jurisdiction of America. These are the prohibited drugs. The punitive approach has been pursued more or less continuously in this country since the passage of the Harrison Act of 1914 and subsequent Supreme Court interpretations of this act during the 1920s. In a nutshell, the punitive policy toward drug use is this: To solve the "drug problem," its proponents argue, we must arrest sellers and users, prosecute them to the full extent of the law, and incarcerate them. If any nonusers contemplate taking up the habit, the example of what happens to those who get caught should dissuade them from such foolish behavior. Of course, as I said earlier, there are variations on a punitive theme.

In short, regardless of how severe or mild the penalties proposed, arrest and incarceration—punishment—remain the cornerstones of the punitive approach to drug abuse. It is our current policy for many drugs, and it is a policy that most Americans support. Public opinion polls find that roughly 90 percent of all Americans believe that the possession and sale of the hard drugs should remain illegal, and 75 percent support such a policy even for marijuana—marijuana as medicine excepted. However, the latter opinion depends on the way the question is worded; a majority of the population agrees with the proposition that marijuana users "should not be arrested." In the 2002 elections, three state decriminalization bills—in Arizona, Nevada, and South Dakota—were supported by a minority of the electorate of only 43, 39, and 38 percent, respectively. Only a temporary setback? Or evidence of permanent public opposition to decriminalization? The coming years will answer these questions. As an aside, in 2003, America's neighbor to the north, Canada, voted to decriminalize small-quantity marijuana possession.

## The Bottom Line

At present, then, the United States follows the maintenance model for 150,000 or so narcotics addicts who are enrolled in methadone programs; the partial decriminalization model (following state, not federal, law) for small-quantity marijuana possession in 12 states; the legalization model for alcohol and tobacco; the medical or prescription model for psychoactive pharmaceuticals such as Valium, Halcion, morphine, Prozac, and Thorazine; and a criminalization or punitive model for illegal drugs such as marijuana (completely illegal in 38 states), crack, Ecstasy, PCP, LSD, and heroin (completely illegal), and a variety of prescription drugs, such as barbiturates, amphetamines, and cocaine, which are completely illegal if used recreationally or without benefit of prescription.

To put the matter another way: *All recreational drug use in America is prohibited unless otherwise exempted*. The exceptions are alcohol and cigarettes. Marijuana is a partial exception in that, even in the decriminalized states, the user cannot possess above a given quantity and, even if he or she does possess less than that, may receive a fine similar to a traffic ticket. (The prescription drugs do not represent an exception to this rule since, in principle, they are to be used exclusively for therapeutic, not recreational, purposes.) In effect, in the United States, the only drugs that users are completely free to take legally for pleasure (caffeine excepted) are alcohol and tobacco.

## THE DRUG WAR AS IDEOLOGY

Peter Kraska (1997, 2003) forcefully argues that current law enforcement policy toward illicit drugs has moved substantially beyond simple prohibition. Our punitive policy toward drugs, he says, began with a military *metaphor*—"fighting the drug war"—and evolved into a military *reality,* that is, using actual military personnel to fight a literal war against drug users.

A metaphor is a verbal image of something that suggests that it is similar to something else. For instance, "A Mighty Fortress Is Our God" is a metaphor that suggests that God, or a belief in God, protects us in much the same way that a fortress protects persons who are within its walls. Metaphors force us—if we accept them—to think of reality in a certain way. Very often, when metaphors are used, people begin to think of the verbal images as if they were the real thing. And they begin to treat the people the images apply to as if they corresponded to the metaphor.

In other words, we can take metaphors too far, Kraska argues. So, for instance, if we think of the enemy during war as rats or as snakes in the grass, that gives us the license to exterminate them as if they were vermin. In other words, metaphors give us license to demonize the enemy, to turn them into the embodiment of evil. When we use or accept the metaphor of "the drug war," what is being implied? The implication is that the drug laws and their enforcement are very much like a war, and that we should think of them *as* a war. It's a very powerful, dramatic metaphor, and it is very expressive of a particular perspective toward the so-called drug problem. Kraska invites us to consider the implications of this metaphorical war.

Kraska calls the military metaphor—thinking of fighting the drug problem as a "war" on drugs—**militarism**. It means using the military metaphor in the fight against illegal drugs, thinking of the processes of punishing drug offenders as if they were an "enemy" that has to be "destroyed." Such a metaphor justifies extreme measures against drug users and sellers.

Kraska says that the issue has moved considerably beyond the verbal or metaphorical stage, however. Militarism (the ideology of the drug war) has become **militarization** (the use of the military to help fight the drug war). In 1981, Congress approved the revision of a 100-year-old law that prohibited the military from engaging in civilian law enforcement (2003, p. 301). This revision allowed the military "to loan equipment to the civilian police, train law enforcement personnel, and directly assist in some aspects of interdiction efforts" (p. 301). While the new law did not authorize the military to arrest or search suspects or to seize suspected illicit drugs within U.S. borders, it did authorize the military to arrest traffickers in other countries. (The invasion of Panama, which resulted in the arrest of dictator Manuel Noriega on drug-trafficking charges, proved to be so unpopular that these arrests were suspended.) The program was funded by President Reagan's diversion of over $700 million away from drug treatment and education to law enforcement (p. 301).

In other words, after 1981, the police were not merely like or similar to the military, they were being backed up by the military. Actual military personnel are being used as drug law enforcers. Militarism is now the spirit that energizes militarization, or the mobilization of troops to wage the drug war.

Interestingly, at first, the Pentagon was extremely reluctant to become involved in drug eradication, seizure, and arrest operations, because they viewed it as a losing proposition, a quagmire, a hopeless cause—as another Vietnam. But the federal government in the 1980s channeled so much money into the military's budget that the program began to seem more attractive to top brass. And with the collapse of the Soviet Union in 1991, there was no single enemy regarded as dangerous to the republic. According to Kraska, in order to achieve the objective of sustaining militarization toward illicit drugs, drug abuse has to be demonized in the public mind to be as threatening as the Soviet Union had been to U.S. national security. Drug dealers have to be depicted as "ruthless peddlers of death and destruction." Drugs have to be regarded as criminogenic—as directly causing criminal behavior—and their users have to be seen as deserving of harsh punishment. Kraska suggests that the war metaphor has accompanied and energized the growing militarization of the enforcement of the drug laws. And it has been promulgated by politicians as a tactic to convince the public that this policy is not only acceptable and desirable but necessary.

The "war on drugs" metaphor seems to have "fallen out of favor" in recent years, argue Jonathan Caulkins and his colleagues (2005, p. 3). The reasons? In part, it is because the metaphor denies or underplays nonwarlike features of the country's multipronged effort to deal with the drug problem—features that President George W. Bush was careful to emphasize in his 2006 *National Drug Control Strategy,* which stressed education, community initiatives, and treatment ("Healing America's Drug Users"), along with law enforcement.

It is possible that the government's war on terrorism, launched after the September 11, 2001, attacks on the United States, has taken some steam out of the drug war rhetoric. But a case can be made that the war on terrorism has energized at least a portion of the military's literal involvement in the war on drugs. More specifically, in coordination with the Defense Department, the Drug Enforcement Administration (DEA) has inaugurated a program, in the words of the White House's 2006 publication *National Drug Control Strategy,* "designed to identify, target, investigate, disrupt, or dismantle transnational drug trafficking" in Afghanistan and the surrounding regions. This publication lists seizures in 2005 of opium, heroin, morphine, labs, vats, and presses as evidence of the success of that program. Opium poppy cultivation, the White House reports, dropped from 206,700 hectares in 2004 to 107,400 in 2005. (A hectare is about two and a half acres.) The source: a U.S. "government estimate." But whether the eradication of opium in Afghanistan has been a success or failure, in this geopolitical context, the drug war has become an ally in the war on terrorism—and vice versa.

## Drug Asset Forfeiture

The 1988 Anti-Drug Abuse Bill increased federal funding for equipment and personnel to fight drug traffickers and stiffened penalties for illicit drug distribution. In addition, it created the Asset Forfeiture Fund, modeled after the 1984 Criminal Forfeiture Act, which legitimated seizing assets earned by criminal conspiracies. The Asset Forfeiture Fund has two components. The first is the authorization of the seizure and liquidation of the ill-gotten drug assets themselves: cash, automobiles, boats, real estate, jewelry, and anything else of value. The second is the use of the funds created by such seizure and liquidation specifically to combat drug-trafficking operations. More specifically—and this is the key to the new law—the fund authorized a percentage of the funds generated by asset seizures to go directly into the budgets of drug law enforcement agencies.

At first glance, the implementation of this bill might seem to be an extremely effective means of fighting the distribution and use of illicit substances. But the drug forfeiture program has its critics, who insist that it has done more harm than good. Mitchell Miller and Lance Selva (1994), among others (for instance, Worrall, 2003), argue that drug forfeiture programs are counterproductive. They've backfired, these authors argue; they are not doing the job they were presumably designed for.

Miller and Selva base their conclusion on research that is referred to as **participant observation.** During an entire year, one of the authors was in the presence of and accompanied the police in the planning and execution stages of their operations. He sat with them as they discussed strategy and went out with them when they carried out their busts. He was a party to 28 narcotics cases in cooperation with officers from state, county, and local or municipal jurisdictions. He was, in other words, conducting "complete member research."

A key aspect of the research, however, was that he was engaged in deception, or **disguised observation.** In other words, he did not tell the officers who conducted these operations that he was conducting research and would eventually write about it. As the authors admit, disguised observation is extremely controversial. Some criminologists and other social scientists think that researchers should always make their presence and research intentions known to their subjects and informants (Erikson, 1967). Others believe that some deception is acceptable as long as it results in useful or important findings (Douglas, 1976). Without drawing a conclusion one way or the other, it is important to keep in mind that certain kinds of information cannot be obtained in any way other than through the deception of research informants. (In the spirit of full disclosure, I have argued in favor of conducting disguised observation; see Goode, 1996.)

Miller and Selva argue that drug dealer asset forfeiture is a good example of what social scientists refer to as the **law of unanticipated consequences.** Given what law enforcement representatives claim, the stated goals of **drug asset forfeiture** programs are fourfold: (1) Take drugs off the street, (2) disrupt or terminate the sale of illegal drugs, (3) reduce the use/abuse of illegal drugs, and (4) reduce the social problems that illegal drug abuse causes. Instead, as Miller and Selva point out, the programs have gone astray from these original goals or intentions. The efforts of the police are now much more directed toward "asset hunting" than toward taking drugs off the street and reducing drug abuse and its problems.

That is, asset forfeiture is being used by law enforcement agencies to supplement their budgets. It has become an entity that feeds off itself. Assets are seized so that law enforcement agencies can then turn around and seize more assets. Says one California undercover narcotics agent, drug enforcement success "is measured by the amount of money seized: You see that there's big money out there, you want to seize the big money for your department. For our unit, the sign of whether you were doing good or poorly was how much money you seized. . . . And my supervisor made it extremely clear that big money cases were a lot more favorable for your overall evaluation than big dope cases." In other words, "when narcotics officers become revenue producers, the system itself becomes corrupt."

Miller and Selva are not saying that this tactic is being used by officers to line their own personal pockets, to buy million-dollar houses and Mercedes and yachts. It's not personal corruption; It's organizational corruption—the corruption of a worthwhile organizational goal resulting in a misdirection of priorities. It results, for instance, in a substantial number of drug dealers being allowed to go free because they don't have sizable enough assets, even though they may be important kingpins in a drug operation. Because narcotics law enforcement is becoming an enterprise to maximize profits, its job of eradicating drugs is being subverted in case after case. When the police face two cases, one of which is likely to yield a seizure of drugs but very little cash and the other of which is likely to yield little in the way of drugs but a lot of cash, they consistently go after the operation that yields the cash or other assets and not the drugs. The operational goal of their efforts seems to be profit rather than an incapacitation of drug operations. And in their quest for profit, the police often permit drugs to continue to be sold and circulated so that they can nab the dealers when they have earned enough cash to make their own efforts worthwhile. In other words, their pursuit of their stated goals has been undermined, short-circuited, subverted, and even abandoned.

Not surprisingly, police officers who are involved in asset forfeiture have a different opinion of the program. Gregory Vecci and Robert Sigler (2001) interviewed 45 officers whose units regularly engage in asset forfeiture of drug dealers. On a 10-point scale, these officers assigned a score to the effectiveness of the forfeiture program with respect to seven goals. The two that ranked the highest were that the program "deprives drug traffickers of their comfortable life style which they can afford because of drug profits" (a mean score of 7.73) and that it "punishes drug traffickers" (7.53). No other goals came close to these two in effectiveness; "assisting the funding of my entire agency" ranked far down the scale (4.43), suggesting that Miller and Selva's analysis, while probably accurate for some agencies, may not apply to all. Interestingly, "deterring people from committing future drug crimes" (3.91) was near the bottom of the scale (p. 322).

Vecci and Sigler also asked their police respondents to rank the most important functions of forfeiture; here, a "1" rather than a "10" is a high score. Again, punishing drug traffickers (1.67) and depriving drug traffickers of their lifestyle (2.41) were regarded as crucial. Likewise, earning money for the agency (4.12) and deterring drug users (4.83) were toward the low end of the scale (p. 323). Interestingly, the authors found some differences between different types of agencies—federal versus local, and, among federal agencies, the FBI, a multipurpose agency, versus the DEA, a specialized, single-purpose agency (pp. 324–325). To local agencies, which are much more dependent on forfeiture for their budgetary strength, earning assets for their units ranked much higher (3.27) than was true for federal agencies, whose budgets are secure regardless of the size of their seizures (4.57). Nonetheless, Vecci and Sigler conclude that drug asset seizures "can become dysfunctional from a law enforcement perspective when forfeiture becomes more important than deterrence, particularly if targets are selected based on the potential for asset forfeiture rather than for the degree of criminal involvement" (p. 328).

## PROACTIVE POLICING AGAINST STREET-LEVEL TRAFFICKING

Traditionally, the police have been **reactive** to crime; that is, they are deployed when a criminal act takes place and a citizen reports it to them. Roughly seven out of eight arrests take place as a result of a citizen complaint. As a general rule, if there is no citizen complaint, there is no police investigation and no arrest. Only a small proportion of arrests result from **proactive** police efforts, that is, neighborhood patrol and surveillance—such as undercover work, a report by a paid police informant (or "snitch"), or direct observation by an officer. Sociologist Lynn Zimmer (1990) discusses the impact of a systematic, concerted program of proactive policing against street-level drug dealing. Interestingly, before the 1960s, proactive policing was the rule. But during that decade, in reaction to charges of police brutality, corruption, and favoritism, a wave of police professionalization and bureaucratization led to the ascendance of reactive over proactive policing. For some crimes, it also resulted in less effective policing. Apparently, the baby had been thrown out with the bathwater.

By the early 1980s, Manhattan's Lower East Side, a poor, predominantly minority neighborhood below 14th Street, had become an open drug market. Buyers milled around waiting to purchase heroin and cocaine; sellers openly and vociferously shouted out brand names to hawk their products; and long lines of double-parked cars snaked around the block. On some blocks, vendors set up carts, selling hot dogs and sodas, so festive were the streets during peak selling periods. The reasons for the open sale of drugs were not difficult to fathom. A nationwide recession had hit cities especially hard, and the minority communities of these cities doubly so. New York City's municipal government was in deep trouble.

The city's bond rating had been downgraded, the city found it difficult to borrow money against its growing debt, and at one point, it faced the possibility of bankruptcy. In response, the city cut the personnel of the New York Police Department by 7,000 officers and directed the department to focus only on high-priority arrests. Hence, drug crimes were practically ignored. Between 1970 and 1980, drug arrests had plummeted from 50,000 to an average of 17,000–18,000 per year. As a consequence, drug dealers realized that their risk of arrest was minimal—hence their blatant presence on the street. Open dealing was the rule in a community such as the Lower East Side, where a number of drug dealers resided and where a high proportion of the community used. Moreover, the reduced police presence attracted buyers from other communities—New Jersey, Long Island, Staten Island, and Westchester County—who flocked to the neighborhood because of the low risk of arrest. And keep in mind what was happening nationally: 1979 and 1980 were all-time highs for drug use in the United States.

Local residents complained to City Hall, demanding that something be done about the grotesque, carnival-like atmosphere on their streets. Community protests led the municipal government to set up "Operation Pressure Point," launched in 1984. This program represented a shift away from reactive and toward proactive drug law enforcement. The police swept through the neighborhood in large numbers, mostly on foot, dispersing crowds, handing out tickets to double-parked cars, conducting searches, and making drug arrests. Canine units were sent into abandoned buildings, sniffing for drugs. Mounted patrols rode though the streets, reminding would-be offenders of a strong police presence. Buy-and-bust operations were initiated and carried out. The police stopped suspicious-looking loiterers in known drug-selling neighborhoods and questioned them, searched them, and either told them to move on or arrested them. Helicopters hovered over the streets, discouraging open drug selling.

What was the impact of Operation Pressure Point? Zimmer (1990) characterizes its achievements as limited and modest. All observers agree that there was a decrease in the volume of open, blatant street trafficking on the Lower East Side. The program's success in clearing out outsiders who came to the neighborhood to buy drugs was especially marked. For instance, the number of cars with New Jersey license plates plummeted to insignificance, and the number of white faces in all-minority neighborhoods also declined precipitously. The decline in the crime rate, especially money-making, drug-related crime such as burglary, declined more sharply on the Lower East Side than it did in the city as a whole. To the superficial gaze, the program seemed to be a success. But Zimmer is careful to qualify the successes of Operation Pressure Point, which were less impressive than they appear at first glance.

In neighborhoods where the police presence was maximized, drug sale declined, but it hardly disappeared. And there was something of a drug displacement in drug sales from neighborhoods that were targeted to those that were less intensely patrolled. And in the poorest and least "gentrified" blocks, where drug dealing was most deeply entrenched and where drug dealers tended to live (and hence blended in), the police found it difficult to spot and apprehend dealers. As a consequence, on such blocks, Operation Pressure Point had little impact. In the more middle-class or gentrified areas, dealing, especially street-level selling, was sharply reduced. In other words, where the nation's urban drug dealing takes place, the police are all but powerless to reduce the sale of drugs because both selling and using are so deeply entrenched. Perhaps the program's most clear-cut victory was in reducing the most publicly visible street-level dealing and, as a result, giving the community's residents a feeling that something was being done about a serious problem. Perhaps in the world of drug control, that is no small victory (Zimmer, 1990).

## DOES PROHIBITION WORK?

In their book *Drug War Heresies,* Robert MacCoun and Peter Reuter (2001) undertook the most thorough and systematic evaluation of drug prohibition ever attempted. They address the question of whether prohibition works—and in what ways—as well as whether legalization would work better. (We'll have a lot more to say about legalization and decriminalization, or what MacCoun and Reuter call "depenalization," in Chapter 15.) In other words, is law enforcement effective in deterring drug use? Their answer is not likely to please either the prohibitionists (the hawks) or the legalizers (the doves). After assembling and evaluating the available empirical evidence, MacCoun and Reuter conclude: "It is plausible that drug penalties could be substantially reduced without significantly increasing use" *and* that "legalization might lead to sizeable increases in use" (p. 74).

In assessing the data on fear of legal sanction as a deterrent to illegal behavior, MacCoun and Reuter conclude that perceived severity "plays virtually no role in explaining deviant/criminal conduct" (p. 83). Variations in marijuana use, they suggest, are not influenced by perceived severity. In the United States, the Netherlands, and Australia, the elimination of or reduction in criminal penalties for small-quantity marijuana possession has had little or no impact on use (p. 96). Almost none of MacCoun's undergraduates at Berkeley even knew that California had decriminalized the possession of small amounts of marijuana a quarter century ago (p. 97).

MacCoun and Reuter also examined the objective likelihood of drug arrest and incarceration. As we saw, between 1980 and 2004, state and local arrests on drug charges rose from 581,000 to 1.745 million—an increase from 5 percent to 12 percent of all arrests. In 1980, marijuana arrests were 70 percent of the total; in 2004, they made up 44 percent of the total, and heroin and cocaine arrests, 30 percent. Over that same time, the number of commitments to state and federal prison increased ten times; over a fifth of state and over half of federal commitments are for drug offenses. Do these arrests and incarcerations argue for or against the effectiveness of law enforcement in reducing illicit drug use?

While it is true that drug arrests and convictions have increased over the past generation, drug transactions have increased as well. And the risk of arrest for a given transaction is actually quite low. Given the volume of sales and the number of cocaine transactions, for example, the likelihood of prison for a single episode of sale is roughly 1 out of 10,000—an extremely small risk indeed (p. 27). The cards are enormously stacked against law enforcement. The capacity of law enforcement to stamp out or seriously disrupt the drug supply by seizing supplies and arresting traffickers is extremely limited. The reasons are many and varied, and include the following:

- The drug trade is a multinational enterprise—the drugs sold on the streets of American cities have their origin in dozens of countries around the world. Decentralization means that stemming the drug tide in one country results in smugglers from other countries stepping in and supplying the shortfall. This has been referred to as "push down/pop up" (Nadelmann, 1988, p. 9). The elimination of one competitor means greater sales for those that remain.

- Illicit drugs can be produced in extremely small spaces in many different locales around the globe. The world's total supply of illicit heroin comes from only 5 percent of the world's opium, most of which is legal. The heroin can be grown on roughly 50 square miles of poppy fields, in tens or hundreds of thousands of scattered fields that are virtually immune to surveillance. Less than 1,000 square miles of land is devoted to the world's illicit coca production, and its production can be shifted around to avoid detection.
- The drug trade is a major employer: It makes a significant contribution to the economy. Considered strictly in terms of its economic impact, selling drugs is no different from any legal business. And it isn't just the top distributors who profit, it is anyone who derives employment from it. The "ripple effect" is enormous; that is, when drug dealers spend money in the legal sector, they generate jobs for the entire economy. If the drug trade were wiped out in countries in which it is a major part of the economy, billions of dollars and millions of jobs would be lost.
- The drug trade is a violent enterprise. Major smugglers command armies that are larger in personnel than many U.S. drug agencies, such as the DEA. Judges and police are bribed or intimidated into cooperating with illicit operations. In some countries, individual reformers are killed, indeed, their entire families are killed, resulting in compliance that is simply not possible in the legal sector.
- Intercepting a substantial proportion of the illegal drugs at the border of the United States is a virtual impossibility. According to the DEA in its publication "Drug Trafficking in the United States," 60 million people enter the United States by air on 675,000 flights; 6 million come from abroad by sea on 90,000 merchant and passenger ships that contain 400 million tons of cargo; and 370 million people enter by land in 116 million vehicles. Counting the many inlets, islands, and harbors, there are 90,000 miles of coastline where small, drug-laden boats can dock surreptitiously, without attracting attention. Moreover, smugglers are extremely inventive in hiding illicit cargo (Goode, 1997, pp. 87–102).

Officials at the Department of Defense commissioned a study by the RAND Corporation to evaluate the feasibility of "sealing" off the borders from incoming illegal drugs (Reuter, Crawford, and Cave, 1988). The report concludes that it would be "extremely difficult" to reduce cocaine consumption in the United States by as little as 5 percent, even if the government were to put into operation the most stringent and thorough interdiction program possible. Drug smuggling, the report states, is too sophisticated, decentralized, diversified, flexible, versatile, adaptable, resourceful, and intelligent an operation to be slowed down by a few—or many—seizures and arrests. It simply can't be done, the RAND report says.

In the past quarter century, given huge increases in expenditures for law enforcement and the higher incidence of drug arrests and incarceration, it might come as a surprise that for cocaine and heroin at least, prices have decreased and purity—and hence, in all likelihood, availability—has increased. We looked at drug supply in more detail in Chapter 13, on the illicit drug industry. We saw that the price of a gram of cocaine purchased at the less-than-one-gram level declined by half, and purity increased from 36 percent to 61 percent; for heroin, the cost of a gram at the one-tenth-of-a-gram level price decreased by over a third, from $3,295 to $2,088, and purity increased from 4 percent to 25 percent (Rhodes, Johnston, and Kling, 2001, p. 43).

Once again, we are forced to face the distinction between absolute and relative deterrence. "Absent law enforcement," says the RAND report, "the cost of moving a kilogram of cocaine [for instance] from the wholesale to the retail level" is "close to the cost of marketing aspirin." The huge difference between the cost of a drug at its point of origin to the ultimate customer "is presumably a consequence of domestic law enforcement" (p. 2). In other words, "most studies have only examined variations in levels of enforcement, rather than compare enforcement to its absence." The fact is, "though the availability and price of drugs are only modestly affected by variations in the current levels of enforcement or interdiction, they would likely be more dramatically affected by the complete elimination of enforcement brought about by legalization or by substantial reductions in the penalties for use" (MacCoun and Reuter, 2001, p. 78). Full legalization, decriminalization, or depenalization, most observers agree, is almost certain to produce substantially lower prices, greater availability, and higher levels of use for most of the currently illicit drugs. In that respect, relative deterrence works.

To the extent that law enforcement can influence price, contrary to what some drug legalization advocates have claimed, both legal and illegal drug use is *not* completely inelastic and *is* sensitive to price. In other words, the higher the price, the lower the levels of use—although for each substance or product, the elasticity index is somewhat different. For instance, for cars, it is −1.5, which means that for every 1 percent increase in price, automobile sales decrease 1.5 percent; for movies, the elasticity index is −3.5 (p. 76). Closer to home, estimates for cigarettes "cluster around" −0.4, and for alcohol, −0.7. Cigarettes, the most compulsively consumed of these products, are least sensitive to price—but sensitive nonetheless.

Obviously, for legal products, price can be set by the market. Do illegal drugs obey a different economic law? Is the demand for heroin and cocaine completely inelastic, totally unrelated to cost? The fact is, though law enforcement does not prevent or seriously disrupt the illicit drug supply, it does make obtaining illegal drugs more difficult and more expensive. And, remarkably, demand for illegal drugs *is* sensitive to price. For a highly addictive illegal drug such as heroin, elasticity is lower than for the legal drugs—in the −0.2 to −0.3 range. And for marijuana, a drug "with much lower dependency potential," this figure is in the −1.0 to −1.5 range (p. 76). Estimates for cocaine exhibit a much wider range from one study to another, from −0.7 to −2.0 (p. 77). To the extent that law enforcement can influence price, clearly, price can influence demand—that is, extent and volume of use.[1]

In short, we are forced to return to our distinction between relative and absolute deterrence. If there were no arrests, no seizures, no inspections at the border, and no eradication programs, the availability of drugs certainly would be vastly greater than it is currently—and, in all likelihood, use would be greater as well. (Yes, relative deterrence does work.) But relying on arrests, seizures, and inspections to eradicate or drastically reduce availability, and hence use, is a fool's errand, a delusional enterprise. The legalizer's argument expresses this position well: The punitive drug policy has been in place since the 1920s; law enforcement has consumed hundreds of billions of dollars in federal, state, and local funds investigating,

---

[1]Since the 1980s, the price of heroin and cocaine has decreased, but use has not only not increased, it has decreased. One explanation for this seeming paradox: Factors other than price enter into the use equation. It is likely that, independent of price, over the past quarter century, social and cultural changes have had an impact on drug use. It is even possible that increases in incarceration have removed the highest-risk drug users from the street, lowering the population's rates of heroin and cocaine use.

arresting, and incarcerating millions of users—a quarter of all prison inmates—and yet the nation has a core of nearly 20 million current illicit drug users. (No, absolute deterrence does not work.) Once again, law enforcement cannot possibly "wipe out" or drastically reduce illicit drug supply or demand. To the extent that law enforcement "works," it prevents a flood from becoming a tidal wave (Goode, 1997, p. 97).

## DRUG COURTS: TREATMENT, NOT PUNISHMENT

In 1989, during the crack epidemic, at a time when the criminal courts were being swamped with cases, Dade County, Florida, officials decided to adjudicate some of their drug defendants in a separate court system. The county instituted a **drug court** to divert defendants charged with narcotics offenses away from the penal system and into an alternate program of counseling, therapy, education, job training, close monitoring—including regular urine tests—and threats of return to jail or prison if conditions of the program were not met. Drug courts bypass the usual adversarial system, with defense and prosecution, creating a system in which the judge "addresses each defendant directly," requiring each to respond directly to him or her. In drug court, "all the justice players are on the same team, making the same demands on the defendant and standing ready to impose the same penalties for noncompliance" (Finn and Newlyn, 1997, p. 360).

In recent decades, according to the National Drug Court Institute, the number of drug diversion courts has grown from the one in Dade County to 1,557 across the country (as of April 2006); 400 more are in the planning stages. Do drug courts work? Do they reduce drug abuse among defendants? Are they more effective than a jail or prison sentence? Do they save taxpayers money? Do they reduce the crime rate? Should the drug court program be expanded? Many researchers have examined the effectiveness of drug courts empirically and in great detail. In June 2006, the U.S. Department of Justice's National Institute of Justice issued a summary report, *Drug Courts: The Second Decade,* and in May 2004, the National Drug Court Institute published its findings in *Painting the Picture: A National Report Card on Drug Courts* (Huddleston, Freeman-Wilson, and Boone, 2004). The conclusions of the studies these reports discuss are fairly consistent; although variation exists with respect to rigorousness of these programs, well-run drug court programs are cost-effective in reducing recidivism, criminal behavior, and cost to the community.

Still, the program has its critics. One group is the conservatives, who believes that all drug offenders should be punished with incarceration and that alternative programs of therapy and counseling are simply a way of letting criminals "off the hook." The second group is drug legalizers, who believe that the state has no right to hold the threat of imprisonment over the head of the user; after all, do we threaten the alcoholic with imprisonment if he or she doesn't comply with the mandates of a treatment program? (Many radicals believe that, by their very nature, any programs sponsored or endorsed by the government are suspect and probably harmful.) The addict needs treatment in the same way the cancer patient does, says the legalizer. Treatment should be voluntary not coerced, and prison should not hang over the head of the addict like the proverbial Sword of Damocles.

At the beginning of this chapter, I referred to drug courts as a "crack" in the armor of drug law enforcement. Drug courts represent "a paradigm shift away from a predominantly punitive approach to one that focuses on treatment, investment in human potential, second (and third) chances, and restoration" (Goldkamp, White, and Robinson, 2001, p. 28).

How should we evaluate the drug court program? What constitutes success? The drug court program can be evaluated with respect to the achievement of two goals—individual and organizational. Individual goals are those that the program sets for the arrestee; they include reducing drug use and abuse and criminal behavior, and obtaining some form of employment. Organizational goals include reduced communitywide rates of criminal recidivism and savings to society in the form of the lower cost of treatment in comparison with incarceration. Have drug courts met these goals?

Drug courts are municipal and countywide entities, and hence unstandardized and highly variable from one jurisdiction to another. As a consequence, it is difficult to characterize their operation and effectiveness, taken as a whole. Available descriptions and evaluations tend to focus on specific drug courts rather than drug courts generally. Nonetheless, enough programs have been described and analyzed by researchers for discernible patterns to emerge.

All drug courts set criteria for eligibility. Miami's drug court is typical. To qualify for the program, arrestees must be charged with possession or purchase of a controlled substance. Defendants charged with trafficking, those with a history of violent crime, or those who have been convicted of more than two nondrug felonies are not eligible (Finn and Newlyn, 1997, p. 358). To the extent that other courts set broader or less stringent criteria for eligibility (accepting dealers, violent offenders, and/or defendants with more felony convictions), they will include in their programs more higher-risk defendants; therefore, officials must be satisfied with correspondingly lower levels of success. Moreover, including higher-risk arrestees in a program will inevitably result in larger numbers who fail, that is, are engaged in crimes in the community rather than being incarcerated. To the extent that the court sets more stringent criteria, its success rate will be higher, but fewer defendants will profit from the program, if it is effective. In short, the community has a stake in and should be aware of the criteria the courts set for program inclusion, because these criteria impact the community.

Measuring the effectiveness of drug courts is not as simple as it sounds. Most studies compare graduates of the program—that is, arrestees diverted from the criminal justice system into the drug court who have completed a year in the program—with drug court dropouts. And in study after study, drug court "graduates" have lower rates of drug and crime recidivism than do drug court dropouts. But since dropouts are already drug court failures, we assume that they will fail in other ways as well, including using illicit drugs and committing crimes. Basically, these studies "show that the successes succeed and the failures fail" (Goldkamp, White, and Robinson, 2001, p. 32). To understand the impact of the drug courts, we need a more meaningful comparison between defendants who have graduated from a drug court and comparable defendants who were subject to more traditional, and punitive, criminal justice treatment.

All qualifications registered, most observers agree that the drug courts have been successful in meeting both their individual and their organizational goals. One study (Peters and Murrin, 2000) examined the recidivism rates of drug court graduates with a matched or comparison sample of probationers and a sample of nongraduates of the drug court program. One measure of success: Six in 10 of the enrollees in the drug court program were retained after a period of a year (p. 74). The average number of arrests per 100 participants in the year following the program "start date" was 22 for drug court graduates, more than 77 for a matched sample of probationers, and over 156 for nongraduates of the program. The number of felony arrests in the 30 months following entry into the program was just under 30 for graduates, 58 for matched probationers, and 109 for nongraduates. The proportions arrested

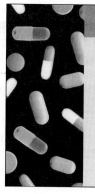

### True-False Quiz

Most of my students were not fooled by the statement "In the United States, drug treatment is a failure; it costs more money to pay for drug treatment programs than these programs save for the society." Only 40 percent agreed with the statement. Still, 4 out of 10 is a substantial minority. In contrast, drug treatment researchers and policy analysts are very clear about the savings these programs deliver to the society; for every dollar spent on them, the society receives four dollars back in an array of economic and social benefits.

in the 12 months following the program start date were 20 percent, 43 percent, and 79 percent, respectively; for the proportion arrested in the 30 months following the start date, the figures were 48 percent, 63 percent, and 86 percent respectively (p. 83).

One of the very few studies of a drug court that randomly assigned eligible clients who were drug-involved, nonviolent offenders to either drug treatment or treatment as usual—jail sentences, parole, and probation—reported that drug court clients were more likely than controls ("treatment as usual") to participate in drug treatment and drug testing and less likely to be rearrested. When "differences in the opportunity to reoffend are taken into consideration, controls were rearrested at a rate nearly three times that of drug treatment clients" (Gottfredson and Exum, 2002, p. 337; Gottfredson, Najaka, and Kearly, 2003).

With some variation in outcomes, and sometimes with slightly less impressive figures when key variables are controlled, a substantial number of other studies have found the same thing. In short, the results of the available research indicate that "the drug court is an effective intervention." Drug court participants tend to have significantly lower re-arrest rates than felony drug offenders who go through "traditional adjudication and sentencing" (Spohn et al., 2001, p. 171). However, programs usually work only if there are frequent urine tests, routine appearances before the judge, active enrollee treatment participation, and the threat of sanctions—jail or prison time—if the enrollee does not meet program goals (Goldkamp, White, and Robinson, 2001, p. 67). And by reducing individual recidivism rates, drug courts also meet collective, organizational, or community goals by lowering the crime rate and, because drug courts are strikingly less costly than incarceration, saving the government and the taxpayers a great deal of money. One estimate has it that drug court costs range from $1,800 to $4,400 per defendant per year, while it costs between $20,000 and $30,000 to incarcerate a convict for a year (Weinstein, 2002). It seems clear that drug courts are an idea whose time has come.

## DRUG TREATMENT

Drug treatment programs represent another "crack" in the armor of a strict "lock 'em up and throw away the key" policy toward illicit drug use. Indeed, drug courts and drug treatment programs are interlocked, since nearly half of all enrollees in treatment programs were referred by the criminal justice system. This means that drug offenders were given ıce: treatment or prison. They are being treated in preference to being incarcerated. e effectiveness of drug courts and drug treatment programs affirm that it is far better o treat drug abusers than to incarcerate them. Many observers view **drug treatment** as an alternative to—indeed, a rejection of—the hawkish arrest-and-incarcerate model.

Drug treatment is based on a pathology or **medical model.** It regards abuse and/or addiction as a disease much like cancer: There's something wrong with the abuser/addict; he or she is "sick" in some way and in need of therapeutic intervention, or "treatment." One set of assumptions held by the medical model is that the drug has seized hold of the abuser, that the abuser has lost control of his or her behavior and is no longer morally responsible for his or her drug use. The medical model contrasts sharply with the moral model, which is the basis of the punitive or prohibitionist policy toward illicit drug use/abuse. Proponents of the moral model argues that the user/abuser/addict is very much responsible for his or her actions and has chosen to engage in behavior that is immoral, a violation of what should be regarded as right, good, and proper. Enactors of such behaviors must be punished to teach them and others a lesson.

Drug abuse may or may not be a disease or something like a disease; the abuser may or may not have lost control of his or her behavior; and the abuser may or may not engage in "immoral" behavior. These considerations are secondary to a far more important issue: Do treatment programs work? That is, do they get abusers and addicts to discontinue behavior that is both self-destructive and harmful to society as a whole? And are they cost-effective? That is, do they save taxpayers money, as compared with the costs of drug-related medical care, crime, and property loss? Speculating on the moral, philosophical, or ideo-logical status of drug use is a separate and independent issue from whether and to what extent drug treatment works. The question of free will is probably unanswerable, and whether addiction is a disease depends on what we mean by "disease" in the first place. But the attempt to unravel and solve these issues is unproductive with respect to assessing the effectiveness of drug treatment programs.

## Evaluating Program Effectiveness

It is something of a cliché that most enrollees in self-help or treatment programs fail to change their behavior. In a given attempt, most cigarette smokers fail to give up cigarette use; over the long run, most weight loss programs fail—that is, the majority of enrollees fail to take and keep off significant poundage; after treatment, most alcoholics go back to compul-sive, destructive drinking; and so on. Careful studies of the majority of treatment programs show that they have a failure rate of 70–90 percent, depending on the criteria used.

Yet, when psychologist Stanley Schachter, a psychologist, interviewed the residents of a village on Long Island, in New York State, three-quarters of those who were smokers in the past had been successful in quitting permanently (Brody, 1983, p. C1). One possi-bility is that these smokers tended to be well educated, and a high level of education is related to successful cessation of smoking. But the experience of the drug-dependent Vietnam veterans, most of whom did not have high levels of education, indicates that abstention is not as difficult as the dismally high rates of failure of treatment programs suggest. Fully 86 percent of soldiers dependent on heroin in Vietnam discontinued their use of the drug (Robins, Davis, and Nurco, 1974, p. 39). Moreover, almost all of them either gave up narcotics voluntarily or did not revert to use after "brief forced detoxification subsequent to their discovery" (p. 43; Robins, 1973). Only 5 percent of the addicts who gave up narcotics did so in a formal treatment program. What these and other findings suggest is that abusers—whether of tobacco, alcohol, food, drugs, or gambling—are a very unrepresentative "tip of the iceberg." That is, they represent only those abusers who were unable to quit on their own, the "dregs" of treatment programs, that segment of the abusing population most resistant to treatment. What about the success rates of drug treatment programs?

Before looking at the findings from the many studies that have examined drug treatment program effectiveness, we must establish several important qualifications. First, reducing drug use or abuse to zero is an extremely unrealistic goal. It is crucial that we measure effectiveness by *reductions* in use, not total abstention. Almost inevitably, if total abstention is the goal, the overwhelming majority—if not all—programs will be found to fail.

Second, there will be some variability in effectiveness from one program to another. Some are better administered, monitor their enrollees more carefully, or are more adequately staffed or better funded than others. Clearly, the big picture is important here—how a program performs around the country rather than in one particular instance.

Third, one type of program may work better for a particular type of client than for another: younger versus older, male versus female, polydrug abuser versus the exclusive heroin or crack addict, educated versus uneducated, and so on. It could be that programs need to be tailored to the characteristics of their clientele.

Fourth, drug treatment programs are not in the business of performing miracles. Their clientele often have medical problems and psychiatric disorders; tend to be relatively uneducated, unemployed, underemployed, or intermittently employed; and are frequently involved in a life of crime. Also, most are polydrug drug users, dropouts or failures at more than one treatment program, and, close to half the time, abusers of alcohol as well as drugs. In short, most of their enrollees are multiproblem clients. In fact, the more severe the client's problems when entering a drug treatment program, the lower the likelihood of success. Drug treatment programs are unlikely to turn people with multiple problems into upstanding, law-abiding, hard-working, responsible, abstemious citizens. Once again, the goal must be a reduction in rather than a complete elimination of problem behavior.

How do we measure drug treatment success? What are the goals we want these programs to accomplish? In the 1800s, countless quack cures for drug abuse were announced, each to be unmasked for the fraud it was. In the 1950s, Synanon, a therapeutic community program, was trumpeted as a cure for many former heroin addicts, who—or so the claim went—were drug-free for a year or more during treatment. The problem with such claims is that they were always made in the absence of control groups, not to mention verifiable evidence. Flawed as they were, during the 1960s, investigations of the pioneering methadone maintenance programs were subject to empirical scrutiny and found to be effective (Dole and Nyswander, 1965). Subsequent research found these early claims to be inflated, due to their selection of clients with an optimistic prognosis and their less-than-careful tabulation of dropouts (Kleinman and Lukoff, 1977). Nonetheless, these early methadone maintenance programs have withstood the challenge; they have grown in enrollments and remain one of several viable treatment options. And the early studies examining these programs have enabled later researchers to establish meaningful criteria with which to evaluate drug treatment programs. What criteria should we use to evaluate the effectiveness of a drug treatment program?

First, clearly, the reduction in the use of illicit drugs must be regarded as paramount here; second, a reduction in the use of alcohol, likewise, is important; third, a reduction in criminal activity, and fourth, the acquisition of an education and marketable skills, along with a rise in employment, certainly must be listed as significant (Hubbard et al., 1989, p. 5). And in an age in which budgetary constraints are ever-present and considerations of the bottom line are deemed essential, we are forced to ask, are these programs cost-effective? Do they save taxpayers money? Does society come out fiscally and economically ahead by funding drug treatment programs?

## Types of Programs

Four principal types of drug treatment programs, or treatment modalities, currently prevail in the United States: (1) methadone maintenance; (2) the therapeutic community (TC); (3) outpatient, drug-free programs; and (4) self-help peer groups, such as Narcotics Anonymous (NA) and Alcoholics Anonymous (AA). Each has strengths and weaknesses; each is appropriate for a somewhat different clientele. The therapeutic community is much more expensive than the other three programs and seems to work best with younger, poly-drug clients. Methadone maintenance is used exclusively for narcotics addicts and seems to work best with older clients who have tried a number of programs but failed to make a go of it. In addition, compared with the other three programs, very few maintenance clients are referrals from the criminal justice system. Drug-free, outpatient programs work best for clients for whom the other three are inappropriate. Clearly, the principle "one size fits all" is wrong. Instead, a "full range of settings is necessary to treat the variety of drug abuse patterns currently prevalent" (Hubbard et al., 1989, p. 98).

**Methadone maintenance** is used solely and exclusive to treat narcotics addicts or abusers, or, in the case of recently released convicts, former narcotics abusers or addicts. (Or polydrug abusers who have a primary dependence on one or more narcotics.) Methadone is a synthetic narcotic that is administered to clients who are dependent on an opiate drug. Enrollees in these treatment programs are either stabilized on a particular dosage of methadone or are withdrawn from methadone, in stages, over a very long period—months, even years. Hence, when they are treated in the program, they are physically dependent on the methadone instead of the narcotic (usually heroin) they were dependent on previously. If patients were to suddenly withdraw from the methadone, they would undergo painful abstinence symptoms, just as they would have previously done had they been withdrawn from heroin. To be plain about it, these clients are methadone addicts. And since methadone is a long-acting drug (unlike heroin, which is a relatively fast-acting drug), the withdrawal symptoms with methadone are likely to be even more prolonged and painful than with heroin. Clearly, if methadone maintenance programs were to be evaluated on the criterion of whether the addict achieves a drug-free existence, they would always and by definition be judged a failure because he or she remains addicted either permanently or for an extremely long time.

Two types of methadone maintenance programs exist. The metabolic or adaptive program administers high doses for long periods of time, in theory, for the remainder of the addict's life; the change or abstinence-oriented program administers smaller doses for shorter periods and aims eventually to withdraw addicts from methadone altogether. According to the Substance Abuse and Mental Health Services Administration (SAMHSA), there are about 150,000–175,000 enrollees in methadone maintenance programs nationwide.

**Therapeutic communities (TCs)** are residential or live-in programs. Phoenix House, Daytop Village, and Odyssey House are some of the hundreds of TC-type programs operating nationally. TCs operate under the assumption that a drug-free existence is not only a realistic goal for recovering drug abusers but an absolutely necessary one. (Tobacco use, presumably, is excluded.) The view of all TC programs is that substance abuse is not the abuser's central problem. Instead, drug abuse is symptomatic of an immature, hedonistic, self-centered personality, a disorder of the whole person, not a single aspect of the person.

Outpatient drug-free programs do not include medication (such as methadone) in their treatment modality; they enroll clients who live in the community; and they administer some form of therapy and counseling as part of treatment.

Peer self-help programs such as **Narcotics Anonymous (NA)** and **Alcoholics Anonymous (AA)** are cost-free, not-for-profit organizations made up of thousands of local, autonomous groups, each of which is self-supporting. AA and NA are based on "the Twelve Steps," which require that members acknowledge powerlessness in the face of substance abuse temptation and submission to the higher power of God.

Do these programs work? Do they help enrollees reduce their current levels of drug abuse? Do they save society money, save lives, and reduce crime in the community? The earliest full-scale evaluation study of the effectiveness of drug treatment programs is referred to as **DARP (Drug Abuse Reporting Program);** it looked at clients enrolled in treatment programs between 1969 and 1972. It concluded that "treatment in methadone maintenance, therapeutic communities, and outpatient drug-free programs [is] effective in improving post-treatment performance with respect to drug use, criminality, and productive activities" (Simpson and Sells, 1982, p. 7). DARP spawned two more recent data collection efforts: TOPS and DATOS.

## TOPS

In the 1980s, a team of researchers (Hubbard et al., 1989) conducted a study that is referred to as **TOPS (Treatment Outcome Prospective Study).** This study examined the treatment outcomes of over 11,000 drug abusers who entered treatment programs nationwide between 1979 and 1981. It was the most thorough, systematic, and detailed investigation ever undertaken on the subject. (TOPS looked only at methadone maintenance, TCs, and outpatient drug-free program outcomes; it did not examine the outcomes of peer-oriented self-help programs such as AA and NA.) Its sample was different from that of DARP's, due in large part to the changing patterns of drug use between the late 1960s and early 1980s. The major difference was that, while half of DARP's sample was made up of daily narcotics abusers, only a fifth of TOPS's sample was, indicating the declining role of heroin over time as the abuser's drug of choice. The study reported the following:

- For all treatment modalities, the longer clients remained enrolled in the program, the greater the likelihood they would discontinue their use of illicit drugs (Hubbard et al., 1989, p. 125).
- Methadone maintenance programs enrolled clients for a significantly longer period than the other programs. The average length of stay of enrollees in methadone maintenance programs was 38 weeks; for TCs, it was only 21 weeks, and for outpatient drug-free programs, it was 15 weeks (Hubbard et al., 1989, p. 95). This suggests that a client's motivation is a crucial factor in achieving treatment goals.

- For all three programs, on average, enrollees reduced their use of illicit substances. There were many failures, of course; in fact, the majority of enrollees failed to be abstinent during and after treatment. But for all three programs, the total volume of illegal drug use was reduced. For methadone maintenance programs, roughly half were abstinent for a year during treatment, and the sample as a whole reduced their illegal drug intake by 70–80 percent compared with pretreatment levels (p. 125). On average, for TC clients, the volume, frequency, and complexity (that is, the use of a variety of drugs) declined substantially. For example, before treatment, more than a quarter of TC enrollees were regular users of cocaine in the year before entering the program; three to five years after treatment, only 1 in 10 were (p. 109). Improvements among participants in outpatient drug-free programs were not quite as impressive but they were significant nonetheless.
- The reduction in predatory crime was significant for all three programs, declining to one-half to one-third of their pretreatment levels. Two-thirds of those who reported engaging in predatory crime before treatment had ceased involvement in the year after treatment (p. 128).
- Employment figures were not nearly as impressive as the reductions in drug use and criminal activity. For methadone maintenance, there was virtually no improvement. For TCs, prior to treatment, 15 percent had been employed for a year; after treatment, this rose to 40 percent. For outpatient drug-free programs, this figure rose from one-quarter to one-half—a significant improvement, but hardly an employment cure-all for the drug abuser (p. 129).
- Changes in levels of alcohol consumption were extremely small and hardly encouraging. One-fourth of methadone maintenance clients used alcohol at abusive levels before treatment; three to five years later, one-fifth did. For TCs, the comparable figures were one-third to one-quarter. And for drug-free, outpatient programs, they were just over 3 in 10 before and just under 3 in 10 after (p. 140). In short, drug treatment programs change the alcohol abuse picture practically not at all for clients.

A consideration of the bottom line emphatically demonstrates that drug treatment *works*. With respect to the total amount of money saved (in terms of productivity, employment, death, disease, hospital care, money stolen, and so on) versus the cost of these programs—*any* and *all* of these programs—society gets back roughly three or four dollars in benefits for every dollar spent (Hubbard et al., 1989, Chapter 7). Viewed in this light, the real bottom line, viewed in cost-benefit analysis terms, is that drug treatment saves much more than it costs. Cutting drug treatment is extremely "penny wise and pound foolish" and costly policy.

## DATOS

**DATOS (Drug Abuse Treatment Outcome Study)** interviewed 10,000 clients between 1991 and 1993 enrolled in 96 programs in 11 cities (Hubbard et al., 1997). The researchers studied enrollees in the same three treatment programs—methadone maintenance, therapeutic communities, and outpatient drug-free programs. In addition, they looked at clients in a new program designed mainly for cocaine abusers, the short-term inpatient program. (Unlike DARP and TOPS, researchers excluded clients enrolled for only a week in a treatment program.) Like the change in sample composition from DARPS to TOPS (that is, in abusers who were in treatment programs in the late 1960s versus those in the early 1980s), DATOS's sample differed from TOPS's. DATOS's clients were older (the majority were over 30), more likely to be female (roughly one-third), more likely to be referred by the criminal justice system (43% versus 31%), and much more likely to use cocaine. Cocaine was the main drug of abuse for DATOS's clients. Compared with the TOPS sample, twice as many methadone maintenance program enrollees and six and a half times as many TC enrollees abused cocaine (Hubbard et al., 1997, pp. 262–263).

With a few exceptions, in general, DATOS's findings confirmed those of TOPS: The longer the client stayed in a program, the more that all forms of drug abuse declined, indicating that motivation plays a powerful role in treatment success. Methadone clients stayed in their programs longer than was true of enrollees in the other treatment programs. Drug use of all kinds declined significantly after treatment as compared with before. Participation in predatory crime declined significantly—by more than half—after treatment. Improvements in levels of employment were modest, and for methadone maintenance (and short-term inpatient therapy) practically nonexistent. Alcohol abuse was reduced not at all for methadone clients, but cut in half for TC, outpatient drug-free, and short-term inpatient program patients (pp. 266–268). One study that focused on cocaine abusers (Simpson, Joe, and Broome, 2002) found that daily alcohol consumption was cut by two-thirds a year (6% versus 22%) five years after leaving the program. Ties to the community (religious, occupational, marital, family, friendship networks) were strongly related to program effectiveness. Once again, the available data suggest that treatment works and that it is cost-effective, saving society and taxpayers *billions* of dollars.

TOPS was conducted in 1979–1981, before the AIDS crisis; DATOS, conducted in the early 1990s, is the first study of the effectiveness of drug treatment after the AIDS epidemic broke. Hence, DATOS included a question on risky sexual behavior as a possible source of AIDS. Clearly, one criterion of an effective drug treatment program is reducing the incidence of risky or HIV/AIDS-causing sexual behavior. The study measured at-risk sexual behavior as "sexual intercourse with two or more partners without always using a condom." For the sample as a whole, risky sexual behavior was cut not quite in half (p. 267), indicating that the effectiveness of treatment extends beyond the usual quartet of drugs, crime, unemployment, and alcohol.

DATOS has continued to collect data into the twenty-first century on the effectiveness of drug treatment programs; the conclusions of these more recent studies, still ongoing, are essentially the same as in the earlier studies. Independently, other researchers (Egertson, Fox, and Leshner, 1997; Leukefeld, Tims, and Farabee, 2002; Simpson, 2003; Tims et al., 1997) have reached precisely the same conclusions. (Findings from 75 DATOS-based publications can be found online at www.datos.org.) In addition, a parallel study conducted in the United Kingdom, NTORS (National Treatment Outcome Study), arrived at essentially the same findings. Drug treatment works, and it is a sound and wise investment.

## SUMMARY

Between 1980 and the early 2000s, on a per population basis, while the crime rate plummeted, the rate of incarceration in the United States increased three and a half times. The reason for the increase is threefold: parole is less likely to be granted; if granted, parole is more likely to be revoked; and drug offenders are more likely to be incarcerated. In recent decades, while most indicators of drug use have declined, arrests and incarceration rates for drug possession and sales have sharply increased. Since 1970, the total number of prisoners in state and federal penitentiaries has increased by seven times, and the number and percentage of drug offenders has increased faster than the total. The length of sentences for nonviolent drug offenses are very similar to those for many violent offenses.

The term "prohibition" refers to a punitive or criminal approach to dealing with troublesome behavior. Under drug prohibition, criminal penalties are applied to the possession and sale of controlled substances. Prohibitionists believe that the application of criminal penalties will reduce or contain drug use. The punitive or prohibitionist argument comes in two very different varieties—the strict and the moderate. The strict punitive version makes use of the logic of *absolute* deterrence, while the moderate punitive version is based on *relative* deterrence. The absolute deterrence argument holds that punishment can wipe out or substantially reduce drug use; the relative deterrence argument holds only that in the absence of punishment—that is, in the absence of drug laws, arrests and incarceration—drug use would be comparatively higher. The moderate deterrence argument holds that the currently high rates of drug use does not provide evidence for the fact that drug prohibition has failed. Indeed, the opposite is the case: The drug laws deter enough drug use to make the enterprise a success.

The United States has a mixture of drug policies for different drugs. The legal drugs, like alcohol and tobacco, are regulated, available to anyone above a certain age but bought and sold under restrictions set by law. The prescription drugs are available with a physician's prescription for specified medical purposes; they are not legal without a prescription or for recreational purposes. The Schedule I drugs are completely outlawed. They include marijuana (legal as medicine under state law in ten states), LSD, heroin (legal in medical treatment in the United Kingdom), and MDMA (Ecstasy). The possession and sale of such drugs is automatically a criminal act. The possession of small quantities of marijuana has been decriminalized in 12 states and in several West European countries.

The current "war on drugs" represents a strong prohibitionist or punitive stance toward the illicit drugs. It makes use of a military metaphor (militarism), a verbal image that has become, in effect, an actual war—that is, the government has approved the use of the resources of the U.S. military in the fight against drugs (militarization). The Army, Navy, and Coast Guard are now loaning equipment to, training, and assisting civilian police forces in enforcing the drug laws, and even accompanying the police on interdiction operations. Some observers question these developments, arguing that they may undermine more reasonable, effective means of dealing with the drug problem. In the United States, the war-on-drugs rhetoric may have diminished, but militarization is still alive and well in American-funded and -led drug-fighting operations in Afghanistan, Colombia, and Mexico.

During the 1980s, several federal bills authorized the seizure of assets—cash, automobiles, boats, real estate, jewelry, and anything else of value—earned by criminal "conspiracies." In the case of accused drug dealers, a portion of these assets, once liquidated, go directly into the budgets of drug enforcement agencies of state, county, and local police departments. Some observers argue that these bills have done more harm than good, that they have backfired and become counterproductive, because asset forfeiture has become the primary goal of antidrug operations. If undercover police work determines that one operation will yield a great deal of cash or property and very little in the way of drugs, while another will yield the opposite, the first will be followed up—even though the second takes a substantial quantity of drugs off the street and the first does not—to fill the coffers of drug units. Some observers argue that this is an example of organization corruption. While these monies do not fill the pockets of individual officers, they do alter the priorities of antidrug operations. The goals of taking drugs off the street, disrupting drug operations, and lowering drug use and drug-related crime become secondary to a quest for cash. Not all observers agree with this critique, however; at least one study has shown that a substantial proportion of police officers rank asset forfeiture as an effective means of combating drug trafficking, at least in some respects. Local police are more subject to cash-seeking antidrug efforts than federal police, since the feds have a steady, mandated drug-fighting budget, while local departments do not.

A program of proactive policing was launched in New York City in 1984. Dubbed "Operation Pressure Point," the program attempted to disrupt the street-level drug dealing that had become emboldened by cuts in police department personnel as a result of the municipal budgetary crisis of the 1970s. Its success was mixed. Overt, open street-level drug dealing diminished, out-of-town buyers were discouraged from making purchases in the community, and trafficking operations in middle-class neighborhoods were displaced. But some of these activities simply moved elsewhere, and in poorer, more heavily minority neighborhoods, where dealers tended to live, the operation had little if any impact. The lesson learned from this program is that the police have a limited impact on the volume of drug sales, though certain forms of dealing may be amenable to law enforcement intervention. The major benefit of Operation Pressure Point was that it gave residents of the community the feeling that something was being done about the drug problem.

An enormous volume of research has been conducted on the impact of drug prohibition. Two policy analysts, Robert MacCoun and Peter Reuter, reviewed, summarized, and analyzed much of this literature. Their conclusions likely are pleasing neither to the staunch advocates of the war on drugs (the hawks) nor to the proponents of legalization (the doves). Severe penalties for drug possession and sales have no deterrent effect whatsoever. And "sealing the borders" of the United States does not reduce consumption because the country's borders are extremely porous.

After 20 years of fighting the drug war, today, heroin and cocaine are both cheaper and purer than they were before the war began. At the same time, criminal penalties for drug trafficking do increase the cost of drugs, and use is responsive to cost. Once again, the distinction between "absolute" and "relative" deterrence is crucial. Full legalization, or a legalization, decriminalization, or depenalization policy of any kind, is almost certain to produce lower drug costs, greater availability, and higher rates of drug use and abuse. But, once again, law enforcement cannot wipe out or even drastically reduce drug use. To the extent that drug law enforcement "works," it merely acts to *contain* drug use.

In jurisdictions around the country, alternatives to incarceration have been instituted. Called "drug courts," they offer the nonviolent drug offender a program of diversion from the criminal justice system into some sort of treatment program. Although the evidence is complex, the results mixed, and the outcomes variable, the available evidence suggests that drug courts are effective in saving the community money and lowering the re-arrest rates of drug offenders.

Drug treatment programs, likewise, have a mixed record of successes and failures. Three waves of research have been conducted, and their findings are more or less consistent. Not all clients who go through a program show improvements; as a general rule, the longer a client remains in a program, the greater the likelihood of improvement. Taken as a whole, drug treatment significantly lowers rates of drug use and criminal behavior, but, for methadone maintenance clients, little improvement is seen in rates of employment or alcohol abuse. In contrast, cocaine samples show marked declines in levels of alcohol consumption. The most recent studies show an improvement in risky, AIDS-related sexual behavior among treatment program graduates.

## KEY TERMS

absolute deterrence   391

Alcoholics Anonymous (AA)   409

Controlled Substances Act   391

criminalization   390

DARP (Drug Abuse Reporting Program)   409

DATOS (Drug Abuse Treatment Outcome Study)   410

disguised observation   397

dove   390

drug asset forfeiture   397

Drug Control Act   391

drug court   403

drug treatment   406

hawk   390

law of unanticipated consequences   397

medical model   406

methadone maintenance   408

militarism   395

militarization   395

Narcotics Anonymous (NA)   409

over-the-counter (OTC) drugs   392

participant observation   396

prescription drugs   392

proactive policing   398

prohibition   389

Prohibition   389

punitive model   389

reactive policing   398

relative deterrence   391

therapeutic community (TC)   409

TOPS (Treatment Outcome Prospective Study)   409

## ACCOUNT: Arrest and Incarceration

*At the time of this interview, the respondent was 21 years old. Sally had been released early after serving one year of a three-year sentence for the sale of a controlled substance. After being out of prison for four weeks, she began working at an office job. She is determined to go straight.*

**Q:** When were you arrested and what was the crime?

**A:** I was arrested two years ago last December. I was 19. The crime was a Class B felony, the sale of a controlled substance in the third degree. The substance was cocaine.

**Q:** To whom did you sell it?

**A:** To friends. We were basically selling to friends because we wanted to do drugs. We'd get a couple of grams extra to sell to our friends. Somehow, the [undercover] police got wind of what we were doing and they wanted ounces. We were just selling maybe five or six grams a week, but the police wanted six ounces. We said we can't get six ounces, that's too much. That's how the police do it—they try to get you to sell a lot so that they have no problem convicting you.

Anyway, the police kept calling us and calling us, they really wanted it, they said, and we thought about it and we thought about it. They really wanted to get us. The police bugged us for about two months, and so finally we said we could get six ounces. We finally sold coke to them, but we had come down to two ounces. They wanted at least that much so they could get a solid conviction. That was the most we could possibly get our hands on. Even when we went around trying to get it, people we dealt with asked us, "What do you want two ounces for?" We had been dealing with our friends for months and months, just small quantities, and all of a sudden, we were asking for two ounces. They figured something was up. But we said, don't worry about it. Being stoned, you're not thinking properly. . . . We made two sales to the cops. The first time was just to see if we could get it for them. That was only half an ounce. They said they wanted to check out what kind of stuff we could get. They didn't arrest us that time. A month later, they called us again, and we got them two ounces. The night we got it, the police came over to our apartment. We weighed out the coke, they snorted a little with us, then they wrapped it up and put it in their pants. One cop told the other to give us the money. The second reached into his pants and instead of coming out with a wallet, he came out with a gun. At first, I thought we were getting ripped off. We had a lot of coke and a lot of jewelry and other valuable stuff in the house. I thought for sure they were going to rip us off. The funny thing is, I was relieved that they were cops. It didn't dawn on me that a ripoff could happen, but at that moment, I thought they were going to take everything we had. . . . The police arrested us about midnight. They took us to [the county seat], down in a basement of some building where they booked us and did all this paper work.

They tried to get us to sign papers stating that we would cooperate with them. I wouldn't sign anything until I talked to my lawyer. . . . My codefendant, who was my boyfriend, was ready to sign anything, he was so scared. He just wanted to get out. My parents came down to the courthouse. . . . The police kept us there overnight. Booked us and kept us in a holding cell. We were arraigned the next morning. Then they let us go in our parents' custody. We went to court on and off for 14 months. Then they incarcerated us. [After 14 months,] we came back and the judge said three years and then they just took me away. I didn't expect to go to prison because I had been out on the street for so long. When I was free, I was scared [about the possibility of being incarcerated], but after more than a year had passed—I had a good job by then—just the arrest alone had scared me enough to stop what I was doing. The one night in jail after our arrest had scared me badly. I thought for sure they were going to give me a second chance. It was my first offense. . . . I went upstate, to [a correctional facility for women]. I was confined for a full year, but I only served nine months there and three months in a much smaller facility near the city. . . .

**Q:** What were the conditions of your release?

**A:** I got two years' parole. The conditions are seek, obtain, and maintain employment. And report to my parole officer twice a month.

**Q:** Do you feel your parole officer is providing you with assistance and guidance?

**A:** Yes. I'm happy to have a very good parole officer. She seems to me to be one of the most caring officers I have met. I have spoken to others on parole and their officers are always threatening to violate them, to send them back [to prison]. My parole officer has not violated me [reported me for a violation], and I've been out for four weeks without finding a job. She could have violated me, but she's not into violating me, she wants to see me make it. We sit down together. I can really talk to her. I put everything on the table with her. We have a good relationship; she wants to help me. . . . She is very supportive.

**Q:** When you returned to your community, what adjustments did you have to make?

**A:** Well, the whole group of friends I had, I can no longer relate to them. Right now, I don't have any friends. . . . They're all doing the same things I was doing before I left. Drugs, drinking, going out all the time. I don't want to do that any more. When you start getting older, there's a lot of responsibility you have to accept, and these people don't see that. I try to talk to them, and all they say is, yeah, yeah, have a drink, do some drugs. I don't want that, but they won't listen. I just can't relate to them any more.

**Q:** What about your parents?

**A:** They are happy to have me home and out of prison. They just want me to stay home all the time, which I don't want to do. I like to go to the movies, I want to go out and see men. I don't want to sit home with my mother all the time. . . .

**Q:** Your father being a retired police officer, what effect did your arrest have on him and the relationship between the two of you?

**A:** He saw it coming. At the time, I wasn't living at home, but when I did come home, I was always stoned. Being a cop, he knew. My boyfriend and I had a brand-new car, a large amount of gold jewelry, new clothes all the time. And I was not working. My father put two and two together and figured out what was going on. I kept saying, don't worry, I'm not doing anything wrong. A month later, I got arrested. He was very upset, but he came to court with me all the time. He thought his being a cop would help me, but it didn't. If anything, everyone thought I should have known better. Your father's a cop, they kept saying. Through it all, my father was very supportive. When I went upstate [to prison], he came to see

me, but the experience upset him so much, I asked him not to come any more. He just sat there, grinding his teeth. I could see by his face it scared him. Seeing all those people I was with, seeing his little daughter there—it didn't fit with him at all. But both my parents could see that I was doing well [in prison]. I had put on weight, I wasn't doing drugs, and I was thinking clearly. In a couple of months, my whole way of thinking was turned around.

**Q:** Do you feel the arresting officers and the district attorney were pushing for a conviction?

**A:** Oh, yes, they were pushing. They love to get convictions. . . . The cops tried to make us look like such big dealers, like we were such dangerous people. In reality, we were dealing a gram here, a gram there, maybe $500 a week. We were dealing so we could snort without paying for it. We were also making a little money on the side. They tried to make us out as big and bad. Yeah, they were really out to arrest us.

**Q:** Did the authorities offer you any plea bargaining?

**A:** Yes, that's how I got the one-to-three years. They wanted my boyfriend and me to cooperate with the police. To go around and set up other dealers. . . . We went to a couple of bars in the area. Getting drugs around here is no problem when you are into it. So we met a couple our age [in a bar], they were turning us on [to cocaine]. But we couldn't rat on them, we couldn't turn them in. I suppose if we could have [ratted on them] we probably would have gotten off [avoided the sentence]. But if you have a reputation of being a rat, this causes a big problem in prison. So we kept lying to the cops, saying we couldn't find anyone [who deals cocaine]. Practically everyone else knew we had been arrested and they wouldn't deal with us. People were avoiding us. Eventually, the cops stopped pushing us to become rats.

**Q:** What is your feeling about the criminal justice system?

**A:** When I was in prison, I was in a program . . . which is a positive alternative type of program. The program offers an environment which gives the inmates training in human development. It helped make my prison experience more rewarding for me. If it had not been for this program, the whole experience would have been very negative. . . . This program encourages inmates to look at themselves, to discover the good stuff about themselves. A lot of people in prison seem to hate themselves. You can see this by the way they treat themselves. Prisons need more programs, more counseling to get inmates to like themselves. To want to get out, to work, to support their kids, make a contribution, realize that they have not done the right thing. Some inmates feel they have not done anything wrong, even though they have shot someone or robbed a little old lady. Through these programs, they learn to get more self-respect. These programs make you think about yourself, your crime and your life. . . .

**Q:** How do you feel about the past and the future?

**A:** I would never want to go back, but it did me good. It took me out of my environment long enough for me to look objectively at everything. What I had been doing and where I was going. It motivated me. I have to be a better . . . worker because of my record. If anything, it gave me motivation. It was a good experience for me, but I would never want to do it again or wish it on anyone. But I tried to make the best of it. I had to. I wouldn't be straight right now [if I hadn't served time in prison]. I would still be out smoking pot, drinking, doing drugs, and not looking for work. I just got a good job. I'm so glad it's all over.

**Q:** Do you feel that through your experience you have found a new you?

**A:** Right. I learned the hard way.

## QUESTIONS

Do you think that Sally's sentence was fair? Would she have served a longer sentence if she had been a racial minority? Did her arrest and incarceration deter her from continuing to sell cocaine? More generally, in the case of drug use and sales, is law enforcement an effective deterrent? Do you think that her reform is permanent? Did she really learn to go straight— in her words, "the hard way"? If so, how is her case different from that of the many other drug arrestees who continue to use and sell even after a jail or prison sentence? Do we learn something from this case about the wisdom of arresting and incarcerating drug sellers and users? Does Sally's success story verify that prohibition is the best policy? Or is Sally an exception to the rule?

# LEGALIZATION, DECRIMINALIZATION, AND HARM REDUCTION

As we've seen throughout this book, the dominant approach in the United States to the control of recreational psychoactive drug use is prohibition. In other words, it is against the law to possess and distribute nearly all substances for the purpose of getting high. Two drugs, alcohol and tobacco, are exceptions to this rule, and tobacco's effects, while recreational, may be described as an extremely "low-key" high (Goldstein, 2001, p. 121). Though the distribution of alcohol and tobacco is controlled by state law, they may be legally purchased by almost anyone above a certain age for any purpose. In addition, thousands of drugs—roughly a fifth of which are psychoactive—are available by a prescription from a physician specifically for medical and psychiatric purposes. However, if these drugs are taken without a prescription, for recreational purposes, their distribution and possession are illegal. Inasmuch as prescription use is not recreational use, these drugs don't count in our equation.

All psychoactive drugs aside from alcohol and tobacco are prohibited by state and federal law. Marijuana is a partial exception, as we've seen, since small-quantity possession has been decriminalized in a dozen states. (The voters of nine states approved medical marijuana initiatives, and the legislatures of two, Vermont and Hawaii, have enacted medical marijuana laws, but this does not count as recreational drug use.) Still, **partial decriminalization** does not mean that the substance is legal, since the police can confiscate the drug and the possessor may be fined. And drug courts and drug treatment, likewise, are "cracks" in the armor of the strict law enforcement model. Peyote is permitted in some states to American Indians for religious ceremonies—another exception to this rule. But the generalization that covers the control of psychoactive substances in the United States is this: The possession and distribution of psychoactive substances for the purpose of recreational use is a crime unless otherwise stipulated.

Critics by the thousands have attacked the current system of prohibition. They believe that criminalizing nearly all drug taking for pleasure has serious negative consequences for users and for the society as a whole. In this chapter, I discuss the proposals for drug legalization, decriminalization, and harm reduction. We'll consider such questions as these: Would a legal change away from our current system of "lock 'em up and throw away the key" be more effective? Is an emphasis on the punitive approach doing more harm than good? Many critics think so. The following sections summarize their reasoning.

## LEGALIZATION: AN INTRODUCTION

Beginning in the late 1980s (Kerr, 1988), critics of the current system began to advance with remarkable frequency and urgency a taboo, almost unthinkable proposal—the decriminalization or legalization of the currently illegal drugs. Since then, dozens of books, hundreds of magazine and newspaper articles, countless editorials and op-ed pieces, and scores of prominent spokespersons have urged the repeal of the drug laws. For a time, drug legalization became a major focus of debate, joining such controversial subjects as abortion, the environment, the economy, gun control, homosexual rights, women's rights, minority rights, and affirmative action as yet another battlefield of controversy. In the past half-dozen years or so, the legalization debate has died down, but the policy's advocates remain.

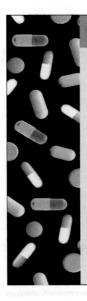

## True-False Quiz

"In public opinion polls, most Americans *oppose* the legalization of marijuana for recreational purposes." This is a true statement; roughly 75 percent of all Americans nationwide are opposed to marijuana legalization. (Marijuana as medicine is a different matter.) Opposition to the legalization of the hard drugs is even stronger—in the 90–95 percent range. Many opponents of drug legalization raise this point in support of their argument; if most Americans oppose drug legalization, legislatively, how can it possibly come about? Any politician who supports the proposal would be committing political suicide. Most of my students (58%) recognized that this statement is true. In 2002, two state initiatives on marijuana decriminalization, one in Arizona and the other in Nevada, were shot down by voters. (The votes in favor were surprisingly strong, however—43 and 39 percent, respectively.) Clearly, that fact poses serious problems for legalizers.

Some observers—Barry McCaffrey, former federal drug "czar" among them—argue that debating drug legalization is a waste of time, little more than cocktail party chatter, since the proposal has no chance of executive, legislative, or judicial approval. I believe, for a variety of reasons outlined in this chapter, that some form of legalization is a program worth discussing. It is true that drug legalization in the United States is a doomed enterprise. But some of its proponents' arguments have influenced less radical proposals elsewhere (Western Europe, for instance) and may do so in the United States in the future. And those opposed to outright drug legalization need to know what critics of the current system are saying to strengthen their own arguments.

It must be emphasized that **legalization** is not a single proposal. Instead, it is a cluster of proposals that stands toward one end of a spectrum of degrees of regulation and availability. Very few, if any, legalization advocates argue that there should be absolutely no controls on the possession and sale of psychoactive drugs—for instance, that minors be allowed to purchase heroin and cocaine from whoever is willing to sell to them. Instead, all agree that *some* sorts of controls are necessary. Hence, the relevant question is, At what point along the spectrum ranging from just shy of complete control to just shy of a complete lack of control makes the most sense? The spectrum is so broad, and the details so crucial, that in many ways the "great divide" between legalization and prohibition is artificial, almost irrelevant. Consequently, both the similarities and the differences between and among the various legalization programs, and those between and among legalization and prohibitionist programs, have to be considered.

To appreciate the import of proposals to legalize the possession and sale of the currently illicit drugs, it is crucial to spell out the reasons why legalizers think the current system of prohibition is fatally flawed and must be changed. According to the legalizers, what's wrong with our current system?

## WHY DO LEGALIZERS BELIEVE CRIMINALIZATION CAN'T WORK?

Proposing that the drug laws and their enforcement be changed implies that the current system of prohibition is ineffective, harmful, and/or unjust. The bulk of the legalizers' writings is devoted to criticizing the current punitive policy; only a very small proportion deal specifically with the particulars of a viable legalization program. Consequently, to fully understand the justifications for drug legalization, it is necessary to explain, in the view of the legalizers, *how* and *why* the current prohibitionist program is a failure. Behind the punitive reasoning of criminalization is the assumption that a drug war can and should be fought, and can be won, and that the principal weapons that must be used in this war are arrest, prosecution, and imprisonment. In other words, the drug warriors believe that drug abuse is primarily a law enforcement matter. In stark contrast, most if not all legalizers agree on one point: They oppose the current punitive system. They insist that drug abuse is not primarily a law enforcement matter. They believe that relying on arrest and incarceration is ineffective, counterproductive—more harmful than beneficial—and unjust. Legalizers oppose the very basis of drug prohibition by means of the law and law enforcement. (DRCNet, a legalization/drug reform organization, publishes an electronic newsletter, the *Drug War Chronicle*, available at www.stopthedrugwar.org.)

Why do the legalizers and decriminalizers believe that our current, mainly punitive approach to drug control doesn't work? In their view, what are some the flaws in attempting to solve the drug problem by criminalizing the sale and possession of drugs? Why don't drug prohibitions work, according to the legalizers? Occasionally, a journalist will argue that the legal ban on drugs actually *stimulates* the desire for the consumption of psychoactive substances (Raver-Lampman, 2003), but hardly anyone who has detailed, systematic knowledge of the impact of legal controls offers such a foolish argument.

Before these questions can be answered, we have to lay down specific criteria as to what constitutes "working" in the first place. No specific drug policy is likely to work best in all important ways. It is entirely possible that a given program may work well in one way but not in another. What do the legalizers mean when they say that the punitive policy toward drug abuse doesn't—and can't—work? In criticizing the current policies and urging drug legalization or decriminalization, they make ten main points.

First criminalization makes illegal drugs expensive, and hence profitable to sell. Because of the profit motive, arresting producers and sellers, and thereby putting them out of business, simply results in other producers and sellers stepping in to supply the shortfall. Therefore, drugs can never be stamped out through the criminal law: The demand for drugs is constant and inelastic; their criminalized status makes them expensive, and so highly profitable to sell. Therefore, it is inevitable that suppliers will remain in business. Ironically, it is criminalization itself that guarantees "business as usual."

Second, the legalizers say, the currently *illegal* drugs are less harmful than the prohibitionists say—less harmful than the currently *legal* drugs. Hence, drug criminalization is both aimed at the wrong target and discriminatory as well. If anything, stricter controls ought to be applied to cigarettes and alcohol—which kill many more people—and not the far safer but currently illegal drugs.

Third, the legalizers insist, prohibition is futile because criminalization does not deter use. Drug abuse is as high now, under a punitive policy, as it would be under a policy of legalization; legalization would not produce an increase in use, or at least not a significant increase. Everyone who wants to use is doing so already. Also, prohibition is a logistical impossibility; there are too many holes in the net of social control, and drugs will always leak through the net. Hence, the very foundation of prohibition is invalid. Moreover, since the demand for drugs is inelastic—users will pay any price, no matter how exorbitant—raising the price through legal harassment cannot work.

Fourth, the legalizers argue, prohibition encourages the distribution and therefore the use of harder, stronger, more dangerous drugs—and discourages the use of softer, weaker, safer drugs. This is the case because criminalization places a premium on selling drugs that are less bulky and easier to conceal, and that show a greater profit margin per operation. This has been referred to as the **Iron Law of Prohibition:** the more intense the law enforcement, the more potent the prohibited substance becomes (Thornton, 1992, p. 70). In contrast, under legalization, they suggest, less potent and less harmful drugs, such as cocaine leaves, cocaine gum, opium, mescaline, psilocybin, and marijuana, will be adopted rather than the more potent, more harmful, and artificial, illicit drugs now in use, such as LSD, crack, heroin, and methamphetamine (Goldstein, 1986).

Fifth, the legalizers say, drug dealers sell in a market in which there are no controls on the purity and potency of their product. Hence, users are always consuming contaminated— and dangerous—substances. In contrast, legalization would enforce strict controls on purity and potency; as a consequence, death by overdose would be virtually eliminated.

Sixth, the legalizers argue, undercutting the profit motive would force organized crime out of the drug trade. As a result, the stranglehold that criminal gangs and mobs have on the throat of the community would be released; residents would be able to reclaim their neighborhoods, and democracy would triumph.

Seventh, the legalizers assert, the current level of drug-related violence is solely a product of the illegality of the drug trade. Drug-related murders are the result of disputes over "turf," robberies of drug dealers, assaults to collect a supposed drug debt, punishment of drug workers, drug thefts, and dealers selling bad or bogus drugs (Goldstein et al., 1989). Eliminate criminalization and the profit motive will be eliminated, and so will drug gangs and the violence they inflict. The murder rate will decline, and neighborhoods and communities will be safer.

Eighth, the legalizers say, by placing such a huge priority on the drug war and encouraging the arrest of dealers, the government has opened the door to the violation of the civil liberties of citizens on a massive scale. False or mistaken arrests and rousts, the seizure of the property of innocent parties, corruption and brutality—these are all legacies of prohibition. Under legalization, such violations would not occur. The police would not be pressured to make questionable arrests, nor be tempted by bribes from dealers; consequently, they would be better able to serve the community (Ostrowski, 1990; Wisotsky, 1990a, 1990b, 1993).

Ninth, the legalizers urge, consider the enormous cost and the staggering tax burden of enforcing prohibition; billions of our tax dollars are being wasted in a futile, harmful endeavor. Currently, the federal government spends $20 billion a year fighting the drug war, and the states spend roughly the same amount. Under legalization, not only would this waste not occur, but the sale of drugs could be taxed, and revenues raised to treat drug abusers. In an era of fiscal austerity, surely the budgetary argument should weigh heavily. Legalization would represent using the tax dollar wisely.

And tenth, the legalizers argue, useful therapeutic drugs that are now banned by the government would be reclassified so as to take their rightful place in medicine. Marijuana, a

Schedule I drug, is useful in reducing the nausea and lack of appetite associated with chemotherapy. Heroin, also completely banned as a Schedule I substance, is an effective analgesic or painkiller. In addition, a Schedule I classification is the kiss of death for scientific experimentation. The book has been prematurely closed on drugs such as MDMA (Ecstasy) and LSD—both Schedule I substances, and both of which have enormous potential for unlocking the secrets of drug mechanisms and, possibly, valuable therapeutic application as well. Our society cannot afford to remain ignorant about drugs with such complex and potentially revealing effects as these (Beck and Rosenbaum, 1994, pp. 146ff; Grinspoon and Bakalar, 1993).

## FOUR PROPOSALS TO REFORM THE DRUG LAWS

The term drug "legalization" has been used to cover a multitude of proposals. Some do not entail real drug legalization at all, but rather offer substantial changes in the drug laws. Proponents of some legalization proposals wish to remove criminal penalties for all psychoactive substances. Others are selective, aiming to legalize some and retain penalties for others. Moreover, legalization is very different from decriminalization. And requiring addicted or drug-dependent individuals to obtain their supply via prescription is not the same thing as permitting drugs to be sold to anyone, without benefit of a prescription. More generally, legalization and prohibition do not represent an either-or proposition. In reality, they form a continuum or spectrum, from a completely libertarian or "hands-off" policy, with no laws governing the possession or sale of any drug at one end, to the most punitive policy imaginable—say, support for the death penalty for users and dealers of every stripe—at the other end, with every conceivable position in between.

In reality, very few commentators advocate a policy of no controls whatsoever on the possession and sale of any and all psychoactive drugs. Nor do many commentators call for the death penalty for the simple possession of the currently illegal drugs, including two joints of marijuana. Hence, what we are discussing in the drug legalization debate is degrees of difference along a spectrum somewhere in between these two extremes. As Ethan Nadelmann (1992, pp. 89–94) persuasively argues, the moderate legalizers and the progressive or reform-minded prohibitionists have more in common than the first group has with the extreme, radical, or hard-core legalizers, or the second has with the harsher, more punitive prohibitionists.

The issue, therefore, is not legalization versus prohibition. Rather, the debate centers around some of the following issues: How much legalization? Which drugs are to be legalized? Under what conditions can drugs be dispensed? Are drugs to be dispensed in approved, licensed clinics? To whom may drugs be dispensed? To addicts and drug abusers only? Or to anyone above a certain age? In what quantity may drugs be dispensed? At what purity? At what price are the legalized drugs to be sold? (For these and other questions that legalizers must answer, see Inciardi and McBride, 1991, pp. 47–49; McBride, Terry, and Inciardi, 1999.)

Each drug policy proposal will answer these questions in a somewhat different way. There are many drug reform proposals, not just one. There are even many different drug legalization proposals. It is naive and fallacious to assume that the broad outlines of drug policy are the only thing that is important, that the details will take care of themselves (Trebach, 1993). Frank Zimring and Gordon Hawkins (1992, pp. 109–110) refer to this view as the "trickle-down fallacy." On both sides of the controversy, observers too often "simply ignore the detailed

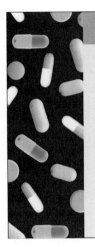

## True-False Quiz

Are the drugs that are illegal in the United States legal elsewhere? I asked my students if the following statement was true: "All the drugs that are illegal in the United States (including cocaine, Ecstasy, and heroin) are *completely legal* in Holland (the Netherlands); there, they can be purchased over the counter or in drug 'bars,' much the way aspirin and alcohol can here." Considerably less than half the students in my course (42%) agreed with this statement, which is false, of course. It is true that marijuana (or cannabis) can be purchased in this way, but other (or "hard") drugs cannot. It is not a plausible statement, and the fact that more than 4 out of 10 of my respondents said that they thought it to be true is revealing.

questions . . . of priority and strategy" (p. 109). A specific policy—what should be done about each and every particular—"cannot be deduced" from a general position (p. 110). At the same time, some points are shared by all legalizers and some points shared by all prohibitionists.

Let's distinguish four drug policy reforms: legalization, decriminalization, the medical or prescription model, and harm reduction.

## Legalization

One common legalization proposal involves placing one or more of the currently illegal and/or prescription drugs under the controls that now apply to alcohol and/or tobacco. (But which is it—alcohol or tobacco? Alcohol is considerably more tightly controlled than tobacco, and controls that apply to alcohol do not apply to tobacco.) Under this proposal, psychoactive drugs could be purchased on the open market, off the shelf, by anyone above a certain age. Since the same controls as on alcohol and tobacco would apply to the currently illicit drugs, a proprietor would not be able to sell to a minor or an intoxicated individual, or to an inmate of a jail or prison or a mental institution, or to sell within a certain distance from a house of worship, a school, or a polling place on election day. Controls would also apply to the establishments that sell the drugs in question. With respect to alcohol, certain types of bars, for instance, must also serve food. Package stores must observe a variety of rules and regulations; some, for instance, are run by (that is, bottled alcoholic products can only be sold by) the government. Even those that are private enterprises are controlled: They cannot be owned and operated by a convicted felon; they cannot be open on Sunday; they cannot sell substances above a certain potency; and so on. Thus, legalization refers to a state licensing system more or less similar to that which prevails for alcohol (again, or tobacco) for the currently illegal drugs. It is difficult to imagine taking seriously a legalization scheme proposing that we control cocaine, heroin, and methamphetamine *less tightly* than we now legally control alcohol (or, even more extremely, tobacco products).

One qualification: Under current policy, manufacturing alcohol (beer and wine, for instance) or growing tobacco for the purpose of *private* consumption—not commercial sale—does not come under state control and is perfectly legal. The state retains the right to step in only when selling (or the presumed intention to sell) takes place. This qualification does not apply to illicit drugs, of course; private production of Schedule I drugs remains illegal. In addition, under legalization, public use is controlled under a variety of circumstances—for instance, driving while intoxicated and public intoxication are illegal. And lastly, for both alcohol and cigarettes, there are restrictions on advertising: Cigarette ads and ads for hard liquor are (voluntarily) banned from television advertising, current athletes are not depicted endorsing alcoholic beverages, and beer is not drunk on camera. Presumably, the drugs that are to be legalized will be controlled, voluntarily or by law, more or less the same way as with alcohol and tobacco—that is, they will be *regulated* but not banned.

In the Netherlands, by law, small-quantity marijuana possession is technically illegal. However, in practice, the drug is sold openly in coffee shops (or "hash bars"), and these transactions are ignored by the police. No advertising of marijuana products is permitted, and sale to minors under 18—even the presence of minors in an establishment—and the sale of hard drugs will cause the police to shut a shop down. Thus, small-quantity marijuana possession and sale have been legalized **de facto,** although **de jure,** or according to the law, they are still technically illegal. The hard drugs are unaffected by this policy; the sale of heroin and cocaine, especially in high volume, remains very much illegal. In the Netherlands, the proportion of prisoners who are convicted drug offenders is the same as in the United States, roughly one-third (Beers, 1991, p. 40). At the same time, possession by the addict or user of small quantities of heroin or cocaine (half a gram or less) tends to be ignored by the police. However, the sale of even small quantities of hard drugs is not permitted to take place openly in legal commercial establishments, as it is with marijuana (Jansen, 1991; Leuw and Marshall, 1994). The Dutch policy toward marijuana represents a variation on legalization.

## Decriminalization

**Decriminalization** refers to the removal of state control over a substance or activity. (Many observers use the term "decriminalization" to refer to what I call "partial decriminalization." **Full decriminalization** is the removal of all—or nearly all—state controls over a given product or activity.) It is a legal hands-off or laissez-faire policy of drug control—that is, no control at all. Under decriminalization, the state no longer has a role in setting rules and regulations concerning the sale, purchase, distribution, and possession of a given drug. Here, the distribution of marijuana, heroin, or cocaine, would no more be the concern of the government than, say, the sale of tomatoes or T-shirts. Of course, no one may sell poisonous tomatoes or dangerously flammable T-shirts. But under a policy of full decriminalization, the rules and regulations that apply to drugs would be even less restrictive than those that now apply to the currently legal drugs alcohol and tobacco.

Under full decriminalization, anyone could manufacture or grow any quantity of any drug and sell it to anybody without restriction. The only factor that might determine the sale of drugs, blatant poisons aside, would be the operation of a free and open economic market (Szasz, 1992). Of course, almost everyone proposing this policy is likely to add one obvious restriction—that sale to a minor be against the law. As noted previously, however, full decriminalization for every currently illegal drug (with the remote possible exception of marijuana) is not a feasible or realistic policy, and so is of theoretical interest only. To expect that legislatures will permit the possession, sale, and distribution of substances that have a powerful effect on the mind and great potential for harm be subject, with government controls no stricter than those that apply to the possession, sale, and distribution of tomatoes, simply beggars the imagination. It is a pie-in-the-sky proposal that has no hope of implementation, at least for the foreseeable future.

There is one partial exception to this rule: Some commentators argue strenuously—and in some quarters, persuasively—that users be permitted to grow certain natural psychoactive plants, such as the opium poppy, the coca bush, the peyote cactus, psychedelic mushrooms, and, of course, the marijuana or cannabis plant, for their own private consumption (Karel, 1991). Thus, one aspect of full decriminalization remains a viable subject of debate, while most of the other particulars do not.

Again, the term "decriminalization" is often used to refer to what is actually partial decriminalization. As also noted previously, in 12 states, someone in possession of a small quantity of marijuana cannot be arrested or imprisoned. Small-quantity marijuana possession is a "violation": The police may confiscate the drug and issue a summons, much like a traffic ticket, which usually entails paying a small fine. Hence, partial decriminalization does not remove any and all legal restrictions on the possession, sale, and/or distribution of a given substance, but it does remove some of them. This is not what advocates of decriminalization mean by the term, although the two terms are often—loosely and inaccurately—equated.

## Prescription and Maintenance Models

The prescription and the maintenance models overlap heavily, although they are conceptually distinct. Both are usually referred to as the **medical approach** to drug abuse, since both see certain conditions as a medical matter and the administration of psychoactive substances as their solution. Currently in the United States, the **prescription model** prevails for pharmaceuticals deemed to have "legitimate" medical utility; hence, certain approved psychoactive substances may be prescribed by physicians for the treatment of their patients' ailments.

Under an expanded prescription or maintenance policy, loosely referred to as legalization, anyone dependent on a given drug would be able to go to a physician or a clinic and, after a medical examination, be duly certified or registered. Certification would enable the drug-dependent person to obtain prescriptions at regular intervals, which, in turn, would make it possible to purchase or obtain the drug in question. Or the drug could be administered directly by a clinic or a physician. Some current prescription models call for an eventual withdrawal of the client or patient from the drug, but they insist that this be done gradually, since that would be both humane and effective. Under the current prescription policy, pharmaceutical companies must test drugs and then submit reports to the **Food and Drug Administration (FDA)** to the effect that they are safe and effective for the ailments for which they would be prescribed. The FDA cannot approve a drug that, tests indicate, is either unsafe or ineffective. Presumably, if the currently illegal drugs are to be prescribed to addicts, they must pass muster as safe and effective medicines. Heroin, cocaine, and methamphetamine are far from safe, and it is difficult to imagine for which ailments they might be effective.

One version of the prescription model is referred to as the **maintenance model** because the addict or drug-dependent person is "maintained" on doses of the drug in question. Currently, in the United States, some form of maintenance is in effect for roughly 175,000 heroin addicts, most of whom are administered methadone. However, methadone maintenance programs are fairly tightly controlled in most jurisdictions, and most addicts nationwide are not enrolled in them, either because they do not wish to be—for instance, because the restrictions are too severe and the quantities administered are too small—or because the clinics do not have room for all who wish to enroll. To set up a full walk-in program for any and all heroin addicts who want to take part in methadone maintenance therapy would require a *quadrupling* of the current operating budget of this treatment modality, and such a program would be extremely controversial. (Currently, legislative critics and supporters of methadone maintenance are in a cease-fire mode: Critics don't try to slash the budget of maintenance programs if supporters don't try to expand them.) In addition, there is no heroin maintenance program in place in the United States, and none for persons dependent on a drug other than a narcotic. Such a program is in effect in Great Britain (in Liverpool) and in Switzerland.

Presumably, a legalizative proposal that relies heavily on the medical model would aim to expand the number of addicts currently on methadone; expand the number of possible narcotics used for maintenance programs, including heroin; and possibly even expand maintenance programs to include non-narcotic drugs, such as cocaine. Again, regardless of the particulars, proponents of drug maintenance programs see drug abuse as a medical, not a criminal, matter, and seek to legalize the administration of psychoactive substances to addicts or abusers. It is not clear what might be done when drug abusers refuse to participate in the program, demand to use other drugs in addition to the legal drugs they are being administered, or insist or a significant escalation in the dose they are administered. Or what might be done when someone who is not chemically or psychologically dependent demands quantities of a given drug from the program, or when someone violates the terms of the program by obtaining illicit supplies of the drug. Proponents sees the primary motivation of drug abusers as maintenance, not recreation, an assumption that many observers view as naive.

## Harm Reduction

**Harm reduction** represents an eclectic or mixed bag of policy proposals. It is a **specifist drug policy:** different programs for different drugs. Harm reduction is the explicit policy that prevails in the Netherlands, Switzerland, and certain jurisdictions in the United Kingdom, such as Liverpool. Its goal is stated in its title: Rather than attempting to wipe out drug distribution, addiction, and use—an impossibility, in any case—its goal is drug policy that minimizes harm. Legal reform, likewise, is secondary; the emphasis is on *practicality*—what works in practice rather than what looks good on paper or in theory. A needle exchange and distribution program stands high on the list of particulars of any harm reduction advocate: Addicts can turn in used needles at distribution centers and receive clean, fresh ones free of charge. This is designed to keep the rate of new AIDS/HIV infections in check. Another particular of the harm reduction advocates relates directly to law enforcement: Make a sharp distinction between "soft" and "hard" drugs, and between users and small-time, low-level sellers on the one hand and high-level, high-volume dealers on the other. In practice, this means de facto decriminalization of small-quantity marijuana possession and the routing of addicts into treatment programs without arresting them. Big-time heroin and cocaine dealers, however, are arrested and imprisoned.

In short, harm reduction entails the following:

- Stressing treatment and rehabilitation; underplaying the punitive, penal, or police approach; and exploring nonpenal alternatives for trivial drug offenses
- Expanding drug maintenance, especially methadone, programs; experimenting with or studying the feasibility of heroin maintenance programs; expanding drug education programs; and permitting heroin and marijuana to be used by prescription for medical treatment
- Considering ways of controlling the legal drugs alcohol and tobacco; being flexible and pragmatic: thinking about new programs that might reduce harm from drug abuse, and if one aspect of the program fails, scuttling it and trying something else

Remember: Drugs are not the enemy—harm to the society and its constituent members is the enemy; whatever reduces harm by whatever means necessary is all to the good (Beers, 1991).

No one who supports a harm reduction proposal questions the fact that there would be substantial theoretical and practical difficulties in implementing such a policy. For instance, how do we measure or weigh one harm against another? What if our policy results in fewer deaths but more addicts? Or in less crime but more drug use? If we are truly worried about harm from drug abuse, why concentrate on legalizing or decriminalizing the illegal drugs? Why not focus on ways of reducing the use of, and therefore the harm from, the *legal* drugs? What if our policy improves conditions for one group or category in the population but harms another? And will harm reduction really result in less state control of the drug addict, abuser, and user? Government regulations and programs designed to reduce drug-related harm are likely to result in far *more* state intervention into the lives of persons affected by them. (For a cynical, mechanistic, and ill-conceived critique of harm reduction programs from a radical or left-wing perspective, see Mugford, 1993.) None of the program's advocates suggest that it is a problem-free panacea or cure-all, but all believe that these and other criticisms are not fatal, and that its problems can be resolved with the application of reliable information and common sense.

## WILL DRUG USE/ABUSE RISE UNDER LEGALIZATION?

In the legalization debate, perhaps the key issue is whether drug use and abuse—and hence, medical complications and death—would rise under legalization. Does the current system of prohibition keep drug abuse to tolerable levels? Would legalization open the floodgates to a greater volume of use, and hence immensely greater drug-related social, economic, and health problems?

As we've seen, there is at least one way in which criminalization is a failure. Attacking the supply or manufacture and distribution side of the drug use equation is extremely unlikely to work. Clearly, the profit motive is too great for many people, even with a small measure of risk involved. But what about the demand or user side of the equation? The motives for selling and use, although intertwined, are at least analytically distinct. Can law enforcement deter use?

More generally, does the law and its enforcement deter *any* activity? If there were no laws and no enforcement, would currently illegal activities become more common? Conversely, if a product or service were criminalized, would the demand for it remain constant? Would just as many customers be willing to pay for it regardless of whether it was legal or illegal? Just how inelastic is the demand for certain products and services? The legalizers are insistent that "prohibition doesn't work"—indeed, *can't* work (Hyse, 1994; Morgan, 1991). Is this true for all products and services, under all circumstances? More specifically, is it true for the currently illegal drugs?

As we've already seen, there are two entirely different arguments underpinning prohibiting or outlawing an activity, and many observers confuse the two. They are the hard or strict, and the soft or moderate, versions of the **punitive model.** The strict punitive version makes use of the logic of absolute deterrence, while the moderate punitive version makes use of the logic of relative deterrence. According to the hard or strict punitive argument, a given activity can be reduced or eliminated by law enforcement; that is, crime is deterred or discouraged in some absolute or abstract sense by law enforcement. In contrast, the soft or moderate punitive position does not see a defeat of or even a drastic reduction in drug use or abuse as feasible. According to this argument, in the absence of law enforcement, a given activity would be much more common than it is with law enforcement. It relies on the logic of relative deterrence because it asserts that with law enforcement—as compared with no law enforcement—certain kinds of crime take place less often. If there were no laws or penalties against robbing or assaulting others, more people would engage in such behavior. (Not most people—*more* people.) Law enforcement does not reduce the incidence of these acts so much as contain them. It's the same thing with drug use: Punishing the drug violator is not, and under most circumstances cannot be, a means of drastically reducing or eliminating drug use. But if there were no drug laws, and no penalties for the production, importation, possession, and sale of the presently illegal substances, use would be considerably higher than it is now.

## Does Criminalization Ever Lower Demand?

I suspect that criminalization actually does lower the demand—as well as the supply—of certain products and services. To put the matter another way, legalization would result in an increase in the incidence of many activities. As a general rule, the more elastic, substitutable, and sensitive to price is the demand for a given product or service, the more effective criminalization is in discouraging its satisfaction; the less elastic, substitutable, and insensitive to price that demand is, the less effective criminalization is (Wisotsky, 1990b, p. 8).

Outlawing leaded gasoline, for instance, has not produced a huge illegal market for it—customers willing to pay many times its previous, legal price, and manufacturers willing to supply it, thereby risking arrest. For practically all motorists, an adequate substitute exists in unleaded gas; hardly any customers are willing to pay huge price increases for marginally superior performance. The sale of automobiles in the United States is restricted to those that meet certain standards, for instance, with respect to emission controls. Has that resulted in a huge underground market for cars that do not meet these standards? No; in this case, the prohibition of nonstandard cars works, more or less.

The number of times customers visit prostitutes, and hence the number of prostitutes, is almost certainly smaller, all other things being equal, where prostitution is illegal than

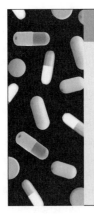

### True-False Quiz

In this section, I distinguish between absolute and relative deterrence—a distinction captured in this statement: "The fact that law enforcement has not been able to stamp out drug abuse shows us that in *all* ways, the drug laws have been a failure." The relative deterrence argument rejects the validity of this statement, as I do, and as most drug researchers and policy analysts do as well. Not many of my students were taken in by this statement; in fact, over three-quarters (77%) said that they thought the statement is false. Clearly, my students have a more sophisticated grasp on the relevant issues than many proponents of drug legalization.

where it is legal. Can anyone seriously doubt that a substantial proportion of men would visit prostitutes more frequently if the public sale of sex were completely legalized? Prostitution is a major business in Nevada, where it is legal; elsewhere in the country, studies show, sex with prostitutes is only a minor sexual outlet for men (Michael et al., 1994, p. 63). For many men, where it is illegal, sex with a prostitute affords a sordid, even risky sexual option, as the "Johns" who have been arrested in street sweeps have discovered. Risks come not only in the form of arrest (an extremely low likelihood, although with sporadic police campaigns it happens) but also in the form of criminal victimization from the prostitute and her colleagues and from denizens of the environs in which prostitution is likely to take place, and, for some, the social stigma in the event of discovery following arrest. Hence, the prohibition of prostitution must be counted as at least a partial success.

### National Alcohol Prohibition (1920–1933)

Some legalizers argue that no ban or prohibition on an activity or substance that is desired by a sizable number of citizens can ever be successful. The legalizers may be referred to as "anti-prohibitionists." Most adopt a broad, sweeping view of the failure of prohibitions in general. And their guiding model for this position is national alcohol prohibition (1920–1933). The Eighteenth Amendment, also referred to as the Volstead Act, is the only constitutional amendment to have been repealed in U.S. history.

Everyone knows that Prohibition was a catastrophic failure—very possibly the biggest domestic legal mistake in the federal government's history. We've all heard about the history of Prohibition—including Al Capone, organized crime, gangland violence, bootleg liquor, bathtub gin, speakeasies and illegal nightclubs. Since Prohibition was such a disastrous failure, it follows as night follows day that our current policy of drug prohibition will also fail. "Prohibition can't work, won't work, and has never worked" (Carter, 1989). True or false?

Keep in mind that policies may work well in one way but badly in another. Prohibition is an excellent example of this principle. Interestingly, as we've discovered, national alcohol prohibition did work in at least one sense: It reduced the level of alcohol consumption in the American population. Historians, medical authorities, and policy analysts have put together indicators from a variety of sources—arrests, automobile fatalities, hospital admissions, medical examiners' reports, as well as legal sales before and after Prohibition—and concluded that the consumption of alcohol declined significantly between 1920, when the Eighteenth Amendment took effect, and 1933, when it was repealed. The conclusion is inescapable: In the narrow sense of reducing alcohol consumption, Prohibition did work. Far from being a failure, in this one respect, it was a resounding success.

But again, in most other important respects, Prohibition was a disaster; in this sense, the anti-prohibitionists are correct. It may have switched millions of drinkers from beer, a less potent beverage, to distilled spirits, a far more potent and more harmful beverage; it encouraged the sale and consumption of harmful, poisonous substitutes, such as methyl alcohol; it certainly gave organized crime an immense boost, pouring billions of dollars into the hands of criminal gangs, consolidating their power, and effectively capitalizing their other illegal enterprises; it encouraged corruption and brutality on the part of politicians and the police on a massive scale; and the homicide rate rose during the 1920s and fell after 1933. In these crucial respects, Prohibition did not work; indeed, it was clearly a colossal failure. It was also a failure from the point of view of absolute deterrence: Many Americans still managed to get their hands on illegal alcoholic beverages.

The lesson from Prohibition should not be that drug prohibitions cannot work; it should be that, in instituting a drug policy, impacts come in packages. Some of the contents in a given package may be desirable, whereas others may be distinctly undesirable. Another package will contain a different mix, with entirely different positives and negatives. Which package one selects depends on values, not science—that is, it depends on a preference for certain results over others. There is no policy that will yield results that everyone—or anyone—will regard as entirely or uniformly positive. As the saying goes, you pay your money and you take your chances.

## Legalization and Use: Two Issues

The question of the impact of legalization on the incidence and frequency of use pivots on two separate questions, one empirical and the second moral and ideological. The empirical question is familiar to us all and can be stated simply: What evidence do we have on the impact of legalization on use? The moral question is a bit harder to spell out, but need not detain us here, since it is essentially unanswerable: If legalization does result in an increase in use, how many more users and abusers represent an acceptable increase, given the benefits that this change will bring about? Richard Dennis (1990, pp. 128–129) estimates that legalization will result in a 25 percent increase in the number of abusers and addicts. Even if the figure were to double, he finds this acceptable, considering that legalization will unburden us from criminalization's enormous monetary and human costs. I suspect that even if we were all to agree with Dennis's numerical prediction, not all of us would accept his conclusion. Again, the moral issue has to be disentangled from the empirical one. Empirically, what is likely to happen under legalization? Will the use of the presently illegal drugs rise or remain at about the same level?

## Worst-Case Scenario

One critic of the drug laws, mocking opponents of the legalization argument, claims that supporters of the current laws argue that legalization will mean that "countries will plunge into anarchy, families will disintegrate, and most of us will become drugged zombies"

(Mitchell, 1990, p. 2). Some supporters of the drug laws actually do believe in this **worst-case scenario.** Former drug czar William Bennett estimates that under legalization—a plan he vigorously opposes—some 40–50 million Americans would become hard-core heroin and cocaine abusers. William Pollin, former director of the National Institute of Drug Abuse (NIDA), argues that cocaine is the most pleasurable (or reinforcing) drug in current use. Therefore, it makes sense that if there were no law enforcement, "the number of cocaine users would be right up there with smokers and drinkers. . . . We'd have 60 to 100 million cocaine users instead of the 6 to 10 million current users we now have. . . . Viewed in this light," Pollin adds, our punitive law enforcement policy "is 90 percent effective" (Brinkley, 1984, p. A12). Would we become a nation of "drugged zombies" under legalization?

In reality, it is highly unlikely that the use or abuse of cocaine or heroin would increase ten times if any of the currently debated legalization plans were put in place. In other words, Bennett's 40–50 million addict estimate for heroin and cocaine and Pollin's 60–100 million regular cocaine user estimate are seriously wide of the mark. Regardless of how alluring, seductive, or reinforcing these drugs are, the tens of millions of Americans Bennett and Pollin project would become involved in the use of these seriously mind-transforming drugs for the pleasure they afford—and risk destroying everything they now value, including job and career, marriage and family, money, possessions, and their freedom—simply do not exist. At the same time, if one or another legalizative proposal were to be instituted, the number of Americans who would take, and become seriously involved with, the currently illegal drugs, including heroin and cocaine, would increase more than modestly, even dramatically, along the lines of two to three times. In other words, there would be a significant increase, but the worst-case scenario would not come to pass. My estimate contradicts both the legalizers, who argue that there would be no, or an extremely modest, increase, and the criminalizers, who argue that the increase would be monstrous, almost uncontrollable. Here, I am a firm believer in relative deterrence: Yes, use is lower than would be the case without law enforcement, but no law enforcement would not and could not eliminate or drastically reduce use. Perhaps some justification of my estimate is in order.

## Factors in the Legalization–Use/Abuse Equation

Three different sets of evidence can be used to address the question of the impact of legalization on frequencies of use. The first is related to what we know about human nature generally. The second is related to the intrinsic nature of each drug—how it is used, and what its effects are. And the third involves what is known about actual or concrete frequencies of use under more, and less, restrictive conditions. In addition, important considerations include the so-called hassle factor, cost, and continuance rates.

### Human Nature

All predictions of what is likely to happen under certain conditions are based on assumptions about human nature—a theory of behavior, if you will. Legalizers and prohibitionists hold contrasting assumptions about human nature. Let's look at each one.

Legalizers see human nature as basically rational, sane, temperate, and wise. "Inform a normally intelligent group of people about the tangible hazards of using a particular substance and the vast majority of them will simply stop" (Gazzaniga, 1990, p. 39). That is, the reason why drug abuse would not rise sharply under legalization is that most people are cautious and not willing to take risks; since the use of the currently illegal drugs entails a certain likelihood of harm, their use is extremely unlikely to be taken up by many people who are not already using. In contrast, one of the reasons that prohibitionists cite in support of their argument is their assumption—as we saw with Bennett's and Pollin's predictions—that many people are not nearly so rational and moderate in their behavior as the legalizers believe. Many Americans would experiment with and use heroin and cocaine, the prohibitionists believe; of this total, a substantial proportion would become compulsively involved with them to the point of abuse and addiction. The reason this would happen, prohibitionists believe, is that many of us are willing to take dangerous risks; a substantial number of us believe that bad things happen only to other people, that we somehow are lucky enough to do risky things, yet not get hurt. A lot more people are reckless risk takers than the legalizers think, the prohibitionists argue; in fact, they say, this is precisely why we have criminal laws outlawing certain activities: By introducing the risk of arrest, the *slightly* foolhardy will be dissuaded from engaging in them, while only a fairly small number of *very* foolhardy souls will be willing to do so.

In my view, the argument between the criminalizers and the legalizers is misplaced. To put it another way, both sides are partly right—and partly wrong. And while most Americans are not risk takers, this is irrelevant. The crucial issue is not the orientation of *most* Americans, but the orientation of a minority. There are enough hedonistic risk takers in this society who, under the right social and legal conditions, would be inclined to experiment with drugs and seriously disrupt the lives of the rest of us. In spite of the practical, hard-working, sober veneer of most Americans, many of us are less sober, traditional, and orderly than we are willing to admit. Deep down, many of us want to drive fast cars, get intoxicated on psychoactive drugs, engage in a variety of sexual adventures, neglect our workaday and family obligations, eat fattening foods without restraint, dance until dawn, and commit a wide range of criminal acts, but we are afraid of the consequences—social, monetary, and, for some of these actions, legal. The removal of legal penalties outlawing one of them—obtaining and getting intoxicated on drugs—would make it more attractive to a substantial number of Americans. My contention is that the threat of arrest and imprisonment is one of the mechanisms that keeps the wilder side of the moderate risk takers in check, while the small minority of extreme risk takers remain undeterred by any manner of risk, legal or otherwise.

But here's an extremely important point: The legalizers are correct in assuming that most of us are not true risk takers. Under legalization, most Americans would not experiment with heroin or cocaine, and of those who did, most would not become unwisely and abusively involved with them. There is practically no chance that, with decriminalization, heroin or cocaine would ever become as popular as cigarettes or alcohol. The vast majority of Americans would shun the recreational use of the currently illegal drugs, and the vast majority of those who used them would be temperate and moderate in their use. Comments one critic of the current policy: "While certain drugs can produce physical dependence, most individuals *will not willingly take* those drugs, even after experiencing their effects" (Gonzales, 1985, p. 105). Still, this is irrelevant. What is important is that more people would use drugs under legalization than is true today, and more would use compulsively and abusively.

Most people do not want to harm themselves. The evidence shows that, however inaccurately, people do calculate costs and benefits before engaging in certain actions. (Indeed, this is one of the reasons behind enacting and enforcing criminal laws.) But risk is not the same thing as harm; risk entails taking chances—it is not a guarantee of being harmed.

In states without helmet laws, a certain proportion of motorcyclists refuse to wear helmets. For most of them who take that risk, not wearing helmets will make no difference to their life or limbs, because most will not get into a serious accident. The same applies to motorists who refuse to wear a seat belt; for most of them, not wearing a seat belt is not harmful. Harm enters into the picture not in each and every case but in the overall picture. Injury and fatality statistics are very clear about this: You are more likely to be seriously injured and die if you do not wear a helmet or a seat belt. *Some* (not all, not even most) motorcyclists are harmed because they didn't wear a helmet; *some* motorists are harmed because they didn't wear a seat belt. The law convinces a substantial proportion of motorcyclists and motorists to wear protective devices; even more persuasive than a law by itself is a law with real penalties and vigorous enforcement.

Again, it is simply irrelevant to argue that most "normally intelligent people" will give up an activity or substance if they are aware of the "tangible hazards" associated with them (Gazzaniga, 1990, p. 39). The fact is, the risk an activity entails is not always clear-cut, obvious, or immediately apparent. Indeed, the danger in question may never manifest itself because, once again, risk is a statistical, not an absolute, affair. Most people are not harmed at all by a great many very risky activities. The two crucial issues are (1) the absolute number who are harmed, not the proportion, and (2) the number who are persuaded not to take a given physical risk because of an entirely separate risk—the likelihood of arrest. If that second risk were removed, a substantial number of people would engage in harmful, abusive drug taking. (Why do the legalizers emphasize the dissuasive power of physical risk but ignore the power of the threat of arrest and imprisonment?) Not a majority, not even remotely close to Bennett and Pollin's tens of millions of Americans, but a substantial number would do so. Seeing the American population as far more risk taking than the legalizers do leads me to conclude that legalization would result in a significant rise in drug use and abuse.

### Drug Use and Effects

A second piece of evidence relevant to the question of the impact of legalization on drug use bears on the effects of the drugs under consideration and the ways they are used. Although all drugs are by definition psychoactive, not all drugs are used in the same way; while all recreational drugs are used for their pleasurable effects, the way that pleasure is experienced and integrated into the lives of users is far from identical for all drugs. Although all the psychoactive drugs possess a potential to generate a dependence in users, that potential varies enormously from drug to drug. And although all the drugs that are taken recreationally are potentially harmful, the ratio of harm to pleasure varies from one drug to the next.

The mechanics, logistics, and effects of each drug influence the degree to which it can be woven into everyday activities. The effects of cigarettes, as they are currently used, are mildly stimulating. Most users can continue to puff cigarettes more or less throughout the day without disruption—while working, studying, interacting, talking, driving a car, walking about, and so on (Kaplan, 1988, p. 41). Only (as it turns out, a growing) social disapproval cuts smokers off from nonsmokers; in other words, the intrinsic nature of the use of the drug and its effects do not preclude their integration into routine living. Although alcohol is not quite so readily integrated into everyday life, in moderation, it is compatible with a wide range of pleasurable activities. For instance, it tastes good to most of us, it goes well with food, and it is typically a lubricator of sociability; it does not usually isolate most drinkers from most nondrinkers except at the point of heavy consumption. Unlike with many drugs, the effects of alcohol are linear: The user does not have to be intoxicated to enjoy its effects. A person can enjoy mild effects of alcohol, whereas for some drugs (heroin, for instance), achieving only subeuphoric effects are more likely to be experienced as frustrating than enjoyable. Most of the currently illegal drugs are taken specifically to get *high;* the user must attain at least a minimal desired threshold of pleasure to make taking them worthwhile.

As a hypothesis, we can state that the more readily a given form of drug use can be adapted to everyday life, other things being equal, the more popular it is likely to be. Contrarily, the more disruptive its use is, the less potential it has for widespread popularity. In contrast to cigarettes and, to a lesser extent, alcohol and, to an even lesser extent, marijuana, drugs such as heroin, crack cocaine, and especially psychedelics like LSD are *highly* disruptive; their effects jolt the users out of routine activities and away from sociability with others, particularly nonusers. Using these drugs requires a much greater commitment to use and a much greater willingness to suspend whatever else one may wish to do, at least for a time. We can place marijuana and powder cocaine midway along a continuum between cigarettes at one end and heroin, crack, and LSD at the other. Smoking marijuana and snorting powder cocaine are only moderately disruptive, and are usually confined to periods when the focus is on getting high and enjoying oneself and socializing with other users who are also high. Again, few users seek a mildly pleasurable sensation comparable to a cigarette or two or half a glass of wine; most wish to become high or intoxicated. Hence, the use of these drugs will create an interactional barrier between users and nonusers—and often among users themselves. Thus, with respect to the connection between the way these drugs are used and their effects, tobacco is least disruptive to everyday life and requires the least commitment to use, while a truly effective dose of heroin, crack cocaine, and LSD stand at the opposite end of the continuum: They are highly disruptive and require a great deal of commitment to use regularly and frequently. Hence, legalizers predict, under legalization, heroin, cocaine (especially crack), and LSD and the other psychedelics could never attain the popularity of the currently legal drugs. Given the basic fact of the socially disruptive nature of heroin, crack cocaine, and LSD, it is almost inconceivable that they would be taken up on an abusive scale by more than a small fraction of users, even if they were to be legalized. Their use would remain marginalized and indulged in by a very small minority (Nadelman, 1989, p. 945).

On the other hand, there is the issue of how reinforcing the drugs in question are, a factor that Bennett and Pollin stress in their predictions of use patterns after legalization. We reviewed some of the research on this issue in Chapter 2. With respect to drugs, **reinforcement** refers, roughly, to how enjoyable a substance is, to its capacity to deliver an orgasmlike jolt or "rush" of unmodified, undiluted, unsocialized pleasure. Reinforcement refers to the reward an organism achieves upon taking the drug and the commitment it has to continue taking it. To put the matter in more formal terms, the more reinforcing a drug, the harder an organism will work to continue taking it. The reinforcing potential of drugs can be determined even among nonhumans; rats, mice, and monkeys find cocaine (and, to a lesser degree, heroin and amphetamines) immensely pleasurable; they will press a bar hundreds of times in order to receive a single dose of the drug. In a laboratory setting, they will take it as much as they can and will even risk their lives to do so. They will take cocaine in preference to food and water, and will even kill themselves self-administering cocaine. Moreover, if they have taken cocaine over a period of time, and the drug is suddenly discontinued, they will continue doing whatever they did previously that rewarded them with doses of cocaine, even as it now goes unrewarded, for a longer time than for any other drug, including heroin (Bozarth and Wise, 1985; Clouet, Asghar, and Brown, 1988; Eckholm, 1986; Johanson, 1984). Psychologists regard whatever produces such slow-to-extinguish, previously rewarded behavior as extremely reinforcing. In this respect, then, cocaine stands at the top of the list of widely used psychoactive drugs. Most pharmacologists and psychologists now argue that psychological reinforcement is the key to dependence, not addiction or physical dependence. Drugs that are highly pleasurable in a direct, immediate, sensual way are most likely to produce addictlike behavior in users, whether or not these drugs produce a literal, physical addiction (Ksir, Hart, and Ray, 2006, pp. 36–39). In this respect, then, among all widely used psychoactive drugs, cocaine possesses the greatest potential for producing dependence.

At the same time, we must be skeptical of any automatic extrapolations from laboratory experiments, whether on humans or animals, to real life. William Wilbanks (1992) warns us against the **monkey model of addiction**—the fallacy of thinking that what monkeys in cages do with drugs automatically tells us everything we need to know about what humans will do on the street. After all, animals do not like the effects of alcohol or tobacco; it is difficult to induce them to take these drugs, use them regularly, or become dependent on them. Yet we know that alcohol and tobacco are extremely widely used—and abused— among humans in their natural habitat.

Still, laboratory experiments cannot be dismissed out of hand. They remind us of the *potential* for dependence that specific drugs possess. And cocaine possesses that potential in greatest abundance: It is highly reinforcing—pleasurable, appealing, sensual, and seductive. Remember, this is only one factor in a range of factors that influence use. By itself, it does not dictate the popularity of drugs. But knowing this one fact about cocaine should make Bennett's and Pollin's prediction understandable. They may be wrong in the *magnitude* of that prediction (again, they leave out the social disruptiveness factor), but it is not difficult to see how they came up with it. Regardless of the size of the predicted increase, other things being equal, the pharmacological properties of cocaine (and, to a lesser extent, heroin) should lead anyone to predict an increase in use under some form of legalization. There are, in other words, sufficient grounds for genuine concern when it comes to sharply reducing the cost and increasing the availability of cocaine—as any legalization scheme is bound to do—given its intrinsically pleasure-inducing and reinforcing properties. A great deal of contrary evidence would have to be marshaled to convince evidence-minded observers that cocaine abuse would not sharply rise under legalization—and, as yet, no such evidence has been forthcoming. In the absence of such evidence, most of us will have to remain convinced that, in the words of John Kaplan (1988, p. 33), any policy of legalization "ignores basic pharmacology."

### Frequencies of Use

What direct evidence do we have that bears on the impact of legalization on drug use? Contrarily, what evidence bears on the impact of the criminalization of drugs and enforcement of the drug laws on use? Does drug use/abuse rise when drugs are legalized and fall when they are criminalized? Or, as the legalizers assume, does law enforcement have little or no impact on the incidence and volume of use? What circumstances make drugs more, or less, available? Are there a variety of controls that influence use, and not merely legal ones? What does the use picture under *nonlegal* controls tell us about the impact of *legal* controls?

We already know that national alcohol prohibition in the United States (1920–1933) *did* discourage use: Fewer Americans drank and fewer contracted cirrhosis of the liver during Prohibition than before or afterwards. (Prohibition brought about a number of other changes, as we saw, but they are separate from the issue of volume of alcohol consumption.) We also know that the partial decriminalization of small quantities of marijuana in the United States has not resulted in a significant increase in the use of this drug (Cuskey, Berger, and Richardson, 1978; Single, 1981). It is entirely possible that marijuana is a case apart from cocaine and heroin. At any rate, cocaine and heroin are the drugs most Americans fear and worry about the most. A number of observers have endorsed the legalization of marijuana and yet oppose the legalization of hard drugs such as heroin and/or cocaine (Kaplan, 1970, 1983; Kleiman, 1992b). And the Dutch policy (often mistakenly referred to as "legalization") is based on making a sharp distinction between soft drugs such as marijuana and hashish and hard drugs such as cocaine and heroin (Beers, 1991; Jansen, 1991; Leuw and Marshall, 1994). Hence, the case for or against heroin and/or cocaine legalization will have to be made separately from the case for or against the legalization of marijuana.

Several pieces of evidence suggest (but do not definitively demonstrate) that when the *availability* of certain drugs increases, their *use* increases as well. It has been something of a cliché among legalizers that criminalization doesn't work. Look around you, they say. Go to certain neighborhoods and see drugs openly sold on the street. Drugs are getting into the hands of addicts and abusers right now. How could the situation be any worse under legalization? Those who want to use are already using; selling drugs to addicts, abusers, and users legally would not change anything.

The fallacy in this line of reasoning is that, currently, under our punitive policy, addicts and abusers are not using as much as they would like to. Under almost any proposed legalization plan, the currently illegal drugs would be more available; if that were so, addicts and abusers would use a great deal more cocaine and heroin than they do now. The fact that we can look around on the streets of the country's largest cities and see drug selling taking place means next to nothing. Most addicts and drug abusers say that they want to use more than they are currently using, and if illicit drugs were cheaper, more readily available, and less difficult to obtain, they would use a great deal more.

### The Hassle Factor

The fact is, there is the **hassle factor** to consider. Addicts are pulled into use by the fact that they enjoy getting high, but they are pushed away from use by the fact that they have to commit crime to do so. Street crime is a difficult, risky, and dangerous enterprise; use is held down by that fact. If drugs were less of a hassle to obtain, most addicts and abusers would use them more. The vast majority of heroin and cocaine abusers want to get high, are forced to commit a great deal of crime to do so, and are not getting as high, or high as often, as they want because their drugs of choice are too expensive and the crimes they commit are too much of a hassle. Mark Moore (1973, 1976) refers to this as the "search time" for illegal drugs; says Moore, as search time goes up, demand decreases. Careful ethnographic and interview studies of street addicts and abusers have shown that getting high—not mere maintenance—is their prime motivation. Most are *not* technically addicted, their day-to-day use varies enormously, and most would use *much more* frequently if they could (Johnson et al., 1985; McAuliffe and Gordon, 1974).

In this sense, then, the drug laws and their enforcement have cut down on the volume of drug use among a substantial proportion—very possibly a majority—of our heaviest users and abusers. Again, the distinction between relative and absolute deterrence comes into play here; these addicts and abusers use a substantial quantity of illegal drugs—but a great deal less than they would if these drugs were legal or freely available to them.

George Rengert (1996) argues that drug use is extremely elastic, depending (among other things) on supply. And if supply is ineffective or inefficient in reaching its ultimate customers, if a given product or service is inconvenient or risky or dangerous to obtain or engage in, use will decline. Customers have to be willing to put up with a certain level of hassle to get what they want; beyond that threshold, they give up. If it is too much trouble to obtain a drug, the number of users taking it will decline. Some drug markets are easier for law enforcement to disrupt. If a chain of drug supply from grower to user is comprised entirely of intimates, under most circumstances, law enforcement cannot (and under most circumstances, should not) attempt to infiltrate it. On the other hand, most drug markets are made up of more public exchanges, and exchanges among nonintimates, and can be disrupted far more easily. When illicit drug exchanges are public, blatant, and located in fixed neighborhoods, they tend to attract customers who are strangers, and a variety of police tactics can be effective in convincing those customers to give up their efforts to purchase the product or service they seek. Some of these tactics include blocking off or rerouting streets, arresting customers, targeting customers who come to a given community from other areas, confiscating customers' cars, and embarrassing customers for whom arrest represents a substantial embarrassment. Law enforcement controls major aspects of the hassle factor, and drug use is most decidedly elastic with respect to hassle.

## Cost

We've already seen in the previous chapter, based on the extensive summary of the literature by Robert MacCoun and Peter Reuter (2001), that drug use is at least moderately elastic— that is, the higher the cost, the lower the use of drugs, both licit and illicit. This equation works better with nonaddicting drugs such as marijuana and less well with addicting drugs such as heroin and tobacco, but the evidence on the strong relationship between cost and use is robust and incontrovertible. And it is prohibition that keeps the cost of illicit drugs high. In the absence of prohibition, heroin and cocaine are as cheap as aspirin to manufacture, and under any conceivable or proposed legalization plan, they would be vastly less expensive than they are now. Indeed, it is their very cost under prohibition that the legalizers criticize; in proposing to make them cheaper, without realizing it, they are intimating that their use should correspondingly increase, and significantly.

Avran Goldstein and Harold Kalant (1990) base their opposition to legalization on the observation that use is directly related to availability, and availability can be influenced by a variety of controls, including criminalization and cost. Under any and all legalization plans, the currently illegal drugs would be sold or dispensed at a fraction of their present price. Indeed, that is the advantage of this plan, say its supporters, because the high cost of drugs leads to crime, which, in turn, leads to a panoply of social harms, costs, and problems.

But Goldstein and Kalant argue exactly the opposite: The high cost of the illegal drugs is precisely what keeps their use down. If drugs were sold or dispensed at low prices, use would almost inevitably rise—in all likelihood, dramatically. This relationship is demonstrated, they say, with a variety of drugs in a variety of settings. For instance, as measured by constant dollars, cost and the per capita consumption of alcohol—and the rate of cirrhosis of the liver—were almost perfectly correlated in a negative fashion in the Canadian province of Ontario between 1928 and 1974: During periods when the price of alcohol was low, the use of alcohol was relatively high; when the price of alcohol was high, use was relatively low. Price and use were mirror reflections of one another.

In addition, observe Goldstein and Kalant, the purchase of cigarettes, and therefore smoking, varies directly and negatively with the level of taxation on cigarettes: the higher the taxes on cigarettes, the lower their sales. "These data suggest that anything making drugs less expensive, such as legal sale at lower prices, would result in substantial increases in use and in the harmful consequences of heavy use" (p. 1515).

There are two additional pieces of evidence bearing on the relationship between the availability of psychoactive drugs and their use: (1) the immense increase in the use of and addiction to narcotics among servicemen stationed in Vietnam, and their sharp decline upon their return to the United States, and (2) the higher rates of certain types of psychoactive drug use among physicians and other health workers—who have greater access to drugs—than is true of the population as a whole.

Lee Robins (1973) reports that almost half of a sample of U.S. military personnel serving in Vietnam in the 1970s had tried one or more narcotic (opium, heroin, and/or morphine), and 20 percent were addicted to opiates. Prior to their arrival in Vietnam, however, only a small fraction had ever been addicted, and after their return to the United States, use and addiction resorted to their pre-Vietnam levels. (This study cross-checked self-reports on drug use with urine tests; hence, we can have a high degree of confidence in the data on use and addiction.) This study's findings are significant for at least two reasons.

First, the fact that the vast majority of addicted returning veterans discontinued their dependence on and use of narcotics on their own, without going through a formal therapeutic program, has major implications for the issue of drug treatment. Second, and more central for our purposes, the fact that use and addiction increased massively in Vietnam, where drugs were freely available (although technically illegal), and returned to their previous, extremely low levels when these veterans returned to the United States, gives us a glimpse of what may happen under legalization. The fact is, 95 percent of those who became addicted in Vietnam had not been addicted in the United States, and a similar 95 percent who became addicted there ceased their addiction when they returned to the United States from Vietnam. This suggests that there must have been something about the conditions that prevailed in Vietnam that encouraged use and addiction, as well as something about those that prevailed in the United States that discouraged them. Some observers have attributed the high levels of drug abuse in Vietnam to the combat stress that these servicemen experienced (Gazzaniga, 1990), but this is unlikely to be the whole explanation. It seems almost incontestable that the greater availability of drugs in Vietnam induced an enormous number of servicemen to use, and become addicted to, narcotics who otherwise would not have become involved. Their low level of narcotics addiction in the United States, both before and after their Vietnam experience, was influenced by the fact that the laws outlawing opiates are enforced here.

There are three aspects pertaining to physician drug use, which is significantly higher than is true for the population at large. First, as a number of studies have shown, recreational drug use among medical students and younger physicians is strikingly higher than among their age peers in the general population; again, availability is related to the likelihood of use. In one study, 73 percent of medical students had at least one recreational experience with at least one illegal psychoactive drug (McAuliffe et al., 1986). In comparison, for 18- to 25-year-olds in the general population at roughly the same time, the figure was 55 percent, and for 26- to 34-year-olds, it was 62 percent. For cocaine, the comparable figures were 39 percent for medical students and, in the general population, 18 percent for 18- to 25-year-olds and 26 percent for 26- to 34-year-olds (NIDA, 1991, pp. 25, 31).

Second, rates of self-medication among physicians are strikingly higher than is true among the general population. In the study of physician drug use cited above, 4 out of 10 physicians (42%) said that they had treated themselves with one or more psychoactive drugs one or more times, and 7 percent said that they had done so on 60 or more occasions; one-third of medical students had done so once or more, and 5 percent had done so on 60 or more occasions (McAuliffe et al., 1986, p. 807). This represents an extraordinarily high rate of self-medication with psychoactive drugs.

Third, the proportion of physicians reporting drug dependence is extraordinarily high— 3 percent of physicians and 5 percent of medical students said that they were currently dependent on a psychoactive drug (McAuliffe et al., 1986, p. 808), far higher than for the population as a whole. Other surveys have produced similar results (Epstein and Eubanks, 1984; McAuliffe et al., 1984; Sethi and Manchanda, 1980). Whereas occupational stress has often been cited as the culprit in high levels of physician drug use, abuse, and dependence (Stout-Wiegand and Trent, 1981), as with the Vietnam situation, it is difficult to deny that availability plays a substantial role.

### Continuance Rates

As we saw earlier, legal drugs tend to have high **continuance rates,** while illegal drugs tend to have far lower continuance rates. That is, out of all the people who have ever taken a given drug, the proportion who continue to use it (say, who used it once or more in the past month) tends to be fairly high for the legal drugs and fairly low for the illegal drugs. As we've learned, 6 out of 10 of all at-least one-time drinkers consumed alcohol during the previous month (61%); for tobacco, the comparable figure is 1 in 3 (37%). In contrast, for marijuana, the continuance rate is only 15 percent, and for most other illegal drugs, it is considerably less than 10 percent; for PCP and LSD, the figure is less than 1 percent. The same relationship holds in Amsterdam, where marijuana (but not the hard drugs) is de facto decriminalized, and users and small-time dealers of the hard drugs are rarely arrested. There, alcohol's continuance rate is 80 percent, tobacco's is 63 percent, and marijuana's is 24 percent; the recreational use of most prescription drugs falls somewhere in between tobacco's and marijuana's rates, and for the illicit, criminalized drugs, it is under 10 percent (Sandwijk, Cohen, and Musterd, 1991, pp. 20–21).

The fact is, although many factors influence a drug's continuance rate, other things being equal, if a drug is legal, users tend to stick with it longer; if it is illegal, they tend to use it less frequently and more sporadically, and they are more likely to give up using it altogether. Clearly, then, it is not true that, under criminalization, illegal drugs are as freely available as are the legal drugs. Criminalization makes drugs more difficult to obtain and use on an ongoing basis; for many would-be regular users, the hassle factor makes use simply not worth it.

# Progressive Legalizers versus Progressive Prohibitionists

The debate between advocates of drug legalization and advocates of prohibition might seem to be where we ought to direct our attention. But the debate between the advocates of two positions that share a great deal in common yet stand on opposite sides of the "great divide" may yield proposals that will prove to be workable a decade or two down the road. Precisely this debate is taking place in Western Europe right now; the majority of Western European nations have adopted or are moving toward adopting some form of a harm reductionist policy. The debate taking place there is between the progressive legalizers and the progressive prohibitionists. Although, for the most part, drug laws remain on the books, law enforcement in most Western European countries ignores small-quantity marijuana possession and sharply distinguishes between possession and possession of substantial qualities of hard drugs for the intention of sale and distribution.

Politically, the term "progressive" refers to an ideology that seeks to achieve equalitarian and humanistic goals, one that favors reform instead of a return to traditional, authoritarian values. In the sphere of drug legislation, progressives seek a solution to the drug problem by acknowledging that punishing drug offenders may have harmful, unintended consequences; consequently, the drug laws and their enforcement are very much in need of a drastic overhaul. Though they have the same goals in mind, the progressive legalizers and the progressive prohibitionists have somewhat different sets of legal proposals for the drug problem.

## Progressive Legalizers

**Progressive legalizers** have a **generalist drug policy;** they hold a definition of drugs that is based on their psychoactive quality, not their legality. The progressive legalizer wishes to dismantle or at least radically restructure the legal-illegal distinction. Unlike the free-market libertarian, who believes in a total decriminalization, hands-off, or laissez-faire policy for all drugs, hard or soft, the progressive legalizer believes in state control of the dispensation of psychoactive substances. Unlike the political leftist or radical, who argues that both the drug problem and the drug laws are a reflection of the inequalities in the class structure, the progressive legalizer argues that the drug laws *are* the problem. Matters of reforming the economy and the political system and redistributing society's resources are important in themselves, but the reform of drug policy is a crucial issue in its own right. Progressive legalizers are more concerned with what to do about drugs than with reformulating the political and economic system generally. They think that there are many things seriously wrong with the present system, and the laws prohibiting drugs represent one of them; they wish to reform them, so that there will be less pain and suffering in the world (Nadelmann, 1988, 1989, 1992, 1995).

How does the progressive formulate or frame the drug legalization issue? What is the nature of the drug problem, and what is the solution? For the most part, progressive legalizers see the drug problem as a human rights issue. When they discuss drug reforms, they mean treating drug addiction as a health problem, much like schizophrenia or alcoholism—not as a crime or law enforcement problem. Above all, society should, in Ethan Nadelmann's words, "stop demonizing illicit drug users"; "they are citizens and human beings." Criminalizing the possession and use of the currently illegal drugs is unjust, oppressive, and inhumane; it has no moral justification. It represents a kind of witch hunt, and it penalizes the unfortunate. Innumerable young lives are being ruined by imprisonment for what are essentially victimless crimes. It is the suffering of the drug user that is foremost on the progressive legalizer's mind in demanding a reform of drug policy. Says Nadelmann, the progressive legalizers' foremost and best-known spokesperson: "Harm reduction means leaving casual drug users alone and treating addicts like they're still human beings" (1995, p. 38). "My strongest argument for legalization," he adds, "is a moral one. Enforcement of drug laws makes a mockery of an essential principle of a free society—that those who do no harm to others should not be harmed by others, particularly by the state." Adds Nadelmann: "To me, [this] is the greatest societal cost of our current drug prohibition system" (1990).

A key to the progressive legalizers' thinking is their belief that drug use is a sphere of behavior that is influenced by much the same rules of human nature as any other activity. They believe that drug users are no more irrational or self-destructive than are participants in such routine—and far less legally controlled—activities as skiing, boating, eating, drinking, walking, and talking. There is, in other words, no special or unique power in psychoactive drugs that makes it necessary for society to enact laws to control and penalize their use. Why do we penalize people who use drugs and harm no one (perhaps not even themselves), but leave the stamp-collecting, chess-playing, and television-watching addict untouched? It is a philosophical tenet of progressive legalizers that it is unjust to penalize one activity in which the participant harms no one while, at the same time, other, not significantly safer, activities are left legally uncontrolled. The assumption that drugs possess uniquely enslaving and uniquely damaging qualities is widely held in American society, but it is sharply challenged by the progressive legalizer. No special or uniquely negative qualities means that there are no extraordinarily compelling reasons why drugs should be singled out to be criminalized or prohibited. Most drug users are every bit as rational as, say, chess players; society has no more cause to penalize the former for their pursuits than the latter (Nadelmann, 1988, 1989).

Another point: Progressive legalizers seriously consider a cost-benefit analysis, but insist that others who also make that claim leave out at least one crucial element in this equation: pleasure. Other perspectives that claim to weigh losses and gains are usually not willing to count the psychoactive effects that users seek—and attain—when they get high as a benefit. But why don't they? Sheer bias, the progressive legalizer would say. Most people take drugs because they enjoy their effects; this must be counted as a benefit to the society. If we are serious about counting positives and negatives, why ignore the most central positive of all— the enjoyment of drug taking? It is what motivates users, and it must be counted as a plus. Clearly, such a consideration would outrage political conservatives, who see hedonism and the pursuit of pleasure as signs of decay and degeneracy—part of what's wrong with this country.

The position of progressive legalizers can best be appreciated by a contrast with that of the progressive prohibitionists, a position we'll examine in the next section. Advocates of both positions urge reforms in the drug laws; both are, or claim to be, concerned with harm reduction; both attempt to weigh costs and benefits carefully and empirically in any evaluation of drug policy; and both believe that users of illegal drugs are treated too harshly, and that the legal drugs are too readily available. But the differences between these two positions are as important as their similarities.

There are three major and profound dissimilarities between the progressive legalizers and the progressive prohibitionists (Nadelmann, 1992, pp. 89–94). First, in their evaluation of costs and benefits, progressive legalizers weigh the moral values of individual liberty, privacy, and tolerance of the addict very heavily, while the progressive prohibitionists to some degree set these values aside and emphasize concrete, material values—specifically, public health—much more heavily.

Second, in considering the impact of legalization—more specifically, whether it will increase use—progressive legalizers are optimists (they believe that use will not increase significantly), while progressive prohibitionists are pessimists (they believe that use will increase, possibly even dramatically). Even if use does increase, the progressive legalizers say, legalization is likely to result in increased use of less harmful drugs and decreased use of more harmful substances.

Third, progressive legalizers believe that most of the harms from the use of the currently illegal drugs stems from criminalization, while progressive prohibitionists believe that such harms are more a product of use per se than of the criminalization of those drugs. Harm from contaminated drugs, the grip of organized crime, the crime and violence that infects the drug scene, HIV/AIDS, and medical maladies from addiction are all secondary, not primary, effects of drugs. And all will decline or disappear under legalization. Progressive prohibitionists are skeptical of these arguments.

With a very few exceptions, progressive legalizers have not spent a great deal of time or space spelling out what their particular form of legalization would look like. Still, they do not mean by legalization what free-market libertarians mean by decriminalization—that is, a complete laissez-faire program—nor, indeed, what their critics mean by legalization. "When we talk about legalization, we don't mean selling crack in candy stores," says Nadelmann (Schillinger, 1995, p. 21). Many progressive legalizers point to harm reduction strategies that seem (to some observers) to have worked in the Netherlands, Switzerland, and the United Kingdom. All support steps in that direction: Decriminalize marijuana, expand methadone maintenance programs, reschedule many Schedule I drugs (such as LSD, Ecstasy, and heroin) that may have therapeutic utility, get addicts into treatment programs instead of arresting them, and so on. However, progressive legalizers see these as only stopgap or transitional steps. If not the candy store or supermarket model, then what would full legalization look like? Nadelmann suggests that the mail order model might work: Sell drugs in limited quantities through the mail (Nadelmann, 1992, pp. 111–113). While not the ideal solution, it is the best compromise "between individual rights and communitarian interests." It must be noted that, while all progressive legalizers emphasize the unanticipated consequences of prohibition, they do not spend much time or space considering the possible unanticipated consequences of legalization.

## Progressive Prohibitionists

**Progressive prohibitionists** (Currie, 1993; Kaplan, 1983, 1988; Kleiman, 1992b; Zimring and Hawkins, 1992) urge many of the same reforms as progressive legalizers; most of them, for instance, would support much of the following programs: needle exchange, condom distribution, an expansion of methadone maintenance, no incarceration of the addict, the rescheduling of many Schedule I drugs, a consideration of decriminalization of marijuana, and higher taxes and more controls on alcohol and tobacco. The progressive prohibitionists draw the line, however, at legal over-the-counter or even mail order sale of drugs such as heroin, cocaine, and amphetamine.

Progressive prohibitionists are not as distressed by the moral incongruity of criminalizing the possession and sale of powerful psychoactive agents and legally tolerating substances or activities that also cause harm. Once again, to demarcate their position from that of the progressive legalizers, they argue that there is a special and unique quality in certain drugs that compels some users of them to become abusers. Not a majority of the society, they say, but a sufficiently sizeable minority to warrant concern for the public health of the collective as a whole. To step back and look at their political, ideological, and moral position more generally, progressive prohibitionists are far more communitarian than individualistic. While the touchstone of the progressive legalizer is the rights of the individual, for the progressive prohibitionist, the guiding principle is the health of the community. The individual, they suggest, does not have the right to harm the society; certain rights have to be curbed for the good of the society as a whole. If injured, the individual has to be cared for by the community; foolish acts engaged in by the individual are purchased at the price of a very substantial cost to the rest of us. The individual does not have the legal or moral right to ignore the seat belt law, the helmet law, or rules and regulations against permitting him or her to be placed in extreme danger—or any other laws, rules, or regulations designed to protect individuals from harming themselves. Any humane society must balance freedom against harm, and in this equation, quite often, certain freedoms must be curtailed. In short, compared with progressive legalizers, progressive prohibitionists are much more concerned with a potential gain in public health as with the moral issue of human rights that are supposedly abridged by certain laws. For instance, coercing addicts and drug abusers into treatment programs by arresting them for possession and giving them a choice between imprisonment and treatment is not a moral problem for the progressive prohibitionist, whereas for the progressive legalizer, it is.

It is almost in the very nature of the progressive prohibitionist's argument that there is an assumption of greater use under any possible legalization plan. (Marijuana may well represent an exception.) The American population—or a segment of it, at any rate—is seen as being vulnerable to the temptation of harmful psychoactive drugs. Progressive prohibitionists are pessimists when it comes to contemplating the extent of use under legalization. They do not necessarily see the dire worst-case scenario predicted by the conservatives— for instance, the tens of millions of new cocaine and heroin addicts and abusers predicted by William Bennett under legalization. But many progressive prohibitionists do see a doubling, tripling, or even quadrupling of hard-drug abuse in the United States as an entirely possible outcome of many of the currently proposed legalization schemes. And they find that unacceptable. Most Americans will resist the temptations and blandishments of these seductive, dependency-producing substances. But focusing on the potential behavior of "most" Americans is a distraction and an irrelevancy. What counts is whether the small minority who use destructively is likely to grow. More distressing is the fact that the volume of drug abuse of current addicts and abusers is likely to increase, and along with it, the harm that flows from it.

And last, the progressive prohibitionists see more direct harm from use of the hard drugs, such as cocaine, amphetamine, and heroin, than the progressive legalizers. There are, they say, significant secondary harms and complications caused mainly by the legal status of these drugs; certainly, HIV/AIDS ranks high among them. But most of these secondary or indirect harms can be addressed through modifications of the current system that fall far short of outright legalization. Certainly, needle exchange and condom distribution programs would go a long way in combating the problem of HIV contamination. The fact is, cocaine and heroin are a great deal more harmful than the legalizers claim, say the prohibitionists.

Harm has been kept low by the very fact of the drug laws, because far fewer people currently use than would be the case with legalization. Alcohol and tobacco kill many Americans in part because their use is intrinsically harmful (at least, given the way we use them) and in part because they are widely used. Cocaine and heroin—considering the many possible ways that drugs can be harmful—are also intrinsically harmful drugs. (Although they are harmful in very different respects.) And they are used, recklessly, by segments of the population who are far more likely to take extreme risks with their health than the rest of us. If they were to be as widely and as commonly used as alcohol and tobacco—not a real possibility—many users would die as a result. It is foolish and unrealistic, the progressive legalizer says, to imagine that these illegal drugs are harmful entirely or even mainly because they are illegal. While the progressive legalizer stresses the secondary harms and dangers of the illegal drugs, the progressive prohibitionist stresses their primary harms and dangers.

Again, while the progressive prohibitionists and the progressive legalizers share many items in their drug policy agenda, they differ on these three major issues: (1) their valuation of individual liberty versus public health, (2) their prediction of whether drug abuse and its attendant harms will increase significantly under legalization, and (3) their notion of whether the currently illegal drugs are more harmful intrinsically or directly, or indirectly, that is, mainly because they are illegal. Ironically, although the progressive legalizers and the progressive prohibitionists stand on opposite sides of the great legalization divide, they share more particulars of their drug policy proposals than any two other major positions in this debate. If major changes in drug policy do take place in the coming decades, they are likely to be drawn from the substantial overlap in these two positions.

It is foolish to picture the drug legalization debate as an either-or proposition. What counts are the particulars of a given proposal; the position taken by some observers—Arnold Trebach (1993) is an outstanding example—that nothing could be worse than what we've got now, is mistaken. The position that we should legalize at once and take care of the specifics as we go along, is irresponsible in the extreme. All policy changes represent a minefield of potential unanticipated—and undesired—consequences. Both God and the devil are in the details.

## SUMMARY

Many critics and observers argue that the system of prohibition that currently prevails in the United States doesn't work and is counterproductive, doing more harm than good. The very nature of legal prohibition makes obtaining a banned product or a service expensive, and hence profitable to supply. Because of the profit motive, the arrest of one purveyor does not result in a disruption in the supply of illicit goods and services. Instead, another purveyor steps in and maintains business as usual. Moreover, the illicit drug business breeds corruption, brutality, violence, and crime, not to mention tainted drugs of unpredictable quality. These critics have proposed that the current system of prohibition be replaced with a system of drug legalization, in one form or another.

Three major changes have been proposed—legalization, decriminalization, and a policy of harm reduction. With legalization, the currently illicit drugs would be regulated by the state in much the same way alcohol or tobacco are. Drugs would be taxed. The state would set limits on their potency and purity, and would determine to whom they may be sold. Presumably, the government would control issues such as drug advertising and determine who may sell drugs and in what sort of establishment, who is permitted to manufacture them, where and under what circumstances they may be used, and so on.

Decriminalization is a very different proposal from legalization. Full decriminalization entails no state regulation or control whatsoever. ("Full" decriminalization should be distinguished from "partial" decriminalization, which currently prevails in 12 states for marijuana, which permits small-quantity possession without arrest.) It is a laissez-faire or hands-off policy of virtually no regulation or control whatsoever. Under this program, anyone may manufacture and distribute any psychoactive substance for any reason. (The sale to and use by minors is presumably an exception, as are being under the influence while flying a plane, driving a car, or handling dangerous machines and equipment, and, in the case of a drug like cigarettes, public use that results in others being forced to inhale the drug's fumes.) Complete decriminalization is not a serious proposal and has no hope of implementation at any time in the foreseeable future.

Some observers argue that drug abuse should be regarded as a medical matter and that Schedule I drugs should be rescheduled as Schedule II drugs, that is, be made available to addicts and abusers by prescription. By the lights of this proposal, they would be controlled in the same way that psychoactive medications such as Xanax, lorazepam, and morphine are, the difference being that maintaining the abuser on the drug would be legally permitted. The "condition" that would be treated is the abuse of the drug, and the "treatment" would be the administration of the abused drug. This proposal assumes that abusers and addicts take drugs not to get high but because they are dependent and cannot control their use.

Harm reduction is a pragmatic or consequentialist proposal rather than a moralistic or ideological one. It argues that the purpose of the law is not to wipe out drug use or abuse—for that is an impossibility—but to reduce the total volume of harm to the society, including death, disease, declines in productivity, educational deficits, and monetary costs. Harm reductionists treat each drug on a case-by-case basis and each detail of every proposal on a case-by-case basis. A major element of the harm reductionist's program is to reduce the harm from the legal drugs; in the case of tobacco, that means drastically lowering its use, period. Harm reductionists are also tinkerers; they believe that any proposal that doesn't work should be scuttled and any proposal that does should be retained. Some elements of a harm reduction policy are currently being instituted in Western Europe, with some success.

A major plank of the legalizer's platform is that drug use/abuse will not rise significantly under legalization. Legalizers reason that prohibition is inherently and fatally flawed because if there is demand for a service or a product, purveyors will find a way to distribute it and consumers will find a way to purchase it. But in actuality, many services and products exist whose availability and consumption are strongly reduced by their illegality and law enforcement—national alcohol prohibition being a major example. While there were other harmful consequences of Prohibition, alcohol consumption declined by half between 1920 and 1933. On the other hand, the "doomsayers" who argue that the worst-case scenario would come about as a result of legalization are completely wrong; under any conceivable form of legalization, most Americans would not use the currently illicit drugs. The regular use of many now-illicit drugs would require a drastically disruptive change in the user's day-to-day lifestyle, and that is extremely unlikely to happen. On the other hand, a great deal of evidence indicates that availability strongly encourages use for a substantial percentage of the population. Moreover, today, the heaviest, most chronic abusers do not use as much as they'd like; legalization would increase their use, as well as the harm such use causes.

## KEY TERMS

continuance rates 440

decriminalization 425

de facto legalization 425

de jure legalization 425

Food and Drug Administration (FDA) 426

full decriminalization 425

generalist drug policy 441

harm reduction 427

hassle factor 437

Iron Law of Prohibition 422

legalization 420

maintenance model 427

medical model 426

monkey model of addiction 436

partial decrim- inalization 419

prescription model 426

progressive legalizers 441

progressive prohibi- tionists 443

punitive model (strict/hard, soft/moderate) 429

reinforcement 435

specifist drug policy 427

worst-case scenario 432

# GLOSSARY

*Note:* Specific drugs are not listed here; they are categorized in "A Classification of Psychoactive Drugs and Their Effects" in Chapter 2. If directly relevant, definitions of terms will be focused primarily on their applicability to drugs and drug use.

**AA** *See* **Alcoholics Anonymous.**

**absolute deterrence** The view that punishing a given activity will eliminate or drastically reduce the incidence of the activity.

**acute effects** With reference to drugs, the rapid or short-term effects of taking a given drug, that is, those that take place during a single episode of administration; *see also* **chronic effects.**

**ADAM** *See* **Arrestee Drug Abuse Monitoring Program.**

**additive effects** A characteristic with two drugs such that when both are taken together, the effects are the same as if twice as much of either had been taken *ad libitum:* at will, at one's own pleasure.

**Alcoholics Anonymous (AA)** A peer-oriented, self-help organization dedicated to weaning alcoholics off their dependence on alcohol; based on the theory that alcoholics cannot drink moderately.

**amphetamines** CNS stimulants, chemically, Alpha + methyl + phenyl + ethyl + amine; examples: Desoxyn, Adderall, Dexedrine; related to but less potent than methamphetamine.

**analgesics** A category of drugs whose primary effect is the alleviation of pain; painkillers.

**anesthetic** A substance with painkilling properties; example: narcotics.

**anomie ("strain") theory of deviant behavior** An explanation which argues that "nonconforming" behavior is the product of a "malintegrated" society whose culture encourages material achievement but whose social and economic structure denies that same achievement to most members, thus leading to "strain," which results in deviant "adaptations," including "retreatism" (such as drug addiction and alcoholism) and "innovation" (such as drug dealing).

**antagonistic effects** Two drugs that, when taken together, cancel out or nullify the effects of each other.

**antidepressant drugs** Mood elevators, a category of substances used to combat clinical depression, including Prozac, Xanax, Paxil, and Zoloft; they do not produce a pleasurable intoxication in nondepressed individuals and are not used recreationally.

**antipsychotic drugs** Substances used to treat mental disorder; they include the phenothiazines; haloperidol (Haldol); and risperidone (Risperdal); they do not produce a pleasurable sensation and are not used recreationally.

**Arrestee Drug Abuse Monitoring (ADAM) Program** A federally sponsored, ongoing data collection program that drug tests and interviews a sample of persons in jails located in metropolitan areas; since there are no legal consequences of testing positive for or admitting drug use, the response rate is very high.

**asset forfeiture (drug)** A program, authorized by the law, that calls for seizing the property of arrestees of drug crimes, even if they are not convicted in court.

**ataxia** Motor discoordination.

**availability (drug)** The presence of one or more substances in a given area such that potential users may obtain them.

**availability heuristic** The widespread tendency to believe that phenomena that readily come to mind are more common or frequent than they actually are.

**BAC** *See* **blood alcohol concentration.**

**BAL** blood alcohol level; *see* **blood alcohol concentration.**

**balloon effect** A metaphor indicating that when arrests for drug sale take place in one area, they open up opportunities in, and expand in another, much the way squeezing a balloon contracts one area and expands another.

**barbiturates** CNS depressants derived from barbituric acid; examples: Seconal, Tuinal, Amytal.

**behavioral dependence** The compulsive use of a substance or an activity, which is continued in spite of harmful consequences and repeated attempts to abstain.

**benzodiazipines** A category of sedative drugs that includes Valium and Ativan; commonly referred to as "tranquilizers" or anti-anxiety agents.

**bias** As it pertains to a perspective or point of view, oriented in a particular direction without regard to the facts; as it pertains to research, *see* **biased sample.**

**biased sample** A subset of a population that was selected by researchers in such a way that each member of the population did not have an equal chance of appearing in the sample.

**bioavailability** The capacity of the body to absorb and metabolize a specific drug, given the form in which it is taken, and deliver it to the relevant receptor sites.

**biological theories of drug use** Explanations for the consumption of psychoactive substances that are based on physical causes, such as genes, hormones, and neurological factors.

**bipolar disorder** A manic-depressive condition that causes periods of depression alternating with periods of mania, that is, extreme, dysfunctional elation.

**blood alcohol concentration** The percentage, by volume, that alcohol comprises of the total content of blood in the body; 0.08 percent is commonly defined as legal intoxication in states throughout the United States.

**brain stem** The "primitive" portion of the brain, located just above the top of the spinal cord, that regulates basic functions such as breathing and swallowing.

**cannabis** The scientific name for the marijuana plant.

**capable guardian** A hypothetical actor in routine activities theory, an agent that discourages crime from taking place by protecting a "suitable target."

**carcinogen** An agent that causes cancer.

**Centers for Disease Control (CDC)** A federal agency that collects and tabulates nationwide data on sources and consequences of death, disease, and accident, and disseminates information on disease and accident prevention.

**central nervous system** The brain and spinal cord, which send signals to other parts of the body to perform organic functions; usually expressed as CNS.

**cerebellum** A part of the brain involved with motor activity and coordination.

**cerebrum** The major part of the brain, involved with cognitive functioning as well as the regulation of most organ activity.

**chemicalistic fallacy** The theory or view that we can predict how people will act under the influence of a drug or as a result of taking a drug simply from the pharmacological actions of the drug.

**chipping** Using an addicting drug on an episodic, sporadic, once-in-a-while basis.

**chippying** *See* **chipping.**

**chronic effects** Drug effects that take place over a long period of time; *see also* **acute effects.**

**club drugs** Informal term for substances used recreationally during "raves," concerts, parties, and clubs; includes Ecstasy, GHB, ketamine, Rohypnol, and, sometimes, methamphetamine.

**CNS** Central nervous system.

**cognitive guidedness model** The argument that behavior under the influence of alcohol is "guided" by cultural norms, rarely straying far from what is culturally acceptable.

**conduce** Lead to, potentiate, contribute, as in, "high levels of alcohol consumption conduce to crime and victimization."

**conflict theory** A "macro" or structural explanation which argues that social behavior is the outcome of differences among groups and categories in the population in power, wealth and resources; hence, drug abuse and drug selling tend to be more entrenched in poorer, more disorganized neighborhoods because viable economic options for residents are limited and community members find it difficult to combat the power of drug dealers.

**constructionism** The approach to reality that defines phenomena subjectively, that is, by how they are seen, regarded, conceptualized, or dealt with by the members of a society (such as, "A drug is whatever the members of a society or the law *define* as a drug").

**consumption levels** The total volume of a given drug that is used during a given time.

**continuance rate** For a given drug, a figure calculated on the basis of comparing the proportion of at-least one-time users who have also taken that drug within a more recent time, usually during either the past month or the past year.

**Controlled Substances Act** Passed in 1970, the federal Comprehensive Drug Abuse Prevention and Controlled Substances Act increased funding for the Public Health Services hospitals; authorized the National Commission on Marihuana and Drug Abuse, a detailed, wide-ranging study of drug use; and established penalties for the possession and sale of drug categories or "schedules" based, supposedly, on a drug's "potential for abuse" and medical utility, as deemed by the federal government.

**criminalization** The process of passing and enforcing a law that makes an activity illegal; with respect to drugs, the process of passing and enforcing a law that makes the possession and sale of a particular drug illegal.

**criminogenic** Having the capacity to cause or influence the commission of criminal behavior.

**cross-dependence** The administration of a particular drug preventing withdrawal from another drug to which the person is addicted.

**cross-tolerance** Tolerance to one drug resulting in diminished effects of another drug.

**DARP** Drug Abuse Reporting Program, a study conducted between 1969 and 1973, to determine the effectiveness of drug treatment programs.

**DATOS** Drug Abuse Treatment Outcome Study, conducted between 1991 and 1993, to determine the effectiveness of drug treatment programs.

**DAWN** *See* **Drug Abuse Warning Network.**

**decriminalization** A legal "hands-off" policy toward the possession and sale of drugs; usually refers to *partial* decriminalization.

**de facto legalization** A "hands-off" practice of not enforcing a law, making the criminalized practice in effect legal.

**de jure legalization** Passing a law that renders a given activity, previously against the law, now legal by law.

**demonology** The practice of portraying certain people as demons or evil spirits, the epitome of evil.

**Department of Health and Human Services** A federal agency that includes the NIDA, NIMH, and NIAAA.

**depenalization** Removing criminal penalties against any activity; here, removing criminal penalties against drug possession and/or sale.

**dependence, drug** Compulsive, repeated use of a substance whose basis is positive reinforcement.

**dependence, physical** *See* **drug addiction.**

**dependent variable** A factor that is caused by another factor, the independent variable; example: age (the independent variable) causes drug use (the dependent variable); *see also* **independent variable.**

**depressant** A substance that "depresses" (or lowers the rate of) a wide range of organs and functions of the body.

**descriptive statistics** Numbers or figures that depict the basic characteristics of a phenomenon, such as "63 percent of persons who die of drug-related causes are white"; *see also* **inferential statistics.**

**deterrence argument/model** The view that punishing a given activity will deter or decrease its incidence.

**direct drug effects** The consequences of taking a given drug that are caused by the drug itself, as opposed by economic, legal, and other circumstances of taking the drug; *see also* **indirect drug effects.**

**disassociative anesthetic** Drugs that have the capacity both to reduce the perception of pain and to generate a psychological state that makes the user feel removed from the reality of the immediate setting; examples: PCP and ketamine.

**disguised observation** A research technique that involves deception by "disguising" from research subjects the fact that the researcher is engaged in a study.

**disinhibition model** The argument that it is the direct effect of alcohol that causes drinkers to be liberated from society's norms and leads to a substantial volume of dangerous, violent behavior while under the influence.

**dopamine** An important neurotransmitter; among other things, it regulates the effects of stimulants such as cocaine and amphetamine.

**dose-response curve** A graph that depicts the relationship between the quantity of a drug that is taken and the measurable magnitude of a specific effect that each quantity produces.

**dove** Someone who believes that drugs should be legalized, that the war on drugs should no longer be fought.

**drug, legal definition** A substance whose possession and sale is against the law.

**drug, medical definition** A substance that is used for the purpose of healing the body or mind.

**drug, psychoactivity definition** A substance whose use generates significant changes in the workings of the mind—mood, emotion, feeling, and cognitive processes.

**drug abuse** (1) "Objective" definition: the use of a substance to the point that is harmful or dangerous to the user's life, where the user threatens or undermines previously held values, including health, safety, schooling, job, relations with loved ones; (2) "biased" or subjective definition: the use of an illicit drug for nonmedical purposes.

**Drug Abuse Warning Network (DAWN)** An ongoing, federally sponsored data collection program that tabulates the number of drug-related admissions to emergency departments (ED reports), as reported by metropolitan hospitals and clinics, and the number of drug-related deaths, as reported by metropolitan medical examiners (ME reports).

**drug action** A specific reaction that takes place at the molecular level between a chemical that is introduced into the body and the body's neurochemical system; sometimes referred to as the "direct" effect of drugs; *see also* **drug effects.**

**drug addiction** The use of a drug to the point where an abrupt discontinuation would cause withdrawal symptoms.

**Drug Control Act** *See* **Controlled Substances Act.**

**drug courts** Diversion of drug offenders away from the penal system into treatment programs.

**drug effects** The direct and indirect physical and psychic consequences of taking a specific drug; *see also* **drug actions.**

**drug fate** The outcome of a process by which a given drug is broken down in the body and, eventually, eliminated from the body.

**drug treatment** A program designed to reduce drug use, or the harm associated with drug use, through a means other than law enforcement.

**Drug Use Forecasting (DUF)** ADAM's name before 1997.

**drugs–violence nexus** The connection between drug use and drug-related activity and violent behavior; researchers attempt to explain why the connection between the two is so strong.

**drunken comportment** Behavior under the influence of alcohol.

**DUF** *See* **Drug Use Forecasting.**

**economic-compulsive model** The view that the connection between drug use and violence is so strong because users need money to maintain their habit and, while committing money-making crimes, engage in such behavior, such as robbery and burglary, which often turns violent (for instance, when the victim resists or struggles); related to **medical model.**

**ED** Effective dose, the quantity of a given drug that produces a specific effect in a percentage of a designated group of subjects.

**ED episode** A specific incident reported to the DAWN program of an untoward, drug-related experience that results in the user presenting him- or herself to metropolitan clinics and hospitals for medical or psychiatric treatment.

**ED mention** The mention of a specific drug in a specific incident reported to the DAWN program.

**ED reports** Reports issued by DAWN emergency departments on drug "episodes," that is, untoward, drug-related experiences that result in users presenting themselves to metropolitan hospitals and clinics for medical or psychiatric treatment.

**ED/LD ratio** The difference between the quantity that it requires to achieve a specific effect in a specific proportion of a designated group of subjects and the quantity it requires to kill that same proportion; also referred to as **safety margin** and **therapeutic margin** (note: most pharmacology textbooks present this as **LD/ED ratio**).

**effective dose** *See* **ED.**

**eidetic imagery** Closed-eye visions or "eyeball movies"; one of the principal psychic effects of LSD.

**emergency department episode/mention/report** *See* **ED episode, ED mention,** and **ED report.**

**empathogen** A drug that has the quality of fostering closeness, intimacy, and compassion for others; said to be the principal effect of MDMA (Ecstasy).

**endogenous drug** A chemical substance, with pharmacological effects, produced entirely within the body.

**enslavement model** The argument that more or less accidental or fortuitous narcotics addiction causes a life that revolves around money-making crimes; it is drug addiction that causes criminal behavior; *see also* **predisposition model** and **intensification model;** consistent with the **medical model.**

**enzyme** An organic chemical, found in the brain and the liver, that speeds up interactions between and among drugs.

**equivalency, rule of** *See* **rule of equivalency.**

**essentialism** The approach to reality that defines phenomena by pregiven or "objective" properties, such as "a drug is any substance with psychoactive effects"; *see also* **constructionism.**

**ethical drug** *See* **pharmaceutical drug.**

**exogenous drugs** Pharmacologically active substances that originate from outside the body.

**Families in Action** An antidrug, mainly anti-marijuana, lobby.

**Federal Bureau of Narcotics (FBN)** The law enforcement agency that regulated illicit drugs prior to the Drug Control Act of 1970.

**Food and Drug Administration (FDA)** Created by the Pure Food and Drug Act of 1906, the agency that regulates the distribution of prescription drugs.

**full decriminalization** A complete "hands-off" or laissez-faire policy toward drugs; anyone above a certain age may legally possess or sell any quantity of any drug without legal penalty.

**gateway hypothesis** The view that certain drugs—and here, marijuana is usually designated as the gateway drug—are *precursors* to the use of other, more dangerous drugs later in life.

**general depressants** *See* **sedative drugs.**

**generalist drug policy** A program of drug regulation based on the notion that "one size fits all," that all drugs should be governed equally by the same laws.

**genetic theories of drug use** Explanations that rely on chromosomal differences in the population, which influence the predisposition to take or abuse psychoactive substances.

**globalization** The worldwide interconnectedness of all nations into an international economic, communications, and legal web; a major factor in the decentralization of drug distribution.

**Golden Crescent** A region of Western Asia in which opium poppies are grown; includes northern Turkey, Iran, Afghanistan, Pakistan, and India.

**Golden Triangle** The area of Southeast Asia in which opium poppies grow; includes northern Burma (Myanmar), Laos, and Thailand.

**grassroots theory of the media** The argument that the slant and content of the mass media are a product of the interests and beliefs of the majority of the population.

**guidedness model** *See* **cognitive guidedness model.**

**habituation** The process by which a given user becomes used to the effects of a given drug.

**Hague Conference** An international meeting on drug control held in the Netherlands in 1911, which produced a treaty that led to the Harrison Act; formal name: International Conference on Opium.

**half-life** The period of time during which 50 percent of a given drug remains in the body after ingestion.

**hallucinogen** A category of drugs whose effects include profound sensory dislocation; often referred to as "psychedelics"; examples: LSD and mescaline.

**harm reduction** A policy toward drug distribution and sale that is governed solely or mainly by lowering those consequences that are widely agreed to be harmful, even if that policy is not concerned about eliminating drug use or addressing the ideological issues of fairness or morality.

**Harrison Act** A federal law, passed in 1914, that required a prescription written by licensed physicians to be obtained for the sale of narcotics and cocaine, and that such sale be registered, recorded, and taxed; the act did not directly criminalize addiction per se, but during a series of Supreme Court rulings between 1919 and 1923, maintaining the addict on a narcotic was declared an improper medical practice, and hence illegal.

**hassle factor** The trouble or difficulty of obtaining illicit drugs.

**hawk** Someone who believes that the drug war should be fought, that illicit drugs should remain illegal and should not be legalized.

**hegemony** Institutional dominance, control by the most powerful segments of the society of the major institutions in a society, such as the media, education, and politics.

**hemp** The marijuana plant; usually refers to plants that are harvested for their fiber and other nonpsychoactive products rather than for their buds and flowering tops, that is, for psychoactive purposes.

**hydroponic** A method of growing plants in water rather than soil; a common technique of growing high-potency marijuana.

**iatrogenic** Medical intervention that itself causes disease or death.

**immediate sensual appeal** Having the quality of eliciting a positive, pleasurable reaction in organisms upon taking a given drug for the first time, without the mediation of learning to recognize that reaction; applies primarily to cocaine and the amphetamines.

**inadequate personality, theories of drug use based on** Explanations for the consumption, usually the abuse, of psychoactive substances that are based on the notion that young people who lack self-esteem, are unable to cope with life, and are failures turn to drugs to drown out the feelings of failure.

**independent variable** A causal factor, one that has an effect on another factor; example: age (the independent variable) causes drug use (the dependent variable); *see also* **dependent variable.**

**indirect drug effects** Consequences of taking drugs that are not caused by the drugs themselves but by the circumstances of use, such as using contaminated needles and contracting HIV.

**individualistic theories of drug use** Explanations for the consumption of psychoactive substances that ignore larger, structural, or "big-picture" factors and focus exclusively on factors relating specifically to the characteristics of users themselves.

**inferential statistics** Numbers or figures that help uncover the cause-and-effect relationships between two or more variables, such as "50 percent of the cause of drug addiction in the United States can be traced to poverty"; *see also* **descriptive statistics.**

**innovation** A "mode of adaptation" in anomie or strain theory that entails seeking culturally approved goals (mainly affluence) through "deviant" or illicit means (such as drug dealing).

**instrumental drug use** The use of a substance for the purpose not of achieving intoxication but of achieving a goal, such as medical therapy or studying for an exam.

**intensification model** The argument that drug addiction *accelerates* but does not *generate* money-making criminal behavior, and that the predisposition to engage in both compulsive drug use and criminal behavior explains part but not all of the connection between the two.

**intoxication** The state of being under the influence of a drug, usually to the point of being exhilarated, disordered, and/or stupefied.

**intramuscular administration** Injecting a drug directly into a muscle.

**intranasal administration** Sniffing or "snorting" a powdered substance into a nasal passage, where it is absorbed into the mucous membranes and from there into the bloodstream.

**intrinsic school** The argument that the "intrinsic" or pharmacological properties of drugs inevitably lead to specific consequences; example: taking marijuana inevitably leads to the use and abuse of harder drugs.

**Iron Law of Prohibition** The theory that the harsher the penalties for the possession and sale of a given drug, the greater the use of more potent drugs.

**IV administration** Injecting a drug directly into a vein.

**IV injection** Using a syringe (or needle) to introduce a liquid solution of a substance directly into a vein.

**judgmental heuristics** Flawed, informal rules of thumb people use to reach conclusions.

**law of unanticipated consequences** The high likelihood that good-intentioned plans will have repercussions that even the planners not only did not intend but regard as undesirable.

**LD** Lethal dose, the quantity of a given drug that produces death in a designated group of subjects, usually expressed as a proportion, as in "LD50," meaning 50 percent of the designated subjects will die if administered the designated dose of the designated drug.

**LD/ED ratio** *See* **ED/LD ratio.**

**legalization** A policy permitting the possession and sale of drugs under a government licensing system similar to that controlling the distribution of alcohol and/or cigarettes.

**lethal dose** *See* **LD.**

**life cycle rates**  Varying likelihoods of using drugs at different ages in the life span.

**lifetime prevalence rates**  The proportion of the population that has used a given drug at least once during their lifetimes.

**longitudinal studies**  Surveys based on studying the same respondents at different points in time.

**loyalty rate**  *See* **continuance rates.**

**macro-level theories**  Explanations of anything—and here drug use is relevant—based on larger structures, such as income distribution, racism, and community disorganization, rather than individual factors; *see also* **micro-level theories, structural theories.**

**maintenance model**  The view that the drug problem could be solved or alleviated if users, abusers, and/or addicts were maintained on their drug of choice; the model may be applied to a specific drug or drug type, or to drugs in general.

**manic-depressive disorder**  *See* **bipolar disorder.**

**Marihuana Tax Act**  A federal law, passed in 1937 and modeled after the Harrison Act, that effectively banned all possession and sale of marijuana until it was superseded by the Controlled Substances Act of 1970.

**ME episode**  A specific incident reported to DAWN of a drug-related death.

**ME mention**  The mention of a specific drug in a specific incident reported to DAWN of a drug-related death.

**ME reports**  Reports issued by medical examiners on the number of drug-related deaths that took place in a given metropolitan area; *see also* **Drug Abuse Warning Network (DAWN).**

**medical examiners episodes/mentions/reports**  *See* **ME episode, ME mention, ME reports.**

**medical model**  The argument that the problem of all drug use—illicit drug use included—is a medical problem and should be dealt with by medical means; usually entails a proposal to emphasize treatment over incarceration.

**metabolic imbalance**  A theory that opiate addiction is caused by an incomplete biochemical makeup, which narcotics "complete."

**metabolite**  The chemical a given drug is broken down into after entering the body; the product of the body's enzymes interacting with the drug.

**methadone maintenance**  A program of "maintaining" narcotics, mainly heroin, addicts on a drug (methadone) that reduces their craving for, and makes it difficult for them to become high on, recreational doses of narcotics.

**methodology**  A research technique.

**micro-level theories**  Explanations of anything—and here, drug use is relevant—that are individualistic rather than structural; *see also* **macro-level theories, structural theories.**

**militarism**  Adopting military metaphors to describe enforcing drug laws.

**militarization**  Using the military to enforce the drug laws.

**mixed model**  A pattern of drug distribution involving both growing a drug-bearing plant in an agricultural setting and chemically extracting its drug for distribution and sale.

**mixing, drug**  Taking two or more substances at the same time.

**money machine theory of the media**  The view that the mass media are primarily motivated by profit and only secondarily or not at all by other factors, such as political indoctrination.

**Monitoring the Future**  (MTF)  A federally sponsored, ongoing data collection program that entails administering questionnaires on drug use to high school seniors (since 1975), young adults not in college (since 1977), college students (since 1980), and eighth- and tenth-graders (since 1991).

**monkey model of addiction**  The view that to understand human drug taking, it is possible to reason directly from the findings of animal studies.

**mood disorder**  A severe disturbance in emotional state, leading to prolonged periods of depression, sometimes accompanied by the alternation of periods of dysfunctional elation.

**motivated offender**  In routine activities theory, the hypothetical actor who is likely to commit a crime if conditions were right.

**MTF**  *See* **Monitoring the Future.**

**multiple confirmation**  Verifying that a given proposition is true through the use of two or more data sources.

**multiplier drug effect**  *See* **synergy.**

**mutagen**  An agent that has the capacity to alter or transform genes and chromosomes.

**narcotics**  Potent, addicting CNS depressants with strong analgesic or painkilling properties; some are semisynthetic, derived from natural products such as opium, while others are created entirely in the laboratory.

**Narcotics Anonymous (NA)**  A peer-oriented, self-help program to wean users off the use of drugs; based on Alcoholics Anonymous.

**National Commission on Marihuana and Drug Abuse**  A panel, authorized by the Controlled Substances Act, to sponsor studies on drug use and to make recommendations based on those studies' findings; produced a multivolume report in 1972 and 1973 recommending the decriminalization of marijuana.

**National Household Survey on Drug Use and Health**  An ongoing, federally sponsored door-to-door or telephone interview and questionnaire study on drug use of a representative sample of the American population ages 12 and older.

**National Institute on Alcohol Abuse and Alcoholism (NIAAA)**  A federal agency that gathers and disseminates information on alcohol abuse and the treatment of alcoholism.

**National Institute on Drug Abuse (NIDA)**  A federal agency that gathers and disseminates information on drug use and drug treatment.

**National Institute of Mental Health (NIMH)**  A federal agency.

**negative reinforcement**  *See* **reinforcement, negative.**

**neuron**  A nerve cell.

**neurotransmitter**  A chemical "messenger," released from one nerve cell to another, that transforms activity in the nerve cell next to it.

**nonspecific effect, drug**  Effects that are not produced directly by the action of drugs.

**objective/objectivistic approach to reality**  *See* **essentialism.**

**Operation Pressure Point**  An experimental law enforcement project that took place in Lower East Side of Manhattan in the 1980s, which entailed saturation enforcement and maximum proactive policing of the drug laws.

**opiates**  A narcotic product of opium; examples: opium itself, morphine, codeine, and heroin.

**opioids**  Synthetic narcotics; examples: fentanyl, oxycodone, Demerol, Percodan, and methadone.

**Opium Wars**  Two wars (1839–1842 and 1856–1860) fought by Great Britain to force China to open that country to the opium trade, which China had outlawed; the sale of opium was enormously profitable to the British government.

**OTC drugs**  Over-the-counter drugs.

**over-the-counter drugs**  Substances that may be purchased off the shelf, without a prescription from a physician; examples: aspirin, Tylenol, Sominex.

**partial decriminalization**  A policy whereby the possession of a small quantity of a controlled drug results not in arrest but, if the possessor is apprehended by law enforcement, a small fine and confiscation of the substance.

**participant observation**  A research technique that involves close, intimate, and prolonged contact between the researcher and his or her subjects and informants.

**passive smoke**  Smoke that issues from the cigarettes of smokers into the air, which nonsmokers are forced to inhale because they are in close proximity.

**patent medicines**  Quack cure-alls or panaceas sold during the 1800s and early 1900s that often contained potent and addicting psychoactive drugs (such as opium and morphine); for the most part, they were neither patented nor medicinal.

**pathology theories/orientations**  The view that illicit drug use is caused by a defect, usually of psychological origin, in the user.

**pharmaceutical drug**  A prescription drug.

**pharmacological school**  The belief that the properties of drugs dictate drug-related behavior; for instance, the belief that the use of marijuana automatically "leads to" the use and abuse of harder drugs.

**pharmacology**  The study of the effects of drugs on organisms.

**phenothiazines**  A category of drugs used to combat psychosis, especially schizophrenia; includes Mellaril, Thorazine, and Stelazine; they do not produce a pleasurable intoxication in nonpsychotic persons and are not used recreationally.

**polydrug use**  The use of more than one drug, whether at the same time or during a given period of time.

**populist theory of the media**  *See* **grassroots theory of the media.**

**positive reinforcement**  *See* **reinforcement, positive.**

**potency**  Refers to the quantity of a given drug that is required to produce a given effect; the smaller the quantity, the more potent the drug.

**predisposition**  The preexisting tendency to do something; relevant to the subject at hand, the tendency to use or abuse one or more psychoactive substances.

**predisposition model/school** The argument that the explanation for the connection between drug addiction and criminal behavior is that the kinds of people who are likely to engage in compulsive drug-taking behavior are also the kinds who are likely to engage in criminal behavior.

**prescription drugs** Drugs that can be obtained, usually at a licensed pharmacy, only by first getting a written, signed document from a licensed physician.

**prescription model** A drug policy that proposes that drugs be administered by prescription.

**prevalence rate** The percentage of a given population that has used a specific drug within a specific time.

**proactive policing** A style of law enforcement that entails close monitoring of the community by the police, the extensive use of informants and undercover agents, and attempts by the police to prevent crime rather than react to it only after it occurs.

**problem behavior proneness, theory of drug use based on** An explanation of the recreational use of psychoactive substances that argues that drug use is simply one specific manifestation of a wide range of problematic behaviors, such as early sex, juvenile delinquency, conflict with and alienation from parents, and impulsivity.

**professional subculture theory of the media** The argument that the content and slant of the media are a product of the norms and ethics of journalists.

**progressive legalizers** Persons who believe that penalties for the possession and sale of drugs should be removed, based on humane values that seek to reduce the suffering of the user, abuser, and addict.

**progressive prohibitionists** Persons who favor retaining and enforcing the drug laws for humane reasons, that is, to protect the common good; usually favor a program of harm reduction.

**Prohibition** The period in the United States (1920–1933) during which it was illegal to sell alcoholic beverages.

**prohibition** Generally, legally banning any activity, including the possession and sale of psychoactive substances.

**proprietary drug** A prescription drug.

**pseudohallucination** An image, vision, or perception by a user of a hallucinogenic drug that the user knows isn't real.

**psychedelics** A category of drugs that causes profound sensory alterations, including synesthesia (translation of one sense into another), eidetic or closed-eye imagery, and "virtual" hallucinations.

**psychoactive** Having the property of influencing the workings of the mind, that is, having an effect on mood, emotions, feelings, and cognitive processes.

**psychodynamic theories of drug use** Explanations that argue that drug use, abuse, and/or addiction are caused by psychological factors.

**psychological theories of drug use** Explanations for the consumption of psychoactive substances that are based either on reinforcement, whether positive or negative, or personality type.

**psychopharmacological model** The argument that drugs, specifically cocaine, and violence, specifically murder, are strongly connected because the direct effects of cocaine conduce or cause violent behavior.

**psychopharmacological revolution** The growing use of psychoactive drugs to treat psychological disorder, rather than relying on other methods, especially "talking" cures.

**psychopharmacology** The study of the effects of drugs on the mind, that is, the CNS, mainly the brain.

**psychosocial unconventionality** A behavioral and attitudinal orientation that is said to be strongly correlated with and causative of experimentation with and use of psychoactive drugs.

**psychotherapeutics** Controlled substances used to treat psychological disorders; examples: antipsychotics and antidepressants.

**punding** A pattern, caused by administration of amphetamine, of engaging in a compulsive, repetitive action.

**punitive approach to drugs** The policy that is directed toward reducing drug use and sales by punishing offenders with legal penalties.

**punitive argument/model** The argument on which the punitive drug policy is based.

**pure agricultural model** A pattern of drug distribution that applies to substances grown and harvested from plants that contain drugs, requiring little or no preparation or transformation; applies mainly to marijuana and opium.

**pure chemical model** A pattern of drug distribution that applies to substances produced entirely in the lab; examples: Ecstasy, LSD, methamphetamine.

**Pure Food and Drug Act** A federal law, passed in 1906, that required distributors to list the ingredients of products on their packaging; may have influenced the subsequent decline in popularity of patent medicines.

**purity** The percentage of a given drug that a given sample contains.

**push down/pop up factor** *See* **balloon effect.**

**reactive policing** Law enforcement that takes place only after a crime has been committed.

**receptors** Locations in neurons at which neurotransmitters bind, hence producing (or blocking) a given action.

**recidivism** Committing a crime or engaging in drug use after correctional intervention.

**recreational drug use** Taking a substance for the purpose of achieving its effects for their own sake, that is, for pleasure, for the purpose of getting high.

**recriminalization** Passing a law against a given activity after the repeal of a law outlawing that same activity.

**reinforcement** Usually refers to positive reinforcement.

**reinforcement, negative** The motivation to continue using a drug to avoid withdrawal symptoms.

**reinforcement, positive** The motivation to continue using a drug to pursue pleasurable sensations attendant upon administration.

**reinforcement theories of drug abuse** Explanations based on the idea that drug abuse is caused by the reinforcing effects of psychoactive substances.

**relative deterrence** The view that, *in the absence of law enforcement,* the incidence of given activity would be greater than it is, given law enforcement.

**retreatism** Withdrawing from society's quest for material success, an adaptation proposed by anomie or strain theory as a consequence of being a "double failure," that is, failing to achieve success by both legitimate and illegitimate means, resulting in alcoholism or drug addiction.

**retrospective estimates** Calculations, based on the recall of interviewees, of drug use during earlier periods.

**route of administration** The way a given drug is taken—that is, orally, via smoking, IV injection, dermal patch, intranasally, or other means.

**rule of equivalency** The principle that the effects of alcohol are related solely and exclusively to the total volume of absolute alcohol in the body, and not the type of alcoholic beverage or the mixing of different kinds of alcoholic beverages.

**ruling elitist theory of the media** The belief that the elite, the most powerful social class in society, control the content and slant of the mass media.

**safety margin** *See* **ED/LD ratio.**

**SAMHSA** The Substance Abuse and Mental Health Service Administration, a federal agency authorized to study, treat, and disseminate information about alcohol and drug abuse, and mental disorder.

**sampling** Systematically selecting a subset of a population that looks like or "represents" that population with respect to important characteristics.

**sedative/hypnotics** A category of drugs that produce a calming, soothing effect.

**selective interaction/socialization theory of drug use** An explanation of drug use which argues that young people use recreational drugs because they gravitate toward social circles whose members are compatible in a range of ways, drug use included, and because these social circles further socialize them into the desirability of using drugs; the theory further argues that different factors are more influential at different stages of the young person's life, that is, as he or she moves from younger to older adolescence into young adulthood.

**self-control theory** An explanation which argues that deviant, criminal, and delinquent behavior—including recreational drug use—are caused by low self-control, which, in turn, is caused by poor, inadequate parenting.

**self-derogation theories of drug use** A theory of drug abuse which argues that young people take drugs as a "crutch," to escape from the fact that they are failures in life.

**sensationalism in the media** The view that the mass media present stories in an exaggerated, biased, and lurid fashion, designed to stimulate interest and excitement in the media-consuming public.

**sensory overload** A consequence of taking a psychedelic drug; being bombarded by an excess of stimuli as a result of being incapable of filtering out those that are relevant.

**serotonin** An important neurotransmitter that regulates sleep, appetite, body temperature, and mood.

**Shanghai Commission** An international meeting on drug control, held in China in 1909, which produced a treaty that eventually led to the Harrison Act; formal name: International Opium Commission.

**social control theory**  A theory of deviance which argues that violations of norms, particularly juvenile delinquency, take place to the extent that bonds to conventional others, conventional beliefs, and conventional activities are weak or absent; also applies to drug use.

**social learning theory**  A theory of deviance which argues that deviant, criminal, and delinquent behavior are learned in a more or less straightforward manner, as a result of exposure to social circles whose members define engaging in non-normative activity in positive terms; also applies to recreational drug use.

**sociocultural school**  An explanation of drug use which argues that drug-related behavior is influenced by the norms users acquire through contact with specific social circles or groups; this school would argue that the "stepping-stone" theory is false because the "progression" from marijuana to harder drugs is a product not of the effects of marijuana but of the norms promulgated by marijuana-using social circles.

**sociological theories of drug use**  Explanations of use, abuse, or addiction that make use of broader structural, cultural, or institutional factors and variables.

**specifist drug policy**  A program of drug control based on the notion that each drug or drug type should be controlled in a somewhat different way.

**stepping-stone hypothesis**  The view that the use of certain drugs (and here, marijuana is often the designated drug) literally cause the use of other, more dangerous drugs.

**stimulant**  A category of drugs that produce a speeding up of signals passing through the central nervous system.

**structural theories of drug use**  Explanations for the consumption of psychoactive substances which focus on factors that characterize entire systems within which people live, such as a society's income distribution, a neighborhood's social disorganization, or a region's rate of unemployment.

**subcultural theories of drug use**  Explanations of use, abuse, or addiction based on the notion that group-based norms, values, beliefs, and behavior influence drug taking.

**subcutaneous administration**  Injecting a drug directly beneath the skin.

**subjective/subjectivistic approach to reality** *See* **constructionism.**

**suitable target**  According to the routine activities theory, anything a motivated offender might seek to acquire illegally.

**survey**  A research technique that entails asking a sample of respondents' questions.

**synapse**  The space between neurons, across which neurotransmitters pass.

**synergistic effects**  A characteristic of two drugs such that if they are taken together, their combined effects will be more than twice as great as if twice the quantity of either had been taken by itself.

**synesthesia**  The translation of one sense into another, such as "seeing" sound and "tasting" color; one of the principal psychic effects of LSD.

**systemic model**  The argument that the reason the connection between drugs and violence is so strong is because the world of cocaine dealing is inherently conflictual, confrontational, and exploitative—and not because of the direct effects of cocaine.

**TC**  *See* **therapeutic community.**

**THC**  Tetrahydrocannabinol, the primary active chemical in marijuana.

**theory**  An explanation, whether confirmed or unconfirmed, of a general class or category of phenomena; hence, a "theory" of drug use would attempt to explain why people, or some people, use or abuse psychoactive substances.

**therapeutic community (TC)**  A live-in drug treatment program that seeks abstinence as its goal.

**therapeutic dose**  Usually refers to effective dose; *see* **ED.**

**therapeutic margin**  *See* **ED/LD ratio.**

**thirty-day prevalence rates**  The proportion of the population that has used a given drug during the past 30 days.

**thought disorder**  A disturbance in cognitive functioning such that delusions, such as hearing voices where none exist, are often regarded as true and may be acted upon; schizophrenia is the most common thought disorder.

**tolerance**  Over time, repeated administration of a particular drug results in diminished effects of that drug, or higher doses to achieve the same effect.

**tolerance, behavioral**  A form of diminishing effects that takes place because the user becomes accustomed to the effects of a given drug and how to act under its influence; *see also* **tolerance (drug).**

**tolerance, drug** Diminishing effects after repeated administration of a given drug.

**tolerance, pharmacological** A form of diminishing effects that takes place because of the interaction, at the molecular level, between a given drug and the body's neurochemistry; *see also* **tolerance (drug).**

**TOPS** The Treatment Outcome Prospective Study (conducted 1979–1981), a study to determine the effectiveness of drug treatment programs.

**toxicity** The quality of a drug that refers to how harmful or deadly it is, usually with respect to its capacity to produce death by overdose.

**tranquilizers** A term that is sometimes used to describe sedatives; formerly, it applied to the benzodiazepines and benzodiazepine-type drugs such as Valium.

**triangulation** Examining a phenomenon by using two or more independent data sources.

**UCR** The Uniform Crime Reports, a yearly publication by the Federal Bureau of Investigation, a federal agency that records the number and rate of crimes, arrest figures, and organizational information about law enforcement.

**vasoconstrictor** A chemical substance that contracts the blood vessels and decreases the volume of blood passing through them.

**vasodilator** A chemical substance that expands the blood vessels and increases the volume of blood passing through them.

**virtual hallucination** *See* **pseudohallucination.**

**Volstead Act** The Eighteenth Amendment, which outlawed the sale and distribution of alcoholic beverages in the United States (1920–1933).

**withdrawal symptoms** Physical reactions, including vomiting, muscular twitching, gooseflesh, and pain in the joints and bones, attendant upon discontinuing the use of a drug to which a person is addicted.

**worst-case scenario** The prediction that, under, and as a consequence of, drug legalization, tens of millions of Americans will become dependent on hard drugs such as heroin, cocaine, and methamphetamine.

**yearly prevalence rates** The proportion of the population that has used a given drug during the past year.

**zero tolerance** A policy guided by the motivation to punish and stamp out illicit drug use in all contexts.

# REFERENCES

*Note:* The pages in a few of the cited newspapers and journals are not standardized nationwide. For instance, *The New York Times* publishes regional editions that vary with respect to inclusion, content, and pagination. I cite the pages of the edition published for the Washington DC, area.

Abel, Ernest L. 1985. "Effects of Prenatal Exposure to Cannabinoids." In T.M. Pinkert (ed.), *Current Research on Consequences of Maternal Drug Abuse.* Rockville, MD: 20–35.

Adams, Edgar H., et al. 1989. "Overview of Selected Drug Trends." Rockville, MD: Division of Epidemiology and Prevention Research, National Institute on Drug Abuse, unpublished paper.

Adler, Freda, and William S. Laufer (eds.). 1995. *The Legacy of Anomie Theory.* New Brunswick, NJ: Transaction.

Agar, Michael. 1973. *Ripping and Running: A Formal Ethnography of Urban Heroin Addicts.* New York: Academic Press.

Akers, Ronald L. 1990. "Scary Drug of the Year: Myths and Realities in the Changing Drug Problem." Paper presented at the meetings of the American Society of Criminology, Baltimore, November.

Akers, Ronald L. 1992. *Drugs, Alcohol, and Society: Social Structure, Process, and Policy.* Belmont, CA: Wadsworth.

Akers, Ronald L., Marvin D. Kron, Lonn Lanza-Kaduce, and Marcia Radosevich. 1979. "Social Learning and Deviant Behavior: A Specific Test of a General Theory." *American Sociological Review,* 44 (August): 636–655.

Anderson, Elijah. 1999. *Code of the Street: Decency, Violence, and the Moral Life of the Inner City.* New York: W.W. Norton.

Andrews, George, and David Solomon (eds.). 1975. *The Coca Leaf and Cocaine Papers.* New York: Harcourt Brace Jovanovich.

Anglin, M. Douglas, Yih-Ing Hser, and Christine E. Grella. 1997. "Drug Addiction and Treatment Careers Among Clients in the Drug Abuse Treatment Outcome Study (DATOS)." *Psychology of Addictive Behaviors,* 11 (4): 308–323.

Anglin, M. Douglas, and George Speckart. 1988. "Narcotics Use and Crime: A Multisample, Multimethod Analysis." *Criminology,* 26 (May): 197–232.

Anonymous. 1996. "A Clearer Picture of Marijuana." *The Sun* (Baltimore), December 27, p. 2A.

Anslinger, Harry J., with Courtney Riley Cooper. 1937. "Marihuana—Assassin of Youth." *American Magazine,* July, pp. 18–19, 150–153.

Armor, David J., J. Michael Polich, and Harriet B. Stambul. 1976. *Alcoholism and Treatment.* Santa Monica: RAND Corporation.

Ashley, Richard. 1975. *Cocaine: Its History, Uses, and Effects.* New York: St. Martin's Press.

Ausubel, David P. 1980. "An Interactionist Approach to Narcotic Addiction." In Dan J. Lettieri et al. (eds.), *Theories on Drug Abuse.* Rockville, MD: National Institute on Drug Abuse, pp. 4–7.

Avalania, Rebecca. 2003. "In the Wake of a Major Retraction of a Report That Linked Parkinson's Disease to Ecstasy Use, Some Critics Wonder If Politics Is Poisoning Science," *Baltimore City Paper,* December 10–16.

Bachman, Jerald G., et al. 1997. *Smoking, Drinking, and Drug Use in Young Adolescence: The Impacts of New Freedoms and New Responsibilities.* Mahwah, NJ: Lawrence Erlbaum.

Bachman, Jerald G., et al. 2002. *The Decline of Substance Use in Young Adulthood: Changes in Social Activities, Roles, and Beliefs.* Mahwah, NJ: Lawrence Erlbaum.

Bachman, Jerald G. Lloyd D. Johnston, and Patrick M. O'Malley. 1981. "Smoking, Drinking, and Drug Use Among American High School Students: Correlates and Trends, 1975–1979." *American Journal of Public Health*, 71 (1): 59–69.

Baker, Russell. 2002. "What Else Is News?" *The New York Review of Books*, July 18, pp. 4, 6, 8.

Ball, John C., Lawrence Rosen, John A. Flueck, and David N. Nurco. 1981. "The Criminality of Heroin Addicts When Addicted and Off Opiates." In James A. Inciardi (ed.), *The Drugs–Crime Connection*. Newbury Park, CA: Sage, pp. 39–65.

Ball, John C., John W. Shaffer, and David N. Nurco. 1983. "The Day-to-Day Criminality of Heroin Addicts in Baltimore—A Study in the Continuity of Offense Rates." *Drug and Alcohol Dependence*, 12 (October): 119–142.

Barnett, Gene, Vojtech Licko, and Travis Thompson. 1985. "Behavioral Pharmacokinetics of Marijuana." *Psychopharmacology*, 85 (1): 51–56.

Barry, Dan, et al. 2003. "Times Reporter Who Resigned Leaves Long Trail of Deception." *The New York Times*, May 11, pp. 1, 20–23.

Beck, Jerome, and Marsha Rosenbaum. 1994. *Pursuit of Ecstasy: The MDMA Experience.* Albany: State University of New York Press.

Becker, Howard S. 1953. "Becoming a Marijuana User." *American Journal of Sociology*, 59 (November): 235–242.

Becker, Howard S. 1955. "Marijuana Use and Social Control." *Social Problems*, 3 (July): 35–44.

Becker, Howard S. 1963. *Outsiders: Studies in the Sociology of Deviance.* New York: Free Press.

Becker, Howard S. 1967. "History, Culture, and Subjective Experiences: An Exploration of the Social Bases of Drug-Induced Experiences." *Journal of Health and Social Behavior*, 8 (September): 163–167.

Beers, David. 1991. "Just Say Whoa!" *Mother Jones*, July/August 1991, pp. 36–43.

Bejerot, Nils. 1972. *Addiction: An Artificially Induced Drive.* Springfield, IL: Charles C Thomas.

Bejerot, Nils. 1980. "Addiction to Pleasure: A Biological and Social-Psychological Theory of Addiction." In Dan J. Lettieri et al. (eds.), *Theories on Drug Abuse*. Rockville, MD: National Institute on Drug Abuse, pp. 246–255.

Best, Joel. 2001. *Damned Lies and Statistics: Untangling Numbers from the Media, Politicians, and Activists.* Berkeley: University of California Press.

Best, Susan. 1990. "We Can't Do Worse by Legalizing Drugs." *The New York Times*, October 3, p. A32.

Blakeslee, Sandra. 1997. "Brain Studies Tie Marijuana to Other Drugs." *The New York Times*, June 17, p. A16.

Bonnie, Richard J., and Charles H. Whitebread II. 1974. *The Marihuana Conviction: A History of Marihuana Prohibition in the United States.* Charlottesville: University Press of Virginia.

Bourgois, Philippe. 1995. *In Search of Respect: Selling Crack in El Barrio.* Cambridge, UK, and New York: Cambridge University Press.

Bozarth, Michael A., and Ray A. Wise. 1985. "Toxicity Associated with Long-Term Intravenous Heroin and Cocaine Self-Administration." *Journal of the American Medical Association*, 254 (July 5): 81–84.

Braden, William. 1970. "LSD and the Press." In Bernard Aaronson and Humphrey Osmond (eds.), *Psychedelics*. Garden City, NY: Anchor Books/Doubleday, pp. 401–418.

Brady, Joseph V., and Scott E. Lucas (eds.). 1984. *Testing Drugs for Physical Dependence Potential and Abuse Liability.* Rockville, MD: National Institute on Drug Abuse.

Brecher, Edward M., and the Editors of Consumer Reports. 1972. *Licit and Illicit Drugs.* Boston: Little, Brown.

Brinkley, Joel. 1984. "The War on Narcotics: Can It Be Won?" *The New York Times*, September 14, pp. A1, A12.

Brody, Jane E. 1983. "New Therapies for the Addict Go Far Beyond Mere Abstinence." *The New York Times,* February 1, pp. C1, C2.

Brownstein, Henry H. 1991. "The Media and the Construction of Random Drug Violence." *Social Justice*, 18 (4): 85–103.

Brownstein, Henry H. 1996. *The Rise and Fall of a Violent Crime Wave: Crack Cocaine and the Social Construction of a Crime Problem.* Guilderland, NY: Harrow & Heston.

Bruen, Anne-Marie, Patrick Johnston, William Rhodes, Mary Layne, and Ryan Kling. 2002. *The Estimation of Heroin Availability: 1996–2000.* Washington, DC: Executive Office of the President, Office of National Drug Control Policy.

Brunvand, Jan Harold. 1999. *Too Good to Be True: The Colossal Book of Urban Legends.* New York: W.W. Norton.

Budd, Robert D. 1989. "Cocaine Abuse and Violent Death." *American Journal of Drug and Alcohol Abuse*, 15 (4): 375–382.

Butterfield, Fox. 2004. "Home-Making Laboratories Expose Children to Toxic Fallout." *The New York Times,* February 23.

Callaway, Enoch, III. 1958. "Institutional Use of Antarctic Drugs." *Modern Medicine, 1958 Annual*, Part I (January 1–June 15): 26–29.

Campbell, A.M.G., et al. 1971. "Cerebral Atrophy in Young Cannabis Smokers," "Cerebral Atrophy in Young Cannabis Users." *The Lancet*, December 4, pp. 1219–1224.

Canadian Commission of Inquiry into the Non-Medical Use of Drugs. 1972. *Cannabis*. Ottawa: Information Canada.

Carey, Shannon M., and Michael W. Finigan. 2006. "Detailed Cost-Benefit Analysis in a Mature Drug Court Setting." www.ncjrs.org/pdffiles1/nij/grants/ 203558.pdf.

Carter, Hodding, III. 1989. "We're Losing the War on Drugs Because Prohibition Never Works." *The Wall Street Journal*, July 13, p. A15.

Cashman, Sean. 1981. *Prohibition*. New York: Free Press.

Cassidy, John. 1995. "Who Killed America's Middle Class?" *The New Yorker*, October 16, pp. 113–124.

Catalano, Shannan M. 2005. "Criminal Victimization, 2004." *Bureau of Justice Statistics National Crime Victimization Survey*, September, pp. 1–12.

Caulkins, Jonathan P., Patricia A. Ebener, and Daniel F. McCaffrey. 1995. "Describing DAWN's Dominion." *Contemporary Drug Problems*, 22 (Fall): 547–567.

Caulkins, Jonathan P., Peter Reuter, Martin Y. Iguchi, and James Chiesa. 2005. *How Goes the "War on Drugs": An Assessment of U.S. Drug Problems and Policy*. Santa Monica, CA: RAND Corporation.

Chaikin, Marcia R. 1986. "Crime Rates and Substance Abuse Among Types of Offenders." In Bruce D. Johnson and Eric Wish (eds.), *Crime Rate Among Drug-Using Offenders*. New York: Narcotic & Drug Research, pp. 12–54.

Chatlos, Calvin. 1987. *Crack: What You Should Know About the Cocaine Epidemic*. New York: Perigee Books.

Chavkin, Wendy. 2001. "Cocaine and Pregnancy—Time to Look at the Evidence." *Journal of the American Medical Association*, 285 (March 28): 1626–1628.

Clouet, Doris, Khursheed Asghar, and Roger Brown (eds.). 1988. *Mechanisms of Cocaine Abuse and Toxicity*. Rockville, MD: National Institute on Drug Abuse.

Cloward, Richard A., and Lloyd E. Ohlin. 1960. *Delinquency and Opportunity*. New York: Free Press.

Co, Ben T., et al. 1977. "Absence of Cerebral Atrophy in Chronic Cannabis Users." *Journal of the American Medical Association*, 237 (March 21): 1229–1230.

Cohen, Maimon M., Michelle J. Marinello, and Nathan Back. 1967. "Chromosomal Damage in Human Leukocytes Induced by Lysergic Acid Diethalymide." *Science*, 155 (17 March): 1417–1419.

Cohen, Sidney. 1987. "Marijuana and the Cannabinoids." In *Drug Abuse and Drug Abuse Research*. The Second Triennial Report from the Secretary, Department of Health and Human Services. Rockville, MD: National Institute on Drug Abuse, pp. 77–91.

Cole, David. 1999. *No Equal Justice: Race and Class in the American Criminal Justice System*. New York: New Press.

Cooke, Janet. 1980. "Jimmy's World—8-Year-Old Heroin Addict Lives for a Fix." *The Washington Post*, September 28, pp. A1ff.

Courtwright, David T. 1982. *Dark Paradise: Opiate Addiction in America Before 1940*. Cambridge, MA: Harvard University Press.

Cowley, Geoffrey, et al. 1991. "A Prozac Backlash." *Newsweek*, April 1, pp. 64–67.

Crancer, Alfred Jr., et al. 1969. "Comparison of the Effects of Marihuana and Alcohol on Simulated Driving Performance." *Science*, 164 (16 May): 851–854.

Currie, Elliott. 1993. *Reckoning: Drugs, the Cities, and the American Future*. New York: Farrar, Straus & Giroux.

Curtis, Henry Pierson. 2000. "Bad Research Clouds State Death Reports," *The Orlando Sentinel*, May 21, pp. 1ff.

Cuskey, Walter R., Lisa H. Berger, and Arthur H. Richardson. 1978. "The Effects of Marijuana Decriminalization on Drug Use Patterns." *Contemporary Drug Problems*, 7 (Winter): 491–532.

Davison, Bill. 1967. "The Hidden Evils of LSD." *Saturday Evening Post*, August 12, pp. 19–23.

DAWN (*see* Drug Abuse Warning Network).

Deadwyler, S.A., C.J. Heyser, R.C. Michaelis, and R.E. Hampson. 1990. "The Effects of Δ-9-THC on the Mechanisms of Learning and Memory." In *Neurobiology of Drug Abuse: Learning and Memory*. Rockville, MD: National Institute on Drug Abuse, pp. 79–93.

Dennis, Richard J. 1990. "The Economics of Legalizing Drugs." *The Atlantic Monthly,* November, pp. 126–132.

Department of Health and Human Services, Centers for Disease Control, 2001. *HIV/AIDS Surveillance Report,* 13 (1), tables 5, 9.

Deutscher, Irwin, Fred P. Pestello, and H. Frances H. Pestello. 1993. *Sentiments and Acts.* New York: Aldine de Gruyter.

DiFranza, Joseph R., and Robert A. Lew. 1995. "Effects of Maternal Cigarette Smoking on Pregnancy Complications and Sudden Death Syndrome." *The Journal of Family Practice*, 40 (April): 385–394.

Dishotsky, Norman I., William D. Loughman, Robert E. Mogar, and Wendell R. Lipscomb. 1971. "LSD and Genetic Damage." *Science,* 172 (30 April): 431–440.

Doblin, Richard E., and Mark A.R. Kleiman. 1991. "Marijuana as Antiemetic Medicine: A Survey of Oncologists' Experiences and Attitudes." *Journal of Clinical Oncology*, 9 (July): 1314–1319.

Dole, Vincent P. 1980. "Addictive Behavior." *Scientific American*, 243 (December): 138–154.

Dole, Vincent P., and Marie E. Nyswander. 1965. "A Medical Treatment for Diacetylmorphine (Heroin) Addiction." *Journal of the American Medical Association*, 193 (August 23): 646–650.

Dole, Vincent P., and Marie E. Nyswander. 1980. "Methadone Maintenance: A Theoretical Perspective." In Dan J. Lettieri, Mollie Sayers, and Henel Wallenstein Pearson (eds.), *Theories on Drug Abuse: Selected Contemporary Perspectives*. Rockville, MD: National Institute on Drug Abuse, pp. 256–261.

Douglas, Jack D. 1976. *Investigative Social Research: Individual and Team Field Research*. Thousand Oaks, CA: Sage.

Downie, Leonard, Jr., and Robert G. Kaiser. 2002. *The News About the News: American Journalism in Peril*. New York: Alfred Knopf.

Drug Abuse Warning Network. 1987. "Trends in Drug Abuse Related Hospital Emergency Room Episodes and Medical Examiner Cases for Selected Drugs, DAWN, 1975–1985." Rockville, MD: National Institute on Drug Abuse, unpublished paper.

Drug Abuse Warning Network. 2002. "Club Drugs: 2001 Update." Rockville, MD: National Institute on Drug Abuse.

Dunlap, Eloise, Bruce D. Johnson, and Ali Manwar. 1994. "A Successful Female Crack Dealer: Case Study of a Deviant Career." *Deviant Behavior*, 15 (1): 1–25.

DuPont, Robert L. 1997. *The Selfish Brain: Learning from Addiction*. Center City, MN: Hazelden.

Duster, Troy. 1995. "The New Crisis of Legitimacy in Controls, Prisons, and Legal Structures." *The American Sociologist*, 26 (Spring): 20–31.

Earleywine, Mitch. 2002. *Understanding Marijuana: A New Look at the Evidence*. Oxford, UK, and New York: Oxford University Press.

Eastland, James O. (Chair). 1974. *Marihuana-Hashish Epidemic and Its Impact on United States Security*. Washington, DC: U.S. Government Printing Office.

Eckholm, Erik. 1986. "Cocaine's Vicious Spiral: Highs, Lows, and Desperation." *The New York Times,* August 17, p. E2.

Egan, Timothy. 2002. "The Seeds of Decline." *The New York Times*, December 8, pp. 1WK, 3WK.

Eisner, Bruce. 1989. *MDMA: The Ecstasy Story*. Berkeley, CA: Ronin.

Epstein, Roberta, and Eugene E. Eubanks. 1984. "Drug Use Among Medical Students." *New England Journal of Medicine*, 311 (October 4): 923.

Erickson, Patricia G., Edward M. Adlaf, Glenn F. Murray, and Reginald G. Smart. 1987. *The Steel Drug: Cocaine in Perspective*. Lexington, MA: Lexington Books.

Erikson, Kai T. 1967. "A Comment on Disguised Observation in Sociology." *Social Problems*, 14 (Spring): 366–373.

Feder, Barnaby J. 1997. "Surge in Teen-Age Smoking Left an Industry Vulnerable." *The New York Times*, April 20, pp. 1, 28.

Felson, Marcus. 1991. "Blame Analysis: Accounting for the Behavior of Protected Groups." *The American Sociologist*, 22 (Spring): 5–23.

Fendrich, Michael, et al. 1999. "Validity of Drug Use Reporting in a High-Risk Community Sample: A Comparison of Cocaine and Heroin Survey Reports with Hair Tests." *American Journal of Epidemiology*, 149 (10): 955–962.

Ferdinand, Pamela. 2003. "Drug Is Making Deadly Inroads in New England." *The Washington Post*, February 8, p. A3.

Fiddle, Seymour. 1967. *Portraits from a Shooting Gallery*. New York: Harper & Row.

Fine, Gary Alan, and Patricia E. Turner. 2001. *Whispers on the Color Line: Rumor and Race in America*. Berkeley: University of California Press.

Finestone, Harold. 1957a. "Cats, Kicks, and Color." *Social Problems*, 5 (July): 3–13.

Finestone, Harold. 1957b. "Narcotics and Criminality," *Law and Contemporary Problems*, 22 (Winter): 69–85.

Finn, Peter, and Andrea K. Newlyn. 1997. "Miami's Drug Court: A Different Approach." In Larry K. Gaines and Peter B. Kraska (eds.), *Drugs, Crime, and Justice:*

*Contemporary Perspectives*. Prospect Heights, IL: Waveland Press, pp. 357–374.

Fishburne, Patricia M., Herbert I. Abelson, and Ira Cisin, 1980. *National Survey on Drug Abuse: Main Findings, 1979*. Rockville, MD: National Institute on Drug Abuse.

Fitzpatrick, Joseph P. 1974. "Drugs, Alcohol, and Violent Crime." *Addictive Diseases*, 1 (3): 353–367.

Flynn, Patrick M., et al. 1997. "Methodological Overview and Research Design for the Drug Abuse Treatment Outcome Study (DATOS)." *Psychology of Addictive Behaviors*, 11 (4): 230–243.

Flynn, Stephen. 1993. "Worldwide Drug Scourge: The Expanding Trade in Illicit Drugs." *The Brookings Review*, Winter, pp. 6–11.

Frank, Deborah A., et al. 2001. "Growth, Development, and Behavior in Early Childhood Following Prenatal Cocaine Exposure." *Journal of the American Medical Association*, 285 (March 28): 1613–1625.

Fuerbringer, Jonathan. 1986. "Wide Bill on Drugs Pressed." *The New York Times,* September 11, p. A24.

Gahlinger, Paul M. 2001. *Illegal Drugs: A Complete Guide to Their History, Chemistry, Use and Abuse*. Las Vegas: Sagebrush Press.

Gazzaniga, Michael S. 1990. "The Federal Drugstore." *National Review*, February 5, pp. 34–41.

Gieringer, Dale. 1990. "How Many Crack Babies?" *The Drug Policy Letter*, 11 (March/April): 4–6.

Gold, Mark S. 1984. *800-COCAINE*. New York: Bantam Books.

Goldberg, Bernard. 2002. *Bias: A CBS Insider Exposes How the Media Distort the News*. Washington, DC: Regnery.

Golden, Tim. 1996. "Though Evidence Is Thin, Tale of C.I.A. and Drugs Has Life of Its Own." *The New York Times*, October 21, p. A14.

Goldkamp, John S., Michael D. White, and Jennifer B. Robinson. 2001. "Do Drug Courts Work? Getting Inside the Drug Court Black Box." *Journal of Drug Issues*, 31 (1): 27–72.

Goldman, Douglas. 1955. "Treatment of Psychotic States with Chlorpromazine." *Journal of the American Medical Association*, 157 (April 9): 1274–1278.

Goldstein, Avram. 1994. *Addiction: From Biology to Drug Policy*. New York: W.H. Freeman.

Goldstein, Avram. 2001. *Addiction: From Biology to Drug Policy* (2nd ed.). New York: Oxford University Press.

Goldstein, Avram, and Harold Kalant. 1990. "Drug Policy: Striking the Right Balance." *Science*, 249 (28 September): 1513–1521.

Goldstein, Paul J. 1985. "The Drugs/Violence Nexus: A Tripartite Conceptual Framework." *Journal of Drug Issues*, 15 (Fall): 493–506.

Goldstein, Paul J., Patricia A. Bellucci, Barry J. Spunt, and Thomas Miller. 1991. "Volume of Cocaine Use and Violence: A Comparison Between Men and Women." *Journal of Drug Issues,* 12 (Spring): 345–367.

Goldstein, Paul J., Henry H. Brownstein, and Patrick J. Ryan. 1992. "Drug-Related Homicide in New York: 1984 and 1988." *Crime and Delinquency*, 38 (October): 459–476.

Goldstein, Paul J., Henry H. Brownstein, Patrick Ryan, and Patricia A. Bellucci. 1989. "Crack in Homicide in New York City, 1988: A Conceptually Based Event Analysis." *Contemporary Drug Problems*, 16 (Winter): 651–687.

Goldstein, Richard. 1986. "Getting Real About Getting High: An Interview with Andrew Weil." *The Village Voice,* September 30, pp. 21–22, 24.

Golub, Andrew, and Bruce D. Johnson. 2001. "The Rise of Marijuana as the Drug of Choice Among Youthful Adult Arrestees." *Research in Brief,* National Institute of Justice, June, pp. 1–19.

Gonzales, Laurence. 1984. "Cocaine: A Special Report." *Playboy*, April, pp. 134–137, 158, 200–216.

Gonzales, Laurence. 1985. "Why Drug Enforcement Doesn't Work." *Playboy*, December, pp. 104–105, 238–249.

Goode, Erica. 2002. "Deflating Self-Esteem's Role in Society's Ills." *The New York Times*, October 1, pp. D1, D6.

Goode, Erich. 1969. "Multiple Drug Use Among Marijuana Smokers." *Social Problems,* 17 (Summer): 48–64.

Goode, Erich. 1970. *The Marijuana Smokers*. New York: Basic Books.

Goode, Erich. 1972a. "Drug Use and Sexual Activity on a College Campus." *American Journal of Psychiatry*, 128 (April): 1272–1276.

Goode, Erich. 1972b. *Drugs in American Society*. New York: Alfred Knopf.

Goode, Erich. 1974. "Marijuana and the Progression to Dangerous Drugs." In Loren L. Miller (ed.), *Marijuana: Effects on Human Behavior*. New York: Academic Press, pp. 303–338.

Goode, Erich. 1996. "The Ethics of Deception in Social Research: A Case Study." *Qualitative Sociology*, 19 (1): 11–33.

Goode, Erich. 1997. *Between Politics and Reason: The Drug Legalization Debate*. New York: St. Martin's Press.

Goode, Erich. 2002. "Drug Arrests at the Millennium." *Society*, July/August, pp. 41–45.

Goode, Erich, and Nachman Ben-Yehuda. 1994. *Moral Panics: The Social Construction of Deviance*. London: Blackwell.

Goodman, Ellen. 1992. "Panic over 'Crack Babies' Conceals Real Issue: Neglect." *Boston Globe*, January 12, p. 69.

Gootenberg, Paul. 2004. "Secret Ingredients: The Politics of Coca in US-Peruvian Relations, 1915–65." *Journal of Latin American Studies*, (May): 233–265.

Gottfredson, Denise C., and M. Lyn Exum. 2002. "The Baltimore City Drug Treatment Court: One-Year Results from a Randomized Study." *Journal of Research in Crime and Delinquency*, 39 (August): 337–356.

Gottfredson, Denise C., Stacy S. Najaka, and Brook Kearly. 2003. "Effectiveness of Drug Treatment Courts: Evidence from a Randomized Trial." *Criminology and Public Policy*, 2 (2): 171–196.

Gottfredson, Michael R., and Travis Hirschi. 1990. *A General Theory of Crime*. Stanford, CA: Stanford University Press.

Gould, Leroy, Andrew L. Walker, Lansing E. Crane, and Charles W. Lidz. 1974. *Connections: Notes from the Heroin World*. New Haven, CT: Yale University Press.

Grant, Bridget F., John Noble, and Henry Malin. 1986. "Decline in Liver Cirrhosis Mortality and Components of Change." *Alcohol Health and Research World*, 10 (Spring): 66–69.

Gravelle, Jane, and Dennis Zimmerman. 1994. "The Marlboro Math." *Outlook (The Washington Post)*, June 5, pp. C1, C4.

Green, Bill. 1981. "Janet's World: The Story of a Child Who Never Existed—How and Why It Came to Be Published." *The Washington Post*, April 19, pp. A1ff.

Grinspoon, Lester, and James B. Bakalar. 1976. *Cocaine: A Drug and Its Social Evolution*. New York: Basic Books.

Grinspoon, Lester, and James B. Bakalar. 1979. *Psychedelic Drugs Reconsidered*. New York: Basic Books.

Grinspoon, Lester, and James B. Bakalar. 1993. *Marihuana: The Forbidden Medicine*. New Haven, CT: Yale University Press.

Grinspoon, Lester, and James B. Bakalar. 1997. *Marihuana: The Forbidden Medicine* (rev. & exp. ed.). New Haven, CT: Yale University Press.

Grinspoon, Lester, and Peter Hedblom. 1975. *The Speed Culture: Amphetamine Use and Abuse in America*. Cambridge, MA: Harvard University Press.

Gruber, Amanda J., Harrison G. Pope, Jr., and Paul Oliva. 1997. "Very Long-Term Users of Marijuana in the United States." *Substance Abuse and Misuse*, 32 (3): 249–264.

Guttman, Erich. 1936. "Artificial Psychosis Produced by Mescaline." *The Journal of Mental Science*, 82: 203–221.

Haddad, Anne. 1996. "More MD. Children Are Using Tobacco." *The Sun* (Baltimore), August 25, pp. 1B, 4B.

Hamid, Ansley. 1990. "The Political Economy of Crack-Related Violence." *Contemporary Drug Problems*, 17 (Spring): 31–78.

Hamid, Ansley. 1998. *Drugs in America: Sociology, Economics, and Politics*. Gaithersburg, MD: Aspen.

Hanson, Bill, George Beschner, James M. Walters, and Eliott Bovelle. 1985. *Life with Heroin: Voices from the Inner City*. Lexington, MA: Lexington Books.

Harclerode, Jack. 1984. "Endocrine Effects of Marijuana in the Male: Preclinical Studies." In Monique C. Braude and Jacqueline C. Luford (eds.), *Marijuana Effects on the Endocrine and Reproductive Systems*. Rockville, MD: National Institute on Drug Abuse, pp. 46–64.

Heath, Robert G. 1981. "Marijuana and the Brain" (pamphlet). New York: American Council on Marijuana and Other Drugs.

Himmelstein, Jerome L. 1979. "The Fetishism of Drugs." *International Journal of the Addictions*, 14 (8): 1083–1101.

Himmelstein, Jerome L. 1983. *The Strange Career of Marihuana*. Westport, CT: Greenwood Press.

Hingson, Ralph, and Michael Winter. 2003. "Epidemiology and Consequences of Drinking and Driving." *Alcohol Research and Health*, 27 (1): 63–78.

Hirschi, Travis. 1969. *Causes of Delinquency*. Berkeley: University of California Press.

Hochman, Joel Simon. 1972. *Marijuana and Social Evolution*. Englewood Cliffs, NJ: Prentice-Hall/Spectrum.

Hochman, Joel Simon, and Norman Q. Brill. 1971. "Chronic Marihuana Usage and Liver Function." *The Lancet*, October 9, pp. 918–919.

Hochman, Joel Simon, and Norman Q. Brill. 1973. "Marijuana Use and Psychosocial Adaptation." *American Journal of Psychiatry*, 130 (February): 132–140.

Hodgson, Barbara. 1999. *Opium: A Portrait of the Heavenly Demon*. San Francisco: Chronicle Books.

Hofmann, Albert. 1980. *LSD, My Problem Child* (trans. Jonathan Ott). New York: McGraw-Hill.

Hollister, Leo E. 1988. "Marijuana and Immunity." *Journal of Psychoactive Drugs*, 20 (1): 3–8.

Holmes, Oliver Wendell, Sr. 1891. *Medical Essays: 1842–1882*. Boston: Houghton Mifflin.

Holmes, Steven A. 1997. "Accusations of C.I.A. Ties to Drug Ring Are Being Renewed." *The New York Times*, May 15, p. B15.

Hoover, Eric. 2002. "Binge Thinking." *The Chronicle of Higher Education*, November 8, pp. A34–A37.

Hubbard, Robert L., et al. 1989. *Drug Abuse Treatment: A National Study of Effectiveness*. Chapel Hill: University of North Carolina Press.

Hubbard, Robert L., et al. 1997. "Overview of 1-Year Follow-Up Outcomes in the Drug Abuse Treatment Outcome Study (DATOS)." *Psychology of Addictive Behaviors*, 11 (4): 261–278.

Huddleston, C. West, III, Karen Freeman-Wilson, and Donna L. Boone. 2004. *Painting the Current Picture: A National Report Card on Drug Courts*. Alexandria, VA: National Drug Court Institute.

Hughes, Helen MacGill (ed.). 1961. *The Fantastic Lodge: The Autobiography of a Girl Addict*. Boston: Houghton Mifflin.

Hyse, Richard. 1994. "Prohibition, for Drugs as for Alcohol, Only Fails." *The New York Times*, February 11, p. 44.

Inciardi, James A. 1987. "Beyond Cocaine: Basuco, Crack, and Other Coca Products."*Contemporary Drug Problems*, 14 (Fall): 461–492.

Inciardi, James A. 1992. *The War on Drugs II: The Continuing Epic of Heroin, Cocaine, Crack, AIDS, and Public Policy*. Mountain View, CA: Mayfield.

Inciardi, James A. 2002. *The War on Drugs III: The Continuing Saga of the Mysteries and Miseries of Intoxication, Addiction, Crime, and Public Policy*. Boston: Allyn & Bacon.

Inciardi, James A., and Duane C. McBride. 1991. "The Case *Against* Legalization." In James A. Inciardi (ed.), *The Drug Legalization Debate*. Newbury Park, CA: Sage, pp. 45–79.

Jansen, A.C.M. 1991. *Cannabis in Amsterdam: A Geography of Hashish and Marihuana*. Muiderberg, The Netherlands: Dick Coutinho.

Jefferson, David J. 2005. "America's Most Dangerous Drug." *Newsweek,* August 8.

Jessor, Richard. 1979. "Marihuana: A Review of Recent Psychological Research." In Robert I. DuPont et al. (eds.), *Handbook on Drug Abuse*. Washington, DC: U.S. Government Printing Office, pp. 337–355.

Jessor, Richard. 1983. "A Psychological Perspective on Adolescent Substance Abuse." In I.F. Litt (ed.), *Adolescent Substance Abuse*. Columbus, OH: Ross Laboratories, pp. 21–28.

Jessor, Richard. 1998. *New Perspectives on Adolescent Risk Behaviors*. New York: Academic Press.

Jessor, Richard, John E. Donovan, and Frances Costa. 1986. "Psychosocial Correlates of Marijuana Use in Adolescence and Young Adulthood: The Past as Prologue." *Alcohol, Drugs, and Driving*, 2 (3/4): 31–49.

Jessor, Richard, and Shirley L. Jessor. 1977. *Problem Behavior and Psychosocial Development: A Longitudinal Study of Youth*. New York: Academic Press.

Jessor, Richard, and Shirley L. Jessor. 1980. "A Social-Psychological Framework for Studying Drug Use." In Dan J. Lettieri et al. (eds.), *Theories on Drug Abuse*. Rockville, MD: National Institute on Drug Abuse, pp. 54–71.

Johanson, Chris E. 1984. "Assessment of the Abuse Potential of Cocaine in Animals." In John Grabowski (ed.), *Cocaine: Pharmacology, Effects, and Treatment of Abuse*. Rockville, MD: National Institute on Drug Abuse, pp. 54–71.

Johnson, Bruce D. 1973. *Marihuana Users and Drug Subcultures*. New York: Wiley-Interscience.

Johnson, Bruce D. 1978. "Once an Addict, Seldom an Addict." *Contemporary Drug Problems*, 7 (Spring): 35–53.

Johnson, Bruce D. 1980. "Toward a Theory of Drug Subcultures." In Dan J. Lettieri et al. (eds.), *Theories on Drug Abuse*. Rockville, MD: National Institute on Drug Abuse, pp. 110–119.

Johnson, Bruce D., et al. 1985. *Taking Care of Business: The Economics of Crime by Heroin Abusers*. Lexington, MA: Lexington Books.

Johnson, Bruce D., Elsayed Elmoghazy, and Eloise Dunlap. 1990. "Crack Abusers and Noncrack Abusers: A Comparison of Drug Use, Drug Sales, and Nondrug Criminality." Unpublished paper.

Johnson, Bruce D., Andrew Golub, and Eloise Dunlap. 2000. "The Rise and Decline of Hard Drugs, Drug Markets, and Violence in Inner-City New York." In Alfred Blumstein and Joel Waldman (eds.), *The Crime Drop in America*. Cambridge, UK & New York: Cambridge University Press, pp. 164–206.

Johnson, Bruce D., and Mitchell Kaplan. 1989. "The Diversity and Frequency of Criminality Among Drug-Abusing Offenders." In Ragner B. Waalberg (ed.), *Prevention and Control/Realities and Aspirations*. Proceedings of the 35th International Congress on

Alcoholism and Drug Dependence, Oslo, Norway: National Directorate for the Prevention of Alcohol and Drug Problems, pp. 524–540.

Johnston, David Cay. 2003. "Very Richest Share of Income Grew Even Bigger, Data Show." *The New York Times*, June 26, pp. A1, C2.

Johnston, Lloyd D., Patrick M. O'Malley, Jerald G. Bachman, and John E. Schulenberg. 2005. *National Survey Results on Drug Use, 1975–2004*, vol. II, College Students and Adults Ages 19–45. Bethesda, MD: National Institute on Drug Abuse.

Johnston, Lloyd D., Patrick M. O'Malley, Jerald G. Bachman, and John E. Schulenberg. 2006. *Monitoring the Future National Results on Adolescent Drug Use: Overview of Key Findings, 2005*. Bethesda, MD: National Institute on Drug Abuse.

Jones, Hardin. 1974. "Testimony of Hardin B. Jones." In James O. Eastland (Chairman), *Marihuana-Hashish Epidemic and Its Impact on United States Security*. Washington, DC: U.S. Government Printing Office, pp. 265ff.

Jones, Hardin, and Helen Jones. 1977. *Sensual Drugs*. Cambridge, UK: Cambridge University Press.

Jones, James H. 1981. *Bad Blood: The Tuskegee Syphilis Experiment, a Tragedy of Race and Medicine*. New York: Free Press.

Jordan, Mary. 2004. "Pit Stop on the Cocaine Highway," *The Washington Post*, October 6, p. A20.

Joy, Janet E., Stanley J. Watson, Jr., and John A. Benson, Jr. (eds.) 1999. *Marijuana and Medicine: Assessing the Science Base*. Washington, DC: National Academy Press.

Julien, Robert M. 1995. *A Primer of Drug Action* (9th ed.). New York: W.H. Freeman.

Kahneman, Daniel, Paul Slovic, and Amos Tversky (eds.). 1982. *Judgment Under Uncertainty: Heuristics and Biases*. Cambridge, UK, and New York: Cambridge University Press.

Kalish, Carol B., and Wilfred T. Matsumura. 1983. "Prisoners and Drugs." *Bureau of Justice Statistics Bulletin*, March, pp. 1–6.

Kandel, Denise B. 1973. "Adolescent Marijuana Use: Role of Parents and Peers." *Science*, 181 (September 14): 1067–1070.

Kandel, Denise B. 1974. "Inter-Generational and Intragenerational Influences on Adolescent Marijuana Use." *Journal of Social Issues,* 30 (2): 107–135.

Kandel, Denise B. 1980a. "Drug and Drinking Behavior Among Youth." *Annual Review of Sociology*, 6: 235–285.

Kandel, Denise B. 1980b. "Developmental Stages in Adolescent Drug Involvement." In Dan J. Lettieri et al. (eds.), *Theories of Drug Abuse*. Rockville, MD: National Institute on Drug Abuse, pp. 120–127.

Kandel, Denise B. 1984. "Marijuana Users in Young Adulthood." *Archives of General Psychiatry*, 41 (February): 202–209.

Kandel, Denise B., and Mark Davies. 1991. "Friendship Networks, Intimacy, and Drug Use in Young Adulthood: A Comparison of Two Competing Theories." *Criminology*, 29 (August): 441–467.

Kandel, Denise B., Ronald C. Kessler, and Rebecca Z. Margulies. 1978. "Antecedents of Adolescent Initiation into Stages of Drug Use: A Developmental Analysis." *Journal of Youth and Adolescence*, 7 (1): 13–40.

Kandel, Denise B., Kazuo Yamaguchi, and Kevin Chen. 1992. "Stages of Progression in Drug Involvement from Adolescence to Adulthood: Further Evidence for the Gateway Theory." *Journal of Studies on Alcohol*, 53 (September): 447–457.

Kaplan, Howard B. 1975. *Self-Attitudes and Deviant Behavior*. Pacific Palisades, CA: Goodyear.

Kaplan, Howard B. 1980. "Self-Esteem and Self-Derogation Theory of Drug Abuse." In Dan J. Lettieri et al. (eds.), *Theories on Drug Abuse*. Rockville, MD: National Institute on Drug Abuse, pp. 128–131.

Kaplan, John. 1970. *Marijuana: The New Prohibition*. New York: World.

Kaplan, John. 1983. *The Hardest Drug: Heroin and Public Policy*. Chicago: University of Chicago Press.

Kaplan, John. 1988. "Taking Drugs Seriously." *The Public Interest*, 98: 32–50.

Karel, Richard B. 1991. "A Model Legalization Proposal." In James A. Inciardi (ed.), *The Drug Legalization Debate*. Newbury Park, CA: Sage, pp. 80–102.

Katz, Jack. 1988. *Seductions of Crime: Moral and Sensuous Attractions of Doing Evil*. New York: Basic Books.

Keating, Brian. 1970. "Four Junkies." *The Village Voice*, April 2, p. 30.

Kennedy, Randall. 1997. *Race, Crime, and the Law*. New York: Pantheon Books.

Kerr, Peter. 1986. "Anatomy of a Drug Issue: The Drugs, the Evidence, the Reaction." *The New York Times*, November 17, pp. A1, B6.

Kerr, Peter. 1988. "The Unspeakable Is Debated: Should Drugs Be Legalized?" *The New York Times*, May 15, pp. 1, 24.

Kew, M.C., et al. 1969. "Possible Hepatoxicity of Cannabis." *The Lancet*, March 15, pp. 578–579.

King, Rufus. 1972. *The Drug Hang-Up: America's Fifty-Year Folly*. Springfield, IL: Charles C Thomas.

King, Ryan S. 2006. *The Next Big Thing? Methamphetamine in the United States*. Washington, DC: Sentencing Project.

Klee, G.D. 1963. "Lysergic Acid Diethylamide (LSD-25) and Ego Function." *Archives of General Psychiatry*, 8: 461–474.

Klein, Joe. 1985. "The New Drug They Call 'Ecstasy.'" *New York*, May 20, pp. 38–43.

Kleiman, Mark A.R. 1992a. "Neither Prohibition nor Legalization: Grudging Toleration in Drug Control Policy." *Daedalus*, 121 (Summer): 53–83.

Kleiman, Mark A.R. 1992b. *Against Excess: Drug Policy for Results*. New York: Basic Books.

Kleinman, Paula Holzman, and Irving K. Lukoff. 1977. "The Magic Fix: A Critical Analysis of Methadone Maintenance Treatment." *Social Problems*. 25 (December): 208–214.

Kolata, Gina. 1987. "Alcoholism: Genetic Links Grow Clearer." *The New York Times*, November 10, pp. C1, C10.

Kolata, Gina. 1990. "Old, Weak, and a Loser: Crack Users' Image Falls." *The New York Times*, July 23, pp. A1, B4.

Kolodny, Robert C., et al. 1974. "Depression of Plasma Testosterone Levels After Chronic Intensive Marijuana Use." *New England Journal of Medicine*, 290 (April 18): 872–874.

Kornhauser, Ruth. 1978. *Social Sources of Delinquency: An Appraisal of Analytic Models*. Chicago: University of Chicago Press.

Kramer, John. 1969. "An Introduction to Amphetamine Abuse." *Journal of Psychedelic Drugs*, 2 (Spring): 8–13.

Kramer, Peter D. 1993. *Listening to Prozac*. New York: Penguin Books.

Kraska, Peter B. 1997. "The Military as Drug Police: Exercising the Ideology of War." In Larry K. Gaines and Peter B. Kraska (eds.), *Drugs, Crime, and Justice: Contemporary Perspectives*. Prospect Heights, IL: Waveland Press, pp. 297–320.

Kraska, Peter B. 2003. "The Military as Drug Police: Exercising the Ideology of War." In Larry K. Gaines and Peter B. Kraska (eds.), *Drugs, Crime, and Justice: Contemporary Perspectives* (2nd ed.). Prospect Heights, IL: Waveland Press, pp. 288–308.

Krohn, Christopher. 2002. "Why I'm Fighting Federal Drug Laws from City Hall." *The New York Times*, September 21, p. A27.

Krug, Etienne G., Linda L. Dahlberg, James A. Mercy, Anthony B. Zwi, and Rafael Lozano (eds.). 2002. *World Report on Violence and Health*. Geneva: World Health Organization.

Krugman, Paul. 2002. "For Richer: How the Permissive Capitalism of the Boom Destroyed American Equality." *The New York Times Magazine*, October 20, pp. 62–67, 76–77, 141–142.

Ksir, Charles, Carl L. Hart, and Oakley Ray. 2006. *Drugs, Society, and Human Behavior* (9th ed.). New York: McGraw-Hill.

Kuehnle, John. 1977. "Computer Tomographic Examination of Heavy Marijuana Smokers." *Journal of the American Medical Association*, 237 (March 21): 1231–1232.

Labianca, Dominick A. 1992. "The Drug Scene's New 'Ice' Age." *USA Today Magazine*, July 28, pp. 48–49.

Lakins, Nekisha E., Gerald D. Williams, Hsiao-ye Yi, and Michael E. Hilton. 2005. "Apparent per Capita Alcohol Consumption: National, State, and Regional Trends, 1977–2003." Rockville, MD: National Institute on Alcohol Abuse and Alcoholism Surveillance Report #73.

Lang, John S., with Ronald A. Taylor. 1986. "America on Drugs." *U.S. News & World Report*, July 28, pp. 48–49.

Lasagna, Louis J., J.M. von Felsinger, and H.K. Beecher. 1955. "Drug-Induced Changes in Man." *Journal of the American Medical Association*, 157 (March 19): 1006–1020.

Lau, R. Jane, et al. 1976. "Phytohemagglutin-Induced Lymphocyte Transformation in Humans Receiving $\Delta$-9-Tetrahydrocannabinol." *Science*, 192 (21 May): 805–807.

Layne, Mary, Patrick Johnston, and William Rhodes. 2002. *Estimation of Cocaine Availability, 1996–2000*. Washington, DC: Executive Office of the President, National Office of Drug Control.

Lazare, Daniel. 1990. "The Drug War Is Killing Us." *The Village Voice*, January 23, pp. 22–29.

Lee, Felicia R. 1994. "Data Show Needle Exchange Curbs H.I.V. Among Addicts." *The New York Times*, November 26, pp. 1, 26.

Lemberger, Louis, et al. 1970. "Marijuana: Studies on the Disposition and Metabolism of Delta-9-Tetrahydrocannabinol." *Science*, 170 (December): 1320–1322.

Lemberger, Louis, et al. 1971. "Delta-9-Tetrahydrocannabinol." *Science*, 173 (July): 72–74.

Lender, Mark Edward, and James Kirby Martin. 1987. *Drinking in America: A History* (rev. & exp. ed.). New York: Free Press.

Lerner, Michael A. 1989. "The Fire of 'Ice.'" *Newsweek,* November 27, pp. 37, 38, 40.

Lettieri, Dan J., Millie Sayers, and Helen Wallenstein Pearson (eds.). 1980. *Theories on Drug Abuse: Selected Comparative Perspectives*. Rockville, MD: National Institute on Drug Abuse.

Leuw, Ed, and I. Haen Marshall (eds.). 1994. *Between Prohibition and Legalization: The Dutch Experiment in Drug Policy*. Amsterdam and New York: Kugler.

Levine, Harry Gene. 1991. "Just Say Poverty: What Causes Crack and Heroin Abuse." Paper delivered at the Annual Meeting of the Drug Policy Foundation, Washington, DC, November.

Levitt, Steven D., and Sudhir Alladi Venkatesh. 1998. "An Economic Analysis of a Drug-Related Selling Gang's Finances." Cambridge, MA: National Bureau of Economic Research, NBER Working Paper Series, Working Paper 6592, www.nber.org/papers/w6592.

Lewis-Williams, J. David, and Thomas A. Dowson. 1988. "The Sign of All Times: Entoptic Phenomena in Upper Paleolithic Art." *Current Anthropology*, 29 (April): 201–245.

Lindesmith, Alfred R. 1947. *Opiate Addiction*. Bloomington, IN: Principia Press.

Lindesmith, Alfred R. 1965. *The Addict and the Law*. Bloomington: Indiana University Press.

Lindesmith, Alfred R. 1968. *Addiction and Opiates*. Chicago: Aldine.

Lindesmith, Alfred R., and John H. Gagnon. 1964. "Anomie and Drug Addiction." In Marshall B. Clinard (ed.), *Anomie and Deviant Behavior: A Discussion and Critique*. New York: Free Press, pp. 158–188.

Lule, Jack. 2001. *Daily News, Eternal Stories: The Mythological Role of Journalism*. New York: Guilford Press.

Lyons, Richard D. 1983. "Physical and Mental Disabilities in Newborns Doubled in 25 Years." *The New York Times*, July 18, pp. A1, A10.

MacAndrew, Craig, and Robert B. Edgerton. 1969. *Drunken Comportment*. Chicago: Aldine.

MacCoun, Robert J., and Peter Reuter. 2001. *Drug War Heresies: Learning from Other Vices, Times, and Places*. Cambridge, UK, and New York: Cambridge University Press.

Massing, Michael. 1998. *The Fix*. New York: Simon & Schuster.

McAuliffe, William E. 1975. "A Second Look at First Effects: The Subjective Effects of Opiates on Nonaddicts." *Journal of Drug Issues*, 5 (Fall): 369–399.

McAuliffe, William E., et al. 1984. "Psychoactive Drug Use by Young and Future Physicians and Medical Students" *Journal of Health and Social Behavior*, 25 (March): 34–54.

McAuliffe, William E., et al. 1986. "Psychoactive Drug Use Among Practicing Physicians and Medical Students." *The New England Journal of Medicine*, 315 (September 25): 805–810.

McAuliffe, William E., and Robert A. Gordon. 1974. "A Test of Lindesmith's Theory of Addiction: The Frequency of Euphoria Among Long-Term Addicts." *American Journal of Sociology*, 79 (January): 795–840.

McAuliffe, William E., and Robert A. Gordon. 1980. "Reinforcement and the Combination of Effects: Summary of a Theory of Opiate Addiction." In Dan J. Lettieri et al. (eds.), *Theories of Drug Addiction*. Rockville, MD: National Institute on Drug Abuse, pp. 137–141.

McBride, Duane C., and James A Swartz. 1990. "Drugs and Violence in the Age of Crack Cocaine." In Ralph Weisheit (ed.), *Drugs, Crime, and the Criminal Justice System*. Cincinnati, OH: Anderson, pp. 141–169.

McBride, Duane C., Yvonne M. Terry, and James A. Inciardi. 1999. "Alternative Perspectives on the Drug Policy Debate." In James A. Inciardi (ed.), *The Drug Legalization Debate* (2nd ed.). Thousand Oaks, CA: Sage, pp. 9–54.

McCoy, Alfred W. 1991. *The Politics of Heroin: CIA Complicity in the Global Drug Trade*. New York: Lawrence Hill.

McKim, William A. 2007. *Drugs and Behavior: An Introduction to Behavioral Pharmacology* (6th ed.). Upper Saddle River, NJ: Prentice-Hall.

McNeil, Donald G., Jr. 2002. "Study in Primates Shows Brain Damage from Doses of Ecstasy." *The New York Times*, September 27, p. A26.

Mencher, Melvin. 1997. *News Reporting and Writing* (7th ed.). Madison, WI: Brown & Benchmark.

Mendelson, Jack H., et al. 1974. "Plasma Testosterone Levels Before, During, and After Chronic Marijuana Smoking." *New England Journal of Medicine*, 291 (November): 1051–1055.

Merton, Robert K. 1938. "Social Structure and Anomie." *American Sociological Review*, 3 (October): 672–682.

Merton, Robert K. 1957, 1968. *Social Theory and Social Structure* (rev. ed., rev. & enlarged ed.). New York: Free Press.

Messner, Steven F., and Richard Rosenfeld. 1997. *Crime and the American Dream* (2nd ed.). Belmont, CA: Wadsworth.

Michael, Robert T., John H. Gagnon, Edward O. Laumann, and Gina Kolata. 1994. *Sex in America: A Definitive Survey.* Boston: Little, Brown.

Mikuriya, Tod (ed.). 1973. *Marijuana: Medical Papers, 1839–1972.* Oakland: MediComp.

Miller, J. Mitchell, and Lance H. Selva. 1994. "Drug Enforcement's Double-Edged Sword: An Assessment of Asset Forfeiture Programs." *Justice Quarterly,* 11 (June): 313–335.

Miller, Judith Droitcour, et al. 1983. *National Survey on Drug Abuse: Main Findings, 1982.* Rockville, MD: National Institute on Drug Abuse.

Miller, Judith Droitcour, and Ira H. Cisin. 1980. *Highlights from the National Survey on Drug Abuse: 1979.* Rockville, MD: National Institute on Drug Abuse.

Mills, James. 1987. *The Underground Empire: Where Crime and Governments Embrace.* New York: Dell.

Mitchell, Chester Nelson. 1990. *The Drug Solution: Regulating Drugs According to Principles of Efficiency, Justice, and Democracy.* Ottawa: Carleton University Press.

Monteforte, J.R., and W.U. Spitz. 1975. "Narcotics Abuse Among Homicides in Detroit." *Journal of Forensic Sciences,* 20 (January): 186–190.

Mooney, Linda A., Robert Grambling, and Craig Forsyth. 1992. "Legal Drinking Age and Alcohol Consumption." *Deviant Behavior,* 13 (1): 59–71.

Moore, Mark. 1973. "Achieving Discrimination on the Effective Price of Heroin." *American Economic Review,* 63 (2): 270–277.

Moore, Mark. 1976. *Buy and Bust: The Effective Regulation of an Illicit Market in Heroin.* Lexington, MA: D.C. Heath.

Morgan, John P. 1991. "Prohibition Is Perverse Policy: What Was True in 1933 Is True Now." In Melvyn B. Krauss and Edward P. Lazaer (eds.), *Searching for Alternatives: Drug Control Policy in the United States.* Stanford, CA: Hoover Institution Press, pp. 405–423.

Morgan, John P., and Doreen Kagan. 1980. "The Dusting of America: The Image of Phencyclidine (PCP) in the Popular Media." *Journal of Psychedelic Drugs,* 12 (July–December): 195–204.

Morishima, Akira. 1984. "Effects of Cannabis and Natural Cannabinoids on Chromosomes and Ova." In Monique C. Braude and Jacqueline P. Luford (eds.), *Marijuana Effects on the Endocrine and Reproductive Systems.* Rockville, MD: National Institute on Drug Abuse, pp. 25–45.

Morral, Andrew R., Daniel F. McCaffrey, and Susan M. Paddock. 2002. "Reassessing the Marijuana Gateway Effect." *Addictions,* 97 (December): 1493–1504.

Morris, Robert R. 1985. "Human Pulmonary Histopathological Changes from Marijuana Smoking." *Journal of Forensic Sciences,* 30 (April): 345–349.

Morrow, Lance, et al. 1996. "Kids & Pot." *Time,* December 9, pp. 26–30.

Mugford, Stephen. 1993. "Harm Reduction: Does It Lead Where Its Proponents Imagine?" In Nick Heather et al. (eds.), *Psychoactive Drugs and Harm Reduction: From Faith to Science.* London: Whurr, pp. 21–33.

Murdock, Catherine Gilbert. 1998. *Domesticating Drink: Women, Men, and Alcohol in America, 1870–1940.* Baltimore: Johns Hopkins University Press.

Murphy, Sheigla, Craig Reinarman, and Dan Waldorf. 1986. "An 11-Year Follow-Up of Twenty-Seven Cocaine Users." Unpublished paper presented at the 36th Annual Meeting of the Society for the Study of Social Problems, New York City, August.

Musto, David F. 1991. "Opium, Cocaine, and Marijuana in American History." *Scientific American,* July, pp. 40–47.

Musto, David F. 1999. *The American Disease: Origins of Narcotic Control* (3rd ed.). New York: Oxford University Press.

Nadelmann, Ethan A. 1988. "The Case for Legalization." *The Public Interest,* 92 (1): 3–31.

Nadelmann, Ethan A. 1989. "Drug Prohibition in the United States: Costs, Consequences, and Alternatives." *Science,* 245 (1 September): 939–947.

Nadelmann, Ethan. 1990. "Should Some Drugs Be Legalized? Legalization Is the Answer." *Issues in Science and Technology,* 6 (Summer): 43–46.

Nadelmann, Ethan A. 1992. "Thinking Seriously About Alternatives to Drug Prohibition." *Daedalus,* 121: 85–132.

Nadelmann, Ethan A. 1995. "Europe's Drug Prescription." *Rolling Stone,* January 26, pp. 38–39.

Nahas, Gabriel G. 1973, 1975. *Marihuana–Deceptive Weed* (1st ed., 2nd ed.). New York: Raven Press.

Nahas, Gabriel G. 1990. *Keep off the Grass.* Middlebury, VT: Paul S. Erickson.

Nahas, Gabriel G., et al. 1974. "Inhibition of Cellular Immunity in Marihuana Smokers." *Science,* 183 (1 February): 419–420.

National Institute on Alcoholism and Alcohol Abuse (NIAAA). 1987, 1997, 2000. *Alcohol and Health.* Sixth, Ninth, and Tenth Special Reports to the U.S. Congress from the Secretary of Health and Human Services. Rockville, MD: NIAAA.

National Institute on Drug Abuse. 1986. "Highlights of the 1985 National Household Survey on Drug Abuse." Rockville, MD: NIDA.

National Institute on Drug Abuse (NIDA). 1991. *National Household Survey on Drug Abuse: Population Estimates, 1991.* Rockville, MD: NIDA.

Nephew, Thomas M., et al. 2003. *Apparent per Capita Alcohol Consumption: National, State, and Regional Trends, 1977–2000.* Rockville, MD: National Institute on Alcohol Abuse and Alcoholism.

Newes-Adeyi, Gabriella, Chiung M. Chen, Gerald D. Williams, and Vivian B. Faden, "Trends in Underage Drinking in the United States, 1991–2003." Rockville, MD: National Institute on Alcohol Abuse and Alcoholism (NIAAA), Surveillance Report #74.

Newmeyer, John A. 1980. "The Epidemiology of PCP in the Late 1970s." *Journal of Psychedelic Drugs,* 12 (July–December): 211–215.

NIAAA (*see* National Institute of Alcohol Abuse and Alcoholism).

Nicholl, Charles. 2000. "Keep Taking the Tablets." *Times Literary Supplement,* February 25, pp. 8–9.

Nichols, Kendra. 2004. "The Other Performance-Enhancing Drugs." *The Chronicle of Higher Education,* December 17, pp. A41–A42.

Nichols, W.W., et al. 1974. "Cytogenic Studies on Human Subjects Receiving Marijuana and 9-Tetrahydrocannabinol." *Mutation Research,* 26: 413–417.

NIDA (*see* National Institute on Drug Abuse).

O'Donnell, John A., and Richard R. Clayton. 1982. "The Stepping-Stone Hypothesis—Marijuana, Heroin, and Causality." *Chemical Dependencies: Behavioral and Biomedical Issues,* 4 (3): 229–241.

Ostrowski, James. 1990. "Has the Time Come to Legalize Drugs?" *USA Today,* July pp. 27–30.

Palmer, Stuart, and Arnold S. Linsky (eds.). 1972. *Rebellion and Retreat: Readings in the Forms and Processes of Deviance.* Columbus, OH: Charles E. Merrill.

Parenti, Michael. 1993. *Inventing Reality: The Politics of News Media* (2nd ed.). New York: St. Martin's Press.

Parker, Robert Nash. 1995. *Alcohol and Homicide: A Deadly Combination of Two American Traditions.* Albany: State University of New York Press.

Paul, D.M. 1975. "Drugs and Aggression." *Medicine, Science, and Law,* 15 (1): 16–21.

Pernanen, Kai. 1991. *Alcohol in Human Violence.* New York: Guilford Press.

Pollan, Michael. 1995. "How Pot Has Grown." *The New York Times Magazine,* February 19, pp. 31–35, 44, 50, 56–57.

Preble, Edward, and John J. Casey, Jr. 1969. "Taking Care of Business—The Heroin Addict's Life on the Street." *International Journal of the Addictions,* 4 (March): 145–169.

Purdum, Todd S. 1997. "Exposé on Crack Was Flawed, Paper Says." *The New York Times,* May 13, pp. A1, A16.

Quindlen, Anna. 1990. "Hearing the Cries of Crack." *The New York Times,* October 7, p. E19.

Quinney, Richard. 1979. *Criminology* (2nd ed.) Boston: Little, Brown.

Radosevich, Marcia, Lonne Lanza-Kaduce, Ronald L. Akers, and Marvin D. Kron. 1980. "The Sociology of Adolescent Drug and Drinking Behavior: Part II." *Deviant Behavior,* 1 (January–March): 145–169.

Ravenholt, R.T. 1984. "Addiction Mortality in the United States, 1980: Tobacco, Alcohol, and Other Substances." *Population and Developmental Review,* 10 (December): 697–724.

Raver-Lampman, Greg. 2003. "The Trouble with Ecstasy." *Washingtonian,* 38 (April): 35–41.

Ravo, Nick. 1987. "Drinking Age Is Said to Fail for Students." *The New York Times,* December 21, pp. A1, B15.

Reeves, Jimmie L., and Richard Campbell. 1994. *Cracked Coverage: Television News, the Anti-Cocaine Crusade, and the Reagan Legacy.* Durham, NC: Duke University Press.

Reinarman, Craig, and Ceres Duskin. 1999. "Dominant Ideology and Drugs in the Media." In Jeff Ferrell and Neil Websdale (eds.), *Making Trouble: Cultural Constructions of Crime, Deviance, and Control.* New York: Aldine de Gruyter, pp. 73–87.

Reinarman, Craig, and Harry Gene Levine. 1995. "The Crack Attack: America's Latest Drug Scare, 1986–1992." In Joel Best (ed.), *Images of Issues: Typifying Contemporary Drug Problems* (2nd ed.). New York: Aldine de Gruyter, pp. 147–186.

Reinarman, Craig, and Harry Gene Levine (eds.). 1997. *Crack in America: Demon Drugs and Social Justice.* Berkeley: University of California Press.

Rengert, George F. 1996. *The Geography of Illegal Drugs.* Boulder, CO: Westview Press.

Reuter, Peter. 1992. "Hawks Ascendant: The Punitive Trend of American Drug Policy." *Daedalus*, 121 (Summer): 15–52.

Reuter, Peter. 1996. "The Mismeasure of Illegal Drug Markets: The Implications of Its Irrelevance." In Susan Pozo (ed.), *The Underground Economy: Studies of Illegal and Unreported Activity*. Kalamazoo, MI: Upjohn Institute for Employment Research, pp. 63–80.

Reuter, Peter. 2001. "The Limits of Supply-Side Drug Control." *The Milken Institute Review*, First Quarter, pp. 14–23.

Reuter, Peter, Gordon Crawford, and Jonathan Cave. 1988. *Sealing the Borders: The Effects of Increased Military Preparation in Drug Interdiction*. Santa Monica, CA: RAND Corporation.

Rhodes, William, Patrick Johnston, and Ryan Kling. 2001. *The Price of Illicit Drugs: 1981 Through the Second Quarter of 2000*. Washington, DC: Executive Office of the President, Office of National Drug Control Policy.

Rhodes, William, Mary Layne, Anne-Marie Bruen, Patrick Johnston, and Lisa Becchetti. 2001. *What America's Users Spend on Illegal Drugs*. Washington, DC: Executive Office of the President, Office of National Drug Control Policy.

Ricaurte, George A., et al. 2002. "Severe Dopaminergic Neurotoxicity in Primates After a Common Recreational Dose Regimen of MDMA ("Ecstasy")." *Science,* 297 (September): 2260–2263.

Rickert, William S., Jack Robinson, and Byron Rogers. 1982. "A Comparison of Tar, Carbon Monoxide, pH Levels in Smoke from Marihuana and Tobacco Cigarettes." *Canadian Journal of Public Health,* 73 (November/December): 386–391.

Roberts, Majory. 1986. "MDMA: Madness, not Ecstasy." *Psychology Today,* June, pp. 14–15.

Robins, Lee N. 1973. *The Vietnam Veteran Returns*. Washington, DC: U.S. Government Printing Office.

Robins, Lee N. 1979. "Addict Careers." In Robert I. DuPont et al. (eds.), *Handbook on Drug Abuse*. Washington, DC: U.S. Government Printing Office, pp. 325–336.

Robins, Lee N. 1980. "The Natural History of Drug Abuse." In Dan J. Lettieri et al. (eds.), *Theories on Drug Abuse*. Rockville, MD: National Institute on Drug Abuse, pp. 215–224.

Robson, Philip. 1994. *Forbidden Drugs: Understanding Drugs and Why People Take Them*. Oxford, UK: Oxford University Press.

Rodriguez de Fonseca, Fernando, et al. 1997. "Activation of the Corticotripin-Releasing Factor in the Limbic System During Cannabinoid Withdrawal." *Science,* 276 (27 June): 2050–2054.

Rosenbaum, Marsha. 2002. "Ecstasy: America's New 'Reefer Madness.'" *Journal of Psychoactive Drugs,* 34 (June): 137–142.

Ross, John F. 1999. *Living Dangerously: Navigating the Risks of Everyday Life*. Cambridge, MA: Perseus.

Rumbarger, John J. 1989. *Profits, Power, and Prohibition: Alcohol Reform and the Industrializing of America, 1800–1930*. Albany: State University of New York Press.

Russell, Katheryn K. 1998. *The Color of Crime*. New York: New York University Press.

Ryan, William. 1976. *Blaming the Victim* (2nd ed.). New York: Vintage Books.

SAMHSA (*see* Substance Abuse and Mental Health Services Administration).

Sandwijk, J.P, Peter D.A. Cohen, and S. Musterd. 1991. *Licit and Illicit Drug Use in Amsterdam*. Amsterdam: Institute for Social Geography.

Schillinger, Liesl. 1995. "The Drug Peacenik." *New York,* January 23, pp. 20–21.

Schmalleger, Frank. 1996. *Criminology Today*. Upper Saddle River, NJ: Prentice-Hall.

Schuckit, Marc A. 1980. "The Theory of Alcohol and Drug Abuse: A Genetic Approach." In Dan J. Lettieri et al. (eds.), *Theories on Drug Abuse*. Rockville, MD: National Institute on Drug Abuse, pp. 297–302.

Schuckit, Marc A. 1984. *Drug and Alcohol Abuse: A Clinical Guide to Diagnosis and Treatment* (2nd ed.). New York: Plenum.

Schur, Edwin M. 1962. *Narcotic Addiction in Britain and America: The Impact of Public Policy*. Bloomington: Indiana University Press.

Seligman, Jean, et al. 1992. "The New Age of Aquarius," *Newsweek,* February 28, pp. 66–67.

Sethi, B.B., and R. Manchanda. 1980. "Drug Use Among Recent Doctors." *Acta Psychiatrica Scandinavica,* 62 (November): 447–455.

Seymour, Richard B. 1986. *MDMD*. San Francisco: Haight-Ashbury Publications.

Shafer, Jack. 2005. "Crack Then. Meth Now: What the Press *Didn't* Learn from the Last Drug Panic." *Slate,* posted August 23.

Shafer, Jack. 2006. "Methamphetamine Propaganda: The Government and the Press are Addicted." *Slate,* posted March 3.

Sherman, Lawrence W., Leslie Steele, Deborah Laufersweiler, Nancy Hoffer, and Sherry A. Julian. 1989. "Stray Bullets and 'Mushrooms': Random Shootings of Bystanders in Four Cities, 1977–1988." *Journal of Quantitative Criminology,* 5 (2): 297–316.

Sidney, Stephen, et al. 1997. "Marijuana Use and Mortality." *American Journal of Public Health,* 87 (April): 585–590.

Siegel, Ronald K. 1982. "Cocaine and Sexual Dysfunction: The Curse of Mama Coca." *Journal of Psychoactive Drugs*, 14 (January–June): 71–74.

Siegel, Ronald K. 1984. "Changing Patterns of Cocaine Use: Longitudinal Observations, Consequences, and Treatment." In John Grabowski (ed.), *Cocaine: Pharmacology, Effects, and Treatment of Abuse*. Rockville, MD: National Institute on Drug Abuse.

Siegel, Ronald K. 1989. *Intoxication: Life in Pursuit of Artificial Paradise*. New York: E.P. Dutton.

Simpson, D. Dwayne. 2003. "Introduction to 5-Year Follow-up Treatment Outcome Studies." *Journal of Substance Abuse Treatment*, 25 (3): 123–124.

Simpson, D. Dwayne, George W. Joe, and Kirk M. Broome. 2002. "A National 5-Year Follow-up of Treatment Outcomes for Cocaine Dependence." *Archives of General Psychiatry*, 59 (June): 538–544.

Simpson, D. Dwayne, and S.B. Sells. 1982. "Effectiveness of Treatment for Drug Abuse: An Overview of the DARP Research Program." *Advances in Alcohol and Drug Abuse*, 2 (1): 7–29.

Single, Eric W. 1981. "The Effect of Marijuana Decriminalization." In Yedy Israel et al. (eds.), *Research Advances in Alcohol and Drug Problems,* vol. 6. New York: Plenum Press, pp. 405–424.

Slater, Philip. 1970. *The Pursuit of Loneliness*. Boston: Beacon Press.

Smith, Gene, and Charles P. Fogg. 1977. "Psychological Antecedents of Teenage Drug Use." In Roberta G. Simmons (ed.), *Research in Community Mental Health: An Annual Compilation of Research,* vol. 1: Greenwich, CT: JAI Press, pp. 87–102.

Smith, Gene, and Charles P. Fogg. 1978. "Psychological Predictors of Early Use, Late Use, and Nonuse of Marijuana Among Teenage Students." In Denise B. Kandel (ed.), *Longitudinal Research on Drug Use: Empirical Findings and Methodological Issues*. Washington, DC: Hemisphere, pp. 101–113.

Spillane, Joseph F. 2000. *Cocaine: From Medical Marvel to Modern Menace in the United States, 1884–1920*. Baltimore: Johns Hopkins University Press.

Stafford, Peter. 1989. "Introduction" to Bruce Eisner, *Ecstasy: The MDMA Story*. Berkeley, CA: Ronin, pp. xv–xxiii.

Stares, Paul B. 1996. *Global Habit: The Drug Problem in a Borderless World*. Washington, DC: Brookings Institution.

Stenchever, Morton A., Terry J. Kunycz, and Marjorie A. Allen. 1974. "Chromosome Breakage in Users of Marijuana." *American Journal of Obstetrics and Gynecology,* 118 (January): 106–118.

Stephens, Richard C., and Rosalind D. Ellis. 1975. "Narcotic Addicts and Crime: Analysis of Recent Trends." *Criminology,* 12 (February): 474–488.

Stout-Weigand, Nancy, and Roger B. Trent. 1981. "Physician Drug Use: Availability or Occupational Stress?" *International Journal of the Addictions,* 16 (2): 317–330.

Streatfeild, Dominic. 2001. *Cocaine: An Unauthorized Biography*. New York: Thomas Dunne Books/St. Martin's Press.

Substance Abuse and Mental Health Services Administration (SAHMSA). 2001. *Summary of Findings from the 2000 National Household Survey on Drug Abuse*. Rockville, MD: U.S. Department of Health and Human Services.

Substance Abuse and Mental Health Services Administration (SAMHSA). 2002. *Results from the 2001 National Household Survey on Drug Abuse:* vol. I, *Summary of National Findings*. Rockville, MD: U.S. Department of Health and Human Services.

Substance Abuse and Mental Health Administration (SAMHSA). 2003. *Results from the 2002 National Survey on Drug Use and Health: National Findings*. Rockville, MD: U.S. Department of Health and Human Services.

Substance Abuse and Mental Health Services Administration (SAMHSA). 2004. *Results from the 2003 National Survey on Drug Use and Health: National Findings*. Rockville, MD: U.S. Department of Health and Human Services.

Substance Abuse and Mental Health Services Administration. 2006. *Results from the 2005 National Survey on Drug Use and Health: National Findings*. Rockville, MD: U.S. Department of Health and Human Services.

Sunstein, Cass R. 2003. *Why Societies Need Dissent*. Cambridge, MA: Harvard University Press.

Sutherland, Edwin H. 1939. *Principles of Criminology* (3rd ed.). Philadelphia: Lippincott.

Sutter, Alan G. 1966. "The World of the Righteous Dope Fiend." *Issues in Criminology*, 2 (Fall): 177–222.

Sutter, Alan G. 1969. "Worlds of Drug Use on the Street Scene." In Donald D. Cressey and David A. Ward (eds.), *Delinquency, Crime, and Social Process.* New York: Harper & Row, pp. 802–829.

Swann, Neil. 1995. "Marijuana Antagonist Reveals Evidence of THC Dependence in Rats," *NIDA Notes,* November/December, pp. 1–2.

Szasz, Thomas S. 1992. *Our Right to Drugs: The Case for a Free Market.* New York: Praeger.

Tanda, Gianluigi, Francesco E. Pontieri, and Gaetano Di Chiara. 1997. "Cannabinoid and Heroin Activation of Mesolimbic Dopamine Transmission by a Common Opioid Receptor Mechanism." *Science,* 276 (June): 299–302.

Tart, Charles T. 1971. *On Being Stoned: A Psychological Study of Marijuana Intoxication.* Palo Alto, CA: Science and Behavior Books.

Tashkin, Donald P., et al. 1976. Subacute Effects of Heavy Marihuana Smoking on Pulmonary Functioning in Healthy Men." *New England Journal of Medicine,* 294 (January 15): 125–129.

Tennes, K., et al. 1985. "Marijuana: Prenatal and Postnatal Exposure in the Human." In T.M. Pinkert (ed.), *Current Research on Consequences of Maternal Drug Abuse.* Rockville, MD: National Institute on Drug Abuse, pp. 48–60.

Thornton, E.M. 1984. *The Freudian Fallacy: An Alternative View of Freudian Theory.* Garden City, NY: Dial Press.

Thornton, Mark. 1992. "Prohibition's Failure: Lessons for Today." *USA Today,* March, pp. 70–73.

Tonry, Michael. 1995. *Malign Neglect: Race, Crime, and Punishment in America.* New York: Oxford University Press.

Torregrossa, Luisita Lopez. 1996. "Up in Smoke." *The New York Times Magazine,* August 25, pp. 40–46.

Toufexis, Anastasia. 1991. "Innocent Victims." *Time,* May 13, pp. 56–60.

Treaster, Joseph B. 1990. "Help Is at Hand, but the Mad Revelry Grinds On." *The New York Times,* September 27, p. A4.

Treaster, Joseph B. 1992. "Agency Says Marijuana Is Not Proven Medicine." *The New York Times,* March 19, p. B11.

Trebach, Arnold S. 1993. "For Legalization of Drugs." In Arnold S. Trebach and James A. Inciardi, *Legalize It? Debating American Drug Policy.* Washington, DC: American University Press.

Tsou, Kang, Sandra L. Patrick, and J. Michael Walker. 1995. "Physical Withdrawal in Rats Tolerant to Δ-9-Tetrahydrocannabinol Precipitated by a Cannabinoid Receptor Antagonist," *European Journal of Pharmacology,* 280: R13–R15.

Turner, Patricia A. 1993. *I Heard It Through the Grapevine: Rumor in African-American Culture.* Berkeley: University of California Press.

Ungerleider, J. Thomas, George D. Lundberg, Irving Sunshine, and Clifford B. Walberg. 1980. "The Drug Abuse Warning Network (DAWN) Program." *Archives of General Psychiatry,* 37 (January): 106–109.

United Nations. 2006. *Global Illicit Drug Trends 2005.* New York: United Nations Office for Drug Control and Crime Prevention.

Valdez, Angela. 2006. "Meth Madness: How *The Oregonian* Manufactured an Epidemic, Politicians Bought It and You're Paying." *wweek.com* (Willamette Week Online), posted June 16.

Van Dyke, Craig, and Robert Byck. 1982. "Cocaine." *Scientific American,* March, pp. 128–141.

Vecci. Gregory M., and Robert T. Sigler. 2001. "Economic Factors in Drug Law Enforcement Decisions." *Policing,* 24 (3): 310–329.

Viscusi, W. Kip, 2002. *Smoke-Filled Rooms: A Postmortem on the Tobacco Deal.* Chicago: University of Chicago Press.

Waldorf, Dan, Craig Reinarman, and Sheigla Murphy. 1991. *Cocaine Changes: The Experience of Using and Quitting.* Philadelphia: Temple University Press.

Walker, Samuel, Cassie Spohn, and Miriam DeLone. 1996. *The Color of Justice: Race, Ethnicity, and Crime in America.* Belmont, CA: Wadsworth.

Webb, Gary. 1998. *Dark Alliance: The CIA, the Contras, and the Crack Cocaine Explosion.* New York: Seven Stories Press.

Weinstein, Susan P. 2002. "Dealing with the District's Drug Users." *The Washington Post,* November 2, p. A24.

Wesson, Donald R., and David E. Smith. 1977. "Cocaine: Its Use for Central Nervous System Stimulation Including Recreational and Medical Use." In Robert C. Petersen and Robert C. Stillman (eds.), *Cocaine 1977.* Rockville, MD: National Institute on Drug Abuse, pp. 137–155.

White, Jack E. 1996. "Crack, Contras, and Cyberspace." *Time,* September 30, p. 59.

White, Stephen C., et al. 1975. "Mitogen-Induced Blastogenic Responses Lymphocytes from Marijuana Smokers." *Science,* 188 (4 April): 71–72.

White House. 2006. *National Drug Control Strategy.* Washington, DC: White House.

Wickelgren, Ingrid. 1997. "Marijuana: Harder Than Thought?" *Science,* 276 (June): 1967–1968.

Wikler, Abraham. 1980. "A Theory of Opioid Dependence." In Dan J. Lettieri et al. (eds.), *Theories on Drug Abuse.* Rockville, MD: National Institute on Drug Abuse, pp. 174–178.

Wilbanks, William. 1987. *The Myth of a Racist Criminal Justice System.* Monterey, CA: Brooks/Cole.

Wilbanks, William. 1992. "The 'Monkey Model' of Addiction: A Dangerous Myth." In Erich Goode (ed.), *Drugs, Society, and Behavior 92/93* (7th ed.). Guilford, CT: Annual Editions/Dushkin, pp. 63–65.

Williams, A.F., M.A. Peat, and D.S. Crouch. 1985. "Drugs in Fatally Injured Young Male Drivers." *PharmChem Newsletter,* 14 (1): 1–11.

Williams, David. 2006. "Meth Makes Its Way to Top of Drug Chart." *Anderson Independent Mail* (South Carolina), February 23.

Wilson, William Julius. 1987. *The Truly Disadvantaged: The Inner City, the Underclass, and Public Policy.* Chicago: University of Chicago Press.

Wilson, William Julius. 1997. *When Work Disappears: The World of the New Urban Poor.* New York: Vintage Books.

Wish, Eric D. 1995. "The Drug Use Forecasting (DUF) Program." In Jerome H. Jaffe (ed.), *Encyclopedia of Drugs and Alcohol.* New York: Simon & Schuster/Macmillan, pp. 432–434.

Wish, Eric D., J.A. Hoffman, and S. Nemes. 1997. "The Validity of Self-Reports of Drug Use at Treatment Admission and Follow-Up: Comparisons with Urinalysis and Hair Assays." In L. Harrison and A. Hughes (eds.), *The Validity of Self-Reported Drug Use: Improving the Accuracy of Survey Estimates.* Rockville, MD: U.S. Department of Health and Human Services, pp. 200–226.

Wisotsky, Steven. 1990a. *Beyond the War on Drugs.* Buffalo: Prometheus Books.

Wisotsky, Steven. 1990b. "Rethinking the War on Drugs." *Free Inquiry,* Spring, pp. 7–12.

Wisotsky, Steven. 1993. *Beyond the War on Drugs: Overcoming a Failed Public Policy.* Buffalo: Prometheus Books.

Worrall, John. 2003. "Civil Asset Forfeiture: Past, Present, and Future." In Larry K. Gaines and Peter B. Kraska (eds.), *Drugs, Crime, and Justice: Contemporary Perspectives* (2nd ed.). Prospect Heights, IL: Waveland Press, pp. 268–287.

Wurmser, Leon. 1980. "Drug Use as a Protective System." In Dan J. Lettieri et al. (eds.), *Theories on Drug Abuse.* Rockville, MD: National Institute on Drug Abuse, pp. 71–74.

Yacoubian, George S., Jr. 2000. "Assessing ADAM's Domain: Past Problems and Future Prospects." *Contemporary Drug Problems,* 2 (Spring): 121–135.

Yesavage, Jerome A., Von Otto Leirer, Mark Denari, and Leo Hollister. 1985. "Carry-Over Effects of Marijuana Intoxication on Aircraft Pilot Performance: A Preliminary Study." *American Journal of Psychiatry,* 142 (November): 1325–1329.

Yett, Andrew. 1990. "All Agree on Failure of Our Drug Strategy." *The New York Times,* January 1, p. 24.

Young, Stanley. 1989. "Zing! Speed: The Choice of a New Generation." *Spin Magazine,* July, pp. 83–84, 124–125.

Zador, Paul L. 1991. "Alcohol-Related Risk of Fatal Driver Injuries in Relation to Age and Sex." *Journal of Studies on Alcohol,* 52 (4): 302–310.

Zahn, Margaret A., and Mark Bencivengo. 1974. "Violent Death: A Comparison Between Drug Users and Nondrug Users." *Addictive Diseases,* 1 (3): 283–296.

Zernike, Kate. 2005. "A 21st-Birthday Drinking Game Can Be a Deadly Rite of Passage." *The New York Times,* March 12, pp. A1, A12.

Zimmer, Lynn. 1990. "Proactive Policing Against Street-Level Drug Trafficking." *American Journal of Police,* 9 (1): 43–74.

Zimring, Frank E., and Gordon Hawkins. 1992. *The Search for a Rational Drug Policy.* Cambridge, UK: Cambridge University Press.

Zinberg, Norman E. 1984. *Drug, Set, and Setting: The Basis for Controlled Intoxicant Use.* New Haven, CT: Yale University Press.

Zuger, Abigail. 2002. "The Case for Drinking (All Together Now: In Moderation!)." *The New York Times,* December 31, p. D1, D6.

# PHOTO CREDITS

# NAME INDEX

## A

Abel, E.L., 246
Abelson, H.I., 186, 213, 279
Adams, E.H., 312
Adlaf, E.M., 288, 292
Adler, F., 69
Agar, M., 341
Agnew, S., 111
Akers, R.L., 128, 247
Allen, M.A., 245
American Council on Marijuana, 245
Anderson, E., 379
Andrews, G., 285
Anglin, M. D., 336
Anonymous 1996, 246
Anslinger, H.J., 107, 128, 129, 332, 337
Armor, D.J., 215
Asghar, K., 42, 288, 436
Ashley, R., 93, 102, 285, 286, 293
Ausubel, D.P., 65
Avalania, R., 270

## B

Bachman, J.G., 19, 249, 287
Back, N., 130, 264
Bakalar, J., 4, 44, 93, 131, 257, 265, 277, 285
Baker, R., 125
Ball, J.C., 336
Barnett, G., 242
Barry, D., 124
Bechetti, L., 357, 364, 401
Becker, H.S., 7, 74–75, 97, 130
Beecher, H.K., 44, 277
Beers, D., 390, 425, 437
Bejerot, N., 63

Bellucci, P.A., 141, 142, 338, 340, 347, 442
Ben-Yehuda, N., 137
Bencivengo, M., 342
Bennett, W., 134, 390, 432, 436, 444
Benson, J.A., 258, 259
Berger, L.H., 437
Beschner, G., 314
Best, S., 391
Blakeslee, S., 246
Blandon, D., 299
Bonner, R., 258
Bonnie, R.J., 106, 107
Boone, D.L., 403
Bourgois, P., 297, 376, 377–378
Bovelle, E., 314
Bozarth, M.A., 42, 436
Braden, W., 129–130
Bradler, B., 139
Brady, J.V., 42, 288
Brecher, E.M., 91, 93, 104, 130
Breecher, E.M., 92, 104
Brill, N.Q., 244, 251
Brinkley, J., 432
Brody, J.E., 406
Broome, K.M., 411
Brown 2002, 207
Brown, R., 42, 288, 436
Brownstein, H.H., 140, 141, 143
Brownstein, P.R., 141, 142, 338, 347, 442
Bruen, A.M., 308, 357, 364, 401
Brunvand, J.H., 132
Bryant, W.J., 102
Budd, R.D., 337
Bureau of Narcotics, 94
Burns, R., 390
Butterfield, F., 137
Byck, R., 284, 288, 290, 293

## C

Callaway, E., 229
Campbell, A.M.G., 244
Campbell, R., 122
Canadian Commission of Inquiry into the Non-Medical Use of Drugs 1972, 242
Canadian Senate Special Committee on Illegal Drugs, 256
Capone, A., 430
Carter, H., 430
Cashman, S., 97
Cassidy, J., 80
Caulkin, J., 396
Caulkins, J.P., 289
Centers for Disease Control (CDC), 212, 219, 222
Cepos, J., 300
Chaiken, M.R., 343
Chatlos, C., 292, 294, 296
Chavkin, W., 136
Chiara, G.D., 49, 246
Cisin, I., 186, 213, 259, 279
Clayton, R.R., 253
Clouet, D., 42, 288, 436
Cloward, R.A., 68, 69, 319, 375
Co, B.T., 245
Cohen, D.A., 170, 173, 440
Cohen, M., 263–264
Cohen, M.M., 130, 264
Cohen, P.D.A., 170, 440
Cohen, S., 246
Cole, D., 379
Cooke, J., 138–140, 144
Cooper, C.R., 128, 129, 332, 337
Costa, F., 251
Courtwright, D.T., 94, 99, 104, 105
Cowley, G., 231

# SUBJECT INDEX

## A

Absolute alcohol, 178
Absolute alcohol per day, 212
Absolute deterrence, 391, 402–403, 412
Abstinence-oriented maintenance
 programs, 408
Abt Associates, 175–176, 308, 310,
 312, 357, 364
Acetaminophen, 15, 308
Active dose, 34
Acute effects, 34, 158
 of alcohol, 208–210
 of marijuana, 242–244
 of nicotine, 217
Acute-chronic distinction, 51
Adam, 269. *See also* Ecstasy
ADAM Program.*See* Arrestee Drug
 Abuse Monitoring (ADAM)
 program
Adaptive methadone maintenance
 programs, 408
Adderall, 4–5, 25–28, 223
Addiction. *See also* Withdrawal
 symptoms
 to alcohol, 41
 to amphetamines, 280
 to cocaine, 290–293
 to crack, 133
 dependence and, 43
 euphoria-seekers, 64–65
 to heroin, 316–320, 325
 maintainers, 64
 to methamphetamines, 137
 monkey model of, 436
 myth and reality of, 319–320
 to narcotics, 309
 to nicotine, 217–218
 to OxyContin, 326–328

 to tranquilizers, 228
*Addiction* (Goldstein), 43
Addiction model, 51
Addicts. *See also* Drug treatment
 euphoria seeking, 64–65
 Harrison Act (1914) and, 103–105
 *junkie* and, 106
 media on marijuana, 128–129
 money earned from heroin
  dealing by, 375
 number of, in nineteenth century,
  94–95
 surveys and, 164–165
Additive effects, 40
Adolescents. *See* Monitoring the Future
 (MTF) survey; Youth
Adopted children, 61
Advertising
 cigarette, 425
 media sensationalism and, 127
Afghanistan, 301, 308, 364,
 372–373, 396
African Americans. *See also*
 Minorities; Race issues
 AIDS and, 323, 324
 cocaine and, 102, 284–285
 crack, the CIA and, 297–302
 drug overdoses and, 159
 economic inequalities and, 80–81
 incarceration of, 23, 378, 387
 marijuana use by, 106
 social marginalization of, 377–378
Afri-Cola, 93
Age
 alcohol use and, 215–216
 drug-induced deaths and, 159
 marijuana use and, 247–249
 rate of illicit drug use and,
  176, 177

AIDS/HIV
 effectiveness of drug treatment
  and, 411
 harm reduction approach and, 427
 heroin and, 34, 322–324, 325–326
 progressive prohibitionists on, 444
Akers, Ronald, 282
*Alamosa Daily Courier,* 107
Alaska, 258
Alcohol
 addiction to, 41
 advertising of, 425
 barbiturates taken with, 224
 classification of, 45, 206
 correlation between illegal drugs
  and, 207
 as a depressant, 46
 distillation of, 19–20
 as a drug, 11
 effects of, 47, 231–232
 emergency department
  beverages on, 161
 illicit drugs *vs.,* 205–206
 learning to appreciate, 44
 legal aspects of drug use and, 13
 legal instrumental use of, 16–17
 in medical examiner reports,
  160, 161
 nature of drug-crime link and,
  333–334
 overdoses with, 22
 potency and, 40
 prevalence rate *vs.* consumption
  level of, 175
 as risk factor for premature
  deaths, 207
Alcohol use/abuse. *See also* Prohibition
 (alcohol)
 acute effects of, 208–210